Lecture Notes in Computer Science 13837

The series Lecture Notes in Computer Science (LNCS), including its subseries Lecture Notes in Artificial Intelligence (LNAI) and Lecture Notes in Bioinformatics (LNBI), has established itself as a medium for the publication of new developments in computer science and information technology research, teaching, and education.

LNCS enjoys close cooperation with the computer science R & D community, the series counts many renowned academics among its volume editors and paper authors, and collaborates with prestigious societies. Its mission is to serve this international community by providing an invaluable service, mainly focused on the publication of conference and workshop proceedings and postproceedings. LNCS commenced publication in 1973.

Yi Deng · Moti Yung
Editors

Information Security and Cryptology

18th International Conference, Inscrypt 2022
Beijing, China, December 11–13, 2022
Revised Selected Papers

Editors
Yi Deng
Institute of Information Engineering, CAS
Beijing, China

Moti Yung
Columbia University
New York, NY, USA

ISSN 0302-9743 ISSN 1611-3349 (electronic)
Lecture Notes in Computer Science
ISBN 978-3-031-26552-5 ISBN 978-3-031-26553-2 (eBook)
https://doi.org/10.1007/978-3-031-26553-2

This Springer imprint is published by the registered company Springer Nature Switzerland AG
The registered company address is: Gewerbestrasse 11, 6330 Cham, Switzerland

Preface

The 18th International Conference on Information Security and Cryptology (Inscrypt 2022) was held on-line on December 11–13, 2002. It was organized by the State Key Laboratory of Information Security, Chinese Academy of Sciences, in cooperation with the IACR.

Inscrypt is an annual international conference held in China, covering all research areas of information security, cryptology, and their applications. The program committee of Inscrypt 2022 was composed of 51 members, and received 69 submissions from China, Japan, the UK, Australia, Romania, Belgium, and the USA, from which 23 submissions were selected as regular papers and 3 papers as short papers. All anonymous submissions were reviewed by at least three PC members each, or aided by external reviewers in the relevant areas. Papers were selected to the program based on their rankings, discussions, and technical remarks.

The program of Inscrypt 2022 included four excellent invited keynote talks by Huaxiong Wang (Singapore), Juan Garay (USA), Yu Yu (China), and Yilei Chen (China). Furthermore, the program included 9 regular sessions on the subjects of block ciphers, public-key encryption and signature, quantum cryptography, multi-party computations, cryptanalysis, mathematical aspects of cryptography, stream ciphers, malware, and lattices.

Many people helped in making the conference a reality. We would like to take this opportunity to thank the Program Committee members and the external reviewers for their invaluable help in producing the conference program. We would like to further thank the honorary chairs, Xiaofeng Wang and Dongdai Lin, for their helpful advice, and the general chairs, Wenhao Wang and Guozhu Meng, for their excellent help in organizing the conference and the proceedings. Finally, we wish to thank all the authors who submitted papers to the conference, the invited speakers, the session chairs, and all the conference attendees.

November 2022

Yi Deng
Moti Yung

Organization

Honorary Chairs

XiaoFeng Wang	Indiana University Bloomington, USA
Dongdai Lin	Institute of Information Engineering, CAS, China

General Chairs

Wenhao Wang	Institute of Information Engineering, CAS, China
Guozhu Meng	Institute of Information Engineering, CAS, China

Program Chairs

Yi Deng	Institute of Information Engineering, CAS, China
Moti Yung	Columbia University, USA

Program Committee

Ghous Amjad	Google LLC, USA
Man Ho Au	The University of Hong Kong, China
Bo Chen	Michigan Technological University, USA
Jie Chen	East China Normal University, China
Kai Chen	Institute of Information Engineering, CAS, China
Rongmao Chen	National University of Defense Technology, China
Sanchuan Chen	Fordham University, USA
Sen Chen	Tianjin University, China
Yu Chen	Shandong University, China
Xiaofeng Chen	Xidian University, China
Yilei Chen	Tsinghua University, China
Yueqiang Cheng	NIO Security Research, USA
Michele Ciampi	The University of Edinburgh, UK
Yi Deng	Institute of Information Engineering, CAS, China
Wenrui Diao	Shandong University, China
Xiong Fan	Rutgers University, USA

Ruitao Feng	The University of New South Wales, Australia
Nicholas Genise	Duality Technologies, USA
Chun Guo	Shandong University, China
Debiao He	Wuhan University, China
Xinyi Huang	Fujian Normal University, China
Miroslaw Kutylowski	Wroclaw University of Technology, Poland
Junzuo Lai	Singapore Management University, Singapore
Jingqiang Lin	University of Science and Technology of China, China
Meicheng Liu	Institute of Information Engineering, CAS, China
Zhen Liu	Shanghai Jiao Tong University, China
Xianhui Lu	Institute of Information Engineering, CAS, China
Yuan Lu	Institute of Information Engineering, CAS, China
Weizhi Meng	Technical University of Denmark, Denmark
Khoa Nguyen	University of Wollongong, Australia
Longjiang Qu	National University of Defense Technology, China
Wenbo Shen	Zhejiang University, China
Bing Sun	National University of Defense Technology, China
Mingshen Sun	Intel, USA
Siwei Sun	University of Chinese Academy of Sciences, China
Qiang Tang	University of Sydney, Australia
Ivan Visconti	University of Salerno, Italy
Ding Wang	Nankai University, China
Qian Wang	Wuhan University, China
Weijia Wang	Shandong University, China
Xiang Xie	Shanghai Qi Zhi Institute, China
Luyi Xing	Indiana University Bloomington, USA
Yang Yu	Tsinghua University, China
Yong Yu	Shaanxi Normal University, China
Yu Yu	Shanghai Jiao Tong University, China
Moti Yung	Columbia University, USA
Chao Zhang	Tsinghua University, China
Jiang Zhang	Institute of Software, CAS, China
Jiliang Zhang	Hunan University, China
Changan Zhao	Sun Yat-sen University, China
Hong-Sheng Zhou	Virginia Commonwealth University, USA
Haojin Zhu	Shanghai Jiao Tong University, China

Contents

MPC

Cryptanalysis

Mathematical Aspects of Crypto

Stream Ciphers

Malware

Lattices

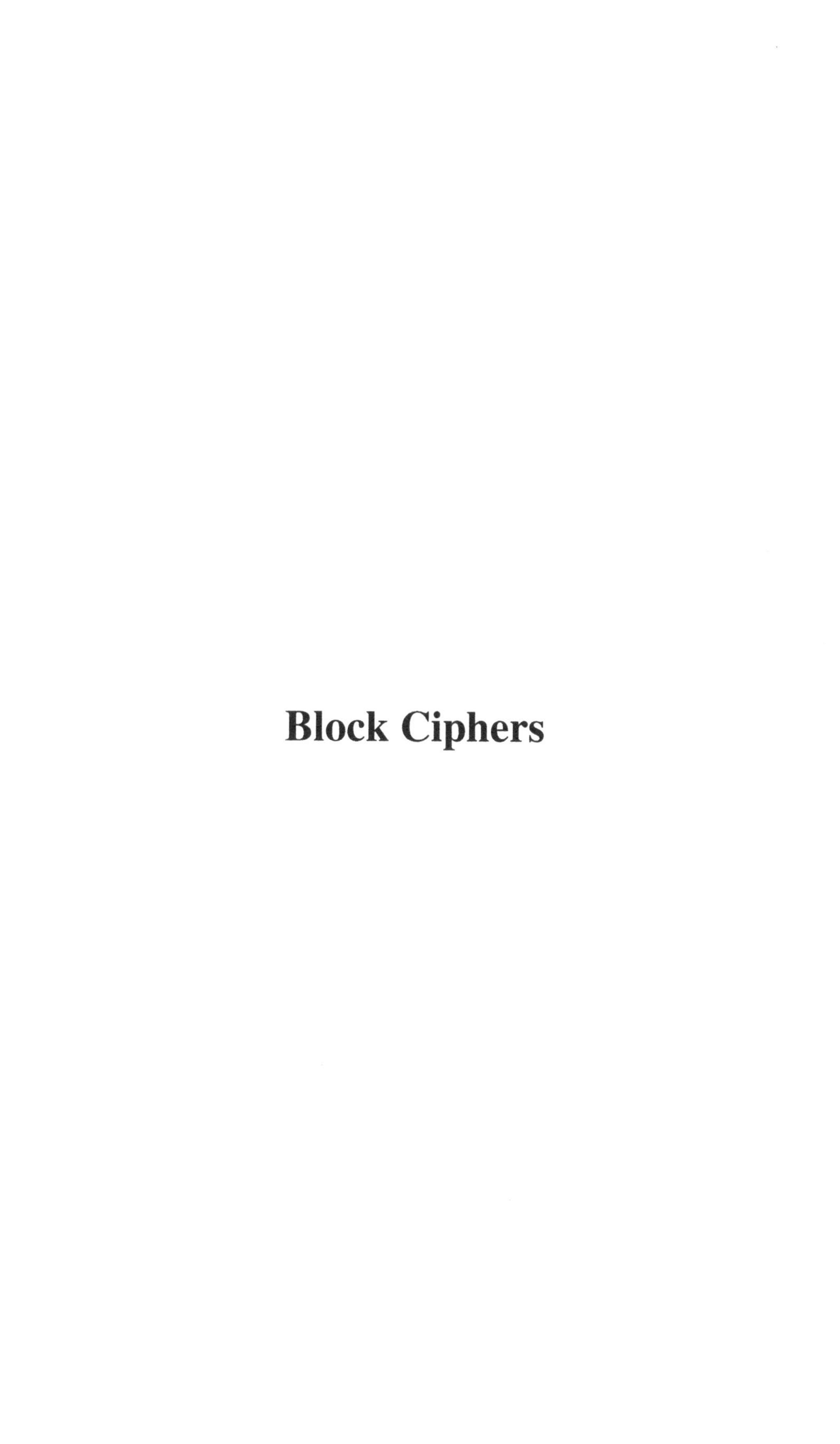

Block Ciphers

How Fast Can SM4 be in Software?

Xin Miao[1], Chun Guo[1,2,3], Meiqin Wang[1,2,4], and Weijia Wang[1,2,4](✉)

[1] School of Cyber Science and Technology, Shandong University, Qingdao 266237, Shandong, China
xin.miao@mail.sdu.edu.cn, {chun.guo,mqwang,wjwang}@sdu.edu.cn
[2] Key Laboratory of Cryptologic Technology and Information Security of Ministry of Education, Shandong University, Qingdao 266237, Shandong, China
[3] Shandong Research Institute of Industrial Technology, Jinan 250102, Shandong, China
[4] Quancheng Laboratory, Jinan 250103, China

Abstract. SM4 is a popular block cipher issued by the Office of State Commercial Cryptography Administration (OSCCA) of China. In this paper, we use the bitslicing technique that has been shown as a powerful strategy to achieve very fast software implementations of SM4. We investigate optimizations on multiple frontiers. First, we present an efficient bitsliced representation for SM4, which enables running 64 blocks in parallel with 256-bit registers. Second, we adopt Boyar's combinational logic optimization method for a more optimal SM4 S-box. The above optimizations contribute to an ≈6 times performance gain on one core compared with the state-of-the-art result. As the bitsliced implementation requires a non-standard input/output data form compatible with existing parallel modes of operation, we present the algorithms for data form transformations in different cases, allowing efficient implementations of SM4 under Counter (CTR) mode and Galois/Counter Mode (GCM). Furthermore, since the overhead on (even optimized) data form transformations is non-negligible, we suggest some adjustments of CTR mode and GCM with respect to the bitsliced implementation, resulting in bitslicing-friendly variants thereof.

Keywords: SM4 · Bitsliced implementation · CTR mode · GCM

1 Introduction

The SM4 block cipher is a symmetric-key cryptographic algorithm issued by the Office of State Commercial Cryptography Administration (OSCCA) of China and was identified as the national cryptographic industry-standard in March 2012 [1,2]. It was incorporated into the ISO/IEC 18033-3 international standard in June 2021 [3]. As the only OSCCA-approved symmetric encryption algorithm for use in China, SM4 has been applied to many industries such as protection for wireless network data transmission.

An appropriate implementation is a very important requirement for cryptographic algorithms. In this paper, we focus on investigating the fast implementation of SM4 on high-end platforms. To speed up SM4 block cipher, a natural

Y. Deng and M. Yung (Eds.): Inscrypt 2022, LNCS 13837, pp. 3–22, 2023.
https://doi.org/10.1007/978-3-031-26553-2_1

thought is to use the instruction set extension. A typical example is the Advanced Encryption Standard New Instructions (AES-NI) [4], which has been integrated into many processors and has significantly improved the speed and security of applications with AES. However, few processors integrate instructions specially for SM4, which largely restricts the speed of applications collocating with it and then naturally raises a question: how fast can SM4 be in software?

1.1 Contributions

In this paper, we describe a fine-grained bitsliced implementation of SM4 based on an enhanced single instruction multiple data (SIMD) instruction set AVX2 (a.k.a, Haswell New Instructions) [5], which runs at a speed of ≈2.48 cycles per byte (cpb) and ≈15.26 Gbits per second (Gbps) on one core with disabled hyper-threading and enabled turbo boost. To the best of our knowledge, it is a new speed record and outperforms state-of-the-art software implementation [6] by a factor of more than 6, and also it operates in constant time. Indeed, the bitsliced SM4 can be further improved using AVX-512 with ultra-wide 512-bit vector operations capabilities to back up higher performance computing in theory. We still choose to consider AVX2 now since it is much more widely deployed (than AVX-512). To get a remarkable performance gain, we investigate optimizations on the following frontiers.

- First of all, we propose a bitsliced representation (that is the way to pack internal states of multiple blocks within the YMM registers) allowing to process 64 SM4 blocks efficiently with 256-bit registers.
- As the nonlinear layer S-box is the toughest part to handle that affects the entire performance when implementing in bitsliced style, we use the decomposition by tower field architecture and adopt Boyar's logic minimization technique [7] to find a highly optimized implementation of S-box.

Finally, by analyzing the performance of current bitsliced implementations, we note that the overhead on transforming data from the block-wise form to the bitslicing-compatible form is non-negligible. Hence, we present the algorithms for data form transformations in different cases, and then wrap them up to give complete implementations of SM4 under Counter (CTR) mode and Galois/Counter Mode (GCM). Besides, in order to reduce the impact of data form transformations, we suggest adjusting CTR mode and GCM to the bitsliced style, resulting in more efficient and bitslicing-friendly variants of these two modes.

1.2 Related Works

The fast software implementations of SM4 have been investigated for several years, due to the wide applications such as networking software and operating system modules. Zhang et al. [6] presented a fast software implementation of SM4 by exploiting bitslicing technique with AVX2, where 256 blocks are processed in parallel. Their bitsliced SM4 code ran at the throughput of 2580 Mbps on an

Intel 2.80 GHz processor. Lang et al. [8] presented an enhanced software implementation of SM4 with the performance of 1795 Mbps and 2437 Mbps on different Intel processors respectively. Zhang et al. [9] proposed a bitsliced software implementation of SM4 and detailed how to implement efficient transformation from original storage form to bitsliced storage form on a 64-bit machine and carry out parallel encryption of multiple blocks. A brief comparison between our bitsliced implementation and state-of-the-art works on Intel platforms is shown in Table 1 where we do not mark the cost of transformations, and more details will be given in Sect. 6. Last but not least, compared with the known bitsliced implementations [6,9], ours (in addition to the significantly faster speed) is the first design able to run n blocks in parallel by using $4n$-bit registers.

Table 1. Comparison results of software implementations on Intel platforms.

Platform	Throughput [Gbps]	Method
Intel Xeon E5-2620 @2.40 GHz [9]	0.054	Bitslicing
Intel Core i3-4160 @3.60 GHz [8]	1.67	Look-up table
Intel Core i7-5500U @2.40 GHz [8]	1.75	Look-up table
Intel Core i7-6700 @3.40 GHz [8]	2.38	Look-up table
Intel Core i7-7700HQ @2.80 GHz [6]	2.52	Bitslicing
Ours (Intel Core i7-8700 @3.20 GHz)	**15.26**	Bitslicing

Liu et al. [10] cracked the algebraic structure of the SM4 S-box, and published its logical expression and specific parameter settings. We recall the state-of-the-art results of logical operations towards the SM4 S-box. Abbasi et al. [11] proposed a compact design for S-box which contained 134 XOR and 36 AND operations. Saarinen et al. [12] also proposed an optimized implementation with 81 XOR, 14 XNOR, and 34 AND operations. The best case of logical gates used by S-box from Gong et al. [13] was 115, including XOR, OR, AND and NOT. By contrast, our SM4 S-box costs a total of 120 bit operations (75 XOR, 13 XNOR, and 32 AND operations).

1.3 Limitations

As our bitsliced implementation runs many (e.g., 64) SM4 blocks in parallel, it benefits the applications encrypting a relatively large amount of bits using SM4, but not quite suitable for the encryption of short messages. The limitation concerning the short messages is due to the nature of the bitsliced implementation. Nevertheless, we believe that, in the case of encrypting a relatively large amount of bits, a fast implementation of encryption is usually significant for the performance of the application as well.

1.4 Organizations

Below we first present backgrounds in Sect. 2. We then present our strategy of bitslicing SM4 in Sect. 3. The implementation of the SM4 S-box is given in

Sect. 4. In Sect. 5, we describe the implementations of modes. The results and comparisons are shown in Sect. 6. Finally, Sect. 7 concludes the whole paper.

2 Backgrounds

2.1 Notations

In the following, we agree on the conventions used throughout the rest of this paper, mainly focussing on the block cipher encryption and its modes of operation. All operations of SM4 are defined over 8-bit, 32-bit, or 128-bit quantities so that 8-bit values can simply be called bytes, 32-bit values words and 128-bit values blocks. The symbol $\oplus$ denotes the bitwise exclusive-or operation and $\lll$ means a left circular rotation by bits in a 32-bit word vector which is different from its specific definitions in Sect. 3. The block cipher encryption with the key k is denoted as Enc_k. The multiplication of two elements $X, Y \in GF(2^{128})$ is denoted as $X \cdot Y$, and the field multiplication operation is defined in Sect. 2.4. The expression $\{0,1\}^m$ denotes the bits string with length m and 0^{128} represents a string of 128 zero bits. The concatenation of two bit strings A and B is represented as $A \| B$.

2.2 The SM4 Block Cipher

SM4 is a block cipher algorithm whose block size and key length are both 128 bits. It adopts an unbalanced Feistel structure and iterates its round function 32 times during the encryption phase, where $X_i \in Z_2^{32}, i = 0, 1, \ldots, 35$ represents a bit string of length 32 bits respectively. Finally, SM4 applies the reverse transformation to produce the corresponding output ciphertext. The 32 round keys are generated in turn by the key expansion algorithm with the original 128-bit key. The decryption phase has a similar structure except that the order of round keys needs to be reversed [2].

Round Function F: Suppose the input to the round function is $(X_0, X_1, X_2, X_3) \in (Z_2^{32})^4$, and the round key is $rk \in Z_2^{32}$, then the round function F can be expressed as:

$$F(X_0, X_1, X_2, X_3) = (X_1, X_2, X_3, X_0 \oplus T(X_1 \oplus X_2 \oplus X_3 \oplus rk)). \quad (1)$$

Mixed Substitution T: $Z_2^{32} \to Z_2^{32}$ is an invertible transformation, composed of a nonlinear transformation τ and a linear transformation L. That is, $T(\cdot) = L(\tau(\cdot))$.

Nonlinear Transformation τ: τ is composed of 4 S-boxes in parallel. Suppose $A = (a_0, a_1, a_2, a_3) \in (Z_2^8)^4$ is the input to τ, and $B = (b_0, b_1, b_2, b_3) \in (Z_2^8)^4$ is the corresponding output, then

$$(b_0, b_1, b_2, b_3) = \tau(A) = (Sbox(a_0), Sbox(a_1), Sbox(a_2), Sbox(a_3)).$$

Linear Transformation L: The 32-bit output from the nonlinear transformation τ is the input to the linear transformation L. Suppose the input to L is $B \in Z_2^{32}$, and the corresponding output is $C \in Z_2^{32}$, then

$$C = L(B) = B \oplus (B \lll 2) \oplus (B \lll 10) \oplus (B \lll 18) \oplus (B \lll 24).$$

2.3 The Counter (CTR) Mode

The Counter (CTR) mode is a confidentiality mode of operation that features the application of the forward cipher to a set of input blocks, called counter blocks, to produce a sequence of output blocks that are XORed with the plaintext to produce the ciphertext, and vice versa [14]. The "nonce" portion and the "counter" portion should be concatenated together to constitute counter blocks (e.g., storing the nonce in the upper 96 bits and the counter in the lower 32 bits of a 128-bit counter block). The sequence of counter block values must be different from every other one of them. This condition is not restricted to a single message, but all of the counter blocks should be distinct. Given a range of counter blocks $T_0, T_1, \ldots, T_{n-1}$ and plaintext $P_0, P_1, \ldots, P_{n-1}$, CTR encryption leaving out padding can be defined as follows:

1. Forward cipher $O_j = Enc_k(T_j)$, for $j = 0, 1, \ldots, n-1$.
2. Ciphertext $C_j = P_j \oplus O_j$, for $j = 0, 1, \ldots, n-1$.

In CTR encryption, the forward cipher functions can be performed in parallel. Moreover, the forward cipher functions can be applied to the counter block values prior to the availability of the plaintext data.

2.4 The Galois/Counter Mode (GCM)

Galois/Counter Mode (GCM) is one of the most widely used authenticated encryption schemes designed by McGrew and Viega [15]. It is constructed from a block cipher with a block size of 128 bits, such as the Advanced Encryption Standard (AES) algorithm. It combines the Counter mode with a block cipher-based Wegman-Carter MAC in an Encrypt-then-MAC manner. The MAC employs a universal hash function defined over a binary Galois field [16]. However, GCM does not follow generic composition, and the establishment of its provable security is the outcome of an intricate line of works [17–19].

We focus on the (authenticated) encryption function of GCM. In addition, we mainly focus on the GCM variant with (fixed-length) 96-bit nonces.[1] In this respect, the encryption function GCM.Enc$_k(N, M)$ takes a nonce $N \in \{0,1\}^{96}$ and a message $M \in \{0,1\}^*$ as the inputs. It first encrypts M to C with CTR mode $GCTR_k(N, M)$, where the initial counter block value is the concatenation of N and the integer 2. Then, it invokes hash function $GHASH_H(C)$ to have

[1] It is mandated (e.g., RFC 4106 or IPsec [20], RFC 5647 or SSH [21], RFC 5288 or SSL [21]) or recommended (e.g., RFC 5084 [22] and 5116 [23]) in many standards to use fixed-length nonces with 96 bits.

the digest of C, where $H := Enc_k(0^{128})$ is the secret hash key generated by encrypting the zero block.

Write C as multiple 128-bit blocks $C = (C_1, C_2, \ldots, C_n)$. Then,

$$GHASH_H(C) = \sum_{j=1}^{n} C_j H^{n-j+1} = C_1 \cdot H^n \oplus C_2 \cdot H^{n-1} \oplus \ldots \oplus C_n \cdot H, \quad (2)$$

where $\cdot$ stands for multiplications over the field $GF(2^{128})$ constructed by the irreducible polynomial $P = x^{128} + x^7 + x^2 + x + 1$ [24]. Also in [24], appropriate methods are provided for us to directly invoke and calculate $GHASH_H$ of GCM.

Alternatively, $GHASH_H(C)$ can be computed by repeating

$$Y_i = [(C_i \oplus Y_{i-1}) \cdot H] \mod P \quad (P = x^{128} + x^7 + x^2 + x + 1), \quad (3)$$

for $i = 1, \ldots, n$, where $Y_i, i = 1, \ldots, n$ are outputs of the function $GHASH_H$, and modular is taken over the aforementioned field $GF(2^{128})$. Eventually, the authentication tag T with the length of t bits is derived by truncating $Enc_k(N\|1) \oplus GHASH_H(C)$ to t bits.

3 Bitslicing SM4

The concept of bitsliced implementation is to convert the algorithm into a series of logical bit operations (e.g., XOR and AND gates) and process multiple encryption blocks in parallel. In this section, we attempt to enhance the software performance of SM4 when implemented in a bitsliced style on 256-bit platforms. We consider a new bitsliced representation of the SM4 state (i.e. block), start with discussing the simple application of SM4 round functions to one single block, and then move to the applications to multiple bitsliced blocks.

3.1 A New Bitliced Representation of SM4

Before introducing the new bitsliced representation, we consider one SM4 state (128-bit) as a bit cuboid, just as shown in Fig. 1(a). We term the yellow edge as "column", the blue edge as "row", and the red edge as "line", where we also mark numbers for locating different small cubes (i.e. bits) and describing the application of round functions. As a result, each column is placed in one slice for our bitsliced representation and each line can represent one byte involved in the classic S-box computation. They are indicated with four small cubes filled with yellow and red frame lines respectively for example. As for any 32-bit vector appearing in Sect. 2.2, it can be defined as column × line.

Different bits of one byte could be rarely placed within the same slice (i.e. register) so that the round function with logical operations can be easily calculated. Therefore, we separate the bits of the same line. Besides, we construct the slices of our new bitsliced representation by separating the bits of the same row as well as packing the bits of the same column. This kind of design is mainly based on the unbalanced Feistel structure of SM4, which has decided that a Mixed Substitution T only works on a part of the data. We do not refer to the so-called conventional bitsliced representation, in which a single N-bit processor can handle N parallel encryptions [25]. There is no doubt that this kind of bitsliced representation needs a large number of registers or plenty of memory accesses since the bits just at the absolutely same position of all blocks are set in the same register. However, our new bitsliced representation prefers to use general-purpose registers available as few as possible with paying necessary memory accesses.

Then, according to our new bitsliced representation, we explain the application of the round function with the pre-computed (and stored in the memory) round keys, which firstly considers one single block for the sake of simplicity. The round encryption function F as shown in Fig. 1(b) comprises XOR operations and Mixed Substitution T made up of a nonlinear layer τ (4 S-boxes in parallel) and a linear transformation L.

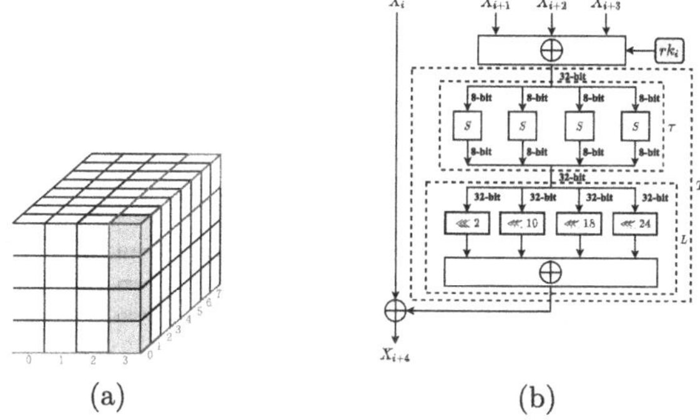

Fig. 1. The State of one block (a) and the round function of SM4 (b).

The former XOR operations with the round keys are properly aligned with regard to the SubBytes operations [26]. That is, the XOR operations get ready for four parallel 8-bit S-boxes with the fixed 8-bit input and 8-bit output. With the help of the assisted numbers marked beside the edges, for each byte of the whole state, bit 0 is placed in line 0, bit 1 in line 1, bit 2 in line 2, and so on. These two operations can be achieved in Fig. 2. We defer the optimization and implementation of S-box as a bitsliced style in Sect. 4.

The linear transformation L in a bitsiced style after S-box is different from the original one which contains left circular rotations within a 32-bit vector. It needs to find corresponding bits and perform circular rotations sometimes. Lastly, we consider the latter XOR operations between the output of the linear transformation L and the part of the unencrypted bits. These two operations are detailed in Fig. 3.

$$
\begin{aligned}
R_7 &= Sbox\,(R_7^1 \oplus R_7^2 \oplus R_7^3 \oplus rk_7)\\
R_6 &= Sbox\,(R_6^1 \oplus R_6^2 \oplus R_6^3 \oplus rk_6)\\
R_5 &= Sbox\,(R_5^1 \oplus R_5^2 \oplus R_5^3 \oplus rk_5)\\
R_4 &= Sbox\,(R_4^1 \oplus R_4^2 \oplus R_4^3 \oplus rk_4)\\
R_3 &= Sbox\,(R_3^1 \oplus R_3^2 \oplus R_3^3 \oplus rk_3)\\
R_2 &= Sbox\,(R_2^1 \oplus R_2^2 \oplus R_2^3 \oplus rk_2)\\
R_1 &= Sbox\,(R_1^1 \oplus R_1^2 \oplus R_1^3 \oplus rk_1)\\
R_0 &= Sbox\,(R_0^1 \oplus R_0^2 \oplus R_0^3 \oplus rk_0)
\end{aligned}
$$

Fig. 2. Calculations of key XORing and the SubBytes operations, where rk_i refers to the bits located at position i of the bitsliced round keys and R_i^j refers to the column corresponding to row j and line i, updated to R_i

$$
\begin{aligned}
R_7' &= R_7^0 \oplus [\,R_7 \oplus R_5 \oplus (R_5 \lll 1) \oplus (R_5 \lll 2) \oplus (R_7 \lll 3)\,]\\
R_6' &= R_6^0 \oplus [\,R_6 \oplus R_4 \oplus (R_4 \lll 1) \oplus (R_4 \lll 2) \oplus (R_6 \lll 3)\,]\\
R_5' &= R_5^0 \oplus [\,R_5 \oplus R_3 \oplus (R_3 \lll 1) \oplus (R_3 \lll 2) \oplus (R_5 \lll 3)\,]\\
R_4' &= R_4^0 \oplus [\,R_4 \oplus R_2 \oplus (R_2 \lll 1) \oplus (R_2 \lll 2) \oplus (R_4 \lll 3)\,]\\
R_3' &= R_3^0 \oplus [\,R_3 \oplus R_1 \oplus (R_1 \lll 1) \oplus (R_1 \lll 2) \oplus (R_3 \lll 3)\,]\\
R_2' &= R_2^0 \oplus [\,R_2 \oplus R_0 \oplus (R_0 \lll 1) \oplus (R_0 \lll 2) \oplus (R_2 \lll 3)\,]\\
R_1' &= R_1^0 \oplus [\,R_1 \oplus (R_7 \lll 1) \oplus (R_7 \lll 2) \oplus (R_7 \lll 3) \oplus (R_1 \lll 3)\,]\\
R_0' &= R_0^0 \oplus [\,R_0 \oplus (R_6 \lll 1) \oplus (R_6 \lll 2) \oplus (R_6 \lll 3) \oplus (R_0 \lll 3)\,]
\end{aligned}
$$

Fig. 3. Calculations of the linear transformation L and the XOR operations at the end of round function, where $\lll$ refers to the circular rotation within a slice, and R_i^0 refers to the column corresponding to row 0 and line i, updated to R_i'.

3.2 The Applications to Multiple SM4 Blocks

We then generalize the bitsliced representation for a single block to multiple ones. As shown in Fig. 4, we do not put multiple blocks in tandem directly but at regular intervals. We use this representation because most AVX2 instructions are strict with the operations crossing lanes freely but can manipulate quadword (64-bit) values as individual processing units. This arrangement is similar to the barrel shifter design [26] enabling efficient circular rotations with PERMUTE instruction instead of SHIFT instruction which is incapable of circular rotating within the whole register.

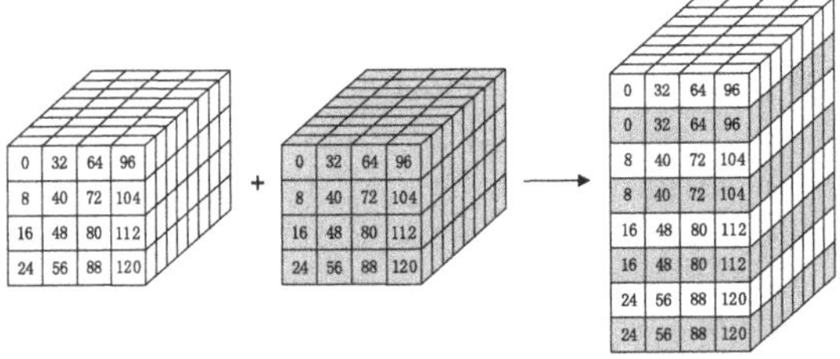

Fig. 4. The bitsliced representation of two SM4 blocks, where we use numbers to mark the bits just at position 0 of each byte from both two blocks.

The round functions for multiple bitsliced blocks have not changed a lot, except for the linear transformation L, where we should pay attention to the bits of circular rotations. On the 256-bit platform which can process 64 blocks in parallel, the operations of L are described in Fig. 5.

$$
\begin{aligned}
R_7^{'} &= R_7 \oplus R_5 \oplus (R_5 \lll 64) \oplus (R_5 \lll 128) \oplus (R_7 \lll 192) \\
R_6^{'} &= R_6 \oplus R_4 \oplus (R_4 \lll 64) \oplus (R_4 \lll 128) \oplus (R_6 \lll 192) \\
R_5^{'} &= R_5 \oplus R_3 \oplus (R_3 \lll 64) \oplus (R_3 \lll 128) \oplus (R_5 \lll 192) \\
R_4^{'} &= R_4 \oplus R_2 \oplus (R_2 \lll 64) \oplus (R_2 \lll 128) \oplus (R_4 \lll 192) \\
R_3^{'} &= R_3 \oplus R_1 \oplus (R_1 \lll 64) \oplus (R_1 \lll 128) \oplus (R_3 \lll 192) \\
R_2^{'} &= R_2 \oplus R_0 \oplus (R_0 \lll 64) \oplus (R_0 \lll 128) \oplus (R_2 \lll 192) \\
R_1^{'} &= R_1 \oplus (R_7 \lll 64) \oplus (R_7 \lll 128) \oplus (R_7 \lll 192) \oplus (R_1 \lll 192) \\
R_0^{'} &= R_0 \oplus (R_6 \lll 64) \oplus (R_6 \lll 128) \oplus (R_6 \lll 192) \oplus (R_0 \lll 192)
\end{aligned}
$$

Fig. 5. The calculation of L for 64 SM4 blocks, where $R_i \lll j$ refers to a circular rotation of j bits to the left for all bits within R_i, updated to $R_i^{'}$.

4 The Implementation of S-Box

The section focuses on optimizing the implementation of nonlinear layer τ with its algebraic structure which drops out of the use of the look-up table.

4.1 Decomposing the SM4 S-Box

We give the algebraic structure of the SM4 S-box suggested by Erickson et al. [27] as shown in the expression $S(X) = A_2 \cdot (A_1 \cdot X + C_1)^{-1} + C_2$. X is an 8-bit input of S-box,

$$
A_1 = A_2 = \begin{bmatrix} 1\,1\,0\,1\,0\,0\,1\,1 \\ 1\,1\,1\,0\,1\,0\,0\,1 \\ 1\,1\,1\,1\,0\,1\,0\,0 \\ 0\,1\,1\,1\,1\,0\,1\,0 \\ 0\,0\,1\,1\,1\,1\,0\,1 \\ 1\,0\,0\,1\,1\,1\,1\,0 \\ 0\,1\,0\,0\,1\,1\,1\,1 \\ 1\,0\,1\,0\,0\,1\,1\,1 \end{bmatrix}, \tag{4}
$$

$$
C_1 = C_2 = \begin{bmatrix} 1\,1\,0\,1\,0\,0\,1\,1 \end{bmatrix}. \tag{5}
$$

The irreducible primitive polynomial in $GF(2^8)$ is $f(x) = x^8 + x^7 + x^6 + x^5 + x^4 + x^2 + 1$. It is obvious that there are both the nonlinear component in charge of computing an inverse in $GF(2^8)$ and the linear components responsible for affine transformations.

We first put the emphasis on the nonlinear component and we would simplify the inverse operation using the tower field architecture $GF(2^8) \rightarrow GF(((2^2)^2)^2)$

by consulting the normal inverter from Canright et al. [28]. The nonlinear component actually, has nonlinear connected portions as well as linear connected portions. To facilitate the discussion of the next subsection, we would keep nonlinear connected portions and linear connected portions apart, and meanwhile, we should identify linear connected portions as large as possible while still being linear. As a consequence, we constitute the nonlinear component of the SM4 S-box with an initial linear expansion L_1 from 8 to 22 bits, a nonlinear contraction F from 22 to 18 bits, and a final linear contraction L_2 from 18 to 8 bits [7]. So far, we have gotten a new expression of S-box $S(X) = A_2 \cdot L_2 \cdot F\ [L_1 \cdot (A_1 \cdot X + C_1)] + C_2$.

For the initial linear expansion L_1, in consideration of decomposing $GF(2^8)$ into $GF(((2^2)^2)^2)$, we choose one set of normal basis $[Y^{16}, Y] = [0x94, 0x95]$, $[X^4, X] = [0x50, 0x51]$, and $[W^2, W] = [0x5D, 0x5C]$ presented by Fu et al. [29] from only eight sets of normal bases which can achieve the right encryption. The isomorphic matrix M mapping from the composite field $GF(((2^2)^2)^2)$ to the standard polynomial representation based on this set of normal basis can be constructed easily, as shown below.

$$M = \begin{bmatrix} 0\,0\,0\,1\,0\,0\,0\,1 \\ 1\,1\,0\,0\,0\,1\,0\,1 \\ 1\,1\,1\,1\,0\,0\,0\,0 \\ 0\,0\,0\,1\,1\,0\,0\,0 \\ 0\,0\,0\,0\,0\,0\,1\,1 \\ 1\,0\,1\,1\,0\,1\,1\,1 \\ 1\,0\,0\,1\,0\,1\,1\,0 \\ 0\,1\,0\,1\,1\,0\,0\,0 \end{bmatrix} \tag{6}$$

Both the isomorphic matrix M^{-1} calculated by the matrix reverse method (*modulo* 2) and the former linear connected portions of the normal inverter are used to build the initial linear layer L_1. For the nonlinear contraction F, SM4 shares the same nonlinear middle layer with AES [12] so that we omit a full explanation of it. It is inevitable that XOR operations still occur in F here and there. For the final linear contraction L_2, it includes the isomorphic matrix M to accomplish the basis conversion as well as the latter linear connected portions of the normal inverter.

Moreover, when we take the affine transformations (i.e. the linear components) into consideration, we could combine L_1 with A_1, the same with L_1 and C_1, L_2 and A_2, for reasons of further optimizing the linear components of the whole S-box. Although $L_1 \cdot C_1$ is a 22-bit constant vector longer than the original 8-bit constant vector C_1, it will not hit the result at all. What's more, performing XOR operations with a constant 0 can also be omitted directly. At this point, the latest expression of the SM4 S-box is $S(X) = B \cdot F\ (U \cdot X + C) + C_2$, where U is equal to $L_1 \cdot A_1$, C equal to $L_1 \cdot C_1$, and B equal to $L_2 \cdot A_2$. The matrix U, the 22-bit constant vector C, and the matrix B are given in Appendix A. Last but not least, we should be aware of the bit order every time we input or output.

4.2 Optimizing the Linear Components

As the structure of S-box has been decomposed into fresh linear and nonlinear components, it is necessary to find an implementation of linear components with the smallest number of XOR operations. The above optimization can be formulated as a problem of finding the smallest number of linear operations necessary to compute a set of linear forms, which is called the Shortest Linear Program (SLP) problem and is essentially NP-hard [30]. In this subsection, we adopt the heuristic optimization by Boyar et al. [7] to achieve an efficient implementation of the linear components (corresponding to matrices U and B). The concrete steps of this new technique for combinational logic optimization can be found in Sect. 3.2 "A New Heuristic" of [7].

Eventually, the resulted implementations using the Boyar et al.'s heuristic are given in Fig. 6(a) and Fig. 6(b). The middle nonlinear transformation F is identical with AES, where inputs are $y_0, y_1, \ldots, y_{21}$ and outputs are $z_0, z_1, \ldots, z_{17}$. Therefore, we omit the specific bit operations of the shared nonlinear mapping from 22 bits to 18 bits, but they can be easily found in Sect. 4 "A Circuit for the S-Box of AES" Fig. 11 of [7]. In a nutshell, the total number of logical gates for our S-box is 75 XOR gates, 13 XNOR gates, and 32 AND gates, which has also taken the XOR operations with constant vectors into consideration.

$n_1 = x_4 + x_2$	$n_2 = x_3 + x_0$	$n_3 = n_2 + x_1$
$y_{10} = n_1 + x_7$	$y_3 = n_3 + x_5$	$n_4 = y_{10} + x_5$
$y_5 = x_6 + x_2$	$n_5 = x_7 + x_4$	$y_{21} = y_3 + n_1$
$y_{14} = n_4 + x_6$	$n_6 = n_5 + x_6$	$n_7 = x_1 + x_0$
$y_6 = y_{21} + n_7$	$y_{17} = n_3 + x_7$	$y_0 = y_{17} + x_0$
$y_1 = y_{10} + y_6$	$y_2 = y_5 + x_1$	$y_7 = y_{10} + x_0$
$y_8 = y_5 + y_3$	$y_9 = n_5 + n_3$	$y_4 = y_9 + y_2$
$y_{11} = n_3 + n_1$	$y_{12} = y_{14} + x_1$	$y_{15} = n_4 + x_1$
$y_{16} = y_{21} + x_1$	$y_{18} = n_7 + n_6$	$y_{19} = y_3 + n_6$
$y_{20} = x_7 + x_2$		

(a) Top linear transformation U with inputs $x_0, x_1, \ldots, x_7$ and outputs $y_0, y_1, \ldots, y_{21}$. $y_{13} = x_1$, which does not need to consider any other operation.

$g_1 = z_9 + z_{15}$	$g_2 = z_6 + z_{10}$	$g_3 = z_{13} + z_{14}$
$g_4 = g_2 + g_3$	$g_5 = z_0 + z_1$	$g_6 = g_1 + z_{17}$
$g_7 = g_4 + z_7$	$g_8 = z_4 + z_5$	$g_9 = g_5 + z_8$
$g_{10} = g_6 + g_7$	$g_{11} = g_8 + z_{11}$	$g_{12} = g_1 + z_{16}$
$g_{13} = g_9 + g_{12}$	$g_{14} = g_8 + g_{13}$	$g_{15} = z_3 + z_4$
$g_{16} = z_{12} + z_{13}$	$g_{17} = z_{15} + z_{16}$	$g_{18} = z_0 + z_2$
$g_{19} = z_7 + z_{10}$	$S_7 = g_{16} + g_{17}$	$g_{20} = g_{11} + g_{18}$
$S_6 = g_7 + g_{20}$	$S_5 = g_5 + g_{10}$	$S_4 = g_2 + g_{14}$
$S_3 = g_6 + z_{11}$	$S_2 = g_{10} + g_{15}$	$g_{21} = g_9 + g_{11}$
$S_1 = g_4 + g_{21}$	$g_{22} = g_{14} + g_{15}$	$S_0 = g_{19} + g_{22}$

(b) Bottom linear transformation B with inputs $z_0, z_1, \ldots, z_{17}$ and outputs $S_0, S_1, \ldots, S_7$.

Fig. 6. The resulted logical bit operations for matrices U and B.

5 Implementations of SM4-CTR, SM4-GCM, and More

The bitslicing technique can benefit modes that support the parallel implementation of block ciphers such as CTR mode and GCM, moreover, this bitsliced implementation needs a non-standard data form. Hence, additional transformations of the data between the block-wise form and the bitslicing-compatible form are required and considered to be expensive [31], which we call the *data form transformation* in the rest of this paper. For example, as shown in Fig. 7(a), the

128-bit counter block values are first transformed (by the short-cut data form transformation detailed in Sect. 5.1) to fully comply with the bitsliced encryption and then transformed (by the general data form transformation detailed in Sect. 5.1) back. GCM with the bitsliced encryption is similar. In this respect, we present our algorithms for data form transformations, where we term the block-wise data into the bitsliced representations as *forward transformation* and its inverse as *backward transformation*. Besides, considering that the overheads of data form transformations are non-negligible, we also propose the variants of CTR and GCM that do not require the backward transformation. For instance, the variant CTR$^+$ is shown in Fig. 7(b).

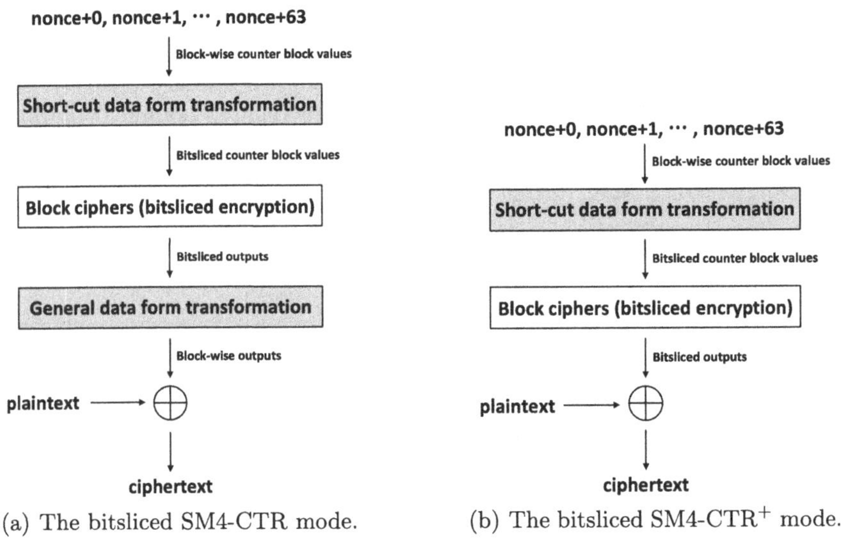

(a) The bitsliced SM4-CTR mode. (b) The bitsliced SM4-CTR$^+$ mode.

Fig. 7. The implementations of the SM4-CTR mode and its variant.

5.1 Data Form Transformation Algorithms

In this subsection, we first present the general algorithm that performs the transformation of any 128-bit block and also its inverse. Then, we consider the common setting under CTR mode for single use, where the 96-bit "nonce" portions of 128-bit counter block values are fixed, and meanwhile, the 32-bit "counter" portions are incremented (block-by-block) from 0 or 1. Hence, we present a much more efficient short-cut transformation algorithm employing the look-up table specific to the above setting.

The General Data Form Transformation Algorithm. We present the forward transformation algorithm that transforms any block-wise (with 128-bit blocks) data into the bitsliced representations. This transformation firstly relies on an in-place transpose of the bit matrix as shown in Fig. 8. Then, with the help of SHIFT instruction which performs within four individual lanes and AND instruction, we perform an extract operation of the most significant bits from four individual quadword values on 256-bit platforms. As a result, the full form transformation for any 128-bit block (also suitable for any 128-bit counter block) can be done by repeating the foregoing extract operation 32 times, where the 4 bits from each of these extractions should be placed in different 256-bit variables and stored for future use. Combined with SHIFT instruction and also XOR instruction, we put extracted bits of 64 different blocks into the appropriate positions of 256-bit variables as detailed in Sect. 3.

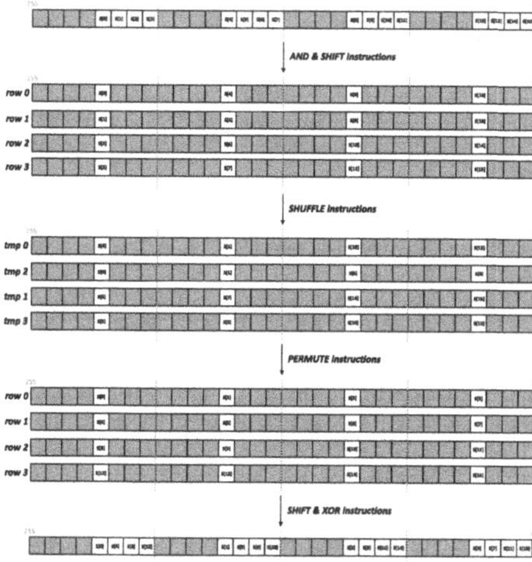

Fig. 8. Steps to transpose a bit matrix, where AND, SHIFT, SHUFFLE, PERMUTE and XOR represent the AVX2 instructions that are mainly used for different operations. The gray area is filled up with zeroes.

Noting that, the general backward transformation is important as well. For example, in CTR mode, the bitsliced representations that have been encrypted should transform back into the initial data form of 128-bit blocks and then perform XOR operations with the plaintext to generate the final ciphertext. The only difference between the two directions of transformation is just to reverse the order of the bit-wise transpose process and the extract operations.

The Short-Cut Data Form Transformation Algorithm. For the short-cut algorithm, we only consider the forward transformation. It is because the inputs of the backward transformation are usually the outputs of parallel block ciphers and thus do not have the pattern of the fixed nonce and incremented counters.

To improve the efficiency of the forward transformation, we build a look-up table about an extension on account of only one form of the 96-bit nonce for CTR mode. This look-up table is an array of one 256-bit data type whose subscripts vary from 0 to 15. The striking feature of all array elements is that there are only two cases for each 64-bit quadword value, either all ones or all zeroes. That is to say, when we extract four bits respectively from random but the same position of four various quadword values within one 256-bit array element, the decimal result of these four bits exactly corresponds to the array subscript of that 256-bit array element. Therefore, in fact, we do not need to execute the general data form transformation algorithm for all counter block values but to use the look-up table after applying the general data form transformation algorithm to only one counter block. Moreover, as the 256-bit general-purpose registers process 64 blocks in parallel, the value of counters could be denoted by $0, 1, \ldots, 63$ or $1, 2, \ldots, 64$ in decimal form. Hence, as for the remaining fixed 32-bit counters, it is easy to transform them into bitsliced representations directly.

So far, we have constituted the inputs of bitslicing SM4. However, the outputs of the forward cipher must be too irregular to predict so that we are not permitted to use the similar short-cut data form transformation algorithm to transform back.

5.2 Bitslicing-Friendly Variants of CTR Mode and GCM

As the general data form transformation has a large overhead, we propose a variant of CTR mode shown in Fig. 7(b) that omits the data form transformation at the outputs of parallel block ciphers, namely the backward transformation. The outputs of the parallel block ciphers, whether the bitsliced representation or the block-wise representation, are uniformly distributed. Therefore, the security of the variant should be the same as the original CTR mode. We adopt the same strategy to GCM, resulting in a variant called GCM$^+$, for which we elaborate more formal details and its security proof in Appendix B. As for the implementation of the GHASH step of GCM, namely the polynomial operations of GCM, we mainly refer to the code samples given by [24] which have already detailed the computation of Galois Hash.

6 Implementation Results and Comparisons

6.1 The Implementation of S-Box for SM4

We present an improved design of the SM4 S-box with a small number of logical operations based on the composite field $GF(((2^2)^2)^2)$ and the pair normal basis $[Y^{16}, Y] = [0x94, 0x95]$, $[X^4, X] = [0x50, 0x51]$, $[W^2, W] = [0x5D, 0x5C]$ respectively. Specifically, our most compact S-box of SM4 comprises 75 XOR, 13 XNOR, and 32 AND gates, as illustrated in Table 2.

Table 2. Logical gates for our designed S-box of SM4.

Mathematical operation	XOR	XNOR	AND
Affine Trans. $(A_1 \cdot X + C_1)$ Map $GF(2^8) \rightarrow GF(((2^2)^2)^2)$	20	8	–
Inversion algorithm	30	–	32
Map inv. $GF(((2^2)^2)^2) \rightarrow GF(2^8)$ Affine Trans. $(A_2 \cdot X + C_2)$	25	5	–
Total	75	13	32

6.2 The Comparison of SM4 Software Implementations

Evaluations are conducted separately for different modes as shown in Table 3. The criteria of these performances are clock cycles per byte (cpb) and 2^{30} bits per second (Gbps). Our bitsliced SM4 enabled running in constant time and processing 64 blocks (1 KB) in parallel achieves 15.26 Gbps for throughput and 2.48 cpb for timing without considering any data form transformations. Additionally, our software performances are obtained when we disable the hyper-threading but enable the turbo boost. Moreover, we can see that the performances of SM4-CTR$^+$ and SM4-GCM$^+$ with only forward transformation are significantly faster than those of SM4-CTR and SM4-GCM with both forward and backward transformation.

Table 3. Our results of different modes for software implementations.

Mode	Timing [cpb]	Throughput [Gbps]
SM4	2.48	15.26
SM4-CTR	8.14	3.81
SM4-CTR$^+$	2.70	11.44
SM4-GCM	10.35	2.29
SM4-GCM$^+$	5.10	5.72

7 Conclusions and Future Works

In this paper, we push the software implementation of SM4 to its limits with AVX2 instructions by investigating optimizations on multiple frontiers. First, we present a new bitsliced representation for SM4 that enables running 64 blocks in parallel with 256-bit registers efficiently. Second, by adopting Boyar's combinational logic optimization method, we obtain the lower number of bit operations

(75 XOR, 13 XNOR, and 32 AND) constructed for the SM4 S-box. Thanks to those optimizations, we can report our new bitsliced SM4 to reach at the speed of ≈2.48 cpb for timing and ≈15.26 Gbps for throughput (by assuming pre-computed round keys and omitting data form transformations), becoming the performance record of SM4 ever made on Intel platforms. These significant improvements also demonstrate that the bitslicing technique is actually promising on platforms with the enhanced SIMD architecture from practical points of view.

We also propose the data form transformation algorithms in different cases for complete and efficient bitsliced implementations of SM4, keeping full compatibility with existing parellel modes of operation, for example, the CTR mode and GCM. Furthermore, the expensive overhead on transforming data from the bitslicing-compatible form to the block-wise form motivates us to adjust CTR mode and GCM to the bitsliced implementation, resulting in bitslicing-friendly variants of these two modes with an essential security proof.

Whilst our work only concentrates on the platform with AVX2 instructions, we believe our optimizations for SM4 could bring about improvements on other architectures as well. Also, the number of general-purpose registers is limited (16 general-purpose registers available on our target platform), and thus numerous memory accesses dominate the entire SM4 processing. In this respect, we deem optimizing the number of memory accesses for the bitsliced implementation as a valuable future study. We are also fired up about the implementation of SM4 on different platforms such as ARMv8/v9 for wider applicability of these techniques, and we will incorporate this throughout our following works. Another interesting topic might be the power analysis of our implementation, i.e., investigating the impact of the bitsliced structure to the known attacking methods such as the chosen plaintext differential power analysis [32].

Acknowledgements. This work was supported by the National Key Research and Development Program of China (Nos. 2021YFA1000600, 2018YFA0704702), the Program of Qilu Young Scholars (Grant Nos. 61580089963177, 61580082063088) of Shandong University, the Program of Taishan Young Scholars of the Shandong Province, the National Natural Science Foundation of China (Grant Nos. 62002202, 62002204, 62032014), the Major Basic Research Project of Natural Science Foundation of Shandong Province, China (Grant No. ZR202010220025).

Appendix

A The Matrices $\boldsymbol{U}$, $\boldsymbol{C}$ and $\boldsymbol{B}$ in S-Box Decomposition

$$
U = \begin{bmatrix}
1&0&0&0&1&0&1&0\\
1&0&1&0&1&0&0&0\\
0&1&0&0&0&1&1&0\\
0&0&1&0&1&0&1&1\\
1&1&0&1&1&1&0&1\\
0&1&0&0&0&1&0&0\\
0&0&1&1&1&1&0&0\\
1&0&0&1&0&1&0&1\\
0&1&1&0&1&1&1&1\\
1&0&0&1&1&0&1&1\\
1&0&0&1&0&1&0&0\\
0&0&0&1&1&1&1&1\\
1&1&1&1&0&1&1&0\\
0&0&0&0&0&0&1&0\\
1&1&1&1&0&1&0&0\\
1&0&1&1&0&1&1&0\\
0&0&1&1&1&1&0&1\\
1&0&0&0&1&0&1&1\\
1&1&0&1&0&0&1&1\\
1&1&1&1&1&0&1&1\\
1&0&0&0&0&1&0&0\\
0&0&1&1&1&1&1&1
\end{bmatrix}
\quad
C = \begin{bmatrix}
0\\1\\0\\0\\0\\0\\1\\1\\0\\0\\0\\1\\0\\0\\0\\1\\0\\1\\1\\0\\1\\0
\end{bmatrix}
\quad
B = \begin{bmatrix}
0&0&0&0&0&0&0&0&0&0&0&0&1&1&0&1&1&0\\
1&0&1&0&1&1&1&1&0&0&1&1&0&1&1&0&0&0\\
1&1&0&0&0&0&1&1&0&1&1&0&0&1&1&1&0&1\\
1&1&0&0&1&1&1&0&1&1&1&0&0&0&0&1&1&0\\
0&0&0&0&0&0&0&0&0&1&0&1&0&0&0&1&0&1\\
0&0&0&1&1&0&1&1&0&1&1&0&0&1&1&1&0&1\\
1&1&0&0&1&1&1&0&1&0&1&1&0&1&1&0&0&0\\
1&1&0&1&0&1&0&1&1&1&1&0&0&0&0&1&1&0
\end{bmatrix}
\tag{7}
$$

B The AEAD Scheme GCM$^+$ and Its Security Proof

B.1 Security Definitions

We follow [33] and consider the all-in-one security definition for nonce-based AEAD. In detail, the advantage of an adversary $\mathcal{A}$ against the AEAD security of GCM^{+E} is

$$
\mathbf{Adv}^{\mathrm{aead}}_{\mathrm{GCM}^{+E}}(\mathcal{A}) := \Pr\left[k \xleftarrow{\$} \mathcal{K} : \mathcal{A}^{\mathrm{Enc}_K(\cdot,\cdot,\cdot),\mathrm{Dec}_K(\cdot,\cdot,\cdot,\cdot)} = 1\right] - \Pr\left[\mathcal{A}^{\$(\cdot,\cdot,\cdot),\perp(\cdot,\cdot,\cdot,\cdot)} = 1\right],
$$

where Enc_K and Dec_K are the GCM$^+$ encryption and decryption oracles respectively, \$ is the random-bits oracle taking (N, A, M) as input and returns $(C, T) \xleftarrow{\$} \{0,1\}^{|M|+\tau}$, and $\perp$ is the rejection oracle taking (N, A, C, T) as input and (always) returns $\perp$. If $\mathcal{A}$ makes a query (N, A, M) to Enc_K and receives (C, T), then we assume that $\mathcal{A}$ does not subsequently make a query (N, A, C, T) to Dec_K. The adversary must be nonce-respecting with respect to encryption queries, i.e., the nonces $N_1, \ldots, N_q$ used in the q encryption queries must be pairwise distinct. On the other hand, decryption queries can reuse nonces that have appeared in earlier encryption or decryption queries.

Meanwhile, the advantage of an adversary $\mathcal{A}$ against the PRP security of a block cipher E is

$$\mathbf{Adv}_E^{\mathrm{prp}}(\mathcal{A}) := \Pr\left[k \xleftarrow{\$} \mathcal{K} : \mathcal{A}^{E_k} = 1\right] - \Pr\left[\mathcal{A}^{\mathbf{P}} = 1\right],$$

where $\mathbf{P}$ is a truly random n-bit permutation.

B.2 GCM$^+$ and Its Security

We refer to Sect. 2.4 for the definition of the standard GCM scheme. This section considers a variant GCM$^{+\pi}$ parameterized by a public, efficient, variable-input-length permutation $\pi : \{0,1\}^* \rightarrow \{0,1\}^*$. In detail, the encryption GCM$^{+\pi}_k$.Enc(N, M) returns (C, T) with $C = \pi(GCTR_k(N, M))$ and $T = \mathsf{msb}_\tau(E_k(N\|1) \oplus GHASH_H(C))$, where $\mathsf{msb}_\tau(X)$ returns the most significant τ bits of X. Namely, GCM$^{+\pi}_k$.Enc(N, M) can be viewed as the standard GCM$^\pi_k$.Enc(N, M) augmented with π.

Theorem 1. *Let τ be the parameters of GCM$^+$. Then for any $\mathcal{A}$ that runs in time t and makes at most q encryption queries and q' decryption queries, where the total plaintext length is at most σ blocks, the maximum nonce length is at most ℓ_N blocks, and the maximum input length is at most ℓ_A blocks, there exists an adversary $\mathcal{A}'$ against the PRP security of the block cipher E, such that $\mathcal{A}'$ makes at most $q + \sigma$ queries and runs in time $O(t + \sigma + q\ell_A)$, and*

$$\mathbf{Adv}^{aead}_{GCM^{+E,\pi}}(\mathcal{A}) \leq \mathbf{Adv}^{prp}_E(\mathcal{A}) + \frac{(\sigma + q + q')^2}{2^{n+1}} + \frac{q'(\ell_A + 1)}{2^\tau}. \quad (8)$$

Let GCM^{+E} be the GCM$^+$ scheme built upon a block cipher E, and let GCM$^{+\mathbf{F}}$ be the idealized GCM$^+$ in which calls to E_K is replaced by a truly random function $\mathbf{F}$. By [18, Eq. (23)] (which is somewhat standard), it holds

$$\mathbf{Adv}^{\mathrm{priv}}_{\mathrm{GCM}^{+E}}(\mathcal{A}) \leq \mathbf{Adv}^{\mathrm{prp}}_E(\mathcal{A}') + \frac{(\sigma + q + q')^2}{2^{n+1}} + \mathbf{Adv}^{\mathrm{aead}}_{\mathrm{GCM}^{+\mathbf{F}}}(\mathcal{A}). \quad (9)$$

Then, since nonces $N_1, \ldots, N_q$ used in the q encryption queries are distinct, the derived counter block values $N_1\|2, N_1\|3, \ldots, N_q\|2, \ldots$ are also distinct, giving rise to σ distinct random function evaluations. Thus, the produced key stream blocks $\mathbf{F}(N_1\|2), \ldots, \mathbf{F}(N_q\|2), \ldots$ are random and independent. This means the ciphertexts obtained by XORing these key stream blocks with the message blocks are truly random, and the outputs of Enc$_K$ (in the real world) and \$ (in the ideal world) have the same distribution.

To bound the gap between the second oracles Dec$_K$ and $\bot$, we consider the probability that a query to Dec$_K(N', A', C', T')$ returns $M' \neq \bot$ in the real world. If so, then it holds $\mathsf{msb}_\tau(\mathbf{F}(N'\|1) \oplus \mathsf{GHASH}_L(A', C')) = T'$: this is essentially the event bad_2 defined in [18, Appendix E]. By [18, Eq. (35)], it holds

$$\Pr[\mathsf{bad}_2] \leq \frac{q'(\ell_A + 1)}{2^\tau}. \quad (10)$$

Gathering Eq. (9) and (10) yields Eq. (8).

References

1. GM/T 0002-2012: SM4 block cipher algorithm. State Cryptography Administration of the People's Republic of China (2012)
2. Tse, R.H., Wong, W.K., Saarinen, M.J.O.: The SM4 blockcipher algorithm and its modes of operations (2018). https://datatracker.ietf.org/doc/html/draft-ribose-cfrg-sm4-10. Internet Engineering Task Force (IETF)
3. ISO/IEC 18033-3:2010/AMD1: 2021 Information Technology - Security techniques - Encryption Algorithms - Part3: Block Ciphers - Amendment1: SM4 (2021). https://www.iso.org/standard/81564.html
4. Gueron, S.: Intel advanced encryption standard (AES) new instructions set. Intel White Paper Rev. **3**, 1–81 (2010)
5. Intel Corporation: Intel C++ Compiler Classic Developer Guide and Reference. https://www.intel.com/content/www/us/en/docs/intrinsics-guide/index.html
6. Zhang, X., Guo, H., Zhang, X., Wang, C., Liu, J.: Fast software implementation of SM4. J. Cryptol. Res. **7**(6), 799–811 (2020)
7. Boyar, J., Matthews, P., Peralta, R.: Logic minimization techniques with applications to cryptology. J. Cryptol. **26**(2), 280–312 (2013). https://doi.org/10.1007/s00145-012-9124-7
8. Lang, H., Zhang, L., Wu, W.: Fast software implementation of SM4. J. Univ. Chin. Acad. Sci. **35**(2), 180 (2018)
9. Zhang, J., Ma, M., Wang, P.: Fast implementation for SM4 cipher algorithm based on bit-slice technology. In: Qiu, M. (ed.) SmartCom 2018. LNCS, vol. 11344, pp. 104–113. Springer, Cham (2018). https://doi.org/10.1007/978-3-030-05755-8_11
10. Liu, F., Ji, W., Hu, L., Ding, J., Lv, S., Pyshkin, A., Weinmann, R.-P.: Analysis of the SMS4 block cipher. In: Pieprzyk, J., Ghodosi, H., Dawson, E. (eds.) ACISP 2007. LNCS, vol. 4586, pp. 158–170. Springer, Heidelberg (2007). https://doi.org/10.1007/978-3-540-73458-1_13
11. Abbasi, I., Afzal, M.: A compact S-Box design for SMS4 block cipher. IACR Cryptology ePrint Archive, p. 522 (2011). http://eprint.iacr.org/2011/522
12. Saarinen, M.O.: A lightweight ISA extension for AES and SM4. CoRR abs/2002.07041 (2020). https://arxiv.org/abs/2002.07041
13. Gong, Z., et al.: Parallel implementation of SM4 based on optimized S-box under tower field. CN 114244496 A, China National Intellectual Property Administration, CNIPA (2022)
14. Dworkin, M.: Recommendation for Block Cipher Modes of Operation: Methods and Techniques. National Institute of Standards and Technology (2001)
15. Bogdanov, A., Lauridsen, M.M., Tischhauser, E.: AES-based authenticated encryption modes in parallel high-performance software. IACR Cryptology ePrint Archive, p. 186 (2014). http://eprint.iacr.org/2014/186
16. Dworkin, M.: Recommendation for Block Cipher Modes of Operation: Galois/-Counter Mode (GCM) and GMAC. National Institute of Standards and Technology (2007)
17. McGrew, D.A., Viega, J.: The security and performance of the Galois/counter mode (GCM) of operation. In: Canteaut, A., Viswanathan, K. (eds.) INDOCRYPT 2004. LNCS, vol. 3348, pp. 343–355. Springer, Heidelberg (2004). https://doi.org/10.1007/978-3-540-30556-9_27
18. Iwata, T., Ohashi, K., Minematsu, K.: Breaking and repairing GCM security proofs. In: Safavi-Naini, R., Canetti, R. (eds.) CRYPTO 2012. LNCS, vol. 7417, pp. 31–49. Springer, Heidelberg (2012). https://doi.org/10.1007/978-3-642-32009-5_3

19. Niwa, Y., Ohashi, K., Minematsu, K., Iwata, T.: GCM security bounds reconsidered. In: Leander, G. (ed.) FSE 2015. LNCS, vol. 9054, pp. 385–407. Springer, Heidelberg (2015). https://doi.org/10.1007/978-3-662-48116-5_19
20. Viega, J., McGrew, D.: The use of Galois/counter mode (GCM) in IPsec encapsulating security payload (ESP). Technical report, RFC 4106 (2005)
21. Igoe, K., Solinas, J.: AES Galois counter mode for the secure shell transport layer protocol. IETF Request for Comments **5647** (2009)
22. Housley, R.: Using AES-CCM and AES-GCM authenticated encryption in the cryptographic message syntax (CMS). Technical report, RFC 5084 (2007)
23. McGrew, D.: An interface and algorithms for authenticated encryption. Technical report, RFC 5116 (2008)
24. Gueron, S., Kounavis, M.E.: Intel Carry-Less Multiplication Instruction and its Usage for Computing the GCM Mode. Intel Corporation (2010)
25. Rebeiro, C., Selvakumar, D., Devi, A.S.L.: Bitslice implementation of AES. In: Pointcheval, D., Mu, Y., Chen, K. (eds.) CANS 2006. LNCS, vol. 4301, pp. 203–212. Springer, Heidelberg (2006). https://doi.org/10.1007/11935070_14
26. Adomnicai, A., Peyrin, T.: Fixslicing AES-like ciphers new bitsliced AES speed records on arm-cortex M and RISC-V. IACR Trans. Cryptogr. Hardw. Embed. Syst. **2021**(1), 402–425 (2021). https://doi.org/10.46586/tches.v2021.i1.402-425
27. Erickson, J., Ding, J., Christensen, C.: Algebraic cryptanalysis of SMS4: Gröbner basis attack and SAT attack compared. In: Lee, D., Hong, S. (eds.) ICISC 2009. LNCS, vol. 5984, pp. 73–86. Springer, Heidelberg (2010). https://doi.org/10.1007/978-3-642-14423-3_6
28. Canright, D.: A very compact Rijndael S-box. Technical report, Naval Postgraduate School Monterey, CA Department of Mathematics (2004)
29. Fu, H., Bai, G., Wu, X.: Low-cost hardware implementation of SM4 based on composite field. In: 2016 IEEE Information Technology, Networking, Electronic and Automation Control Conference, pp. 260–264 (2016). https://doi.org/10.1109/ITNEC.2016.7560361
30. Boyar, J., Matthews, P., Peralta, R.: On the shortest linear straight-line program for computing linear forms. In: Ochmański, E., Tyszkiewicz, J. (eds.) MFCS 2008. LNCS, vol. 5162, pp. 168–179. Springer, Heidelberg (2008). https://doi.org/10.1007/978-3-540-85238-4_13
31. Matsui, M., Nakajima, J.: On the power of bitslice implementation on Intel Core2 processor. In: Paillier, P., Verbauwhede, I. (eds.) CHES 2007. LNCS, vol. 4727, pp. 121–134. Springer, Heidelberg (2007). https://doi.org/10.1007/978-3-540-74735-2_9
32. Wang, S., Gu, D., Liu, J., Guo, Z., Wang, W., Bao, S.: A power analysis on SMS4 using the chosen plaintext method. In: Ninth International Conference on Computational Intelligence and Security, CIS 2013, Emei Mountain, Sichan Province, China, 14–15 December 2013, pp. 748–752. IEEE Computer Society (2013). https://doi.org/10.1109/CIS.2013.163
33. Rogaway, P., Shrimpton, T.: A provable-security treatment of the key-wrap problem. In: Vaudenay, S. (ed.) EUROCRYPT 2006. LNCS, vol. 4004, pp. 373–390. Springer, Heidelberg (2006). https://doi.org/10.1007/11761679_23

LLLWBC: A New Low-Latency Light-Weight Block Cipher

Lei Zhang[1,2](✉), Ruichen Wu[1], Yuhan Zhang[1], Yafei Zheng[1,2], and Wenling Wu[1]

[1] Institute of Software, Chinese Academy of Sciences, Beijing 100190, China
zhanglei@iscas.ac.cn

[2] State Key Laboratory of Cryptology, P. O. Box 5159, Beijing, China

Abstract. Lightweight cipher suitable for resource constrained environment is crucial to the security of applications such as RFID, Internet of Things, etc. Moreover, in recent years low-latency is becoming more important and highly desirable by some specific applications which need instant response and real-time security. In this paper, we propose a new low-latency block cipher named LLLWBC. Similar to other known low-latency block ciphers, LLLWBC preserves the important α-reflection property, namely the decryption for a key K is equal to encryption with a key $K \oplus \alpha$ where α is a fixed constant. However, instead of the normally used SP-type construction, the core cipher employs a variant of generalized Feistel structure called extended GFS. It has 8 branches and employs byte-wise round function and nibble-wise round permutation iterated for 21 rounds. We choose the round permutations carefully together with a novel key schedule to guarantee the α-reflection property. This allows an efficient fully unrolled implementation of LLLWBC in hardware and the overhead of decryption on top of encryption is negligible. Moreover, because of the involutory property of extended GFS, the inverse round function is not needed, which makes it possible to be implemented in round-based architecture with a competitive area cost. Furthermore, our security evaluation shows that LLLWBC can achieve enough security margin within the constraints of security claims. Finally, we evaluate the hardware and software performances of LLLWBC on various platforms and a brief comparison with other low-latency ciphers is also presented.

Keywords: Block cipher · Low-latency · Lightweight · Extended GFS

1 Introduction

Lightweight cryptography has drawn a lot of attention since it was proposed and has become one of the hotspots in symmetric-key cryptography. A variety of lightweight ciphers aiming at various goals have been proposed in the last few years. The earliest lightweight block ciphers such as RRESENT [5] and KATAN [8], mainly focused on hardware implementation performance such as area cost. Then software-oriented designs such as LBlock [17], TWINE [16] and

Y. Deng and M. Yung (Eds.): Inscrypt 2022, LNCS 13837, pp. 23–42, 2023.
https://doi.org/10.1007/978-3-031-26553-2_2

bit-slice cipher RECTANGLE [18] have emerged, which take into account not only hardware platform but also 8/16/32-bit software platforms. Furthermore, there are lightweight ciphers capable of serialized implementation such as Piccolo [13] and SIMON [3], which can achieve ultra lightweight with a very small hardware footprint compared to the standard round-based implementations but at the cost of more cycles. On the other hand, lightweight block ciphers aiming at other goals such as low-latency and low-energy, have also been studied.

Low-latency block cipher is aiming at the need of real-time security. For some special applications, such as instant authentication, memory encryption, and automatic drive, low-latency and instant response are highly desirable. For these cases, the cipher should be optimized for latency and the entire encryption and decryption should be completed within the shortest delay. Moreover, for embedded applications where lightweight block ciphers are implemented in traditional round-based architecture, the needed high clock rates are usually not supported by the system. Therefore, a fully unrolled implementation which allows encryption of data within one clock cycle with competitive area costs will be a possible solution. However, this may be a huge challenge for traditional lightweight block ciphers, in particular if encryption and decryption should both be available on a given platform. Several new designs optimized for low-latency have been proposed recently, including PRINCE [6], MANTIS [4], QARMA [1], PRINCEv2 [7], Orthros [2], and SPEEDY [11].

PRINCE [6] is the first low-latency block cipher proposed by Borghoff *et al.* at ASIACRYPT 2012. It is a 64-bit block cipher with a 128-bit key and its overall structure is based on the FX construction. Its core cipher is a 12-round block cipher named $\texttt{PRINCE}_{core}$ whose round function basically follows the AES structure and the main difference is symmetric around an involutory linear layer in the middle. This special construction together with carefully chosen round constants makes $\texttt{PRINCE}_{core}$ satisfy an interesting property called α-reflection, namely the decryption for a key K is equal to encryption with a key $K \oplus \alpha$ where α is a fixed constant. This is the main feature for low-latency design and is crucial for efficient unrolled implementation. As the first low-latency encryption scheme, PRINCE has already been deployed in a number of products including LPC55S of NXP Semiconductors. Recently, Bozilov *et al.* improved the design of PRINCE to increase its security with almost no overhead and proposed the version of PRINCEv2 [7]. The main difference is a new key schedule with a single XOR in the middle round instead of the unkeyed middle round of PRINCE. Without changing the number of rounds or round functions they try to improve the security level and reach the required security claim set by NIST [12].

Inspired by the design of PRINCE, Beierle *et al.* proposed a low-latency tweakable block cipher named MANTIS in [4]. It is a 64-bit block cipher with 128-bit key and 64-bit tweak. MANTIS basically employs the same structure of PRINCE together with a suitable tweak-scheduling. It simply replaces the PRINCE-round function with the MIDORI-round function while keeping the entire design symmetric around the middle to keep the α-reflection property. The MIDORI-round function consists of involutory S-box specially optimized for small area and low circuit depth, cell permutation of internal state, and multiplication by a binary matrix. These choices result in improved latency and security.

Qualcomm company also proposed a low-latency block cipher family called QARMA [1] which targets at applications such as memory encryption and pointer authentication. It employs a three-round Even-Mansour scheme instead of the FX-construction. QARMA supports 64-bit and 128-bit block sizes, where block and tweak sizes are equal, and key size is twice as long as the block size. The round function of QARMA is also SP-type construction. Two central rounds use the whitening key instead of the core key and the middle permutation is non-involutory and keyed. QARMA only satisfies a property similar to α-reflection where the central permutation is Pseudo-Reflector which can be inverted by means of a simple transformation of the key. QARMA is used in the pointer authentication deployed in the products of ARMv8.3. In these applications, a very short keyed and tweaked tag of the pointer is computed by truncating QARMA's output. It can achieve *control flow integrity* (CFI) by verifying the tagged pointer before use for hardware-assisted prevention of software exploitation.

On the other hand, there are also a few schemes which ignore the support of decryption to achieve ultra low-latency. Orthros [2] is a low-latency pseudorandom function (PRF) proposed by Banik *et al.* at FSE 2021. It is a 128-bit block PRF with a 128-bit key. The overall structure is a sum of two parallel SPN-type keyed permutations. Since it does not support decryption, there is no need to use involutory components and ultra low-latency S-box can be used. SPEEDY [11] is another ultra low-latency block cipher family proposed at CHES 2021. It primarily targets at secure process architectures embedded in high-end CPUs, where area and energy restrictions are secondary. It achieves ultra low-latency in single-cycle encryption speed, while the decryption is less efficient.

It is noteworthy that nearly all of the low-latency block ciphers proposed so far utilize similar structures and preserve the α-reflection property. For the core cipher they all employ SP-type round function which are relatively complex compared to traditional lightweight block ciphers. Moreover, a special middle round and its inverse should also be implemented. Therefore, they only focus on fully unrolled implementation in hardware. However, this will be un-friendly and sometimes difficult for round-based hardware implementation and software implementations on platforms such as 8-bit AVR, etc. Moreover, the number of rounds for low-latency block cipher should be as small as possible to decrease the delay, which brings in more risk in the security aspect. For example, there exists an effective reflection attack [14] on full-round core cipher of PRINCE. In [10] a practical clustering differential attack on full-round $\texttt{MANTIS}_5$ was reported. Therefore, new design of low-latency block cipher with enough security margin against known attacks will be important and desirable. Moreover, in addition to the fully unrolled hardware implementation optimized for latency, the capability of being implemented efficiently on various platforms should also be interesting and valuable.

Our Contribution. We propose a new low-latency block cipher named LLLWBC. Its block size is 64-bit and key size is 128-bit. Similar to other known low-latency block ciphers, LLLWBC preserves the α-reflection property. However, instead of the normally used SP-type construction, its core cipher employs a variant of generalized Feistel structure (GFS) which can be called extended GFS. It is basically a Type-2 GFS with 8 branches, and it employs byte-wise round function and nibble-wise round permutation which will be iterated for 21 rounds. We choose the round permutations carefully together with a novel key schedule to guarantee the α-reflection property. Specifically, LLLWBC consists of odd number of rounds with a nibble-wise permutation P used in the first half rounds and its inverse P^{-1} used in the last half rounds. Moreover, for even rounds, some special constants are XORed to the subkey so as to construct the α-reflection property. This allows an efficient fully unrolled implementation of LLLWBC and the overhead for decryption on top of encryption is negligible. Moreover, because of the involutory property of extended GFS, the inverse of round function is needless, which makes LLLWBC can also be implemented in round-based architecture with competitive area costs. We explicitly state that we do not have security claims in related-key, known-key and chosen-key models, and the time complexity for an adversary with 2^n data should be less than 2^{127-n}. Our security evaluation shows that LLLWBC can achieve enough security margin within the constraints of security claims. Moreover, in the middle round (namely Round-11), the addition of subkey helps to prevent the reflection attack. The round function and permutations are carefully chosen to achieve a good tradeoff between security and performance on various platforms (including ASIC, x86/64, 8-bit AVR, etc.). In the end, we provide detailed implementation results on various platforms and give a brief comparison with other known low-latency block ciphers.

Organization of the Paper. We present the specification of LLLWBC in Sect. 2. Design rationales are explained in Sect. 3. We provide a brief security evaluation of LLLWBC against known attacks in Sect. 4. Implementation results including hardware and software performances and comparisons with other low-latency block ciphers are given in Sect. 5. Finally, Sect. 6 concludes the paper.

2 Specification of LLLWBC

LLLWBC is a 64-bit block cipher with a 128-bit key. Its structure is a special kind of extended GFS and it consists of 21 rounds. The specification of LLLWBC consists of three parts: key schedule, encryption algorithm, and decryption algorithm.

2.1 Key Schedule

The master key of LLLWBC is 128-bit and it is used to generate two 64-bit whitening keys and twenty-one 32-bit round subkeys. First of all, the 128-bit master key K is split into two parts of 64-bit each,

$$K = k_w || k_e.$$

The pre-whitening key k_w^b and post-whitening key k_w^e are defined as follows:

$$k_w^b = k_w, \quad k_w^e = (k_w >>> 1) \oplus (k_w \gg 63)$$

For the odd rounds $r = 1, 3, \ldots, 21$, the higher 32-bit of k_e is used as the round subkey. While for the even rounds $r = 2, 4, \ldots, 20$, the lower 32-bit of k_e is XORed with some constants ck^r to produce the round subkey. The procedure can be expressed as the following equations.

- Denote $k_e = K_1 || K_2$:
- For $r = 1, 3, \ldots, 21$, $k^{r-1} = K_1 \oplus ck^r$.
- For $r = 2, 4, \ldots, 20$, $k^{r-1} = K_2 \oplus ck^r$.

The 32-bit constants $ck^r = (c_0^r || c_1^r || c_2^r || c_3^r)$ used in LLLWBC are listed in Table 1. In order to preserve the α-reflection property of LLLWBC, it satisfies that $ck^r = ck^{22-r}$ for $(r = 1, 3, \ldots, 9)$ and $ck^r \oplus ck^{22-r} = \alpha$ for $(r = 2, 4, \ldots, 10)$. Similar to the other low-latency block ciphers such as PRINCE, the constants α and $ck^r (r = 1, 2, \ldots, 11)$ are derived from the fraction part of $\pi = 3.141\ldots$.

Table 1. Constants used in LLLWBC (in hexadecimal).

$\alpha =$ c0ac29b7	$ck^{11} =$ c97c50dd
$ck^1 = ck^{21} =$ 13198a2e	$ck^2 =$ 03707344
	$ck^{20} = ck^2 \oplus \alpha =$ c3dc5af3
$ck^3 = ck^{19} =$ a4093822	$ck^4 =$ 299f31d0
	$ck^{18} = ck^4 \oplus \alpha =$ e9331867
$ck^5 = ck^{17} =$ 082efa98	$ck^6 =$ ec4e6c89
	$ck^{16} = ck^6 \oplus \alpha =$ 2ce2453e
$ck^7 = ck^{15} =$452821e6	$ck^8 =$ 38d01377
	$ck^{14} = ck^8 \oplus \alpha =$ f87c3ac0
$ck^9 = ck^{13} =$be5466cf	$ck^{10} =$ 34e90c6c
	$ck^{12} = ck^{10} \oplus \alpha =$ f44525db

2.2 Encryption Algorithm

The block size and key size of LLLWBC are 64-bit and 128-bit respectively, which can be denoted as LLLWBC-64/128. First of all, the 64-bit plaintext is XORed with a 64-bit pre-whitening key k_w^b. Then, a special kind of extended generalized Feistel structure (GFS) is iterated 21 rounds. For the r-th round, the 64-bit input is split into 16 nibbles and the 32-bit round subkey is split into 4 bytes, and then after going through a traditional type-2 GFS transformation with round function F, the 16 nibbles are permuted according to a nibble-wise permutation P to produce the round output. Note that as usual the last nibble-wise permutation in Round-21 is omitted. Moreover, in order to preserve the reflection property, the nibble-wise permutation P is used in the first 10 rounds and P^{-1} is used in the last 10 rounds. At last, a 64-bit post-whitening key k_w^e is XORed to get the ciphertext.

Denote M and C as the 64-bit plaintext and ciphertext, $(x_0^{r-1}||x_1^{r-1}||\ldots||x_{15}^{r-1})$ as the 64-bit round input, and $(k_0^{r-1}||k_1^{r-1}||k_2^{r-1}||k_3^{r-1})$ as the 32-bit round subkey. The encryption procedure of LLLWBC can be expressed as follows.

1. $M \oplus k_w^b = x_0^0||x_1^0||\ldots||x_{15}^0$.
2. For $r = 1, 2, \ldots, 10$:

$$\begin{aligned} x_0^r, x_1^r, \ldots, x_{15}^r = P(&x_0^{r-1}, x_1^{r-1}, F((x_0^{r-1}||x_1^{r-1}) \oplus k_0^{r-1}) \oplus (x_2^{r-1}||x_3^{r-1}), \ldots, \\ &x_{12}^{r-1}, x_{13}^{r-1}, F((x_{12}^{r-1}||x_{13}^{r-1}) \oplus k_3^{r-1}) \oplus (x_{14}^{r-1}||x_{15}^{r-1})). \end{aligned}$$

3. For $r = 11, 12, \ldots, 20$:

$$\begin{aligned} x_0^r, x_1^r, \ldots, x_{15}^r = P^{-1}(&x_0^{r-1}, x_1^{r-1}, F((x_0^{r-1}||x_1^{r-1}) \oplus k_0^{r-1}) \oplus (x_2^{r-1}||x_3^{r-1}), \ldots, \\ &x_{12}^{r-1}, x_{13}^{r-1}, F((x_{12}^{r-1}||x_{13}^{r-1}) \oplus k_3^{r-1}) \oplus (x_{14}^{r-1}||x_{15}^{r-1})). \end{aligned}$$

4. For $r = 21$:

$$\begin{aligned} x_0^r, x_1^r, \ldots, x_{15}^r = &x_0^{r-1}, x_1^{r-1}, F((x_0^{r-1}||x_1^{r-1}) \oplus k_0^{r-1}) \oplus (x_2^{r-1}||x_3^{r-1}), \ldots, \\ &x_{12}^{r-1}, x_{13}^{r-1}, F((x_{12}^{r-1}||x_{13}^{r-1}) \oplus k_3^{r-1}) \oplus (x_{14}^{r-1}||x_{15}^{r-1}). \end{aligned}$$

5. $C = (x_0^{21}||x_1^{21}||\ldots||x_{15}^{21}) \oplus k_w^e$.

Specifically, the components used in each round are defined as follows.

Round Function F. The non-linear function F operates on 8-bit which consists of an S-box layer S, a linear layer A and a second S-box layer S. It can be expressed as the following equation, and Fig. 1 illustrates the structure of round function F in detail.

$$\begin{aligned} F : \{0,1\}^8 &\rightarrow \{0,1\}^8 \\ (u_0, u_1) &\rightarrow S(A(S(u_0, u_1))) \end{aligned}$$

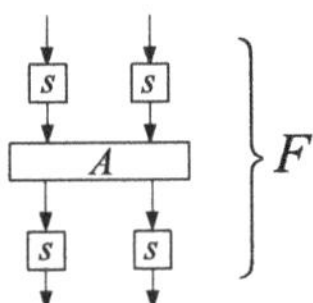

Fig. 1. Round function F.

The S-box layer S consists of two 4-bit S-boxes s in parallel, and the contents of 4-bit S-box are listed in Table 2. Note that for a fair comparison, here we apply the same 4-bit S-box used in PRINCE [6].

Table 2. Contents of the 4-bit S-box.

u	0	1	2	3	4	5	6	7	8	9	A	B	C	D	E	F
$s(u)$	B	F	3	2	A	C	9	1	6	7	8	0	E	5	D	4

The linear layer A consists of matrix multiplication with 2×2 MDS matrix over $GF(2^4)$, and the irreducible polynomial used is $x^4 + x + 1$. The linear function can be expressed as the following equation.

$$\begin{aligned} &A : \{0,1\}^8 \rightarrow \{0,1\}^8 \\ &(u_0, u_1) \rightarrow \begin{pmatrix} 0x2 & 0x3 \\ 0x1 & 0x1 \end{pmatrix} \cdot \begin{pmatrix} u_0 \\ u_1 \end{pmatrix} \end{aligned}$$

Note that the round function F can also be considered as an 8-bit non-linear S-box. Its contents can be precomputed and stored in a table.

Permutation P. Permute all the 16 nibbles according to the nibble-wise permutation P, and it can be expressed as follows.

$$\begin{aligned} &P : \{0,1\}^{64} \rightarrow \{0,1\}^{64} \\ &Y = (y_0, y_1, \ldots y_{15}) \rightarrow Z = (z_0, z_1, \ldots z_{15}) \end{aligned}$$

$$\begin{aligned} &z_0 = y_6,\ z_1 = y_{11},\ z_2 = y_0,\ z_3 = y_{12},\ z_4 = y_{10},\ z_5 = y_7,\ z_6 = y_{13},\ z_7 = y_1, \\ &z_8 = y_3,\ z_9 = y_{15},\ z_{10} = y_4,\ z_{11} = y_9,\ z_{12} = y_2,\ z_{13} = y_{14},\ z_{14} = y_5,\ z_{15} = y_8. \end{aligned}$$

Inverse Permutation P^{-1}. Permute all the 16 nibbles according to the nibble-wise permutation P^{-1}, which is the inverse of permutation P. It can also be expressed as the following equations.

$$\begin{aligned} &P^{-1} : \{0,1\}^{64} \rightarrow \{0,1\}^{64} \\ &Z = (z_0, z_1, \ldots z_{15}) \rightarrow Y = (y_0, y_1, \ldots y_{15}) \end{aligned}$$

$$\begin{aligned} &y_0 = z_2,\ y_1 = z_7,\ y_2 = z_{12},\ y_3 = z_8,\ y_4 = z_{10},\ y_5 = z_{14},\ y_6 = z_0,\ y_7 = z_5, \\ &y_8 = z_{15},\ y_9 = z_{11},\ y_{10} = z_4,\ y_{11} = z_1,\ y_{12} = z_3,\ y_{13} = z_6,\ y_{14} = z_{13},\ y_{15} = z_9. \end{aligned}$$

2.3 The Decryption Algorithm

From the fact that LLLWBC employs a novel construction of extended GFS with permutations P, P^{-1} and the special subkey settings, we can deduce that LLLWBC satisfies the α-reflection property. Namely, the decryption algorithm parameterized with $(k_w^b || K_1 || K_2 || k_w^e)$ is equal to the encryption algorithm parameterized with $(k_w^e || K_1 || K_2 \oplus \alpha || k_w^b)$, which can be expressed as the following equation.

$$D_{(k_w^b || K_1 || K_2 || k_w^e)}(\cdot) = E_{(k_w^e || K_1 || K_2 \oplus \alpha || k_w^b)}(\cdot)$$

where α is the 32-bit constant $\alpha =$ `C0 AC 29 B7`. Thus, decryption only has to change the master key slightly and reuse the exact same encryption algorithm.

3 Design Rationale

3.1 Cipher Structure

LLLWBC employs a special kind of extended generalized Feistel structure (GFS). Usually in the standard Type-2 GFS structure with k branches, a single round can be described as the following equation:

$$\textbf{GFS:}\ (X_0^{r+1}, \ldots, X_{k-1}^{r+1}) = F(X_0^r) \oplus X_1^r, X_2^r, \ldots, F(X_{k-2}^r) \oplus X_{k-1}^r, X_0^r$$

where F is a non-linear function applied on even-number branches.

Later in FSE 2010, Suzaki *et al.* [15] proposed a kind of improved GFS. Their main idea was to replace the cyclic shift of branches with a different permutation, which could improve the diffusion and security strength efficiently. A single round of improved GFS can be described as the following equation:

$$\textbf{GFS}_{\text{imp}}:\ (X_0^{i+1}, \ldots, X_{k-1}^{i+1}) = \pi(X_0^i, F(X_0^i) \oplus X_1^i, \ldots, X_{k-2}^i, F(X_{k-2}^i) \oplus X_{k-1}^i)$$

where $\pi : (\{0,1\}^t)^k \rightarrow (\{0,1\}^t)^k$ is a deterministic permutation, i.e., a shuffle of k branches and each branch t-bit (corresponding to the size of round function F). Furthermore, their analysis showed that optimum permutation had the property that any even-number input branch should be mapped to an odd-number output branch, and vice versa, which they referred as even-odd permutation.

Extended GFS Structure. Notice that in the analysis of these structures, the round function F is usually considered as a whole and its internal property is ignored. Then it is a direct idea to propose an extended GFS structure with permutation operating on smaller unit, which can further enhance the diffusion effect and obtain more accurate security evaluation by utilizing the internal property of round function F. For the extended GFS structure used in LLLWBC, a single round can be described as the following equation:

$$(x_0^{r+1}, x_1^{r+1}, \ldots, x_{15}^{r+1}) = P(x_0^r, x_1^r, \ldots, F(x_{12}^r || x_{13}^r) \oplus (x_{14}^r || x_{15}^r))$$

where P is a permutation applied on 4-bit nibbles and F is a non-linear function applied on 8-bit bytes. The sizes of F and P are carefully chosen so as to achieve good tradeoff between security and implementation costs on various platforms (including ASIC, x86/64, 8-bit AVR, etc.).

Permutation Choices. The choice of nibble-wise permutation P is essential for the security of extended GFS structure used in LLLWBC. In this part we explain several criterions of the permutation choices. First of all, following the observation of even-odd shuffle in [15], we also restrict the permutation P to be an active-passive shuffle, namely it maps an active input nibble to a passive output nibble and vice versa, where active nibble means a nibble going through F and passive nibble means the opposite case. This can make sure that every nibble will go through F once in two rounds. Secondly, divide the input nibbles into four groups as follows $(x_0, x_1, x_2, x_3)||(x_4, x_5, x_6, x_7)||(x_8, x_9, x_{10}, x_{11})||(x_{12}, x_{13}, x_{14}, x_{15})$, and the permutation P satisfies that it maps four nibbles from one group into four different groups respectively. Thirdly, the permutation P should achieve best full diffusion, namely each output bit is influenced by all the input bits in shortest rounds. We have searched all the possible permutations and obtained 1609728 candidates satisfying all the above requirements. On this basis, we further filter the candidate permutations based on the minimum number of active F in truncated differential/linear characteristics using MILP method. The nibble-wise permutation P used is one of the optimal permutations we found.

At last, we give a brief comparison of extended GFS with improved GFS and Type-2 GFS structures. For the sake of fairness, all the structures are under the same parameters of 8-branch GFS and 8-bit round function F. In Table 3, we list the security evaluation results including full diffusion round (DR_{max}), minimum number of active F for 20-round differential and linear trails (AF_D and AF_L), and the impossible differential and integral distinguishers (IDC and SC). We can see that extended GFS tends to achieve better diffusion and security appearances with a carefully chosen F ($S \circ \mathtt{MDS} \circ S$) at the expense of more costs.

Table 3. Comparison of security evaluation results.

`GFS with` $k = 8$ `branches`	`Source`	DR_{max}	AF_D	AF_L	IDC	SC
`Type-2 GFS`	[19]	8	27	27	17	16
`Improved GFS` (No.1*)	[15]	6	30	30	11	11
`Improved GFS` (No.2+)	[15]	6	26	26	10	11
`Extended GFS`	`This paper`	5	32	32	9	8

*: sub-block-wise shuffle $\tau = (3, 0, 1, 4, 7, 2, 5, 6)$
+: sub-block-wise shuffle $\tau = (3, 0, 7, 4, 5, 6, 1, 2)$

Moreover, in the implementation aspect, extended GFS shares the advantages of GFS-type structure. For example, the same procedure can be used in both encryption and decryption and there is no need to implement the inverse round function F^{-1}. The round function F is applied on small branch which is much easier to construct and cheaper to implement. Based on the active-passive property of nibble-wise permutation P, we can separate the active and passive nibbles to left and right half branches respectively, and get an equivalent structure which can be implemented efficiently in software. Furthermore, in order to preserve the α-reflection property of `LLLWBC`, we employ permutations P and P^{-1} instead of an involutory permutation which can not achieve optimal diffusion and security properties.

3.2 Round Function F

The round function F can be considered as an 8-bit non-linear S-box constructed by SPS structure. It consists of an S-box layer S, a linear layer A and a second S-box layer S. The S-box layer consists of two 4-bit S-boxes s in parallel and the linear layer A consists of matrix multiplication with a 2×2 MDS matrix over $GF(2^4)$. This is a commonly used method to generate 8-bit S-box with smaller 4-bit S-boxes, which can achieve good cryptographic properties and relatively low implementation costs.

The 4-Bit S-Box. Since two layers of 4-bit S-boxes are used in round function F, its area and critical path is a substantial part of the overall cost. However, as the cost of an S-box depends on various parameters, such as the technology, the synthesis tool, and the library used, it is very difficult to construct an optimal 4-bit S-box for all environments. Therefore, for a fair comparison, we apply the same 4-bit S-box used in PRINCE, which can achieve low-latency and small area cost. It also fulfills the optimal cryptographic properties such that its maximal differential probability is 1/4 and its maximal absolute linear bias is 1/4.

Linear Layer A. For the matrix multiplication in linear layer A, the 2×2 MDS matrix is carefully chosen so that its elements can be implemented efficiently by SHIFT and XOR operations. Moreover, the MDS matrix guarantees that the nibble-wise branch number of round function F is 3, namely except the zero difference there should be at least 3 non-zero nibbles for the input and output differences of F. This is crucial for the security analysis. Based on this property, the lower bound for minimum number of active F in nibble-wise truncated differential/linear characteristics can be improved significantly.

Overall speaking, the round function F provides a good tradeoff between security and implementation cost. It can be considered as an 8-bit S-box with maximal differential probability of $14/256 \approx 2^{-4.2}$, maximal absolute linear bias of 2^{-4}, algebraic degree of 6, and nibble-wise branch number of 3. In the implementation aspect, it can be decomposed to smaller 4-bit S-boxes based on the SPS construction. All the components can be implemented efficiently in hardware and in software the SIMD Vector Permutation Instruction ((v)pshufb) can be directly applied. It can also be precomputed and stored as an 8-bit S-box for 8-bit AVR implementation. Moreover, LLLWBC employs a kind of GFS-type structure where its inverse function F^{-1} is not needed.

3.3 Key Schedule

The key schedule of LLLWBC should be carefully designed in order to satisfy the α-reflection property. Similar to other low-latency ciphers such as PRINCE, MANTIS and QARMA, we simply employ the same method to generate the whitening keys used outside the core function. For round subkeys used in the core function, we alternately choose the upper and lower half of the 64-bit key $K_1||K_2$ in odd and even rounds. Since LLLWBC utilizes an extended GFS structure with odd number of rounds (resp. 21 rounds), together with a nibble-wise permutation P used in the first half rounds and P^{-1} used in the last half rounds, it can preserve the encryption and decryption symmetry property completely. Moreover, for even rounds, some special constants ck^r are XORed to the subkey K_2 so as to construct the α-reflection property. According to the construction of constants ck^r defined in Sect. 2.1, it can be seen that for the core function the decryption parameterized with $(K_1||K_2)$ is equal to the encryption parameterized with $(K_1||K_2 \oplus \alpha)$. Moreover, for the middle round (namely Round-11), the addition of subkey K_1 serves to prevent the reflection attacks which are particularly efficient against PRINCE-like ciphers [14].

From the aspect of implementation, the simple key schedule of LLLWBC is particularly beneficial to unified Enc and Dec circuits, because additional hardware is not required to construct the inverse key schedule. Moreover, the order of upper/lower half of keys used in successive rounds is exactly the same for encryption and decryption, thus no additional overhead is needed to implement decryption alongside the encryption. In addition, all the subkeys are directly obtained from the master key requiring no additional register to store and update the key, which is costly in terms of area and energy consumption.

4 Security Analysis

4.1 Differential Cryptanalysis

For differential cryptanalysis, the minimum number of active S-boxes for the differential trail is usually used to evaluate the security against differential attack. For LLLWBC, the round function F can be considered as an 8-bit S-box. Moreover, considering the extended GFS structure of LLLWBC, the non-linear round function F operates on 8-bit while the nibble-wise permutation P operates on 4-bit. Therefore, we have to search the minimum number of active F for the nibble-wise truncated differential characteristics.

In order to model the truncated differential characteristic more concisely, we analyze the difference propagation property of F. Based on the construction of F specified in Sect. 2.2, the linear layer A employs an MDS matrix whose branch number is 3. Therefore, if the input difference of F is non-zero, there should be at least 3 nibbles with non-zero difference for the input and output of F. Table 4 illustrates this propagation property in detail, where '0' denotes zero difference nibble and '1' denotes non-zero difference nibble.

In our nibble-wise truncated differential characteristics search program the above property is utilized. We have searched the lower bound of the number of active F with an MILP-aided search method. Table 5 shows the minimum number of active F (denoted as AF_D) for up to 21 rounds in the single-key setting. It can be observed that LLLWBC has more than 16 active F after 11 rounds. Since the maximum differential probability of F is $14/256 \approx 2^{-4.2}$, then the maximum probability of differential characteristics satisfies $DCP_{\max}^{11r} \leq 2^{16\times(-4.2)} = 2^{-67.2}$.

Table 4. Difference propagation property of round function F.

Input difference (ΔX_0, ΔX_1)	Output difference (ΔY_0, ΔY_1)
(0, 0)	(0, 0)
(0, 1)	(1, 1)
(1, 0)	(1, 1)
(1, 1)	(0, 1), (1, 0), (1, 1)

Table 5. The minimum number of active F for the differential trail.

Rounds	$\mathbf{AF_D}$	Rounds	$\mathbf{AF_D}$	Rounds	$\mathbf{AF_D}$
1	0	**8**	12	**15**	23
2	1	**9**	13	**16**	25
3	2	**10**	14	**17**	27
4	4	**11**	16	**18**	29
5	6	**12**	18	**19**	30
6	8	**13**	20	**20**	32
7	10	**14**	22	**21**	33

Moreover, since LLLWBC employs permutation P in the first 10 rounds and P^{-1} in the last 10 Rounds, we have also searched reduced rounds of LLLWBC starting from middle round with different combinations of permutations P and P^{-1}. Results of the minimum number of active F for all kinds of reduced 11-round LLLWBC are listed in Table 6. It can be seen that there are at least 16 active F and hence there is no useful differential characteristic for more than 11-round LLLWBC. Considering that LLLWBC requires 5-round to achieve full diffusion, we expect that there is no effective key-recovery attack and the full 21-round LLLWBC is secure against differential cryptanalysis.

4.2 Linear Cryptanalysis

Similar to the differential cryptanalysis, we have also evaluated the minimum number of active F by searching for nibble-wise truncated linear characteristics using MILP method. The linear approximation propagation property also holds for round function F, namely if the input linear mask of F is non-zero, there should be at least 3 nibbles with non-zero linear mask. The results show that the minimum number of active F are exactly the same for the linear and differential trails, and hence for all kinds of reduced rounds of LLLWBC there are at least 16 active F for the linear trail after 11 rounds. Since the maximum linear bias of F is 2^{-4}, the maximum bias of linear approximations for 11-round LLLWBC satisfies $LCP_{\max}^{11r} \leq 2^{16\times(-4)} = 2^{-64}$. As a result, there is no useful linear characteristic for more than 11-round and we expect that the full 21-round LLLWBC is secure against linear cryptanalysis.

Table 6. The minimum number of active F for all kinds of 11-round LLLWBC.

Starting round	# of P	# of P^{-1}	$\mathbf{AF_D}$
1	10	–	16
2	9	1	16
3	8	2	16
4	7	3	17
5	6	4	17
6	5	5	17
7	4	6	17
8	3	7	17
9	2	8	16
10	1	9	16
11	–	10	16

4.3 Impossible Differential Cryptanalysis

Impossible differential cryptanalysis is one of the most powerful techniques and its key point is to find an impossible differential distinguisher as long as possible. We have searched the longest impossible differential distinguisher of LLLWBC using MILP method. Specifically, we evaluate the search space such that the input difference and output difference are active only in one nibble, respectively. As a result, we find the best impossible differential distinguisher can reach up to 9 rounds and there are 14 different distinguishers. Take the following 9-round impossible differential as example, where zero difference is denoted as '0', non-zero difference as '$*$' and unknown difference as '?'.

$$(0,0,*,0,0,0,0,0,0,0,0,0,0,0,0,0) \rightarrow (*,0,0,0,0,0,0,0,0,0,0,0,0,0,0,0)$$

Choose the input difference ΔX_0 as $(0,0,*,0,0,0,0,0,0,0,0,0,0,0,0,0)$, with only the third nibble is active. Then after 4-round encryptions the output difference ΔX_4 should be $(?,?,0,0,?,*,*,*,*,*,*,*,*,*,0,*)$ with probability 1. On the other hand, set the output difference as $(*,0,0,0,0,0,0,0,0,0,0,0,0,0,0,0)$, and then after 4-round decryptions the output difference of $P^{-1}(\Delta X_5)$ should be $(*,?,0,0,*,*,0,*,*,*,*,*,?,?,*,*)$ with probability 1. Therefore, considering the first F in Round-5, there is a contradiction since its input difference is non-zero and its output difference is zero.

Similarly, since LLLWBC employs permutation P in the first 10 rounds and P^{-1} in the last 10 Rounds, we have also evaluated reduced rounds of LLLWBC starting from middle round with different combinations of P and P^{-1}. The best impossible differential distinguishers found are all 9-round. Therefore, considering that LLLWBC requires 5 rounds to achieve full diffusion, based on the above 9-round impossible differential distinguisher we expect that an effective key-recovery attack cannot reach up to full 21-round.

4.4 Integral Attack

Since LLLWBC is a nibble oriented block cipher, integral attack may also be one of the most powerful cryptanalytic methods. We define the notations of four integral states as follows: for a set of 2^n n-bit cell, C denoting a constant set (if $\forall i, j, i \neq j \Leftrightarrow x_i = x_j$), A denoting an active set (if $\forall i, j, i \neq j \Leftrightarrow x_i \neq x_j$), B denoting a balance set ($\oplus_i^{2^n-1} x_i = 0$), and U denoting the other cases. Note that the integral attack was further generalized to the division property by Todo, which can exploit some hidden features and find better integral distinguisher especially for ciphers with low algebraic degree. Considering that LLLWBC employs an 8-bit non-linear round function F with algebraic degree of 6, the division property search may be consuming and achieving limited benefit. Therefore, we search the traditional nibble-based integral property to evaluate the security of LLLWBC against integral attack roughly.

The nibble-based integral property propagation of LLLWBC are as follows.

$$\mathtt{C} \oplus \mathtt{S} = \mathtt{S},\ \mathtt{A} \oplus \mathtt{A} = \mathtt{B},\ \mathtt{A} \oplus \mathtt{B} = \mathtt{B},\ \mathtt{B} \oplus \mathtt{B} = \mathtt{B},\ \mathtt{U} \oplus \mathtt{S} = \mathtt{U},$$

$$F(\mathtt{C}||\mathtt{C}) = \mathtt{C}||\mathtt{C},\ F(\mathtt{C}||\mathtt{A}) = \mathtt{A}||\mathtt{A},\ F(\mathtt{A}||\mathtt{C}) = \mathtt{A}||\mathtt{A},$$

$$F(\mathtt{A}||\mathtt{A}) = \mathtt{U}||\mathtt{U},\ F(\mathtt{B}||\mathtt{S}) = \mathtt{U}||\mathtt{U},\ F(\mathtt{U}||\mathtt{S}) = \mathtt{U}||\mathtt{U}$$

where S denotes an arbitrary state. In this way, we give an 8-round integral distinguisher (CAAAACAACAAAAAAA) $\longrightarrow$ (UUBUUUBBUUBBUUBU). Namely, the set of plaintexts are chosen to be C in $j = (0, 5, 8)$-th nibble and A in all the other nibbles. Then after 8-round encryption, the set of ciphertexts should be B in $j = (2, 6, 7, 10, 11, 14)$-th nibble. Similarly, by traversing the positions of C in plaintexts, we can obtain other 8-round integral distinguisher and there are 16 different distinguishers in all.

Moreover, we have also evaluated reduced rounds of LLLWBC starting from middle round with different combinations of P and P^{-1}. The best integral distinguishers found are all 8-round. Therefore, considering that LLLWBC requires 5 rounds to achieve full diffusion, based on the above 8-round integral distinguisher we expect that a key-recovery attack cannot reach up to full 21-round.

4.5 Meet-in-the-Middle Attack

We evaluate the security of LLLWBC against δ-set meet-in-the-middle attack and the best distinguisher found is 6-round. Denote the input of j-th nibble as $x_j^r (j = 0, 1, \ldots, 15)$ and the input of k-th round function F as $y_k^r (k = 0, 1, \ldots, 3)$ for the r-th round. Choose a set of plaintexts active at nibble x_3^0, namely the δ-set contains 16 plaintexts $(M[0], M[1], \ldots, M[15])$ which traverse all the possible values at nibble x_3^0 and stay constants at all the other nibbles. Then after 6 rounds encryption, the difference sequence of the output sets at nibble x_2^6 can be fully determined by 6 bytes $(y_2^1[0], y_0^2[0], y_1^2[0], y_1^3[0], y_2^3[0], y_1^4[0])$. It means that there are 2^{48} possible values of $(x_2^6[0] \oplus x_2^6[1], x_2^6[0] \oplus x_2^6[2], ..., x_2^6[0] \oplus x_2^6[15])$, while for the random case there should be 2^{60} possible values. Therefore, we can construct a 6-round δ-set meet-in-the-middle distinguisher with filter probability of 2^{-12}. Based on this distinguisher, we can mount at most an 11-round meet-in-the-middle attack by adding two rounds before and three rounds after the distinguisher. Hence we can expect that the full 21-round LLLWBC is secure against meet-in-the-middle attack.

4.6 Other Attacks

Similar to other low-latency ciphers, we do not have security claims in related-key or known-key and chosen-key models. Therefore, related-key attacks should be out of consideration. Since differential attack seems to be the most effective technique according to the above evaluation results, we also evaluate some variants of differential attack such as boomerang attack. The result shows that the best boomerang distinguisher for LLLWBC should not exceed 10 rounds. At last, for the reflection attack, the main step is to find some fix points of the unkeyed central rounds. In the design of LLLWBC, extended GFS structure with special round permutations together with a novel key schedule are used to guarantee the α-reflection property, meanwhile the middle round also contains a round subkey addition. The keyed middle round helps to prevent this type of reflection attack because of the difficulty to find fix points and the impossibility to control the self-differentials when round subkey used in middle round is unknown.

5 Implementations

5.1 Hardware Implementation

Similar to other low-latency block ciphers, the fully unrolled hardware implementation performance should be considered as a major result. We use Xilinx ISE 14.7 for simulation and Synopsys Design Compiler for synthesis. The performance of LLLWBC in ENC/DEC mode has been synthesized in NanGate 45 nm Open Cell Library technology. The unrolled implementation of LLLWBC is a direct mapping to hardware based on the specification in Sect. 2.

The performance results of LLLWBC together with other low-latency block ciphers are listed in Table 7. All the ciphers are analyzed in ENC/DEC mode and the results of PRINCE, MANTIS and QARMA are provided by previous works. Obviously, the comparison is difficult since gate count and delay parameters are heavily technology dependent.

On the other hand, we also analyze the traditional round-based hardware implementation of LLLWBC and the performance results are listed in Table 8. We compare the results with available existing designs with the same parameter. Note that in the round-based version of PRINCE, symmetry around the middle should be kept and rounds are added in an inside-out fashion, i.e. its inverse is also added.

Table 7. Performance results of fully unrolled version of LLLWBC and other ciphers.

Cipher	Technology	Latency(ns)	Area(GE)	Source
LLLWBC	NanGate 45 nm Generic	11.76	8226.85	This paper
PRINCE	NanGate 45 nm Generic	–	8263	[6]
$MANTIS_7$	UMC L180 0.18 μm 1P6M	20.50	11209	[4]
$QARMA_7$	FinFet 7 nm	6.04	17109	[1]

Table 8. Performance results of round-based version of LLLWBC and PRINCE.

Cipher	Technology	Latency(ns)	Area(GE)	Source
LLLWBC	NanGate 45 nm Generic	0.64	1024.10	This paper
PRINCE	NanGate 45 nm Generic	–	3779	[6]

5.2 Software Implementation

On High-End Processors. LLLWBC can be implemented efficiently by the Single Instruction Multiple Data (SIMD) instruction commonly provided on modern high-end processors. For example, Intel and AMD CPUs both provide SSE/AVX2 instruction sets, which can support 128/256-bit registers and corresponding instructions. Specifically, the SIMD instruction Vector Permutation Instruction (VPI) (named `(v)pshufb` for Intel CPUs) can perform a vector permutation providing a look-up table representation of the permutation offsets. Therefore, both the 4-bit S-box and the nibble-wise permutations used in LLLWBC can be implemented directly using `(v)pshufb` instruction. Moreover, for the matrix multiplication used in the linear layer, the multiplication by 0×2 over $GF(2^4)$ can be pre-computed as a 4-bit look-up table and implemented by the `(v)pshufb` instruction too. Therefore, LLLWBC can be implemented efficiently in software by using only a few `(v)pxor` and `(v)pshufb` instructions.

We explain the software implementation of LLLWBC briefly as follows. First of all, an equivalent structure of LLLWBC is introduced. The input is rearranged into two branches, and the even (resp. odd) bytes are separated to the left (resp. right) half branch. Accordingly, the nibble-wise permutations P and P^{-1} are transformed into nibble-wise permutations PL, PR, PL^{-1} and PR^{-1} operating on left and right branches respectively. The contents of the equivalent nibble-wise permutations are listed in Table 9. Thc left (resp. right) branch is stored within one 128/256-bit register separately. Because of the byte-orientate character of the `(v)pshufb` instruction, in each byte of the register, only the lower 4 bits are used. Therefore, the plaintext and ciphertext should be packed and unpacked accordingly. Moreover, in order to make full use of the 128/256-bit register, for some parallelizable operating modes such as ECB and CTR, we can process double and even quadruple blocks in parallel using SSE/AVX2 instructions so as to achieve more performance benefit.

Table 9. Nibble-wise permutations used in equivalent structure of LLLWBC.

	$\{0,1\}^{32} \to \{0,1\}^{32}: \ (y_0, y_1, \dots y_7) \to (z_0, z_1, \dots z_7)$
PL	$z_0 = y_0,\ z_1 = y_6,\ z_2 = y_7,\ z_3 = y_1,\ z_4 = y_2,\ z_5 = y_5,\ z_6 = y_3,\ z_7 = y_4$
PR	$z_0 = y_2,\ z_1 = y_5,\ z_2 = y_4,\ z_3 = y_3,\ z_4 = y_1,\ z_5 = y_7,\ z_6 = y_0,\ z_7 = y_6$
PL^{-1}	$z_0 = y_0,\ z_1 = y_3,\ z_2 = y_4,\ z_3 = y_6,\ z_4 = y_7,\ z_5 = y_5,\ z_6 = y_1,\ z_7 = y_2$
PR^{-1}	$z_0 = y_6,\ z_1 = y_4,\ z_2 = y_0,\ z_3 = y_3,\ z_4 = y_2,\ z_5 = y_1,\ z_6 = y_7,\ z_7 = y_5$

We evaluate the software performance of LLLWBC on Intel Core I7-10700 CPU@2.90 GHz, 16.0 GB RAM, Windows 7 Pro 64-bit. We test the average encryption time (ENC) and decryption time (DEC) using 10000 samples of messages of a particular length in ECB mode. We present the benchmark results of our performance evaluation of LLLWBC with various length of messages in Table 10.

Table 10. Software performance of LLLWBC with various message length (Cycles/Byte).

|**M**| (Bytes)	2-block parallel SSE		4-block parallel AVX2	
	Enc	Dec	Enc	Dec
32	10.44	10.99	5.93	7.24
64	9.89	10.10	5.37	5.97
128	9.15	9.26	5.02	5.36
256	9.02	9.11	4.86	5.02
512	8.81	8.92	4.79	4.86
1024	8.76	8.81	4.70	4.73
2048	8.73	8.74	4.64	4.66
4096	8.65	8.66	4.60	4.61

On 8-Bit AVR Microcontrollers. We also evaluate the performances of LLLWBC on Atmel 8-bit AVR. Our test settings are similar to the commonly used benchmarking framework FELICS [9]. The target device is ATmega128 and the scenario is encryption/decryption of 128 bytes of data in CBC mode. The implementations are written in assembly and compiled in Atmel Studio 6.2. The performance results include code size (ROM), RAM usage (RAM), execution time (Cycles) and the speed (Cycles/Byte) of ENC (encryption including key schedule), DEC (decryption including key schedule) and ENC+DEC (encryption and decryption including key schedule).

The implementations can be directly obtained according to the cipher specification in Sect. 2. Note that, we can pre-compute and store the round function F as an 8-bit S-box to reduce the execution time significantly. For the nibble-wise permutation, it can be implemented efficiently by the assembly instructions `swap` and `andi`. For the low-latency design rationale, we first evaluate the fully unrolled implementation of LLLWBC. Then, in order to trade-off between ROM and Cycles, we evaluate a two-round unrolled implementation which consists of odd-round and even-round. We compare the differences introduced by storing the look-up table of 8-bit round function F and constants in RAM or ROM. We have analyzed different trade-offs between ROM/RAM/Cycles, and Table 11 summarizes the results in detail.

Table 11. Software performance results of LLLWBC on 8-bit AVR.

Unroll	Features	Function	ROM (Bytes)	RAM (Bytes)	Time (Cycles)	Speed (C/B)
Fully unrolled	8-bit Sbox and Const. in ROM	ENC	1820	0	34112	266.50
		DEC	1864	0	34544	269.88
		ENC+DEC	1990	0	68656	536.38
Fully unrolled	8-bit Sbox and Const. in RAM	ENC	1520	320	32286	252.23
		DEC	1564	320	32714	255.58
		ENC+DEC	1690	320	65000	507.81
Two-round	8-bit Sbox and Const. in ROM	ENC	1034	0	39812	311.03
		DEC	1058	0	40224	314.25
		ENC+DEC	1188	0	80036	625.28
Two-round	8-bit Sbox and Const. in RAM	ENC	650	320	37102	289.86
		DEC	674	320	37531	293.21
		ENC+DEC	804	320	74633	583.07

Moreover, we compare the representative performance results of LLLWBC with other low-latency block ciphers in Table 12. Available performance results of PRINCE are from https://www.cryptolux.org/index.php/FELICS. Note that the RAM required for storing the data to be processed, the master key, and the initialization vector are subtracted for consistence.

Table 12. Comparisons with other low-latency block cipher on 8-bit AVR.

Cipher	Function	ROM (Bytes)	RAM (Bytes)	Time (Cycles)
LLLWBC	ENC+DEC	1990	0	68656
LLLWBC	ENC+DEC	1690	320	65000
PRINCE	ENC+DEC	1930	205	300799

6 Conclusion

We have introduced a new low-latency block cipher called LLLWBC, whose block size is 64-bit and key size is 128-bit. LLLWBC employs a variant of generalized Feistel structure called extended GFS. It utilizes byte-wise round function and nibble-wise round permutations. The round permutations are carefully chosen together with a novel key schedule so as to satisfy the α-reflection property. The keyed middle round helps to prevent the reflection attack. A brief security evaluation of the cipher has been provided and we believe it can achieve enough security margin with the recommended number of rounds under the constraints of security claim. LLLWBC can achieve good performances on various platforms. Results show that LLLWBC is not only competitive in fully unrolled low-latency implementation, but also it can be implemented efficiently in traditional round-based architecture with a relatively small area. The software performances of LLLWBC on 8-bit microcontrollers and high-end processors are both very efficient. Moreover, the overhead for decryption on top of encryption is negligible.

Acknowledgements. This work is supported by the National Natural Science Foundation of China (No. 62072445), and National Cryptography Development Fund (MMJJ20180205). Moreover, the authors are very grateful to the anonymous referees for their comments and editorial suggestions.

Appendix

Test vectors of LLLWBC (in hexadecimal).

- **Plaintext**: `01 23 45 67 89 ab cd ef`
- **Key**: `01 23 45 67 89 ab cd ef fe dc ba 98 76 54 32 10`
- **Ciphertext**: `4d ac 97 75 8b 96 f3 83`

References

1. Avanzi, R.: The QARMA block cipher family. IACR Trans. Symmetric Cryptol. **2017**(1), 4–44 (2017)
2. Banik, S., Isobe, T., Liu, F., Minematsu, K., Sakamoto, K.: Orthros: a low-latency PRF. IACR Trans. Symmetric Cryptol. **2021**(1), 37–77 (2021)
3. Beaulieu, R., Shors, D., Smith, J., Treatman-Clark, S., Weeks, B., Wingers, L.: SIMON and SPECK: block ciphers for the internet of things (2015). https://eprint.iacr.org/2015/585
4. Beierle, C., et al.: The SKINNY family of block ciphers and its low-latency variant MANTIS. In: Robshaw, M., Katz, J. (eds.) CRYPTO 2016. LNCS, vol. 9815, pp. 123–153. Springer, Heidelberg (2016). https://doi.org/10.1007/978-3-662-53008-5_5
5. Bogdanov, A., et al.: PRESENT: an ultra-lightweight block cipher. In: Paillier, P., Verbauwhede, I. (eds.) CHES 2007. LNCS, vol. 4727, pp. 450–466. Springer, Heidelberg (2007). https://doi.org/10.1007/978-3-540-74735-2_31

6. Borghoff, J., et al.: PRINCE – a low-latency block cipher for pervasive computing applications. In: Wang, X., Sako, K. (eds.) ASIACRYPT 2012. LNCS, vol. 7658, pp. 208–225. Springer, Heidelberg (2012). https://doi.org/10.1007/978-3-642-34961-4_14
7. Božilov, D., et al.: PRINCEv2. In: Dunkelman, O., Jacobson, Jr., M.J., O'Flynn, C. (eds.) SAC 2020. LNCS, vol. 12804, pp. 483–511. Springer, Cham (2021). https://doi.org/10.1007/978-3-030-81652-0_19
8. De Cannière, C., Dunkelman, O., Knežević, M.: KATAN and KTANTAN — a family of small and efficient hardware-oriented block ciphers. In: Clavier, C., Gaj, K. (eds.) CHES 2009. LNCS, vol. 5747, pp. 272–288. Springer, Heidelberg (2009). https://doi.org/10.1007/978-3-642-04138-9_20
9. Dinu, D., Corre, Y.L., Khovratovich, D., Perrin, L., Groschadl, J., Biryukov, A.: FELICS - fair evaluation of lightweight cryptographic systems (2015). https://www.cryptolux.org/index.php/FELICS
10. Dobraunig, C., Eichlseder, M., Kales, D., Mendel, F.: Practical key-recovery attack on MANTIS5. IACR Trans. Symmetric Cryptol. **2016**(2), 248–260 (2016)
11. Leander, G., Moos, T., Moradi, A., Rasoolzadeh, S.: The SPEEDY family of block ciphers - engineering an ultra low-latency cipher from gate level for secure processor architectures. IACR Trans. Cryptograph. Hardware Embedded Syst. **2021**(4), 510–545 (2021)
12. NIST: Submission requirements and evaluation criteria for LWC standardization process. https://csrc.nist.gov/projects/lightweight-cryptography
13. Shibutani, K., Isobe, T., Hiwatari, H., Mitsuda, A., Akishita, T., Shirai, T.: *Piccolo*: an ultra-lightweight Blockcipher. In: Preneel, B., Takagi, T. (eds.) CHES 2011. LNCS, vol. 6917, pp. 342–357. Springer, Heidelberg (2011). https://doi.org/10.1007/978-3-642-23951-9_23
14. Soleimany, H., et al.: Reflection cryptanalysis of PRINCE-like ciphers. J. Cryptol. **28**(3), 718–744 (2015)
15. Suzaki, T., Minematsu, K.: Improving the generalized feistel. In: Hong, S., Iwata, T. (eds.) FSE 2010. LNCS, vol. 6147, pp. 19–39. Springer, Heidelberg (2010). https://doi.org/10.1007/978-3-642-13858-4_2
16. Suzaki, T., Minematsu, K., Morioka, S., Kobayashi, E.: *TWINE*: a lightweight block cipher for multiple platforms. In: Knudsen, L.R., Wu, H. (eds.) SAC 2012. LNCS, vol. 7707, pp. 339–354. Springer, Heidelberg (2013). https://doi.org/10.1007/978-3-642-35999-6_22
17. Wu, W., Zhang, L.: LBlock: a lightweight block cipher. In: Lopez, J., Tsudik, G. (eds.) ACNS 2011. LNCS, vol. 6715, pp. 327–344. Springer, Heidelberg (2011). https://doi.org/10.1007/978-3-642-21554-4_19
18. Zhang, W., Bao, Z., Lin, D., Rijmen, V., Yang, B., Verbauwhede, I.: RECTANGLE: a bit-slice ultra-lightweight block cipher suitable for multiple platforms. Sci. China Inf. Sci. **58**(122103), 1–15 (2015)
19. Zheng, Y., Matsumoto, T., Imai, H.: On the construction of block ciphers provably secure and not relying on any unproved hypotheses. In: Brassard, G. (ed.) CRYPTO 1989. LNCS, vol. 435, pp. 461–480. Springer, New York (1990). https://doi.org/10.1007/0-387-34805-0_42

New Automatic Search Tool for Searching for Impossible Differentials Using Undisturbed Bits

Weiwei Cao[1,2], Wentao Zhang[1,2](✉), and Chunning Zhou[1,2]

[1] State Key Laboratory of Information Security, Institute of Information Engineering, Chinese Academy of Sciences, Beijing, China
{caoweiwei,zhouchunnin}@iie.ac.cn

[2] School of Cyber Security, University of Chinese Academy of Sciences, Beijing, China
zhangwentao@iie.ac.cn

Abstract. Impossible differential cryptanalysis is a powerful tool for analyzing the security of symmetric-key primitives. At first, the attacker must finds some impossible differentials as long as possible. There are many tools to automatically search for the longest impossible differentials. In all of these search tools, the input and output differences are fixed before searching, which leads to some limitations. The first limitation is that the number of impossible differentials that can be found is very small. The second limitation is that the existing tools are ineffective in searching for truncated impossible differentials. For some symmetric-key primitives, these tools can only find short round truncated impossible differentials, and for others they can't even find truncated impossible differentials. As we all know, the number of impossible differentials is also very important because it can improve the data complexity and time complexity of impossible differential cryptanalysis in some cases. In addition, using truncated impossible differentials can usually get better results when impossible differentials are of the same length. In this paper, we propose a new automatic search tool that can overcome the above two limitations. The tool can not only find a large number of impossible differentials in a short time, but also can get truncated impossible differentials of bit-level primitives. It uses undisturbed differential bits, that is, the differential bits with probability 1 in differential propagation, and is based on mixed-integer linear programming (MILP) and meet-in-the-middle technology. We applied the tool to ASCON, SIMON, LBlock and LEA. For each of the four primitives, we found many new impossible differentials. For SIMON and LBlock, we found some related-key impossible differentials longer than the best-known results.

Keywords: Impossible differential · Undisturbed bits · MILP · ASCON · SIMON · LEA · LBlock · Automatic search tool

1 Introduction

Impossible differential cryptanalysis was first independently introduced by Biham et al. [6] to attack Skipjack and Knudsen [15] to attack DEAL. As a

Y. Deng and M. Yung (Eds.): Inscrypt 2022, LNCS 13837, pp. 43–63, 2023.
https://doi.org/10.1007/978-3-031-26553-2_3

variant of differential analysis, impossible differential cryptanalysis is not to use the differentials that occur in high probability but to use the differentials never occur. So one can use impossible differentials to discard some wrong keys because the differentials never occur under the right key. In impossible differential cryptanalysis, the first step is to find some impossible differentials as long as possible, and then use a sieving method to filter some wrong keys.

There are many tools to automatically search for impossible differentials, such as μ-Method [14], UID-Method [13] and WW-Method [24]. The above three search tools can only be used to search for truncated impossible differentials. Any input and output difference pairs of S-boxes are assumed to be possible in the search tools. This leads to the fact that some impossible differences are possible under these tools, so that the searched impossible differentials may be shorter than they actually are. To overcome the above limitations, Sasaki et al. [18] and Cui et al. [10] independently proposed a new tool based on the mixed-integer linear programmer(MILP) for searching for impossible differentials, it can be used to search for bit-level impossible differentials. The tool uses a MILP model to characterize the differential propagation of linear layer and S-boxes at the bit level, so longer impossible differentials can be found.

In the search tool of Sasaki et al. and Cui et al. [10,18], they firstly model the differential propagation of a symmetric-key primitive, then fix the values of input and output difference pair and then solve the model to test wether the given input-output difference pair is an impossible differential. In theory, if we can traverse all input-output difference pairs, we can find the longest impossible differential that exists in a symmetric-key primitive. However, this is not possible because it means that we need to solve 2^{2n} models, where n is the block size of the cipher. This is a very huge number, so we can only traverse a few input-output difference pairs. This leads to the following limitations.

The first limitation is that the number of impossible differentials that can be searched is very small. The number of impossible differentials can significantly improve impossible differential cryptanalysis in some cases. Take the impossible differential cryptanalysis [2] of SIMON as an example, the time complexity and data complexity of the attack are both inversely proportional to the number of impossible differentials, or as in paper [9], multiple impossible differentials can be used to reduce the amount of plaintext required. The second limitation is that the truncated impossible differentials found by this tool are short, or the tool cannot be used to search for truncated differentials for some symmetric primitives. Using truncated impossible differentials can usually get a better attack result since the probability of a plaintext(ciphertext) pair propagating to a truncated impossible differential is usually higher than that of a non-truncated impossible differential. Furthermore, in the search tools [10,18,24], it is hard to know whether it is the model's error or if there really is an impossible differential when the model is infeasible. It will take a lot of effort to verify.

For the related-key setting, searching for impossible differentials is more complex and time-consuming. Under the single-key setting, the difference of the key is set to zero, so we don't need to consider the key schedule. Under the related-key setting, we need to consider the key schedule, and the input and output difference space of traversal will also become larger. Generally, only a single active bit of input and output difference can be traversed. Also, if the key schedule is too complex, then the search time will become infeasible. As in searching for related-key impossible differentials of SIMON, Kondo et al. [16] concluded that *the tool* [18] *did not stop even for 13 rounds* to search for the related-key impossible differentials of SIMON32/64.

To overcome the above limitations, inspired by meet-in-the-middle technology, we propose a new tool to search for impossible differentials. This tool uses the MILP model to characterize the differential propagation with probability 1 of cipher primitives. The model of such differential propagation will be much simpler and the search efficiency will be much higher. Compared with the tool [10,18], a large number of impossible differentials can be searched in a short time and truncated impossible differentials of the bit-level cipher primitives can be searched by our tool.

Our Contributions. In the search of impossible differentials, meet-in-the-middle technology is one of the most important method. Many impossible differentials are found by this method. Based on the technology, we propose a new impossible differential search tool by characterizing the undisturbed differential bits in differential propagation with the MILP model in this paper. We first introduce in detail how to use the MILP model to characterize the propagation of undisturbed differential bits of XOR, S-box, modular addition and other operations. Then we use the tool to search for impossible differentials of ASCON [11], SIMON [4], LBlock [25] and LEA [12]. Our works are summarized as follows:

- **For ASCON.** In the paper [21], Tezcan et al. found 2^{63} 5-round impossible differentials of ASCON. However, we found that the impossible differentials they found are actually wrong. In this paper, we found 2^{161} new 5-round impossible differentials by using our tool.
- **For SIMON.** The current longest impossible differentials of SIMON32/48/64 /96/128 are 11, 12, 13, 16 and 19 rounds, respectively. Only a few impossible differentials can be found with tool [10,18]. Using our tool, although no longer impossible differentials were found, we found a lot of new impossible differentials and truncated impossible differentials. For the search of related-key settings, the best results at present are only the search of SIMON32/64 and SIMON48/96 [23]. It is very difficult to search for large versions. Using our tool, we found some new longer related-key impossible differentials of SIMON48/96, SIMON64/128 and SIMON128/256.
- **For LBlock.** In [10], Cui et al. found six 16-round related-key impossible differentials. Using our tool, we found a 17-round related-key impossible differential. This new related-key impossible differential holds on 2^{-2} key space.
- **For LEA.** The longest impossible differential is 10 rounds, which was found in [10] by Cui et al. They found only one impossible differential using the tool [10,18], we found six new 10-round impossible differentials using our tool.

All the search results obtained by our tool are shown in Table 1:

Paper Outline. In Sect. 2, we firstly detail how to characterize the propagation of undisturbed differential bits for operations such as XOR, S-box, AND, and modulo addition, and then introduce the framework of our tool to search for impossible differentials. In Sect. 3, we apply our tool to search for impossible differentials and related-key impossible differentials of four symmetric-key primitives ASCON, SIMON, LBlock and LEA. In Sect. 4, we conclude this paper.

Table 1. Summary of the results obtained by our tool

Type	Cipher	Round	Num. of Imp.diff.	Ref	Improve
Imp.diff.	ASCON	5	2^{63}	[21]	
		5	$\approx \mathbf{2^{161}}$**(64 T.ID.)**	Sect. 3.1	**Truncated and new Imp.diff.**
	SIMON32	11	48	[22]	
		11	**352**	Sect. 3.2	**Truncated and new Imp.diff.**
	SIMON48	12	360	[22]	
		12	**3072**	Sect. 3.2	**Truncated and new Imp.diff.**
	SIMON64	13	64	[9]	
		13	$\approx \mathbf{2^{24}}$**(64 T.ID.)**	Sect. 3.2	**Truncated and new Imp.diff.**
	SIMON96	16	768	[9]	
		16	$\approx \mathbf{2^{37.585}}$**(96 T.ID.)**	Sect. 3.2	**Truncated and new Imp.diff.**
	SIMON128	19	1024	[9]	
		19	$\approx \mathbf{2^{53}}$**(128 T.ID.)**	Sect. 3.2	**Truncated and new Imp.diff.**
	LEA	10	1	[10]	
		10	**6**	Sect. 3.4	**New Imp.diff.**
RK Imp.diff.	SIMON48/96	13	1	[23]	
		14	**1**	Sect. 3.2	**Longer**
	SIMON64/128	**14**	**1**	Sect. 3.2	**First Found**
	SIMON128/256	**20**	**6**	Sect. 3.2	**First Found**
	LBlock	16	6	[10]	
		17	**1**	Sect. 3.3	**Longer**

[a] All the results can be obtained within few hours with Intel(R) Core(TM) i7-6700 CPU @ 3.40 GHz.
[b] TID: Truncated impossible differential.
[c] (RK)Imp.diff.: (related-key) impossible differential.

2 The New Tool to Search for Impossible Differentials

In this section, we briefly introduce the principle of impossible differential search and clarify the search principle of our new search tool. Then we introduce and extend the definition of undisturbed differential bits and detail the model characterization of undisturbed differential bits for basic operations. Finally, we give the overall framework of our impossible differential search tool.

The Principle of Searching for Impossible Differentials. For a symmetric-key primitive, there is an input difference α and an output difference β of the cipher. All possible output differences can be propagated to after R_f-round encrypting for input α is a set $\mathbb{A}$. All possible input differences that can propagate to β after R_b-round encrypting is a set $\mathbb{B}$. If $\mathbb{A} \cap \mathbb{B} = \emptyset$, it means that the pair (α, β) is an impossible differential. In the previous search tools [10,14,17,18,24], the job of these tools is to search for the existence of $\mathbb{A} \cup \mathbb{B} = \emptyset$. From another point of view, the principle of searching for impossible differentials is if we already know the set $\mathbb{A}$ and the set $\mathbb{B}$ with $\mathbb{A} \cap \mathbb{B} = \emptyset$, all difference pairs that can only propagate to sets $\mathbb{A}$ and $\mathbb{B}$ respectively constitute a set of impossible differentials. The new search tool we proposed is based on the second principle.

In [20], Tezcan introduced the concept of undisturbed differential bits: for an S-box, when a specific difference is given to the input (resp. output), the bits that can be guessed with probability 1 of output can be characterized (resp. input) difference are called undisturbed differential bits. This is very important in the search for impossible differentials. However, it is impossible to use this definition to characterize the propagation of undisturbed differential bits with the MILP model. So we extend the concept of undisturbed differential bits.

Definition 1 (Undisturbed differential bits). *For a bit-oriented operation, the bits whose value in the output (resp. input) difference are constant under a certain input(resp. output) difference set are called undisturbed differential bits.*

Different from [20], our definition of undisturbed differential bits contains not only S-boxes but also all operation primitives. In addition, the undisturbed output differential bits are not only the bits with the probability of 1 under a specific input difference but also the bits with the probability of 1 in the output difference under a group of input differences.

Undisturbed differential bits are useful for search for impossible differentials. It is usually combined with meet-in-the-middle technology to search for impossible differentials. In some previous security analysis of symmetric cipher, the author designed a proprietary algorithm or used handwriting calculations to search for impossible differentials using the meet-in-the-middle technology, which makes the meet-in-the-middle technology not effective. So we proposed a generalized tool that combines MILP, undisturbed differential bits and meet-in-the-middle technology to search for impossible differentials.

When we consider undisturbed differential bits, one bit will have three values 0,1 and ? (unknown bit). So we use two variables to represent the value of a bit. There we agree to use (0,0), (0,1) and (1,1) to represent 0,1 and ? respectively.

In our MILP model, what is characterized is not the propagation of a single differential characteristic but the propagation of a set of differential characteristics. The propagation of the difference in a certain round can be expressed as $\Delta_{in} \rightarrow \Delta_{out}$. Assume that the actual set of output differences under the set of input differences Δ_{in} is Δ'_{out}, according to the definition of undisturbed differential bits, there are $\Delta'_{out} \in \Delta_{out}$. If the value of a bit in Δ_{out} is a definite 0 or 1, then the probability of all output differences under the input difference set Δ_{in} is 0 or 1 at the position of this bit is 1. Therefore, the principle of our MILP model searching for impossible differentials is: first, we establish two independent models M_0 and M_1 to characterize the differential propagation of the undisturbed differential bits of the encrypted part and the decrypted part, respectively. Then we assign contradictory values to one bit at the same positions in the output of the two models. According to the previous analysis, suppose that after assigning contradictory values to these two models, the sets of input differences obtained by solving are Δ_X and Δ_Y. We have $\Delta_X \nrightarrow \Delta_Y$. So we get a set of impossible differentials $\Delta_X \nrightarrow \Delta_Y$ by solving these two models.

2.1 Modeling Undisturbed Differential Bits Propagation of Basic Operations

For a symmetric-key primitive, the basic operations are usually XOR, AND, Modular addition, Permutation and S-box. Next, we will introduce the propagation of undisturbed differential bits of these operations one by one and the inequalities used to characterize the propagation of undisturbed differential bits.

Modeling XOR: When both input differences bits are determined values, the output difference is the exclusive OR of the input differences. When any bit of input difference is unknown, the output difference is unknown. All of these propagations hold with probability 1. Since each bit has three values, there are a total of 9 possible input difference for 2 bits. The input and output difference of the XOR operation is shown in Table 2.

Table 2. Undisturbed differential bits of XOR operation

Input difference	Output difference
00	0
01	1
0?	?
10	1
11	0
1?	?
?0	?
?1	?
??	?

We use two variables to represent 1 bit value, which are 0(0,0), 1(0,1) and ?(1,1). So the input and output difference of XOR can be represented by 6 variables. According to Table 2, there are 9 possible values of these 6 variables, which are (0, 0, 0, 0, 0, 0), (0, 0, 0, 1, 0, 1), (0, 0, 1, 1, 1, 1), (0, 1, 0, 0, 0, 1), (0, 1, 0, 1, 0, 0), (0, 1, 1, 1, 1, 1), (1, 1, 0, 0, 1, 1), (1, 1, 0, 1, 1, 1) and (1, 1, 1, 1, 1, 1). These points on F_2^6 can be represented by logical condition modeling in [1] to convert these points into a set of inequalities with 6 variables (x_0, x_1, x_2, x_3, x_4, x_5). Through the above steps, the input and output difference of XOR can be represented by the following set of inequalities.

$$\begin{cases} (0,1,0,-1,0,1)x+0\geq 0 \\ (0,-1,0,1,0,1)x+0\geq 0 \\ (0,0,-1,0,1,0)x+0\geq 0 \\ (-1,0,0,0,1,0)x+0\geq 0 \\ (0,1,0,1,0,-1)x+0\geq 0 \\ (-1,1,0,0,0,0)x+0\geq 0 \\ (0,0,-1,1,0,0)x+0\geq 0 \\ (1,0,1,0,-1,0)x+0\geq 0 \\ (0,0,0,0,-1,1)x+0\geq 0 \\ (0,-1,0,-1,1,-1)x+2\geq 0 \end{cases} \tag{1}$$

where $(0,1,0,-1,0,1)x+0\geq 0$ represents $x_1-x_3+x_5+0\geq 0$.

Modeling AND: When the input difference is (0,0), the output difference is 0. In other cases, the output differences are unknown (Table 3).

Table 3. Undisturbed differential bits of & operation

Input difference	Output difference
00	0
Others	?

The input and output difference of AND can be characterized by inequalities 2.

$$\begin{cases} (-1,1,0,0,0,0)x+0\geq 0 \\ (0,0,-1,1,0,0)x+0\geq 0 \\ (0,0,0,-1,0,1)x+0\geq 0 \\ (0,0,0,0,1,-1)x+0\geq 0 \\ (0,-1,0,0,0,1)x+0\geq 0 \\ (0,1,0,1,-1,0)x+0\geq 0 \end{cases}. \tag{2}$$

Modeling Modular Addition: For a modular addition operation $Y=A\boxplus B$, where $A=(a_n,\ldots,a_1), B=(b_n,\ldots,b_1), Y=(y_n,\ldots,y_1)$, a_n, b_n, c_n are MSB respectively. The modulo addition operation can be written as follows:

$$
\begin{aligned}
&y_1 = a_1 \oplus b_1,\ c_1 = f_1(a_1, b_1)\\
&y_2 = a_2 \oplus b_2 \oplus c_1,\ c_2 = f_2(a_2, b_2, c_1)\\
&\vdots\\
&y_{n-1} = a_{n-1} \oplus b_{n-1} \oplus c_{n-2},\ c_{n-1} = f_2(a_{n-1}, b_{n-1}, c_{n-2})\\
&y_n = a_n \oplus b_n \oplus c_{n-1}
\end{aligned}
\tag{3}
$$

Here c_i means carry, and f_1 and f_2 are non-linear functions. Their input and output differences are shown in Table 4 and Table 5:

Table 4. Undisturbed differential bits of f_1

Input difference	Output difference
00	0
Others	?

Table 5. Undisturbed differential bits of f_2

Input difference	Output difference
000	0
111	1
Others	?

According to Eq. 3, we can decompose the modulo addition operation into three small operations: XOR, f_1 and f_2. We can model these three operations separately when modeling the modulo addition operation. In differential propagation, since we regard these three operations as independent of each other and do not consider the correlation among them, the model will lead to some impossible differences that can be propagated in the model. This will cause us to search for fewer impossible differentials, that is, $\Delta \in \Delta'$, where Δ is the set of impossible differentials that the model can search for, and Δ' is all the impossible differentials of a block cipher with modulo addition. This ensures that the impossible differentials searched by our model built in this way are always correct.

Modeling S-box: Sun et al. [19] proposed the method of using Convex Hulls(CH) to characterize the difference/linear propagation of S-box in 2014. However, the method is not correct in some cases. In [3], the author finds there can be points outside set which also satisfy all the inequalities of the CH are generated from the set. We tested the model of undisturbed differential bits of some S-box and found that the inequalities of the CH are incorrect in all of them.

So we use the logical condition modeling proposed in [1] to model S-box. For more details, please refer to [1]. Since we use two variables to represent one bit, it means that we have to model a set of 4n-bit points for an n-bit S-box. When n is larger than 4, it is hard to compute the minimum set of linear inequalities of the logical condition modeling, such as the software Logic Friday supports up to 16 input variables while the input variable number is 20 when n is 5. So we use Property 1 to reduce the dimension of points.

Property 1. For a mapping $X \to Y$, $x \in X, y \in Y$. The binary representations of x and y are $(x_{n-1}, \cdots, x_0), (y_{n-1}, \cdots, y_0)$ respectively. Then y_i is independent of each other because y_i is only determined by x_i, and this mapping can be represented by $f_i((x_{n-1}, \cdots, x_0), y_i)$, Where f_i is a set of inequalities.

In the case of undisturbed differential bits only being considered, the difference distribution of an S-box is a mapping. This is to say, when the input difference is determined, the output difference is determined and unique. According to Property 1, we can model every output bit independently. This means that we can use several sets of inequalities that can be at least $2n + 1 = 11$ variables to characterize the undisturbed differential bit's propagation of a 5-bit S-box.

2.2 Framework for Impossible Differential Searches

Searching for the Longest Impossible Differentials. We firstly construct two set of models $(M0, M1)_i$, where M_0 is the model characterizing the propagation of undisturbed differential bits of the encryption part and M_1 is the model of decryption part. We agree that the input and output difference variables corresponding to a couple of given models $(M0, M1)_i$ are $(x_i,\ y_i)$ and $(x\prime_i,\ y\prime_i)$ respectively. The number of the longest rounds of (M_0, M_1) has undisturbed differential bits are R0 and R1 respectively. $constr1(a, x)$ represents the constraints of assigning value a to variables x, $constr2(a, x)$ represents the constraint that exclude value a of variables x. We use Algorithm 1 to search for the longest impossible differentials. The process of the Algorithm 1 is as follows:

Step 1. We use the variable "longestID" to store the number of rounds that we are currently searching for whether there is an impossible differential. The initial value of "longestID" is set to 2.

Step 2. Searching whether there is an impossible differential when the number of rounds is "longestID". Firstly, We fix the number of rounds r for M0 to 1; the number of rounds of M1 will be "longestID"-r. Then traverse the output variables at the same position of M0 and M1 and fix their values to contradictory values, respectively. If the two models have solutions simultaneously, it means that there is an impossible differential; otherwise, we increase the value of r until to "longestID"-1. Repeat the above steps; if M0 and M1 still do not have solutions at the same time, it means that there is no impossible differential.

Step 3. Increasing the value of "longestID" until all the positions are traversed and there is still no solution simultaneously, this indicates there is no impossible differential of "longestID"-round. So the longest impossible differential round number is "longestID"-1. See Algorithm 1 for more details.

Algorithm 1: Searching for longest impossible differential

```
1  Flag←1
2  longestID←2
3  while Flag=1 do
4      Flag=0
5      for r=1 to longestID-1 do
6          for index=0 to blocksize-1 do
7              Create encryption model M0_r and decryption model M1_{longestID-r}
8              for value=0 to 1 do
9                  Generate constraint constr1_0(y_index = value) and add it to M0_r
10                 Generate constraint constr1_1(y_index = value ⊕ 1) and add it to
                   M1_{longestID-r}
11                 if M0_r and M1_{longestID-r} both have solution then
12                     Flag←1
13                     longestID←longestID+1
14                     Goto line 3
15                 end
16                 else
17                     Remove constraint constr1_0 and constr1_1
18                 end
19             end
20         end
21     end
22 end
23 return longestID-1
```

Searching for All Longest Impossible Differentials. In impossible differential cryptanalysis, the more impossible differentials, the more likely we are able to reduce the data and time complexity of impossible differential attacks, and the more likely to attack for longer rounds. So we can use Algorithm 2 to search for as many impossible differentials as possible under a given number of rounds. When we search for all r-round impossible differentials. We first generate a set of models $(M0_1, M1_{r-1}), (M0_2, M1_{r-2}), \cdots, (M0_{r-1}, M1_1)$, then traverse the output variables y_i and y'_{r-i} of $M0_i$ and $M1_{r-i}$ and assign contradictory values to them. If $M0_i$ and $M1_{r-i}$ have solutions simultaneously and the corresponding input difference of $M0_i$ is `X`, it means that there is an impossible differential of r rounds under the input difference `X`. Then we use function `AlloutputID(X)` to search for all impossible differentials of round r under the input difference `X`. After we have searched out all the impossible output differences under the input difference `X`, then add the constraints constr1 to all model M0 to exclude the values we have searched in the following search.

`AlloutputID(X)`: We have known that the longest rounds of $M0$ and $M1$ have undisturbed differential bits are $R0$ and $R1$ respectively. Impossible differentials can only be existed in $(M0_{r-R1}, M1_{R1})$, $(M0_{r-R1+1}, M1_{R1-1})$, $\cdots$, $(M0_{R0}, M1_{r-R0})$. Firstly we generate a set of models $(M0_{r-R1}, M1_{R1})$, $(M0_{r-R1+1}, M1_{R1-1})$, $\cdots$, $(M0_{R0}, M1_{r-R0})$ and assign `X` to the input variables x_i of $M0_i$, then we traverse and fix the same positional variables of the output variables (y_i, y'_{r-i}) of $(M0_i, M1_{r-i})$ to contradictory values and solve the two models at the same time. If they both have solutions, the value of the input variables x'_{r-i} of $M1_{r-i}$ is X_{m1}, then $(\texttt{X}, X_{m1})$ is a pair of impossible differences. Then add the constraint $constr2$ to all model M1 to exclude X_{m1}. Repeat the above steps until $(M0_i, M1_{r-i})$ does not have a solution simultaneously, which means that we have found out all impossible output differences whose input difference is `X`. See Algorithm 2 for more details.

The Technique for Searching for as Many as Possible Impossible Differentials by Solving the Models Once. For many symmetric-key primitives, the number of impossible differentials is very large. It is impossible to search them all, so we can only search out part of them. Since we don't need to fix the value of the input and output differences, the input and output differences can be ?. This means the more ?, the more impossible differentials. If we solve the model once, the number of ? is b, it means that we can get 2^b impossible differentials at a time. We use an additional variable d_i to indicate whether a bit of input(resp output) difference is ?, if yes, $d_i = 1$, else $d_i = 0$. Two variables (x_0, x_1) representing a bit have the following relationship with d_i.

$$\begin{cases} x_0 \geqslant d_i \\ x_1 \geqslant d_i \\ x_0 + x_1 - d_i \leqslant 1 \end{cases} \tag{4}$$

To make the input and output differential bits have more ?, we only need to set an objective function:

$$obj = d_0 + d_1 +, \cdots, + d_{2n-1}$$

Searching for Related-Key Impossible Differentials. Under the single key settings, the models of the encryption part and the decryption part are independent, so we build the models of these two parts separately. Under the related-key settings, we need to build a model of key schedule, which connects the encryption part and the decryption part together, so the models of the encryption part and the decryption part are no longer independent, thus only one model needs to be used to characterize the differential propagation. After the differential propagation model is built, the output differences of the decryption part and the encryption part are set to contradictory values. If the model has a solution, there are at least one related-key impossible differential; if there is no solution, there are no related-key impossible differentials.

3 Applying the Tool to Four Primitives

In this section, we applied our search tool to four symmetric-key primitives ASCON, SIMON, LEA and LBlock. Under the single key settings, we searched for the impossible differentials of ASCON, SIMON, and LEA, and found many new impossible differentials. Under the related-key settings, we searched for the related-key impossible differentials of SIMON and LBlock, and found some longer related-key impossible differentials.

3.1 ASCON

ASCON was proposed by Dobraunig et al. [11]. Its mode of operation is based on duplex sponge modes like MonkeyDuplex [5]. The block size is 320 bits and is divided into five 64-bit word $x_0, \cdots, x_4$. The permutation p is an SPN-based round transformation using a 5-bit S-box and the bit XOR operation is used as linear layer. The permutation is composed as follows:

$$p = p_L \circ p_S \circ p_C$$

where p_C, p_S and p_L represent addition of constants, substitution layer and linear diffusion layer, respectively.

S-box of ASCON. The 5-bit S-box is shown in Table 6.

Tezcan [21] found 2^{63} 5-round impossible differentials using undisturbed differential bits. However, the impossible differentials he found were wrong because the output difference of the fourth row in S_4 after passing through linear layer should be "1110101101001000 0110011110111101110111001010100111000100001 00101" instead of "0110101101001000011 0011110111101110111001010100111000 010000100101", and he only considered the undisturbed differential bits under a single input difference of the S-box when searching. In our model, we consider the undisturbed differential bits of the S-box and inverse S-box, and then build two sets of models. By the solution of the models, we have found sixty-four 4.5-round truncated impossible differentials and there are no longer impossible differentials in our model; each truncated differential includes 2^{155} 5-round impossible differentials, a total number of 2^{161} 5-round impossible differentials.

Undisturbed Differential Bits of ASCON's S-box: There are many input differences that their output differences have undisturbed differential bits. They are shown in Table 7:

Undisturbed Differential Bits of Invert S-box of ASCON: When the input differences of the invert S-box of ASCON are (0,2,8), the output differences have undisturbed differential bits, and the output difference under the other input difference does not have undisturbed differential bits (Table 8).

One of 4.5-round truncated impossible differential:

Algorithm 2: Searching all impossible differentials

```
IDS← ϕ is a dict
INPUTDIFF← ϕ
for i = r − R_1 to R_0 do
    Generate i rounds model of encryption and r-i rounds model of decryption (M0, M1)_i
end
for index=0 to n-1 do
    for i=r-R_1 to R_0 do
        for each v in INPUTDIFF do
            Add constraints constr2(v, x) to M0_i
        end
        for value=0 to 1 do
            Add constraints constr1_1(y_i[index] = value, y'_i[index] = value ⊕ 1) to (M0, M1)_i
            while (M0, M1)_i both has solution and the value of x_i is X do
                IDS[X]← AlloutputID(X)
                Add constraints constr2(X,x_i) to M0_i
                INPUTDIFF← X
            end
            Remove constraint constr1_1
        end
    end
end

Function AlloutputID(X)
begin
    for i = r − R_1 to R_0 do
        Generate i rounds model of encryption and r-i rounds model of decryption (M0, M1)_i
    end
    ID← ϕ
    for i = r − R_1 to R_0 do
        Generate constraints of constr1_0(X,x_i) and add it to M0_i
        M0_i.optimize()
        The output difference of model M0_i is obtained as Y_m0
        for each v in ID do
            Generate constraints of constr2_0(v, x') and add to M1_i
        end
        for index=0 to n-1 do
            if Y_m0[index] ≠? then
                Add constraint constr1_1(Y_m0[index] ⊕ 1, y'_i[index]) to M1_i
                M1_i.optimize()
                while M1_i has solution and it's input difference is X_m1 do
                    Generate constraint of constr2_1(X_m1, x'_i) and add it to M1_i
                    ID.append(X_m1)
                end
                Remove constraint constr1_1
            end
        end
    end
    return ID
end
return IDS
```

Table 6. S-box of ASCON

x	0	1	2	3	4	5	6	7	8	9	10	11	12	13	14	15
S(x)	4	11	31	20	26	21	9	2	27	5	8	18	29	3	6	28
x	16	17	18	19	20	21	22	23	24	25	26	27	28	29	30	31
S(x)	30	19	7	14	0	13	17	24	26	12	1	25	22	10	15	23

Table 7. Undisturbed differential bits of ASCON's S-box

Input difference	Output difference	Input difference	Output difference
00000	00000	10011	0???0
00001	?1???	10100	0?1??
00010	1???1	10101	????1
00011	???0?	10110	1????
00100	??110	10111	????0
00101	1????	10?01	????1
00110	????1	10?11	????0
00111	0??1?	11000	??1??
00?00	????0	11100	??0??
00?10	????1	11110	?1???
01000	??11?	11111	?0???
01011	???1?	?0000	??0??
01100	??00?	?0100	??1??
01110	?0???	?1000	??1??
01111	?1?0?	?1100	??0??
10000	?10??	others	?????
10001	10??1		

$$000000000\alpha 000000000000000000000000000000000000000000000000000000 \overset{4.5r}{\nrightarrow}$$
$$??88??8?888?8??08?888???8???8????8888?888?8?8??8?08?8??8???88888$$

where $\alpha = 0\text{x}13$. ? indicates that this S-box can take any value. We can use the 4.5 rounds truncated impossible differentials to generate 2^{155} 5-round bit-oriented impossible differentials. We found 64 such truncated differentials in total, so we got 2^{161} bit-oriented impossible differentials.

3.2 SIMON

SIMON [4] is a family of lightweight block ciphers released by the National Security Agency (NSA) in June 2013. The design of SIMON is a classical Feistel structure. To optimize both hardware and software in mind, SIMON has only three operations: AND, left rotation, and XOR. The 2n-bit input is operated in each round and the input is divided into left and right halves. After passing the F function, the left half is XORed with the right half as the left half of the output. The right half of the output is the same as the left half of the input. The F function is defined as:

$$F(x) = (x \lll 8) \odot (x \lll 1) \oplus (x \lll 2)$$

Table 8. Undisturbed differential bits of invert S-box of ASCON

Input difference	Output difference
00000	00000
00010	???1?
01000	?1???
Others	?????

SIMON's key schedule is composed of linear feedback shift registers(LFSR). For different versions, its subkey generation algorithm is shown as follows:

$$k_{i+a} = \begin{cases} c \oplus (z_j)_i \oplus k_i \oplus (I \oplus S^{-1})S^{-3}k_{i+1} & \text{if a} = 2, \\ c \oplus (z_j)_i \oplus k_i \oplus (I \oplus S^{-1})S^{-3}k_{i+2} & \text{if a} = 3, \\ c \oplus (z_j)_i \oplus k_i \oplus (I \oplus S^{-1})(S^{-3}k_{i+3} \oplus k_{i+1}) & \text{if a} = 4. \end{cases}$$

where $a = (n/m) \times 2$ and the corresponding version is SIMONn/m. c is a constant and $(z_j)_i$ is generated from a known sequence.

For SIMON, bit-oriented impossible differentials are much longer than word-oriented impossible differentials. Under single-key settings, all versions of SIMON have at least 2n impossible differentials in round lengths of 11, 12, 13, 16, 19 (respectively corresponded to n = 16, 24, 32, 48, 64). In [22], Wang et al. found 48 and 360 impossible differentials of SIMON32 and SIMON48, respectively. In our work, we build MILP models for encryption and decryption parts with rounds R_0 and R_1, respectively. Then assign contradictory values to the output differences of these two models and solve the two models. If both models have solutions at the same time, then we have found a $(R_0 + R_1)$-round impossible differentials. In order to find more impossible differentials at a time, we follow the method described in Sect. 2.2, adding an extra variable d_i and setting a objective function. Finally, We did not find longer differentials than the best-known, but we found a large number of new impossible differentials. Some of them are shown in Table 9.

Under the setting of the related-key, it is difficult to search with the tool [10,18], because the key schedule of SIMON is linear and relatively complex, which leads to a long solution time. The best related-key impossible differentials searched at present are Kondo et al. [16] find some 15-round related-key impossible differentials of SIMON32/64 by using iterative key difference, and Wang et al. [23]. find some 13-round related-key impossible differentials of SIMON48/96 by using MILP model. Using our tool, we did not find longer related-key impossible differential for SIMON32/64, while found some (14,14,20)-round related-key impossible differentials of SIMON48/96, SIMON64/128 and SIMON128/256, respectively. The related-key impossible differentials of SIMON48/96 and SIMON64/128 are shown in Table 10 and Table 11.

Table 9. Some impossible differentials of SIMON

Cipher	Num. of Imp.diff.	ID
SIMON32	1	00000000000000000100000000000001 $\overset{r11}{\nrightarrow}$ 00000000000000000100000010000001
SIMON48	1	000000000000000000000000000000000000000001000000 $\overset{r12}{\nrightarrow}$ 000000000000000001000000000000000101000111100000
SIMON64	2^{18}	00^{22}000000000000000000000000000000000000001 $\overset{r13}{\nrightarrow}$?0^{22}?0?000???0?0000001000000?0?000???00?????
SIMON96	2^{31}	0^{94}10 $\overset{r16}{\nrightarrow}$ 0^{28}?0?000???00?????0?0^{21}?0?000???00?????0????????01
SIMON128	2^{46}	0^{124}1000 $\overset{r19}{\nrightarrow}$ 0^{34}?0?000???00?????0????????0^{30}?0?000???00?????0???????????????1?000

Table 10. 14-round related-key impossible differential of SIMON48/96

Impossible difference	SubKey
0000000000000000000000000000100011000?1010000100 $\nrightarrow$	0x08C2840118000A48010D9D38
011111000110010000100000000000000000000000000000	

Table 11. 14-Round related-key impossible differential of SIMON64/128

Impossible difference	SubKey
0000000000000000000000000000000011101011111110011111111110011000 $\nrightarrow$	0xBBF9FF9840000010902050E66081861E
1001111000100110001011011010010100010000000000000000000000000000	

3.3 LBlock

LBlock is a lightweight block cipher proposed by Wu and Zhang [25]. Its block size and key size are 64 and 80 bits, respectively. The structure of LBlock is a 32-round classical Feistel structure. In the round function, the plaintext is divided into left and right parts in the round function. Firstly, the left half is XORed with the round subkey and then through eight different S-boxes, and then through a nibble permutation. Finally, the left half is XORed with the right half that has been rotated left by 8 bits.

The key schedule is simple. The master key is 80 bits and denoted by $K = k_{79}, k_{78}, \cdots, k_0$. The leftmost 32 bits of the master key are used as the subkey sk_0 of the first round, and the generation of the remaining subkey sk_i is shown in Algorithm 3.

Under the related-key setting, the current best search result is Cui et al.'s search for the related-key impossible differentials in [10]. They found six 16-round related-key impossible differentials by using the MILP model. In our search, two different modeling approaches were used to search for the related-key impossible

Algorithm 3: Key Schedule of LBlock Cipher

```
sk_0 = K_{79~48};
for 1 ≤ i ≤ 31 do
    k_{79~0} ← k_{79~0} ⋘ 29;
    k_{79~76} ← S_9(k_{79~76}); k_{75~72} ← S_8(k_{75~72});
    k_{50~47} ← k_{50~47} ⊕ [i]_2;
    sk_i ← k_{79~48};
end
```

differentials of LBlock. One is that the model of the key schedule is a model that characterizes the propagation of undisturbed differential bits. Using this method, as long as the model has a solution, the impossible differentials found must exist in the entire key space. We searched for some 16 rounds of related-key impossible differentials using this approach. Another way is that the model of the key schedule is a model that characterizes differential propagation. Using this method, when the model has a solution, the impossible differentials found may not necessarily hold over the entire key space. Finally, we found a new 17-round related-key impossible differentials holds on 2^{-2} key space. It is one round longer than Cui et al.'s [10], as shown in Table 12.

Table 12. 17-Round related-key impossible differential of LBlock

Rounds	Left	Right	Subkey
0	0000 0000 0000 0000 0000 0000 0000 0000	0000 0000 0000 0000 0000 0011 0000 0000	00000000
1	0000 0000 0000 0011 0000 0000 0000 0000	0000 0000 0000 0000 0000 0000 0000 0000	00030000
2	0000 0000 0000 0000 0000 0000 0000 0000	0000 0000 0000 0011 0000 0000 0000 0000	00000000
3	0000 0011 0000 0000 0000 0000 0000 0000	0000 0000 0000 0000 0000 0000 0000 0000	00000000
4	??01 0000 0000 0000 0000 0000 0000 0000	0000 0011 0000 0000 0000 0000 0000 0000	01800000
5	??1? 0000 ???? ?1?? 0000 0000 0000 0011	??01 0000 0000 0000 0000 0000 0000 0000	00000000
6	0000 ???? ???? ???? 0000 ??10 ??01 0000	??1? 0000 ???? ?1?? 0000 0000 0000 0011	00000006
7	???? ???? 0000 ???? ???? ???? ??1? ????	0000 ???? ???? ???? 0000 ??10 ??01 0000	?0000000
8	???? ???? ???? ??10 ???? ???? ???? ????	???? ???? 0000 ???? ???? ???? ??1? ????	00000000
9	???? ???? ???? ???? ???? ???? ???? ????	???? ???? ???? ??**1**0 ???? ???? ???? ????	
9	???? 0000 ???? 0000 ???? ???? ???? 0000	???? ???? ???? ??**0**1 ???? ???? ???? 0000	
10	???? ??01 ?1?0 0000 ???? 0000 0000 0000	???? 0000 ???? 0000 ???? ???? ???? 0000	$00000\alpha\beta0$
11	???? 0000 0000 0000 ???? 0000 0011 0000	???? ??01 ?1?0 0000 ???? 0000 0000 0000	00000000
12	?1?0 0000 0000 0000 0000 0000 0000 0000	???? 0000 0000 0000 ???? 0000 0011 0000	00000000
13	0000 0000 0000 0000 0011 0000 0000 0000	?1?0 0000 0000 0000 0000 0000 0000 0000	$0000\gamma\delta000$
14	0000 0000 0000 0000 0000 0000 0000 0000	0000 0000 0000 0000 0011 0000 0000 0000	00000000
15	0000 0000 0011 0000 0000 0000 0000 0000	0000 0000 0000 0000 0000 0000 0000 0000	00000000
16	0000 0000 0000 0000 0000 0000 0000 0000	0000 0000 0011 0000 0000 0000 0000 0000	00?00000
17	0011 0000 0000 0000 0000 0000 0000 0000	0000 0000 0000 0000 0000 0000 0000 0000	00000000

Where $\alpha \in \{0, 1, 2, 3\}$, $\beta \in \{0, 4, 8, 12\}$, $\gamma \in \{0, 1\}$, $\delta \in \{0, 2, 4, 6, 8, 10, 12, 14\}$.

3.4 LEA

LEA is a lightweight cipher proposed by Hong et al. [12], its block size is 128 bits, and the key size has three versions of 128,192 and 256 bits. According to different key sizes, the number of rounds is 24, 28 and 32, respectively. The input of LEA is divided into four 32-bit words, and these words are outputted after XORed with the round subkey, modulated and cyclic shift. The operation of the round function is shown in Fig. 1, where ROL_i and ROR_j means the left rotation of 32-bit value by i-bit and right rotation of 32-bit value by j-bit, respectively. In [10], the author did not find any new impossible differentials using the MILP model. This is because, for the block cipher of the ARX structure, the longest impossible differentials may not be the case where the number of active bits is 1. Since the input and output differences need to be determined before the search, if the input and output active bits are more than 2, it is almost impossible to complete the search. Using our tool, as mentioned earlier, the search is more advantageous because the values of the input and output differences are not to be fixed. We first build the propagation model of the undisturbed differential bits of the encryption part and the decryption part, and then use Algorithm 2 to search for all impossible differentials. Finally, six new 10-round impossible differentials are found. They are shown as follows:

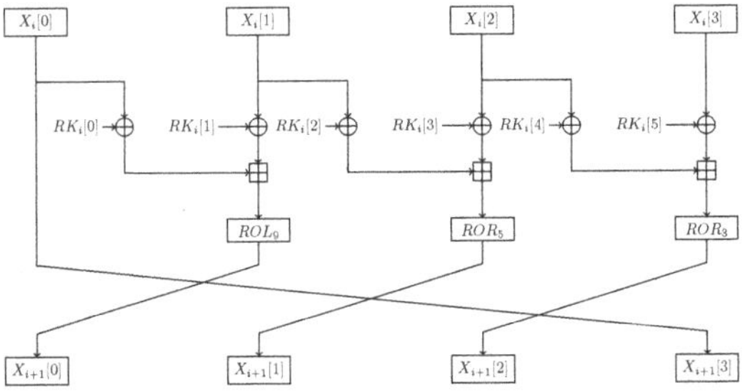

Fig. 1. The LEA round function

$$\mathrm{ID0}: 10^{31}10^{31}10^{31} \nrightarrow 0^{68}10^{59} \quad \mathrm{ID1}: 10^{31}10^{31}10^{31} \nrightarrow 0^{67}110^{59}$$
$$\mathrm{ID2}: 10^{31}10^{31}10^{31} \nrightarrow 0^{69}10^{58} \quad \mathrm{ID3}: 10^{31}10^{31}10^{31} \nrightarrow 0^{67}1110^{58}$$
$$\mathrm{ID4}: 10^{31}10^{31}10^{31} \nrightarrow 0^{68}110^{58} \quad \mathrm{ID5}: 10^{31}10^{31}10^{31} \nrightarrow 0^{67}1010^{58}$$

4 Conclusion

In this paper, we proposed a new tool for searching impossible differentials. This tool can find more impossible differentials, which can improve impossible differential attacks. Besides, this tool has a faster search speed than the previous tools and can output where there are contradictions, eliminating the process of manual checking. It is greatly reducing the workload. Then, we applied the tool to search for impossible differentials of ASCON, SIMON, LEA and related-key impossible differentials of SIMON and LBlock. Under the single key settings, we found many new impossible differentials. For SIMON and LBlock, we found some related-key impossible differentials longer than the best-known result.

Due to the duality of zero-correlation linear attacks and impossible differential attacks, our tool can also be used to search for zero-correlation linear approximations. In zero-correlation linear attacks, multiple zero-correlation cryptanalysis [8] and multidimensional zero-correlation cryptanalysis [7] can reduce the amount of data required. However, using the previous search tools, the number of zero-correlation linear approximations can be searched for the symmetric-key primitives that linear layer is bit-oriented is very small, and it is difficult to apply multiple zero-correlation cryptanalysis and multidimensional zero-correlation cryptanalysis to these symmetric-key primitives. Using the tool we proposed, we can search for more zero-correlation linear approximations, thus extending the multiple zero-correlation cryptanalysis and multidimensional zero-correlation cryptanalysis to this type of symmetric-key primitives. This can improve the zero-correlation linear cryptanalysis for some symmetric-key primitives.

Acknowledgements. The authors would like to thank the anonymous reviewers for their helpful comments and suggestions. This work was supported by the National Natural Science Foundation of China (Grant No. 61379138).

References

1. Abdelkhalek, A., Sasaki, Y., Todo, Y., Tolba, M., Youssef, A.M.: MILP modeling for (large) s-boxes to optimize probability of differential characteristics. IACR Trans. Symmetric Cryptol. **2017**(4), 99–129 (2017)
2. Alkhzaimi, H., Lauridsen, M.: Cryptanalysis of the simon family of block ciphers. IACR Cryptology ePrint Archive (2013)
3. Baksi, A.: New insights on differential and linear bounds using mixed integer linear programming. In: Maimut, D., Oprina, A.-G., Sauveron, D. (eds.) SecITC 2020. LNCS, vol. 12596, pp. 41–54. Springer, Cham (2021). https://doi.org/10.1007/978-3-030-69255-1_4
4. Beaulieu, R., Shors, D., Smith, J., Treatman-Clark, S., Weeks, B., Wingers, L.: The SIMON and SPECK lightweight block ciphers. In: 2015 52nd ACM/EDAC/IEEE Design Automation Conference (DAC), pp. 1–6. IEEE (2015)
5. Bertoni, G., Daemen, J., Peeters, M., Van Assche, G.: Permutation-based encryption, authentication and authenticated encryption. In: Directions in Authenticated Ciphers, pp. 159–170 (2012)
6. Biham, E., Biryukov, A., Shamir, A.: Cryptanalysis of skipjack reduced to 31 rounds using impossible differentials. In: Stern, J. (ed.) EUROCRYPT 1999. LNCS, vol. 1592, pp. 12–23. Springer, Heidelberg (1999). https://doi.org/10.1007/3-540-48910-X_2
7. Bogdanov, A., Leander, G., Nyberg, K., Wang, M.: Integral and multidimensional linear distinguishers with correlation zero. In: Wang, X., Sako, K. (eds.)

ASIACRYPT 2012. LNCS, vol. 7658, pp. 244–261. Springer, Heidelberg (2012). https://doi.org/10.1007/978-3-642-34961-4_16

8. Bogdanov, A., Wang, M.: Zero correlation linear cryptanalysis with reduced data complexity. In: Canteaut, A. (ed.) FSE 2012. LNCS, vol. 7549, pp. 29–48. Springer, Heidelberg (2012). https://doi.org/10.1007/978-3-642-34047-5_3
9. Boura, C., Naya-Plasencia, M., Suder, V.: Scrutinizing and improving impossible differential attacks: applications to CLEFIA, camellia, LBlock and SIMON. In: Sarkar, P., Iwata, T. (eds.) ASIACRYPT 2014. LNCS, vol. 8873, pp. 179–199. Springer, Heidelberg (2014). https://doi.org/10.1007/978-3-662-45611-8_10
10. Tingting, C.U.I., Shiyao, C.H.E.N., Kai, F.U., Meiqin, W.A.N.G., Keting, J.I.A.: New automatic tool for finding impossible differentials and zero-correlation linear approximations. Inf. Sci. **64**(129103), 1–129103 (2021)
11. Dobraunig, C., Eichlseder, M., Mendel, F., Schläffer, M.: Ascon v1. 2. Submission to the CAESAR Competition (2016)
12. Hong, D., Lee, J., Kim, D., Kwon, D., Ryu, K.H., Lee, D.: LEA: a 128-bit block cipher for fast encryption on common processors. In: Workshop on Information Security Applications, pp. 3–27 (2013)
13. Hong, D., et al.: HIGHT: a new block cipher suitable for low-resource device. In: Goubin, L., Matsui, M. (eds.) CHES 2006. LNCS, vol. 4249, pp. 46–59. Springer, Heidelberg (2006). https://doi.org/10.1007/11894063 4
14. Kim, J., Hong, S., Sung, J., Lee, S., Lim, J., Sung, S.: Impossible differential cryptanalysis for block cipher structures. In: Johansson, T., Maitra, S. (eds.) INDOCRYPT 2003. LNCS, vol. 2904, pp. 82–96. Springer, Heidelberg (2003). https://doi.org/10.1007/978-3-540-24582-7_6
15. Knudsen, L.: Deal-a 128-bit block cipher. Complexity **258**(2), 216 (1998)
16. Kondo, K., Sasaki, Yu., Todo, Y., Iwata, T.: Analyzing key schedule of SIMON: iterative key differences and application to related-key impossible differentials. In: Obana, S., Chida, K. (eds.) IWSEC 2017. LNCS, vol. 10418, pp. 141–158. Springer, Cham (2017). https://doi.org/10.1007/978-3-319-64200-0_9
17. Luo, Y., Wu, Z., Lai, X., Gong, G.: Unified impossible differential cryptanalysis on block cipher structures. Report, Cryptology ePrint Archive, Report 2009/627 (2009)
18. Sasaki, Yu., Todo, Y.: New impossible differential search tool from design and cryptanalysis aspects. In: Coron, J.-S., Nielsen, J.B. (eds.) EUROCRYPT 2017. LNCS, vol. 10212, pp. 185–215. Springer, Cham (2017). https://doi.org/10.1007/978-3-319-56617-7_7
19. Sun, S., Hu, L., Wang, P., Qiao, K., Ma, X., Song, L.: Automatic security evaluation and (related-key) differential characteristic search: application to SIMON, PRESENT, LBlock, DES(L) and other bit-oriented block ciphers. In: Sarkar, P., Iwata, T. (eds.) ASIACRYPT 2014. LNCS, vol. 8873, pp. 158–178. Springer, Heidelberg (2014). https://doi.org/10.1007/978-3-662-45611-8_9
20. Tezcan, C.: Improbable differential attacks on present using undisturbed bits. J. Comput. Appl. Math. **259**, 503–511 (2014)
21. Tezcan, C.: Truncated, impossible, and improbable differential analysis of ASCON. In: Camp, O., Furnell, S., Mori, P. (eds.) Proceedings of the 2nd International Conference on Information Systems Security and Privacy, ICISSP 2016, Rome, Italy, 19–21 February 2016, pp. 325–332. SciTePress (2016)
22. Wang, Q., Liu, Z., Varıcı, K., Sasaki, Yu., Rijmen, V., Todo, Y.: Cryptanalysis of reduced-round SIMON32 and SIMON48. In: Meier, W., Mukhopadhyay, D. (eds.) INDOCRYPT 2014. LNCS, vol. 8885, pp. 143–160. Springer, Cham (2014). https://doi.org/10.1007/978-3-319-13039-2_9

23. Wang, X., Baofeng, W., Hou, L., Lin, D.: Searching for related-key impossible differentials for SIMON. J. Cryptol. Res. **8**(5), 881–893 (2021)
24. Wu, S., Wang, M.: Automatic search of truncated impossible differentials for word-oriented block ciphers. In: Galbraith, S., Nandi, M. (eds.) INDOCRYPT 2012. LNCS, vol. 7668, pp. 283–302. Springer, Heidelberg (2012). https://doi.org/10.1007/978-3-642-34931-7_17
25. Wu, W., Zhang, L.: LBlock: a lightweight block cipher. In: Lopez, J., Tsudik, G. (eds.) ACNS 2011. LNCS, vol. 6715, pp. 327–344. Springer, Heidelberg (2011). https://doi.org/10.1007/978-3-642-21554-4_19

Public Key Encryption & Signature

You Can Sign but Not Decrypt: Hierarchical Integrated Encryption and Signature

Min Zhang[1,2,3,4,5], Binbin Tu[1,2,3,4,5], and Yu Chen[1,2,3,4,5](✉)

[1] School of Cyber Science and Technology, Shandong University, Qingdao 266237, China
{zm_min,tubinbin}@mail.sdu.edu.cn, yuchen@sdu.edu.cn
[2] State Key Laboratory of Cryptology, P.O. Box 5159, Beijing 100878, China
[3] Key Laboratory of Cryptologic Technology and Information Security of Ministry of Education, Shandong University, Qingdao 266237, China
[4] Quancheng Laboratory, Jinan 250103, China
[5] Shandong Institute of Block-chain, Jinan 250101, China

Abstract. Recently, Chen et al. (ASIACRYPT 2021) introduced a notion called hierarchical integrated signature and encryption (HISE), which provides a new principle for combining public key schemes. It uses a single public key for both signature and encryption schemes, and one can derive a decryption key from the signing key but not vice versa. Whereas, they left the dual notion where the signing key can be derived from the decryption key as an open problem.

In this paper, we resolve the problem by formalizing the notion called hierarchical integrated encryption and signature (HIES). Similar to HISE, it features a unique public key for both encryption and signature components and has a two-level key derivation mechanism, but reverses the hierarchy between signing key and decryption key, i.e. one can derive a signing key from the decryption key but not vice versa. This property enables secure delegation of signing capacity in the public key reuse setting. We present a generic construction of HIES from constrained identity-based encryption. Furthermore, we instantiate our generic HIES construction and implement it. The experimental result demonstrates that our HIES scheme is comparable to the best Cartesian product combined public-key scheme in terms of efficiency, and is superior in having richer functionality as well as retaining merits of key reuse.

Keywords: Hierarchical integrated signature and encryption · Hierarchical identity-based encryption · Key delegation

1 Introduction

Combined usage of public key schemes is a practically relevant topic in the context of public key cryptography, especially combining public key encryption (PKE) and signature schemes. In many real-word applications, the two primitives

Y. Deng and M. Yung (Eds.): Inscrypt 2022, LNCS 13837, pp. 67–86, 2023.
https://doi.org/10.1007/978-3-031-26553-2_4

are commonly used in combination to guarantee confidentiality and authenticity simultaneously, such as secure communication software (like PGP [2], WhatsApp [5]) and privacy-preserving cryptocurrency (like Zether [10], PGC [13]).

Typically, there are two principles for combining these two schemes, *key separation* and *key reuse*, each of which has its own strengths and weaknesses. Key separation, which means using two independent key pairs for two schemes, supports secure escrow[1] for both signing key and decryption key, while the key management and certificate costs[2] are doubled. Key reuse, which means using a unique key pair for both PKE and signature schemes, can reduce key management and certificate costs, but it does not support secure key escrow, and its joint security is not immediate.

Recently, Chen et al. [14] proposed a new notion called *hierarchical integrated signature and encryption* (HISE), which strikes a sweet balance between key separation and key reuse. It employs a single public key for both encryption and signature schemes, and allows one to derive a decryption key from signing key. This feature gives HISE advantages that (i) key management and certificate costs are reduced by half and (ii) secure delegation of decryption capacity is admitted.

Nevertheless, since the signing key is regarded as the master key in HISE, it is not applicable to some scenarios such as where one wants to delegate his signing capacity while retaining his decryption capacity. Chen et al. remarked that it is possible to consider a dual version of HISE, and it could be useful in scenarios where decryption capability is a first priority. However, they did not give the formal definition, construction and applications of it, and left it as an open problem. Therefore, the motivation for this work is two-fold: (i) find a proper key usage strategy for scenarios where key management costs are desired to be cheap, and signature delegation is needed; (ii) solve the open problem left in [14], and complete the key usage strategies.

1.1 Our Contributions

In this work, we resolve the open problem in [14] and our contributions can be summarized as follows:

Formal Definition of HIES. We start off by formalizing the definition and the joint security of the dual notion of HISE, called hierarchical integrated encryption and signature (HIES). It allows one to derive a signing key from the decryption key, such that secure delegation of signature capacity is allowed. In terms of joint security, the PKE component is IND-CCA secure even when the adversary is given the signing key and the signature component is EUF-CMA secure in the presence of an additional decryption oracle.

---

[1] Key escrow means that the owner delegates his decryption/signing capacity to the escrow agent simply through sharing his decryption/signing key with the agent.

[2] A public key certificate which signed by a certificate authority (CA) is an electronic document used to validate the public key. Its costs include but not limited to registration, issuing, storage, transmission, verification, and building/recurring fees.

Generic Construction from CIBE. We present a generic construction of HIES from constrained identity-based encryption (CIBE) and give a rigorous proof of its joint security.

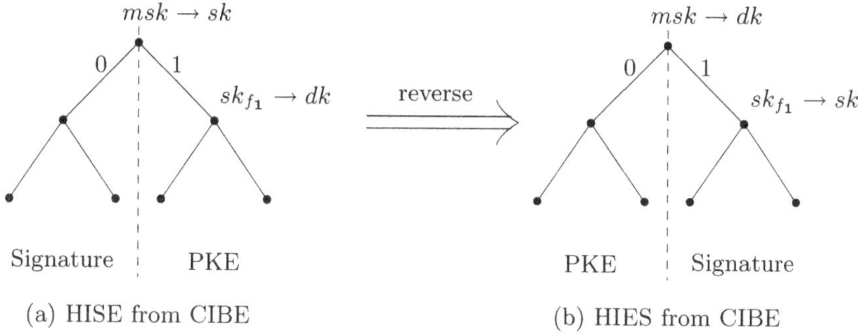

Fig. 1. HISE and HIES from CIBE

Our generic construction is inspired by HISE from CIBE. We notice that CIBE inherently implies a binary tree, where the root node is served as Private Key Generator (PKG) who possesses the master secret key, and each leaf node is viewed as a user, specified by an ID, who owns an ID-based private key. Indeed, each ID can be interpreted as identifying a unique path from root node to corresponding leaf node. We refer the reader to Sect. 2.3 for formal definition of CIBE. As for HISE from CIBE (shown as Fig. 1(a)), users each forms a CIBE binary tree, employs the master secret key of the root node as the signing key, and lets the secret key of its right child node be the decryption key, i.e. sk_{f_1}, the secret key for prefix predicate f_1, from which all secret keys for ID prefixed with "1" can be derived (we use $sk_{f_\mathbf{v}}$ to denote the constrained secret key for prefix predicate $f_\mathbf{v}$, where $f_\mathbf{v}(\text{ID}) = 1$ iff ID prefixed with $\mathbf{v}$). Thus, the whole tree is divided into two parts. The left one containing IDs prefixed with "0" is used for PKE component and the right one containing IDs prefixed with "1" is used for signature component. Based on above observations, we naturally get a construction of HIES by switching the roles the two secret keys play (shown in Fig. 1(b)).

Extensions. We propose three extensions with different purposes. The first one is for flexible delegation, with which the user is able to delegate his/her decryption and signing capacities separately to different entities. It is actually the combination of HISE and HIES. The second is for limited delegation, with which the user can limit the decryption or signing capacity given to the escrow. The last one is for finegrained delegation, which is designed to generate keys labeled by time or identifier information. We believe these extensions is useful in scenarios where delegation is not straightforward.

Applications. We give several scenarios where HIES is useful. *The first one* is a concern reported in [7]. In a confidential payment system like Zether [10] and PGC [13], which currently is equipped with a key reuse mechanism, if the signing key needs to be revoked or rotated, then all encrypted assets of an account need to be transferred to a new account, which leads to high overhead. While there is no such trouble if HIES is used, in which one can derive time labeled signing keys. *The second one* is the following scenario discussed in Viafirma [4]. In a company, the president needs to deal with multifarious documents everyday, including but not limited to commercial contracts, applications for the procurement of goods and so on. It is quite necessary to delegate his signing right to assistant presidents so that they can help settle documents which are less important. Meanwhile, the president may require keeping the decryption key secret for the security of some confidential business documents. Many similar scenarios where signature delegation is needed widely appear in other institutions, such as schools and government departments [1,3].

Indeed, signature delegation, also known as *Proxy Signature* which was first introduced by Mambo et al. [28], has numerous applications, such as distributed systems [29], mobile agent [26] and electronic commerce [16]. Various schemes and extensions of it were proposed during the last few decades [8,12,22–24,34]. In contrast to these schemes, HIES not only considers delegating signing right, but also combines an additional PKE scheme without increasing the size of public key, yielding a scheme with richer functionality. In general, HIES is suitable for the scenarios where low key management costs are desired, while the signing key is not permanent, or the signature delegation is needed.

Instantiation and Implementation. We instantiate our HIES and implement it with 128-bit security. The performance of our HIES scheme is comparable to the best Cartesian product combined public-key scheme [30] in terms of efficiency, and is superior in having richer functionality as well as retaining merits of key reuse.

1.2 Related Works

Here we briefly review the works related to combined usage of public key schemes.

Key Separation. It is the folklore principle for combining PKE and signature schemes, which indicates using two independent key pairs for two public key schemes. Paterson et al. formalized it via the notion of "Cartesian product" combined public key scheme (CP-CPK) [30], which means using arbitrary encryption and signature schemes as components, and combining two key pairs into one simply through concatenating the public/private keys of the component schemes. They pointed out that CP-CPK provides a benchmark by which other constructions can be judged, so we use it as a baseline.

Key Reuse. The first work to formally study the security of key reuse was by Haber and Pinkas [20]. They introduced the concept of a combined public key (CPK) scheme, where an encryption scheme and a signature scheme are combined. CPK preserves the existing algorithms of sign, verify, encrypt and decrypt, while the two key generation algorithms are modified into a single algorithm, which outputs two key pairs for PKE and signature components respectively, with the key pairs no longer necessarily being independent. In addition, they formalized the joint security of CPK scheme, i.e., the encryption component is IND-CCA secure even in the presence of an additional signing oracle, and the signature component is EUF-CMA secure even in the presence of an additional decryption oracle. Integrated signature and encryption (ISE) is an extreme case of CPK. It uses an identical key pair for both PKE and signature components, which in turn makes it not support key delegation. In subsequent works, both Coron et al. [15] and Komano et al. [25] considered building ISE from trapdoor permutations in the random oracle model. Paterson et al. [30] gave an ISE construction from identity-based encryption.

Hierarchical Integrated Signature and Encryption. It is a new notion presented by Chen et al. in [14]. HISE employs a unique public key for both PKE and signature components, and serves the signing key as the master secret key from which the decryption key can be derived. Thus, HIES supports secure delegation of decryption power and achieves stronger joint security than ISE, that is, the encryption component is IND-CCA secure even in the presence of an additional signing oracle, while the signature component is EUF-CMA secure even in the presence of the decryption key.

Our notion is dual to HISE, where the hierarchy between signing key and decryption key is reversed. It completes the last piece of the key usage strategy puzzle, as shown in Fig. 2. We use index e to indicate keys for PKE component and s to signature component.

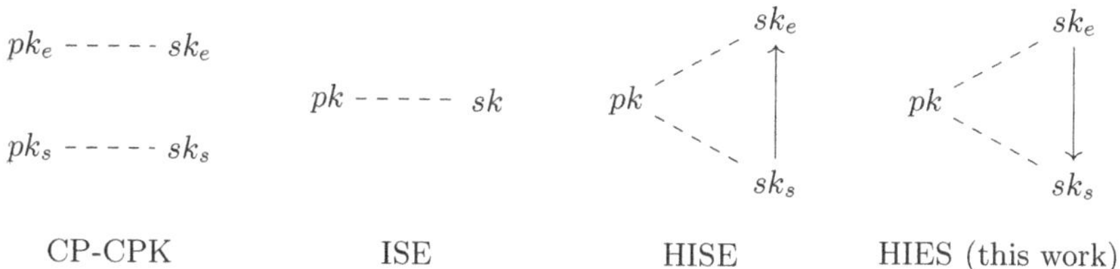

Fig. 2. Different key usage strategies

2 Preliminaries

Notations. We use $m \xleftarrow{R} M$ to denote that m is sampled uniformly at random from a set M and $y \leftarrow A(x)$ to denote the algorithm A that on input x outputs y. We use the abbreviation PPT to indicate probabilistic polynomial-time. We denote by $\mathsf{negl}(\lambda)$ a negligible function in λ. Let tuple $(\mathbb{G}_1, \mathbb{G}_2, \mathbb{G}_T, p, g_1, g_2, e)$ denote the descriptions of asymmetric pairing groups where $\mathbb{G}_1$, $\mathbb{G}_2$ and $\mathbb{G}_T$ are cyclic groups of the same prime order p, and g_1, g_2 are generators of $\mathbb{G}_1, \mathbb{G}_2$ respectively, and $e : \mathbb{G}_1 \times \mathbb{G}_2 \rightarrow \mathbb{G}_T$ is the bilinear map.

2.1 Public Key Encryption

Definition 1. *A public key encryption (PKE) scheme consists of four polynomial-time algorithms:*

- $\mathsf{Setup}(1^\lambda)$: *on input a security parameter* λ, *outputs public parameters* pp, *including the descriptions of plaintext space* $\mathcal{M}$, *ciphertext space* $\mathcal{C}$, *and randomness space* $\mathcal{R}$.
- $\mathsf{KeyGen}(pp)$: *on input public parameters* pp, *outputs a public encryption key* ek *and a secret decryption key* dk.
- $\mathsf{Enc}(ek, m)$: *on input an encryption key* ek *and a plaintext* m, *outputs a ciphertext* c.
- $\mathsf{Dec}(dk, c)$: *on input a decryption key* dk *and a ciphertext* c, *outputs a plaintext* m *or a special reject symbol* $\perp$ *denoting failure. This algorithm is typically deterministic.*

Correctness. For any $pp \leftarrow \mathsf{Setup}(1^\lambda)$, any $(ek, dk) \leftarrow \mathsf{KeyGen}(pp)$, any $m \in \mathcal{M}$ and any $c \leftarrow \mathsf{Enc}(ek, m)$, it holds that $\mathsf{Dec}(dk, c) = m$.

Security. Let $\mathcal{O}_{\mathsf{dec}}$ be a decryption oracle that on input a ciphertext, outputs a plaintext. A public key encryption scheme is IND-CCA secure if for any PPT adversary $\mathcal{A}$ there is a negligible function $\mathsf{negl}(\lambda)$ such that:

$$\Pr\left[\beta = \beta' : \begin{array}{l} pp \leftarrow \mathsf{Setup}(1^\lambda); \\ (ek, dk) \leftarrow \mathsf{KeyGen}(pp); \\ (m_0, m_1) \leftarrow \mathcal{A}^{\mathcal{O}_{\mathsf{dec}}}(pp, ek); \\ \beta \xleftarrow{\text{R}} \{0,1\}, c^* \leftarrow \mathsf{Enc}(ek, m_\beta); \\ \beta' \leftarrow \mathcal{A}^{\mathcal{O}_{\mathsf{dec}}}(c^*); \end{array}\right] \leq \frac{1}{2} + \mathsf{negl}(\lambda).$$

$\mathcal{A}$ is not allowed to query $\mathcal{O}_{\mathsf{dec}}$ for c^* in the guess stage. The IND-CPA security can be defined similarly by denying the decryption oracle.

2.2 Digital Signature

Definition 2. *A digital signature scheme consists of four polynomial-time algorithms:*

- $\mathsf{Setup}(1^\lambda)$: *on input the security parameter* λ, *outputs public parameters* pp, *including the descriptions of message space* $\mathcal{M}$ *and signature space* Σ.
- $\mathsf{KeyGen}(pp)$: *on input* pp, *outputs a public verification key* vk *and a secret signing key* sk.
- $\mathsf{Sign}(sk, m)$: *on input a signing key* sk *and a message* m, *outputs a signature* σ.
- $\mathsf{Vrfy}(vk, m, \sigma)$: *on input a verification key* vk, *a message* m, *and a signature* σ, *outputs a bit* b, *with* $b = 1$ *meaning valid and* $b = 0$ *meaning invalid.*

Correctness. For any $(vk, sk) \leftarrow \mathsf{KeyGen}(pp)$, any $m \in \mathcal{M}$ and any $\sigma \leftarrow \mathsf{Sign}(sk, m)$, it holds that $\mathsf{Vrfy}(pk, m, \sigma) = 1$.

Security. Let $\mathcal{O}_{\mathsf{sign}}$ be a signing oracle that on input a message, outputs a signature. A digital signature scheme is EUF-CMA secure if for any PPT adversary $\mathcal{A}$ there is a negligible function $\mathsf{negl}(\lambda)$ such that:

$$\Pr\left[\begin{array}{c}\mathsf{Vrfy}(vk, m^*, \sigma^*) = 1 \\ \wedge\ m^* \notin \mathcal{Q}\end{array} : \begin{array}{l} pp \leftarrow \mathsf{Setup}(1^\lambda); \\ (vk, sk) \leftarrow \mathsf{KeyGen}(pp); \\ (m^*, \sigma^*) \leftarrow \mathcal{A}^{\mathcal{O}_{\mathsf{dec}}}(pp, vk); \end{array}\right] \leq \mathsf{negl}(\lambda).$$

The set $\mathcal{Q}$ records queries to $\mathcal{O}_{\mathsf{sign}}$. The *strong* EUF-CMA security can be defined similarly by asking $\mathcal{A}$ to output a fresh valid message-signature tuple. The one-time signature can also be defined similarly by restricting the adversary to access $\mathcal{O}_{\mathsf{sign}}$ only once.

2.3 Constrained Identity-Based Encryption

We recall the definition of constrained IBE introduced by Chen et al. [14] below.

Definition 3. *A constrained identity-based encryption (CIBE) scheme consists of seven polynomial-time algorithms:*

- $\mathsf{Setup}(1^\lambda)$*: on input a security parameter λ, outputs public parameters pp. Let $\mathcal{F}$ be a family of predicates over identity space $\mathcal{I}$.*
- $\mathsf{KeyGen}(pp)$*: on input public parameters pp, outputs a master public key mpk and a master secret key msk.*
- $\mathsf{Extract}(msk, id)$*: on input a master secret key msk and an identity $id \in \mathcal{I}$, outputs a user secret key sk_{id}.*
- $\mathsf{Constrain}(msk, f)$*: on input a master secret key msk and a predicate $f \in \mathcal{F}$, outputs a constrained secret key sk_f.*
- $\mathsf{Derive}(sk_f, id)$*: on input a constrained secret key sk_f and an identity $id \in \mathcal{I}$, outputs a user secret key sk_{id} if $f(id) = 1$ or $\perp$ otherwise.*
- $\mathsf{Enc}(mpk, id, m)$*: on input mpk, an identity $id \in \mathcal{I}$, and a message m, outputs a ciphertext c.*
- $\mathsf{Dec}(sk_{id}, c)$*: on input a user secret key sk_{id} and a ciphertext c, outputs a message m or a special reject symbol $\perp$ denoting failure.*

Correctness. For any $pp \leftarrow \mathsf{Setup}(1^\lambda)$, any $(mpk, msk) \leftarrow \mathsf{KeyGen}(pp)$, any identity $id \in \mathcal{I}$, any $sk_{id} \leftarrow \mathsf{Extract}(msk, id)$, any message m, and any $c \leftarrow \mathsf{Enc}(mpk, id, m)$, it always holds that $\mathsf{Dec}(sk_{id}, c) = m$. Besides, for any $f \in \mathcal{F}$ such that $f(id) = 1$, the outputs of $\mathsf{Extract}(msk, id)$ and $\mathsf{Derive}(sk_f, id)$ have the same distribution.

Security. Let $\mathcal{O}_{\mathsf{extract}}$ be an oracle of $\mathsf{Extract}$ that on input an identity id outputs sk_{id}. Let $\mathcal{O}_{\mathsf{constrain}}$ be an oracle of $\mathsf{Constrain}$ that on input a predicate f outputs sk_f. A CIBE scheme is IND-CPA secure, if for all PPT adversary $\mathcal{A}$ there is a negligible function $\mathsf{negl}(\lambda)$ suth that:

$$\Pr\left[\beta = \beta' : \begin{array}{l} pp \leftarrow \mathsf{Setup}(1^\lambda); \\ (mpk, msk) \leftarrow \mathsf{KeyGen}(pp); \\ (id^*, (m_0, m_1)) \leftarrow \mathcal{A}^{\mathcal{O}_{\mathsf{extract}}, \mathcal{O}_{\mathsf{constrain}}}(pp, mpk); \\ \beta \xleftarrow{R} \{0,1\}, c^* \leftarrow \mathsf{Enc}(mpk, id^*, m_\beta); \\ \beta' \leftarrow \mathcal{A}^{\mathcal{O}_{\mathsf{extract}}, \mathcal{O}_{\mathsf{constrain}}}(c^*); \end{array}\right] \leq \frac{1}{2} + \mathsf{negl}(\lambda).$$

$\mathcal{A}$ is not allowed to query the $\mathcal{O}_{\mathsf{extract}}$ with id^* or query the $\mathcal{O}_{\mathsf{constrain}}$ with f such that $f(id^*) = 1$. Meanwhile, two weaker security notions can be defined similarly. One is OW-CPA security, in which the adversary is required to recover the plaintext from a random ciphertext. The other is selective-identity IND-CPA security, in which the adversary must commit ahead of time (non-adaptively) to the identity it intends to attack before seeing the mpk.

3 Hierarchical Integrated Encryption and Signature

3.1 Definition of HIES

As mentioned in the introduction, HIES allows one to derive the signing key from the decryption key, which is opposite to HISE. Next, we give a self-contained description of the formal definition of HIES.

Definition 4. *A hierarchical integrated encryption and signature (HIES) scheme is defined by seven polynomial-time algorithms:*

- $\mathsf{Setup}(1^\lambda)$: *on input a security parameter λ, outputs public parameters pp including the description of plaintext space $\mathcal{M}$ and message space $\widetilde{\mathcal{M}}$.*
- $\mathsf{KeyGen}(pp)$: *on input public parameters pp, outputs a public key pk and a decryption key dk. Here, dk serves as a master secret key, which can be used to derive signing key.*
- $\mathsf{Derive}(dk)$: *on input a decryption key dk, outputs a signing key sk.*
- $\mathsf{Enc}(pk, m)$: *on input a public key pk and a plaintext $m \in \mathcal{M}$, outputs a ciphertext c.*
- $\mathsf{Dec}(dk, c)$: *on input a decryption key dk and a ciphertext c, outputs a plaintext m or a special reject symbol $\perp$ denoting failure.*
- $\mathsf{Sign}(sk, \widetilde{m})$: *on input a signing key sk and a message $\widetilde{m} \in \widetilde{\mathcal{M}}$, outputs a signature σ.*
- $\mathsf{Vrfy}(pk, \widetilde{m}, \sigma)$: *on input a public key pk, a message $\widetilde{m}$, and a signature σ, outputs a bit b, with $b = 1$ meaning valid and $b = 0$ meaning invalid.*

Correctness. The correctness of HIES is divided into two parts, the correctness of PKE and signature components: (i) the PKE component satisfies correctness if for any $pp \leftarrow \mathsf{Setup}(1^\lambda)$, any $(pk, dk) \leftarrow \mathsf{KeyGen}(pp)$, any $m \in \mathcal{M}$ and any $c \leftarrow \mathsf{Enc}(pk, m)$, it holds that $\mathsf{Dec}(dk, c) = m$; (ii) the signature component satisfies correctness if for any $pp \leftarrow \mathsf{Setup}(1^\lambda)$, any $(pk, dk) \leftarrow \mathsf{KeyGen}(pp)$, any $sk \leftarrow \mathsf{Derive}(dk)$, any $\widetilde{m} \in \widetilde{\mathcal{M}}$ and any $\sigma \leftarrow \mathsf{Sign}(sk, \widetilde{m})$, it holds that $\mathsf{Very}(pk, \widetilde{m}, \sigma) = 1$.

Security. (Joint security) The joint security for HIES needs to be considered from two aspects as well. The PKE component requires to satisfy IND-CCA security in the presence of a signing key and the signature component requires to satisfy EUF-CMA security in the presence of a decryption oracle. Let $\mathcal{O}_{\mathsf{dec}}$ be the decryption oracle and $\mathcal{O}_{\mathsf{sign}}$ be the signing oracle. The formal security notion is defined as below.

Definition 5. *HIES is joint secure if its encryption and signature components satisfy the following security notions:*

(i) The PKE component is IND-CCA secure in the presence of a signing key, if for any PPT adversary $\mathcal{A}$ there is a negligible function $\mathsf{negl}(\lambda)$ *such that:*

$$\Pr\left[\beta = \beta' : \begin{array}{l} pp \leftarrow \mathsf{Setup}(1^\lambda); \\ (pk, dk) \leftarrow \mathsf{KeyGen}(pp); \\ sk \leftarrow \mathsf{Derive}(dk); \\ (m_0, m_1) \leftarrow \mathcal{A}^{\mathcal{O}_{\mathsf{dec}}}(pp, pk, sk); \\ \beta \xleftarrow{R} \{0,1\}, c^* \leftarrow \mathsf{Enc}(pk, m_\beta); \\ \beta' \leftarrow \mathcal{A}^{\mathcal{O}_{\mathsf{dec}}}(c^*); \end{array}\right] \leq \frac{1}{2} + \mathsf{negl}(\lambda).$$

$\mathcal{A}$ is not allowed to query $\mathcal{O}_{\mathsf{dec}}$ with c^* in the guess stage.

(ii) The signature component is EUF-CMA secure in the presence of a decryption oracle, if for all PPT adversary $\mathcal{A}$ there is a negligible function $\mathsf{negl}(\lambda)$ *such that:*

$$\Pr\left[\begin{array}{c} \mathsf{Vrfy}(pk, m^*, \sigma^*) = 1 \\ \wedge m^* \notin \mathcal{Q} \end{array} : \begin{array}{l} pp \leftarrow \mathsf{Setup}(1^\lambda); \\ (pk, dk) \leftarrow \mathsf{KeyGen}(pp); \\ (m^*, \sigma^*) \leftarrow \mathcal{A}^{\mathcal{O}_{\mathsf{dec}}, \mathcal{O}_{\mathsf{sign}}}(pp, pk); \end{array}\right] \leq \mathsf{negl}(\lambda).$$

The set $\mathcal{Q}$ records queries to $\mathcal{O}_{\mathsf{sign}}$.

3.2 HIES from Constrained IBE

In this section, we give a generic construction of HIES from constrained identity-based encryption. Let CIBE be a constrained IBE scheme and OTS be a strong one-time signature scheme, then an HIES scheme can be created as Fig. 3. We assume the identity space of CIBE is $\mathcal{I} = \{0,1\}^{\ell+1}$, and the verification space of OTS is $\{0,1\}^\ell$.

The correctness of the scheme follows directly from the correctness of CIBE and OTS. The joint security of the HIES scheme is formalized as below.

$\mathsf{Setup}(1^\lambda)$:
$pp_{\text{cibe}} \leftarrow \text{CIBE.}\mathsf{Setup}(1^\lambda)$
$pp_{\text{ots}} \leftarrow \text{OTS.}\mathsf{Setup}(1^\lambda)$
Return $pp = (pp_{\text{cibe}}, pp_{\text{ots}})$

$\mathsf{KeyGen}(pp)$:
Parse $pp = (pp_{\text{cibe}}, pp_{\text{ots}})$
$(mpk, msk) \leftarrow \text{CIBE.}\mathsf{KeyGen}(pp_{\text{cibe}})$
Return $(pk, dk) = (mpk, msk)$

$\mathsf{Derive}(dk)$:
Parse $dk = msk$
$sk_{f_1} \leftarrow \text{CIBE.}\mathsf{Constrain}(msk, f_1)$
$(f_1(id) = 1 \text{ iff } id[1] = 1)$
Return $sk = sk_{f_1}$

$\mathsf{Enc}(pk, m)$:
Parse $pk = mpk$
$(ovk, osk) \leftarrow \text{OTS.}\mathsf{KeyGen}(pp_{\text{ots}})$
Set $id = 0||ovk$
$c_{\text{cibe}} \leftarrow \text{CIBE.}\mathsf{Enc}(mpk, id, m)$
$\sigma_{\text{ots}} \leftarrow \text{OTS.}\mathsf{Sign}(osk, c_{\text{cibe}})$
Return $c = (ovk, c_{\text{cibe}}, \sigma_{\text{ots}})$

$\mathsf{Dec}(dk, c)$:
Parse $c = (ovk, c_{\text{cibe}}, \sigma_{\text{ots}})$
If $\text{OTS.}\mathsf{Vrfy}(ovk, c_{\text{cibe}}, \sigma_{\text{ots}}) \neq 1$
return $\perp$
Parse $dk = msk$
Set $id = 0||ovk$
$sk_{id} \leftarrow \text{CIBE.}\mathsf{Extract}(msk, id)$
$m \leftarrow \text{CIBE.}\mathsf{Dec}(sk_{id}, c_{\text{cibe}})$
Return m

$\mathsf{Sign}(sk, \widetilde{m})$:
Parse $sk = sk_{f_1}$
Set $id = 1||\widetilde{m}$
$sk_{id} \leftarrow \text{CIBE.}\mathsf{Derive}(sk_{f_1}, id)$
Return $\sigma = sk_{id}$

$\mathsf{Vrfy}(pk, \widetilde{m}, \sigma)$:
Parse $pk = mpk$ and $\sigma = sk_{id}$
Set $id = 1||\widetilde{m}$
$m \xleftarrow{\text{R}} M$
$c_{\text{cibe}} \leftarrow \text{CIBE.}\mathsf{Enc}(mpk, id, m)$
If $\text{CIBE.}\mathsf{Dec}(c_{\text{cibe}}, sk_{id}) = m$
Return 1, else return 0

Fig. 3. A generic construction of HIES from CIBE

Theorem 1. *Assume CIBE satisfies IND-CPA security and OTS satisfies strong EUF-CMA security, then the HIES scheme constructed as Fig. 3 satisfies joint security.*

This theorem comes straightforwardly from two lemmas.

Lemma 1. *If CIBE scheme is OW-CPA secure, then the signature component is EUF-CMA secure in the presence of the decryption oracle.*

Proof. If there exists a PPT adversary $\mathcal{A}$ against the signature component, we can construct a PPT adversary $\mathcal{B}$ that uses $\mathcal{A}$ as a subroutine and attacks the CIBE. $\mathcal{B}$ is given public parameters pp_{cibe}, public key mpk and access to $\mathcal{O}_{\mathsf{extract}}$ and $\mathcal{O}_{\mathsf{constrain}}$ by its own challenger $\mathcal{CH}_{\text{cibe}}$, then it simulates $\mathcal{A}$'s challenger $\mathcal{CH}_{\text{sign}}$ as below.

- Setup: $\mathcal{B}$ runs $pp_{\text{ots}} \leftarrow \text{OTS.}\mathsf{Setup}(1^\lambda)$, sets $pp = (pp_{\text{cibe}}, pp_{\text{ots}})$ and $pk = mpk$, then sends (pp, pk) to $\mathcal{A}$.
- Signing query: when $\mathcal{A}$ requests a signature on message $\widetilde{m}$, $\mathcal{B}$ queries $\mathcal{O}_{\mathsf{extract}}$ with identity $id = 1||\widetilde{m}$ to obtain sk_{id}, outputs $\sigma = sk_{id}$.
- Decryption query: when $\mathcal{A}$ requests the plaintext of a ciphertext c, $\mathcal{B}$ first parses c as $(ovk, c_{\text{cibe}}, \sigma_{\text{ots}})$, then checks whether $\text{OTS.}\mathsf{Vrfy}(ovk, c_{\text{cibe}}, \sigma_{\text{ots}}) =$

1, and returns $\perp$ if not; else it queries $\mathcal{O}_{\mathsf{extract}}$ for $id = 0||ovk$ to obtain sk_{id} and returns the plaintext $m \leftarrow$ CIBE.$\mathsf{Dec}(sk_{id}, c_{\mathrm{cibe}})$ to $\mathcal{A}$.
- Forgery: when $\mathcal{A}$ outputs a forged message-signature pair $(\widetilde{m}^*, \sigma^*)$, $\mathcal{B}$ first submits $id^* = 1||\widetilde{m}$ as the target identity to $\mathcal{CH}_{\mathrm{cibe}}$ and receives back $c^*_{cibe} \leftarrow$ CIBE.$\mathsf{Enc}(mpk, id^*, m)$ for a random plaintext $m \xleftarrow{\mathrm{R}} \mathcal{M}$, then it parses $\sigma^* = sk_{id^*}$, and computes $m' \leftarrow$ CIBE.$\mathsf{Dec}(sk_{id^*}, c^*_{cibe})$. $\mathcal{B}$ wins if $m' = m$.

The view of $\mathcal{A}$ when it interacts with $\mathcal{B}$ is identical to the view of $\mathcal{A}$ interacting with a real challenger, which implies the simulation of $\mathcal{B}$ is perfect. If no PPT adversary $\mathcal{B}$ has non-negligible probability to break the OW-CPA security of the CIBE scheme, then no PPT adversary $\mathcal{A}$ has non-negligible probability to break the EUF-CMA security of signature component. This proves Lemma 1.

Lemma 2. *If the OTS scheme satisfies strong EUF-CMA security and the CIBE scheme satisfies selective-identity IND-CPA security, then the encryption component PKE satisfies IND-CCA security even in the presence of signing key.*

Proof. Consider following games. Let $\mathcal{A}$ be an adversary against the PKE component and S_i be the event that $\mathcal{A}$ wins in Game i.

Game 0. This is the standard IND-CCA security experiment for PKE component in the presence of a signing key, $\mathcal{CH}_{\mathrm{pke}}$ interacts with $\mathcal{A}$ as below.

- Setup: $\mathcal{CH}_{\mathrm{pke}}$ runs $pp_{\mathrm{cibe}} \leftarrow$ CIBE.$\mathsf{Setup}(1^\lambda)$ and $pp_{\mathrm{ots}} \leftarrow$ OTS.$\mathsf{Setup}(1^\lambda)$, sets $pp = (pp_{\mathrm{cibe}}, pp_{\mathrm{ots}})$, then runs $(mpk, msk) \leftarrow$ CIBE.$\mathsf{KeyGen}(pp_{\mathrm{cibe}})$, sets $pk = mpk$ and $dk = msk$, runs $sk \leftarrow \mathsf{Derive}(dk)$, and gives (pp, pk, sk) to $\mathcal{A}$.
- Decryption query: upon receiving a ciphertext c, $\mathcal{CH}_{\mathrm{pke}}$ first parses $c = (ovk, c_{\mathrm{cibe}}, \sigma)$, checks if OTS.$\mathsf{Vrfy}(ovk, c_{\mathrm{cibe}}, \sigma) = 1$, outputs $\perp$ if not; else sets $id = 0||ovk$, parses $dk = msk$, runs $sk_{id} \leftarrow$ CIBE.$\mathsf{Extract}(msk, id)$ and outputs $m \leftarrow$ CIBE.$\mathsf{Dec}(sk_{id}, c_{\mathrm{cibe}})$.
- Challenge: $\mathcal{A}$ outputs a pair of messages (m_0, m_1). $\mathcal{CH}_{\mathrm{pke}}$ chooses a random bit $b \xleftarrow{\mathrm{R}} \{0,1\}$, runs $(ovk^*, osk^*) \leftarrow$ OTS.$\mathsf{KeyGen}(pp_{\mathrm{ots}})$, sets $id^* = 0||ovk^*$, computes $c^*_{\mathrm{cibe}} \leftarrow$ CIBE.$\mathsf{Enc}(mpk, id^*, m_b)$, and $\sigma^* \leftarrow$ OTS.$\mathsf{Sign}(osk^*, c^*_{\mathrm{cibe}})$, outputs $c^* = (ovk^*, c^*_{\mathrm{cibe}}, \sigma^*)$ to $\mathcal{A}$. Then $\mathcal{A}$ can continue to query the decryption oracle, but it is not allowed to query for c^*.
- Guess: Eventually, $\mathcal{A}$ outputs a bit b'. $\mathcal{A}$ wins if $b' = b$.

Game 1. Same as Game 0 except that $\mathcal{CH}_{\mathrm{pke}}$ generates the OTS keypair $(ovk^*, osk^*) \leftarrow$ OTS.$\mathsf{KeyGen}(pp_{\mathrm{ots}})$ in the setup stage rather than in the challenge stage. The modification is only conceptual and does not affect the advantage of $\mathcal{A}$, so we have:

$$\Pr[S_1] = \Pr[S_0].$$

Game 2. Same as Game 1 except that the experiment directly aborts when one of following two events happens:

E_1: in phase 1, $\mathcal{A}$ queries the decryption oracle with $c = (ovk^*, c_{\mathrm{cibe}}, \sigma)$ such that OTS.$\mathsf{Vrfy}(ovk^*, c_{\mathrm{cibe}}, \sigma) = 1$.

E_2: in phase 2, $\mathcal{A}$ queries the decryption oracle with $c = (ovk^*, c^*_{\text{cibe}}, \sigma)$ such that $\text{OTS.}\mathsf{Vrfy}(ovk^*, c^*_{\text{cibe}}, \sigma) = 1$ and $\sigma \neq \sigma^*$.

Let E be the event that E_1 or E_2 happens, then we have (Game $1 \wedge \neg E$) = (Game $2 \wedge \neg E$). According to the difference lemma, we have:

$$|\Pr[S_2] - \Pr[S_1]| \leq \Pr[E].$$

Actually, the two events mean a successful attack on the OTS, while the strong EUF-CMA security of OTS ensures that for any PPT $\mathcal{A}$, it holds that $\Pr[E] = \mathsf{negl}(\lambda)$.

Claim 1. *If the CIBE scheme is selective-identity IND-CPA secure, then for any PPT adversary $\mathcal{A}$, there is a negligible function* $\mathsf{negl}(\lambda)$ *such that:*

$$\left|\Pr[S_2] - \frac{1}{2}\right| \leq \mathsf{negl}(\lambda).$$

Proof. Let $\mathcal{B}$ be an adversary against CIBE scheme. It is given public param eters pp_{cibe} and access to $\mathcal{O}_{\mathsf{extract}}$ and $\mathcal{O}_{\mathsf{constrain}}$ by its own challenger $\mathcal{CH}_{\text{cibe}}$. $\mathcal{B}$ simulates $\mathcal{A}$'s challenger as below.

- Setup: $\mathcal{B}$ runs $pp_{\text{ots}} \leftarrow \text{OTS.}\mathsf{Setup}(1^\lambda)$, $(ovk^*, osk^*) \leftarrow \text{OTS.}\mathsf{KeyGen}(pp_{\text{ots}})$, sets $id^* = 0||ovk^*$, then commits to id^* and sends the commitment to its own challenger $\mathcal{CH}_{\text{cibe}}$ as the target identity and receives back public key $pk = mpk$. Next, $\mathcal{B}$ queries $\mathcal{O}_{\mathsf{constrain}}$ with f_1, and obtains the signing key $sk = sk_{f_1}$. $\mathcal{B}$ gives $pp = (pp_{\text{cibe}}, pp_{\text{ots}})$, $pk = mpk$ and $sk = sk_{f_1}$ to $\mathcal{A}$.
- Decryption query: When $\mathcal{A}$ queries for a ciphertext $c = (ovk, c_{\text{cibe}}, \sigma)$, $\mathcal{B}$ first checks whether $\text{OTS.}\mathsf{Vrfy}(ovk, c_{\text{cibe}}, \sigma) = 1$, if not, outputs $\perp$; else if $ovk = ovk^*$ which means event E_1 happens, $\mathcal{B}$ aborts; otherwise it must have $ovk \neq ovk^*$, $\mathcal{B}$ queries $\mathcal{O}_{\mathsf{extract}}$ with $id = 0||ovk$ to obtain sk_{id}, and outputs $m \leftarrow \text{CIBE.}\mathsf{Dec}(sk_{id}, c_{\text{cibe}})$.
- Challenge: $\mathcal{A}$ submits two messages (m_0, m_1) to $\mathcal{B}$. $\mathcal{B}$ sends the two messages to its own challenger and receives back a ciphertext c^*_{cibe} which is a ciphertext of m_b under the target identity $id^* = 0||ovk^*$. $\mathcal{B}$ proceeds to compute a signature σ^* on c^*_{cibe}, then sends $c^* = (ovk^*, c^*_{\text{cibe}}, \sigma^*)$ to $\mathcal{A}$.
- Guess: Upon receiving c^*, $\mathcal{A}$ continues to query decryption oracle but is not allowed to query it with c^*. If E_2 happens, $\mathcal{B}$ aborts. Else it answers the query as before. Finally, $\mathcal{A}$ outputs b', and $\mathcal{B}$ uses b' as its own guess.

The view of $\mathcal{A}$ when it interacts with $\mathcal{B}$ is identical to the view of $\mathcal{A}$ in experiment Game 2 which implies the simulation of $\mathcal{B}$ is perfect. Due to the selective-identity IND-CPA security of CIBE, the advantage of $\mathcal{A}$ wins in Game 2 is negligible. This proves Claim 1.

Therefore, the proof of Lemma 2 is completed.

Remark 1. We strengthen PKE component to IND-CCA security via the Canetti-Halevi-Katz (CHK) transform [11] with the help of a one-time signature. To enhance the efficiency, we can get rid of OTS and use an $id_0 = 0^{\ell+1}$ as a fixed target identity for encryption, then apply the Fujisaki-Okamoto transformation [17] to achieve the IND-CCA security in the random oracle model.

4 Further Discussion

In this section, we discuss three simple extensions of HIES for different delegation purposes and each of them is in the public key reuse setting. The key observation is that the prefix predicates in a constrained IBE can be assigned different and specific meanings.

Flexible Delegation. One delegation function is insufficient sometimes, such as the cases when the president wants to give his signing right to his assistants and give his decryption right to vice president. Thus, it is attractive to give a more flexible notion that enables the secret key owner to delegate these two types of authorities to different entities. The key technique is equalizing two secret keys by deriving them both from the master secret key as shown in Fig. 4(a). It is evident that the extended version satisfies united joint security as long as the two agents are not in collusion, namely the PKE/signature component is IND-CCA secure even when the adversary is given the signing/decryption key.

Limited Delegation. In the signature proxy function introduced by Mambo et al. [27], the full delegation (giving the full original secret key to the proxy signer) requests the proxy is authentic, since the proxy signer has the ability to sign any message and the proxy signature is indistinguishable from the created by the original signer. The decryption proxy suffers the similar discomfort if the decryption key is disclosed. In order to limit the decryption and signing capacity of proxy, we consider an extension which supports partial delegation. It divides the decryption/signing capacity into two parts so that the original user can retain the higher power while delegating partial power to agents as shown in Fig. 4(b).

Finegrained Delegation. Giving the prefix predicates with more specific meanings such as the ID (identifier information such as email address) of a person or the number of a department, more finegrained delegation keys can be derived.

5 Instantiation and Implementation

5.1 Instantiation of HIES

Towards efficient realizations, we choose the hierarchical IBE (cf. Appendix A.1) rather than the constrained IBE to instantiate our HIES scheme, where the security can be similarly demonstrated. By choosing Boneh-Boyen two-level hierarchical IBE scheme (BB_1-IBE, cf. Appendix A.2), we instantiate our HIES scheme as below.

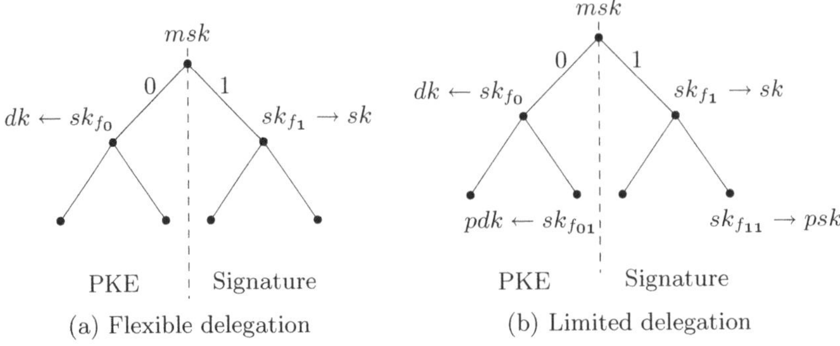

Fig. 4. Extensions of HIES from constrained IBE

- $\mathsf{Setup}(1^\lambda)$: on input the security parameter λ, generates an asymmetric pairing tuple $(\mathbb{G}_1, \mathbb{G}_2, \mathbb{G}_T, p, g_1, g_2, e)$, picks two collision resistant hash functions $\mathsf{H}_j : \{0,1\}^* \rightarrow \mathbb{G}_2$ for $j = 1, 2$, sets $\mathsf{ID}_0 = 0^n$ and $\mathsf{ID}_1 = 1^n$ with $n = \Theta(\lambda)$. The public parameter $pp = ((\mathbb{G}_1, \mathbb{G}_2, \mathbb{G}_T, p, g_1, g_2, e), \mathsf{H}_1, \mathsf{H}_2, \mathsf{ID}_0, \mathsf{ID}_1)$. The plaintext space is $\mathbb{G}_T$. The message space is $\{0,1\}^*$.
- $\mathsf{KeyGen}(pp)$: on input the public parameters pp, picks a random $\alpha \in \mathbb{Z}_p$, sets $f_1 = g_1^\alpha$ and $f_2 = g_2^\alpha$, sets public key $mpk = f_1 = g_1^\alpha$ and decryption key $dk = msk = f_2 = g_2^\alpha$.
- $\mathsf{Derive}(dk)$: on input the decryption key dk, picks a random $r' \in \mathbb{Z}_p$, computes $d_0' = dk \cdot \mathsf{H}_1(\mathsf{ID}_1)^{r'}$ and $d_1' = g_1^{r'}$, outputs $sk = (d_0', d_1') \in (\mathbb{G}_2, \mathbb{G}_1)$.
- $\mathsf{Enc}(pk, m)$: on input the public key $pk = mpk$ and a plaintext $m \in \mathbb{G}_T$, firstly picks a random $s \in \mathbb{Z}_p$ and computes $A = e(f_1, g_2)^s \cdot m$, $B = g_1^s$ and $C_1 = \mathsf{H}_1(\mathsf{ID}_0)^s$, outputs $c = (A, B, C_1) \in (\mathbb{G}_T, \mathbb{G}_1, \mathbb{G}_2)$.
- $\mathsf{Dec}(dk, c)$: on input $dk = f_2 = g_2^\alpha$ and a ciphertext $c = (A, B, C_1)$, picks a random $r'' \in \mathbb{Z}_p$, computes $d_0'' = dk \cdot \mathsf{H}_1(\mathsf{ID}_0)^{r''}$ and $d_1'' = g_1^{r''}$, outputs $A \cdot e(d_1'', C_1)/e(B, d_0'') = m$.
- $\mathsf{Sign}(sk, \widetilde{m})$: on input a signing key $sk = sk_{\mathsf{ID}_1} = (d_0', d_1')$ and a message $\widetilde{m} \in \{0,1\}^*$, first picks a random $r \in \mathbb{Z}_p$, computes $d_0 = d_0' \cdot \mathsf{H}_2(\widetilde{m})^r$, $d_1 = d_1'$ and $d_2 = g_1^r$, outputs $\sigma = sk_{\mathsf{ID}} = (d_0, d_1, d_2) \in (\mathbb{G}_2, \mathbb{G}_1, \mathbb{G}_1)$.
- $\mathsf{Vrfy}(pk, \widetilde{m}, \sigma)$: on input the public key $pk = mpk = f_1$, a message $\widetilde{m} \in \{0,1\}^*$ and a signature $\sigma = sk_{\mathsf{ID}} = (d_0, d_1, d_2)$, outputs 1 if following equation holds, otherwise outputs 0.

$$e(f_1, g_2) \cdot e(d_1, \mathsf{H}_1(\mathsf{ID}_1)) \cdot e(d_2, \mathsf{H}_2(\widetilde{m})) = e(g_1, d_0).$$

Remark 2. We simplify the Vrfy algorithm based on the fact that if σ is a valid signature for $\widetilde{m}$, then it can be used as the secret key for user $\mathsf{ID} = \langle \mathsf{ID}_1, \widetilde{m} \rangle$ to successfully decrypt any ciphertext $c = (A, B, C_1, C_2)$ for any plaintext m encrypted by mpk via BB_1-IBE. Specifically, for any randomness s, it always holds that $e(f_1, g_2)^s \cdot e(d_1, C_1) \cdot e(d_2, C_2) = e(B, d_0)$.

5.2 Implementation

Since our HIES is a newly proposed notion, there is no similar schemes can be used to judge its performance. As mentioned before (see Sect. 1.2), the "Cartesian product" construction of combined public key (CP-CPK) scheme introduced by Paterson et al. [30], which uses arbitrary public key encryption and signature schemes as components, provides a benchmark for any bespoke construction. Thus, we build a concrete CP-CPK scheme by choosing the most efficient encryption and signature schemes, i.e. ElGamal PKE and Schnorr signature and use it as a baseline.

We implement the concrete CP-CPK scheme atop elliptic curve `secp256k1` with 128-bit security in which $|\mathbb{G}| = 256$ bits and $|\mathbb{Z}_p| = 256$ bits, and implement our HIES scheme atop pairing-friendly curve `bls12-381` with 128-bit security level [32] in which $|\mathbb{G}_1| = 381$ bits, $|\mathbb{G}_2| = 762$ bits, $|\mathbb{Z}_p| = 256$ bits, and $|\mathbb{G}_T| = 1524$ bits (by exploiting compression techniques [31]).

Both of them are implemented in C++ based on the `mcl` library [33], and all the experiments are carried out on a MacBook Pro with Intel i7-9750H CPU (2.6 GHz) and 16 GB of RAM. Our implementation is released on GitHub and is available on https://github.com/yuchen1024/HISE/tree/master/hies. The code follows KEM-DEM paradigm.

Table 1. Efficiency comparison between CP-CPK and our HIES scheme

Functionality	strong joint security		individual escrow	key reuse		certificate costs
CP-CPK	✓		✓	✗		×2
HIES	✓		✓	✓		×1
Sizes (bits)	$\|pk\|$		$\|sk\|$	$\|c\|$		$\|\sigma\|$
CP-CPK	512		512	512		512
HIES	381		762	2667		1524
Efficiency (ms)	KeyGen	Derive	Enc	Dec	Sign	Vrfy
CP-CPK	0.015	⊘	0.118	0.056	0.064	0.120
HIES	0.111	0.116	0.500	0.621	0.117	1.022

In the paradigm of KEM-DEM, we test the efficiency of algorithms of key generation, key derivation, encryption, decryption, signing and verification as well as the sizes of public key, secret key, ciphertext and signature. Symbol ⊘ means no corresponding algorithm.

Table 1 offers a comparison of HIES against the previous CP-CPK. In terms of functionality, it shows that HIES is in the public key reuse setting while CP-CPK is not. Moreover, HIES reduces the key management and key certificate costs. In terms of the experimental results, we admit the efficiency of our HIES scheme is slower than CP-CPK, but it is fortunately still considerable.

6 Conclusion

In this work, we resolve the problem left in [14] by formalizing the definition and the joint security of HIES. Similar to HISE, HIES also has a two-level key derive system, but the hierarchy between signing key and decryption key are reversed, thus it enables secure delegation of signature capacity. In addition, we present a generic construction of HIES from constrained identity-based encryption and give a rigorous proof of its joint security. Furthermore, we discuss three simple extensions of HIES for different delegation purposes. In the end, we implement our HIES scheme with 128-bit security. Though the construction here is a straightforward variant of HISE from constrained IBE, we emphasize the theoretical significance of HIES for completing the last piece of the key usage strategy puzzle. We leave the more ingenious and efficient constructions for future work.

Acknowledgements. We thank the anonymous reviewers for their helpful feedback. This work is supported by the National Key Research and Development Program of China (Grant No. 2021YFA1000600), the National Natural Science Foundation of China (Grant No. 62272269), and the Taishan scholar program of Shandong Province.

A Hierarchical Identity-Based Encryption

Hierarchical identity-based encryption (HIBE) is first introduced in [19,21]. We formally describe the definition of HIBE below. In an HIBE scheme, users having a position in the hierarchy, are specified by an ID-tuple $\mathsf{ID} = (I_1, \cdots, I_j)$, where I_i corresponds to the identity at level i.

A.1 Definition of HIBE

Definition 6. *A hierarchical identity-based encryption scheme consists of five polynomial-time algorithms:*

- $\mathsf{Setup}(1^\lambda)$*: on input a security parameter* λ*, outputs public parameters* pp*, including the plaintext space* $\mathcal{M}$*, the ciphertext space* $\mathcal{C}$ *and the identity space* $\mathcal{I}$ *in every level.*
- $\mathsf{KeyGen}(pp)$*: on input the public parameters* pp*, outputs a public key* mpk *and a master secret key* msk *(i.e. root secret in level-*0*).*
- $\mathsf{Extract}(mpk, sk_{\mathsf{ID}}, \langle \mathsf{ID}, I \rangle)$*: on input the public key* mpk*, a secret key for ID-tuple* ID*, and an ID-tuple* $\langle \mathsf{ID}, I \rangle$ *which is a child node of* ID*, outputs* $sk_{\langle \mathsf{ID}, I \rangle}$*.*
- $\mathsf{Enc}(mpk, \mathsf{ID}, m)$*: on input public key* mpk*, the ID-tuple of the intended message recipient* ID *and a message* $m \in \mathcal{M}$*, outputs a ciphertext* $c \in \mathcal{C}$*.*
- $\mathsf{Dec}(sk_{\mathsf{ID}}, c)$*: on input a secret key* sk_{ID} *and a ciphertext* c*, outputs a message* m *or a special reject symbol* $\perp$ *denoting failure.*

Correctness. An HIBE scheme is correct, if encryption algorithm Enc and decryption algorithm Dec satisfy the standard consistency constraint, namely, when sk_{ID} is the secret key generated by the extraction algorithm $\mathsf{Extract}$ for user ID, then for any $m \in \mathcal{M}$ and $c \leftarrow \mathsf{Enc}(mpk, \mathsf{ID}, m)$, it always holds that $\mathsf{Dec}(sk_{\mathsf{ID}}, c) = m$.

Security. Let $\mathcal{O}_{\mathsf{extract}}$ be an oracle of $\mathsf{Extract}$ that on input an ID-tuple ID and outputs sk_{ID}. An HIBE scheme is IND-CPA secure, if for all PPT adversary $\mathcal{A}$ there is a negligible function $\mathsf{negl}(\lambda)$ such that:

$$\Pr\left[b = b' : \begin{array}{l} pp \leftarrow \mathsf{Setup}(1^{\lambda}); \\ (mpk, msk) \leftarrow \mathsf{KeyGen}(pp); \\ (\mathsf{ID}^*, (m_0, m_1)) \leftarrow \mathcal{A}^{\mathcal{O}_{\mathsf{extract}}}(pp, mpk); \\ b \xleftarrow{R} \{0,1\}, c^* \leftarrow \mathsf{Enc}(mpk, \mathsf{ID}^*, m_b); \\ b' \leftarrow \mathcal{A}^{\mathcal{O}_{\mathsf{extract}}}(c^*); \end{array}\right] \le \frac{1}{2} + \mathsf{negl}(\lambda).$$

In guess stage, $\mathcal{A}$ is not allowed to query the $\mathcal{O}_{\mathsf{extract}}$ for ID^* or the ancestor nodes of it (i.e. IDs which are prefixed with ID^*). Meanwhile, two weaker security notions can be defined similarly. One is OW-CPA security, in which the adversary is required to recover the plaintext from a random ciphertext. The other is selective-identity IND-CPA security, in which the adversary must commit ahead of time (non-adaptively) to the identity it intends to attack before seeing the mpk.

A.2 Boneh-Boyen HIBE Scheme

We review the ℓ-HIBE scheme of Boneh-Boyen (BB_1-IBE) [9] as below. As [6,18] noticed, compared to symmetric pairings, asymmetric pairings yield schemes having more efficiency in terms of both bandwidth and computation time. Therefore, we adjust the original Boneh-Boyen HIBE with asymmetric pairings.

- $\mathsf{Setup}(1^{\lambda})$: on input the security parameter λ, generates an asymmetric pairings tuple $(\mathbb{G}_1, \mathbb{G}_2, \mathbb{G}_T, p, g_1, g_2, e)$, and picks a family of collision resistant hash functions $\mathsf{H}_j : \{0,1\}^* \to \mathbb{G}_2$ for $j \in [0, \ell]$. The public parameters pp include the description of bilinear groups and the hash functions $\{\mathsf{H}_j\}_{j \in [0,\ell]}$. The ID at level-j is $\mathcal{I}^j = (\{0,1\}^*)^j$. The plaintext space is $\mathcal{M} = \mathbb{G}_T$.
- $\mathsf{KeyGen}(pp)$: on input the public parameters pp, picks a random $\alpha \in \mathbb{Z}_p$, sets $f_1 = g_1^{\alpha}$ and $f_2 = g_2^{\alpha}$, sets public key $mpk = f_1 = g_1^{\alpha}$ and master secret key $msk = f_2 = g_2^{\alpha}$.
- $\mathsf{Extract}(mpk, sk_{\mathsf{ID}}, \langle \mathsf{ID}, I \rangle)$: on input the public key mpk, a level-j private key $sk_{\mathsf{ID}} = (d_0, \ldots, d_j) \in \left(\mathbb{G}_2, \mathbb{G}_1^j\right)$ and a level-$(j+1)$ ID-tuple $\langle \mathsf{ID}, I \rangle = (I_1, \ldots, I_j, I_{j+1}) \in (\{0,1\}^*)^{j+1}$, first picks a random $r \in \mathbb{Z}_p$ and outputs

$$sk_{\langle \mathsf{ID}, I \rangle} = (d_0 \cdot \mathsf{H}_{j+1}(I_{j+1})^r, d_1, \ldots, d_j, g_2^r) \in \left(\mathbb{G}_2, \mathbb{G}_1^{j+1}\right)$$

Note that (1) when ID is an empty set denoted as ϵ, sk_{ID} is exactly the master secret key msk, that is $sk_{\epsilon} = f_2 = g_2^{\alpha}$. (2) all the private keys can be also extracted directly from the master secret key msk through computing $sk_{\langle \mathsf{ID}, I \rangle} = \left(g_2^{\alpha} \cdot \prod_{k=1}^{j+1} \mathsf{H}_k(I_k)^{r_k}, g_1^{r_1}, \ldots, g_1^{r_{j+1}} \right)$ with random elements $r_1, \ldots, r_{j+1} \in \mathbb{Z}_p$.

- $\mathsf{Enc}(mpk, \mathsf{ID}, m)$: on input the public key mpk, an ID-tuple $\mathsf{ID} = (I_1, \ldots, I_j) \in (\{0,1\}^*)^j$ and a message $m \in \mathbb{G}_T$, picks a random $s \in \mathbb{Z}_p$ and outputs

$$C = (e(f_1, g_2)^s \cdot m, g_1^s, \mathsf{H}_1(I_1)^s, \ldots, \mathsf{H}_j(I_j)^s) \in \left(\mathbb{G}_T, \mathbb{G}_1, \mathbb{G}_2^j \right).$$

- $\mathsf{Dec}(sk_{\mathsf{ID}}, c)$: on input a private key $sk_{\mathsf{ID}} = (d_0, d_1, \ldots, d_j)$ and a ciphertext $C = (A, B, C_1, \ldots, C_j)$, outputs

$$A \cdot \frac{\prod_{k=1}^{j} e\left(d_k, C_k\right)}{e\left(B, d_0\right)} = m.$$

References

1. Government of Canada. https://www.canada.ca/en/shared-services/corporate/transparency/briefing-documents/ministerial-briefing-book/delegation.html
2. PGP. https://www.openpgp.org
3. The University of Iowa. https://opsmanual.uiowa.edu/administrative-financial-and-facilities-policies/facsimile-signatures-and-signature-assignment-2
4. Viafirma. https://www.viafirma.com/blog-xnoccio/en/signature-delegation/
5. WhatsApp. https://www.whatsapp.com
6. Akinyele, J.A., Garman, C., Hohenberger, S.: Automating fast and secure translations from type-i to type-iii pairing schemes. In: ACM CCS 2015, pp. 1370–1381 (2015)
7. Alimi, P.: On the use of pedersen commitments for confidential payments. https://research.nccgroup.com/2021/06/15/on-the-use-of-pedersen-commitments-for-confidential-payments/
8. Boldyreva, A.: Secure proxy signature scheme for delegation of signing rights (2003). http://eprint.iacr.org/2003/096/
9. Boneh, D., Boyen, X.: Efficient selective-id secure identity based encryption without random oracles. Cryptology ePrint Archive, Report 2004/172 (2004). https://ia.cr/2004/172
10. Bünz, B., Agrawal, S., Zamani, M., Boneh, D.: Zether: towards privacy in a smart contract world. In: Bonneau, J., Heninger, N. (eds.) FC 2020. LNCS, vol. 12059, pp. 423–443. Springer, Cham (2020). https://doi.org/10.1007/978-3-030-51280-4_23
11. Canetti, R., Halevi, S., Katz, J.: A forward-secure public-key encryption scheme. In: Biham, E. (ed.) EUROCRYPT 2003. LNCS, vol. 2656, pp. 255–271. Springer, Heidelberg (2003). https://doi.org/10.1007/3-540-39200-9_16
12. Cao, F., Cao, Z.: A secure identity-based multi-proxy signature scheme. Comput. Electr. Eng. **35**(1), 86–95 (2009)
13. Chen, Y., Ma, X., Tang, C., Au, M.H.: PGC: pretty good confidential transaction system with auditability. In: ESORICS 2020, pp. 591–610 (2020)
14. Chen, Y., Tang, Q., Wang, Y.: Hierarchical integrated signature and encryption. Cryptology ePrint Archive, Report 2021/1237 (2021). https://ia.cr/2021/1237
15. Coron, J.-S., Joye, M., Naccache, D., Paillier, P.: Universal padding schemes for RSA. In: Yung, M. (ed.) CRYPTO 2002. LNCS, vol. 2442, pp. 226–241. Springer, Heidelberg (2002). https://doi.org/10.1007/3-540-45708-9_15

16. Dai, J.Z., Yang, X.H., Dong, J.X.: Designated-receiver proxy signature scheme for electronic commerce. In: SMC 2003 Conference Proceedings. 2003 IEEE International Conference on Systems, Man and Cybernetics. Conference Theme - System Security and Assurance (Cat. No.03CH37483) (2003)
17. Fujisaki, E., Okamoto, T.: Secure integration of asymmetric and symmetric encryption schemes. In: Wiener, M. (ed.) CRYPTO 1999. LNCS, vol. 1666, pp. 537–554. Springer, Heidelberg (1999). https://doi.org/10.1007/3-540-48405-1_34
18. Galbraith, S.D., Paterson, K.G., Smart, N.P.: Pairings for cryptographers. Discret. Appl. Math. **16**, 3113–3121 (2008)
19. Gentry, C., Silverberg, A.: Hierarchical ID-based cryptography. In: Zheng, Y. (ed.) ASIACRYPT 2002. LNCS, vol. 2501, pp. 548–566. Springer, Heidelberg (2002). https://doi.org/10.1007/3-540-36178-2_34
20. Haber, S., Pinkas, B.: Securely combining public-key cryptosystems. In: ACM CCS 2001, pp. 215–224 (2001)
21. Horwitz, J., Lynn, B.: Toward hierarchical identity-based encryption. In: Knudsen, L.R. (ed.) EUROCRYPT 2002. LNCS, vol. 2332, pp. 466–481. Springer, Heidelberg (2002). https://doi.org/10.1007/3-540-46035-7_31
22. Huang, X., Mu, Y., Susilo, W., Zhang, F., Chen, X.: A short proxy signature scheme: efficient authentication in the ubiquitous world. In: Enokido, T., Yan, L., Xiao, B., Kim, D., Dai, Y., Yang, L.T. (eds.) EUC 2005. LNCS, vol. 3823, pp. 480–489. Springer, Heidelberg (2005). https://doi.org/10.1007/11596042_50
23. Huang, X., Susilo, W., Mu, Y., Wu, W.: Proxy signature without random oracles. In: Cao, J., Stojmenovic, I., Jia, X., Das, S.K. (eds.) MSN 2006. LNCS, vol. 4325, pp. 473–484. Springer, Heidelberg (2006). https://doi.org/10.1007/11943952_40
24. Kim, S., Park, S., Won, D.: Proxy signatures, revisited. In: Han, Y., Okamoto, T., Qing, S. (eds.) ICICS 1997. LNCS, vol. 1334, pp. 223–232. Springer, Heidelberg (1997). https://doi.org/10.1007/BFb0028478
25. Komano, Y., Ohta, K.: Efficient universal padding techniques for multiplicative trapdoor one-way permutation. In: Boneh, D. (ed.) CRYPTO 2003. LNCS, vol. 2729, pp. 366–382. Springer, Heidelberg (2003). https://doi.org/10.1007/978-3-540-45146-4_22
26. Lee, B., Kim, H., Kim, K.: Secure mobile agent using strong non-designated proxy signature. In: Varadharajan, V., Mu, Y. (eds.) ACISP 2001. LNCS, vol. 2119, pp. 474–486. Springer, Heidelberg (2001). https://doi.org/10.1007/3-540-47719-5_37
27. Mambo, M., Usuda, K., Okamoto, E.: Proxy signatures: delegation of the power to sign messages. IEICE Trans. Fundam. Electron. Commun. Comput. Sci. **79**(9), 1338–1354 (1996)
28. Mambo, M., Usuda, K., Okamoto, E.: Proxy signatures for delegating signing operation. In: Proceedings of the 3rd ACM Conference on Computer and Communications Security, pp. 48–57. CCS 1996, Association for Computing Machinery, New York, NY, USA (1996)
29. Neuman, B.: Proxy-based authorization and accounting for distributed systems. In: 1993 Proceedings. The 13th International Conference on Distributed Computing Systems, pp. 283–291 (1993)
30. Paterson, K.G., Schuldt, J.C.N., Stam, M., Thomson, S.: On the joint security of encryption and signature, revisited. In: Lee, D.H., Wang, X. (eds.) ASIACRYPT 2011. LNCS, vol. 7073, pp. 161–178. Springer, Heidelberg (2011). https://doi.org/10.1007/978-3-642-25385-0_9
31. Rubin, K., Silverberg, A.: Compression in finite fields and torus-based cryptography. SIAM J. Comput. **37**(5), 1401–1428 (2008)

32. Sakemi, Y., Kobayashi, T., Saito, T., Wahby, R.S.: Pairing-Friendly Curves. Internet-Draft draft-irtf-cfrg-pairing-friendly-curves-09, Internet Engineering Task Force (2020). https://datatracker.ietf.org/doc/html/draft-irtf-cfrg-pairing-friendly-curves-09
33. Shigeo, M.: A portable and fast pairing-based cryptography library. https://github.com/herumi/mcl
34. Shim, K.A.: Short designated verifier proxy signatures. Comput. Electr. Eng. **37**(2), 180–186 (2011)

SR-MuSig2: A Scalable and Reconfigurable Multi-signature Scheme and Its Applications

Wenqiu Ma[1,2] and Rui Zhang[1,2](✉)

[1] State Key Laboratory of Information Security, Institute of Information Engineering, Chinese Academy of Sciences, Beijing 100093, China
{mawenqiu,zhangrui}@iie.ac.cn

[2] School of Cyber Security, University of Chinese Academy of Sciences, Beijing 100049, China

Abstract. Multi-signature is a kind of digital signature with a wide range of uses, such as certificate authorities signing certificates, which can enable a group of signers to sign the same message in a very short period, thereby aggregating a compact signature. In this work, we propose SR-MuSig2, a multi-signature scheme with scalability and reconfigurability. First of all, we use a tree structure to significantly improve the efficiency of computation and communication of signers, so that the scheme can support a large number of participants signing simultaneously and has better scalability. For the reconfigurability, SR-MuSig2 supports the signers to revoke passively or actively from the signer group, while can effectively generate the signature and complete the verification. Then we implement a prototype system in Python, and evaluate our scheme in the simulation network environment. The experimental results show that SR-MuSig2 is able to generate aggregated signature in an acceptable time with up to thousands of signers, and it can complete the signing process in only 12 s when there are 2^{11} signers. In addition, when 5% of the nodes in the signer group (up to 2^{11} signers) go offline, SR-MuSig2 only needs to update the values of 2.6% of the remaining nodes (nearly 66 s) instead of updating the values of all the remaining nodes to recover signing process.

Keywords: Multi-signature · Tree structure · Scalability · Reconfigurability

1 Introduction

Multi-signature, which was first proposed by K. Itakura and K. Nakamura [7] in 1983, is a special digital signature scheme that allows multiple signers to sign a public message in a short period, thereby generating an independent aggregated signature. The verifier can confirm the validity of it by verifying the aggregated signature. This is more compact and convenient than verifying a list of signatures generated by all the signers. The multi-signature scheme has a wide range of applications, especially in critical network authorities, such as certificate authorities, timestamping authorities, and directory authorities.

Y. Deng and M. Yung (Eds.): Inscrypt 2022, LNCS 13837, pp. 87–107, 2023.
https://doi.org/10.1007/978-3-031-26553-2_5

Multi-signature schemes can be obtained from general signature schemes, but require the underlying signature scheme to be aggregatable. Many proposed multi-signature schemes [1,3–6,8,10–13,16,17] are based on Schnorr signature [15], since it has good aggregability and can be well used in some distributed scenarios. However, Syta et al. [17] pointed out that multi-signature schemes are only used or considered practical in small groups (less than 10 signers), because the time cost of signing increases linearly with the number of signers. When the number of signers increases beyond 10, the time to complete a signature increases greatly, which is unacceptable in practice. Therefore, some scholars proposed multi-signature schemes based on tree structure [6,19] to reduce time consumption caused by the increase in the number of signers. However, these schemes are only theoretically feasible, because the case where nodes in the tree go offline is not considered, so the actual network environment needs to be taken into account when it is used. CoSi scheme proposed by Syta et al. [17] in 2016 is based on a tree structure. Although it considers the influence of the network environment, Drijvers et al. [6] proposed an attack on CoSi in 2019, so the scheme is insecure. To sum up, the multi-signature scheme based on tree structure needs further exploration and innovation. In this paper, we propose SR-MuSig2, a multi-signature scheme with scalability and reconfigurability. The specific contributions of this paper are as follows:

- Based on MuSig2 [12], we propose a trivial tree-based MuSig2 scheme. By introducing a tree structure, we allocate the computation and communication costs of signing to each node of the tree, which improves the efficiency of signing while not losing security and makes the scheme no longer restricted by the increasing number of signers. Namely, the trivial tree-based MuSig2 scheme has scalability;
- Based on the above scheme, we propose a scalable and reconfigurable multi-signature scheme named SR-MuSig2, which not only has the property of scalability, but also supports signers passively or actively revoke from the signer group while it still can generate multi-signatures and be verified correctly. Namely, the SR-MuSig2 scheme has scalability and reconfigurability;
- We implement the proposed SR-MuSig2 signature system in Python, and compare it with Schnorr and tree-based Schnorr multi-signature schemes. Experimental results show that SR-MuSig2 is able to generate aggregated signature in an acceptable time with up to thousands of signers, and it can complete the signing process in only 12 s when there are 2^{11} signers. In addition, when 5% of the nodes in the signer group (up to 2^{11} signers) go offline, SR-MuSig2 only needs to update the values of 2.6% of the remaining nodes (nearly 66 s) instead of updating the values of all the remaining nodes to recover signing process.

2 Related Work

Multi-signature was first proposed by K. Itakura and K. Nakamura [7] in 1983, which aims to emphasize that signatures of different signers on the same message can be combined into an independent signature and verified correctly.

2.1 Multi-signature Scheme Based on Schnorr

Schnorr signature algorithm has natural aggregation advantages, so it is very suitable as the underlying scheme of multi-signature. Scholars have designed a large number of multi-signature schemes based on Schnorr signature.

Based on Schnorr signature, Bellare and Neven [4] added a round to signature, requiring all participating signers exchange their own commitments, thus proposing a three-round multi-signature scheme BN [4], which is match to the standard Schnorr signature. Bagherzandi et al. proposed BCJ [3] scheme based on BN [4], which reduces the number of rounds from 3 to 2 by using multiplicative homomorphic commitments, but increases the signature size and computational cost of signing and verifying phases.

Ma et al. [9] proposed a variant MWLD based on Okamoto [14] signature scheme in 2010, which makes the scheme continue to execute in two rounds and reduces the size of the signature compared to Bagherzandi [3] scheme. However, both schemes above (Bagherzandi [3] and Ma [9]) don't support key aggregation.

In 2019, Maxwell et al. [10] extended BN [4] scheme and proposed a new Schnorr-based multi-signature scheme MuSig. A notable feature of this scheme is that it supports public key aggregation, and the verifier only needs a short aggregated key instead of an explicit list of all n public keys. The scheme is proven secure under the assumptions of the plain public-key model and discrete logarithm. However, whether their scheme can be proven safe under different assumptions or in a generic group model is currently an open question.

Drijvers et al. [6] showed that all previously proposed two-round multi-signature schemes (BN [4], BCJ [3], MWLD [9], MuSig [10]) in a pure DL setting are insecure under concurrent signing sessions. Therefore, Drijvers et al. [6] presented a two-round scheme mBCJ in 2019, which is safe under discrete logarithm assumption. However, this two-round scheme is more than twice as efficient as Schnorr signatures, and the resulting signature format is custom made.

In 2020, Nick et al. [13] proposed a variant of MuSig, MuSig-DN, which is the first Schnorr multi-signature scheme with deterministic nonces. In this scheme, signers deterministically generate the nonces in the form of a pseudorandom function of the message and public keys of all signers, and prove that they do so by providing NIZK to the co-signers, but NIZK is expensive and hurts the performance of signers, making MuSig-DN, which requires only two rounds of interactions, less efficient than three rounds of MuSig in common settings.

Therefore, Nick et al. [12] proposed a simple and practical two-round multi-signature scheme MuSig2 under the one-more discrete logarithm assumption. This is the first multi-signature scheme that simultaneously has several advantages: i) is secure under concurrent signing sessions, ii) supports key aggregation, iii) outputs standard Schnorr signatures, iv) requires only two communications, v) has signer complexity similar to standard Schnorr signatures. Alper and Burdges [2] used the idea of a linear combination of multiple random numbers to obtain a two-round multi-signature scheme DWMS, which is very similar to MuSig2, but lacks some optimizations present in MuSig2.

2.2 Multi-signature Scheme Based on Tree Structure

Syta et al. [17] designed CoSi using Schnorr multi-signature scheme, which organizes all cosigners into a tree structure, thereby realizing the rapid generation of multi-signatures, which is a highly scalable multi-signature scheme that allows a tree of 8192 signers to sign in less than two seconds. However, CoSi is vulnerable to rogue-key attack and k-sum problem, and an overpowering leader in this scheme may replace message m to create a different challenge, which will pose a threat to its security.

In 2018, Alangot et al. [1] showed through practical analysis that when using spanning tree topology of CoSi to extend Schnorr multi-signature, an average of 10–30% of the protocols failed. Therefore, they proposed a robust spanning tree topology and an implementation of BLS multi-signature, the enhanced topology successfully solves the reliability problem, and BLS multi-signature reduces the number of messages exchanged compared to Schnorr signature, thereby reducing failures and improving performance.

After tree-based multi-signature schemes being proposed, some practical problems come up, such as whether the unreliability of network will affect the structure of communication tree, thereby affecting communication efficiency between signing nodes; how to ensure that the signature is re-generated in the case of minimally affecting other nodes when nodes drop out of the signer group, etc., the above problems are all that need to be studied and solved.

Xiao Yue et al. [19] proposed a multi-signature scheme GMS based on Gamma signature [20], which is resistant to rogue-key attack and k-sum problem attack. This scheme also solves the problem of excessive power of CoSi leader and achieves provable security. To further improve online performance of GMS, Xiao Yue et al. [19] proposed a more efficient scheme, Advanced Gamma Multi-Signature (AGMS), which reduces the computational steps after the message arrives by changing the running order of the stages in the signature algorithm.

3 Preliminaries

In this section we briefly recall some important components needed in the rest of the paper, which are multi-signature scheme MuSig2 [12] and tree structure.

3.1 Notation and Definitions

Notation. Given a sampleable set S, we denote $s \xleftarrow{\$} S$ the operation of sampling an element of S uniformly at random and assigning it to s. In the following, λ is the security parameter. $\mathbb{G}$ be a cyclic group of order p, where p is a λ-bit prime, and g be a generator of $\mathbb{G}$. The triplet $(\mathbb{G}, p, g)$ are group parameters.

Definition 1 ***(Multi-signature Scheme).*** *A multi-signature scheme Π consists of three algorithms $(KeyGen, Sign, Ver)$. Public parameters are selected by a setup algorithm taking as input the security parameter. The randomized key generation algorithm takes no input and returns a private/public key pair $(sk, pk) \xleftarrow{\$} KeyGen()$. The signing algorithm Sign is run by every signer on* *input their key pair* (sk, pk)*, a multiset of public keys* $L = pk_1, ..., pk_n$*, and a message* m*, and returns a signature* σ *for* L *and* m*. The deterministic verification algorithm* Ver *takes as input a multiset of public keys* $L = pk_1, ..., pk_n$*, a message* m*, and a signature* σ*, and returns 1 if the signature is valid for* L *and* m *and 0 otherwise.*

3.2 Multi-Signature Scheme MuSig2

The multi-signature scheme MuSig2 [12] is characterized as follows:

Parameters setup (*Setup*). On input 1^λ, *Setup* runs $(\mathbb{G}, p, g) \leftarrow GrGen(1^\lambda)$, chooses three hash functions $H_{agg} : \{0,1\}^* \rightarrow \mathbb{Z}_p$, $H_{non} : \{0,1\}^* \rightarrow \mathbb{Z}_p$ and $H_{sig} : \{0,1\}^* \rightarrow \mathbb{Z}_p$, and returns $par := ((\mathbb{G}, p, g), H_{agg}, H_{non}, H_{sig})$.

Key generation (*KeyGen*). Each signer chooses a secret key $x \xleftarrow{\$} \mathbb{Z}_p$ randomly and computes a public key $X := g^x$ corresponding to its secret key x.

Key aggregation (*KeyAgg*). The multiset of public keys is $L = \{X_1, X_2, ..., X_n\}$. *KeyAgg* runs $KeyAggCoef(L, X) := H_{agg}(L, X)$ to generate key aggregation coefficient, in which X are public keys in multiset L. Then *KeyAgg* generates aggregated key $\tilde{X} := \prod_{i=1}^{n} X_i^{a_i}$, where $a_i := KeyAggCoef(L, X_i)$.

First signing round (*Sign* and *SignAgg*). Each signer can perform *Sign* before the cosigners and the message have been determined.

Sign: Integer v specifies the number of nonces generated by each signer, integer n specifies the number of signers. For each $j \in \{1, ..., v\}$, each signer i generates random $r_{i,j} \xleftarrow{\$} \mathbb{Z}_p$ and computes $R_{i,j} := g^{r_{i,j}}$ and then outputs v nonces $(R_{i,1}, ..., R_{i,v})$. Note that in all the schemes below, we set $v = 2$.

SignAgg: Aggregator receives outputs $(R_{1,1}, ..., R_{1,v}), ..., (R_{n,1}, ..., R_{n,v})$ from n signers and aggregates them by computing $R_j := \prod_{i=1}^{n} R_{i,j}$ for each $j \in \{1, ..., v\}$ and outputting $(R_1, ..., R_v)$.

Second signing round (*Sign'*, *SignAgg'*, and *Sign''*). Let m be the message to sign, (X_1, x_1) be the key pairs of a specific signer, $X_2, ..., X_n$ be the public keys of cosigners, and $L = \{X_1, ..., X_n\}$ be the multiset of all public keys.

Sign': Signers execute *KeyAgg* to compute $\tilde{X}$ and store their own key aggregation coefficient $a_i := KeyAggCoef(L, X_i)$. Upon receiving of aggregated public nonces $(R_1, ...R_v)$, signers compute $b := H_{non}(\tilde{X}, (R_1, ..., R_v), m)$, $R := \prod_{j=1}^{v} R_j^{b^{j-1}}$, $c := H_{sig}(\tilde{X}, R, m)$, $s_i := ca_i x_i + \sum_{j=1}^{v} r_{i,j} b^{j-1} \bmod p$, and each signer outputs s_i.

SignAgg': The aggregator receives individual signatures $(s_1, ..., s_n)$ from all signers, then aggregates them and outputs the sum $s := \sum_{i=1}^{n} s_i \bmod p$.

Sign'': Signers receive s and output the final signature $\sigma := (R, s)$.

Verification (Ver) . Given an aggregated public key $\tilde{X}$, a message m, and a signature $\sigma := (R, s)$, the verifier accepts the signature if $g^s = R\tilde{X}^c$.

3.3 Tree Structure

In this paper, tree structure is introduced into multi-signature schemes, which can spread the communication and calculation costs of signing across each signer, so that the cost of each signer node is at most logarithmic level. The introduction of tree structure does not change the security, but it makes the multi-signature scheme have better scalability and higher efficiency.

The tree structure used here is a binary tree. When constructing it in the preparation stage, all the layers are full except the last one, that is, a binary tree of height h has at least 2^{h-1} nodes and at most $2^h - 1$ nodes.

4 Trivial Tree-Based MuSig2 Scheme

In order to make MuSig2 scheme scalable, we try to introduce tree structure into the scheme to make it no longer restricted by the number of signers, and also to improve signing efficiency, while not losing security of the original scheme.

The leader organizes N signers into a balanced binary tree, whose depth is $\mathcal{O}(\log N)$, thus spreads the communication and computation costs evenly across each node. A round of MuSig2 protocol consists of four phases, as shown in Fig. 1, including two round-trips of communication in a tree:

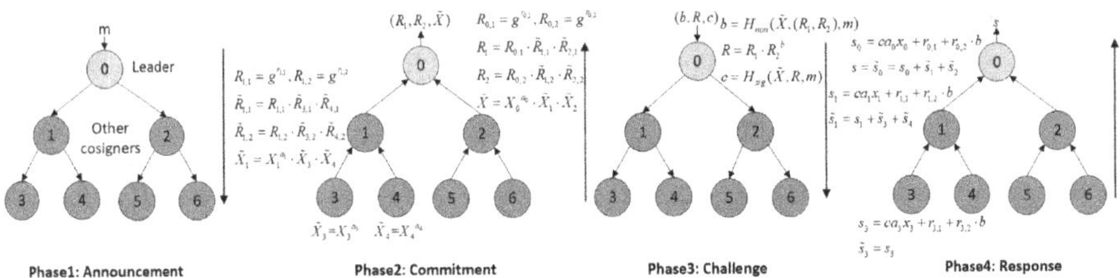

Fig. 1. MuSig2 uses four communication phases for scalable construction of a Schnorr multi-signature over a spanning tree.

1) Announcement: The leader (root node) broadcasts down the tree, declaring the start of signing, along with the message m to be signed.
2) Commitment: Each node i computes ${X_i}^{a_i}$, generates random secrets $r_{i,1}, r_{i,2}$ and computes its individual commits $R_{i,1}, R_{i,2}$. It then outputs two nonces $(R_{i,1}, R_{i,2})$. In the bottom-up process, each node i waits for two aggregated commits $(R_{j,1}, R_{j,2})$ and one aggregated public key $\tilde{X}_j$ from each immediate child node j. Node i then computes its own aggregated commit $\tilde{R}_{i,1} = R_{i,1} \prod_{j \in C_i} \tilde{R}_{j,1}$, $\tilde{R}_{i,2} = R_{i,2} \prod_{j \in C_i} \tilde{R}_{j,2}$ and public key $\tilde{X}_i = {X_i}^{a_i} \prod_{j \in C_i} \tilde{X}_j$, where C_i is the set of i's immediate child nodes. Finally, i passes $((\tilde{R}_{i,1}, \tilde{R}_{i,2}), \tilde{X}_i)$ up to its parent, unless i is the leader.

3) Challenge: Upon receiving the commitments and public keys from its two child nodes, the leader first computes the aggregated public key $\tilde{X} = {X_0}^{a_0} \cdot \tilde{X}_1 \cdot \tilde{X}_2$, where 0 indicates the leader, and 1 and 2 are two child nodes of the leader. In order to compute $b = H_{non}(\tilde{X}, (R_1, R_2), m)$, the leader first needs to compute final commitments of two nonces (R_1, R_2), which R_1 indicates the final commitment of the first nonces of all signers, and R_2 indicates the final commitment of the second nonces of all signers. After computing (R_1, R_2) and thus the value of b, the leader computes the aggregated commitment of two nonces $R = R_1 \cdot {R_2}^b$, and finally generates the challenge $c = H_{sig}(\tilde{X}, R, m)$. The root node then broadcasts the challenge c down to each node in the tree.
4) Response: In the final bottom-up phase, each node i waits to receive a partial aggregated response $\tilde{s}_j$ from each of its immediate child nodes $j \in C_i$. Node i computes its individual response $s_i = ca_ix_i + r_{i,1} + r_{i,2}b$, and then computes its partial aggregated response $\tilde{s}_i = s_i + \sum_{j \in C_j} \tilde{s}_j$. Node i finally passes $\tilde{s}_i$ up to its parent, unless i is the root node.

The final signature is $\sigma := (R, s)$, which any third party can verify as a standard Schnorr signature given an aggregated public key $\tilde{X}$ and a message m, the verifier accepts the signature iff $g^s = R\tilde{X}^c$.

By applying the tree structure to the signing process, a multi-signature can be generated more efficiently. The generated multi-signature is calculated and aggregated by a group of signers, so the multi-signature is compact and cannot be separated from individual signatures. However, if some signers drop out of the signer group due to network reasons or voluntarily quit because of their own subjective reasons, then it is a question of whether the signature is reconfigurable without starting a new signing round. We will first analyze the feasibility of the problem and then discuss its solution.

5 SR-MuSig2 Scheme

We have made MuSig2 scalable by introducing tree structure, and in this section we will focus on reconfigurability, thus proposing a scalable and reconfigurable multi-signature scheme, SR-MuSig2. First, we improve the original MuSig2, making it more applicable to reconfiguring. In addition, we discuss what steps should be taken when nodes go offline due to network problems. Finally, the solutions after nodes actively revoke from the signer group will also be discussed.

5.1 Advanced MuSig2 Scheme

Before discussing the reconfigurability of multi-signatures, we first consider the potential problems in signature generation. In the actual signing process, due to the uncertainty of the network environment, there may be problems such as node disconnection. The drop of a node will affect the communication between it and other directly connected nodes in the tree structure, thus affecting the signature generation process. How to complete the original signing process without restarting a new round when some nodes go offline is the problem to be solved.

By analyzing MuSig2, we can conclude that once a node drops due to network failure or subjective reasons, $L = \{X_1, ...X_n\}$ will be affected, and then $a_i = H_{agg}(L, X_i)$ will change. At this time, all signers need to update $X_i{}^{a_i}$, which will bring huge computation overhead. Introducing the concept of **key tree** and modifying the rules of computing a_i of the original scheme can effectively solve the above problems without affecting the security of the original scheme.

Definition 2. *The* **key tree** *is a binary tree composed of the signers' public keys. The topology of the key tree is exactly the same as the topology of the signing tree described above, and each layer of the tree is connected by hash functions.*

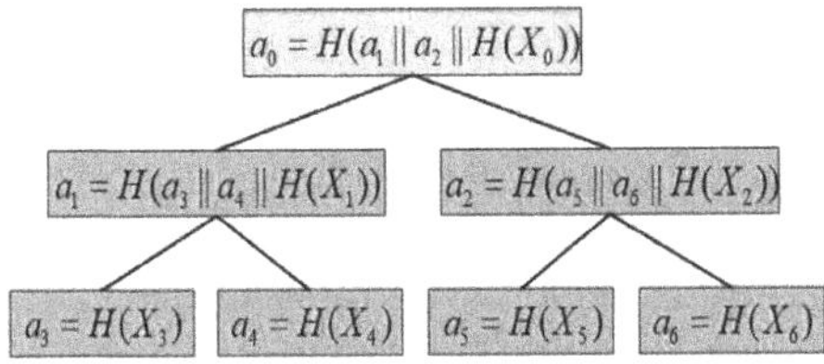

Fig. 2. The logical structure of the key tree (Take a seven-node tree as an example).

The logical structure of the key tree is shown in Fig. 2. Based on the key tree, we can redefine the computing rule of a_i:

$$a_i = H(a_{i_{j1}} || a_{i_{j2}} || H(X_i)) \tag{1}$$

Note that i_{j1} and i_{j2} are the immediate child nodes of i.

Now we have a new scheme, advanced MuSig2. In this scheme, the exit of any signer will affect a_i of only his direct and indirect parent nodes, on the other hand, it ensures that the exit of any signer will not affect a_i of all nodes which are not in the same subtree with it.

Now we discuss the correctness and security of the advanced MuSig2 scheme after changing the computing rule of a_i.

Correctness requires that for all $m \in \{0,1\}^*$ it holds that $Ver(\tilde{X}, m, \sigma) = 1$ with probability one when $\tilde{X} = KeyAgg(L)$, $L = \{X_1, X_2, ..., X_n\}$, $\sigma = (R, s)$ and $s = SignAgg(s_1, s_2, ..., s_n)$. If every signer produces his individual signature honestly, it is not hard to see that the scheme is correct:

$$\begin{aligned} g^s = g^{\sum_{i=1}^{n} s_i} = \prod_{i=1}^{n} g^{s_i} = \prod_{i=1}^{n} g^{ca_i x_i + r_{i,1} + r_{i,2} \cdot b} = \prod_{i=1}^{n} X_i{}^{a_i c} \cdot R_{i,1} \cdot R_{i,2}{}^{b} \\ = \prod_{i=1}^{n} R_{i,1} \cdot (\prod_{i=1}^{n} R_{i,2})^b \cdot (\prod_{i=1}^{n} X_i{}^{a_i})^c = (R_1 \cdot R_2{}^b) \cdot (\prod_{i=1}^{n} X_i{}^{a_i})^c = R\tilde{X}^c \end{aligned} \tag{2}$$

Now we analyze the **security** of the scheme. First, we will introduce the k-sum problem, and secondly, how to use the Wagner algorithm to solve the k-sum problem to attack the old version of MuSig scheme. Then, we will explain why Wagner's algorithm cannot be applied to attack MuSig2, thus proving that MuSig2 is resistant to k-sum attacks. Finally, we explain that our advanced MuSig2 scheme only changes the computing rule of a_i and does not affect the security of MuSig2, so it is still resistant to k-sum attacks.

Definition 3 ***(k-Sum Problem).*** *Given a constant $t \in \mathbb{Z}_p$, an integer k_m, and a random oracle $H : \mathbb{Z}_p \to \{0,1\}^n$, find a set $\{q_1, ..., q_{k_m}\}$ satisfying $\sum_{k=1}^{k_m} H(q_k) = t$ through k_m queries. As k_m increases, the difficulty of the problem gradually becomes lower. Wagner et al. [18] give a sub-exponential level algorithm without limiting k_m.*

The process of using the Wagner algorithm [18] to attack the old version of MuSig is as follows: the adversary, who acts as the signer holding the public key $X_2 = g^{x_2}$ in the session process, opens k_m signature sessions at the same time, and obtains a total of k_m nonces $R_1^1, ..., R_1^{k_m}$ from the honest signer with the public key $X_1 = g^{x_1}$. Let $\widetilde{X} = X_1^{a_1} X_2^{a_2}$ denote the aggregated public key, where $a_i = H(\langle X_1, X_2 \rangle, X_i)$. Given a forged message m^*, the adversary calculates $R^* = \prod_{k=1}^{k_m} R_1^{(k)}$, and then uses Wagner's algorithm to find $R_2^{(k)}$ that satisfies the following conditions:

$$\sum_{k=1}^{k_m} H_{sig}(\widetilde{X}, R_1^{(k)} R_2^{(k)}, m^{(k)}) = H_{sig}(\widetilde{X}, R^*, m^*) \tag{3}$$

where the left-hand side of the equation is equivalent to the sum of $c^{(k)}$, and the right-hand side of the equation is equivalent to the challenge value c^*.

After finding all $R_2^{(k)}$ that meet the above conditions, the adversary sends all $R_2^{(k)}$ to the honest signer, and the honest signer will feed back all $s_1^{(k)} = r_1^{(k)} + c^{(k)} \cdot a_1 x_1$ to the adversary after receiving $R_2^{(k)}$. Let $r^* = \sum_{k=1}^{k_m} r_1^{(k)} = DL(R^*)$, the adversary can obtain:

$$s_1^* = \sum_{k=1}^{k_m} s_1^{(k)} = \sum_{k=1}^{k_m} r_1^{(k)} + (\sum_{k=1}^{k_m} c^{(k)}) \cdot a_1 x_1 = r^* + c^* \cdot a_1 x_1 \tag{4}$$

The adversary can further construct the following equation based on s_1^*:

$$s^* = s_1^* + c^* \cdot a_2 x_2 = r^* + c^* \cdot (a_1 x_1 + a_2 x_2) \tag{5}$$

(R^*, s^*) is the legal signature of m^*, where the signature hash is $c^* = H_{sig}(\widetilde{X}, R^*, m^*)$. Although the forged message here is only legal for the public key $\widetilde{X}$ obtained by the aggregation of X_1 and X_2, as long as the public key X_1 of the honest signer is aggregated with the public key set of the adversary, the attack can forge legitimate messages with just a few adjustments.

Therefore, from the perspective of the above attack, the old version of MuSig is vulnerable to k-sum attack. The new version of MuSig adds an additional commitment round in the process of exchanging the public nonces R_1 to prevent the adversary from calculating the required R_2 after obtaining all R_1.

The following analyzes whether the MuSig2 scheme is vulnerable to k-sum attacks. The ingenuity of MuSig2 is that each signer i needs to send a list of nonces $R_{i,1},...,R_{i,v}(v \geq 2)$, and use their linear combination $\hat{R}_i = \prod_{j=1}^{v} R_{i,j}^{b^{j-1}}$ as their final nonce instead of a single nonce R_i like the MuSig scheme, where $b = H_{non}(\tilde{X}, (\prod_{i=1}^{n} R_{i,1},...,\prod_{i=1}^{n} R_{i,v}), m)$ and $H_{non} : \{0,1\}^* \to \mathbb{Z}_p$. In this way, each time the adversary tries a different $R_2^{(k)}$, the coefficient $b^{(k)}$ will change accordingly, which in turn changes the $\hat{R}_1 = \prod_{j=1}^{v} R_{1,j}^{b^{j-1}}$ of the honest signer, and finally changes the $R^* = \prod_{k=1}^{k_m} \hat{R}_1^{(k)}$ on the right-hand side of the equation. This also causes the right-hand side of the equation to be no longer a constant, thereby destroying the necessary prerequisites for the k-sum problem, and the Wagner algorithm is no longer applicable. Therefore, to sum up, the MuSig2 algorithm is also resistant to k-sum attacks.

Finally, we explain that changing the computing rule of a_i will not affect the security of the original scheme. To be specific, the generation of a_i in the original scheme is calculated through the public key list and users' public keys, that is to say, the calculation of a_i does not rely on private values, so neither the calculation nor the result of a_i need to be kept secret. After changing the computing rule of a_i, a_i can also be calculated using only public keys. From another aspect, the security of the scheme lies in the confidentiality of the private key x_i and the private nonces $(r_{i,1}, r_{i,2})$. In summary, changing computing rule of a_i doesn't affect the security of the original scheme. Therefore, our advanced MuSig2 is also resistant to k-sum attacks.

Given the tree-based advanced MuSig2, which has scalability and is more applicable to reconfiguring, we further propose SR-MuSig2 which has reconfigurability, and discuss it in two separate cases.

5.2 SR-MuSig2 in Case of Network Failure

During communication between tree nodes, if a node i does not receive a message from its child node j in a certain period, or the child node j does not receive the message from its parent node i, we can think of it as network failure. Combined with the above analysis of the tree-based MuSig2 scheme, we mainly focus on two phases, commitment and response.

In commitment phase, when a node goes offline, the first thing that comes to mind is to create a missing list to include the ID of the offline node, and then the verifier calculates the aggregated public keys of the remaining signers through modular inverse calculation. However, we already know that the final aggregated public key is in the form of $\tilde{X} := \prod_{i=1}^{n} X_i^{a_i}$. After careful analysis, we can see that if the modular inverse $\tilde{X}' := \tilde{X} \cdot (X_j^{a_j})^{-1}$ is used directly, the aggregated public key of the remaining signers is not correct. Because as long as a node is offline, a_i of its parent node and all indirect parent nodes will change, so it is necessary to recalculate new a_i, $\tilde{X}_i$, and $(R_{i,1}, R_{i,2})$, and upload from the bottom up. During this process, two issues need to be discussed respectively:

- How to adjust tree structure after nodes go offline due to network failure?

- Is the set of nodes whose a_i are changed and the set whose $(\tilde{R}_{i,1}, \tilde{R}_{i,2})$ are changed the same set?

We start with the **first question**. The commitment and response phases of signing are bottom-up value transfer processes. If a node drops, its parent node will not be able to receive the message from it, and the parent node communicates up to inform the leader that its child node is offline. The leader adjusts the tree structure and re-broadcasts the tree topology down, so that each node updates the tree topology. In this process, the rules for adjusting the tree structure should meet the goal of minimizing the number of other nodes affected as much as possible. If multiple nodes drop, the leader should follow the rules described in Algorithm 1. Before describing the pseudocode, we first give five definitions.

Definition 4. *When the nodes are offline, the previous tree will be broken down into many trees. The tree containing the root node is called the* **main tree**, *and the remaining trees not connected to the root node are called* ***free subtrees***.

Definition 5. *The* ***dyed node*** *is the node that needs to be recalculated after the nodes go offline.*

Definition 6 ***Height Priority Criteria. (HPC)*** *If there is a dyed node in the free subtree, then calculate the height between the vacant position closest to the dyed node and the dyed node; if there is no dyed node in the free subtree, then assume that the parent node of the root node of the free subtree is a dyed node, then calculate the height between the vacant position closest to the dyed node and the dyed node. The smaller the height, the higher the priority.*

Definition 7 ***Vacancy Priority Criteria. (VPC)*** *If the two trees have the same priority according to the height priority criteria, then compare the number of vacant positions in the layer where the vacant position closest to the dyed node in the two trees. The higher the number, the higher the priority.*

Definition 8 ***Optimal Insertion Node. (OIN)*** *The optimal insertion node is the one that requires the least number of recalculated nodes when inserting a subtree under it.*

After the nodes are offline, make the parent nodes of all the offline nodes become dyed nodes.

Given the pseudocode of tree adjustment rules for network failure in commitment phase, we further explain with a specific example. From Fig. 3, we can find that Node 2, 4, 10, 12 are offline. First, dye the parent nodes of all the offline nodes, and dye the parent nodes of all the dyed nodes until the root is dyed. The drop of four nodes caused the previous tree to be split into a main tree and three free subtrees. Prioritize the three free subtrees, the vacant position of the second subtree is only one level away from the dyed node, and the remaining two are all two layers away, so the second subtree has the highest priority. There are two vacant positions in the layer closest to the dyed node in the first subtree, but only one in the last tree, so the priority of the last tree is at the end. Finally,

Algorithm 1. Adjustment rules of tree structure in commitment phase.

Input: A main tree and many free subtrees
Output: A new tree

Traverse the entire ***main tree*** from bottom to top, and dye the parent nodes of all ***dyed nodes*** until the root node is dyed
Prioritize all ***free subtrees*** according to ***HPC*** and ***VPC***, and store them in a list called ***Priority List***
for *subtree* in ***Priority List*** **do**
  get ***OIN*** from the ***main tree*** as ***OIN_node***
  insert ***subtree*** into ***OIN_node***
  dye all the nodes on the path from ***OIN_node*** to the root node
end for
return A new tree

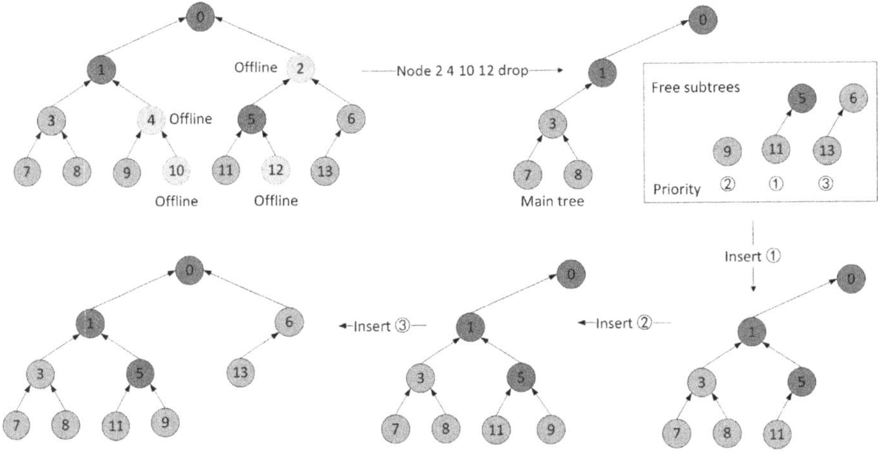

Fig. 3. An example of adjustment rules of tree structure in commitment phase.

insert the free subtrees into the main tree in sequence according to the order of priority, and the adjustment of the tree structure is completed.

Then, we analyze the **second question**. Based on Fig. 3, we analyze the nodes who need to update a_i and $(R_{i,1}, R_{i,2})$ after network failure. It is not difficult to see from Fig. 3 that the nodes need to update a_i are Node 0, 1, 5, and the nodes need to update $(R_{i,1}, R_{i,2})$ are the same.

Through the above analysis, we can conclude that the nodes need to recalculate a_i and $(R_{i,1}, R_{i,2})$ are completely equivalent. Each time the leader adjusts the topology of the tree, it only needs to adjust the subtree rooted at the offline nodes, and the nodes of other subtrees remain unchanged, so the previously calculated values of these nodes do not need to be updated. To a certain extent, the time cost of signing can be saved a lot.

The solution of network failure problems in commitment stage have been discussed. Next, we will discuss the problems that should be dealt with when network failure occurs **in the response phase**, which is the last stage of signing.

If a node goes offline at this stage, the cost of recalculation will be very large because the previously calculated values need to be recomputed, that is to say, the commitment, challenge and response phase should all be re-executed, thus the cost is close to that of a new signing round. Therefore, we make a compromise here. Since the goal of signature is to authenticate the identity of the signer, if authentication is passed, the verifier can believe that the message has been signed by the signer group. Therefore, if a signer drops at this stage, we will not adjust the tree structure first, but to continue the signing process, and use a special method to verify the signature, which can save a lot of time cost. After verification is passed, we will adjust the tree structure to facilitate subsequent signature operations. Below, we use a concrete example to illustrate the special method for verifying signatures and then give a general rule.

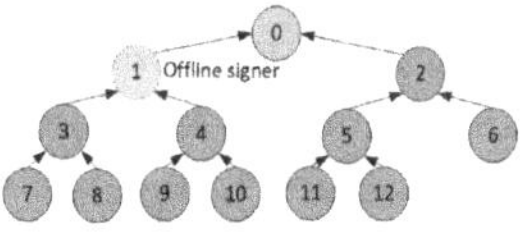

Fig. 4. Nodes go offline in the response phase.

As shown in Fig. 4, if node 0 has not received the message from node 1 in the response phase, then we can consider that node 1 is offline. At this time, the root node does not need to adjust the tree structure, but first plays the role of node 1 to collect signature information of its child nodes (node 3 and node 4), and integrates it with the information of node 2 and its own information, then generate an aggregated signature excluding information of node 1. At the same time, the root node calculates the following values:

$$a_1 = Hash(a_3||a_4||Hash(X_1)) \tag{6}$$

$$s^{'} = s_0 + \tilde{s}_3 + \tilde{s}_4 + \tilde{s}_2 \tag{7}$$

The root node passes $s^{'}$, b, c, $\tilde{X}$, R, $(R_{1,1}, R_{1,2})$, X_1, a_1 to the verifier.

The verifier does the following verification to check if the equation holds:

$$g^{s'} \cdot (X_1{}^{a_1})^c \cdot R_{1,1} \cdot R_{1,2}{}^b = R\tilde{X}^c \tag{8}$$

If the above equation holds, the signature verification passes.

Now we summarize a general rule for generating and verifying the final multi-signature when nodes go offline at response phase. Whenever root node receives information about dropped nodes, it adds them to a **missing list** until it receives everyone's signature s_i. At this point, the root node calculates a_j of all the nodes in the missing list, and the corresponding signature verification value $verifyVal[j] = (X_j{}^{a_j})^c \cdot R_{j,1} \cdot R_{j,2}{}^b$ of each node in this list, the root node calculates the aggregated signatures $s' = \sum s_i$ of all the remaining signers, and outputs the final multi-signature which contains three main components:

$$\sigma = ((R, s'), verifyVal, proof) \tag{9}$$

In which R is the aggregated public nonces of all signers, s' is multi-signature of the remaining signers, $verifyVal$ is the list of verification value for missing signers in the response phase used for verifying, while $proof$ is used for proving that R and $\tilde{X}$ are fixed before challenge c was generated.

Upon receiving the final multi-signature σ, anyone can verify by checking the equation $g^{s'} \cdot \prod verifyVal[j] = R\tilde{X}^c$ holds or not.

5.3 SR-MuSig2 in Case of Signers' Active Revocation

After discussing the situation which nodes may drop due to network problems during signing, we will further analyze another question. After the signature is generated and even verified, if there is a signer wants to revoke his signature, how to deal with it efficiently and make the new signature still be verified. This question also belongs to the reconfigurable problem of multi-signature.

If a signer wants to revoke his signature after the multi-signature is generated, then there is no need to re-execute signing, because if it is really necessary to re-execute signing, then nonces need to be re-selected, and all intermediate values need to be re-calculated, which will bring huge computation cost. The signer only needs to provide some information to the root node before he revokes his signature, and then the root generates a new signature through modular inverse operation. The specific process is as follows.

The signer i who wants to revoke his own signature needs to provide the root node with $({X_i}^{a_i}, R_i, s_i)$, then the root node updates the final multi-signature:

$$s' = s - s_i \tag{10}$$

$$R' = R \cdot (R_i)^{-1} \tag{11}$$

$$\tilde{X}' = \tilde{X} \cdot ({X_i}^{a_i})^{-1} \tag{12}$$

In which $R_i = R_{i,1} \cdot {R_{i,2}}^b$, the verifier checks whether the equation $g^{s'} = R' \cdot \tilde{X}'^c$ holds or not.

Here we have to note that during verification, if we want to verify c, it will not pass, because at this time $\tilde{R}'$ and $\tilde{X}'$ have been changed, $c' = H_{sig}(\tilde{R}', \tilde{X}', m)$ also has changed, thus the verification of challenge c will not pass. To alleviate this problem, we recommend adding an component called evidence, which will prove that the missing node has participated in the calculation of the challenge c, which will not be modified after signing.

6 Evaluation

Based on MuSig2 scheme proposed by Nick et al. [12], the implementation of SR-MuSig2 proposed in this paper is written in Python, and its main algorithm consists of 1300 lines of code. SR-MuSig2 implements tree-based multi-signature, including exception handling for signer disconnection due to network failure and active revocation due to individual reasons.

The main aspect we wish to evaluate is whether SR-MuSig2 proposed in this paper has good scalability and reconfigurability. Other issues to consider include the impact of changing the computing rule of a_i on signing efficiency, the impact of different network environments (i.e., latency) on signing efficiency, and so on.

We implement SR-MuSig2 proposed in this paper, and compare it with the basic Schnorr scheme used in SP'16 [17] and MuSig2 scheme when necessary, then give the experimental results and analysis.

6.1 Experimental Setup

We use 3 physical machines (Intel Xeon Gold 6248R@3.0GHz) with an 8-core processor and 32 GB of RAM to test SR-MuSig2 proposed in this paper. At the same time, we control the communication delay to simulate different network environment. Except for the experiments on communication delay, all other experiments are done in the environment where the communication delay is 50 ms (average delay of network communication in China). To simulate as many signing participants as possible, we assign up to 8192 nodes to 3 machines for signing experiments, corresponding to a binary tree with a depth of $\lfloor \log_2 8192 \rfloor + 1$. For each group of experiments, we conduct 10 tests and calculate the average value.

6.2 Performance of Different Stages

The first experiment we do is to compare which phase occupies the main time cost in the entire signing process, including the preparation stage before signing, that is, the construction of tree, the generation of the aggregated public key, the signing stage, and verification after the signature is generated. It is not difficult to see from Table 1 that tree construction becomes the most time-consuming phase. When there are as many as 8192 signers, the time to construct the tree structure is as high as nearly 7 min. However, this phase can be counted as the offline preparation stage of signing, for multiple signatures of the same signer group, the construction of tree only needs to be done once. For the signing process which contains 4 phases, 2048 signers can reach the level of 12 s, which is a considerable result.

Table 1. Time cost of 4 stages versus number of signers (seconds)

Stages	Num of signers					
	8	32	128	512	2048	8192
Tree construction	0.6992	1.8961	6.7002	25.9696	103.1132	415.5308
Public key aggregation	0.6265	1.0431	1.6183	2.1926	3.7886	12.0023
Signing (4 phases)	1.2911	2.1639	3.3024	5.2775	12.6945	58.3020
Verification	0.0120	0.0117	0.0114	0.0114	0.0397	0.2814

6.3 Performance of Aggregating Public Keys

The second experiment we need to do is to test whether the change in computing rule of a_i has a huge impact on efficiency of the signature scheme, particularly, the process of aggregating public keys. We compare the time required for this process with and without tree structure respectively. The experimental data is shown in Fig. 5. It is not difficult to see from the figure that whether the scheme is tree-based or trivial, after changing the computing rule of a_i, the efficiency of aggregating public keys does not change significantly when the number of signers is less than 2048, and surprisingly, when the number of signers is more than 2048, the new a_i computing rule will improve the efficiency of this process for both tree-based schemes and trivial ones.

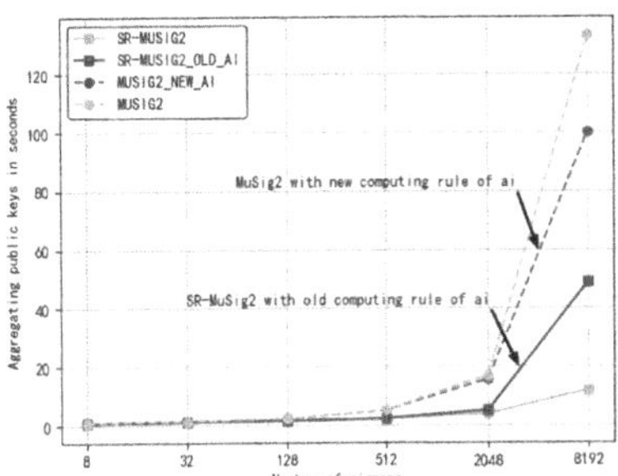

Fig. 5. Time cost of aggregating public keys versus number of signers.

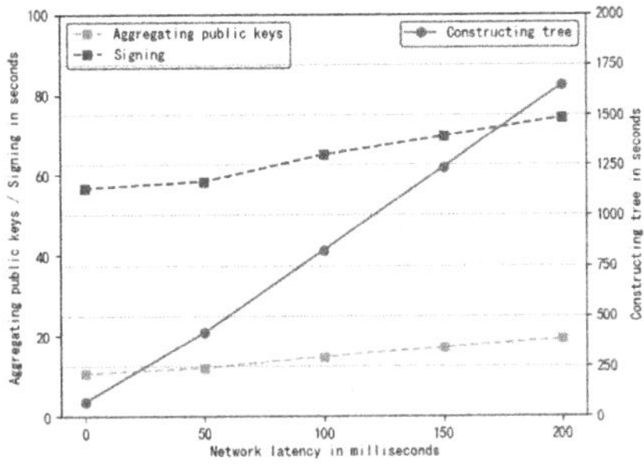

Fig. 6. Time cost of three phases versus network latency.

6.4 Impact of Network Environments

In the following experiment, we analyze the influence of communication delay on the efficiency of constructing trees and generating signatures. We use 0ms to simulate local network environment, 50ms to simulate average delay of network communication in China, and 200ms to that of international environment. In order to make experimental results clearer and more appreciable, we conduct experiments in a scenario where 8192 participants co-sign, and the results are shown in Fig. 6.

It is not difficult to see from the figure that although the time cost of aggregating public keys and signing increases linearly with the increase of delay, the growing rate is not large. This is because in these two phases, the process of passing values in the tree is a one-time bottom-up or top-down transfer, and the amount of data transmitted is small, so the increase in communication delay does not have a great impact on signing efficiency, thus we can implement SR-MuSig2 scheme in an international network environment, that is, signers can be dispersed all over the world.

It can also be seen from the figure that although the time spent on constructing tree also increases linearly with the increase of delay, the growing rate is relatively larger. When all the signers co-sign locally, the time to build the tree is about 70 s. When they co-sign in China, the time to build the tree is about 7 min, and when they are in different countries, the time is as high as 27 min. This phenomenon is attributable to the fact that information is repeatedly transmitted when constructing tree, and the amount of data transmitted is relatively larger. Therefore, the construction of tree is indeed a step that needs to be optimized. However, for the same signer group, if it performs multiple signing operations, it is enough to build a tree structure only once.

6.5 Scalability

In the next experiment we evaluate the scalability of implementing SR-MuSig2 among up to 8192 signers. We compare this scheme with 3 other schemes. The first is an advanced MuSig2 scheme without a tree structure, in which the aggregator collects their public nonces and standard individual signatures through direct communication with all other signers, and then aggregates them. The second is the tree-based Schnorr scheme, which implements the Schnorr multi-signature scheme through a tree structure. The third is the naïve Schnorr multi-signature scheme without a tree structure, which also relies on direct communication between the aggregator and other signers to pass values. We extract the process of aggregating public keys and signing in these four schemes for comparison.

After introducing tree structure into multi-signature, aggregation that originally needs to be calculated by a specific node (i.e., aggregator) is now allocated to each node of the tree, thus saving a lot of computation and communication cost, and improving the signing efficiency. The experimental results are shown in Fig. 7 and Fig. 8. It is not difficult to see that under the same signature algorithm, the introduction of the tree structure is much more efficient than that in the naïve case. As the number of signers increases, the naïve signature is not so efficient. This experiment shows from a practical point of view that introducing tree structure will indeed bring about an improvement in efficiency.

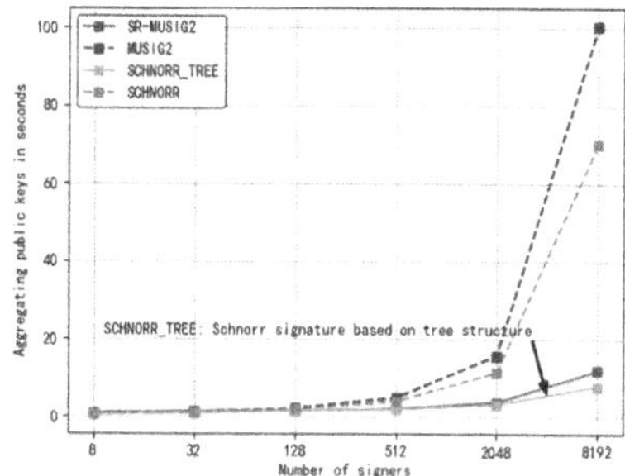

Fig. 7. Time cost of aggregating public keys versus number of signers.

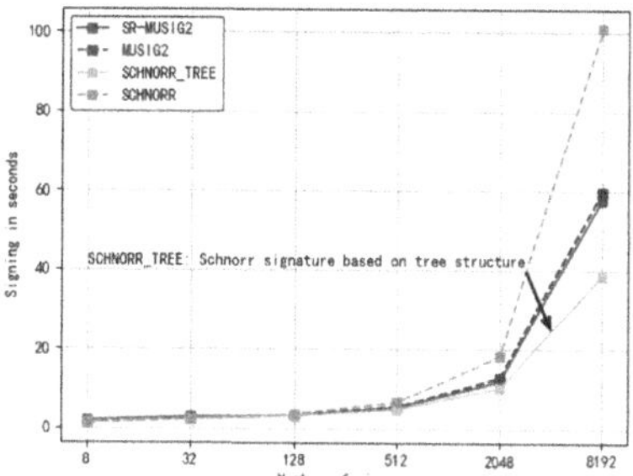

Fig. 8. Time cost of signing versus number of signers.

6.6 Reconfigurability

Finally, we conduct experiments on the reconfigurability of SR-MuSig2. The key to reconfigurability is that after the node is offline, the scheme can quickly adjust the tree structure and continue to sign, while the trivial tree-based MuSig2 scheme can only go back to the first step of signing, rebuild tree structure for the remaining nodes, and then start a new round of signing. See Fig. 9 for the processing logic of these two schemes when the node is offline. Our experiments focus on analyzing the extra time it takes for trivial tree-based MuSig2 to generate the final signature compared to SR-MuSig2 scheme after the node is offline, which shows that SR-MuSig2 can be more efficient than the trivial tree-based MuSig2 scheme. We have a convention in controlling the number of disconnected nodes. It is assumed that 5% of the nodes in each layer of the tree drop due to network failure, and the root node will never be disconnected. The experimental results are shown in Fig. 10 and Fig. 11.

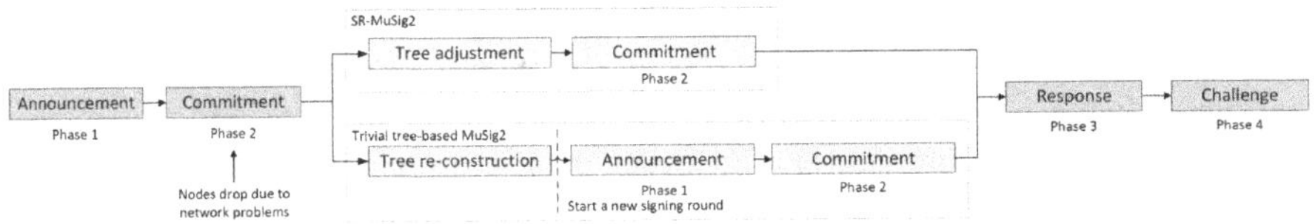

Fig. 9. Process of SR-MuSig2 and trivial tree-based MuSig2 after nodes go offline.

Figure 10 counts the number of two types of nodes in the tree after the node drops. The first type is **re-calculate nodes**, which represent the number of nodes that need to recalculate public nonces after adjusting the tree structure, that is, the number of affected nodes. The second type of node is **remaining nodes**, that is, the number of nodes remaining in the tree after the node drops. We can easily know that if the trivial tree-based MuSig2 scheme is used to deal with the node disconnection problem, then all the remaining nodes in the tree need to recalculate the nonces, because they need to re-execute signing. However, the number of nodes to be recalculated required in SR-MuSig2 is very small, which undoubtedly saves a lot of computation and communication overhead.

Figure 11 counts the time it takes to reconstruct tree and recalculate aggregated nonces after the node goes offline in commitment phase. In SR-MuSig2, the first thing to do is to adjust the tree structure. After this process is completed, the calculation in the commitment phase can be directly continued. In this process, the intermediate values generated by a large number of nodes before disconnection can be used directly, and only a small number of nodes need to re-aggregate public nonces due to changes in the tree structure. Since the trivial tree-based MuSig2 scheme has no reconfigurability, after the node drops, it must go back to the first step of signing, reconstruct a new tree for the remaining nodes, and then start signing from announcement phase, which will cause large communication and computation overhead. It is not difficult to see from

Fig. 11 that as the number of signers increases, the efficiency gap between SR-MuSig2 and trivial tree-based MuSig2 in dealing with network failure increases. Therefore, reconfigurability is a crucial property for tree-based multi-signature schemes.

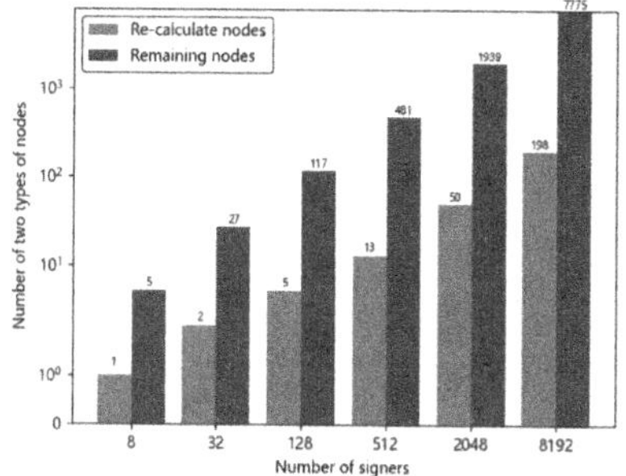

Fig. 10. Number of two types of nodes versus number of signers.

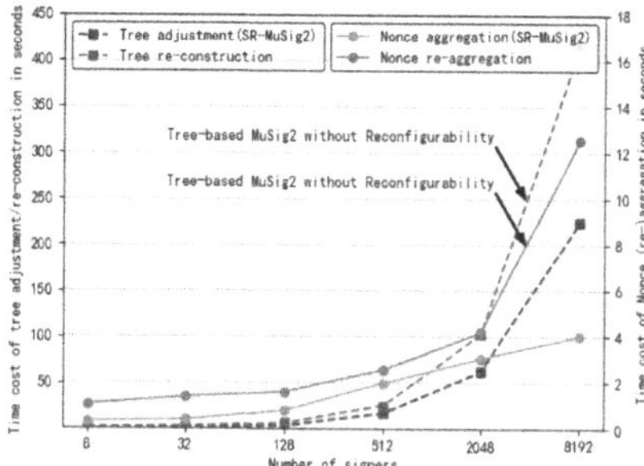

Fig. 11. Time cost of four phases versus number of signers.

7 Applications

In the process of information transmission, in order to verify the identity of the sender, the public key of the sender is usually sent to the receiver, the sender uses the private key to encrypt the content and then sends it to the receiver, and the receiver decrypts the public key to verify the sender's identity.

The client obtains the public key through distribution by the server. If this process is hijacked by a third party, then the third party forges a pair of keys and sends the public key to the client. When the server sends data to the client, the middleman hijacks the information, decrypts it with the hijacked public key, and then uses its own private key to encrypt the data and send it to the client, and the client uses the public key to decrypt it, which forms a middleman attack.

In order to prevent this situation, digital certificate plays an important role. Digital certificate is issued to the server by authoritative Certificate Authority (CA). CA generates the certificate through the information provided by the server. The certificate mainly includes the identity information of the certificate owner, the signature of CA, the public and private key. CA certificate is a string of numbers that can indicate the identity information of a network user, and provides a way to verify the identity of a network user on a computer network.

Since CA itself has a pair of public and private keys, this often becomes the main target of attackers. In order to prevent malicious third parties from using stolen CA private keys to sign some illegal documents, the traditional single CA signature mode can be transformed into a multi-certificate authority signature mode. That is, a large number of authoritative CAs are called together to sign documents. In this case, the attacker can only sign the document after stealing all the private keys. The attack difficulty is significantly increased, and the security of the CA is protected to a certain extent.

Combined with the above discussion on the application of multi-signatures in certificate authority, we can well apply SR-MuSig2 proposed in this paper to CA, so as to perform efficient signing operations of the signature authority group around the world. At the same time, when nodes are offline due to network failure or revoke their signatures out of individual reasons, the scheme can quickly recover the original signing process and thus has certain reconfigurability.

8 Conclusion

This paper proposes SR-MuSig2 scheme based on MuSig2 signature. Compared to MuSig2, a simple and practical two-round multi-signature scheme under the one-more discrete logarithm assumption, SR-MuSig2 has scalability and reconfigurability. Compared to CoSi, the tree-based multi-signature based on Schnorr, SR-MuSig2 has advanced security.

It is worth mentioning that tree construction is a time-consuming process. Although this time cost will not be counted in the real signing time, its huge time consumption brings a certain burden to the whole system. Therefore, how to construct a tree structure more efficiently so that the scheme can quickly come into the signing phase is one of our future work.

References

1. Alangot, B., Suresh, M., Raj, A.S., Pathinarupothi, R.K., Achuthan, K.: Reliable collective cosigning to scale blockchain with strong consistency. In: Proceedings of the Workshop Decentralized IoT Security Standards, pp. 1–6 (2018)
2. Kılınç Alper, H., Burdges, J.: Two-round trip schnorr multi-signatures via delinearized witnesses. In: Malkin, T., Peikert, C. (eds.) CRYPTO 2021. LNCS, vol. 12825, pp. 157–188. Springer, Cham (2021). https://doi.org/10.1007/978-3-030-84242-0_7
3. Bagherzandi, A., Cheon, J.H., Jarecki, S.: Multisignatures secure under the discrete logarithm assumption and a generalized forking lemma. In: CCS (2008)
4. Bellare, M., Neven, G.: Multi-signatures in the plain public-key model and a general forking lemma. In: CCS 2006 (2006)
5. Castelluccia, C., Jarecki, S., Kim, J., Tsudik, G.: A robust multisignature scheme with applications to acknowledgement aggregation. In: Blundo, C., Cimato, S. (eds.) SCN 2004. LNCS, vol. 3352, pp. 193–207. Springer, Heidelberg (2005). https://doi.org/10.1007/978-3-540-30598-9_14
6. Drijvers, M., Edalatnejad, K., Ford, B., Kiltz, E., Loss, J., Neven, G., Stepanovs, I.: On the security of two-round multi-signatures. In: 2019 IEEE Symposium on Security and Privacy SP, pp. 1084–1101 (2019)
7. Itakura, K.: A public-key cryptosystem suitable for digital multisignatures. NEC Res. Devel. (71), 1-8 (1983)
8. Kogias, E.K., Jovanovic, P., Gailly, N., Khoffi, I., Gasser, L., Ford, B.: Enhancing bitcoin security and performance with strong consistency via collective signing. In: Usenix Security 16, pp. 279–296 (2016)

9. Ma, C., Weng, J., Li, Y., Deng, R.H.: Efficient discrete logarithm based multi-signature scheme in the plain public key model. DCC **54**, 121–133 (2010)
10. Maxwell, G., Poelstra, A., Seurin, Y., Wuille, P.: Simple schnorr multi-signatures with applications to bitcoin. Des. Codes Crypt. **87**(9), 2139–2164 (2019). https://doi.org/10.1007/s10623-019-00608-x
11. Micali, S., Ohta, K., Reyzin, L.: Accountable-subgroup multisignatures: extended abstract. In: CCS 2001 (2001)
12. Nick, J., Ruffing, T., Seurin, Y.: MuSig2: simple two-round schnorr multi-signatures. In: Malkin, T., Peikert, C. (eds.) CRYPTO 2021. LNCS, vol. 12825, pp. 189–221. Springer, Cham (2021). https://doi.org/10.1007/978-3-030-84242-0_8
13. Nick, J.D., Ruffing, T., Seurin, Y., Wuille, P.: Musig-dn: schnorr multi-signatures with verifiably deterministic nonces. In: Proceedings of the 2020 ACM SIGSAC Conference on Computer and Communications Security(2020)
14. Okamoto, T.: Provably secure and practical identification schemes and corresponding signature schemes. In: Brickell, E.F. (ed.) CRYPTO 1992. LNCS, vol. 740, pp. 31–53. Springer, Heidelberg (1993). https://doi.org/10.1007/3-540-48071-4_3
15. Schnorr, C.P.: Efficient signature generation by smart cards. J. Cryptol. **4**(3), 161–174 (1991). https://doi.org/10.1007/BF00196725
16. Syta, E., et al.: Scalable bias-resistant distributed randomness. In: In 2017 IEEE Symposium on Security and Privacy SP, pp. 444–460. IEEE (2017)
17. Syta, E., et al.: Keeping authorities "honest or bust" with decentralized witness cosigning. In: 2016 IEEE Symposium on Security and Privacy SP, pp. 526–545 (2016)
18. Wagner, D.: A generalized birthday problem. In: Yung, M. (ed.) CRYPTO 2002. LNCS, vol. 2442, pp. 288–304. Springer, Heidelberg (2002). https://doi.org/10.1007/3-540-45708-9_19
19. Xiao, Y.L., Zhang, P., Liu, Y.: Secure and efficient multi-signature schemes for fabric: an enterprise blockchain platform. TIFS **16**, 1782–1794 (2021)
20. Yao, A.C.C., Zhao, Y.: Online/offline signatures for low-power devices. TIFS **8**, 283–294 (2013)

McEliece-Type Encryption Based on Gabidulin Codes with No Hidden Structure

Wenshuo Guo(✉) and Fang-Wei Fu

Chern Institute of Mathematics and LPMC, Nankai University, Tianjin, China
ws_guo@mail.nankai.edu.cn, fwfu@nankai.edu.cn

Abstract. This paper presents a new McEliece-type public key encryption scheme based on Gabidulin codes, which uses linearized transformations to disguise the private key. When endowing this scheme with the partial cyclic structure, we obtain a public key of the form GM^{-1}, where G is a partial circulant generator matrix of Gabidulin code and M as well as M^{-1} is a circulant matrix of large rank weight. Another difference from Loidreau's proposal at PQCrypto 2017 is that both G and M are publicly known. Recovering the private key is equivalent to deriving from M a linearized transformation and two circulant matrices of small rank weight. This scheme is shown to resist some well-known distinguisher-based attacks, such as the Overbeck attack and Coggia-Couvreur attack, and also has a very small public key size. For instance, 2592 bytes are enough for our proposal to achieve the security of 256 bits, which is around 400 times smaller than Classic McEliece that has been selected into the fourth round of the NIST Post-Quantum Cryptography (PQC) standardization process.

Keywords: Post-quantum cryptography · Code-based cryptography · Gabidulin codes · Partial cyclic codes · Linearized transformations

1 Introduction

Over the past decades, post-quantum cryptosystems (PQCs) have been drawing more and more attention from the cryptographic community. The most remarkable advantage of PQCs over classical cryptosystems is their potential resistance against attacks from quantum computers. In the area of PQC, cryptosystems based on coding theory are one of the most promising candidates. Apart from resisting quantum attacks, these cryptosystems also have faster encryption

This research was supported by the National Key Research and Development Program of China (Grant No. 2018YFA0704703), the National Natural Science Foundation of China (Grant No. 61971243), the Natural Science Foundation of Tianjin (20JCZDJC00610), and the Fundamental Research Funds for the Central Universities of China (Nankai University).

Y. Deng and M. Yung (Eds.): Inscrypt 2022, LNCS 13837, pp. 108–126, 2023.
https://doi.org/10.1007/978-3-031-26553-2_6

and decryption procedures. The first code-based cryptosystem was proposed by McEliece [32] in 1978. However, this scheme has never been used in practice due to the drawback of large key size. For instance, Classic McEliece [3] submitted to the NIST PQC project [33] requires 255 kilobytes of public key for the 128-bit security. To overcome this drawback, various improvements have been proposed one after another.

Gabidulin, Paramonov and Tretjakov (GPT) [16] proposed a rank-based encryption scheme by using Gabidulin codes in the McEliece setting. Research results show that the complexity of decoding general rank metric codes is much higher than that for Hamming metric codes. Rank-based cryptosystem, therefore, have a more compact representation of public keys. Unfortunately, the GPT cryptosystem was broken by Gibson [21,22] and then by Overbeck [37]. To resist these attacks, some reparations of GPT were proposed [14,15,17,40]. However, because of Gabidulin codes being highly structured, all these variants are still vulnerable to structural attacks [24,34,38]. Specifically, Gabidulin codes contain a large subspace invariant under the Frobenius transformation, which makes Gabidulin codes distinguishable from general linear codes.

Loidreau [29] proposed a McEliece-type cryptosystem using Gabidulin codes, whose public key is a matrix of the form GM^{-1}. The right scrambler matrix is chosen such that M has a small rank weight of λ. The public code then cannot be distinguished from random ones and therefore, Loidreau's proposal can prevent the Overbeck attack [38]. However, by operating the dual of the public code Coggia and Couvreur [12] presented an effective distinguisher and gave a practical key recovery attack for $\lambda = 2$. This attack was extended by Ghatak [20] to the case of $\lambda = 3$ and then by Pham and Loidreau [39]. Let H_{pub} be a parity-check matrix of the public code, then $H_{pub} = HM^T$ where H forms a parity-check matrix of Gabidulin code. Although Loidreau [31] claimed that one can publish G without losing security, one cannot derive H from H_{pub} because of M being kept secret. For this reason we still view this scheme as one with hidden structure.

Lau and Tan [25] (LT18) proposed a scheme based on Gabidulin codes with hidden structure. The public key consists of two matrices $G + UT$ and U, where G is a generator matrix of Gabidulin code and U is a partial circulant matrix, scrambled by a matrix T over the base field. Recently Guo and Fu [23] showed that one can recover T in polynomial time and completely break this scheme. By modifying the idea of LT18, Lau and Tan [26] (LT19) designed another scheme based on the so-called partial cyclic Gabidulin codes, also with hidden structure. The public key of LT19 consists of two vectors and therefore has a quite small size. This scheme can prevent the Guo-Fu attack and remains secure until now for properly chosen parameters.

Our Contributions. Firstly, we introduce and investigate the properties of linearized transformations over linear codes. Secondly, we propose a McEliece-type encryption scheme, where linearized transformations are utilized to disguise the private key. The public matrix in our proposal appears quite random and consequently, some well-known distinguisher-based attacks do not work any longer.

Besides, the use of the partial cyclic structure greatly reduces the public key size.

Recently NIST has completed the third round of the PQC standardization process. Three key-establishment mechanisms (KEMs) based on coding theory have been selected into the fourth round. These algorithms are Classic McEliece [3] based on Goppa codes, and HQC [1] as well as BIKE [4] based on quasi-cyclic moderate density parity check (QC-MDPC) codes. In contrast to these NIST PQC submissions and Loidreau's proposal, our scheme has the following innovations and advantages:

- The use of linearized transformations enhances the security against structural attacks. Before our work in the present paper, most known approaches used to disguise the private key are based on linear or affine transformations. That is, the public key has the form of $S(G+M)P$, which has been shown to fail in most cases.
- In the partial cyclic version, the algebraic structure of Gabidulin code can be published without reducing the security. This enables our proposal to be a McEliece-type encryption scheme with no hidden structure.
- The use of the partial cyclic structure greatly shrinks the public key. However, one cannot use this technique in Loidreau's proposal, otherwise one can easily deduce an equivalent private key from the public information.
- The advantage over HQC and BIKE is that the decryption algorithm in our proposal is deterministic and therefore, has no decryption failure that the former two ones confront.

The rest of this paper is arranged as follows. Section 2 introduces some notations and preliminaries used throughout this paper. Section 3 presents the RSD problem in coding theory and two types of generic attacks. In Sect. 4, we introduce the concept of linearized transformations and investigate their properties over linear codes. Section 5 describes our new proposal and gives some notes on the private key. Security analysis of the new proposal will be given in Sect. 6. In Sect. 7, we suggest some parameters for three security levels and compare the public key size with some other code-based cryptosystems. A few concluding remarks will be made in Sect. 8.

2 Preliminaries

We now present some notations used throughout this paper, as well as some basic concepts of linear codes and rank metric codes. Then we introduce the so-called partial cyclic Gabidulin codes and some related results.

2.1 Notations and Basic Concepts

Let $\mathbb{F}_q$ be the finite field with q elements, and $\mathbb{F}_{q^m}$ an extension of $\mathbb{F}_q$ of degree m. We call $\boldsymbol{a} \in \mathbb{F}_{q^m}^m$ a basis vector of $\mathbb{F}_{q^m}/\mathbb{F}_q$ if the components of $\boldsymbol{a}$ are linearly independent over $\mathbb{F}_q$. We call α a normal element if $(\alpha, \alpha^q, \ldots, \alpha^{q^{m-1}})$ forms a basis vector of $\mathbb{F}_{q^m}$ over $\mathbb{F}_q$. Denote by $\mathcal{M}_{k,n}(\mathbb{F}_q)$ the space of $k \times n$ matrices over $\mathbb{F}_q$, and by $\mathrm{GL}_n(\mathbb{F}_q)$ the space of invertible matrices in $\mathcal{M}_{n,n}(\mathbb{F}_q)$. Let $\langle M \rangle_q$ be the vector space spanned by the rows of $M \in \mathcal{M}_{k,n}(\mathbb{F}_q)$ over $\mathbb{F}_q$.

An $[n, k]$ linear code $\mathcal{C}$ over $\mathbb{F}_q$ is a k-dimensional subspace of $\mathbb{F}_q^n$. The dual code $\mathcal{C}^\perp$ of $\mathcal{C}$ is the orthogonal space of $\mathcal{C}$ under the Euclidean inner product over $\mathbb{F}_q^n$. A matrix $G \in \mathcal{M}_{k,n}(\mathbb{F}_q)$ is called a generator matrix of $\mathcal{C}$ if its rows form a basis of $\mathcal{C}$. A generator matrix of $\mathcal{C}^\perp$ is called a parity-check matrix of $\mathcal{C}$.

The rank support of $\boldsymbol{v} \in \mathbb{F}_{q^m}^n$ with respect to $\mathbb{F}_q$, denoted by $\mathrm{RS}_q(\boldsymbol{v})$, is the linear space spanned by the components of $\boldsymbol{v}$ over $\mathbb{F}_q$. The rank weight of $\boldsymbol{v}$, denoted by $\mathrm{rk}_q(\boldsymbol{v})$, is the dimension of $\mathrm{RS}_q(\boldsymbol{v})$ over $\mathbb{F}_q$. The rank support of $M \in \mathcal{M}_{k,n}(\mathbb{F}_{q^m})$, denoted by $\mathrm{RS}_q(M)$, is the linear space spanned by the entries of M over $\mathbb{F}_q$. The rank weight of M, denoted by $\mathrm{rk}_q(M)$, is the dimension of $\mathrm{RS}_q(M)$ over $\mathbb{F}_q$. For $\boldsymbol{v} \in \mathbb{F}_{q^m}^u, M \in \mathcal{M}_{u,v}(\mathbb{F}_{q^m})$ and $N \in \mathcal{M}_{v,w}(\mathbb{F}_{q^m})$, it is easy to see that $\mathrm{rk}_q(\boldsymbol{v}M) \leqslant \mathrm{rk}_q(\boldsymbol{v}) \cdot \mathrm{rk}_q(M)$ and $\mathrm{rk}_q(MN) \leqslant \mathrm{rk}_q(M) \cdot \mathrm{rk}_q(N)$.

For $\alpha \in \mathbb{F}_{q^m}$ and a positive integer l, we define $\alpha^{[l]} = \alpha^{q^l}$ to be the l-th Frobenius power of α. For $\boldsymbol{v} = (v_1, \dots, v_n) \in \mathbb{F}_{q^m}^n$, let $\boldsymbol{v}^{[l]} = (v_1^{[l]}, \dots, v_n^{[l]})$. For $M = (M_{ij}) \in \mathcal{M}_{u,v}(\mathbb{F}_{q^m})$, let $M^{[l]} = (M_{ij}^{[l]})$. For $\mathcal{V} \subseteq \mathbb{F}_{q^m}^n$, let $\mathcal{V}^{[i]} = \{\boldsymbol{v}^{[i]} : \boldsymbol{v} \in \mathcal{V}\}$. For $M \in \mathcal{M}_{u,v}(\mathbb{F}_{q^m}), N \in \mathcal{M}_{v,w}(\mathbb{F}_{q^m})$, it is clear that $(MN)^{[l]} = M^{[l]}N^{[l]}$. For $M \in \mathrm{GL}_n(\mathbb{F}_{q^m})$, clearly $(M^{[l]})^{-1} = (M^{-1})^{[l]}$.

2.2 Gabidulin Code

Gabidulin codes are actually the rank metric counterpart of Reed-Solomon codes, which can be defined through the so-called Moore matrix.

Definition 1 (Moore matrix). *Let $\boldsymbol{g} = (g_1, g_2, \dots, g_n) \in \mathbb{F}_{q^m}^n$, then the $k \times n$ Moore matrix generated by $\boldsymbol{g}$ is a matrix of the form*

$$\mathrm{Mr}_k(\boldsymbol{g}) = \begin{pmatrix} g_1 & g_2 & \cdots & g_n \\ g_1^{[1]} & g_2^{[1]} & \cdots & g_n^{[1]} \\ \vdots & \vdots & \ddots & \vdots \\ g_1^{[k-1]} & g_2^{[k-1]} & \cdots & g_n^{[k-1]} \end{pmatrix}.$$

Definition 2 (Gabidulin code). *For positive integers $k \leqslant n \leqslant m$ and $\boldsymbol{g} \in \mathbb{F}_{q^m}^n$ with $\mathrm{rk}_q(\boldsymbol{g}) = n$, the $[n, k]$ Gabidulin code $\mathrm{Gab}_k(\boldsymbol{g})$ generated by $\boldsymbol{g}$ is defined to be a linear code that has $\mathrm{Mr}_k(\boldsymbol{g})$ as a generator matrix.*

Remark 1. An $[n, k]$ Gabidulin code $\mathrm{Gab}_k(\boldsymbol{g})$ has minimum rank weight $n-k+1$ [16] and can therefore correct up to $\lfloor \frac{n-k}{2} \rfloor$ rank errors in theory. Several efficient decoding algorithms for Gabidulin code can be found in [13,28,41].

2.3 Partial Cyclic Code

Lau and Tan [26] used partial cyclic Gabidulin codes to reduce the public key size in rank-based cryptography. Now we introduce this family of codes and present some related results.

Definition 3 (Circulant matrix). *For a vector $\boldsymbol{m} \in \mathbb{F}_q^n$, the circulant matrix generated by $\boldsymbol{m}$ is a matrix $M \in \mathcal{M}_{n,n}(\mathbb{F}_q)$ whose first row is $\boldsymbol{m}$ and i-th row is obtained by cyclically right shifting its $(i-1)$-th row for $2 \leqslant i \leqslant n$.*

Definition 4 (Partial circulant matrix). *For $k \leqslant n$ and $\boldsymbol{m} \in \mathbb{F}_q^n$, the $k \times n$ partial circulant matrix $\mathrm{PC}_k(\boldsymbol{m})$ generated by $\boldsymbol{m}$ is defined to be the first k rows of the circulant matrix generated by $\boldsymbol{m}$. Particularly, we denote by $\mathrm{PC}_n(\boldsymbol{m})$ the circulant matrix generated by $\boldsymbol{m}$.*

Remark 2. Let $\mathrm{PC}_n(\mathbb{F}_q)$ be the space of $n\times n$ circulant matrices over $\mathbb{F}_q$. Chalkley [11] proved that $\mathrm{PC}_n(\mathbb{F}_q)$ forms a commutative ring under matrix addition and multiplication. It is easy to see that, for a partial circulant matrix $A \in \mathcal{M}_{k,n}(\mathbb{F}_q)$ and a circulant matrix $B \in \mathrm{PC}_n(\mathbb{F}_q)$, AB forms a $k \times n$ partial circulant matrix.

Now we present a sufficient and necessary condition for a circulant matrix to be invertible, then make an accurate estimation of the number of invertible circulant matrices over $\mathbb{F}_q$.

Proposition 1. [35] *For $\boldsymbol{m} = (m_0, \ldots, m_{n-1}) \in \mathbb{F}_q^n$, let $\boldsymbol{m}(x) = \sum_{i=0}^{n-1} m_i x^i \in \mathbb{F}_q[x]$, then $\mathrm{PC}_n(\boldsymbol{m})$ is invertible if and only if $\gcd(\boldsymbol{m}(x), x^n - 1) = 1$.*

Proposition 2. [27] *For a monic $f(x) \in \mathbb{F}_q[x]$ of degree n, let $g_1(x), \ldots, g_r(x) \in \mathbb{F}_q[x]$ be r distinct monic irreducible factors of $f(x)$, i.e. $f(x) = \prod_{i=1}^{r} g_i(x)^{e_i}$ for some positive integers $e_1, \ldots, e_r$. Let $d_i = \deg(g_i)$ for $1 \leqslant i \leqslant r$, then*

$$\Phi_q(f) = q^n \prod_{i=1}^{r} (1 - \frac{1}{q^{d_i}}), \tag{1}$$

where $\Phi_q(f)$ denotes the number of monic polynomials coprime to $f(x)$ of degree less than n.

The following corollary is drawn directly from Propositions 1 and 2.

Corollary 1. *The number of invertible matrices in $\mathrm{PC}_n(\mathbb{F}_q)$ is $\Phi_q(x^n - 1)$.*

Now we introduce the concept of partial cyclic codes.

Definition 5 (Partial cyclic code). *For $k \leqslant n$ and $\boldsymbol{a} \in \mathbb{F}_q^n$, let $G = \mathrm{PC}_k(\boldsymbol{a})$ be a partial circulant matrix generated by $\boldsymbol{a}$, then $\mathcal{C} = \langle G \rangle_q$ is called an $[n, k]$ partial cyclic code.*

Remark 3. Let $\boldsymbol{g} = (\alpha^{[n-1]}, \alpha^{[n-2]}, \ldots, \alpha)$ be a normal basis vector of $\mathbb{F}_{q^n}/\mathbb{F}_q$ and $G = \mathrm{Mr}_k(\boldsymbol{g})$, then G forms a $k \times n$ partial circulant matrix. We call $\mathcal{G} = \langle G \rangle_{q^n}$ an $[n, k]$ partial cyclic Gabidulin code generated by $\boldsymbol{g}$.

3 RSD Problem and Generic Attacks

Now we introduce the well-known RSD problem in coding theory which lays the foundation of rank-based cryptography, as well as the best known generic attacks that will be useful to estimate the practical security of our proposal later in this paper.

Definition 6 (Rank Syndrome Decoding (RSD) Problem). *Given positive integers m, n, k and t, let H be an $(n-k) \times n$ matrix over $\mathbb{F}_{q^m}$ of full rank and $\boldsymbol{s} \in \mathbb{F}_{q^m}^{n-k}$. The RSD problem with parameters (q, m, n, k, t) is to search for $\boldsymbol{e} \in \mathbb{F}_{q^m}^n$ such that $\boldsymbol{s} = \boldsymbol{e}H^T$ and $\mathrm{rk}_q(\boldsymbol{e}) = t$.*

The RSD problem has been used for designing cryptosystems since the proposal of the GPT cryptosystem in 1991. However, the hardness of this problem had never been proved until the work in [19], where the authors gave a randomized reduction of the RSD problem to an NP-complete decoding problem [9] in the Hamming metric.

Generic attacks on the RSD problem can be divided into two categories, namely the combinatorial attacks and algebraic attacks. The main idea of combinatorial attacks consists in solving a multivariate linear system obtained from the parity-check equation, whose variables are components of e_i under a basis of $\mathrm{RS}_q(\boldsymbol{e})$ over $\mathbb{F}_q$. The complexity mainly consists in enumerating t-dimensional $\mathbb{F}_q$-subspaces of $\mathbb{F}_{q^m}$. The best known combinatorial attacks up to now can be found in [5,18,36], as summarized in Table 1.

The main idea of algebraic attacks consists in converting an RSD instance into a multivariate quadratic system and then solving this system with algebraic approaches, such as the Gröbner basis techniques. Algebraic attacks are generally believed to be less efficient than combinatorial approaches until the work in [7,8], whose complexity and applicable condition are summarized in Table 2, where $\omega = 2.81$ is the linear algebra constant.

Table 1. Best known combinatorial attacks.

Attack	Complexity
[36]	$\mathcal{O}\left(\min\left\{m^3t^3q^{(t-1)(k+1)}, (k+t)^3t^3q^{(t-1)(m-t)}\right\}\right)$
[18]	$\mathcal{O}\left((n-k)^3m^3q^{\min\left\{t\left\lceil\frac{mk}{n}\right\rceil,(t-1)\left\lceil\frac{m(k+1)}{n}\right\rceil\right\}}\right)$
[5]	$\mathcal{O}\left((n-k)^3m^3q^{t\left\lceil\frac{m(k+1)}{n}\right\rceil-m}\right)$

4 Linearized Transformations

Note that $\mathbb{F}_{q^m}$ can be viewed as an m-dimensional linear space over $\mathbb{F}_q$. Let $(\alpha_1, \dots, \alpha_m)$ and $(\beta_1, \dots, \beta_m)$ be two basis vectors of $\mathbb{F}_{q^m}/\mathbb{F}_q$. For any $\alpha =$

Table 2. Best known algebraic attacks.

Attack	Condition	Complexity
[8]	$m\binom{n-k-1}{t} \geqslant \binom{n}{t} - 1$	$\mathcal{O}\left(m\binom{n-p-k-1}{t}\binom{n-p}{t}^{\omega-1}\right)$, where $p = \max\{1 \leqslant i \leqslant n : m\binom{n-i-k-1}{t} \geqslant \binom{n-i}{t} - 1\}$
[7]		$\mathcal{O}\left(\left(\frac{((m+n)t)^t}{t!}\right)^{\omega}\right)$
[8]	$m\binom{n-k-1}{t} < \binom{n}{t} - 1$	$\mathcal{O}\left(q^{at}m\binom{n-k-1}{t}\binom{n-a}{t}^{\omega-1}\right)$, where $a = \min\{1 \leqslant i \leqslant n : m\binom{n-k-1}{t} \geqslant \binom{n-i}{t} - 1\}$
		$\mathcal{O}\left(\frac{B_b\binom{k+t+1}{t}+C_b(mk+1)(t+1)}{B_b+C_b}A_b^2\right)$, where $A_b = \sum_{j=1}^{b}\binom{n}{t}\binom{mk+1}{j}$, $B_b = \sum_{j=1}^{b} m\binom{n-k-1}{t}\binom{mk+1}{j}$, $C_b = \sum_{j=1}^{b}\sum_{i=1}^{j}(-1)^{i+1}\binom{n}{t+i}\binom{m+i-1}{i}\binom{mk+1}{j-i}$, $b = \min\{0 < a < t+2 : A_a - 1 \leqslant B_a + C_a\}$
[7]		$\mathcal{O}\left(\left(\frac{((m+n)t)^{t+1}}{(t+1)!}\right)^{\omega}\right)$

$\sum_{i=1}^{m} \lambda_i \alpha_i \in \mathbb{F}_{q^m}$ with $\lambda_i \in \mathbb{F}_q$, we define a permutation of $\mathbb{F}_{q^m}$ as

$$\psi(\alpha) = \sum_{i=1}^{m} \lambda_i \beta_i.$$

It is easy to see that ψ is $\mathbb{F}_q$-linearized, namely

$$\psi(\gamma_1\alpha + \gamma_2\beta) = \gamma_1\psi(\alpha) + \gamma_2\psi(\beta)$$

holds for any $\alpha, \beta \in \mathbb{F}_{q^m}$ and $\gamma_1, \gamma_2 \in \mathbb{F}_q$. By $\mathrm{LP}_m(\mathbb{F}_q)$ we denote the space of all $\mathbb{F}_q$-linearized permutations of $\mathbb{F}_{q^m}$.

In the sequel we will do further study on this family of permutations. Firstly, we present a basic fact about $\mathbb{F}_q$-linearized permutations of $\mathbb{F}_{q^m}$.

Proposition 3. *The total number of $\mathbb{F}_q$-linearized permutations of $\mathbb{F}_{q^m}$ is*

$$|\mathrm{LP}_m(\mathbb{F}_q)| = \prod_{i=0}^{m-1}(q^m - q^i).$$

Let $\psi \in \mathrm{LP}_m(\mathbb{F}_q)$ be an $\mathbb{F}_q$-linearized permutation of $\mathbb{F}_{q^m}$. For any $\boldsymbol{v} \in \mathbb{F}_{q^m}^n$, let $\psi(\boldsymbol{v}) = (\psi(v_1), \ldots, \psi(v_n))$. For $\mathcal{V} \subseteq \mathbb{F}_{q^m}^n$, let $\psi(\mathcal{V}) = \{\psi(\boldsymbol{v}) : \boldsymbol{v} \in \mathcal{V}\}$. For $M \in \mathcal{M}_{k,n}(\mathbb{F}_{q^m})$, let $\psi(M) = (\psi(M_{ij}))$. In these cases, we call ψ a linearized transformation over $\mathbb{F}_{q^m}/\mathbb{F}_q$.

For $\boldsymbol{v} \in \mathbb{F}_{q^m}^n$ and $\psi \in \mathrm{LP}_m(\mathbb{F}_q)$, a natural question is how the rank weight of $\boldsymbol{v}$ varies under the action of ψ. For this reason, we introduce the following proposition.

Proposition 4. *A linearized transformation over $\mathbb{F}_{q^m}/\mathbb{F}_q$ is an isometry in the rank metric.*

Proof. For $n \leqslant m$, let $\boldsymbol{v} \in \mathbb{F}_{q^m}^n$ with $\mathrm{rk}_q(\boldsymbol{v}) = n$. If $\mathrm{rk}_q(\psi(\boldsymbol{v})) < n$, then there exists $\boldsymbol{b} \in \mathbb{F}_q^n \backslash \{\boldsymbol{0}\}$ such that $\psi(\boldsymbol{v})\boldsymbol{b}^T = \psi(\boldsymbol{v}\boldsymbol{b}^T) = 0$. This implies that $\boldsymbol{v}\boldsymbol{b}^T = 0$, which conflicts with $\mathrm{rk}_q(\boldsymbol{v}) = n$. More generally, suppose $\mathrm{rk}_q(\boldsymbol{v}) = r < n$, then there exist $Q \in \mathrm{GL}_n(\mathbb{F}_q)$ and $\boldsymbol{v}^* \in \mathbb{F}_{q^m}^r$ with $\mathrm{rk}_q(\boldsymbol{v}^*) = r$ such that $\boldsymbol{v} = (\boldsymbol{v}^*|\boldsymbol{0})Q$. It follows that $\psi(\boldsymbol{v}) = (\psi(\boldsymbol{v}^*)|\boldsymbol{0})Q$ and then $\mathrm{rk}_q(\psi(\boldsymbol{v})) = \mathrm{rk}_q(\psi(\boldsymbol{v}^*)) = \mathrm{rk}_q(\boldsymbol{v}^*) = \mathrm{rk}_q(\boldsymbol{v})$.

Remark 4. Let $\mathbb{E}$ be an extension field of $\mathbb{F}_{q^m}$, then a linearized transformation over $\mathbb{E}/\mathbb{F}_{q^m}$ preserves the rank metric over $\mathbb{E}^n$ with respect to $\mathbb{F}_q$.

A permutation of $\mathbb{F}_{q^m}$ leads to a polynomial of degree at most $q^m - 1$, which can be derived from the Lagrange Interpolation Formula [27]. An $\mathbb{F}_q$-linearized permutation ψ of $\mathbb{F}_{q^m}$ leads to a linearized polynomial $L_\psi(x)$ over $\mathbb{F}_{q^m}/\mathbb{F}_q$, which has the form of

$$\gamma_0 x + \gamma_1 x^{[1]} + \cdots + \gamma_{m-1} x^{[m-1]} \in \mathbb{F}_{q^m}[x].$$

Let $\boldsymbol{b}$ be a basis vector of $\mathbb{F}_{q^m}/\mathbb{F}_q$ and $B \in \mathcal{M}_{m,m}(\mathbb{F}_{q^m})$ a Moore matrix generated by $\boldsymbol{b}$. Note that $L_\psi(\boldsymbol{b}) = (\gamma_0, \ldots, \gamma_{m-1})B = \psi(\boldsymbol{b})$, then $(\gamma_0, \ldots, \gamma_{m-1}) = \psi(\boldsymbol{b})B^{-1}$.

Remark 5. For $\psi \in \mathrm{LP}_m(\mathbb{F}_q)$ and a linear code $\mathcal{C} \subseteq \mathbb{F}_{q^m}^n$, it is easy to verify that $\psi(\mathcal{C})$ is $\mathbb{F}_q$-linear, but generally no longer $\mathbb{F}_{q^m}$-linear. However, if $L_\psi(x)$ has the form of $\gamma x^{[j]}$ for $\gamma \in \mathbb{F}_{q^m}^*$ and $0 \leqslant j \leqslant m-1$, namely $L_\psi(x)$ is a monomial, then ψ preserves the $\mathbb{F}_{q^m}$-linearity of all linear codes over $\mathbb{F}_{q^m}$.

5 Our Proposal

This section first presents a formal description of the new proposal, then gives some notes on the private key. It should be noted that the following description and notes are mainly aimed at the partial cyclic version.

5.1 Description of Our Proposal

For a desired security level, choose a field $\mathbb{F}_q$ and positive integers m, n, k, l, λ_1 and λ_2 such that $n = lm$. Let $\boldsymbol{g} = (\alpha^{[n-1]}, \alpha^{[n-2]}, \ldots, \alpha)$ be a normal basis vector of $\mathbb{F}_{q^n}/\mathbb{F}_q$. Let $G = \mathrm{PC}_k(\boldsymbol{g})$, then $\mathcal{G} = \langle G \rangle_{q^n}$ forms an $[n, k]$ partial cyclic Gabidulin code. Our proposal consists of the following three algorithms.

- Key generation
  For $i = 1, 2$, randomly choose an $\mathbb{F}_q$-linear space $\mathcal{V}_i \subseteq \mathbb{F}_{q^n}$ with $\dim_q(\mathcal{V}_i) = \lambda_i$. Randomly choose $\boldsymbol{m}_i \in \mathcal{V}_i^n$ with $\mathrm{rk}_q(\boldsymbol{m}_i) = \lambda_i$ such that $M_i = \mathrm{PC}_n(\boldsymbol{m}_i)$ is invertible. Randomly choose $\psi \in \mathrm{LP}_l(\mathbb{F}_{q^m})$ such that $L_\psi(x)$ is not a monomial. Let $\boldsymbol{g}^* = \psi(\boldsymbol{g}M_1^{-1})M_2^{-1}$, then $\mathrm{PC}_k(\boldsymbol{g}^*) = \psi(GM_1^{-1})M_2^{-1}$. Let $t = \left\lfloor \frac{n-k}{2\lambda_1\lambda_2} \right\rfloor$, then the public key is $(\boldsymbol{g}^*, t)$, and the private key is $(\boldsymbol{m}_1, \boldsymbol{m}_2, \psi)$.

- Encryption
  For a plaintext $\boldsymbol{x} \in \mathbb{F}_{q^m}^k$, randomly choose $\boldsymbol{e} \in \mathbb{F}_{q^n}^n$ with $\mathrm{rk}_q(\boldsymbol{e}) = t$. Then the ciphertext corresponding to $\boldsymbol{x}$ is computed as

$$\boldsymbol{y} = \boldsymbol{x}\mathrm{PC}_k(\boldsymbol{g}^*) + \boldsymbol{e} = \boldsymbol{x}\psi(GM_1^{-1})M_2^{-1} + \boldsymbol{e}.$$

- Decryption
  For a ciphertext $\boldsymbol{y} \in \mathbb{F}_{q^n}^n$, compute

$$\boldsymbol{y}M_2 = \boldsymbol{x}\psi(GM_1^{-1}) + \boldsymbol{e}M_2 = \psi(\boldsymbol{x}GM_1^{-1}) + \boldsymbol{e}M_2,$$

  and

$$\boldsymbol{y}' = \psi^{-1}(\boldsymbol{y}M_2)M_1 = \boldsymbol{x}G + \boldsymbol{e}'$$

  where $\boldsymbol{e}' = \psi^{-1}(\boldsymbol{e}M_2)M_1$. Note that

$$\mathrm{rk}_q(\boldsymbol{e}') \leqslant \mathrm{rk}_q(\psi^{-1}(\boldsymbol{e}M_2)) \cdot \lambda_1 = \mathrm{rk}_q(\boldsymbol{e}M_2) \cdot \lambda_1 \leqslant \mathrm{rk}_q(\boldsymbol{e}) \cdot \lambda_2 \cdot \lambda_1 \leqslant \lfloor \frac{n-k}{2} \rfloor.$$

  Applying the decoder of $\mathcal{G}$ to $\boldsymbol{y}'$ will lead to the plaintext $\boldsymbol{x}$.

Remark 6. For the case where no partial cyclic structure is used, the only difference is that it suffices to choose at random a generator matrix G of Gabidulin code and two matrices M_i with $\mathrm{rk}_q(M_i) = \lambda_i$. On the other hand, the design of the new proposal involves three finite fields, that is $\mathbb{F}_q \subset \mathbb{F}_{q^m} \subset \mathbb{F}_{q^n}$. The reason why $\mathbb{F}_{q^m}$ is chosen to define ψ consists in two aspects. Specifically, if there is no such an intermediate field and ψ is defined over $\mathbb{F}_{q^n}/\mathbb{F}_q$, then the transformation will be $\mathbb{F}_q$-linearized and the plaintext has to be chosen from $\mathbb{F}_q^k$. Consequently, the practical security of this scheme will be bounded from above by $\mathcal{O}(q^k)$ and the transmission rate will be only $\frac{k}{n^2}$, which will greatly weaken the performance of the proposed scheme.

5.2 Why Not Hide Gabidulin Code

Now we explain why Gabidulin code is not used as part of the private key. Firstly, we introduce the following proposition, which reveals the relationship between two normal basis vectors.

Proposition 5. *Let α be a normal element of $\mathbb{F}_{q^n}/\mathbb{F}_q$, then $\beta \in \mathbb{F}_{q^n}$ is normal if and only if there exists $Q \in \mathrm{PC}_n(\mathbb{F}_q) \cap \mathrm{GL}_n(\mathbb{F}_q)$ such that*

$$(\beta^{[n-1]}, \beta^{[n-2]}, \ldots, \beta) = (\alpha^{[n-1]}, \alpha^{[n-2]}, \ldots, \alpha)Q.$$

Proof. Trivial from a direct verification.

Let $\boldsymbol{g}' \in \mathbb{F}_{q^n}^n$ be an arbitrary normal basis vector of $\mathbb{F}_{q^n}/\mathbb{F}_q$. By Proposition 5, there exists a matrix $Q \in \mathrm{PC}_n(\mathbb{F}_q) \cap \mathrm{GL}_n(\mathbb{F}_q)$ such that $\boldsymbol{g}' = \boldsymbol{g}Q$. Let $G' = \mathrm{PC}_k(\boldsymbol{g}')$, then $G' = GQ$ and

$$\psi(GM_1^{-1})M_2^{-1} = \psi(G'Q^{-1}M_1^{-1})M_2^{-1} = \psi(G'M_1^{-1})Q^{-1}M_2^{-1} = \psi(G'M_1^{-1})M_2'^{-1},$$

where $M_2' = M_2Q \in \mathrm{PC}_n(\mathbb{F}_{q^n}) \cap \mathrm{GL}_n(\mathbb{F}_{q^n})$ satisfies $\mathrm{wt}_R(M_2') = \lambda_2$. Furthermore, it is clear that anyone possessing the knowledge of $\psi, \boldsymbol{g}', M_1$ and M_2' can decrypt any ciphertext in polynomial time. This implies that breaking this cryptosystem can be reduced to recovering ψ, M_1 and M_2'. Hence we conclude that it does not make a difference to keep the underlying Gabidulin code secret.

5.3 On the Choice of ψ

We first explain why ψ is chosen such that the associated polynomial $L_\psi(x)$ is not monomial, then investigate the equivalence of linearized transformations.

Why $L_\psi(x)$ cannot be monomial Assume that $L_\psi(x)$ is a monomial, then there exist $\gamma \in \mathbb{F}_{q^n}^*$ and $0 \leqslant j \leqslant l-1$ such that

$$\psi(GM_1^{-1}) = \gamma(GM_1^{-1})^{[mj]} = \gamma G^{[mj]}(M_1^{[mj]})^{-1}.$$

It follows that

$$\psi(GM_1^{-1})M_2^{-1} = G^{[mj]}(\gamma^{-1}M_1M_2^{[mj]})^{-1} = G'M'^{-1},$$

where $G' = G^{[mj]}$ and $M' = \gamma^{-1}M_1M_2^{[mj]}$. Apparently $\mathrm{rk}_q(M') \leqslant \lambda_1\lambda_2$ and G' is a Moore matrix generated by $\boldsymbol{g}' = \boldsymbol{g}^{[mj]}$, a normal basis vector of $\mathbb{F}_{q^n}/\mathbb{F}_q$. Similar to Sect. 5.2, G' is assumed to be known, and therefore one recover M' by computing $\mathrm{PC}_n(\boldsymbol{g}^*)^{-1}\mathrm{PC}_n(\boldsymbol{g}')$. With the knowledge of (G', M'), one can decrypt any ciphertext in polynomial time.

Equivalence of ψ For any $\beta \in \mathbb{F}_{q^n}^*$ and $\psi \in \mathrm{LP}_l(\mathbb{F}_{q^m})$, it is clear that $\beta\psi$ is also a linearized transformation, where $\beta\psi$ is defined by $\beta\psi(\alpha) = \beta \cdot \psi(\alpha)$ for any $\alpha \in \mathbb{F}_{q^n}$. Furthermore, let $\psi' = \beta\psi, M_2' = \beta M_2$, then $\mathrm{rk}_q(M_2') = \mathrm{rk}_q(M_2) = \lambda_2$ and

$$\psi(GM_1^{-1})M_2^{-1} = \beta^{-1}\psi'(GM_1^{-1})M_2^{-1} = \psi'(GM_1^{-1})(\beta M_2)^{-1} = \psi'(GM_1{}^{-1})M_2'^{-1}.$$

In terms of brute-force attack, ψ is said to be equivalent to ψ'. For any two transformations $\psi_1, \psi_2 \in \mathrm{LP}_l(\mathbb{F}_{q^m})$, we have either $\overline{\psi_1} = \overline{\psi_2}$ or $\overline{\psi_1} \cap \overline{\psi_2} = \varnothing$, where $\overline{\psi_i} = \{\beta\psi_i : \beta \in \mathbb{F}_{q^n}^*\}$.

Now we count the nonequivalent linearized transformations. By Proposition 3, the number of $\mathbb{F}_{q^m}$-linearized permutations of $\mathbb{F}_{q^n}$ is

$$|\mathrm{LP}_l(\mathbb{F}_{q^m})| = \prod_{i=0}^{l-1}(q^n - q^{mi}).$$

On the other hand, the number of $\mathbb{F}_q$-linearized transformations with a associated monomial is $l(q^n-1)$. Hence the number of nonequivalent linearized transformations is evaluated as

$$\mathcal{N}(\overline{\psi}) = \frac{|\mathrm{LP}_l(\mathbb{F}_{q^m})| - l(q^n-1)}{q^n-1} = \prod_{i=1}^{l-1}(q^n - q^{mi}) - l.$$

5.4 On the Choice of $(\boldsymbol{m}_1, \boldsymbol{m}_2)$

In this section, we first investigate how to choose $(\boldsymbol{m}_1, \boldsymbol{m}_2)$ to avoid some structural weakness, then investigate the equivalence of $\boldsymbol{m}_1$.

How to choose $(\boldsymbol{m}_1,\boldsymbol{m}_2)$ Note that neither $\boldsymbol{m}_1$ nor $\boldsymbol{m}_2$ should be taken over $\mathbb{F}_{q^m}$, otherwise the proposed scheme will degenerate into a weak instance. This problem is investigated in the following two cases.

(1) If $\boldsymbol{m}_1 \in \mathbb{F}_{q^m}^n$, then $M_1, M_1^{-1} \in \mathrm{GL}_n(\mathbb{F}_{q^m})$. It follows that

$$\psi(GM_1^{-1})M_2^{-1} = \psi(G)M_1^{-1}M_2^{-1} = \psi(G)(M_1M_2)^{-1} = \psi(G)M^{-1},$$

where $M = M_1M_2$ satisfies $\mathrm{rk}_q(M) \leqslant \lambda_1\lambda_2$. A direct verification shows that, if one can recover ψ and M, then one can decrypt any ciphertext in polynomial time. Let $G'_{pub} = \mathrm{PC}_n(\boldsymbol{g}^*)$ and $G' = \mathrm{PC}_n(\boldsymbol{g})$, then it is clear that $G'_{pub} = \psi(G')M^{-1}$. If one can find ψ, then one can recover M by computing ${G'_{pub}}^{-1}\psi(G')$. This implies that breaking this cryptosystem can be reduced to finding the secret ψ.

(2) If $\boldsymbol{m}_2 \in \mathbb{F}_{q^m}^n$, then $M_2, M_2^{-1} \in \mathrm{GL}_n(\mathbb{F}_{q^m})$. It follows that

$$\psi(GM_1^{-1})M_2^{-1} = \psi(GM_1^{-1}M_2^{-1}) = \psi(GM^{-1}),$$

where $M = M_1M_2$ satisfies $\mathrm{rk}_q(M) \leqslant \lambda_1\lambda_2$. A direct verification shows that, one can decrypt any ciphertext with the knowledge of ψ, G and M. If one can find ψ, then one can recover GM^{-1} and hence M as explained above. This implies that breaking this cryptosystem can be reduced to finding the secret ψ.

Equivalence of $\boldsymbol{m}_1$. For $Q \in \mathrm{PC}_n(\mathbb{F}_q) \cap \mathrm{GL}_n(\mathbb{F}_q)$, let $M_1' = M_1Q, M_2' = M_2Q$, then $\mathrm{rk}_q(M_1') = \mathrm{rk}_q(M_1), \mathrm{rk}_q(M_2') = \mathrm{rk}_q(M_2)$. It follows that

$$\psi(GM_1'^{-1})M_2^{-1} = \psi(GQ^{-1}M_1^{-1}){M_2}^{-1} = \psi(GM_1^{-1})Q^{-1}M_2^{-1} = \psi(G{M_1}^{-1})M_2'^{-1}.$$

In terms of brute-force attack on $\boldsymbol{m}_1$, it does not make a difference to multiply $\boldsymbol{m}_1$ with a matrix in $\mathrm{PC}_n(\mathbb{F}_q) \cap \mathrm{GL}_n(\mathbb{F}_q)$. Let $\overline{\boldsymbol{m}}_1 = \{\boldsymbol{m}_1Q : Q \in \mathrm{PC}_n(\mathbb{F}_q) \cap \mathrm{GL}_n(\mathbb{F}_q)\}$. In what follows, we count the number of nonequivalent $\overline{\boldsymbol{m}}_1$'s.

For a positive integer $\lambda < n$, let $\mathcal{V} \subseteq \mathbb{F}_{q^n}$ be an $\mathbb{F}_q$-space of dimension λ. For a matrix $M \in \mathrm{PC}_n(\mathcal{V}) \cap \mathrm{GL}_n(\mathcal{V})$ with $\mathrm{rk}_q(M) = \lambda$, assume that $M = \sum_{j=1}^{\lambda} \alpha_jA_j$, where α_j's form a basis of $\mathcal{V}$ over $\mathbb{F}_q$ and A_j's are nonzero matrices in $\mathrm{PC}_n(\mathbb{F}_q)$. Let $A \in \mathcal{M}_{\lambda,n}(\mathbb{F}_q)$ be a matrix whose j-th row is the first row of A_j, then A has full rank. Denote by $\mathcal{N}(A)$ the number of full-rank matrices in $\mathcal{M}_{\lambda,n}(\mathbb{F}_q)$, and by $\mathcal{N}(\mathcal{V})$ the number of λ-dimensional $\mathbb{F}_q$-subspaces of $\mathbb{F}_{q^n}$. Then

$$\mathcal{N}(A) = \prod_{i=0}^{\lambda-1}(q^n - q^i) \text{ and } \mathcal{N}(\mathcal{V}) = \prod_{j=0}^{\lambda-1}\frac{q^n - q^j}{q^\lambda - q^j}.$$

The number of matrices $M \in \mathrm{PC}_n(\mathbb{F}_{q^n}) \cap \mathrm{GL}_n(\mathbb{F}_{q^n})$ with $\mathrm{rk}_q(M) = \lambda$ can be evaluated as

$$\mathcal{N}(M) = \mathcal{N}(\mathcal{V}) \cdot \mathcal{N}(A) \cdot \xi,$$

where

$$\xi = \frac{|\{M \in \mathrm{PC}_n(\mathcal{V}) \cap \mathrm{GL}_n(\mathcal{V}) : \mathrm{rk}_q(M) = \lambda\}|}{|\{M \in \mathrm{PC}_n(\mathcal{V}) : \mathrm{rk}_q(M) = \lambda\}|}.$$

As for ξ, we have the following proposition (see Appendix A for the proof).

Proposition 6. *If $q^\lambda - q^{\lambda-1} \geqslant 2n$, then $\xi \geqslant \frac{1}{2}$.*

Proposition 6 provides a sufficient condition for $\xi \geqslant \frac{1}{2}$. Actually, this inequality always holds according to our extensive experiments in MAGMA [10], even when the sufficient condition is not satisfied. Hence we suppose $\xi = \frac{1}{2}$ in practice. Finally, the number of nonequivalent $\overline{\boldsymbol{m}}_1$'s is evaluated as

$$\mathcal{N}(\overline{\boldsymbol{m}}_1) = \frac{\mathcal{N}(M_1)}{|\mathrm{PC}_n(\mathbb{F}_q) \cap \mathrm{GL}_n(\mathbb{F}_q)|} \sim q^{(2\lambda_1-1)n}.$$

6 Security Analysis

Attacks in code-based cryptography can be divided into two categories, namely the structural attacks and generic attacks. Structural attacks aim to recover the private key or an equivalent private key from the published information, with which one can decrypt any ciphertext in polynomial time. Generic attacks aim to recover the plaintext directly without knowing the private key. In what follows, we investigate the security of the new cryptosystem from these two aspects.

6.1 Structural Attacks

This section mainly introduces some well-known structural attacks in rank-based cryptography and explains why our scheme can prevent these attacks.

Overbeck Attack. The best known structural attacks on McEliece-type variants using Gabidulin codes are the Overbeck attack [38] and some of its derivations [24, 34]. All these attacks are based on the fact that Gabidulin code contains a large subspace invariant under the Frobenius transformation. To prevent these attacks, Loidreau [29] proposed a cryptosystem that can be seen as a rank metric counterpart of the BBCRS cryptosystem [6] based on generalized Reed-Solomon (GRS) codes. In Loidreau's proposal, the secret code is disguised by right multiplying a matrix whose inverse has a small rank weight. This method of hiding information about the private key, as claimed by Loidreau, is able to resist the structural attacks mentioned above. A similar technique is applied in our proposal, namely the use of the matrix M_2 of rank weight λ_2, which we believe can as well prevent these attacks.

Coggia-Couvreur Attack. Coggia and Couvreur [12] presented an effective distinguisher for the Loidreau cryptosystem, and gave a practical key recovery attack for $\lambda = 2$ and the code rate being greater than 1/2. Instead of operating the public code directly, the Coggia-Couvreur distinguisher considers the dual of the public code. Specifically, let $G_{pub} = GM^{-1}$ be the public matrix, where G is a generator matrix of an $[n, k]$ Gabidulin code $\mathcal{G}$ over $\mathbb{F}_{q^N}$ and M is taken over a λ-dimensional $\mathbb{F}_q$-subspace of $\mathbb{F}_{q^N}$, where $N \geqslant n$. Let H be a parity-check matrix of $\mathcal{G}$, then $H_{pub} = HM^T$ forms a parity-check matrix of the public code $\mathcal{G}_{pub} = \langle G_{pub} \rangle_{q^N}$. As for $\mathcal{G}_{pub}^{\perp} = \langle H_{pub} \rangle_{q^N}$, the Coggia-Couvreur distinguisher states that the following inequality holds

$$\dim_{q^N}(\mathcal{G}_{pub}^{\perp} + \mathcal{G}_{pub}^{\perp}{}^{[1]} + \cdots + \mathcal{G}_{pub}^{\perp}{}^{[\lambda]}) \leqslant \min\{n, \lambda(n-k) + \lambda\}.$$

However, for an $[n, k]$ random linear code $\mathcal{C}_{rand}$ over $\mathbb{F}_{q^N}$, the following equality holds with high probability

$$\dim_{q^N}(\mathcal{C}_{rand}^{\perp} + \mathcal{C}_{rand}^{\perp}{}^{[1]} + \cdots + \mathcal{C}_{rand}^{\perp}{}^{[\lambda]}) = \min\{n, (\lambda+1)(n-k)\}.$$

Now we explain why our scheme can prevent the Coggia-Couvreur attack. For simplicity, we consider the case of $l = 2$. Let $L(x) = \gamma_1 x + \gamma_2 x^{[m]} \in \mathbb{F}_{q^n}[x]$ be the linearized permutation polynomial associated to ψ, then

$$G_{pub} = \psi(GM_1^{-1})M_2^{-1} = (\gamma_1 GM_1^{-1} + \gamma_2 G^{[m]}(M_1^{-1})^{[m]})M_2^{-1}.$$

It is easy to see that there exists $Q \in \mathrm{PC}_n(\mathbb{F}_q) \cap \mathrm{GL}_n(\mathbb{F}_q)$ such that $G^{[m]} = GQ$, then

$$G_{pub} = G(\gamma_1 M_1^{-1} + \gamma_2 Q(M_1^{-1})^{[m]})M_2^{-1} = GM^{-1},$$

where

$$M = (\gamma_1 M_1^{-1} + \gamma_2 Q(M_1^{-1})^{[m]})^{-1}M_2. \tag{2}$$

Although one can recover M directly by computing $\mathrm{PC}_n(\boldsymbol{g}^*)^{-1}\mathrm{PC}_n(\boldsymbol{g})$, it does not mean one can conduct decryption with the knowledge of G and M. This is because M appears quite random and $\mathrm{rk}_q(M)$ can be very large. For instance, we have run 1000 random tests for $q = 2, m = 50, n = 100$ and $\lambda_1 = \lambda_2 = 2$. It turned out that $\mathrm{rk}_q(M) \geqslant 86$ holds in all these tests. By the way, $\mathrm{rk}_q(M^{-1}) \geqslant 90$ holds in 1000 random tests. Consequently, $\mathrm{rk}_q(\boldsymbol{e}M)$ will be far beyond the error correcting capability of Gabidulin code and the dual of $\mathcal{G}_{pub} = \langle G_{pub} \rangle_{q^n}$ appears indistinguishable from random codes. Exactly, the following equality holds with high probability according to our experiments,

$$\dim_{q^n}(\mathcal{G}_{pub}^{\perp} + \mathcal{G}_{pub}^{\perp}{}^{[1]} + \cdots + \mathcal{G}_{pub}^{\perp}{}^{[\lambda]}) = \min\{n, (\lambda+1)(n-k)\}.$$

This convinces us that our proposal can prevent the Coggia-Couvreur attack. It is easy to see that the Coggia-Couvreur attack also does not work for the general case where no partial cyclic structure is used.

Furthermore, we point out that recovering the private key is equivalent to deriving M_1, M_2 and φ, or their equivalent form, from the matrix M in (2). Firstly, it is clear that if one can decompose M as above, then one has found an equivalent private key. Conversely, if one can derive an equivalent private key from the public information, then one is able to get a decomposition of M. Specifically, given a matrix M of the form (2), one randomly chooses a partial circulant matrix G of Gabidulin code, then clearly GM^{-1} forms an instance of our scheme. This implies that recovering the private key leads to a decomposition of M.

Loidreau Attack. In a talk [30] at CBCrypto 2021, Loidreau proposed an attack to recover a decoder of the public code in the Loidreau cryptosystem with a complexity of $\mathcal{O}(((\lambda n + (n-k)^2)N)^{\omega} q^{(\lambda-1)N})$. With this decoder at hand, one can decrypt any ciphertext in polynomial time. Similar to the Coggia-Couvreur attack, this attack also operates the dual of the public code.

Let $M_1' = (\gamma_1 M_1^{-1} + \gamma_2 Q(M_1^{-1})^{[m]})^{-1}$. Notice that the matrix M in our scheme is publicly known, an adversary may try to recover M_2 or its equivalent form. However, due to the randomness of M_1', GM_1' is far from a Moore matrix. This implies that one cannot construct a linear system as Loidreau attack does. Therefore, Loidreau attack is not applicable to our cases.

A Brute-Force Attack. Now we consider a potential brute-force attack against the duple $(\overline{\psi}, \overline{\boldsymbol{m}}_1)$. Notice that for any $\psi' \in \overline{\psi}, \boldsymbol{m}_1' \in \overline{\boldsymbol{m}}_1$, there exists $\boldsymbol{m}_2' \in \mathbb{F}_{q^n}^n$ with $\mathrm{rk}_q(\boldsymbol{m}_2') = \lambda_2$ such that $G_{pub} = \psi(GM_1{}^{-1})M_2^{-1} = \psi'(GM_1'^{-1})M_2'^{-1}$, where $M_1' = \mathrm{PC}_n(\boldsymbol{m}_1'), M_2' = \mathrm{PC}_n(\boldsymbol{m}_2')$. Let $G_{pub}' = \mathrm{PC}_n(\boldsymbol{g}^*), G' = \mathrm{PC}_n(\boldsymbol{g})$, then

$$G_{pub}' = \psi(G'M_1^{-1})M_2^{-1} = \psi'(G'M_1'^{-1})M_2'^{-1}.$$

This implies that one can compute $M_2' = G_{pub}'{}^{-1}\psi'(G'M_1'^{-1})$. Furthermore, a direct verification shows that one can decrypt any ciphertext with the knowledge of $\psi', \boldsymbol{m}_1', \boldsymbol{m}_2'$ and the public $\boldsymbol{g}$. Apparently the complexity of this brute-force attack by enumerating $(\overline{\psi}, \overline{\boldsymbol{m}}_1)$ is $\mathcal{O}(\mathcal{N}(\overline{\psi}) \cdot \mathcal{N}(\overline{\boldsymbol{m}}_1))$.

6.2 Generic Attacks

A legitimate message receiver can always recover the plaintext in polynomial time, while an adversary without the private key has to deal with the underlying RSD problem presented in Sect. 3. Attacks that aim to recover the plaintext directly by solving the RSD problem are called generic attacks, the complexity of which only relates to the parameters of the cryptosystem. In what follows, we will show how to establish a connection between our proposal and the RSD problem.

Let $G_{pub} = \psi(GM_1^{-1})M_2^{-1} \in \mathcal{M}_{k,n}(\mathbb{F}_{q^n})$ be the public matrix, and $H_{pub} \in \mathcal{M}_{n-k,n}(\mathbb{F}_{q^n})$ a parity-check matrix of the public code $\mathcal{G}_{pub} = \langle G_{pub} \rangle_{q^n}$. Let $\boldsymbol{y} = \boldsymbol{x}G_{pub} + \boldsymbol{e}$ be the received ciphertext, then the syndrome of $\boldsymbol{y}$ with respect to H_{pub} can be computed as $\boldsymbol{s} = \boldsymbol{y}H_{pub}^T = \boldsymbol{e}H_{pub}^T$. By Definition 6, one obtains an RSD instance of parameters (q, n, n, k, t). Solving this RSD instance by the combinatorial attacks in Table 1 or the algebraic attacks in Table 2 will lead to the error vector $\boldsymbol{e}$, then one can recover the plaintext by solving the linear system $\boldsymbol{y} - \boldsymbol{e} = \boldsymbol{x}G_{pub}$.

7 Parameters and Public Key Size

In this section, we consider the practical security of our proposal against the generic attacks presented in Sect. 3, as well as a brute-force attack against the duple $(\overline{\psi}, \overline{\boldsymbol{m}}_1)$ in Sect. 6.1 with a complexity of $\mathcal{O}(\mathcal{N}(\overline{\psi}) \cdot \mathcal{N}(\overline{\boldsymbol{m}}_1))$. The public key in our proposal is a vector in $\mathbb{F}_{q^n}^n$, leading to a public key size of $n^2 \log_2(q)$ bits. In Table 3, we give some suggested parameters for security of at least 128 bits, 192 bits, and 256 bits. After that, we compare the public key size with some other code-based cryptosystems in Table 5. It should be noted that, when considering the algebraic attacks in [7,8], the practical security of LT19 under the original parameters in [26] will be lower than 88 bits. The updated parameters of LT19 and corresponding public key size are given in Table 4. It is clear that our proposal has an obvious advantage over other variants in public key representation.

Table 3. Parameters and public key size (in bytes).

Parameters							Public key size	Security
q	m	n	k	l	λ_1	λ_2		
2	55	110	54	2	2	2	1513	139
2	60	120	64	2	2	2	1800	198
2	72	144	72	2	2	2	2592	258

Table 4. Updated parameters and public key size (in bytes) for LT19.

Parameters								Public key size	Security
q	m	n	k	λ_1	λ_2	r	t		
2	167	167	59	3	3	54	9	6973	129
2	194	194	86	3	3	54	9	9409	193
2	203	203	95	3	3	54	9	10303	265

Table 5. Comparison on public key size (in bytes).

Instance	Security		
	128	192	256
Classic McEliece [3]	261120	524160	1044992
Loi17 [31]	34560		59136
LT19 [26]	6973	9409	10303
HQC [1]	2249	4522	7245
BIKE [4]	1541	3083	5122
RQC [2]	1834	2853	4090
Our proposal	1513	1800	2592

8 Conclusion

This paper has presented a new McEliece-type public key encryption scheme based on Gabidulin codes, where we use the so-called linearized transformations to hide the private key. Combining the technique of Loidreau's proposal, this new proposal can resist the existing distinguisher-based attacks. When equipped with the partial cyclic structure, this scheme turns into one with no hidden structure and with a competitive public key size.

A Proof of Proposition 6

Proof. For a λ-dimensional $\mathbb{F}_q$-linear space $\mathcal{V} \subseteq \mathbb{F}_{q^n}$, denote by $\mathcal{M}_\lambda(\mathcal{V})$ the set of all matrices with rank weight λ in $\mathrm{PC}_n(\mathcal{V})$. Let U be the set of all singular matrices in $\mathcal{M}_\lambda(\mathcal{V})$, and $V = \mathcal{M}_\lambda(\mathcal{V}) \cap \mathrm{GL}_n(\mathcal{V})$. In what follows, we will construct an injective mapping σ from U to V. First, we divide U into a certain number of subsets. For a matrix $M \in U$, let $\boldsymbol{m} = (m_0, m_1, \ldots, m_{n-1}) \in \mathcal{V}^n$ be the first row vector of M, namely $M = \mathrm{PC}_n(\boldsymbol{m})$. Let $\overline{M} = \{N \in U : M - N \text{ is a scalar matrix}\}$, a set of matrices in U whose first row resembles M at the last $n-1$ coordinates. Let $\boldsymbol{x} = (x, m_1, \ldots, m_{n-1})$, and $X = \mathrm{PC}_n(\boldsymbol{x})$. Denote by $f(x) \in \mathbb{F}_{q^n}[x]$ the determinant of X, then $f(x)$ is a polynomial of degree n. In the meanwhile, we have that $|\overline{M}|$ equals the number of roots of $f(x) = 0$ in $\mathcal{V}$, which indicates that $|\overline{M}| \leqslant n$. Let $\boldsymbol{m}^* = (m_1, \ldots, m_{n-1})$, then it is easy to see that $\mathrm{rk}_q(\boldsymbol{m}^*) \geqslant \lambda - 1$. Now we establish the mapping σ in the following two cases:

(1) $\mathrm{rk}_q(\boldsymbol{m}^*) = \lambda - 1$.
For a matrix $M_1 \in \overline{M}$, let $\boldsymbol{m}_1 = (\delta_1, \boldsymbol{m}^*)$ be the first row vector of M_1. Let $\mathcal{W} = \langle m_1, \ldots, m_{n-1} \rangle_q$, then $\dim_q(\mathcal{W}) = \lambda - 1$. Because of $q^\lambda - q^{\lambda-1} > n$, there exists $\delta_1' \in \mathcal{V} \backslash \mathcal{W}$ such that $f(\delta_1') \neq 0$, where $f(x)$ is defined as above. Let $\boldsymbol{m}_1' = (\delta_1', \boldsymbol{m}^*)$, then we have $M_1' = \mathrm{PC}_n(\boldsymbol{m}_1') \in \mathrm{GL}_n(\mathcal{V})$, and $\mathrm{rk}_q(\boldsymbol{m}_1') = \lambda$ in the meanwhile. We define $\sigma(M_1) = M_1'$.
For $2 \leqslant i \leqslant n$ and a matrix $M_i \in \overline{M} \backslash \{M_j\}_{j=1}^{i-1}$, if any, let $\boldsymbol{m}_i = (\delta_i, \boldsymbol{m}^*)$ be

the first row vector of M_i. Because of $q^\lambda - q^{\lambda-1} - (i-1) > n$, there exists $\delta_i' \in \mathcal{V}\backslash(\mathcal{W} \cup \{\delta_j'\}_{j=1}^{i-1})$ such that $f(\delta_i') \neq 0$. Let $\boldsymbol{m}_i' = (\delta_i', \boldsymbol{m}^*)$, then we have $M_i' = \mathrm{PC}_n(\boldsymbol{m}_i') \in \mathrm{GL}_n(\mathcal{V})$, and $\mathrm{rk}_q(\boldsymbol{m}_i') = \lambda$ in the meanwhile. We define $\sigma(M_i) = M_i'$.

(2) $\mathrm{rk}_q(\boldsymbol{m}^*) = \lambda$.
For a matrix $M_1 \in \overline{M}$, let $\boldsymbol{m}_1 = (\delta_1, \boldsymbol{m}^*)$ be the first row vector of M_1. Because of $q^\lambda > n$, there exists $\delta_1' \in \mathcal{V}$ such that $f(\delta_1') \neq 0$, where $f(x)$ is defined as above. Let $\boldsymbol{m}_1' = (\delta_1', \boldsymbol{m}^*)$, then we have $M_1' = \mathrm{PC}_n(\boldsymbol{m}_1') \in \mathrm{GL}_n(\mathcal{V})$, and $\mathrm{rk}_q(\boldsymbol{m}_1') = \lambda$ in the meanwhile. We define $\sigma(M_1) = M_1'$.
For $2 \leqslant i \leqslant n$ and a matrix $M_i \in \overline{M}\backslash\{M_j\}_{j=1}^{i-1}$, if any, let $\boldsymbol{m}_i = (\delta_i, \boldsymbol{m}^*)$ be the first row vector of M_i. Because of $q^\lambda - (i-1) > n$, there exists $\delta_i' \in \mathcal{V}\backslash\{\delta_j'\}_{j=1}^{i-1}$ such that $f(\delta_i') \neq 0$. Let $\boldsymbol{m}_i' = (\delta_i', \boldsymbol{m}^*)$, then we have $M_i' = \mathrm{PC}_n(\boldsymbol{m}_i') \in \mathrm{GL}_n(\mathcal{V})$, and $\mathrm{rk}_q(\boldsymbol{m}_i') = \lambda$ in the meanwhile. We define $\sigma(M_i) = M_i'$.

It is easy to see that σ forms an injective mapping from U to V. Apparently $\sigma(U) = \{\sigma(M) : M \in U\} \subseteq V$, which implies that $|U| = |\sigma(U)| \leqslant |V|$. Together with $U \cap V = \varnothing$ and $\mathcal{M}_\lambda(\mathcal{V}) = U \cup V$, we have that

$$\xi = \sum_{\mathcal{V} \subseteq \mathbb{F}_{q^n}, \dim_q(\mathcal{V}) = \lambda} |V| \Big/ \sum_{\mathcal{V} \subseteq \mathbb{F}_{q^n}, \dim_q(\mathcal{V}) = \lambda} |\mathcal{M}_\lambda(\mathcal{V})| \geqslant \frac{1}{2}.$$

References

1. Aguilar-Melchor, C., et al.: Hamming quasi-cyclic (HQC). http://pqc-hqc.org/doc/hqc-specification_2020-10-01.pdf. Accessed 10 Oct 2020
2. Aguilar-Melchor, C., et al.: Rank quasi-cyclic (RQC). Second Round submission to NIST Post-Quantum Cryptography call (2020)
3. Albrecht, M.R., et al.: Classic McEliece: conservative code-based cryptography. https://classic.mceliece.org/nist/mceliece-20201010.pdf. Accessed 10 Oct 2020
4. Aragon, N., et al.: BIKE: bit flipping key encapsulation. https://bikesuite.org/files/v4.1/BIKE_Spec.2020.10.22.1.pdf. Accessed 10 Oct 2020
5. Aragon, N., Gaborit, P., Hauteville, A., Tillich, J.-P.: A new algorithm for solving the rank syndrome decoding problem. In: Proceedings of ISIT 2018, pp. 2421–2425. IEEE (2018)
6. Baldi, M., Bianchi, M., Chiaraluce, F., Rosenthal, J., Schipani, D.: Enhanced public key security for the McEliece cryptosystem. J. Cryptol. **29**(1), 1–27 (2016)
7. Bardet, M., et al.: An algebraic attack on rank metric code-based cryptosystems. In: Canteaut, A., Ishai, Y. (eds.) EUROCRYPT 2020. LNCS, vol. 12107, pp. 64–93. Springer, Cham (2020). https://doi.org/10.1007/978-3-030-45727-3_3
8. Bardet, M., et al.: Improvements of algebraic attacks for solving the rank decoding and MinRank problems. In: Moriai, S., Wang, H. (eds.) ASIACRYPT 2020. LNCS, vol. 12491, pp. 507–536. Springer, Cham (2020). https://doi.org/10.1007/978-3-030-64837-4_17
9. Berlekamp, E.R., McEliece, R.J., van Tilborg, H.: On the inherent intractability of certain coding problems. IEEE Trans. Inf. Theory **24**(3), 384–386 (1978)
10. Bosma, W., Cannon, J., Playoust, C.: The MAGMA algebra system I: the user language. J. Symbolic Comput. **24**(3–4), 235–265 (1997)

11. Chalkley, R.: Circulant matrices and algebraic equations. Math. Mag. **48**(2), 73–80 (1975)
12. Coggia, D., Couvreur, A.: On the security of a Loidreau rank metric code based encryption scheme. Des. Codes Crypt. **88**(9), 1941–1957 (2020). https://doi.org/10.1007/s10623-020-00781-4
13. Gabidulin, E.M.: Theory of codes with maximum rank distance. Prob. Peredachi Inf. **21**(1), 3–16 (1985)
14. Gabidulin, E.M.: Attacks and counter-attacks on the GPT public key cryptosystem. Des. Codes Cryptogr. **48**(2), 171–177 (2008)
15. Gabidulin, E.M., Ourivski, A.V., Honary, B., Ammar, B.: Reducible rank codes and their applications to cryptography. IEEE Trans. Inform. Theory **49**(12), 3289–3293 (2003)
16. Gabidulin, E.M., Paramonov, A.V., Tretjakov, O.V.: Ideals over a non-commutative ring and their application in cryptology. In: Davies, D.W. (ed.) EUROCRYPT 1991. LNCS, vol. 547, pp. 482–489. Springer, Heidelberg (1991). https://doi.org/10.1007/3-540-46416-6_41
17. Gabidulin, E.M., Rashwan, H., Honary, B.: On improving security of GPT cryptosystem. In: Proceedings of ISIT 2009, pp. 1110–1114. IEEE (2009)
18. Gaborit, P., Ruatta, O., Schrek, J.: On the complexity of the rank syndrome decoding problem. IEEE Trans. Inf. Theory **62**(2), 1006–1019 (2016)
19. Gaborit, P., Zémor, G.: On the hardness of the decoding and the minimum distance problems for rank codes. IEEE Trans. Inf. Theory **62**(12), 7245–7252 (2016)
20. Ghatak, A.: Extending Coggia-Couvreur attack on Loidreau's rank-metric cryptosystem. Des. Codes Cryptogr. **90**(1), 215–238 (2022)
21. Gibson, K.: Severely denting the Gabidulin version of the McEliece public key cryptosystem. Des. Codes Cryptogr. **6**(1), 37–45 (1995)
22. Gibson, K.: The security of the Gabidulin public key cryptosystem. In: Maurer, U. (ed.) EUROCRYPT 1996. LNCS, vol. 1070, pp. 212–223. Springer, Heidelberg (1996). https://doi.org/10.1007/3-540-68339-9_19
23. Guo, W., Fu, F.-W.: Polynomial-time key recovery attack on the Lau-Tan cryptosystem based on Gabidulin codes. arXiv:2112.15466 [cs.IT] (2022)
24. Horlemann-Trautmann, A.-L., Marshall, K., Rosenthal, J.: Extension of Overbeck's attack for Gabidulin-based cryptosystems. Des. Codes Cryptogr. **86**(2), 319–340 (2018)
25. Lau, T.S.C., Tan, C.H.: A new technique in rank metric code-based encryption. Cryptography **2**(4), 32 (2018)
26. Lau, T.S.C., Tan, C.H.: New rank codes based encryption scheme using partial circulant matrices. Des. Codes Crypt. **87**(12), 2979–2999 (2019). https://doi.org/10.1007/s10623-019-00659-0
27. Lidl, R., Niederreiter, H.: Finite Fields. Cambridge University Press, Cambridge (1997)
28. Loidreau, P.: A Welch–Berlekamp like algorithm for decoding Gabidulin codes. In: Ytrehus, Ø. (ed.) WCC 2005. LNCS, vol. 3969, pp. 36–45. Springer, Heidelberg (2006). https://doi.org/10.1007/11779360_4
29. Loidreau, P.: A new rank metric codes based encryption scheme. In: Lange, T., Takagi, T. (eds.) PQCrypto 2017. LNCS, vol. 10346, pp. 3–17. Springer, Cham (2017). https://doi.org/10.1007/978-3-319-59879-6_1
30. Loidreau, P.: Analysis of a rank metric codes based encryption scheme. https://drive.google.com/file/d/1FuMgqm0NfGMJOxaZyrIrI1OWn0UICwPo/view. Accessed 1 July 2021

31. Loidreau, P.: Analysis of a public-key encryption scheme based on distorted Gabidulin codes. https://www.wcc2022.uni-rostock.de/storages/uni-rostock/Tagungen/WCC2022/Papers/WCC_2022_paper_5.pdf. Accessed 1 July 2022
32. McEliece, R.J.: A public-key cryptosystem based on algebraic coding theory. Jet Propuls. Lab. DSN Progr. Rep. **42–44**, 114–116 (1978)
33. National Institute of Standards and Technology (NIST), U.S. Department of Commerce: Post-quantum cryptography standardization (2017). https://csrc.nist.gov/Projects/post-quantum-cryptography/Post-Quantum-Cryptography-Standardization
34. Otmani, A., Kalachi, H.T., Ndjeya, S.: Improved cryptanalysis of rank metric schemes based on Gabidulin codes. Des. Codes Cryptogr. **86**(9), 1983–1996 (2018)
35. Otmani, A., Tillich, J.-P., Dallot, L.: Cryptanalysis of two McEliece cryptosystems based on quasi-cyclic codes. Math. Comput. Sci. **3**(2), 129–140 (2010)
36. Ourivski, A.V., Johansson, T.: New technique for decoding codes in the rank metric and its cryptography applications. Prob. Inform. Trans. **38**(3), 237–246 (2002)
37. Overbeck, R.: A new structural attack for GPT and variants. In: Dawson, E., Vaudenay, S. (eds.) Mycrypt 2005. LNCS, vol. 3715, pp. 50–63. Springer, Heidelberg (2005). https://doi.org/10.1007/11554868_5
38. Overbeck, R.: Structural attacks for public key cryptosystems based on Gabidulin codes. J. Cryptol. **21**(2), 280–301 (2008)
39. Pham, B.-D., Loidreau, P.: An analysis of Coggia-Couvreur attack on Loidreau's rank-metric public-key encryption scheme in the general case. arXiv:2112.12445 [cs.CR] (2021)
40. Rashwan, H., Gabidulin, E.M., Honary, B.: Security of the GPT cryptosystem and its applications to cryptography. Secur. Commun. Netw. **4**(8), 937–946 (2011)
41. Richter, G., Plass, S.: Error and erasure decoding of rank-codes with a modified Berlekamp-Massey algorithm. ITG FACHBERICHT, 203–210 (2004)

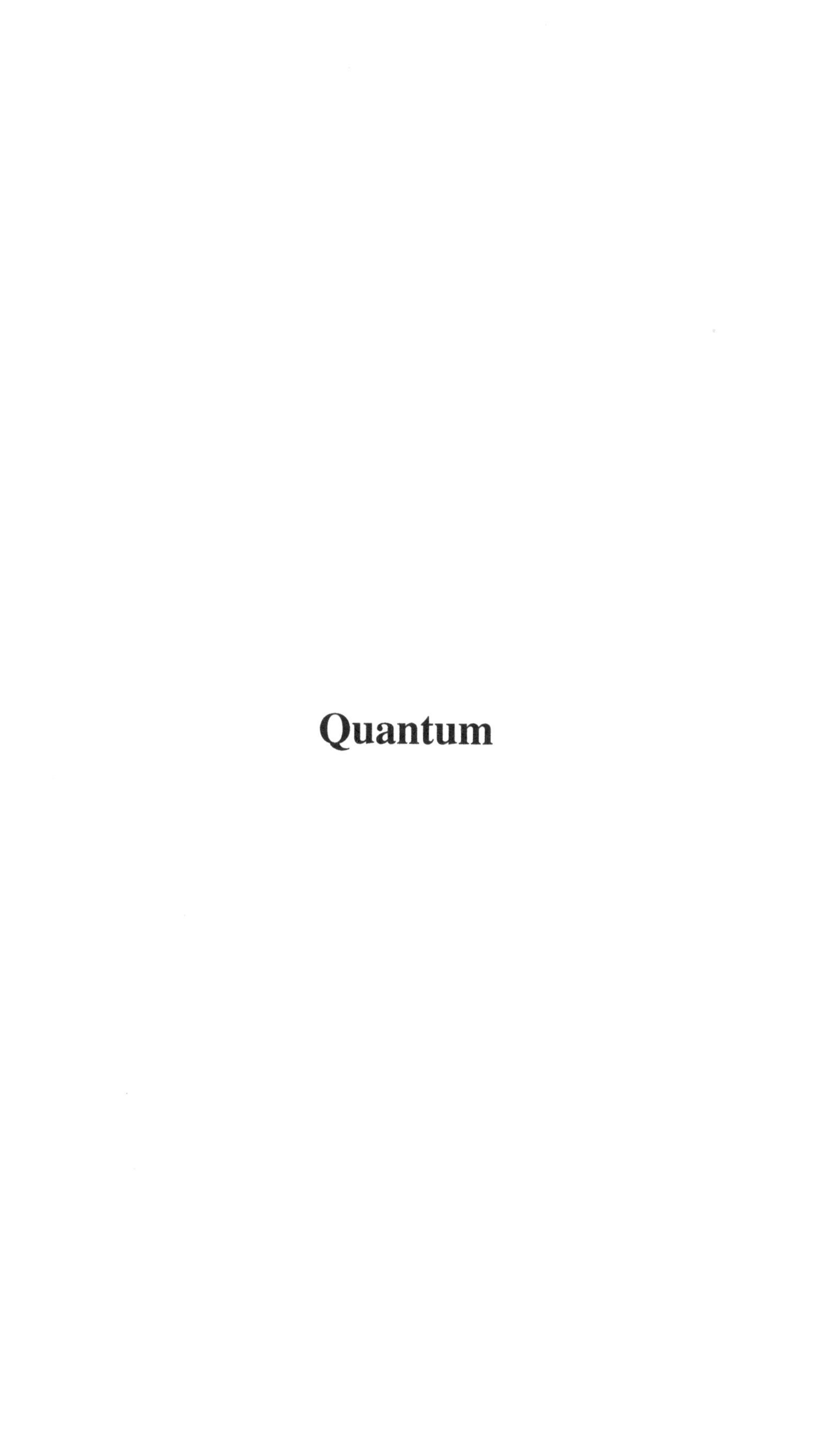

Quantum

Optimizing the Depth of Quantum Implementations of Linear Layers

Chengkai Zhu[1,2] and Zhenyu Huang[1,2](✉)

[1] SKLOIS, Institute of Information Engineering, Chinese Academy of Sciences, Beijing, China
{zhuchengkai,huangzhenyu}@iie.ac.cn

[2] School of Cyber Security, University of Chinese Academy of Sciences, Beijing, China

Abstract. Synthesis and optimization of quantum circuits are important and fundamental research topics in quantum computation, due to the fact that qubits are very precious and decoherence time which determines the computation time available is very limited. Specifically in cryptography, identifying the minimum quantum resources for implementing an encryption process is crucial in evaluating the quantum security of symmetric-key ciphers. In this work, we investigate the problem of optimizing the depth of quantum circuits for linear layers while utilizing a small number of qubits and quantum gates. To this end, we present a framework for the implementation and optimization of linear Boolean functions, by which we significantly reduce the depth of quantum circuits for many linear layers used in symmetric-key ciphers without increasing the gate count.

Keywords: Quantum circuit · Reversible circuit · Linear depth · Symmetric-key ciphers

1 Introduction

With the rapid development of quantum technologies and quantum algorithms such as Grover's algorithm, Simon's algorithm, and Shor's algorithm, the security of modern cryptography has been challenging. It is widely known that Grover's algorithm [22] has a square root speedup over a classical algorithm in terms of the problem of database search, which can be applied to find the key for a symmetric cipher instead of a classical exhaustive key search. Moreover, quantum attacks on symmetric-key schemes are extensively studied these years, including Simon's period-finding algorithm [12,25] and other attacks derived from cryptanalytic techniques [13,14,23,30]. All these works imply that there would be a potential quantum threat to our symmetric encryption system used today.

To actually implement a quantum key search on a symmetric-key encryption scheme, e.g., a block cipher, the encryption process is supposed to be implemented as a *Grover oracle*, meaning that we should be capable of constructing a quantum circuit for the specific encryption algorithm. Meanwhile, in

Y. Deng and M. Yung (Eds.): Inscrypt 2022, LNCS 13837, pp. 129–147, 2023.
https://doi.org/10.1007/978-3-031-26553-2_7

the call for proposals to the standardization of post-quantum cryptography, the National Institute of Standards and Technology (NIST) makes the complexities of the quantum circuit for AES standards to categorize the security strength of post-quantum public-key schemes. All these reasons give rise to the growing appeals for studying the quantum implementation of quantum oracles of iterative symmetric-key ciphers as well as how to optimize the implementation. This has been an important and fruitful topic recently, which helps understand the quantum security of current encryption schemes and guide future post-quantum encryption designs.

Although the circuit implementations of symmetric-key ciphers differ from each other, a recurring theme can be recognized, which is to construct the quantum circuit for each building block of the cipher separately. Then we can do post-optimizations for the circuit to reduce the quantum cost, including the depth, the width (the number of qubits), and the gate count (the number of quantum gates). For the non-linear building blocks, most work has been focusing on reducing the T-depth due to its importance in fault-tolerant quantum computation [21]. The circuits that implement the linear building blocks, are called *linear reversible circuits*, which only consist of CNOT gates. They have many important applications in quantum computation, e.g., stabilizer circuits.

Related Work. Work in quantum implementation of symmetric ciphers mostly focuses on AES due to its popularity and importance. In 2015, Grassl et al. [21] first proposed a quantum circuit of AES and found that the number of logical qubits required to implement a Grover attack on AES is around 3000 to 7000. Followed by their work, Almazrooie et al. [4] gave a more detailed circuit of AES trying to use fewer qubits. In [33] Langenberg et al. presented an improved quantum circuit for the S-box of AES which reduced the numbers of Toffoli gates and qubits. In [48], Zou et al. constructed two quantum circuits for AES S-box and S-box^{-1}, trying to use fewer qubits as well. Except for these works primarily focusing on the number of qubits, Jaques et al. in [25] build circuits for AES and LowMC with the primary goal of reducing the circuit depth. Recently, Huang and Sun [24] proposed a general structure for implementing quantum circuits for the round functions of block ciphers. They utilized some techniques to give the state-of-the-art synthesis of AES, with respect to depth-width trade-offs. Not surprisingly, their strategy for efficient quantum circuit synthesis is also to build linear and non-linear cryptographic building blocks separately. The depth of the linear block is not considered in the first place in their work.

Apart from the efficient quantum implementation of symmetric-key ciphers, the problem of quantum circuit optimization has been studied for many years in the field of synthesis and optimization of reversible logic circuits [5,36,38,41,47], which is historically motivated by theoretical research in low-power electronics transforms in cryptography and computer graphics. The basic task is to use reversible gates to implement a reversible Boolean function, i.e., a permutation. There have been enormous algorithmic paradigms such as search-based, cycle-based, transformation-based, and BDD-based for reversible circuit synthesis, both exact and heuristic. One may refer to [38] for a detailed review. Also, there are some tools developed to study the synthesis of reversible circuits [45].

Specifically for the synthesis and optimization of linear quantum circuits (the CNOT circuits), traditional methods usually yield a circuit with $O(n^2)$ gates based on standard row reduction methods such as Gaussian elimination and LU-decomposition for an $n \times n$ matrix. In [37], Patel et al. present an algorithm that uses $O\left(n^2/\log(n)\right)$ gates, which is the theoretical lower bound, to build an n-qubit linear quantum circuit. This will trivially give a bound of $O\left(n^2/\log(n)\right)$ on the circuit depth. Furthermore, Jiang et al. [28] reduce this bound by a factor of n, achieving an asymptotically optimal depth bound of $O\left(n/\log(n)\right)$. Some other efforts were also made to achieve a more compact circuit of linear layers [17,18]. The synthesis of the CNOT circuits has direct applications to the synthesis of stabilizer circuits, an important class of quantum circuits introduced by Aaronson and Gottesman [2]. However, there is still a lack of practical and efficient strategies for the optimal implementation of the linear components.

Our Contribution. In this work, we first revisit the problem of optimization of a subclass of quantum circuits - CNOT circuits. We give three characterizations of the CNOT circuit depth, i.e., sequence depth, move-equivalent depth, and exchange-equivalent depth. Based on that, we focus on the problem of minimizing the circuit depth while maintaining the gate count of a gate-count-optimized CNOT circuit.

We present a practical and efficient framework in Algorithm 3 for the implementation of linear operators as well as the optimization of their circuits. Consequently, one can construct the quantum circuit for a linear Boolean function with a small number of CNOT gates and lower circuit depth. For a linear Boolean function with n-variables, our depth optimization procedure yields a complexity of $O\left(n^4/\log(n)^2\right)$.

We finally showcase the strength of our framework in quantum implementations of symmetric-key ciphers. For different linear layers used in symmetric-key ciphers, which corresponds to some invertible matrices, our method can always give a considerable reduction in the circuit depths of their implementations, and obtain the state-of-the-art quantum circuits for those linear layers. Notably, for non-invertible linear transformations that appear in the non-linear building blocks or other more complex circuit structures, our method can also make the circuits for these linear part more compact hence reduce the depth of the whole circuit.

2 Preliminaries

2.1 Quantum Circuit

Among the various alternative models used to represent a quantum computer, the circuit model is arguably the most widely used. In the circuit model of quantum computation, a qubit (quantum bit) is a theoretically abstract mathematical object. It has two possible states $|0\rangle$ and $|1\rangle$ that are usually called basis states just as a classical bit has a state of either 0 or 1. The difference between bits and qubits is that a qubit can be in a state other than $|0\rangle$ and $|1\rangle$. It can be a linear combination of basic states, $|\psi\rangle = \alpha|0\rangle + \beta|1\rangle$, where $\alpha, \beta \in \mathbb{C}$ and $|\alpha|^2 + |\beta|^2 = 1$.

Geometrically, $|0\rangle$ and $|1\rangle$ can be represented as two-dimensional vectors $|0\rangle = [1, 0]^T$ and $|1\rangle = [0, 1]^T$. And $|\psi\rangle$ is described by a unit vector in a two-dimensional Hilbert space $\mathcal{H} \cong \mathbb{C}^2$ of which $|0\rangle$ and $|1\rangle$ are known as computational basis states. A system of n-qubits, also called an n-qubit register, has states described by a unit vector in the Hilbert space $\mathcal{H}_n \cong \mathcal{H}^{\otimes n}$. Based on this, the evolution of quantum states is described by unitary transformations, or quantum gates. A quantum gate acting on n qubits is represented by a $2^n \times 2^n$ unitary matrix. For instance, a NOT gate will invert the qubit and has a matrix form $\begin{pmatrix} 0 & 1 \\ 1 & 0 \end{pmatrix}$. There are some important single-qubit gates like the Hadamard gate H, S gate, T gate:

$$H = \frac{1}{\sqrt{2}} \begin{pmatrix} 1 & 1 \\ 1 & -1 \end{pmatrix}, S = \begin{pmatrix} 1 & 0 \\ 0 & i \end{pmatrix}, T = \begin{pmatrix} 1 & 0 \\ 0 & e^{i\pi/4} \end{pmatrix}.$$

For two-qubit gate, one of the most important one is the CNOT gate which is a two qubits (control and target) operation.

$$\mathrm{CNOT} : |x_1\rangle|x_2\rangle \to |x_1\rangle|x_1 \oplus x_2\rangle. \tag{1}$$

It is worth mentioning that CNOT gate, H gate, and S gate generate the Clifford group and Clifford + T forms a universal gate library. Whereas, in the field of cryptography and quantum combined, one mostly works with the Boolean functions, thus is more interested in a gate set called CNTS gate library, consisting of the CNOT, NOT, Toffoli, and SWAP gates.

From (1), we can see that a CNOT gate can be seen as an invertible linear transformation $\begin{pmatrix} 1 & 0 \\ 1 & 1 \end{pmatrix}$ over $\mathbb{F}_2^2$. Similarly, for an n-qubit system, we can characterize a CNOT gate with an $n \times n$ matrix instead of its $2^n \times 2^n$ unitary matrix form for its linearity. In detail, a CNOT gate controlled by the j-th qubit, acting on the i-th qubit $(i \neq j)$ can be written as

$$E_{ij} = I + e_{ij}, \tag{2}$$

where I is the $n \times n$ identity matrix and e_{ij} the elementary matrix with all entries equal 0 but the entry (i, j) equals 1. In fact, E_{ij}'s belong to the *elementary matrices* in linear algebra or matrix theory. Recall that there are three types of elementary matrices, which correspond to three types of row operations (respectively, column operations) and may be interpreted as quantum gates:

1. Row switching: interchange two rows, which will be implemented by renaming or switching the circuit wires[1].

[1] This operation can also be implemented by 3 CNOT gates, but this will cost more quantum resources, since we think the cost of rewiring is free in most cases.

2. Row multiplication: multiply a row with a nonzero number, which is trivial in $\mathbb{F}_2$ and not concerned in this paper.
3. Row addition: add a row to another one multiplied by a nonzero number, which in $\mathbb{F}_2$ will be interpreted as a CNOT gate.

It is a well-known theorem that any linear reversible matrix can be decomposed as a product of elementary matrices. All of these indicate that for any linear Boolean function with n variables, we can use a sequence of CNOT gates on n qubits, referred as a CNOT circuit with n qubits, to implement it.

Theorem 1. *Any invertible matrix A can be decomposed as a product of elementary matrices.*

Two metrics, named width and depth, are often used to characterize the cost of a quantum circuit. Width refers to the number of qubits that comprise the circuit and depth refers to the number of layers of gates that are not executed at the same time. Width and depth are both limiting factors in the execution of quantum algorithms. For CNOT circuits, since it can be easily implemented without auxiliary qubits, hence minimizing its width is an easy problem. Therefore, in this paper, we focus on optimizing the depth of CNOT circuits, by which we can reduce the depth of the quantum implementations of linear components of symmetric-key ciphers.

2.2 Depth of the Quantum Circuits

For the depth of a quantum circuit, one usually refers to the minimal number of stages the hardware needs to execute the gates when we suppose that the gates acting on different qubits are executed simultaneously. For instance, the following circuit (a) in Fig. 1 has depth 3 and the circuit (b) in Fig. 1 has depth 2 since the second and the last CNOT gates on the right circuit can be executed simultaneously. However, when the quantum circuit consists of different kinds of gates and we want to reduce the depth for a particular gate, e.g., the Toffoli depth that refers to the number of stages the hardware needs to execute the Toffoli gates simultaneously, the definition of depth we mentioned should be fixed.

For instance, the two circuits illustrated in Fig. 2 contain the same gates. In circuit (b), in order to execute the two Toffoli gate in parallel, the two CNOT

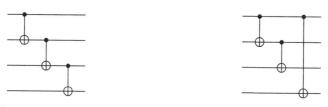

(a) CNOT circuit with depth 3 (b) CNOT circuit with depth 2

Fig. 1. The quantum CNOT circuits with different depth.

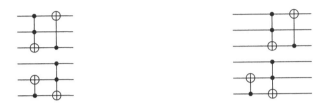

(a) Toffoli depth 2 and circuit depth 2 (b) Toffoli depth 1 and circuit depth 3

Fig. 2. The quantum circuits with different Toffoli depth.

gates should be executed in another two different stages, which makes the circuit has depth 3.

This example shows that the depth of a circuit should be defined based on its building structure. The key issue here is that quantum circuits are written such that the horizontal axis is time, starting at the left hand side and ending at the right. These lines define the sequence of events, and are usually not physical cables, resulting in that these two circuits in Fig. 2 are practically two different events. In this sense, the depth of the quantum circuit actually reveals its execution time. For this reason, in this paper, when we say a circuit with depth d, we mean a circuit is described by d layers of gates, and all gates in each layer can be executed simultaneously.

3 Linear Depth Optimization

Generally for a linear Boolean function or a linear component in symmetric-key ciphers, one may first easily obtain its matrix A from its algebraic normal form. Then implementing A with a CNOT circuit is equivalent to decomposing A into a sequence of elementary matrices and a permutation matrix. Since this permutation matrix corresponds to rewiring operations which are considered as free, we only need to focus on this sequence of elementary matrices. We call it the *decomposition sequence* of A, which is defined formally as follows.

Definition 1. *A decomposition sequence* SEQ *of a matrix* A *is a finite sequence of elementary matrices with a particular order*

$$\mathit{SEQ} = \{E(c_1, t_1), E(c_2, t_2), \cdots, E(c_L, t_L)\}, \tag{3}$$

such that

$$A = P\left(\prod_{k=L}^{1} E(c_k, t_k)\right), \tag{4}$$

where P *is a permutation matrix. Here,* L *is called the length of the sequence, and* $\prod_{k=L}^{1} E(c_k, t_k)$ *is called the output of the sequence.*

In fact, any invertible matrix in $\mathbb{F}_2$ has a decomposition sequence followed by Theorem 1. Each $E(c_k, t_k)$ actually corresponds to a CNOT gate controlled by the line c_k acting on the line t_k in a quantum context. For convenience, we may simply use SEQ to denote the decomposition sequence corresponding to a CNOT circuit for a given linear transformation A. For a SEQ, we say it is divided continuously into D sub-sequences if

$$\begin{aligned}
\mathtt{SEQ}_1 &= \{E(c_1,t_1), E(c_2,t_2), \cdots, E(c_{k_1}, t_{k_1})\},\\
\mathtt{SEQ}_2 &= \{E(c_{k_1+1},t_{k_1+1}), E(c_{k_1+2},t_{k_1+2}) \cdots, E(c_{k_2}, t_{k_2})\},\\
&\cdots \\
\mathtt{SEQ}_D &= \{E(c_{k_{D-1}+1},t_{k_{D-1}+1}), E(c_{k_{D-1}+2},t_{k_{D-1}+2}) \cdots, E(c_{k_D}, t_{k_D})\},
\end{aligned} \tag{5}$$

and $\bigcup_{k=1}^{D} \mathtt{SEQ}_k = \mathtt{SEQ}$, and $\{\mathtt{SEQ}_1, \mathtt{SEQ}_2, \ldots, \mathtt{SEQ}_D\}$ is called a *parallel partition* of SEQ if $\bigcap_i \{c_i, t_i\} = \emptyset$ for any i in each $\mathtt{SEQ}_k$. Then the depth of SEQ is defined as follows.

Definition 2 (Sequence depth). *For a decomposition sequence SEQ, the depth of SEQ is the minimum D such that there is a parallel partition of SEQ with D sub-sequence.*

Notably, as discussed in Sect. 2.2, the depth of a quantum circuit is a circuit-architecture-dependent parameter, and from a parallel partition with D sub-sequences, we can easily achieve a quantum circuit with depth D. Moreover, we always cluster the CNOT gates leftward when considering the depth of a CNOT circuit particularly, making as many gates as possible run simultaneously.

It is straightforward to know that if $\{c_{i-1}, t_{i-1}\} \cap \{c_i, t_i\} = \emptyset$ (or $\{c_i, t_i\} \cap \{c_{i+1}, t_{i+1}\} = \emptyset$), $E(c_i, t_j)$ can be *moved forward (or backward)* without changing the output of the sequence. Then we have the following definition for the equivalence of two decomposition sequences.

Definition 3 (Move-equivalence). *Two decomposition sequences SEQ and SEQ′ are move-equivalent if SEQ′ can be obtained by moving gates in SEQ forward or backward.*

Actually, given a CNOT circuit, which corresponds to a decomposition sequence SEQ, the output of its depth from most quantum resources estimators, for example the Q# resources estimator of Microsoft [1], is the depth of the move-equivalent sequence of SEQ under the strategy that moves all $E(c_i, t_i)$ forward as far as possible. However, we will discuss in the next subsection that for a SEQ, after exchanging some gates that seem can not be further moved forward (or backward), we can obtain a new decomposition sequence which has lower depth than all move-equivalent sequences of SEQ.

3.1 Depth Optimization for Decomposition Sequences

By PLU-decomposition, one can easily obtain a decomposition sequence of a matrix A. However, it is obviously not an optimal implementation when concerning two metrics - the gate count and the circuit depth.

For the gate count, it is pointed out in [46] that there are seven cases where three adjacent elementary operations can be equivalently reduced to two, implementing the same Boolean function. As a result, they built seven rules to optimize a given sequence and here we employ the same method to reduce the gate count of a decomposition sequence.

For the circuit depth, we find that the depth of a CNOT circuit can be further reduced since there are other equivalent decomposition sequences for a SEQ that is shallower. For example, we can swap the order of the second and the third CNOT gates of Circuit (a) in Fig. 3, maintaining the output. Then we obtain Circuit (b), which has circuit depth 2.

(a) CNOT circuit with depth 3 (b) CNOT circuit with depth 2

Fig. 3. The quantum CNOT circuits with different depth by exchanging gates.

Actually we have the following observation for the elementary matrix (the CNOT gate) $E(c_k, j_k)$ in a decomposition sequence:

Observation 1. *For elementary matrices,* $E(c_i, t_i)E(c_j, t_j) = E(c_j, t_j)E(c_i, t_i)$ *if and only if* $t_i \neq c_j$ *and* $c_i \neq t_j$.

Observation 1 is quite obvious from the circuit perspective meaning that two CNOT gates can swap order with each other if and only if the control qubit of the first gate is not the target qubit of the other, and vice versa. In Fig. 3 the first CNOT gate and the second CNOT gate in Circuit (a) can not be exchanged since the target qubit of the first gate is the controlled qubit of the second gate. In this way, we have the following definition for *exchange-equivalence* of two decomposition sequences.

Definition 4 (Exchange-equivalence). *For two adjacent gates* $E(c_k, t_k)$ *and* $E(c_{k+1}, t_{k+1})$ *in SEQ, we can exchange the order of the two if and only if* $t_k \neq c_{k+1}$ *and* $c_k \neq t_{k+1}$. *We say SEQ′ and SEQ are exchange-equivalent if SEQ′ can be obtained by exchanging the order of the gates in SEQ.*

It is worth noting that the move-equivalence is a special case of the exchange-equivalence. Obviously, now we can try to find a shallower circuit for SEQ among all exchange-equivalent decomposition sequences. To this end, we present Algorithm 1 to find the exchange-equivalent SEQ′ that has nearly optimal circuit depth for a given decomposition sequence. Intuitively, we try to apply as many quantum gates as possible in a single sub-sequence. To accomplish this, we search possible swapping between different gates forward and backward as detailed in the function One-way-opt. Algorithm 1 uses One-way-opt twice, and has the following property.

Property 1. Given a decomposition sequence $\texttt{SEQ}$ with L gates, the Algorithm 1 has $O(L^2)$ steps to achieve a stable depth, meaning the depth will not be further reduced by using One-way-opt more.

Proof. Suppose the output of the Algorithm 1 is S_1 which is exchange-equivalent to $\texttt{SEQ}$. If the number of sub-sequences can still be reduced, meaning there is a redundant sub-sequence S_r all of whose gates can be moved equivalently into other sub-sequences in S_1. For any gate E_r in S_r, if the sub-sequence in which E_r can be moved lies before S_r, E_r should have been moved there in Step 1 of the Algorithm 1 by the definition of the One-way-opt procedure. Else if the sub-sequence in which E_r can be moved lies after S_r, E_r should have been moved there in Step 3 of the Algorithm 1. All of which claim that there is no such E_r that can be moved equivalently into other sub-sequences. Thus by applying One-way-opt twice, we achieve a stable depth for implementing $\texttt{SEQ}$ with Algorithm 1. For each gate in $\texttt{SEQ}$, in the worst case, we may iterate through all the gates that lie after A in $\texttt{SEQ}$ twice to check whether they can be executed in parallel and whether they are exchangeable. This will give us a query complexity $O(L^2)$.

Remark 1. For a linear Boolean function $\mathcal{F}$ with n variables, the result in [37] shows that it can be implemented with $O(n^2/\log(n))$ CNOT gates. Hence, by Algorithm 1, we can obtain a low-depth CNOT circuit of $\mathcal{F}$ with complexity $O(n^4/\log(n)^2)$.

Algorithm 1: CNOT depth optimization of $\texttt{SEQ}$

Input: A decomposition sequence $\texttt{SEQ}$.
Output: A low-depth decomposition sequence $\texttt{SEQ}_{\text{opt}}$ which is exchange-equivalent to $\texttt{SEQ}$.

1 $\texttt{SEQ}_{\text{left}} \leftarrow$One-way-opt($\texttt{SEQ}$);
2 Reverse sort the gates in $\texttt{SEQ}_{\text{left}}$ to get $\texttt{SEQ}_{\text{left}}^{\text{rev}}$;
3 $\texttt{SEQ}_{\text{opt}}^{rev} \leftarrow$ One-way-opt($\texttt{SEQ}_{\text{left}}^{\text{rev}}$);
4 Reverse sort the gates in $\texttt{SEQ}_{\text{opt}}^{rev}$ to get $\texttt{SEQ}_{\text{opt}}$;
5 **return** $\texttt{SEQ}_{\text{opt}}$;

Example 1. Here we show a toy example to demonstrate the effectiveness of our algorithm. For a decomposition sequence

$$\texttt{SEQ} = \{E(0,1), E(1,3), E(2,3), E(3,1), E(0,3), E(0,2), E(2,1)\}, \tag{6}$$

its circuit is shown as (a) in Fig. 4 whose sequence depth is obviously 7. After the first step of Algorithm 1, $E(2,3)$ is exchanged with $E(1,3)$ since it can be executed with $E(0,1)$ in parallel and is exchangeable with $E(1,3)$. Then we get an exchanging-equivalent sequence whose circuit is shown as (b) in Fig. 4 with

One-way-opt: One-way-opt CNOT depth optimization of SEQ(A)

```
Input: A decomposition sequence
       SEQ(A) = {E(c_1, t_1), E(c_2, t_2), ··· , E(c_K, t_K)} of an invertible matrix A.
Output: A decomposition sequence SEQ_out(A) of matrix A and the sequence
        depth d.
SEQ_out(A) ← {·};
d = 0;
while length(SEQ(A)) > 1 do
    Layer ← {·};
    d = d + 1;
    Move the first gate in SEQ to Layer;
    i = 1;
    while i <= length(K) do
        if E(c_i, t_i) can be executed simultaneously with all gates in Layer then
            CHANGE ← TRUE;
            for j = 1 : i do
                if E(c_j, t_j) can not swap with E(c_i, t_i) then
                    CHANGE ← FALSE;
                end
            end
            if CHANGE = TRUE then
                Layer ← E(c_i, t_i);
                Remove E(c_i, t_i) from SEQ
            end
            i = i + 1;
        else
            i = i + 1;
        end
    end
    Add all gates in Layer to SEQ_out(A);
end
Add all gates left in SEQ to SEQ_out(A);
return SEQ_out(A), d;
```

depth 5. Furthermore, after Step 3 and Step 4, the order of $E(0,3)$ and $E(0,2)$ are swapped since they are exchangeable and $E(0,3)$ can be executed in parallel with $E(2,1)$, reducing the circuit depth from 5 to 4. Then Algorithm 1 output the sequence

$$\mathtt{SEQ}_{\mathrm{opt}} = \{E(0,1), E(2,3), E(3,1), E(1,3), E(0,2), E(0,3), E(2,1)\}, \quad (7)$$

whose circuit is shown as (c) in Fig. 4.

3.2 Finding Better Gate Sequences

Besides the optimized implementation of a given decomposition sequence as well as all its equivalent sequences, we point out that there are actually other different

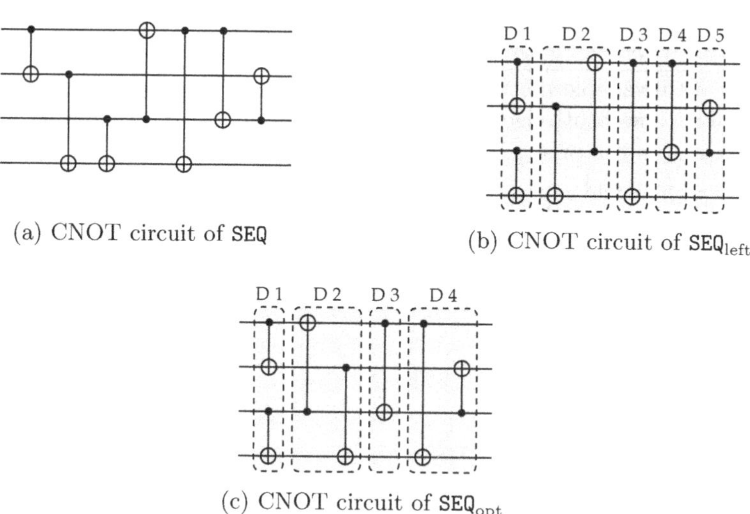

(a) CNOT circuit of SEQ

(b) CNOT circuit of $\texttt{SEQ}_{\text{left}}$

(c) CNOT circuit of $\texttt{SEQ}_{\text{opt}}$

Fig. 4. The quantum CNOT circuit of SEQ and its exchange-equivalent circuits obtained in Algorithm 1.

decomposition sequences that can implement the linear transformation A. As an example shown in Fig. 5, circuit (a) and circuit (b) realize the same Boolean function after we rename (or swap) wire i and wire k, hence $\texttt{SEQ}_a$ for Circuit (a) and $\texttt{SEQ}_b$ for Circuit (b) are two different decomposition sequences for the same matrix. Whereas, circuit (a) has depth 4 and circuit (b) has depth 3 since the second and the third CNOT gates in (b) can be executed simultaneously. Hence, we are inspired to find a shallower implementation, by firstly constructing different decomposition sequences, then applying Algorithm 1 to find a better decomposition sequence whose minimum depth after our optimization method in Sect. 3.1 is lower. We present our framework for searching a depth-optimized linear quantum circuit for a linear building block in Algorithm 3.

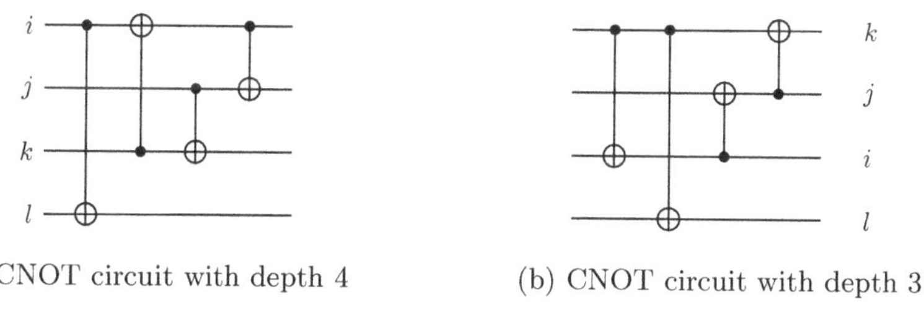

(a) CNOT circuit with depth 4

(b) CNOT circuit with depth 3

Fig. 5. The quantum CNOT circuits with different depth after swapping wires.

Algorithm 3: Search a low-depth implementation of $\texttt{SEQ}(\mathrm{A})$

Input: An invertible matrix $A \in \mathrm{GL}(n, \mathbb{F}_2)$.
Output: A low-depth decomposition sequence $\texttt{SEQ}_{\mathrm{opt}}(A)$ of matrix A.

Translate A into a binary matrix and decompose it into $\{E_t, E_{t-1} \cdots, E_1\}$;
$\texttt{SEQ} \leftarrow \{E_t, E_{t-1} \cdots, E_1\}$;
$\texttt{SEQ}_{\mathrm{opt}}$ is the output of Algorithm 1 ($\texttt{SEQ}$), and $d(\texttt{SEQ}_{\mathrm{opt}})$ is the depth of $\texttt{SEQ}_{\mathrm{opt}}$; `// Initialize the depth`
$g \leftarrow t + 1$;
while $g \geq 2$ **do**
  $g = g - 1$;
  for $i = 0$ *to* $t - g$ **do**
    $\texttt{SEQ}_1 \leftarrow \{E_t, \cdots E_{i+g-1}\}$;
    $\texttt{SEQ}_2 \leftarrow \{E_{i+g}, \cdots E_{i+1}\}$;
    $\texttt{SEQ}_3 \leftarrow \{E_i, \cdots E_1\}$;
    $A' \leftarrow \{E_{i+g}, \cdots E_{i+1}\}$;
    Decompose A' into $\{E'_u, E'_{u-1} \cdots, E_1\}$;
    $\texttt{SEQ}'_2 \leftarrow \{E'_u, \cdots, E_1\}$;
    $\texttt{SEQ}' = \texttt{SEQ}_1 + \texttt{SEQ}'_2 + \texttt{SEQ}_3$; `// New decomposition sequence`
    $\texttt{SEQ}'_{opt}$ is the output of Algorithm 1 ($\texttt{SEQ}'$), and $d(\texttt{SEQ}')$ is the deoth of $\texttt{SEQ}'_{opt}$; `// Minimize depth for SEQ'`
    if $d(SEQ') < d(SEQ_{\mathrm{opt}})$ *and* $|SEQ'| < |SEQ_{\mathrm{opt}}|$ **then**
      $\texttt{SEQ}_{\mathrm{opt}} = \texttt{SEQ}'$;
      $d(\texttt{SEQ}_{\mathrm{opt}}) = d(\texttt{SEQ}')$;
      Break;
    end
  end
end
return $\texttt{SEQ}_{\mathrm{opt}}$;

4 Applications

In this section, we showcase the applications of our algorithm in different linear building blocks. From these experimental results, one can see that our algorithm can not only be applied to optimize invertible linear transformations, but also be extended to optimize non-invertible linear transformations. Consequently, it is helpful for the optimization of the whole circuit depth for some block ciphers such as AES by optimizing some linear sub-structures of the whole circuit.

Optimization for Invertible Linear Transformations. Firstly, we apply our framework to minimize the quantum circuit depth of a large set of invertible cipher matrices. Notice that [46] gave state-of-the-art classical implementations of some cipher matrices to our knowledge in terms of the gate count, which outperform Paar's and Boyar-Peralta's heuristics [32] in most cases. And their implementation can be typically employed to produce a compact CNOT circuit implementing the linear transformation. We therefore compare our result with theirs in Table 1, concerning the circuit depth while maintaining the gate count same.

The depths of the quantum circuits for different cipher matrices optimized by our method are listed in the last column. We can see there is a significant improvement in our synthesis compared with the circuit implementation in [46]. When the matrix size is large such as an 8×8 matrix for KHAZAD [9] (the size is 8×8 in GF(8, $\mathbb{F}_2$) and 64×64 in GF(2, $\mathbb{F}_2$)), our method can give a nearly 75% improvement compared with the naive implementation with sequence depth, and a 45% improvement compared with the usual move-equivalent optimization. Even for 4×4 small matrices, our method still can reduce the depth of the circuits in some cases.

Next, we apply our framework to optimize the depth of the quantum circuit implementation for various invertible matrices, presented in different works [11, 27,35,39,40,43]. All matrices compared can be found in those papers sorted by their size and the finite field they belong to. The experiment results are summarized in Table 2. Notice that for different matrices with different sizes, our method always reduces the circuit depth compared with the previous quantum circuit construction derived from the in-place implementations of classical linear circuits. Generally, the larger the size of the matrix, the greater the advantage of our method.

Optimization for Non-invertible Linear Transformations. Besides, our framework can also be used to optimize the circuit depth of some non-invertible linear transformations, since any non-invertible linear transformation can always be expressed by a sequence as well. For example, we optimized the quantum circuit depth for AES, by reducing the depth of some linear sub-structures in its nonlinear blocks. As shown in [16], when using the tower filed structure, there are two linear components in the implementation of AES S-box, called the *top linear layer* and *bottom linear layer*, respectively. The top linear layer, which is defined as a 22×8 binary matrix, is used to generate desired number of middle variables used for a tower field construction, while the bottom linear layer, which is defined as a 8×18 binary matrix, is used to generate the output of the S-box from the output of the tower field construction. After applying our framework, we can reduce the depth of the top linear layer of the AES S-box circuit from 14 [24,25] to 8, compared with the previous implementations. For the bottom linear layer, we can reduce the depth from 11 to 7. Thus we can reduce the depth of linear layers of an AES S-box by 10. Even though this reduction is not very large, our new implementation will reduce the depth of the whole AES circuit significantly, since the S-box and its inverse are used iteratively in the whole circuit.

Table 1. Quantum circuit depth of cipher matrices under different optimization heuristic

Cipher	Size[a]	# CNOT[b]	Seq D[c]	Move-eq D[d]	Exchange-eq D[e]
KHAZAD [9]	64	366	112	54	30
AES [20]	32	92	41	30	28
ANUBIS [44]	32	98	40	26	20
CLEFIA M0 [42]	32	98	41	30	27
CLEFIA M1 [42]	32	103	41	21	16
FOX MU4 [29]	32	136	75	55	48
QARMA128 [6]	32	48	12	6	5
TWOFISH [31]	32	111	53	37	29
WHIRLWIND M0 [8]	32	183	93	65	51
WHIRLWIND M1 [8]	32	190	90	69	54
JOLTIK [26]	16	44	23	20	17
MIDORI [7]	16	24	9	3	3
SmallScale AES [19]	16	43	26	20	19
PRIDE L0 [3]	16	24	9	3	3
PRIDE L1 [3]	16	24	15	5	5
PRIDE L2 [3]	16	24	12	5	5
PRIDE L3 [3]	16	24	11	5	5
PRINCE M0 [15]	16	24	10	6	6
PRINCE M1 [15]	16	24	10	6	6
QARMA64 [6]	16	24	9	6	5
SKINNY [10]	16	12	3	3	3

[a] The size refers to the degree of the corresponding binary matrix.
[b] The number of CNOT gates of quantum implementation in [46].
[c] Quantum circuit depth with sequence depth.
[d] Quantum circuit depth with minimum move-equivalent depth.
[e] Quantum circuit depth with minimum exchange-equivalent depth.

Table 2. Quantum circuit depth of some invertible matrices with different optimization methods.

Matrices	Size[a]	#CNOT[b]	Seq D[c]	Move-eq D[d]	Exchange-eq D[e]
4×4 matrices in GF(4, $\mathbb{F}_2$)					
[11]	16	41	27	23	21
[27]	16	41	28	24	18
[35]	16	44	29	27	26
[43]	16	44	30	25	22
[34]	16	44	29	29	27
[27] (Involutory)	16	41	25	15	14
[43] (Involutory)	16	44	24	19	16
[34] (Involutory)	16	44	33	27	25
[39] (Involutory)	16	38	19	12	11
4×4 matrices in GF(8, $\mathbb{F}_2$)					
[11]	32	114	72	56	47
[27]	32	82	43	26	22
[35]	32	121	79	67	54
[34]	32	104	69	55	42
[43]	32	90	42	23	20
[39]	32	114	58	47	40
[27] (Involutory)	32	83	34	18	14
[43] (Involutory)	32	91	39	18	16
[34] (Involutory)	32	87	39	19	19
[39] (Involutory)	32	93	42	19	18
8×8 matrices in GF(4, $\mathbb{F}_2$)					
[40]	32	183	83	54	44
[43]	32	170	89	59	49
[43] (Involutory)	32	185	85	47	37
8×8 matrices in GF(8, $\mathbb{F}_2$)					
[43] (Involutory)	64	348	117	50	37

[a] The size refers to the degree of the corresponding binary matrix.
[b] The number of CNOT gates of quantum implementation in [46].
[c] Quantum circuit depth with sequence depth.
[d] Quantum circuit depth with minimum move-equivalent depth.
[e] Quantum circuit depth with minimum exchange-equivalent depth.

5 Conclusion

In this work, we focus on minimizing the depth of a subclass of quantum circuits - the CNOT circuits, especially those for the linear building blocks of symmetric-key ciphers. We are motivated by the quantum security analysis of current symmetric-key encryption systems and end up with a framework for constructing low-depth quantum circuits for linear Boolean functions. We fully characterize the CNOT circuits with decomposition sequence and its two equivalent classes, called move-equivalent sequence and exchange-equivalent sequence. Based on these two classes, we can give a clearer definition for the depth of the CNOT circuits and achieve shallower quantum circuit implementations for a large set of cipher matrices compared with previous results.

Acknowledgements. This work is supported by the National Natural Science Foundation of China (Grant No. 61977060).

Appendix

In the following, we present the CNOT circuit for AES MixColumns using 92 CNOT gates, which keeps the gate count the same as the implementation with classical XOR gates in [46]. After our optimization, the circuit depth is reduced from 41 to 28, compared with direct sequence depth; from 30 to 28, compared with move-equivalent circuit depth (Table 3).

Table 3. A quantum circuit for AES MixColumns with depth 28, where each XOR operation is corresponding to a CNOT gate.

No.	Operation	No.	Operation	No.	Operation	No.	Operation
	Layer 1		Layer 11	44	$x_8 = x_0 \oplus x_8$	68	$x_6 = x_5 \oplus x_6$
0	$x_{14} = x_6 \oplus x_{14}$	21	$x_3 = x_{11} \oplus x_3$	45	$x_{28} = x_{12} \oplus x_{28}$	69	$x_1 = x_{25} \oplus x_1$
	Layer 2	22	$x_{20} = x_{19} \oplus x_{20}$	46	$x_4 = x_{31} \oplus x_4$		Layer 26
1	$x_6 = x_{22} \oplus x_6$	23	$x_{26} = x_{10} \oplus x_{26}$	47	$x_{15} = x_7 \oplus x_{15}$	70	$x_{28} = x_{20} \oplus x_{28}$
	Layer 3		Layer 12		Layer 19	71	$x_{14} = x_{30} \oplus x_{14}$
2	$x_{22} = x_{30} \oplus x_{22}$	24	$x_{11} = x_{10} \oplus x_{11}$	48	$x_{16} = x_0 \oplus x_{16}$	72	$x_{15} = x_7 \oplus x_{15}$
3	$x_{13} = x_{21} \oplus x_{13}$	25	$x_{19} = x_{18} \oplus x_{19}$	49	$x_{12} = x_{15} \oplus x_{12}$	73	$x_5 = x_{29} \oplus x_5$
	Layer 4		Layer 13	50	$x_{27} = x_{31} \oplus x_{27}$	74	$x_0 = x_{24} \oplus x_0$
4	$x_{30} = x_{13} \oplus x_{30}$	26	$x_{10} = x_{18} \oplus x_{10}$		Layer 20	75	$x_{25} = x_9 \oplus x_{25}$
	Layer 5	27	$x_{17} = x_9 \oplus x_{17}$	51	$x_0 = x_{31} \oplus x_0$	76	$x_3 = x_{19} \oplus x_3$
5	$x_{13} = x_{29} \oplus x_{13}$		Layer 14	52	$x_{25} = x_{24} \oplus x_{25}$		Layer 27
6	$x_{21} = x_5 \oplus x_{21}$	28	$x_{18} = x_2 \oplus x_{18}$	53	$x_{11} = x_{15} \oplus x_{11}$	77	$x_{20} = x_4 \oplus x_{20}$
7	$x_{12} = x_4 \oplus x_{12}$	29	$x_9 = x_1 \oplus x_9$		Layer 21	78	$x_{29} = x_{21} \oplus x_{29}$
	Layer 6	30	$x_0 = x_{24} \oplus x_0$	54	$x_{31} = x_7 \oplus x_{31}$	79	$x_6 = x_{14} \oplus x_6$
8	$x_5 = x_{13} \oplus x_5$		Layer 15	55	$x_{24} = x_{15} \oplus x_{24}$	80	$x_7 = x_{23} \oplus x_7$
9	$x_4 = x_{28} \oplus x_4$	31	$x_{18} = x_{17} \oplus x_{18}$		Layer 22	81	$x_1 = x_0 \oplus x_1$
	Layer 7	32	$x_{10} = x_9 \oplus x_{10}$	56	$x_7 = x_{14} \oplus x_7$	82	$x_9 = x_{17} \oplus x_9$
10	$x_{13} = x_{12} \oplus x_{13}$	33	$x_{11} = x_2 \oplus x_{11}$	57	$x_{15} = x_{23} \oplus x_{15}$	83	$x_2 = x_{26} \oplus x_2$
11	$x_{29} = x_4 \oplus x_{29}$	34	$x_{24} = x_8 \oplus x_{24}$	58	$x_{12} = x_{27} \oplus x_{12}$	84	$x_{19} = x_{27} \oplus x_{19}$
12	$x_{11} = x_{27} \oplus x_{11}$		Layer 16		Layer 23		Layer 28
	Layer 8	35	$x_{17} = x_{25} \oplus x_{17}$	59	$x_{14} = x_{21} \oplus x_{14}$	85	$x_4 = x_{12} \oplus x_4$
13	$x_{12} = x_{20} \oplus x_{12}$	36	$x_2 = x_9 \oplus x_2$	60	$x_{31} = x_{22} \oplus x_{31}$	86	$x_{21} = x_{13} \oplus x_{21}$
14	$x_4 = x_{11} \oplus x_4$	37	$x_8 = x_{23} \oplus x_8$	61	$x_{16} = x_{23} \oplus x_{16}$	87	$x_{22} = x_6 \oplus x_{22}$
	Layer 9	38	$x_{24} = x_{16} \oplus x_{24}$	62	$x_{27} = x_{26} \oplus x_{27}$	88	$x_{23} = x_{31} \oplus x_{23}$
15	$x_{20} = x_{27} \oplus x_{20}$	39	$x_{31} = x_{15} \oplus x_{31}$	63	$x_{30} = x_6 \oplus x_{30}$	89	$x_{17} = x_0 \oplus x_{17}$
16	$x_{11} = x_{19} \oplus x_{11}$		Layer 17		Layer 24	90	$x_{26} = x_{18} \oplus x_{26}$
17	$x_{23} = x_{31} \oplus x_{23}$	40	$x_1 = x_{17} \oplus x_1$	64	$x_{22} = x_{21} \oplus x_{22}$	91	$x_{27} = x_{11} \oplus x_{27}$
	Layer 10	41	$x_9 = x_8 \oplus x_9$	65	$x_{23} = x_6 \oplus x_{23}$		
18	$x_{27} = x_3 \oplus x_{27}$	42	$x_{16} = x_{31} \oplus x_{16}$	66	$x_{26} = x_1 \oplus x_{26}$		
19	$x_{19} = x_{23} \oplus x_{19}$		Layer 18		Layer 25		
20	$x_{18} = x_{26} \oplus x_{18}$	43	$x_{17} = x_{16} \oplus x_{17}$	67	$x_{21} = x_{28} \oplus x_{21}$		

References

1. Microsoftt q#. quantum development. https://devblogs.microsoft.com/qsharp/
2. Aaronson, S., Gottesman, D.: Improved simulation of stabilizer circuits. Phys. Rev. A **70**(5), 052328 (2004). https://doi.org/10.1103/physreva.70.052328
3. Albrecht, M.R., Driessen, B., Kavun, E.B., Leander, G., Paar, C., Yaln, T.: Block ciphers - focus on the linear layer (feat. PRIDE). In: Annual Cryptology Conference (2014)
4. Almazrooie, M., Samsudin, A., Abdullah, R., Mutter, K.N.: Quantum reversible circuit of AES-128. Quantum Inf. Process. **17**(5), 1–30 (2018)
5. Amy, M., Maslov, D., Mosca, M., Roetteler, M.: A meet-in-the-middle algorithm for fast synthesis of depth-optimal quantum circuits. IEEE Trans. Comput. Aided Des. Integr. Circuits Syst. **32**(6), 818–830 (2013)
6. Avanzi, R.: The QARMA block cipher family. Almost MDS matrices over rings with zero divisors, nearly symmetric even-mansour constructions with non-involutory central rounds, and search heuristics for low-latency s-boxes. IACR Trans. Symmetric Cryptol. **2017**(1), 4–44 (2017)
7. Banik, S., et al.: Midori: a block cipher for low energy. In: Iwata, T., Cheon, J.H. (eds.) ASIACRYPT 2015. LNCS, vol. 9453, pp. 411–436. Springer, Heidelberg (2015). https://doi.org/10.1007/978-3-662-48800-3_17
8. Barreto, P., Nikov, V., Nikova, S., Rijmen, V., Tischhauser, E.: Whirlwind: a new cryptographic hash function. Des. Codes Crypt. **56**(2–3), 141–162 (2010)
9. Barreto, P., Rijmen, V.: The Khazad legacy-level block cipher. Submission to the NESSIE project (2000)
10. Beierle, C., Jean, J., Kölbl, S., Leander, G., Sim, S.M.: The skinny family of block ciphers and its low-latency variant mantis. In: Annual Cryptology Conference (2016)
11. Beierle, C., Kranz, T., Leander, G.: Lightweight multiplication in $GF(2^n)$ with applications to MDS matrices. In: Robshaw, M., Katz, J. (eds.) CRYPTO 2016. LNCS, vol. 9814, pp. 625–653. Springer, Heidelberg (2016). https://doi.org/10.1007/978-3-662-53018-4_23
12. Bonnetain, X., Leurent, G., Naya-Plasencia, M., Schrottenloher, A.: Quantum linearization attacks. Cryptology ePrint Archive, Paper 2021/1239 (2021). https://eprint.iacr.org/2021/1239
13. Bonnetain, X., Naya-Plasencia, M., Schrottenloher, A.: Quantum security analysis of AES. IACR Trans. Symmetric Cryptol. **2019**(2), 55–93 (2019)
14. Bonnetain, X., Naya-Plasencia, M., Schrottenloher, A.: On quantum slide attacks. Cryptology ePrint Archive, Paper 2018/1067 (2018). https://eprint.iacr.org/2018/1067
15. Borghoff, J., et al.: PRINCE – a low-latency block cipher for pervasive computing applications. In: Wang, X., Sako, K. (eds.) ASIACRYPT 2012. LNCS, vol. 7658, pp. 208–225. Springer, Heidelberg (2012). https://doi.org/10.1007/978-3-642-34961-4_14
16. Boyar, J., Peralta, R.: A small depth-16 circuit for the AES S-box. In: Gritzalis, D., Furnell, S., Theoharidou, M. (eds.) SEC 2012. IAICT, vol. 376, pp. 287–298. Springer, Heidelberg (2012). https://doi.org/10.1007/978-3-642-30436-1_24
17. de Brugiere, T.G., Baboulin, M., Valiron, B., Martiel, S., Allouche, C.: Reducing the depth of linear reversible quantum circuits. IEEE Trans. Quantum Eng. **2**, 1–22 (2021). https://doi.org/10.1109/tqe.2021.3091648

18. Brugière, T.G.D., Baboulin, M., Valiron, B., Martiel, S., Allouche, C.: Gaussian elimination versus greedy methods for the synthesis of linear reversible circuits. ACM Trans. Quantum Comput. **2**(3), 1–26 (2021). https://doi.org/10.1145/3474226
19. Cid, C., Murphy, S., Robshaw, M.: Small scale variants of the AES. In: International Conference on Fast Software Encryption (2005)
20. Daemen, J., Rijmen, V.: The Design of Rijndael: AES - The Advanced Encryption Standard. The Design of Rijndael: AES - The Advanced Encryption Standard (2002)
21. Grassl, M., Langenberg, B., Roetteler, M., Steinwandt, R.: Applying Grover's algorithm to AES: quantum resource estimates. In: Takagi, T. (ed.) PQCrypto 2016. LNCS, vol. 9606, pp. 29–43. Springer, Cham (2016). https://doi.org/10.1007/978-3-319-29360-8_3
22. Grover, L.K.: A fast quantum mechanical algorithm for database search (1996)
23. Hosoyamada, A., Sasaki, Yu.: Quantum Demiric-Selçuk meet-in-the-middle attacks: applications to 6-round generic Feistel constructions. In: Catalano, D., De Prisco, R. (eds.) SCN 2018. LNCS, vol. 11035, pp. 386–403. Springer, Cham (2018). https://doi.org/10.1007/978-3-319-98113-0_21
24. Huang, Z., Sun, S.: Synthesizing quantum circuits of AES with lower T-depth and less qubits. Cryptology ePrint Archive, Paper 2022/620 (2022). https://eprint.iacr.org/2022/620
25. Jaques, S., Naehrig, M., Roetteler, M., Virdia, F.: Implementing Grover oracles for quantum key search on AES and LowMC. In: Canteaut, A., Ishai, Y. (eds.) EUROCRYPT 2020. LNCS, vol. 12106, pp. 280–310. Springer, Cham (2020). https://doi.org/10.1007/978-3-030-45724-2_10
26. Jean, J., Nikolić, I., Peyrin, T.: Joltik. Submission to the CAESAR competition (2014)
27. Jean, J., Peyrin, T., Sim, S.M., Tourteaux, J.: Optimizing implementations of lightweight building blocks. Cryptology ePrint Archive (2017)
28. Jiang, J., Sun, X., Teng, S.H., Wu, B., Wu, K., Zhang, J.: Optimal space-depth trade-off of CNOT circuits in quantum logic synthesis. In: Proceedings of the Fourteenth Annual ACM-SIAM Symposium on Discrete Algorithms, pp. 213–229. SIAM (2020)
29. Junod, P., Vaudenay, S.: FOX: a new family of block ciphers. In: Handschuh, H., Hasan, M.A. (eds.) SAC 2004. LNCS, vol. 3357, pp. 114–129. Springer, Heidelberg (2004). https://doi.org/10.1007/978-3-540-30564-4_8
30. Kaplan, M., Leurent, G., Leverrier, A., Naya-Plasencia, M.: Quantum differential and linear cryptanalysis. arXiv preprint arXiv:1510.05836 (2015)
31. Kelsey, B., Whiting, D., Wagner, D., Hall, C., Ferguson, N.: Twofish: a 128bit block cipher (1998)
32. Kranz, T., Leander, G., Stoffelen, K., Wiemer, F.: Shorter linear straight-line programs for MDS matrices (2017)
33. Langenberg, B., Pham, H., Steinwandt, R.: Reducing the cost of implementing the advanced encryption standard as a quantum circuit. IEEE Trans. Quantum Eng. **1**, 1–12 (2020)
34. Li, Y., Wang, M.: On the construction of lightweight circulant involutory MDS matrices. In: Peyrin, T. (ed.) FSE 2016. LNCS, vol. 9783, pp. 121–139. Springer, Heidelberg (2016). https://doi.org/10.1007/978-3-662-52993-5_7
35. Liu, M., Sim, S.M.: Lightweight MDS generalized circulant matrices. In: Peyrin, T. (ed.) FSE 2016. LNCS, vol. 9783, pp. 101–120. Springer, Heidelberg (2016). https://doi.org/10.1007/978-3-662-52993-5_6

36. Miller, D., Maslov, D., Dueck, G.: A transformation based algorithm for reversible logic synthesis, pp. 318–323 (2003). https://doi.org/10.1109/dac.2003.1219016
37. Patel, K.N., Markov, I.L., Hayes, J.P.: Optimal synthesis of linear reversible circuits. Quantum Inf. Comput. **8**(3), 282–294 (2008)
38. Saeedi, M., Markov, I.L.: Synthesis and optimization of reversible circuits-a survey. ACM Comput. Surv. **45**(2), 1–34 (2013). https://doi.org/10.1145/2431211.2431220
39. Sarkar, S., Syed, H.: Lightweight diffusion layer: importance of Toeplitz matrices (2016)
40. Sarkar, S., Syed, H.: Analysis of Toeplitz MDS matrices. In: Pieprzyk, J., Suriadi, S. (eds.) ACISP 2017. LNCS, vol. 10343, pp. 3–18. Springer, Cham (2017). https://doi.org/10.1007/978-3-319-59870-3_1
41. Shende, V.V., Prasad, A.K., Markov, I.L., Hayes, J.P.: Reversible logic circuit synthesis. In: IEEE/ACM International Conference on Computer-Aided Design, Digest of Technical Papers, pp. 353–360 (2002). https://doi.org/10.1145/774572.774625
42. Shirai, T., Shibutani, K., Akishita, T., Moriai, S., Iwata, T.: The 128-bit blockcipher CLEFIA (extended abstract). In: International Workshop on Fast Software Encryption (2007)
43. Sim, S.M., Khoo, K., Oggier, F., Peyrin, T.: Lightweight MDS involution matrices. In: Leander, G. (ed.) FSE 2015. LNCS, vol. 9054, pp. 471–493. Springer, Heidelberg (2015). https://doi.org/10.1007/978-3-662-48116-5_23
44. Barreto, P., Rijmen, V.: The anubis block cipher (2000)
45. Wille, R., Große, D., Teuber, L., Dueck, G.W., Drechsler, R.: RevLib: an online resource for reversible functions and reversible circuits. In: 38th International Symposium on Multiple Valued Logic (ISMVL 2008), pp. 220–225. IEEE (2008)
46. Xiang, Z., Zeng, X., Lin, D., Bao, Z., Zhang, S.: Optimizing implementations of linear layers. IACR Trans. Symmetric Cryptol. 120–145 (2020)
47. Zakablukov, D.V.: Application of permutation group theory in reversible logic synthesis. In: Devitt, S., Lanese, I. (eds.) RC 2016. LNCS, vol. 9720, pp. 223–238. Springer, Cham (2016). https://doi.org/10.1007/978-3-319-40578-0_17
48. Zou, J., Wei, Z., Sun, S., Liu, X., Wu, W.: Quantum circuit implementations of AES with fewer qubits. In: Moriai, S., Wang, H. (eds.) ASIACRYPT 2020. LNCS, vol. 12492, pp. 697–726. Springer, Cham (2020). https://doi.org/10.1007/978-3-030-64834-3_24

IND-CCA Security of Kyber in the Quantum Random Oracle Model, Revisited

Zhao Chen[1,2], Xianhui Lu[1,2(✉)], Dingding Jia[1], and Bao Li[1]

[1] State Key Laboratory of Information Security, Institute of Information Engineering, Chinese Academy of Sciences, Beijing, China
luxianhui@iie.ac.cn

[2] School of Cyber Security, University of Chinese Academy of Sciences, Beijing, China

Abstract. In this paper, we answer the open question pointed out by Grubbs et al. (EUROCRYPT 2022) and Xagawa (EUROCRYPT 2022), i.e., the *concrete* IND-CCA security proof of Kyber. In order to add robustness, Kyber uses a slightly tweaked Fujisaki-Okamoto (FO) transformation. Specifically, it uses a "double-nested-hash" to generate the final key. This makes the proof techniques (Jiang et al., CRYPTO 2018) of proving standard FO transformation invalid. Hence, we develop a novel approach to overcome the difficulties, and prove that Kyber is IND-CCA secure in the quantum random oracle model (QROM) if the underlying encryption scheme is IND-CPA secure. Our result provides a solid quantum security guarantee for the post-quantum cryptography standard of NIST competition, Kyber algorithm.

Keyword: IND-CCA security, Kyber, Fujisaki-Okamoto transformation, Quantum random oracle model

1 Introduction

With the development of quantum computation [9,21], post-quantum cryptography (PQC) has attracted much attention in the past decade. Particularly, in 2016, National Institute of Standard and Technology (NIST) launched the PQC standardization project, which called for candidates of quantum-resistant public-key cryptographic primitives [17], such as digital-signature, public-key encryption (PKE) and key encapsulation mechanism (KEM). Recently, NIST announced the latest results, and selected Kyber [20] as one of the PQC standards. Kyber is a KEM scheme, the security requirement of which is indistinguishability against chosen-ciphertext attacks (IND-CCA) [18], which is widely accepted as the standard security notion. However, the *concrete* IND-CCA security of Kyber in the quantum setting is currently an open question that pointed out by Grubbs et al. [10] and Xagawa [25]. In this paper, we answer the open question in the affirmative and provide a concrete post-quantum security proof for Kyber.

Y. Deng and M. Yung (Eds.): Inscrypt 2022, LNCS 13837, pp. 148–166, 2023.
https://doi.org/10.1007/978-3-031-26553-2_8

Kyber [20] uses a variant of the KEM version of the Fujisaki-Okamoto (FO) transformation [7,8]. FO transformation was first introduced by Fujisaki and Okamoto [7] in 1999, and it is one of the most important transformations to construct an IND-CCA [18] secure PKE scheme from a weaker secure one in the random oracle model (ROM) [3]. There are many variants [4,6,10,11,13–16,19,25] of FO transformation that are widely used in the submissions to NIST PQC competition [17]. To obtain a concrete cryptographic scheme, the random oracle is replaced by a concrete hash function, which a quantum adversary may evaluate on a quantum superposition of inputs. In order to capture this ability of quantum adversaries, Boneh et al. [5] introduced the quantum random oracle model (QROM), where hash functions are modeled as public random oracles similarly as in the ROM [3] but with *quantum* access. Now, it is generally believed that the security of post-quantum cryptographic schemes should be established in the QROM.

In 2017, Hofheinz et al. [11] first analyzed the KEM version of the FO transformation (FO-KEM) in the QROM. They followed the Targhi and Unruh's proof technique [23] and provided two variants of the standard FO-KEM[1], i.e., $\mathsf{QFO}_m^{\not\perp}$ and $\mathsf{QFO}_m^{\perp}$, which convert a one-way against chosen-plaintext attacks (OW-CPA) secure PKE scheme into an IND-CCA secure KEM scheme in the QROM. Here Q means adding an additional length-preserving hash to the ciphertext and $\not\perp$ ($\perp$) means implicit (explicit) rejection, where a pseudorandom key (a rejection symbol $\perp$) is returned for an invalid ciphertext c in the decapsulation algorithm.

Subsequently, for the FO-KEMs with implicit rejection, Jiang et al. [14] extended the technique in [5] to remove the additional hash, and proved the IND-CCA security of $\mathsf{FO}_m^{\not\perp}$ and $\mathsf{FO}^{\not\perp}$ [11] in the QROM. Unfortunately, although the standard FO-KEMs with implicit rejection, i.e., $\mathsf{FO}_m^{\not\perp}$ and $\mathsf{FO}^{\not\perp}$, can be shown to be IND-CCA secure in the QROM [4,6,10,13–16,19,25], Grubbs et al. [10] and Xagawa [25] recently pointed out that the proof technique does not seem to carry over to Kyber (see Sect. 1.1 for details).

The important trick used by Jiang et al. [14] in their security proofs of $\mathsf{FO}^{\not\perp}$ is to associate the key-derivation-function (KDF) H with a secret random function H_1 by setting $K := \mathsf{H}(m,c) := \mathsf{H}_1(g(m)) = \mathsf{H}_1(c)$, where $g(\cdot) := \mathsf{Enc}(pk, \cdot; \mathsf{G}(\cdot))$. The rationality of this simulation depends on the injectivity of $g(\cdot)$. However, in order to add *robustness* [1], Kyber uses a slightly tweaked $\mathsf{FO}^{\not\perp}$. More concretely, Kyber hash the hash of m and the hash of c (double-nested-hash) into the final key K, i.e., $K := \mathsf{H}(\mathsf{G}_1(m), \mathsf{H}'(c))$. Thus, there are two extra nested hash functions between (m,c) and the computation of K. Since the domain of H' is much larger than the range of H', $\mathsf{H}' \circ g \circ \mathsf{G}_1^{-1}(\cdot)$ is not injective[2]. Therefore, these extra hash functions are a significant barrier to applying the trick used in [14].

Surprisingly, we can easily overcome this barrier in the ROM, where random oracles can be simulated efficiently via lazy sampling. Thus, we can force G_1 and H' to be injective without being noticed by the IND-CCA adversary. However,

[1] The standard FO-KEMs including $\mathsf{FO}^{\not\perp}$, $\mathsf{FO}_m^{\not\perp}$, $\mathsf{FO}^{\perp}$ and $\mathsf{FO}_m^{\perp}$ [11], where m (without m) means $K := \mathsf{H}(m)$ ($K := \mathsf{H}(m,c)$).

[2] $\mathsf{H}' \circ g \circ \mathsf{G}_1^{-1}(\cdot)$ is not even a function.

in the QROM, since quantum adversaries can evaluate the random oracle on a superposition state of all states, it is natural to have many collisions for G_1 and H'. Therefore, the proof trick [14] cannot be used directly to prove the quantum security of Kyber. As a result, the concrete IND-CCA security proof of Kyber in the QROM is currently an open question.

Our Contributions. In this paper, we answer the open question pointed out in [10,25]. We observe that the significant barrier to prove the IND-CCA security of Kyber in the QROM is that it uses a "double-nested-hash" to generate the final key K. This makes the previous proof techniques [14] of proving $\mathsf{FO}^{\not\perp}$ invalid in the QROM. Hence, we develop a novel approach to overcome the barrier, and we prove that Kyber is IND-CCA secure in the QROM if the underlying PKE scheme is IND-CPA secure. Our result provides a solid quantum security guarantee for PQC standard of NIST competition, Kyber algorithm.

1.1 Technical Overview

Before showing our proof, we first review the generic transformation $\mathsf{FO}^{\not\perp}$ [11] and its quantum security proof [4,6,13–16]. $\mathsf{FO}^{\not\perp}$ converts a PKE scheme $\mathsf{PKE} := (\mathsf{Gen}, \mathsf{Enc}, \mathsf{Dec})$ into a KEM scheme $\mathsf{KEM} := \mathsf{FO}^{\not\perp}[\mathsf{PKE}, \mathsf{G}, \mathsf{H}]$ with implicit rejection. The encapsulation of KEM is defined by

$$\mathsf{Encaps}(pk) := (c := \mathsf{Enc}(pk, m; \mathsf{G}(m)), K := \mathsf{H}(m, c)),$$

where m is picked at random from the message space, G and H are hash functions (modeled as random oracles). The decapsulation of KEM is defined by

$$\mathsf{Decaps}^{\not\perp}(sk, c) := \begin{cases} \mathsf{H}(m, c) & c = \mathsf{Enc}(pk, m; \mathsf{G}(m)) \\ \mathsf{H}(s, c) & c \neq \mathsf{Enc}(pk, m; \mathsf{G}(m)), \end{cases}$$

where $m := \mathsf{Dec}(sk, c)$ and s is a random seed as part of the private key.

Security Proof of FO$^{\not\perp}$. In 2018, Jiang et al. [14] first proved the IND-CCA security of $\mathsf{FO}^{\not\perp}$ in the QROM. During the security reduction, the hardest part is that the simulator needs to simulate the oracle $\mathsf{Decaps}^{\not\perp}$ without possessing the secret key. In the ROM, an RO-query list can be used to verify the validity of ciphertexts during the $\mathsf{Decaps}^{\not\perp}$ queries, thus helping the simulator to simulate the oracle $\mathsf{Decaps}^{\not\perp}$. However, such an RO-query list does not exist in the QROM since quantum adversaries can evaluate the random oracle on a superposition state of exponential many states [5]. In order to overcome this obstacle, Jiang et al. [14] presented a novel approach to simulate the oracle $\mathsf{Decaps}^{\not\perp}$.

Specifically, they associated the KDF H with a secret random function H_1 by setting $\mathsf{H}(m, c) := \mathsf{H}_1(c)$ if the input $(m, c) \in \mathcal{S}$[3], where the set $\mathcal{S}$ is defined

[3] The set $\mathcal{S}$ must satisfy public verifiability, i.e., given any input A, there is a polynomial time algorithm that can effectively check whether A belongs to $\mathcal{S}$.

by $\mathcal{S} := \{(m,c)|c = \mathsf{Enc}(pk, m; \mathsf{G}(m))\}$. Since the decryption of PKE is deterministic, it is not possible for two distinct $A_1 \in \mathcal{S}$ and $A_2 \in \mathcal{S}$ to result in a same c. Thus, such a simulation of H is a purely conceptual change and it is still a random oracle in the adversary's view, see Fig. 1. Moreover, we have $\mathsf{Decaps}^{\not\perp}(sk, c) = \mathsf{H}(m, c) = \mathsf{H}_1(c)$ if c is valid[4]. In addition, if c is invalid, we can also use $\mathsf{H}_1(c)$ to simulate the oracle $\mathsf{Decaps}^{\not\perp}$ since s is independent of the adversary's view, and the adversary cannot distinguish $\mathsf{H}(s,c)$ from $\mathsf{H}_1(c)$ for an invalid c. Therefore, the simulator can simulate the decapsulation oracle by only using H_1 whether the ciphertext is valid or not.

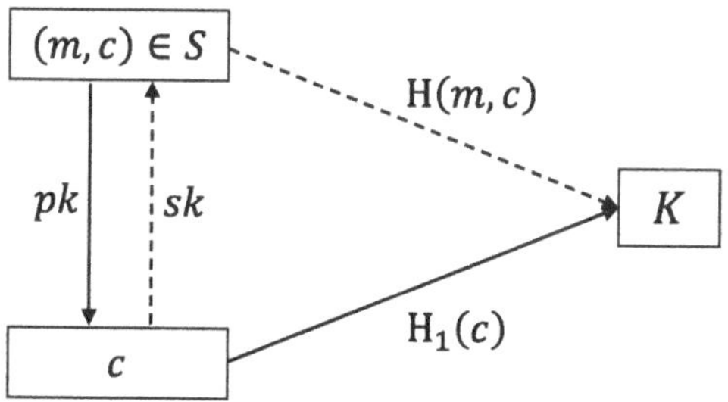

Fig. 1. The proof framework of $\mathsf{FO}^{\not\perp}$. Dashed arrows indicate the real environment and solid arrows indicate the simulated environment.

However, the proof technique above does not carry over to Kyber. In the security proof of $\mathsf{FO}^{\not\perp}$, we utilize an important property that $\mathsf{FO}^{\not\perp}$ satisfies but Kyber does not, i.e., for any $A \in \mathcal{S}$, there exists a polynomial-time algorithm $\mathcal{E}$ such that $c := \mathcal{E}(A)$[5], and A and c are *one-to-one*. This property makes our simulations of H and $\mathsf{Decaps}^{\not\perp}$ perfect. If there exist $A \in \mathcal{S}$ and c that are *many-to-one*, i.e., $c := \mathcal{E}(A_1) = \mathcal{E}(A_2)$, then the distribution of H in the real environment is not equal to that in the simulated environment. If there exist $A \in \mathcal{S}$ and c that are *one-to-many*, i.e., $c_1 \leftarrow \mathcal{E}(A)$ and $c_2 \leftarrow \mathcal{E}(A)$, then $\mathsf{Decaps}^{\not\perp}(c_1) = \mathsf{Decaps}^{\not\perp}(c_2) = \mathsf{H}(A)$ in the real environment, but $\mathsf{Decaps}^{\not\perp}(c_1) := \mathsf{H}_1(c_1)$ is not equal to $\mathsf{Decaps}^{\not\perp}(c_2) := \mathsf{H}_1(c_2)$ in the simulated environment. Next, we try to follow the proof trick of $\mathsf{FO}^{\not\perp}$ to prove the IND-CCA security of Kyber, and explain why Kyber does not satisfy the property.

Security Proof of Kyber, Attempt. Kyber uses a variant of $\mathsf{FO}^{\not\perp}$ (see Fig. 5 for details). In Kyber, the KDF is defined by $K := \mathsf{H}(\hat{k}, \mathsf{H}'(c))$, where $(\hat{k}, r) := \mathsf{G}(\mathsf{H}'(pk), m)$, $c := \mathsf{Enc}(pk, m; r)$ and $\mathsf{H}', \mathsf{H}, \mathsf{G}$ are modeled as random oracles. Following the proof trick of proving $\mathsf{FO}^{\not\perp}$, the simulation of the oracle $\mathsf{Decaps}^{\not\perp}$ can be divided into two steps:

(1) We first modify the simulation of the oracle G. Since $h := \mathsf{H}'(pk)$ is public to adversary, without loss of generality, we can assume that the adversary's

[4] For any fixed (pk, sk), we say that a ciphertext c is valid if $c = \mathsf{Enc}(pk, m; \mathsf{G}(m))$, where $m := \mathsf{Dec}(sk, c)$, and invalid otherwise.

[5] In $\mathsf{FO}^{\not\perp}$, $\mathcal{E}(m, c)$ directly outputs c.

query to oracle G is of the form (h, m) with $h := \mathsf{H}'(pk)$ and $m \in \mathcal{M}$. Then, we can use two independent internal random functions $\mathsf{G}_1 : \mathcal{M} \to \hat{\mathcal{K}}$ and $\mathsf{G}_2 : \mathcal{M} \to \mathcal{R}$ to simulate oracle G, and set $(\hat{k}, r) := \mathsf{G}(h, m) := (\mathsf{G}_1(m), \mathsf{G}_2(m))$. It is obvious that such a simulation of G is a purely conceptual change.

(2) We then modify the simulation of the oracle H. Similar to the proof of $\mathsf{FO}^{\not\perp}$, according to the responses of the decapsulation algorithm to valid ciphertexts, we can define a public verifiable set $\mathcal{S}'$ that contains all possible queries to H during the decapsulation queries for valid ciphertexts:

$$\mathcal{S}' := \{(\hat{k}, b) | b = \mathsf{H}'(c), \textit{where } c := \mathsf{Enc}(pk, m; \mathsf{G}_2(m)) \textit{ and } m := \mathsf{G}_1^{-1}(\hat{k})\}.$$

However, Kyber does not satisfy the *one-to-one* property. (a) If we define the polynomial-time algorithm $\mathcal{E}$ such that $\mathcal{E}(\hat{k}, b)$ outputs c, then $(\hat{k}, b) \in \mathcal{S}'$ and c are *one-to-many* since G_1 and H' are random oracles, see left-hand of Fig. 2. (b) If we define the polynomial-time algorithm $\mathcal{E}$ such that $\mathcal{E}(\hat{k}, b)$ outputs b, then $(\hat{k}, b) \in \mathcal{S}'$ and c are *many-to-one* when c_1 and c_2 are a collision for H', see right-hand of Fig. 2.

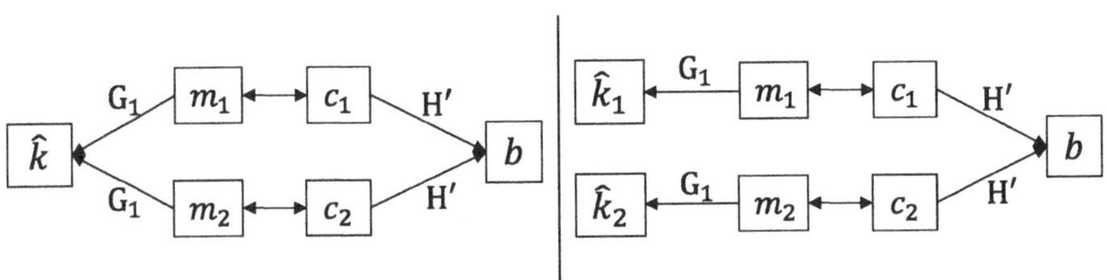

Fig. 2. The relationship between $(\hat{k}, b) \in \mathcal{S}'$ and the corresponding c (and b).

Our Solution. The high-level idea is that we modify the definition of $\mathcal{S}'$ to force Kyber to satisfy the property. From the NIST document of Kyber [17], we have $\mathcal{M} = \hat{\mathcal{K}} = \{0, 1\}^{256}$. Note that a random function $\mathsf{G}_1 : \mathcal{M} \to \hat{\mathcal{K}}$ is indistinguishable from a random permutation $\mathsf{P}_1 : \mathcal{M} \to \hat{\mathcal{K}}$ with probability $\mathcal{O}(q^3/2^{256})$ for any q-query quantum algorithm [27]. Thus, we can replace G_1 with P_1 in the security proof to force Kyber to satisfy the property. Specifically, we define a new set

$$\mathcal{S}'' := \{(\hat{k}, b) | b = \mathsf{H}'(c), \textit{where } c := \mathsf{Enc}(pk, m; \mathsf{G}_2(m)) \textit{ and } m := \mathsf{P}_1^{-1}(\hat{k})\}.$$

In this case, for any $(\hat{k}, b) \in \mathcal{S}''$, there exists a unique m such that $\hat{k} = \mathsf{P}_1(m)$ since P_1 is a permutation. Moreover, there exists a unique c such that $c = \mathsf{Enc}(pk, m; \mathsf{G}_2(m))$ and $b = \mathsf{H}'(c)$. Conversely, for any valid ciphertext c, we can obtain the unique $(\hat{k}, b) \in \mathcal{S}''$ since $\mathsf{Decaps}^{\not\perp}(sk, c)$ is deterministic. Thus, $(\hat{k}, b) \in \mathcal{S}''$ and c are one-to-one, and we can set $\mathsf{H}(\hat{k}, b) := \mathsf{H}_1(c)$ if the input $(\hat{k}, b) \in \mathcal{S}''$ and then simulate the oracle $\mathsf{Decaps}^{\not\perp}$ by only using H_1.

Remark. For the KEM variants with "single-nested-hash", i.e., the KDF is defined by $K := \mathsf{H}(\mathsf{G}_1(m), c)$ or $K := \mathsf{H}(m, \mathsf{H}'(c))$, it is easy to verify that these two KEM variants satisfy the *one-to-one* property. Thus, we can use the proof technique in [14] to prove the IND-CCA security.

1.2 Paper Organization

The rest of this paper is organized as follows. In Sect. 2, some notations and lemmas are introduced. In Sect. 3, we prove that Kyber is IND-CCA secure in the QROM. The conclusions are drawn in Sect. 4.

2 Preliminaries

Notations. For a finite set S, let $|S|$ denotes the cardinality of S, let $x \xleftarrow{\$} S$ denote the sampling of a uniform random element x, while we denote the sampling according to some distribution D by $x \leftarrow D$. For the Boolean statement E, $[\![E]\!]$ denotes the bit that is 1 if E is true, and 0 otherwise. We denote deterministic (probabilistic) computation of an algorithm $\mathcal{A}$ on input x by $y := \mathcal{A}(x)$ ($y \leftarrow \mathcal{A}(x)$). We denote algorithm $\mathcal{A}$ with access to an oracle H by $\mathcal{A}^{\mathsf{H}}$.

2.1 Public-Key Encryption

A public-key encryption $\mathsf{PKE} = (\mathsf{Gen}, \mathsf{Enc}, \mathsf{Dec})$ consists of three polynomial-time algorithms and a finite message space $\mathcal{M}$:

- $\mathsf{Gen}(1^k) \rightarrow (pk, sk)$: a key generation algorithm that on input 1^k, where k is the security parameter, outputs a key pair (pk, sk), where pk defines a randomness space $\mathcal{R} = \mathcal{R}(pk)$.
- $\mathsf{Enc}(pk, m) \rightarrow c$: an encryption algorithm that on input pk and a message $m \in \mathcal{M}$, outputs a ciphertext $c \leftarrow \mathsf{Enc}(pk, m)$. If necessary, we make the used randomness of encryption explicit by writing $c := \mathsf{Enc}(pk, m; r)$, where $r \xleftarrow{\$} \mathcal{R}$ and $\mathcal{R}$ is the randomness space.
- $\mathsf{Dec}(sk, c) \rightarrow m/\bot$: a decryption algorithm that on input decryption key sk and ciphertext c, outputs either a message $m := \mathsf{Dec}(sk, c)$ or a special symbol $\bot \notin \mathcal{M}$ to indicate that c is an invalid ciphertext.

Definition 1 (Correctness [11]). *We call a public-key encryption scheme* PKE *δ-correct if*

$$\mathbf{E}[\max_{m \in \mathcal{M}} \Pr[\mathsf{Dec}(sk, c) \neq m : c \leftarrow \mathsf{Enc}(pk, m)]] \leq \delta,$$

where the expectation is taken over $(pk, sk) \leftarrow \mathsf{Gen}$.

GAME OW-CPA$^{\mathcal{A}}$	**GAME** IND-CPA$^{\mathcal{A}}$
$(pk, sk) \leftarrow \mathsf{Gen}$	$(pk, sk) \leftarrow \mathsf{Gen}$
$m^* \stackrel{\$}{\leftarrow} \mathcal{M}$	$b \stackrel{\$}{\leftarrow} \{0, 1\}$
$c^* \leftarrow \mathsf{Enc}(pk, m^*)$	$(m_0^*, m_1^*, st) \leftarrow \mathcal{A}_1(pk)$
$m' \leftarrow \mathcal{A}(pk, c^*)$	$c^* \leftarrow \mathsf{Enc}(pk, m_b^*)$
return $[\![m' = m^*]\!]$	$b' \leftarrow \mathcal{A}_2(pk, c^*, st)$
	return $[\![b' = b]\!]$

Fig. 3. Games OW-CPA and IND-CPA for PKE.

Security. We now define two security notions for public-key encryption: One-Way against Chosen Plaintext Attacks (OW-CPA) and Indistinguishbility against Chosen Plaintext Attacks (IND-CPA).

Definition 2 (OW-CPA). *For any adversary $\mathcal{A}$, we define its* OW-CPA *advantage against* PKE *as follows:*

$$\mathsf{Adv}_{\mathsf{PKE}}^{\mathsf{OW\text{-}CPA}}(\mathcal{A}) := \Pr\left[\mathsf{OW\text{-}CPA}^{\mathcal{A}} \Rightarrow 1\right],$$

where OW-CPA *game is defined as in the left-hand of Fig. 3.*

Definition 3 (IND-CPA). *For any adversary $\mathcal{A} = (\mathcal{A}_1, \mathcal{A}_2)$, we define its* IND-CPA *advantage against* PKE *as follows:*

$$\mathsf{Adv}_{\mathsf{PKE}}^{\mathsf{IND\text{-}CPA}}(\mathcal{A}) := \left|\Pr\left[\mathsf{IND\text{-}CPA}^{\mathcal{A}} \Rightarrow 1\right] - 1/2\right|,$$

where IND-CPA *game is defined as in the right-hand of Fig. 3.*

2.2 Key Encapsulation Mechanism

A key encapsulation mechanism $\mathsf{KEM} = (\mathsf{Gen}, \mathsf{Encaps}, \mathsf{Decaps})$ consists of three polynomial-time algorithms:

- $\mathsf{Gen}(1^k) \rightarrow (pk, sk)$: a key generation algorithm that on input 1^k, where k is the security parameter, outputs a key pair (pk, sk).
- $\mathsf{Encaps}(pk) \rightarrow (K, c)$: an encapsulation algorithm that on input encapsulation key pk, outputs a tuple (K, c), where c is called an encapsulation of the key K which is contained in the key space $\mathcal{K}$.
- $\mathsf{Decaps}(sk, c) \rightarrow K$: a decapsulation algorithm that on input decapsulation key sk and an encapsulation ciphertext c, outputs a key K associated with c or a pseudorandom key (implicit rejection), which implies that c is an invalid encapsulation ciphertext.

Remark. Implicit (Explicit) rejection means a pseudorandom key K (a rejection symbol $\perp \notin \mathcal{K}$, resp.) is returned for an invalid encapsulation ciphertext. Kyber is a KEM with implicit rejection.

Security. We now define Indistinguishability against Chosen Ciphertext Attacks (IND-CCA) security for key encapsulation mechanism.

GAME $\mathsf{IND\text{-}CCA}^{\mathcal{A}}$	$\mathsf{Decaps}(c)$
$(pk, sk) \leftarrow \mathsf{Gen}$	**if** $c = c^*$
$b \xleftarrow{\$} \{0,1\}$	**return** $\perp$
$(K_0^*, c^*) \leftarrow \mathsf{Encaps}(pk)$	**else return**
$K_1^* \xleftarrow{\$} \mathcal{K}$	$K := \mathsf{Decaps}(sk, c)$
$b' \leftarrow \mathcal{A}^{\mathsf{Decaps}}(pk, c^*, K_b^*)$	
return $[\![b' = b]\!]$	

Fig. 4. Game IND-CCA for KEM.

Definition 4 (IND-CCA). *For any adversary $\mathcal{A}$, we define its* IND-CCA *advantage against* KEM *as follows:*

$$\mathsf{Adv}_{\mathsf{KEM}}^{\mathsf{IND\text{-}CCA}}(\mathcal{A}) := \left|\Pr\left[\mathsf{IND\text{-}CCA}^{\mathcal{A}} \Rightarrow 1\right] - 1/2\right|,$$

where IND-CCA *game is defined as in Fig. 4.*

2.3 Quantum Random Oracle Model

We prove security in the QROM [5] where adversaries are given quantum access to the random oracles, and classical access to all the other oracles.

Simulating Quantum Random Oracle. In 2012, Zhandry [26] proved that for at most q queries, no quantum algorithm $\mathcal{A}^{\mathcal{O}}$ can distinguish a truly random function $\mathsf{H} : \mathcal{X} \rightarrow \mathcal{Y}$ from a $2q$-wise independent function f_{2q}, where $f_{2q} : \mathcal{X} \rightarrow \mathcal{Y}$ is a random polynomial of degree $2q$ over the finite field $F_{|\mathcal{Y}|}$. In 2019, Zhandry [28] developed the compressed oracle technique, which can also be used to simulate quantum random oracle.

Lemmas. Next, we will review several important lemmas, which we will use in our proof. All of the lemmas have been proved in other works.

Lemma 1 (Lemma 4 in [14]). *Let Ω_H and $\Omega_{H'}$ be the sets of all functions $\mathsf{H} : \{0,1\}^{n_1} \times \{0,1\}^{n_2} \rightarrow \{0,1\}^m$ and $\mathsf{H}' : \{0,1\}^{n_2} \rightarrow \{0,1\}^m$, respectively. Let $\mathsf{H} \xleftarrow{\$} \Omega_H$, $\mathsf{H}' \xleftarrow{\$} \Omega_{H'}$, $x \xleftarrow{\$} \{0,1\}^{n_1}$. Let $F_0 = \mathsf{H}(x,\cdot)$, $F_1 = \mathsf{H}'(\cdot)$. Consider an oracle algorithm $\mathcal{A}^{\mathsf{H},F_i}$ that makes at most q quantum queries to H and F_i ($i \in \{0,1\}$). If x is independent from the $\mathcal{A}^{\mathsf{H},F_i}$'s view, then*

$$\left|\Pr[1 \leftarrow \mathcal{A}^{\mathsf{H},F_0}] - \Pr[1 \leftarrow \mathcal{A}^{\mathsf{H},F_1}]\right| \leq 2q/\sqrt{2^{n_1}}.$$

Lemma 2 (Theorem 3.1 in [27]). *There is a universal constant C such that the following holds. Let $\mathsf{H} : \mathcal{X} \rightarrow \mathcal{Y}$ be a random function, then any algorithm making q quantum queries to H outputs a collision for H with probability at most $C(q+1)^3/|\mathcal{Y}|$ (or $\mathcal{O}((q+1)^3/|\mathcal{Y}|)$).*

Lemma 3 (Page 5,6 in [27]). *There is a universal constant C such that the following holds. Let $\mathcal{D}_f$ be a distribution that outputs a truly random function from $\mathcal{N}$ to $\mathcal{N}$, let $\mathcal{D}_p$ be a distribution that outputs a truly random permutation* *from $\mathcal{N}$ to $\mathcal{N}$. Then any q-query*[6] *quantum oracle algorithm can only distinguish the distribution $\mathcal{D}_f$ from $\mathcal{D}_p$ with probability $Cq^3/|\mathcal{N}|$ (or $\mathcal{O}(q^3/|\mathcal{N}|)$).*

Lemma 4 (Theorem 3 in [12]). *Let Π_P be the sets of all permutations $\mathsf{P}: \{0,1\}^n \rightarrow \{0,1\}^n$, let $\mathsf{P} \xleftarrow{\$} \Pi_P$ be a random permutation. Let $\mathsf{LR}_4(f_1, f_2, f_3, f_4)$ be the 4-round Luby-Rackoff construction, where round functions $f_i : \{0,1\}^{n/2} \rightarrow \{0,1\}^{n/2}$ ($i \in \{1,2,3,4\}$) are truly random functions. Then for any q-query quantum oracle algorithm $\mathcal{A}$, we have*

$$\left|\Pr[1 \leftarrow \mathcal{A}^{\mathsf{P}}] - \Pr[1 \leftarrow \mathcal{A}^{\mathsf{LR}_4}]\right| \leq \mathcal{O}\left(\sqrt{q^3/2^{n/2}}\right).$$

Lemma 5 (One-Way to Hiding (OW2H) [24]). *Let Ω_{H} be the set of all functions H: $\mathcal{X} \rightarrow \mathcal{Y}$, and let $\mathsf{H} \xleftarrow{\$} \Omega_{\mathsf{H}}$ be a quantum random oracle. Consider an oracle algorithm $\mathcal{A}^{\mathsf{H}}$ that makes at most q queries to H. Let $\mathcal{B}^{\mathsf{H}}$ be an oracle algorithm that on input x does the following: picks $i \xleftarrow{\$} \{1, \cdots, q\}$ and $y \xleftarrow{\$} \mathcal{Y}$, runs $\mathcal{A}^{\mathsf{H}}(x, y)$ until (just before) the i-th query, measures the argument of the query in the computational basis and outputs the measurement outcome (When $\mathcal{A}$ makes less than i queries to H, $\mathcal{B}$ outputs $\perp \notin \mathcal{X}$.). Let*

$$P_{\mathcal{A}}^1 := \Pr[b' = 1 : \mathsf{H} \xleftarrow{\$} \Omega_{\mathsf{H}}, x \xleftarrow{\$} \mathcal{X}, b' \leftarrow \mathcal{A}^{\mathsf{H}}(x, \mathsf{H}(x))], \tag{1}$$

$$P_{\mathcal{A}}^2 := \Pr[b' = 1 : \mathsf{H} \xleftarrow{\$} \Omega_{\mathsf{H}}, x \xleftarrow{\$} \mathcal{X}, y \xleftarrow{\$} \mathcal{Y}, b' \leftarrow \mathcal{A}^{\mathsf{H}}(x, y)], \tag{2}$$

$$P_{\mathcal{B}} := \Pr[x' = x : \mathsf{H} \xleftarrow{\$} \Omega_{\mathsf{H}}, x \xleftarrow{\$} \mathcal{X}, x' \leftarrow \mathcal{B}^{\mathsf{H}}(x)]. \tag{3}$$

Then $\left|P_{\mathcal{A}}^1 - P_{\mathcal{A}}^2\right| \leq 2q\sqrt{P_{\mathcal{B}}}$.

Lemma 6 (Generic Distinguishing Problem with Bounded Probabilities [6,13]). *Let $\gamma \in [0,1]$, Z be a finite set. Let $F_1 : Z \rightarrow \{0,1\}$ be the following function: for each $z \in Z$, $F_1(z) = 1$ with probability p_z ($p_z \leq \gamma$), and $F_1(z) = 0$ else. Let $F_2 : Z \rightarrow \{0\}$ be the constant zero function. Then, for any (unbounded) algorithm $\mathcal{A}$ issuing at most q quantum queries to F_1 or F_2,*

$$|\Pr[1 \leftarrow \mathcal{A}^{F_1}] - \Pr[1 \leftarrow \mathcal{A}^{F_2}]| \leq 8(q+1)^2 \cdot \gamma.$$

3 IND-CCA Proof for Kyber

According to the NIST document for Kyber [20], we first describe the construction of Kyber, which uses a variant of $\mathsf{FO}^{\not\perp}$ [11]. To a public-key encryption scheme $\mathsf{PKE} = (\mathsf{Gen}, \mathsf{Enc}, \mathsf{Dec})$ with message space $\mathcal{M} := \{0,1\}^{256}$ and randomness space $\mathcal{R} := \{0,1\}^{256}$, hash functions $\mathsf{H}' : \{0,1\}^* \rightarrow \{0,1\}^{256}$, $\mathsf{G} : \{0,1\}^* \rightarrow \{0,1\}^{512}$ and $\mathsf{H} : \{0,1\}^{512} \rightarrow \mathcal{K}$, we associate $\mathsf{Kyber} = \mathsf{FO}^{\not\perp'}[\mathsf{PKE}, \mathsf{H}', \mathsf{H}, \mathsf{G}]$. The algorithms of $\mathsf{Kyber} = (\mathsf{Gen}', \mathsf{Encaps}, \mathsf{Decaps}^{\not\perp})$ are defined in Fig. 5.

The following theorem establish that Kyber is IND-CCA secure in the QROM if PKE is IND-CPA secure.

[6] We say that $\mathcal{A}$ is a q-query oracle algorithm [2] if it performs at most q oracle queries.

Gen′	Encaps(pk)	Decaps$^{\not\perp}(sk', c)$
$(pk, sk) \leftarrow$ Gen	$m \xleftarrow{\$} \mathcal{M}$	$m' :=$ Dec(sk, c)
$h :=$ H′(pk)	$m :=$ H′(m)	$(\hat{k}', r') :=$ G(h, m')
$s \xleftarrow{\$} \{0,1\}^{256}$	$(\hat{k}, r) :=$ G(h, m)	$c' :=$ Enc$(pk, m'; r')$
$sk' := (sk, s, h)$	$c :=$ Enc$(pk, m; r)$	**if** $c = c'$, **then**
return (pk, sk')	$K :=$ H$(\hat{k},$ H′$(c))$	**return** $K :=$ H$(\hat{k}',$ H′$(c))$
	return (K, c)	**else return** $K :=$ H$(s,$ H′$(c))$

Fig. 5. Kyber := FO$^{\not\perp'}$[PKE, H′, H, G], here H′, H, G are hash functions.

Theorem 1. *Given* PKE = (Gen, Enc, Dec) *is* δ*-correct. For any* IND-CCA *adversary* $\mathcal{B}$ *against* Kyber = (Gen′, Encaps, Decaps$^{\not\perp}$) = FO$^{\not\perp'}$[PKE, H′, H, G], *issuing at most* q_{D} *classical queries to the decapsulation oracle* Decaps$^{\not\perp}$ *and at most* $q_{\mathsf{H}'}$ *(resp.* q_{H} *and* q_{G}*) quantum queries to the random oracle* H′ *(resp.* H *and* G*), there exists an* IND-CPA *adversary* $\mathcal{A}$ *against* PKE *such that*

$$\mathsf{Adv}_{\mathsf{KEM}}^{\mathsf{IND-CCA}}(\mathcal{B}) \le 2(q_{\mathsf{H}} + q_{\mathsf{G}})\sqrt{\mathsf{Adv}_{\mathsf{PKE}}^{\mathsf{IND-CPA}}(\mathcal{A}) + \frac{1}{2^{256}}} + \frac{2q_{\mathsf{H}}}{2^{128}} + 16(q_{\mathsf{G}}+1)^2 \cdot \delta + \mathcal{O}\left(\frac{(q_{\mathsf{H}'}+1)^3}{2^{256}}\right) + \mathcal{O}\left(\frac{q_{\mathsf{G}}^3}{2^{256}}\right) + \mathcal{O}\left(\sqrt{q_{\mathsf{G}}^3/2^{128}}\right).$$

and the running time of $\mathcal{A}$ *is that of* $\mathcal{B}$.

The proof can be divided into two steps: we first replace the truly quantum random oracle H with a structured H, then we can simulate the oracle Decaps$^{\not\perp}$ such that it no longer uses secret key. Finally, we apply OW2H lemma [24] to argue key indistinguishability.

Proof. We first define some notations. Let Ω_{H}, Ω_{G} and $\Omega_{\mathsf{G}'}$ be the sets of all functions $\mathsf{H}: \{0,1\}^{512} \to \mathcal{K}$, $\mathsf{G}: \{0,1\}^* \to \{0,1\}^{512}$ and $\mathsf{H}': \{0,1\}^* \to \{0,1\}^{256}$, respectively. Let Ω_a, Ω_b and Ω_c be the sets of all functions $\mathsf{H}_1: \{0,1\}^{256} \to \mathcal{K}$, $\mathsf{H}_2: \mathcal{C} \to \mathcal{K}$ and $\mathsf{G}_2: \{0,1\}^{256} \to \{0,1\}^{256}$, respectively. Let Π_{P} be the sets of all permutations $\mathsf{P}: \{0,1\}^{256} \to \{0,1\}^{256}$. Let $\mathcal{B}$ be an adversary against the IND-CCA security of KEM, issuing at most $q_{\mathsf{H}'}$ (resp. q_{H} and q_{G}) quantum queries to H′ (resp. H and G), and q_{D} classical queries to Decaps$^{\not\perp}$. Consider the games in Fig. 6, we will prove security through a sequences of games.

Game G$_0$: The game G_0 is the original IND-CCA game, then we have

$$|\Pr[G_0 \Rightarrow 1] - 1/2| = \mathsf{Adv}_{\mathsf{KEM}}^{\mathsf{IND-CCA}}(\mathcal{B}).$$

Game G$_1$: The game G_1 is identical to game G_0, except that the oracle Decaps$^{\not\perp}$ is modified such that $\mathsf{H}_1(\mathsf{H}'(c_i))$ is returned instead of $\mathsf{H}(s, \mathsf{H}'(c_i))$ for an invalid encapsulation ciphertext c_i, where $\mathsf{H}_1 \xleftarrow{\$} \Omega_a$ is an internal random function.

Note that the change is quite similar to the game-hop "$G_0 \Rightarrow G_1$" in the proof of Theorem 1 in [14], by Lemma 1, we have

$$|\Pr[G_0 \Rightarrow 1] - \Pr[G_1 \Rightarrow 1]| \le \frac{2q_{\mathsf{H}}}{\sqrt{2^{256}}}.$$

GAMES $G_0 - G_{12}$

$(pk, sk') \leftarrow \mathsf{Gen}'$, $\mathsf{H}' \xleftarrow{\$} \Omega_{\mathsf{H}'}$, $\mathsf{H}_3 \xleftarrow{\$} \Omega_{\mathsf{H}}$
$\mathsf{G}_3 \xleftarrow{\$} \Omega_{\mathsf{G}}$ $//G_0 - G_3$
$\mathsf{H}_1 \xleftarrow{\$} \Omega_a$ $//G_1 - G_2$
$\mathsf{H}_2 \xleftarrow{\$} \Omega_b$ $//G_3 - G_8$
$\mathsf{H}_4 \xleftarrow{\$} \Omega_b$ $//G_8 - G_{12}$
$\mathsf{H}_5 \xleftarrow{\$} \Omega_a$ $//G_{10} - G_{12}$
$\mathsf{G}_1 \xleftarrow{\$} \Omega_c$ $//G_4$
$\mathsf{G}_2 \xleftarrow{\$} \Omega_c$ $//G_4 - G_5, G_{11} - G_{12}$
$\mathsf{G}_2' \xleftarrow{\$} \Omega_{c'}$ $//G_6 - G_{10}$
construct LR_4, LR_4^{-1} $//G_7 - G_{12}$
$\mathsf{P}_1 \xleftarrow{\$} \Pi_{\mathsf{P}}$ $//G_5 - G_6$
$m \xleftarrow{\$} \mathcal{M}$, $m^* := \mathsf{H}'(m)$
$(\hat{k}^*, r^*) := \mathsf{G}(\mathsf{H}'(pk), m^*)$
$r^* \xleftarrow{\$} \mathcal{R}$, $K_0^* \xleftarrow{\$} \mathcal{K}$ $//G_{12}$
$c^* := \mathsf{Enc}'(pk, m^*; r^*)$
$K_0^* := \mathsf{H}(\hat{k}^*, \mathsf{H}'(c^*))$ $//G_0 - G_{10}$
$K_0^* := \mathsf{H}_5(m^*)$ $//G_{11}$
$K_1^* \xleftarrow{\$} \mathcal{K}$, $b \xleftarrow{\$} \{0,1\}$
$b' \leftarrow \mathcal{B}^{\mathsf{Decaps}^{\not\perp}, \mathsf{H}, \mathsf{G}, \mathsf{H}'}(pk, c^*, K_b^*)$
return $[\![b' = b]\!]$

$\mathsf{G}(h, m)$ $//G_0 - G_{12}$

$(\hat{k}, r) := \mathsf{G}_3(h, m)$ $//G_0 - G_3$
$\hat{k} := \mathsf{G}_1(m), r := \mathsf{G}_2(m)$ $//G_4$
$\hat{k} := \mathsf{P}_1(m), r := \mathsf{G}_2(m)$ $//G_5$
$\hat{k} := \mathsf{P}_1(m), r := \mathsf{G}_2'(m)$ $//G_6$
$\hat{k} := \mathsf{LR}_4(m), r := \mathsf{G}_2'(m)$ $//G_7 - G_{10}$
$\hat{k} := \mathsf{LR}_4(m), r := \mathsf{G}_2(m)$ $//G_{11} - G_{12}$
return $(\hat{k}, r)$

$\mathsf{H}(\hat{k}, b)$ $//G_0 - G_{12}$

Define the set $\mathcal{S}$ $//G_8 - G_{12}$
if $(\hat{k}, b) \in \mathcal{S}$ $//G_8 - G_{12}$
  if $c = c^*$ $//G_{10} - G_{12}$
  return $\mathsf{H}_5(m)$ $//G_{10} - G_{12}$
return $\mathsf{H}_4(c)$ $//G_8 - G_{12}$
return $\mathsf{H}_3(\hat{k}, b)$

$\mathsf{Decaps}^{\not\perp}(sk', c_i \neq c^*)$ $//G_0 - G_8$

for $j \in \{1, \cdots, i-1\}$ $//G_2 - G_8$
if $\exists c_j$: $\mathsf{H}'(c_j) = \mathsf{H}'(c_i)$ $//G_2 - G_8$
  QUERY:=true $//G_2 - G_8$
  abort $//G_2 - G_8$
Parse $sk' = (sk, s, h)$
$m' := \mathsf{Dec}(sk, c_i)$
$(\hat{k}', r') := \mathsf{G}(h, m')$
if $\mathsf{Enc}(pk, m'; r') = c_i$
  return $K := \mathsf{H}(\hat{k}', \mathsf{H}'(c_i))$
else return $K := \mathsf{H}(s, \mathsf{H}'(c_i))$ $//G_0$
else return $K := \mathsf{H}_1(\mathsf{H}'(c_i))$ $//G_1 - G_2$
else return $K := \mathsf{H}_2(c_i)$ $//G_3 - G_8$

$\mathsf{Decaps}^{\not\perp}(c_i \neq c^*)$ $//G_9 - G_{12}$

for $j \in \{1, \cdots, i-1\}$
if $\exists c_j$: $\mathsf{H}'(c_j) = \mathsf{H}'(c_i)$
  QUERY:=true
  abort
return $K := \mathsf{H}_4(c_i)$

Fig. 6. Games G_0–G_{12} for the proof of Theorem 1. LR_4 is the 4-round Luby-Rackoff construction $\mathsf{LR}_4(f_1, f_2, f_3, f_4)$, where round functions $f_i : \{0,1\}^{n/2} \to \{0,1\}^{n/2}$ ($i \in \{1,2,3,4\}$) are truly random functions, which can be simulated by using the compressed oracle technique developed by Zhandry [28]. LR_4^{-1} is the inverse permutation of LR_4.

Game $\mathbf{G_2}$: In game G_2, we raise a flag QUERY in the oracle $\mathsf{Decaps}^{\not\perp}$ and abort if there exists c_j for $j \in \{1, \cdots, i-1\}$ such that $\mathsf{H}'(c_j) = \mathsf{H}'(c_i)$, where i means i-th $\mathsf{Decaps}^{\not\perp}$ queries. Obviously, G_1 and G_2 only differ if QUERY is raised, meaning that there exists a quantum algorithm that finds a collision for H'. By the difference lemma [22] and Lemma 2, we have

$$|\Pr[G_1 \Rightarrow 1] - \Pr[G_2 \Rightarrow 1]| \le \Pr[\text{QUERY}] \le \mathcal{O}\left(\frac{(q_{\mathsf{H}'}+1)^3}{2^{256}}\right).$$

Game G₃: In game G_3, we further modify the oracle $\mathsf{Decaps}^{\not\perp}$ such that $\mathsf{H}_2(c_i)$ is returned instead of $\mathsf{H}_1(\mathsf{H}'(c_i))$ for an invalid encapsulation ciphertext c_i, where $\mathsf{H}_2 \xleftarrow{\$} \Omega_b$ is an internal random function. It is not hard to verify that the output distributions of $\mathsf{Decaps}^{\not\perp}$ in G_2 and G_3 are identical. Therefore, we have

$$\Pr[G_2 \Rightarrow 1] = \Pr[G_3 \Rightarrow 1].$$

Game G₄: In game G_4, we modify the simulation of the oracle G. Since $h := \mathsf{H}'(pk)$ is public to adversary, without loss of generality, we can assume that the adversary's query to oracle G is of the form (h, m) with $h := \mathsf{H}'(pk)$ and $m \in \mathcal{M}$. We then simulate the oracle G by setting $\mathsf{G}(h,m) := (\mathsf{G}_1(m), \mathsf{G}_2(m))$, where $\mathsf{G}_1 \xleftarrow{\$} \Omega_{\mathsf{c}}$ and $\mathsf{G}_2 \xleftarrow{\$} \Omega_{\mathsf{c}}$ are two independent internal random functions. It is easy to see that the distributions of the oracle G in G_3 and G_4 are identical. Thus, we have

$$\Pr[G_3 \Rightarrow 1] = \Pr[G_4 \Rightarrow 1].$$

Game G₅: In game G_5, we replace $\mathsf{G}_1 \xleftarrow{\$} \Omega_{\mathsf{c}}$ with $\mathsf{P} \xleftarrow{\$} \Pi_{\mathsf{P}}$. Note that the distinguishing problem between G_4 and G_5 is essentially the distinguishing problem between a random function G_1 and a random permutation P. By Lemma 3, we have

$$|\Pr[G_4 \Rightarrow 1] - \Pr[G_5 \Rightarrow 1]| \le \mathcal{O}\left(\frac{q_{\mathsf{G}}^3}{2^{256}}\right).$$

Remark: Since PKE is non-perfectly correct, there exist "bad" $r := \mathsf{G}_2(m)$ such that $c := \mathsf{Enc}(pk, m; r)$ but $\mathsf{Dec}(sk, c) \neq m$. In order to handle decryption errors, we define a new random oralce G_2', and force $\mathsf{G}_2'(m)$ to be a "good" randomness.

For the fixed $(pk, sk) \leftarrow \mathsf{Gen}$, we define a set of "bad" randomness as follows:

$$\mathcal{R}^{bad}_{(pk,sk),m} := \{r \in R : \mathsf{Dec}(sk, \mathsf{Enc}(pk, m; r)) \neq m\}.$$

By the definitions of δ-correct, we have $\delta_{(pk,sk),m} := |\mathcal{R}^{bad}_{(pk,sk),m}|/|\mathcal{R}|$, $\delta_{(pk,sk)} := \max_{m \in \mathcal{M}} \delta_{(pk,sk),m}$ and $\delta := \mathbf{E}\left[\delta_{(pk,sk)}\right]$, where the expectation is taken over $(pk, sk) \leftarrow \mathsf{Gen}$. Let $\mathcal{R}^{good}_{(pk,sk),m} := \mathcal{R} \backslash \mathcal{R}^{bad}_{(pk,sk),m}$ be the set of "good" randomness, we define G_2' such that $\mathsf{G}_2'(m)$ is sampled according to the uniform distribution in $\mathcal{R}^{good}_{(pk,sk),m}$. Let $\Omega_{c'}$ be the set of all function G_2'.

Game G₆: In game G_6, we replace $\mathsf{G}_2 \xleftarrow{\$} \Omega_{\mathsf{c}}$ with $\mathsf{G}_2' \xleftarrow{\$} \Omega_{c'}$, where $\mathsf{G}_2'(m)$ samples "good" randomness. According to the same analysis as in the proof of [13], the distinguishing problem between G_5 and G_6 is essentially the distinguishing problem between G_2 and G_2', which can be converted into distinguish F_1 from F_2, where F_1 is a function such that $F_1(m)$ is sampled from the *Bernoulli* distribution $B_{\delta_{(pk,sk),m}}$ and F_2 is a constant zero function. Here, we use the generic distinguishing problem proposed in [13] to achieve a better correctness bound than that in [10,14,15][7]. By Lemma 6, for a fixed (pk, sk), we have

$$|\Pr[G_5 \Rightarrow 1 : (pk, sk)] - \Pr[G_6 \Rightarrow 1 : (pk, sk)]| \leq 8(q_{\mathsf{G}} + 1)^2 \cdot \delta_{(pk,sk)}.$$

By averaging over $(pk, sk) \leftarrow \mathsf{Gen}$, we can obtain

$$|\Pr[G_5 \Rightarrow 1] - \Pr[G_6 \Rightarrow 1]| \leq 8(q_{\mathsf{G}} + 1)^2 \cdot \delta.$$

Game $\mathbf{G_7}$: In game G_7, we replace $\mathsf{P} \xleftarrow{\$} \Pi_{\mathsf{P}}$ with the 4-round Luby-Rackoff construction LR_4 [12]. Then the distinguishing problem between G_6 and G_7 is essentially the distinguishing problem between a random permutation P and LR_4. By Lemma 4, we have

$$|\Pr[G_6 \Rightarrow 1] - \Pr[G_7 \Rightarrow 1]| \leq \mathcal{O}\left(\sqrt{q_{\mathsf{G}}^3/2^{128}}\right).$$

Game $\mathbf{G_8}$: In game G_8, we construct a structured H via domain separation to simulate the truly quantum random oracle H. We define a public verifiable set

$$\mathcal{S} := \{(\hat{k}, b) | b = \mathsf{H}'(c), where\ c := \mathsf{Enc}(pk, m; \mathsf{G}_2'(m))\ and\ m := \mathsf{LR}_4^{-1}(\hat{k})\},$$

where LR_4^{-1} is the inverse permutation of LR_4. Let $\mathsf{H}_3 \xleftarrow{\$} \Omega_{\mathsf{H}}$ and $\mathsf{H}_4 \xleftarrow{\$} \Omega_b$ be two independent internal random functions, H is defined by:

$$\mathsf{H}(\hat{k}, b) := \begin{cases} \mathsf{H}_4(c) & (\hat{k}, b) \in \mathcal{S} \\ \mathsf{H}_3(\hat{k}, b) & otherwise. \end{cases}$$

Note that it is not possible for two distinct $(\hat{k}', b') \in \mathcal{S}$ and $(\hat{k}'', b'') \in \mathcal{S}$ to result in a same c. The reason is, as G_2' samples "good" randomness, there exists at most one value m that satisfies $\mathsf{Enc}(pk, m; \mathsf{G}_2'(m)) = c$. And since LR_4 and H'· are deterministic, the above follows. Therefore, the distributions of the oracle H in G_7 and G_8 are identical. Thus we have

$$\Pr[G_7 \Rightarrow 1] = \Pr[G_8 \Rightarrow 1].$$

Remark: For any $(\hat{k}, b) \in \mathcal{S}$, we can compute the unique $m = \mathsf{LR}_4^{-1}(\hat{k})$ and the unique $c = \mathsf{Enc}(pk, m; \mathsf{G}_2'(m))$. Since G_2' samples "good" randomness, the unique c is valid.

Game $\mathbf{G_9}$: This game is identical to game G_8, except that the oracle $\mathsf{Decaps}^{\not\perp}$ is modified such that it does not make use of sk' any more: if QUERY is not raised, then $\mathsf{H}_4(c_i)$ is returned as long as $c_i \neq c^*$. Let $m' := \mathsf{Dec}(sk, c_i)$, $\hat{k}' := \mathsf{LR}_4(m')$ and $r' := \mathsf{G}_2{}'(m')$, we consider the following two case:

[7] In [10,14,15], the correctness bound is $q_{\mathsf{G}}\sqrt{\delta}$, and ours is $q_{\mathsf{G}}{}^2\delta$.

Case1: $\mathsf{Enc}(pk, m'; r') = c_i$. In this case, $\mathsf{H}(\hat{k}', \mathsf{H}'(c_i))$ is returned in G_8 and $\mathsf{H}_4(c_i)$ is returned in G_9. Note that $(\hat{k}, \mathsf{H}'(c_i))$ belongs to $\mathcal{S}$, thus we can rewrite $\mathsf{H}(\hat{k}', \mathsf{H}'(c_i)) = \mathsf{H}_4(c_i)$. Hence, querying $\mathsf{Decaps}^{\not\perp}$ in G_8 and G_9 will return the same value.

Case2: $\mathsf{Enc}(pk, m'; r') \neq c_i$, namely c_i is invalid. In this case, $\mathsf{H}_2(c_i)$ is returned in G_8 and $\mathsf{H}_4(c_i)$ is returned in G_9. In game G_8, since H_2 is independent of all other oracles, the output $\mathsf{H}_2(c_i)$ is uniformly random in $\mathcal{B}$'s view. In game G_9, $\mathcal{B}$'s queries to H can only help him get access to H_4 at valid ciphertexts. Thus, $\mathsf{H}_4(c_i)$ will also be a uniformly random value in $\mathcal{B}$'s view.

As a result, the output distributions of the oracle $\mathsf{Decaps}^{\not\perp}$ in G_8 and G_9 are identical in $\mathcal{B}$'s view. Thus, we have

$$\Pr[G_8 \Rightarrow 1] = \Pr[G_9 \Rightarrow 1].$$

Game $\mathbf{G_{10}}$: In game G_{10}, we make a further modification to the oracle H: if $(\hat{k}, b) \in \mathcal{S}$ and the computed unique $c = c^*$, then $\mathsf{H}_5(m)$ is returned, where $m := \mathsf{LR}_4^{-1}(\hat{k})$ and $\mathsf{H}_5 \xleftarrow{\$} \Omega_a$ is another independent internal random function.

Since it is impossible for two distinct $(\hat{k}', b') \in \mathcal{S}$ and $(\hat{k}'', b'') \in \mathcal{S}$ to result in a same c, this further change to H only affects the H-query at one value $(\hat{k}^*, b^*)$, where $b^* = \mathsf{H}'(c^*)$, $\hat{k}^* = \mathsf{LR}_4(m^*)$ and $\mathsf{Enc}(pk, m^*; \mathsf{G}_2'(m^*)) = c^*$. In this case, $\mathsf{H}_4(c^*)$ is returned in G_9 and $\mathsf{H}_5(m^*)$ is returned in G_{10}. Since c^* is a forbidden decapsulation query, $\mathsf{H}_4(c^*)$ is a uniformly random value in $\mathcal{B}$'s view in G_9. Moreover, since H_5 is independent of all other oracles, the output $\mathsf{H}_5(m^*)$ is also a uniformly random value in $\mathcal{B}$'s view. Therefore, the output distributions of the oracle H in G_9 and G_{10} are identical. Thus, we have

$$\Pr[G_9 \Rightarrow 1] = \Pr[G_{10} \Rightarrow 1].$$

Remark: Following the above modification, we can rewrite the generation of K_0^* in the setup, i.e., "$K_0^* := \mathsf{H}_5(m^*)$" (instead of "$K_0^* := \mathsf{H}(\hat{k}^*, b^*)$"). This change does not affect the game in any way.

Game $\mathbf{G_{11}}$: In game G_{10}, we replace $\mathsf{G_2}' \xleftarrow{\$} \Omega_{\mathsf{c}'}$ with $\mathsf{G}_2 \xleftarrow{\$} \Omega_{\mathsf{c}}$, namely G_2 is reset to be an ideal random function in this game. Similar to the game-hop "$G_5 \Rightarrow G_6$", we can obtain

$$|\Pr[G_{10} \Rightarrow 1] - \Pr[G_{11} \Rightarrow 1]| \leq 8(q_{\mathsf{G}} + 1)^2 \cdot \delta.$$

Game $\mathbf{G_{12}}$: This is identical to game G_{11}, except that we choose r^* and K_0^* uniformly at random from $\mathcal{R}$ and $\mathcal{K}$, respectively. In this game, bit b is independent from $\mathcal{B}$'s view. Hence,

$$\Pr[G_{12} \Rightarrow 1] = 1/2.$$

Next, we use OW2H lemma to bound $|\Pr[G_{11} \Rightarrow 1] - \Pr[G_{12} \Rightarrow 1]|$. Let $(\mathsf{G}_2 \times \mathsf{H}_5)(\cdot) := (\mathsf{G}_2(\cdot), \mathsf{H}_5(\cdot))$. G_2 and H_5 are internal random oracles that $\mathcal{B}$ can access to only by querying the oracle G and H. The number of total queries to $\mathsf{G}_2 \times \mathsf{H}_5$ is at most $q_\mathsf{G} + q_\mathsf{H}$.

$A^{\mathsf{G}_2 \times \mathsf{H}_5}(pk, m^*, (r^*, K_0^*))$	$\mathsf{Decaps}^{\not\perp}(c_i \neq c^*)$
$\mathsf{H}' \xleftarrow{\$} \Omega_{\mathsf{H}'}$	**for** $j \in \{1, \cdots, i-1\}$
construct LR_4, LR_4^{-1}	**if** $\exists c_j$: $\mathsf{H}'(c_j) = \mathsf{H}'(c_i)$
$\mathsf{H}_3 \xleftarrow{\$} \Omega_\mathsf{H}$, $\mathsf{H}_4 \xleftarrow{\$} \Omega_b$	QUERY:=true
$c^* := \mathsf{Enc}(pk, m^*; r^*)$	**abort**
$K_1^* \xleftarrow{\$} \mathcal{K}$, $b \xleftarrow{\$} \{0,1\}$	**return** $K := \mathsf{H}_4(c_i)$
$b' \leftarrow \mathcal{B}^{\mathsf{Decaps}^{\not\perp}, \mathsf{H}, \mathsf{G}, \mathsf{H}'}(pk, c^*, K_b^*)$	
return $[\![b = b']\!]$	

Fig. 7. $A^{\mathsf{G}_2 \times \mathsf{H}_5}$ for the proof of Theorem 1, where oracles $\mathsf{H}, \mathsf{G}, \mathsf{H}'$ are defined as in game G_{12} of Fig. 6.

Let $A^{\mathsf{G}_2 \times \mathsf{H}_5}$ be an oracle algorithm that on input $(pk, m^*, (r^*, K_0^*))$, see Fig. 7. If $r^* := \mathsf{G}_2(m^*)$, $K_0^* := \mathsf{H}_5(m^*)$, then $A^{\mathsf{G}_2 \times \mathsf{H}_5}(pk, m^*, (r^*, K_0^*))$ perfectly simulates G_{11}. If $r^* \xleftarrow{\$} \mathcal{R}$, $K_0^* \xleftarrow{\$} \mathcal{K}$, then $A^{\mathsf{G}_2 \times \mathsf{H}_5}(pk, m^*, (r^*, K_0^*))$ perfectly simulates G_{12}. Let $C^{\mathsf{G}_2 \times \mathsf{H}_5}$ be an oracle algorithm that on input (pk, m^*) does the following: pick $i \xleftarrow{\$} \{1, \cdots, q_\mathsf{G} + q_\mathsf{H}\}$, $r^* \xleftarrow{\$} \mathcal{R}$, $K_0^* \xleftarrow{\$} \mathcal{K}$, run $A^{\mathsf{G}_2 \times \mathsf{H}_5}(pk, m^*, (r^*, K_0^*))$ until (just before) the i-th query, measure the argument of the $\mathsf{G}_2 \times \mathsf{H}_5$ query in the computational basis, output the measurement outcome (when $A^{\mathsf{G}_2 \times \mathsf{H}_5}$ makes less than i queries, $C^{\mathsf{G}_2 \times \mathsf{H}_5}$ outputs $\perp \notin \mathcal{M}$.). Define game G_{13} as in the Fig. 8. Then, $\Pr[C^{\mathsf{G}_2 \times \mathsf{H}_5} \Rightarrow m^*] = \Pr[G_{13} \Rightarrow 1]$.

Remark: Let $\mathsf{H}' \xleftarrow{\$} \Omega_{\mathsf{H}'}$, $m \xleftarrow{\$} \mathcal{M}$, then the distribution of $m^* := \mathsf{H}'(m)$ is equivalent to the distribution of $m^* \xleftarrow{\$} \mathcal{M}$.

Applying Lemma 5 with $x := m^*$ and $y := (r^*, K_0^*)$, we have

$$|\Pr[G_{11} \Rightarrow 1] - \Pr[G_{12} \Rightarrow 1]| \leq 2(q_\mathsf{H} + q_\mathsf{G})\sqrt{\Pr[G_{13} \Rightarrow 1]}.$$

It remains to bound $\Pr[G_{13} \Rightarrow 1]$. To this end, we can construct an OW-CPA adversary $\mathcal{C}(pk, c^*)$ against the underlying PKE scheme that perfectly simulates game G_{13} for $\mathcal{B}$, see Fig. 9.

It is not hard to see that $\Pr[G_{13} \Rightarrow 1] = \mathsf{Adv}_{\mathsf{PKE}}^{\mathsf{OW-CPA}}(\mathcal{C})$. It is well known that IND-CPA[8] security of PKE with sufficiently large message space implies its OW-CPA security. For any OW-CPA adversary $\mathcal{C}$ there exists an IND-CPA adversary $\mathcal{A}$ against PKE with the same running time as that of $\mathcal{C}$ such that

$$\mathsf{Adv}_{\mathsf{PKE}}^{\mathsf{OW-CPA}}(\mathcal{C}) \leq \mathsf{Adv}_{\mathsf{PKE}}^{\mathsf{IND-CPA}}(\mathcal{A}) + 1/2^{256}.$$

[8] Kyber requires the underlying PKE scheme to be IND-CPA secure.

GAME G_{13}

$(pk, sk') \leftarrow \mathsf{Gen}'$
$\mathsf{H}' \xleftarrow{\$} \Omega_{\mathsf{H}'}$, $\mathsf{H}_3 \xleftarrow{\$} \Omega_{\mathsf{H}}$
$\mathsf{H}_4 \xleftarrow{\$} \Omega_b$, $\mathsf{H}_5 \xleftarrow{\$} \Omega_a$
$\mathsf{G}_2 \xleftarrow{\$} \Omega_c$
construct LR_4, LR_4^{-1}
$m^* \xleftarrow{\$} \mathcal{M}$, $r^* \xleftarrow{\$} \mathcal{R}$
$c^* := \mathsf{Enc}(pk, m^*; r^*)$
$K_0^*, K_1^* \xleftarrow{\$} \mathcal{K}$, $b \xleftarrow{\$} \{0,1\}$
$i \xleftarrow{\$} \{1, \cdots, q_{\mathsf{G}} + q_{\mathsf{H}}\}$
run $\mathcal{B}^{\mathsf{Decaps}^{\not\perp}, \mathsf{H}, \mathsf{G}, \mathsf{H}'}(pk, c^*, K_b^*)$
  until the i-th query to $\mathsf{G}_2 \times \mathsf{H}_5$
measure the argument $\hat{m}$
return $[\![\hat{m} = m^*]\!]$

$\mathsf{H}(\hat{k}, b)$

Define the set $\mathcal{S}$
if $(\hat{k}, b) \in \mathcal{S}$
  if $c = c^*$
    return $\mathsf{H}_5(m)$
  return $\mathsf{H}_4(c)$
return $\mathsf{H}_3(\hat{k}, b)$

$\mathsf{Decaps}^{\not\perp}\ (c_i \neq c^*)$

for $j \in \{1, \cdots, i-1\}$
if $\exists c_j$: $\mathsf{H}'(c_j) = \mathsf{H}'(c_i)$
  QUERY:=true
  abort
return $K := \mathsf{H}_4(c_i)$

$\mathsf{G}\,(h, m)$

$\hat{k} := \mathsf{LR}_4(m), r := \mathsf{G}_2(m)$
return $(\hat{k}, r)$

Fig. 8. Games G_{13} for the proof of Theorem 1.

$\mathcal{C}\,(pk, c^*)$

Pick a $2q_{\mathsf{H}'}$-wise independent function to simulate H'
Pick three different $2q_{\mathsf{H}}$-wise independent functions to simulate $\mathsf{H}_3, \mathsf{H}_4$ and H_5, respectively.
Pick a $2q_{\mathsf{G}}$-wise independent function to simulate G_2
construct LR_4, LR_4^{-1}
$K^* \xleftarrow{\$} \mathcal{K}$, $i \xleftarrow{\$} \{1, \cdots, q_{\mathsf{G}} + q_{\mathsf{H}}\}$
run $\mathcal{B}^{\mathsf{Decaps}^{\not\perp}, \mathsf{H}, \mathsf{G}, \mathsf{H}'}(pk, c^*, K^*)$,
  measure the argument $\hat{m}$ of i-th query to $\mathsf{G}_2 \times \mathsf{H}_5$
output $\hat{m}$

Fig. 9. Adversary $\mathcal{C}$ against OW-CPA for the proof of Theorem 1, where oracles $\mathsf{H}, \mathsf{G}, \mathsf{H}'$ and $\mathsf{Decaps}^{\not\perp}$ are defined as in game G_{13} of Fig. 8.

Combining all of the above formulas, we obtain

$$\begin{aligned}\mathsf{Adv}_{\mathsf{KEM}}^{\mathsf{IND-CCA}}(\mathcal{B}) \leq\ & 2(q_{\mathsf{H}} + q_{\mathsf{G}})\sqrt{\mathsf{Adv}_{\mathsf{PKE}}^{\mathsf{IND-CPA}}(\mathcal{A}) + \frac{1}{2^{256}}} + \frac{2q_{\mathsf{H}}}{2^{128}} + 16(q_{\mathsf{G}}+1)^2 \cdot \delta \\ & + \mathcal{O}\left(\frac{(q_{\mathsf{H}'}+1)^3}{2^{256}}\right) + \mathcal{O}\left(\frac{q_{\mathsf{G}}^3}{2^{256}}\right) + \mathcal{O}\left(\sqrt{q_{\mathsf{G}}^3/2^{128}}\right).\end{aligned}$$

4 Conclusions

In order to add robustness, Kyber uses a slightly tweaked FO transformation, i.e., it uses a "double-nested-hash" to generate the final key. This makes the proof techniques [14] of proving standard FO-KEMs with implicit rejection invalid in the QROM. Recently, Grubbs et al. [10] and Xagawa [25] pointed out that the *concrete* IND-CCA security of Kyber is an open question. In this paper, we answer the open question and develop a novel approach to overcome the difficulties in the security proof. We prove that Kyber is IND-CCA secure in the QROM if the underlying encryption scheme is IND-CPA secure. Our result provides a solid quantum security guarantee for the post-quantum cryptography standard of NIST competition, Kyber algorithm.

Acknowledgments. We thank the anonymous Inscrypt 2022 reviewers for their valuable comments and suggestions. This work was supported by the National Natural Science Foundation of China (Grant Nos. 61972391, 62272455).

References

1. Abdalla, M., Bellare, M., Neven, G.: Robust encryption. In: Micciancio, D. (ed.) TCC 2010. LNCS, vol. 5978, pp. 480–497. Springer, Heidelberg (2010). https://doi.org/10.1007/978-3-642-11799-2_28
2. Ambainis, A., Hamburg, M., Unruh, D.: Quantum security proofs using semi-classical oracles. IACR Cryptology ePrint Archive, vol. 2018, p. 904 (2018). https://eprint.iacr.org/2018/904
3. Bellare, M., Rogaway, P.: Random oracles are practical: a paradigm for designing efficient protocols. In: CCS'93, Fairfax, Virginia, USA, November 1993, pp. 62–73 (1993). https://doi.org/10.1145/168588.168596
4. Bindel, N., Hamburg, M., Hövelmanns, K., Hülsing, A., Persichetti, E.: Tighter proofs of CCA security in the quantum random oracle model. In: Hofheinz, D., Rosen, A. (eds.) TCC 2019. LNCS, vol. 11892, pp. 61–90. Springer, Cham (2019). https://doi.org/10.1007/978-3-030-36033-7_3
5. Boneh, D., Dagdelen, Ö., Fischlin, M., Lehmann, A., Schaffner, C., Zhandry, M.: Random oracles in a quantum world. In: Lee, D.H., Wang, X. (eds.) ASIACRYPT 2011. LNCS, vol. 7073, pp. 41–69. Springer, Heidelberg (2011). https://doi.org/10.1007/978-3-642-25385-0_3
6. Duman, J., Hövelmanns, K., Kiltz, E., Lyubashevsky, V., Seiler, G.: Faster lattice-based kems via a generic fujisaki-okamoto transform using prefix hashing. In: Kim, Y., Kim, J., Vigna, G., Shi, E. (eds.) CCS'21, pp. 2722–2737. ACM (2021). https://doi.org/10.1145/3460120.3484819
7. Fujisaki, E., Okamoto, T.: Secure integration of asymmetric and symmetric encryption schemes. In: Wiener, M. (ed.) CRYPTO 1999. LNCS, vol. 1666, pp. 537–554. Springer, Heidelberg (1999). https://doi.org/10.1007/3-540-48405-1_34
8. Fujisaki, E., Okamoto, T.: Secure integration of asymmetric and symmetric encryption schemes. J. Cryptol. **26**(1), 80–101 (2011). https://doi.org/10.1007/s00145-011-9114-1

9. Grover, L.K.: A fast quantum mechanical algorithm for database search. In: Miller, G.L. (ed.) The 28th Annual ACM Symposium on the Theory of Computing, pp. 212–219. ACM (1996). https://doi.org/10.1145/237814.237866
10. Grubbs, P., Maram, V., Paterson, K.G.: Anonymous, robust post-quantum public key encryption. In: Dunkelman, O., Dziembowski, S. (eds.) EUROCRYPT 2022. LNCS, vol. 13277. Springer, Cham (2022). https://doi.org/10.1007/978-3-031-07082-2_15
11. Hofheinz, D., Hövelmanns, K., Kiltz, E.: A modular analysis of the fujisaki-okamoto transformation. In: Kalai, Y., Reyzin, L. (eds.) TCC 2017. LNCS, vol. 10677, pp. 341–371. Springer, Cham (2017). https://doi.org/10.1007/978-3-319-70500-2_12
12. Hosoyamada, A., Iwata, T.: 4-round Luby-rackoff construction is a qPRP. In: Galbraith, S.D., Moriai, S. (eds.) ASIACRYPT 2019. LNCS, vol. 11921, pp. 145–174. Springer, Cham (2019). https://doi.org/10.1007/978-3-030-34578-5_6
13. Hövelmanns, K., Kiltz, E., Schäge, S., Unruh, D.: Generic authenticated key exchange in the quantum random oracle model. In: Kiayias, A., Kohlweiss, M., Wallden, P., Zikas, V. (eds.) PKC 2020. LNCS, vol. 12111, pp. 389–422. Springer, Cham (2020). https://doi.org/10.1007/978-3-030-45388-6_14
14. Jiang, H., Zhang, Z., Chen, L., Wang, H., Ma, Z.: IND-CCA-secure key encapsulation mechanism in the quantum random oracle model, revisited. In: Shacham, H., Boldyreva, A. (eds.) CRYPTO 2018. LNCS, vol. 10993, pp. 96–125. Springer, Cham (2018). https://doi.org/10.1007/978-3-319-96878-0_4
15. Jiang, H., Zhang, Z., Ma, Z.: Tighter security proofs for generic key encapsulation mechanism in the quantum random oracle model. In: Ding, J., Steinwandt, R. (eds.) PQCrypto 2019. LNCS, vol. 11505, pp. 227–248. Springer, Cham (2019). https://doi.org/10.1007/978-3-030-25510-7_13
16. Kuchta, V., Sakzad, A., Stehlé, D., Steinfeld, R., Sun, S.-F.: Measure-rewind-measure: tighter quantum random oracle model proofs for one-way to hiding and CCA security. In: Canteaut, A., Ishai, Y. (eds.) EUROCRYPT 2020. LNCS, vol. 12107, pp. 703–728. Springer, Cham (2020). https://doi.org/10.1007/978-3-030-45727-3_24
17. NIST: National institute for standards and technology. In: Post quantum crypto project (2021). https://csrc.nist.gov/Projects/Post-Quantum-Cryptography
18. Rackoff, C., Simon, D.R.: Non-interactive zero-knowledge proof of knowledge and chosen ciphertext attack. In: Feigenbaum, J. (ed.) CRYPTO 1991. LNCS, vol. 576, pp. 433–444. Springer, Heidelberg (1992). https://doi.org/10.1007/3-540-46766-1_35
19. Saito, T., Xagawa, K., Yamakawa, T.: Tightly-secure key-encapsulation mechanism in the quantum random oracle model. In: Nielsen, J.B., Rijmen, V. (eds.) EUROCRYPT 2018. LNCS, vol. 10822, pp. 520–551. Springer, Cham (2018). https://doi.org/10.1007/978-3-319-78372-7_17
20. Schwabe, P., et al.: Crystals-kyber. In: Technical report, National Institute of Standards and Technology, 2020 (2020). https://csrc.nist.gov/Projects/post-quantum-cryptography/selected-algorithms-2022
21. Shor, P.W.: Polynomial-time algorithms for prime factorization and discrete logarithms on a quantum computer. SIAM J. Comput. **26**(5), 1484–1509 (1997). https://doi.org/10.1137/S0097539795293172
22. Shoup, V.: Sequences of games: a tool for taming complexity in security proofs. IACR CRYPTOL. ePrint Arch, p. 332 (2004). http://eprint.iacr.org/2004/332
23. Targhi, E.E., Unruh, D.: Post-quantum security of the Fujisaki-Okamoto and OAEP transforms. In: Hirt, M., Smith, A. (eds.) TCC 2016. LNCS, vol. 9986, pp.

192–216. Springer, Heidelberg (2016). https://doi.org/10.1007/978-3-662-53644-5_8
24. Unruh, D.: Revocable quantum timed-release encryption. In: Nguyen, P.Q., Oswald, E. (eds.) EUROCRYPT 2014. LNCS, vol. 8441, pp. 129–146. Springer, Heidelberg (2014). https://doi.org/10.1007/978-3-642-55220-5_8
25. Xagawa, K.: Anonymity of NIST PQC round 3 KEMS. In: Dunkelman, O., Dziembowski, S. (eds.) EUROCRYPT 2022. LNCS, vol. 13277, pp. 551–581. Springer, Cham (2022). https://doi.org/10.1007/978-3-031-07082-2_20
26. Zhandry, M.: Secure identity-based encryption in the quantum random oracle model. In: Safavi-Naini, R., Canetti, R. (eds.) CRYPTO 2012. LNCS, vol. 7417, pp. 758–775. Springer, Heidelberg (2012). https://doi.org/10.1007/978-3-642-32009-5_44
27. Zhandry, M.: A note on the quantum collision and set equality problems. Quantum Inf. Comput. **15**, 557–567 (2015). https://doi.org/10.26421/QIC15.7-8-2
28. Zhandry, M.: How to record quantum queries, and applications to quantum indifferentiability. In: Boldyreva, A., Micciancio, D. (eds.) CRYPTO 2019. LNCS, vol. 11693, pp. 239–268. Springer, Cham (2019). https://doi.org/10.1007/978-3-030-26951-7_9

MPC

Practical Multi-party Private Set Intersection Cardinality and Intersection-Sum Under Arbitrary Collusion

You Chen[1], Ning Ding[1(✉)], Dawu Gu[1(✉)], and Yang Bian[2]

[1] School of Electronic Information and Electrical Engineering, Shanghai Jiao Tong University, 800 Dongchuan Road, Shanghai 200240, China
{chenyou99,dingning,dwgu}@sjtu.edu.cn

[2] Fudata Technology, Room 1003, T7, Lane 100, Pingjiaqiao Road, Shanghai 200126, China
douheng@fudata.cn

Abstract. Private set intersection cardinality (PSI-CA) and private intersection-sum with cardinality (PSI-CA-sum) are two primitives that enable data owners to learn the intersection cardinality of their data set, with the difference that PSI-CA-sum additionally outputs the sum of the associated integer values of all the data that belongs to the intersection (i.e., intersection-sum). In this paper, we investigate the practical constructions of these two primitives, focusing on the multi-party setting. To our knowledge, all existing multi-party PSI-CA (MPSI-CA) protocols are either impractical or vulnerable to arbitrary collusion (i.e., the adversary can corrupt any proper subset of all parties), and as for multi-party PSI-CA-sum (MPSI-CA-sum), there is even no formalization for this notion at present, not to mention secure constructions for it.

So in this paper, we first propose the first MPSI-CA protocol that achieves simultaneous practicality and security against arbitrary collusion (in the semi-honest adversary model). We also conduct implementation to verify its practicality (while the previous results under arbitrary collusion only present theoretical analysis of performance, lacking real implementation). Numeric results show that it only takes 12.805 s to finish the online computation by shifting expensive operations to an offline phase, even in the dishonest majority setting with 15 parties each holding 2^{16} data. Among all parties, the cost of clients is especially lower compared to that of the known results, which is only 0.3 s in finishing their tasks.

Second, we formalize the notion of MPSI-CA-sum and give the first realization which admits simultaneous practicality and security against arbitrary collusion as well. The computational complexity of it is roughly double that of our MPSI-CA protocol.

Besides the main results, we introduce the notions and provide efficient constructions of two new building blocks: multi-party secret-shared shuffle and oblivious zero-sum check, which may be of independent interest.

The original version of this chapter was revised: this chapter contained errors on page 8, 9, 10 & 11 in chapter 9 which is indicated in our final book. The correction to this chapter is available at https://doi.org/10.1007/978-3-031-26553-2_27

Y. Deng and M. Yung (Eds.): Inscrypt 2022, LNCS 13837, pp. 169–191, 2023.
https://doi.org/10.1007/978-3-031-26553-2_9

Keywords: Multi-party PSI-CA · Multi-party PSI-CA-sum · Secure multiparty computation

1 Introduction

Motivation. Private set intersection cardinality (PSI-CA) is a cryptographic primitive that enables multiple parties to learn the intersection cardinality of their private data sets without leaking other information beyond the intersection cardinality. PSI-CA can be applied to real-world applications like measuring advertisement conversion rates [10] and so on. Despite its broad usage, nevertheless, PSI-CA is still not sufficient for some applications where each data is associated with an integer value (e.g. payload), like measuring advertisement conversion rates when one person contributes multiple purchases [10]. Thus a variant of PSI-CA is proposed, known as private intersection-sum with cardinality (PSI-CA-sum) [10], which is specified to output the intersection cardinality, as well as the sum of associated payloads for all the elements that belong to the intersection (i.e., intersection-sum).

Besides measuring advertisement conversion rates, we come up with the following possible application of PSI-CA-sum. Consider a score-based voting scenario with multiple voters, where voter P_i can vote for any candidate $s \in \{0,1\}^*$ that he prefers, and the ballot of him is associated with a score for candidate s (s is the candidate's ID). If P_i does not vote for candidate s, then there is no need for him to give s a score. P_i's voting result is represented using a set $S_i = \{(s_{i,1}, v_i(s_{i,1})), ..., (s_{i,m}, v_i(s_{i,m})\}$ of size m, where $s_{i,k}, k \in [m]$ are the IDs of his chosen candidates and $v_i(s_{i,k})$ is his score of candidate $s_{i,k}$. Given the set $S_i, i \in [n]$ of n voters, the set of common candidates supported by all voters is denoted as set intersection IS. The total score of a common candidate s is $\sum_{i=1}^{n} v_i(s)$, which can be used to calculate the average score of every common candidate. In this problem setting, the required information consists of the intersection cardinality $|IS|$ and the sum of common candidates' scores Sum_{IS} (i.e., $Sum_{IS} = \sum_{i=1}^{n} \sum_{x \in IS} v_i(x)$), so that the average score of a common candidate is $Sum_{IS}/|IS|$. Here, PSI-CA-sum can be employed to securely obtain the average score without additional information leakage.

However, most existing PSI-CA protocols work in the two-party setting, while the results of multi-party PSI-CA (MPSI-CA) are either limited by massive computational overhead, or vulnerable to arbitrary collusion (i.e., the adversary can corrupt any proper subset of all parties [15]). Meanwhile, to the best of our knowledge, there has been no work for multi-party PSI-CA-sum (MPSI-CA-sum). Therefore, we will address the problems and aim at formalizing the notion of MPSI-CA-sum, proposing protocols for MPSI-CA and MPSI-CA-sum that can achieve simultaneous practicality and security against arbitrary collusion.

1.1 State of the Art of MPSI-CA

Although there have been some effective two-party PSI-CA schemes [5,7,13], only a small number of works can deal with the multi-party setting [1,2,11,17].

Existing constructions of PSI-CA protocols can be generally classified into three categories, depending on whether the protocol is based on circuits, public key operations, or oblivious transfer (OT) and its extensions, say oblivious programmable pseudorandom function (OPPRF). Previous MPSI-CA schemes secure against arbitrary collusion typically follow public-key-based paradigm, and their computational complexities are determined by the number of expensive public key operations. Kissner and Song [11] proposed the first MPSI-CA protocol in the semi-honest model. This protocol relies on polynomial evaluation and homomorphic encryption (HE), and the overall computational complexity of it is $O\left(n^2 m_{\max}^2\right)$, where n is the number of parties and m_{max} is the maximum set size. Debnath et al. [2] presented an MPSI-CA protocol based on inverse bloom filter (IBF) and HE. The protocols in [2,11] are both proven secure against arbitrary collusion. Despite their good properties in privacy preserving, it is impractical for resource-limited devices with large data sets to carry out these protocols due to the massive computational overhead.

To tackle with this problem, two practical schemes have been proposed. Chandran et al. [1] introduced a circuit-based generic multi-party computation protocol, which can be extended to realize MPSI-CA by modifying the circuit. However, this protocol is only proven secure with honest majority in semi-honest model. Besides, a concurrent work of [17] presented two OPPRF-based MPSI-CA protocols under the additional assumption that specific parties are non-colluding, which deviate from the well-known "threshold security". Although assuming the existence of some specific non-colluding parties can improve the performance, it is believed that the "threshold security" is closer to real life applications for the following reasons: (1) There may not always exist such well-established non-colluding parties to participate in the protocol; (2) The identities of corrupted parties may be kept secret to honest parties, so it is unrealistic to assume that specific parties are non-colluding and to appoint them to perform special tasks.

Therefore, how to design and implement a practical semi-honest secure MPSI-CA scheme under arbitrary collusion is still worth studying.

1.2 State of the Art of Two-Party PSI-CA-Sum

(Since there is no result of PSI-CA-sum in the multi-party setting) we sketch some known results on the two-party PSI-CA-sum [7,9,10]. Motivated by the business problem of online-to-offline advertisement conversions, Ion et al. [10] introduced the first two-party PSI-CA-sum protocol by applying the classic Diffie-Hellman style construction into this new scenario. The protocol then was further polished in [9] and developed into two new constructions, built on modern techniques like random OT, which nevertheless rely on expensive HE as a building block for aggregating intersection-sum. Garimella et al. [7] put forward a lightweight two-party PSI-CA protocol by adopting oblivious switching network and OT to successfully avoid the reliance on HE.

1.3 Our Contributions

In this paper we formalize the notion of MPSI-CA-sum and propose the first MPSI-CA protocol and MPSI-CA-sum protocol that can achieve simultaneous practicality and security against arbitrary collusion. Details are as follows.

MPSI-CA Under Arbitrary Collusion. Our MPSI-CA protocol admits the following properties and advantages.

- It is the first practical realization of MPSI-CA under arbitrary collusion to our knowledge, and we also conduct an implementation to verify its practicality (while the previous results under arbitrary collusion only present theoretical analysis of performance without real implementation).
- The cost of clients is especially lower than the existing schemes with the same security.
- Its computational efficiency is attributed to the element sharing technique and underlying lightweight primitives, which do not require any public key operations besides a set of base OTs.
- In our implementation, most of the expensive operations can be shifted to an offline phase to significantly reduce the running time of online computation. Numeric results show that even in the dishonest majority setting with 15 parties each holding 2^{16} data, it only takes 12.805 s to finish the online computation, which is about one fourth of the original running time.

Table 1 compares our MPSI-CA protocol with current MPSI-CA schemes with respect to security and computational complexity. On one hand, when compared to the existing practical schemes [1,17], our protocol is more secure, since the existing schemes are not resistant to arbitrary collusion (remark that our protocol is also of practicality which is incomparable to the schemes in [1,17] due to different running frameworks). On the other hand, when compared to the existing schemes secure against arbitrary collusion [2,11], our protocol is much more practical, since it adopts a set of base OTs and symmetric key operations to reduce the number of expensive public key operations.

Table 1. Comparison between MPSI-CA schemes

Comparison Between MPSI-CA Schemes		
MPSI-CA Schemes	Techniques	Security Model
[1]	OT+symmetric key operations	Honest majority
Server-aided [17]	OT+symmetric key operations	Two specific parties are non-colluding
Server-less [17]	OT+symmetric key operations	Three specific parties are non-colluding
[11]	HE	Arbitrary collusion
[2]	HE	Arbitrary collusion
Our Protocol 4.2	OT+symmetric key operations	Arbitrary collusion

Computational Complexities of MPSI-CA Schemes Under Arbitrary Collusion (Number of Public Key Operations)				
MPSI-CA Schemes	Primary Leader	Secondary Leader	Client	Total
[11]	/	/	$O(nm_{max}^2)$	$O(n^2m_{max}^2)$
[2]	$O(m_1)$	/	$O(km_{max})$	$O(knm_{max})$
Our Protocol 4.2	$O(t\kappa)$	$O(t\kappa)$	/	$O(t^2\kappa)$

MPSI-CA-sum Under Arbitrary Collusion. We formalize the notion of MPSI-CA-sum and propose the first MPSI-CA-sum protocol that achieves simultaneous practicality and security against arbitrary collusion. Its computational complexity is roughly double that of our MPSI-CA protocol. Compared with most two-party PSI-CA-sum schemes, our protocol avoids the usage of expensive HE in aggregating intersection-sum, thus greatly reducing the computational cost.

Additional Contributions. Besides the main contributions, we also introduce the new notions and efficient constructions of two new building blocks of our MPSI-CA and MPSI-CA-sum protocols: multi-party secret-shared shuffle and oblivious zero-sum check.

- Multi-party secret-shared shuffle helps multiple parties jointly shuffle the sum of their input data in an unknown permutation π and obtain additive secret shares of the result. It is an advancement of the multi-party Permute+Share [14] because it can hide π even when confronted with arbitrary collusion. Our construction is practical since its costly operations can be shifted to an offline phase.
- Oblivious zero-sum check is a primitive that can securely determine whether the sum of multiple parties' inputs is 0 without revealing anything else. Our construction of oblivious zero-sum check employs Beaver triples to reduce online computational overhead.

1.4 High-Level Description

In this part, we present a high-level overview of our MPSI-CA and MPSI-CA-sum protocols. Our protocols involve n parties, including $T = t + 1$ leaders $L_1, ..., L_T$ and $n - T$ clients $P_1, ..., P_{n-T}$, where t is the corruption threshold (t can be up to $n - 1$). In order to differentiate between leaders, leader L_1 is called the primary leader, and the rest of the leaders are called secondary leaders. Each party holds a private set with size m. The data set of the i-th leader L_i is $X_i, i \in [T]$, and that of the j-th client P_j is $S_j, j \in [n - T]$.

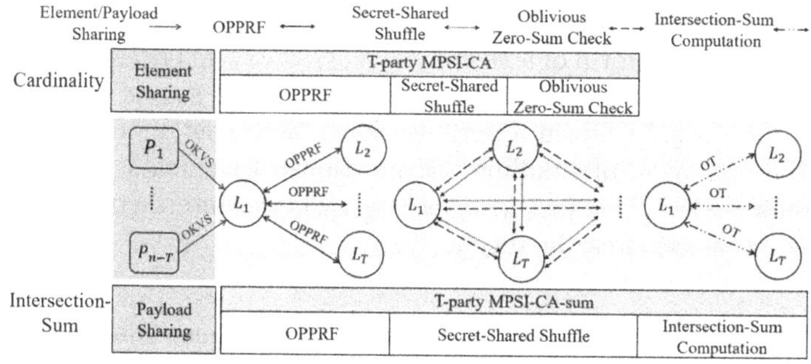

Fig. 1. The overview of our MPSI-CA and MPSI-CA-sum protocols

As shown in Fig. 1, in the setting of MPSI-CA, clients first share their encoded data sets to leaders through element sharing, so that the original n-party MPSI-CA problem can be reduced to T-party MPSI-CA of T leaders, where $T = t + 1$.

Then, primary leader L_1 invokes OPPRFs with all secondary leaders $L_i, i \in [2, T]$ on each element $x_{1,k} \in X_1$. If $x_{1,k}$ belongs to the intersection, then the sum of all leaders' outputs and L_1's element sharing on $x_{1,k}$ equals 0, which is denoted as t_k. After participating in T-party secret-shared shuffle, each leader L_i obtains a random additive share of shuffled set $\{t_{\pi(k)}\}_{k\in[m]}$, where the shuffle order π is kept secret to all parties. Finally, leaders perform oblivious zero-sum check to securely calculate the number of elements that satisfy $\gamma_k t_{\pi(k)} = 0$, where the random value γ_k is unknown to any leader. If $\gamma_k t_{\pi(k)} = 0$, then L_1 adds one to intersection cardinality, otherwise the value of $t_{\pi(k)}$ will not be revealed.

In the setting of MPSI-CA-sum, parties need to perform element sharing (payload sharing), OPPRF and secret-shared shuffle on both elements and their associated payloads. After running oblivious zero-sum check on elements, L_1 can obtain a binary vector $\vec{e}$, which indicates the shuffled indices of elements that belong to the intersection. As for those elements, L_1 invokes OTs with all other leaders using choice string $\vec{e}$ to aggregate the sum of their associated payloads.

1.5 Organizations

Section 2 introduces the preliminaries. In Sect. 3, the notions and constructions of two new building blocks are presented. We propose the practical MPSI-CA and MPSI-CA-sum protocols in Sect. 4 and 5, respectively. The computational complexity of MPSI-CA-sum protocol is roughly double that of our MPSI-CA protocol, therefore we focus on implementing and analyzing the performance of our MPSI-CA protocol in Sect. 6.

2 Preliminaries

Notations. We use κ and λ to denote the computational and statistical security parameters. The set $\{1, 2, \dots, x\}$ is denoted as $[x]$ (thus $\sum_{i=1}^{T}$ is equivalent to $\sum_{i\in[T]}$). If the elements of a set $\{x_1, \dots, x_m\}$ are arranged in order, then this set can be expressed in the form of a vector $\vec{x} = (x_1, \dots, x_m)$. Therefore, $\vec{x} + \vec{y}$ means performing addition on corresponding elements in two sets x and y to obtain $\{x_1 + y_1, \dots, x_m + y_m\}$. Given a permutation π and a set $\vec{x} = (x_1, \dots, x_m)$, we represent the operation of shuffling the positions of elements in this set using permutation π with $\pi(\vec{x}) = (x_{\pi(1)}, \dots, x_{\pi(m)})$. The set intersection is denoted as IS, and the intersection cardinality is $|IS|$.

Security Definitions. The parties corrupted by a semi-honest adversary $\mathcal{A}$ will faithfully follow the protocol, while attempting to learn about other parties' inputs. Moreover, those corrupted parties will collude with each other. By "non-colluding parties", we mean that at most one of those parties can be corrupted by $\mathcal{A}$; while "arbitrary collusion" means that $\mathcal{A}$ may corrupt any proper subset of all parties, which is the most challenging case. The coalition of corrupted parties is denoted as $\mathcal{C}$. Let Π be a protocol and f be a deterministic functionality.

We define the following distributions of random variables and use the real-ideal simulation paradigm to formally define the semi-honest security of Π [6]. In this paper, we prove the security of all the protocols based on Definition 1.

- $\text{Real}_{\Pi}(\kappa, \mathcal{C}; x_1, \ldots, x_n)$: Each party P_i runs the protocol honestly using private input x_i and security parameter κ. Output $\{V_i \mid i \in \mathcal{C}\}, (y_1, \ldots, y_n)$, where V_i and y_i denote the final view and output of party P_i.
- $\text{Ideal}_{f,\mathcal{S}}(\kappa, \mathcal{C}; x_1, \ldots, x_n)$: Compute $(y_1, \ldots, y_n) \leftarrow f(x_1, \ldots, x_n)$. Output $\mathcal{S}(\mathcal{C}, \{(x_i, y_i) \mid i \in \mathcal{C}\}), (y_1, \ldots, y_n)$, where $\mathcal{S}$ is a probabilistic polynomial time (PPT) simulator.

Definition 1. *[6] We say that protocol Π securely computes f in the presence of a semi-honest adversary, if there exists a PPT simulator $\mathcal{S}$ such that for $\mathcal{C}$ and all inputs $x_1, \ldots, x_n$, the distributions* $\text{Real}_{\Pi}(\kappa, \mathcal{C}; x_1, \ldots, x_n)$ *and* $\text{Ideal}_{f,\mathcal{S}}(\kappa, \mathcal{C}; x_1, \ldots, x_n)$ *are computationally indistinguishable in κ.*

Oblivious Key-Value Store (OKVS). The definitions of key-value store (KVS) and OKVS were first given in [8]. An OKVS is a generalized data structure that stores the mapping from keys to their values, and it can be instantiated with polynomial, garbled bloom filter (GBF) [4] and so on.

Definition 2. *[8] A KVS is parameterized by a set $\mathcal{K}$ of keys and a set $\mathcal{V}$ of values, and consists of two algorithms: (1)* Encode *takes as input a set of (k_i, v_i) key-value pairs and outputs an object S (or, with statistically small probability, an error indicator $\perp$); (2)* Decode *takes as input the object S, a key k and outputs a value v. A KVS is correct if, for all $A \subseteq \mathcal{K} \times \mathcal{V}$ with distinct keys:*
$(k, v) \in A$ *and* $\perp \neq S \leftarrow \text{Encode}(A) \Longrightarrow \text{Decode}(S, k) = v$
A KVS is an OKVS if, for any two sets $\mathcal{K}^0, \mathcal{K}^1$ of m distinct keys, the output of $\mathcal{R}(\mathcal{K}^1)$ is computationally indistinguishable to that of $\mathcal{R}(\mathcal{K}^0)$, where:

$\mathcal{R}(\mathcal{K} = (k_1, \ldots, k_m))$
1. For $i \in [m]$: choose uniform $v_i \leftarrow \mathcal{V}$; 2. Return $\text{Encode}(\{(k_1, v_1), \ldots (k_m, v_m)\})$.

Oblivious Programmable Pseudorandom Function (OPPRF, $\mathcal{F}_{\text{opprf}}^{F,m,u}$). The formal definition of OPPRF was first given in [12], which also provided a semi-honest secure realization. An OPPRF takes as input the queries $(q_1, \ldots, q_u)$ from receiver and a programmed set $\mathcal{P} = \{\langle x_i, y_i \rangle\}_{i \in [m]}$ from sender. Then, the receiver's OPPRF outputs satisfy the following property: if the query $q_j = x_i \in \mathcal{P}$, then its OPPRF output equals y_i, otherwise the output is pseudorandom. Generally speaking, receiver's OPPRF outputs are fixed at some selected points.

Functionality 1: OPPRF $\mathcal{F}_{\mathbf{opprf}}^{F,m,u}$
Parameters: A pseudorandom function (PRF) F; upper bound m on the number of points to be programmed, and bound u on the number of queries.
Behaviour: On input $\mathcal{P}$ from the sender and u queries $(q_1,\ldots,q_u)$ from the receiver, where $\mathcal{P}=\{\langle x_1,y_1\rangle,\ldots,\langle x_m,y_m\rangle\}$ is a set of points:
•Run KeyGen $((1^\kappa,\mathcal{P}))\rightarrow(k,hint)$ and give $(k,hint)$ to the sender, where k is the PRF key and $hint$ stores the information of the set $\mathcal{P}$.
•Give $(hint, F(k,hint,q_1),\ldots,F(k,hint,q_u))$ to the receiver.

Multi-party Pemute+Share ($\mathcal{F}_{\text{mPS}}^{T,m,i}$). $\mathcal{F}_{\text{mPS}}^{T,m,i}$ takes as input the vectors $\vec{x_j}$ from all parties $P_j, j\in[T]$ and a permutation π_i from sender P_i, then outputs additive shares of shuffled sum $\pi_i(\sum_{j=1}^{T}\vec{x_j})$ to every party. The functionality of $\mathcal{F}_{\text{mPS}}^{T,m,i}$ was given in [14], along with an realization of $\mathcal{F}_{\text{mPS}}^{T,m,i}$ based on OT and switching network, which is proven secure against a semi-honest adversary which may corrupt up to $T-1$ parties. $\mathcal{F}_{\text{mPS}}^{T,m,i}$ is an essential building block of our multi-party secret-shared shuffle primitive proposed in Sect. 3.

Functionality 2: Multi-party Pemute+Share $\mathcal{F}_{\mathbf{mPS}}^{T,m,i}$
Parameters: T parties $P_j, j\in[T]$; the dimension of vector is m; the sender is P_i.
Behaviour: On input permutation π_i and vector $\vec{x_i}=(x_{i,1},\ldots,x_{i,m})$ from sender P_i, and input vector $\vec{x_j}=(x_{j,1},\ldots,x_{j,m})$ from each receiver $P_j, j\in[T]\backslash\{i\}$:
•Give shuffled share $\vec{x}'_j=(x'_{j,1},\ldots,x'_{j,m})$ to all parties $P_j, j\in[T]$, where

$$\sum_{j\in[T]} x'_{j,k}=\sum_{j\in[T]} x_{j,\pi_i(k)}, k\in[m], \text{namely} \sum_{j\in[T]}\vec{x}'_j=\pi_i(\sum_{j\in[T]}\vec{x_j}).$$

3 Two New Primitives and Constructions

In this section, we present the notions and constructions of two new building blocks for our MPSI-CA and MPSI-CA-sum protocols, namely the multi-party secret-shared shuffle and oblivious zero-sum check.

3.1 Multi-party Secret-Shared Shuffle

We formalize the new notion of multi-party secret-shared shuffle, and give a realization of it. It can help parties shuffle the sum of their inputs in an unknown permutation order π, and obtain additive shares of the result.

Functionality ($\mathcal{F}_{\text{mSS}}^{T,m}$). $\mathcal{F}_{\text{mSS}}^{T,m}$ can be regarded as an advancement of the original $\mathcal{F}_{\text{mPS}}^{T,m,i}$, since it ensures that none of the parties gets to know the permutation π. $\mathcal{F}_{\text{mSS}}^{T,m}$ receives permutations π_i and vectors $\vec{x_i}$ from all parties $P_i, i\in[T]$, and gives them the additive shares of shuffled sum of inputs $\pi(\sum_{i\in[T]}\vec{x_i})$ as outputs.

Functionality 3: Multi-party Secret-Shared Shuffle $\mathcal{F}_{\text{mSS}}^{T,m}$
Parameters: T parties $P_i, i \in [T]$; the dimension of vector is m.
Behaviour: On input permutation π_i and vector $\vec{x}_i = (x_{i,1}, \ldots, x_{i,m})$ from all parties $P_i, i \in [T]$:

- Give each party $P_i, i \in [T]$ an additive share $\vec{x}'_i = (x'_{i,1}, \ldots, x'_{i,m})$, where $\sum_{i\in[T]} x'_{i,k} = \sum_{i\in[T]} x_{i,\pi(k)}, k \in [m]$, namely $\sum_{i\in[T]} \vec{x}'_i = \pi(\sum_{i\in[T]} \vec{x}_i)$. Here, permutation $\pi = \pi_T \circ \ldots \pi_2 \circ \pi_1$ is the composition of T permutations.

Protocol. We propose a protocol to realize $\mathcal{F}_{\text{mSS}}^{T,m}$ as follows. This protocol invokes T rounds of T-party Permute+Share [14] in an iterative way. During the i-th round, P_i acts as the sender who provides permutation π_i and vector $\vec{x}_i^{(i-1)}$, others act as receivers with vectors $\vec{x}_j^{(i-1)}, j \in [T]\backslash\{i\}$ (Here, $\vec{x}_j^{(0)} = \vec{x}_j, j \in [T]$). Then, P_j receives an output $\vec{x}_j'^{(i-1)}$, where $\sum_{j\in[T]} \vec{x}_j'^{(i-1)} = \pi_i(\sum_{j\in[T]} \vec{x}_j^{(i-1)})$, and treats $\vec{x}_j'^{(i-1)}$ as his input vector during the next round. Finally, each party P_j obtains an additive share $\vec{x}_j'^{(T-1)}$ of the shuffled sum $\pi(\sum_{j\in[T]} \vec{x}_j^{(0)})$ with permutation $\pi = \pi_T \circ \cdots \circ \pi_1$. If we adopt the Permute+Share scheme proposed in [14], then our realization of $\mathcal{F}_{\text{mSS}}^{T,m}$ requires $O(T(T-1)m \log m)$ OTs in total.

Correctness. By the definition of $\mathcal{F}_{\text{mPS}}^{T,m,i}$, the sum of all parties' outputs equals $\pi_T(\sum_{j\in[T]} \vec{x}_j^{(T-1)}) = \pi_T(\pi_{T-1}(\sum_{j\in[T]} \vec{x}_j^{(T-2)})) = \cdots = \pi(\sum_{j\in[T]} \vec{x}_j^{(0)})$.

Theorem 1. *This protocol securely computes $\mathcal{F}_{\text{mSS}}^{T,m}$ under a semi-honest adversary which may corrupt up to $T-1$ parties, if $\mathcal{F}_{\text{mPS}}^{T,m}$ is secure against semi-honest adversaries.*

Proof. The views of corrupted parties (i.e., $\mathcal{C}$) consist of their inputs and views during T invocations of $\mathcal{F}_{\text{mPS}}^{T,m}$. As for the first round, simulator $\mathcal{S}$ chooses random vectors as corrupted parties' outputs by the definition of $\mathcal{F}_{\text{mPS}}^{T,m}$, then treats them as inputs into the next round. By following the above strategies for each round of T-party Permuta+Share and leveraging the simulator of subroutine functionality $\mathcal{F}_{\text{mPS}}^{T,m}$ in turn, the view of $\mathcal{C}$ during $\mathcal{F}_{\text{mSS}}^{T,m}$ can be ideally simulated by $\mathcal{S}$.

3.2 Oblivious Zero-Sum Check

We present the notion and construction of the new primitive of oblivious zero-sum check. It can help parties securely determine whether the sum of their inputs is 0 without revealing anything else. It can be employed in the last step of MPSI-CA to obtain the intersection cardinality of shuffled data.

Functionality ($\mathcal{F}_{\text{OZK}}^{T,m}$). $\mathcal{F}_{\text{OZK}}^{T,m}$ receives input additive shares $\langle\vec{x}\rangle_i, i \in [T]$ from all parties, then outputs a binary vector $\vec{e} = (e_1, \ldots, e_m)$ to P_1. If the k-th position of the sum of input vectors $\vec{x} = \sum_{i=1}^{T} \langle\vec{x}\rangle_i$ equals 0, then $e_k = 1$; otherwise $e_k = 0$ (i.e., $e_k = 1$ only when $x_k = 0$). That is to say, $\mathcal{F}_{\text{OZK}}^{T,m}$ ensures that P_1 can not get to know the value of x_k unless it is equal to 0.

Functionality 4: Oblivious Zero-Sum Check $\mathcal{F}_{\mathrm{OZK}}^{T,m}$
Parameters: The number of parties is T; the dimension of input vector is m.
Behaviour: On input vector $\langle\vec{x}\rangle_i$ from $P_i, i \in [T]$, where $\sum_{i=1}^{T}\langle\vec{x}\rangle_i = \vec{x} = (x_1, \ldots, x_m)$:
- Give a binary vector $\vec{e} = (e_1, \ldots, e_m)$ to P_1, where $e_k = 1$ if the k-th position of $\vec{x}$ equals 0 (i.e., $x_k = 0$), otherwise $e_k = 0$.

Protocol. As presented in Protocol 3.2, $\mathcal{F}_{\mathrm{OZK}}^{T,m}$ can be realized using secret sharing mechanism. Since each party holds an additive share of secret $\vec{x}$, parties can obtain their additive shares of the product $\vec{\gamma} \cdot \vec{x}$ using Beaver multiplication triples, where $\vec{\gamma}$ is a "negotiated" random value and notation $\cdot$ denotes component-wise multiplication of two vectors. $\vec{\gamma}$ is kept secret to everyone, since each party P_i only knows an additive share $\langle\vec{\gamma}\rangle_i$ of $\vec{\gamma}$. If $x_k = 0$, it is obvious that the k-th position of $\vec{\gamma} \cdot \vec{x}$ equals 0 (i.e., $\gamma_k x_k = 0$); if $x_k \neq 0$, P_1 can not infer anything about x_k from $\gamma_k x_k$ due to the random value γ_k.

Parties need to interact with each other in order to obtain their additive shares of the product $\vec{\gamma} \cdot \vec{x}$. We note that $\vec{\gamma} \cdot \vec{x} = \sum_{i,j\in[T]}\langle\vec{\gamma}\rangle_i\langle\vec{x}\rangle_j$ can be divided into $\sum_{i\in[T]}\langle\vec{\gamma}\rangle_i\langle\vec{x}\rangle_i$ and $(T^2 - T)/2$ components $\langle\vec{\gamma}\rangle_i\langle\vec{x}\rangle_j + \langle\vec{\gamma}\rangle_j\langle\vec{x}\rangle_i$, where $i < j \in [T]$. For each component $\langle\vec{\gamma}\rangle_i\langle\vec{x}\rangle_j + \langle\vec{\gamma}\rangle_j\langle\vec{x}\rangle_i$, it is feasible for P_i and P_j to securely obtain their additive shares $sh_0^{i,j}$ and $sh_1^{i,j}$ using Beaver triples by following Protocol 3.2. The online pairwise share-based multiplication will be greatly accelerated by consuming the Beaver triples, which have already been prepared in the setup stage. Finally, P_i sends the sum of $\langle\vec{\gamma}\rangle_i\langle\vec{x}\rangle_i$ and his $T-1$ shares of $\sum_{j\in[T]\setminus\{i\}}(\langle\vec{\gamma}\rangle_i\langle\vec{x}\rangle_j + \langle\vec{\gamma}\rangle_j\langle\vec{x}\rangle_i)$ to P_1. So that P_1 can reconstruct $\vec{\gamma} \cdot \vec{x}$. If the k-th position of $\vec{\gamma} \cdot \vec{x}$ equals 0, P_1 sets e_k to 1, otherwise $e_k = 0$.

Correctness. It can be verified that $sh_0^{i,j} + sh_1^{i,j} = \langle\vec{\gamma}\rangle_i\langle\vec{x}\rangle_j + \langle\vec{\gamma}\rangle_j\langle\vec{x}\rangle_i$ based on the property of Beaver triples. Therefore, the sum of all parties' shares equals $\sum_{i\in[T]}\langle\vec{\gamma}\rangle_i\langle\vec{x}\rangle_i + \sum_{1\le i<j\le T}(\langle\vec{\gamma}\rangle_i\langle\vec{x}\rangle_j + \langle\vec{\gamma}\rangle_j\langle\vec{x}\rangle_i) = \vec{\gamma} \cdot \vec{x}$.

Theorem 2. *Protocol 3.2 securely computes* $\mathcal{F}_{\mathrm{OZK}}^{T,m}$ *under a semi-honest adversary which may corrupt up to* $T - 1$ *parties.*

Proof. In the trivial case that $P_1 \notin \mathcal{C}$, the views of corrupted parties $\mathcal{C}$ can be simulated by substituting all shares with random vectors. If $P_1 \in \mathcal{C}$, for those positions where $e_k = 0$, all generated and received shares of randomized $\gamma_k x_k$ are indistinguishable from uniformly random values; for positions where $e_k = 1$, shares can be simulated by choosing random values that sum to zero.

Protocol 3.2: Oblivious Zero-Sum Check
Parameters: The number of parties is T; the dimension of input vector is m.
Initialization: For every two parties P_i and P_j, $i, j \in [T], i < j$, they prepare enough Beaver triples $\langle\vec{a}\rangle_0$,$\langle\vec{b}\rangle_0$,$\langle\vec{c}\rangle_0$ and $\langle\vec{a}\rangle_1$,$\langle\vec{b}\rangle_1$,$\langle\vec{c}\rangle_1$ for online share-based multiplication, where $\vec{c} = \vec{a} \cdot \vec{b}$, $\vec{c} = \langle\vec{c}\rangle_0 + \langle\vec{c}\rangle_1$, $\vec{a} = \langle\vec{a}\rangle_0 + \langle\vec{a}\rangle_1$ and $\vec{b} = \langle\vec{b}\rangle_0 + \langle\vec{b}\rangle_1$. Note that P_i holds $\langle\vec{a}\rangle_0$,$\langle\vec{b}\rangle_0$,$\langle\vec{c}\rangle_0$, and P_j holds $\langle\vec{a}\rangle_1$,$\langle\vec{b}\rangle_1$,$\langle\vec{c}\rangle_1$. $\vec{a}$ and $\vec{b}$ are kept secret to both parties.
Input: Additive share $\langle\vec{x}\rangle_i$ from party P_i, where $\vec{x} = (x_1, \ldots, x_m) = \sum_{i=1}^{T} \langle\vec{x}\rangle_i$.
Output: P_1 outputs a binary vector $\vec{e} = (e_1, \ldots, e_m)$: if $x_k = 0$, then $e_k = 1$, otherwise $e_k = 0$.
Protocol:

1 For $i \in [T]$, each party P_i randomizes his share $\langle\vec{x}\rangle_i$ as follows:
  (a) **(Negotiating Randomness)** P_i locally generates a random vector $\langle\vec{\gamma}\rangle_i$, so that the random vector $\vec{\gamma} = \sum_{i=1}^{T} \langle\vec{\gamma}\rangle_i$ is unknown to everyone.
  (b) **(Pairwise Multiplication)** P_i computes his additive share of $\vec{\gamma} \cdot \vec{x} = \sum_{u,l \in [T]} \langle\vec{\gamma}\rangle_u \langle\vec{x}\rangle_l$. For each component $\langle\vec{\gamma}\rangle_i \langle\vec{x}\rangle_j + \langle\vec{\gamma}\rangle_j \langle\vec{x}\rangle_i, j \in [T] \backslash \{i\}$, P_i needs to interact with P_j as follows:
  - P_i locally computes $\langle\vec{\alpha}\rangle_0 = \langle\vec{x}\rangle_i - \langle\vec{a}\rangle_0$ and $\langle\vec{\beta}\rangle_0 = \langle\vec{\gamma}\rangle_i - \langle\vec{b}\rangle_0$, then announces them to P_j; P_j also locally computes $\langle\vec{\alpha}\rangle_1 = \langle\vec{x}\rangle_j - \langle\vec{a}\rangle_1$ and $\langle\vec{\beta}\rangle_1 = \langle\vec{\gamma}\rangle_j - \langle\vec{b}\rangle_1$, then announces them to P_i.
  - P_i reconstructs $\vec{\alpha}$ and $\vec{\beta}$, computes his additive share of $\langle\vec{\gamma}\rangle_i \langle\vec{x}\rangle_j + \langle\vec{\gamma}\rangle_j \langle\vec{x}\rangle_i$ as $sh_0^{i,j} = \langle\vec{c}\rangle_0 + \vec{\alpha} \cdot \langle\vec{b}\rangle_0 + \vec{\beta} \cdot \langle\vec{a}\rangle_0 + \vec{\alpha} \cdot \vec{\beta} - \langle\vec{\gamma}\rangle_i \langle\vec{x}\rangle_i$. P_j also obtains his additive share of $\langle\vec{\gamma}\rangle_i \langle\vec{x}\rangle_j + \langle\vec{\gamma}\rangle_j \langle\vec{x}\rangle_i$ as $sh_1^{i,j} = \langle\vec{c}\rangle_1 + \vec{\alpha} \cdot \langle\vec{b}\rangle_1 + \vec{\beta} \cdot \langle\vec{a}\rangle_1 + \vec{\alpha} \cdot \vec{\beta} - \langle\vec{\gamma}\rangle_j \langle\vec{x}\rangle_j$, where $sh_0^{i,j} + sh_1^{i,j} = \langle\vec{\gamma}\rangle_i \langle\vec{x}\rangle_j + \langle\vec{\gamma}\rangle_j \langle\vec{x}\rangle_i$.

2 **(Reconstruction)** Each $P_i, i \in [2, T]$ computes the sum of $\langle\vec{\gamma}\rangle_i \langle\vec{x}\rangle_i$ and all his shares of $\sum_{j=1, j \neq i}^{T} (\langle\vec{\gamma}\rangle_i \langle\vec{x}\rangle_j + \langle\vec{\gamma}\rangle_j \langle\vec{x}\rangle_i)$ (obtained in step 1(a)), and then sends the result to P_1, so that P_1 can reconstruct $\vec{\gamma} \cdot \vec{x}$. If the k-th position of $\vec{\gamma} \cdot \vec{x}$ equals 0, P_1 sets e_k to 1, otherwise $e_k = 0$.

4 MPSI-CA Protocol Under Arbitrary Collusion

In this section, we recall the functionality of MPSI-CA and propose a semi-honest secure MPSI-CA protocol under arbitrary collusion. First, we introduce a technique called element sharing to reduce the original n-party MPSI-CA to T-party MPSI-CA of T leaders. Then, a detailed description of our MPSI-CA protocol is presented.

Functionality ($\mathcal{F}_{\mathbf{MPSI-CA}}$). MPSI-CA allows n parties with m items to learn the intersection cardinality of their private sets without revealing anything else.

Functionality 5: MPSI-CA $\mathcal{F}_{\mathbf{MPSI\text{-}CA}}$
Parameters: T leaders $L_1, \ldots, L_T$; $n - T$ clients $P_1, \ldots, P_{n-T}$; the set size is m.
Behaviour: On input data sets X_i from all leaders $L_i, i \in [T]$, and data sets S_j from all clients $P_j, j \in [n - T]$:
- Give leader L_1 the intersection cardinality $|IS| = |(\bigcap_{i=1}^{T} X_i) \cap (\bigcap_{j=1}^{n-T} S_j)|$.

High-Level Description. The fundamental idea of our MPSI-CA protocol is to let all clients share their PRF-encoded data sets to T leaders $L_i, i \in [T]$, and then delegate leaders to complete the task of T-party PSI-CA. T is set to be $t+1$, otherwise the T-party MPSI-CA computation will be vulnerable to collusion attack in the worst case that all leaders are corrupted. Then, L_1 invokes OPPRFs with all secondary leaders. After that, all leaders treat their modified outputs $\vec{t_i}, i \in [T]$ as inputs to the following multi-party secret-shared shuffle and oblivious zero-sum check, so that L_1 can obtain the intersection cardinality.

4.1 Element Sharing

Considering that the overhead of MPSI-CA protocol tends to increase with the number of parties, it is a natural idea to delegate only a small number of parties to engage in expensive interactive procedures by sharing other parties' PRF-encoded data sets to them in the first step. This trick was first adopted by [15] and is called element sharing for short in this paper.

Sub-protocol 4.1: Element Sharing in MPSI-CA
Parameters: The number of parties is n, number of leaders is T; set size is m.
Input: $X_i = \{x_{i,1}, \dots, x_{i,m}\}$ from leader $L_i, i \in [T]$; $S_j = \{s_{j,1}, \dots, s_{j,m}\}$ from client $P_j, j \in [n-T]$.
Protocol:

1. **(Client)** For client $P_j, j \in [n-T]$,
   (a) He sends a random PRF key $K_{j,i}$ to each secondary leader $L_i, i \in [2, T]$.
   (b) For each element $s_{j,k} \in S_j, k \in [m]$, P_j computes the PRF-encoded value of $s_{i,j}$ as $\sum_{i=2}^{T} PRF(K_{j,i}, s_{j,k})$. Then, P_j encodes key-value pairs $\{(s_{j,k}, \sum_{i=2}^{T} PRF(K_{j,i}, s_{j,k}))\}_{k \in [m]}$ into an OKVS D_j and sends D_j to primary leader L_1.
2. **(Primary Leader)** For each element $x_{1,k} \in X_1, k \in [m]$, L_1 decodes all received $D_j, j \in [n-T]$ on $x_{1,k}$ to get $D_j(x_{1,k})$, and then obtains his element sharing of $x_{1,k}$ as $q_1(x_{1,k}) = -\sum_{j=1}^{n-T} D_j(x_{1,k})$.
3. **(Secondary Leader)** Each secondary leader $L_i, i \in [2, T]$ computes the PRF outputs of all his elements $x_{i,k} \in X_i, k \in [m]$ using $n-T$ received keys $K_{j,i}, j \in [n-T]$, then adds the $n-T$ PRF outputs of $x_{i,k}$ together to obtain his element sharing of $x_{i,k}$ as $q_i(x_{i,k}) = \sum_{j=1}^{n-T} PRF(K_{j,i}, x_{i,k})$.

The functionality $\mathcal{F}_{\text{ElemSh}}^{n,T,m}$ of element sharing is that: for an element x, if $x \in IS$, then each leader $L_i, i \in [T]$ holds a random additive share $q_i(x)$ of 0 corresponding to x. The detailed process is shown in Sub-protocol 4.1, its correctness is obvious because if $x \in IS$, then each PRF key $K_{i,j}$ is used twice by both client P_j and leader L_i on the same item x, so that the two PRF outputs cancel out each other and $\sum_{i=1}^{T} q_i(x) = 0$.

We show that Sub-protocol 4.1 can securely compute $\mathcal{F}_{\text{ElemSh}}^{n,T,m}$ under a semi-honest adversary which may corrupt up to t parties ($t < n$) by giving a sketch of how to simulate the views of corrupted parties in the ideal world. The ideal views of corrupted clients are easy to simulate since they receive no messages. For corrupted $L_i, i \in [2, T]$, his received PRF keys can be simulated using random values. For the corrupted L_1, the OKVS D_j (from an honest party P_j)

appears random to him, since all the values encoded in D_j are encrypted using P_j's $T-1$ PRF keys. Therefore, $\mathcal{S}$ can easily simulate the OKVS by generating an OKVS that encode m random key-value pairs, which is computationally indistinguishable from his real view by the obliviousness property of OKVS.

4.2 Detailed Description

Protocol 4.2: MPSI-CA Under Arbitrary Collusion
Parameters: The set size is m; the number of leaders is $T = t+1$; hash functions h_1, h_2, h_3; the number of bins is b.
Input: $X_i = \{x_{i,1}, \ldots, x_{i,m}\}$ from leader L_i; $S_j = \{s_{j,1}, \ldots, s_{j,m}\}$ from client P_j.
Protocol:

1. **(Element sharing)** Run Sub-protocol 4.1 ($\mathcal{F}^{n,T,m}_{\text{ElemSh}}$). For each element $x_{i,k} \in X_i$, leader L_i obtains his element sharing of $x_{i,k}$ as $q_i(x_{i,k})$.
2. **(T-party MPSI-CA)** Leaders $L_i, i \in [T]$ act as follows:
   (a) **(Bucketing)** L_1 does $Table_1 \leftarrow \text{CuckooHash}^b_{h_1,h_2,h_3}(X_1)$, $L_i, i \in [2,T]$ does $Table_i \leftarrow \text{SimpleHash}^b_{h_1,h_2,h_3}(X_i)$.
   (b) **(OPPRF)** L_1 invokes $\mathcal{F}^{F,3m,b}_{\text{opprf}}$ with every $L_i, i \in [2,T]$,
   - Sender L_i provides a programmed set $\mathcal{P} = \{\mathcal{P}_k\}_{k\in[b]}$, where subset $\mathcal{P}_k = \{\langle x, q_i(x) - t_{i,k}\rangle\}_{x\in Table_i[k]}$ stores key-value pairs for the k-th bin $Table_i[k]$, and $t_{i,k}$ is a random value.
   - Receiver L_1 provides b queries $\{Table_1[k]\}_{k\in[b]}$, and outputs $\vec{r_i} = (r_{i,1}, \ldots, r_{i,b})$, where $r_{i,k}$ is the OPPRF output on $Table_1[k]$.

   (c) For each bin $k \in [b]$, L_1 computes $t_{1,k} = q_1(Table_1[k]) + \sum_{i=2}^{T} r_{i,k}$.
   (d) **(T-party Shuffle)** All leaders $L_i, i \in [T]$ jointly invoke $\mathcal{F}^{T,b}_{\text{mSS}}$.
   - Each L_i inputs the vector $\vec{t_i} = (t_{i,1}, \ldots, t_{i,b})$ and a permutation π_i, then outputs an additive share $\vec{t_i'}$ of the shuffled sum $\pi(\vec{t})$ (i.e., $\sum_{i=1}^{T} \vec{t_i'} = \pi(\vec{t})$), where $\vec{t} = \sum_{i=1}^{T} \vec{t_i} = (t_1, \ldots, t_b)$ and $\pi = \pi_T \circ \cdots \circ \pi_1$.

   (e) **(OZK)** All leaders $L_i, i \in [T]$ engage in $\mathcal{F}^{T,b}_{\text{OZK}}$ to securely obtain the number of zeros in the b-dimensional vector $\sum_{i=1}^{T} \vec{t_i'}$.
   - Each leader $L_i, i \in [T]$ inputs his share $\vec{t_i'}$ (obtained in step 2(d)).
   - L_1 outputs a binary vector $\vec{e}$ indicating which positions of $\sum_{i=1}^{T} \vec{t_i'}$ equal 0. If the k-th position is 0, then $e_k = 1$, otherwise $e_k = 0$.

   L_1 outputs the number of 1s in $\vec{e}$ as the intersection cardinality $|IS|$.

As shown in Protocol 4.2, leader L_i utilizes the bucketing technique [12] to hash his elements into a hash table $Table_i$ with b bins using simple hashing (or cuckoo hashing when $i = 1$) with hash functions h_1, h_2, h_3. For cuckoo hash table $Table_1$, each element $x \in X_1$ will be inserted into only one bin, say $Table_1[h_u(x)] = x$ for some $u \in [3]$. Finally, each empty bin will be padded with a dummy element. As for the simple hash table $Table_i, i \in [2,T]$, each $x \in X_i$ will be inserted into three bins $Table_i[h_1(x)]$, $Table_i[h_2(x)]$ and $Table_i[h_3(x)]$. When the number of hash functions is 3, the stash size can be reduced to 0 by setting $b = 1.28m$ while achieving a hashing failure probability of 2^{-40} [16].

After invoking $\mathcal{F}^{F,3m,b}_{\text{opprf}}$ on b queries $Table_1[k], k \in [b]$, if $Table_1[k] \in IS$, then leaders hold additive shares of 0 (i.e., $t_k = \sum_{i\in[T]} t_{i,k} = 0$). In order to obtain the number of k that satisfies $t_k = 0$ without revealing the index k, leaders invoke $\mathcal{F}_{\text{mSS}}^{T,m}$ to obtain additive shares of shuffled $t_{\pi(k)}$, where π is unknown to anyone. Then they engage in $\mathcal{F}_{\text{OZK}}^{T,m}$ to securely aggregate and rerandomize the value of $t_{\pi(k)}$. By the definition of $\mathcal{F}_{\text{OZK}}^{T,m}$, the output $\gamma_k t_{\pi(k)}$ equals 0 only when $t_{\pi(k)} = 0$, therefore L_1 adds one to intersection cardinality $|IS|$.

Correctness. If element $Table_1[k] \in IS$, then from the property of element sharing and OPPRF, we have $\sum_{i\in[T]} q_i(Table_1[k]) = 0$ and $r_{i,k} = q_i(Table_1[k]) - t_{i,k}$, and thus $t_k = 0$. By the correctness of multi-party secret-shared shuffle and oblivious zero-sum check, L_1 successfully reconstructs $\gamma_k t_{\pi(k)} = 0$, and knows there exists one more element that belongs to IS. Otherwise, if $Table_1[k]$ does not belong to some X_i or S_j, then either the OPPRF output $r_{i,k}$ or the OKVS decode output $q_1(Table_1[k])$ is a random value. Therefore, the probability that there exists an element $Table_1[k] \notin IS$ s.t. $\gamma_k t_{\pi(k)} = 0$ is negligible.

Theorem 3. *Protocol 4.2 securely computes $\mathcal{F}_{\text{MPSI-CA}}$ under a semi-honest adversary which may corrupt up to t parties ($t < n$), if $\mathcal{F}_{\text{ElemSh}}^{n,T,m}$, $\mathcal{F}_{\text{opprf}}^{F,3m,b}$, $\mathcal{F}_{\text{mSS}}^{T,b}$ and $\mathcal{F}_{\text{OZK}}^{T,b}$ are secure against semi-honest adversaries.*

Proof. We divide the proof into three cases.
Case1: ($L_i \notin \mathcal{C}, i \in [T]$). In this trival case, the views of corrupted parties (i.e., $\mathcal{C}$) can be easily simulated since they receive no messages.
Case2: ($L_1 \notin \mathcal{C}$). In this case, $\mathcal{C}$ receives no final output. The views of corrupted clients can be simulated in a way similar to Case 1. As for those corrupted $L_i, i \in [2,T]$, simulator $\mathcal{S}$ first chooses a random key k to simulate L_i's output of $\mathcal{F}_{\text{opprf}}^{F,3m,b}$ since $\mathcal{C}$ only sees the senders' views. Then, by the definition of $\mathcal{F}_{\text{mSS}}^{T,b}$, $\mathcal{S}$ chooses a random vector $\vec{t_i'}$ as his output of $\mathcal{F}_{\text{mSS}}^{T,b}$, and leverages the simulators of subroutine functionalities $\mathcal{F}_{\text{ElemSh}}^{n,T,m}$, $\mathcal{F}_{\text{mSS}}^{T,b}$, $\mathcal{F}_{\text{opprf}}^{F,3m,b}$ and $\mathcal{F}_{\text{OZK}}^{T,b}$ to simulate the view of corrupted L_i. The view output by $\mathcal{S}$ is indistinguishable from $\mathcal{C}$'s real view, which is obtained by the underlying simulators' indistinguishability.
Case3: ($L_1 \in \mathcal{C}$). In this case, $\mathcal{C}$ receives $|IS|$ as final output. $\mathcal{S}$ can simulate $\mathcal{C}$'s view as follows. In step 2(b), it simulates L_1's OPPRF outputs $\vec{r_i}, i \in [2,T]$ using uniformly random values while ensuring that: if $L_i \in \mathcal{C}$, then $r_{i,k} = q_i(Table_1[k]) - t_{i,k}$ for every element $Table_1[k]$ that belongs to $X_1 \cap X_i$, otherwise $r_{i,k}$ and $t_{i,k}$ are independent; if $L_i \notin \mathcal{C}$, then L_1's $r_{i,k}$ is picked at random. In step 2(d), by the definition of $\mathcal{F}_{\text{mSS}}^{T,b}$, it simulates corrupted parties' outputs of $\mathcal{F}_{\text{mSS}}^{T,b}$ using uniformly random vectors. In step 2(e), it simulates L_1's output $\vec{e}$ of $\mathcal{F}_{\text{OZK}}^{T,b}$ by uniformly sampling a binary vector with $|IS|$ ones due to the uniformly distributed permutation adopted in $\mathcal{F}_{\text{mSS}}^{T,b}$. After that, $\mathcal{S}$ can leverage the simulators of subroutine functionalities $\mathcal{F}_{\text{ElemSh}}^{n,T,m}$, $\mathcal{F}_{\text{mSS}}^{T,b}$, $\mathcal{F}_{\text{opprf}}^{F,3m,b}$ and $\mathcal{F}_{\text{OZK}}^{T,b}$ to simulate the view of $\mathcal{C}$. The view output by $\mathcal{S}$ is indistinguishable from $\mathcal{C}$'s real view, which is obtained by the underlying simulators' indistinguishability.

5 MPSI-CA-Sum Protocol Under Arbitrary Collusion

In this section, we first introduce a technique called payload sharing to share the payloads of clients to leaders. Then we smoothly extend Protocol 4.2 to provide a practical MPSI-CA-sum protocol that is secure under arbitrary collusion.

Functionality ($\mathcal{F}_{\mathbf{MPSI-CA-sum}}$). To the best of our knowledge, we are the first to formalize the notion of MPSI-CA-sum. The functionality of MPSI-CA-sum is a generalization of the two-party PSI-CA-sum proposed in [10], with some modifications as to the number of parties that hold the payloads. The associated payload of element x is denoted as $v_i(x)$ at leader L_i's side and $w_j(x)$ at client P_j's side, respectively. The purpose of MPSI-CA-sum is to securely output the $|IS|$ and intersection-sum Sum_{IS}, which is shown in Functionality 6.

Functionality 6: MPSI-CA-sum $\mathcal{F}_{\mathrm{MPSI-CA-sum}}$
Parameters: T leaders $L_1, \ldots, L_T$; $n-T$ clients $P_1, \ldots, P_{n-T}$; the set size is m.
Behaviour: On input data set $X_i = \{x_{i,1}, \ldots, x_{i,m}\}$ and payload set $V_i = \{v_i(x_{i,1}), \ldots v_i(x_{i,m})\}$ from leader $L_i, i \in [T]$; data set $S_j = \{s_{j,1}, \ldots s_{j,m}\}$ and payload set $W_j = \{w_j(s_{j,1}), \ldots w_j(s_{j,m})\}$ from client $P_j, j \in [n-T]$:
• Give output $(|IS|, Sum_{IS})$ to leader L_1, where the intersection cardinality is $|IS| = |(\bigcap_{i=1}^{T} X_i) \cap (\bigcap_{j=1}^{n-T} S_j)|$, and the intersection-sum is $Sum_{IS} = \sum_{i=1}^{T} \sum_{x \in IS} v_i(x) + \sum_{j=1}^{n-T} \sum_{x \in IS} w_j(x)$.

High-Level Description. The procedures of our MPSI-CA-sum protocol are similar to those of Protocol 4.2. Parties perform payload sharing, OPPRF and shuffle on their associated payloads of each element, and run Protocol 4.2 in parallel to obtain a binary vector $\vec{e}$, which shows the shuffled indices of elements that belong to IS. As for those shuffled elements that belong to IS, L_1 invokes OTs with all other leaders using choice string $\vec{e}$, in order to aggregate the sum of their associated payloads (i.e., intersection-sum).

5.1 Payload Sharing

Sub-protocol 5.1: Payload Sharing in MPSI-CA-sum
Input: Set $X_i = \{x_{i,1}, \ldots, x_{i,m}\}$ and payload $V_i = \{v_i(x_{i,1}), \ldots v_i(x_{i,m})\}$ of leader L_i; Set $S_j = \{s_{j,1}, \ldots, s_{j,m}\}$ and payload $W_j = \{w_j(s_{j,1}), \ldots w_j(s_{j,m})\}$ of client P_j.
Protocol:

1. **(Client)** For client $P_j, j \in [n-T]$,
   (a) He sends a random PRF key $K'_{j,i}$ to each leader $L_i, i \in [T]$.
   (b) For each element $s_{j,k} \in S_j, k \in [m]$,
   - P_j computes its random mask $\sum_{i=1}^{T} PRF(K'_{j,i}, s_{j,k})$. So his masked payload of $s_{j,k}$ is $\widehat{w}_j(s_{j,k}) = w_j(s_{j,k}) + \sum_{i=1}^{T} PRF(K'_{j,i}, s_{j,k})$.
   - P_j performs (T,T) additive secret sharing on $\widehat{w}_j(s_{j,k})$, where the i-th share is denoted as $\widehat{w}_j^{(i)}(s_{j,k})$ (i.e., $\sum_{i=1}^{T} \widehat{w}_j^{(i)}(s_{j,k}) = \widehat{w}_j(s_{j,k})$).

   (c) For $i \in [T]$, P_j encodes the i-th set of key-value pairs $\{\langle s_{j,k}, \widehat{w}_j^{(i)}(s_{j,k})\rangle\}_{k\in[m]}$ into the i-th OKVS $DW_j^{(i)}$, and sends it to L_i.
2. **(Leader)** For each element $x_{i,k} \in X_i, k \in [m]$, $L_i, i \in [T]$ decodes all received $DW_j^{(i)}, j \in [n-T]$ on $x_{i,k}$ to obtain $DW_j^{(i)}(x_{i,k})$, and computes PRF outputs using all $n-T$ received PRF keys to obtain his payload sharing of $x_{i,k}$ as $\widehat{v}_i(x_{i,k}) = v_i(x_{i,k}) - \sum_{j=1}^{n-T} PRF(K'_{j,i}, x_{i,k}) + \sum_{j=1}^{n-T} DW_j^{(i)}(x_{i,k})$.

Sub-protocol 5.1 presents the steps of payload sharing, which aims to share the payloads of clients to T leaders. The functionality $\mathcal{F}_{\text{PaySh}}^{n,T,m}$ of payload sharing is that: for an element x, if $x \in IS$, then each leader $L_i, i \in [T]$ holds an additive share $\widehat{v}_i(x)$ of the sum of payloads corresponding to x (i.e., $\sum_{i=1}^{T} v_i(x) + \sum_{j=1}^{n-T} w_j(x)$). The procedures of payload sharing are similar to those of element sharing. The correctness of Sub-protocol 5.1 relies on the correctness of (T,T) additive secret sharing scheme and the property that the PRF output of input x with a fixed PRF key $K'_{i,j}$ is deterministic.

We show that Sub-protocol 5.1 can securely compute $\mathcal{F}_{\text{PaySh}}^{n,T,m}$ under a semi-honest adversary which may corrupt up to t parties ($t < n$) by briefly simulating the view of $\mathcal{C}$. The views of corrupted clients can be easily simulated since they receive no messages from the others. For corrupted $L_i, i \in [T]$, his received PRF key and OKVS from an honest party can be simulated using a random value and an OKVS that encodes m random key-value pairs, which are computationally indistinguishable from the real view by the obliviousness property of OKVS.

5.2 Detailed Description

The MPSI-CA-sum protocol under arbitrary collusion is presented in Protocol 5.2. Step 3 and step 4 can be executed in parallel by concatenating each element with its associated payload to avoid the cost of repeatedly invoking $\mathcal{F}_{\text{opprf}}^{F,3m,b}$ and $\mathcal{F}_{\text{mSS}}^{T,b}$. But note that there is no need to perform $\mathcal{F}_{\text{OZK}}^{T,b}$ on additive shares of the shuffled sum of payloads $\pi(\vec{g})$ (i.e., $\vec{g_i'}$, $i \in [T]$). The hash table $Table_i, i \in [T]$ used in step 4 is generated in step 3 by following step 2(a) of Protocol 4.2.

After invoking $\mathcal{F}_{\text{OZK}}^{T,b}$ during step 3, leader L_1 outputs a vector $\vec{e} = (e_1, \ldots, e_b)$. If $e_k = 1$, it means that the element in the $\pi^{-1}(k)$-th bin of $Table_1$ belongs to the intersection IS. Although L_1 can not infer the original index of this element (i.e., $\pi^{-1}(k)$) from k, he knows the existence of such an element. Therefore, he can still aggregate its associated payloads by invoking b OTs with each secondary leader $L_i, i \in [2, T]$. In the k-th OT with L_i, L_1 acts as a receiver with choice bit e_k, L_i acts as a sender who provides two strings $(mk_{i,k}, mk_{i,k} + g'_{i,k})$, where the random masks $mk_{i,k}, i \in [2, T], k \in [b]$ satisfy $\sum_{i=2}^{T} \sum_{k=1}^{b} mk_{i,k} = 0$. Those masks can be generated through additive secret sharing within secondary leaders. First, each secondary leader $L_i, i \in [2, T]$ locally generates a random vector $\vec{mk}'_i = (mk'_{i,1}, \ldots, mk'_{i,b})$ that ensures $\sum_{k=1}^{b} mk'_{i,k} = 0$. Then, $L_i, i \in [2, T]$ performs $(T-1, T-1)$ additive secret sharing on vector $\vec{mk}'_i$, and sends $T-2$ shares to other secondary leaders. Finally, $L_i, i \in [2, T]$ sums all his received shares and his local share together to obtain the new random mask vector $\vec{mk}_i$.

Correctness. Since the correctness of $|IS|$ (obtained in step 3) has already been proven in Section 4.2, here we only prove the correctness of Sum_{IS}. If $e_k = 1$, then we have $Table_1[\pi^{-1}(k)] \in IS$ and $\sum_{i=1}^{T} g'_{i,k} = \sum_{i=1}^{T} \widehat{v}_i(Table_1[\pi^{-1}(k)])$. After invoking OTs with each secondary leader, L_1 adds the $b(T-1)$ OT outputs together to obtain $\sum_{i=2}^{T} \sum_{k=1}^{b} mk_{i,k} + \sum_{e_k=1, k \in [b]} \sum_{i=2}^{T} g'_{i,k} = \sum_{e_k=1, k \in [b]} \sum_{i=2}^{T} g'_{i,k}$. Therefore, we have $\sum_{e_k=1, k \in [b]} \sum_{i=2}^{T} g'_{i,k} + \sum_{e_k=1, k \in [b]} g'_{1,k} = \sum_{x \in IS} \sum_{i=1}^{T} \widehat{v}_i(x) = \sum_{x \in IS} \left(\sum_{i=1}^{T} v_i(x) + \sum_{j=1}^{n-T} w_j(x) \right) = Sum_{IS}$.

Theorem 4. *Protocol 5.2 securely computes $\mathcal{F}_{\text{MPSI-CA-sum}}$ under a semi-honest adversary which may corrupt up to t parties ($t < n$), if $\mathcal{F}_{\text{ElemSh}}^{n,T,m}$, $\mathcal{F}_{\text{PaySh}}^{n,T,m}$, $\mathcal{F}_{\text{opprf}}^{F,3m,b}$, $\mathcal{F}_{\text{mSS}}^{T,b}$ and $\mathcal{F}_{\text{OZK}}^{T,b}$ and OT are secure against semi-honest adversaries.*

Proof. (sketch) The view of $\mathcal{C}$ during step 1–4 can be simulated by following similar strategies given in Theorem 3 of Protocol 4.2. Given $|IS|$, L_1's input choice string $\vec{e}$ can be simulated with a uniform binary vector with $|IS|$ ones. Since $\vec{mk}_i$ is a random mask, $\mathcal{S}$ can simulate corrupted L_i's OT inputs $(mk_{i,k}, mk_{i,k} + g'_{i,k})$ using random values, and simulate corrupted L_1's OT outputs from honest parties using random values, while ensuring that all $b(T-1)$ OT outputs sum to $Sum_{IS} - \sum_{e_k=1, k \in b} g'_{1,k}$. Then, $\mathcal{C}$'s view can be simulated by leveraging the simulator of underlying OT.

Protocol 5.2: MPSI-CA-sum Under Arbitrary Collusion

Parameters: The set size is m; the number of leaders is $T = t + 1$; hash functions h_1, h_2, h_3; the number of bins is b.

Input: Set $X_i = \{x_{i,1}, \ldots, x_{i,m}\}$ and payload $V_i = \{v_i(x_{i,1}), \ldots v_i(x_{i,m})\}$ of leader L_i; Set $S_j = \{s_{j,1}, \ldots, s_{j,m}\}$ and payload $W_j = \{w_j(s_{j,1}), \ldots w_j(s_{j,m})\}$ of client P_j.

Protocol:

1-2 **(Element/Payload Sharing)** Run Sub-protocol 4.1 ($\mathcal{F}^{n,T,m}_{\text{ElemSh}}$) and Sub-protocol 5.1 ($\mathcal{F}^{n,T,m}_{\text{PaySh}}$) in parallel. For each element $x_{i,k} \in X_i$, L_i obtains his element sharing and payload sharing of $x_{i,k}$ as $q_i(x_{i,k})$ and $\widehat{v}_i(x_{i,k})$.

3 **(T-party PSI-CA)** Run step 2 of Protocol 4.2, then L_1 will obtain a binary vector $\vec{e}$, where the number of 1s in $\vec{e}$ equals the intersection cardinality $|IS|$.

4 **(T-party MPSI-CA-sum)**
  (a) In step 3, each leader L_i has already obtained his hash table $Table_i$, so there is no need to repeat the bucketing step here.
  (b) **(OPPRF)** L_1 invokes $\mathcal{F}^{F,3m,b}_{\text{opprf}}$ with every $L_i, i \in [2, T]$,
    - Sender L_i provides a programmed set $\mathcal{P} = \{\mathcal{P}_k\}_{k \in [b]}$, where subset $\mathcal{P}_k = \{\langle x, \widehat{v}_i(x) - g_{i,k} \rangle\}_{x \in Table_i[k]}$ stores key-value pairs for the k-th bin $Table_i[k]$, and $g_{i,k}$ is a random value, $k \in [b]$.
    - Receiver L_1 provides b queries $\{Table_1[k]\}_{k \in [b]}$, and outputs $\vec{p_i} = (p_{i,1}, \ldots, p_{i,b})$, where $p_{i,k}$ is the OPPRF output on $Table_1[k]$,$k \in [b]$.
  (c) For each bin $k \in [b]$, L_1 computes $g_{1,k} = \widehat{v}_1(Table_1[k]) + \sum_{i=2}^{T} p_{i,k}$.
  (d) **(T-party Shuffle)** All leaders $L_i, i \in [T]$ jointly invoke $\mathcal{F}^{T,b}_{\text{mSS}}$.
    - Each L_i inputs the permutation π_i (adopted in step 3) and a vector $\vec{g_i} = (g_{i,1}, \ldots, g_{i,b})$, then outputs an additive share $\vec{g_i'}$ of the shuffled sum $\pi(\vec{g}) = \pi\left(\sum_{i=1}^{T} \vec{g_i}\right)$, where $\sum_{i=1}^{T} \vec{g_i'} = \pi(\vec{g})$ and $\pi = \pi_T \circ \cdots \circ \pi_1$.

5 **(Intersection-sum Computation)**
  (a) L_1 locally computes $\sum_{e_k=1, k \in [b]} g'_{1,k}$.
  (b) $L_2, \ldots, L_T$ jointly generate $T - 1$ random mask vectors $\vec{mk_i} = (mk_{i,1}, \ldots, mk_{i,b}), i \in [2, T]$, which satisfy that $\sum_{i=2}^{T} \sum_{k=1}^{b} mk_{i,k} = 0$.
  (c) For $i \in [2, T]$, L_1 invokes OTs with each secondary leader L_i.
    - Sender L_i inputs a set of strings $\{(mk_{i,k}, mk_{i,k} + g'_{i,k})\}_{k \in [b]}$.
    - Receiver L_1 inputs the choice string $\vec{e}$ and obtains b outputs. If $e_k = 0$, then the k-th output is $mk_{i,k}$, otherwise the k-th output is $mk_{i,k} + g'_{i,k}$.

6 L_1 adds $\sum_{e_k=1, k \in [b]} g'_{1,k}$ and all $b(T-1)$ OT outputs (received in step 5) together to obtain the intersection-sum Sum_{IS}.

6 Experimental Evaluation

Since the operations of computing intersection-sum is similar to those of computing intersection cardinality, the computational complexity of our MPSI-CA-sum protocol is roughly double that of our MPSI-CA protocol. So in this section, we only focus on evaluating the performance of our MPSI-CA protocol.

Parameters and Settings. We set statistical security parameter $\lambda = 40$ and computational security parameter $\kappa = 128$. We run our experiments on a laptop with an Intel i7-12700H 2.30 GHz CPU, 28 GB RAM, and Ubuntu-20.04 system in LAN setting. We instantiate the OPPRF using the realization provided in [12]. In the setup stage, it takes every two parties about 32 s to generate 2^{18} Beaver triples [3]. Each party adopts separated threads to communicate with others to ensure parallelism. Besides, we divide our protocol into offline and online phases in the experiment. The offline phase consists of all base OT operations in secret-shared shuffle, which can be carried out in advance because they are independent of the input sets. The online phase consists of all the remaining operations: element sharing, OPPRF, secret-shared shuffle (without base OT) and oblivious zero-sum check (without Beaver triples generation).

Running Time and Communication Cost of MPSI-CA (Protocol 4.2**).** Table 2 shows the running time of our MPSI-CA protocol in both online and offline phases, as well as its communication cost, which includes both sent and received messages.

We present the performance of clients and primary leader under three different corruption conditions, namely when $t = 1, n/2$ and $n - 1$. Assuming $t = 1$, it takes our MPSI-CA protocol only 27.174 s to compute the multi-party intersection cardinality of 15 parties, each with a large set size of 2^{18}. In the honest majority situation where $t = n/2$, the running time of leaders increases with the number of parties participating in multi-party secret-shared shuffle, and thus the running time is linear in t. When $n = 15$ and $m = 2^{12}$, the total running time is about 4.576 s with the online phase taking only 0.926 s. In the most challenging dishonest majority setting where $t = n - 1$, parties are not allowed to share their sets to leaders for fear of collusion attack, therefore, the number of leaders has to be n. However, since most of the expensive operations of multi-party secret-shared shuffle can be shifted to an offline phase, the total online running time can be reduced to only one fourth of the original time.

With respect to the communication performance of different parties, the cost of client is nearly independent of n and t. Whereas the cost of primary leader not only depends on n, but is also linear in the number of leaders $T = t + 1$. Concretely, when the set size is large (i.e., $m = 2^{18}$), our protocol takes roughly 7KB communication cost per item at each leader's side when $n = 5, t = 4$, which includes both sent and received messages. This cost increases to about 25 KB per item in the most challeging case that $n = 15$, $t = 14$ and $m = 2^{18}$.

Running Time of Different Steps in Protocol 4.2**.** Table 2 lists the running time of different steps in Protocol 4.2 when $t = n - 2$. As shown in the table, the two steps OPPRF and shuffle take a large percentage of the total running time. When n grows, the change in the running time of OPPRF is slight since each party adopts separated threads to communicate with others to ensure parallelism. In the case that $m = 2^{16}$, $n = 15$ and $t = 13$, it only takes 7.881 s to finish the online task of MPSI-CA computation with this simple optimization.

Table 2. The total running time, total communication cost, and the running time of different steps in our MPSI-CA protocol (Protocol 4.2).

n	t	Roles	Total Running Time (Seconds)				Total Communication Cost (MB)			
			$m = 2^{12}$	$m = 2^{14}$	$m = 2^{16}$	$m = 2^{18}$	$m = 2^{12}$	$m = 2^{14}$	$m = 2^{16}$	$m = 2^{18}$
5	1	Client	0.109	0.204	0.272	5.919	0.156265	0.625015	2.50002	10
		Leader	0.718	1.657	5.015	26.620	5.64464	25.4972	113.907	503.547
		Online	**0.467**	**1.354**	**4.433**	**24.110**				
	2	Client	0.110	0.221	2.77	5.921	0.156281	0.625031	2.50003	10
		Leader	1.022	2.339	6.867	36.352	10.6642	48.4943	217.814	967.094
		Online	**0.543**	**1.542**	**5.067**	**26.894**				
	4	Leader	2.650	4.025	12.165	52.312	20.7034	94.4886	425.628	1894.19
		Online	**0.670**	**1.789**	**6.289**	**31.236**				
10	1	Client	0.122	0.224	0.293	5.96	0.156265	0.625015	2.50002	10
		Leader	0.723	1.668	5.126	26.871	6.42595	28.6222	126.407	553.547
		Online	**0.497**	**1.360**	**4.567**	**24.516**				
	5	Client	0.111	2.37	0.309	5.994	0.156326	0.625076	2.50008	10.0001
		Leader	3.302	5.284	15.264	72.882	26.5044	120.611	542.036	2407.74
		Online	**0.844**	**1.890**	**5.733**	**32.764**				
	9	Leader	7.531	10.796	30.254	150.109	46.5828	212.599	957.664	4261.92
		Online	**1.004**	**2.690**	**10.415**	**58.485**				
15	1	Client	0.128	0.245	0.310	5.978	0.156265	0.625015	2.50002	10
		Leader	0.726	1.676	5.177	27.174	7.20725	31.7473	138.907	603.547
		Online	**0.505**	**1.383**	**4.598**	**25.115**				
	7	Client	0.111	0.239	0.349	6.183	0.156357	0.625107	2.50011	10.0001
		Leader	4.576	7.766	21.536	107.927	37.3249	169.73	762.35	3384.83
		Online	**0.926**	**2.257**	**5.955**	**36.913**				
	14	Leader	13.955	22.676	63.061	365.722	72.4621	313.97	1489.7	6629.66
		Online	**1.477**	**4.503**	**12.805**	**95.228**				

Running Time of Different Steps (Seconds)									
Steps	$n = 5, t = 3$			$n = 10, t = 8$			$n = 15, t = 13$		
	2^{12}	2^{14}	2^{16}	2^{12}	2^{14}	2^{16}	2^{12}	2^{14}	2^{16}
Element Sharing	0.119	0.250	0.319	0.109	0.237	0.341	0.103	0.263	0.337
OPPRF	0.473	1.261	5.113	0.566	1.407	4.697	0.942	1.821	5.691
Shuffle (Offline)	1.296	1.432	3.723	4.689	7.467	19.278	10.964	17.459	47.680
Shuffle (Online)	0.024	0.069	0.219	0.041	0.177	0.704	0.065	0.279	1.189
Oblivious Zero-Sum Check	0.006	0.009	0.017	0.013	0.021	0.036	0.019	0.034	0.065
Total	**1.938**	**3.062**	**9.560**	**5.485**	**9.425**	**25.368**	**12.269**	**20.115**	**55.561**
Online	**0.642**	**1.630**	**5.837**	**0.796**	**1.958**	**6.090**	**1.305**	**2.656**	**7.881**

Comparison with Other Works. There are only two MPSI-CA schemes [2,11] secure against arbitrary collusion in the semi-honest adversary model, but they only give theoretic analysis of performance without experimental results. Table 3 compares the performance of them and our MPSI-CA protocol (Protocol 4.2) in terms of computational and communication complexities.

As shown in Table 3, [2,11] both rely on a large number of expensive public key operations, which is linear in the maximal set size m_{max} or even m_{max}^2. Therefore, it is impractical for resource-limited devices with large data sets to carry out these protocols due to the massive computational overhead. Moreover, the efficiency of those schemes remains to be improved in the unbalanced data setting (i.e., the minimal set size $m_{min} \ll m_{max}$), or when the number of corrupted parties t only accounts for a small percentage of n.

By adopting lightweight primitives which do not require any public key operations besides a set of base OTs, the number of public key operations in our MPSI-CA protocols is independent of set size, which is significantly lower than that of [2,11]. At the same time, clients only need to send their PRF-encoded data to leaders instead of participating in expensive cryptographic interactive protocols for themselves, so that the total computational complexity can be significantly reduced especially when t/n is small. Besides, all the OTs required in multi-party secret-shared shuffle can be carried out in an offline phase, thus further decreasing the online computational complexity of our MPSI-CA protocol.

With respect to communication and round complexities, [2,11] both involve $O(n)$ rounds due to the operation of passing on randomized ciphertexts to the next party in a circle. Whereas we only need to perform T-party shuffle within $T = t+1$ leaders, and the round complexity is $O(t)$. Although utilizing expensive HE can save the communication cost during the stage of multi-party shuffle in [2], we reckon that the gap between [2] and our MPSI-CA scheme can be narrowed in an unbalanced setting, for we can designate the party with the smallest data set to be leader L_1 to ensure that $m_1 \ll m < m_{max}$. In this case, the additional communication overhead brought by multi-party secret-shared shuffle and oblivious zero-sum check can be reduced, so that the communication performance of our MPSI-CA scheme is comparable to that of [2].

Table 3. The computational and communication complexities of MPSI-CA schemes, where m is the average set size, m_{max} is the largest set size and m_1 is L_1's set size; k is the ratio of OKVS size to its encoded set size m. In our Protocol 4.2, most of the public key operations can be shifted to the offline phase.

Computational Complexity (Number of Public Key Operations)				
MPSI-CA Scheme	Primary Leader	Secondary Leader	Client	Total
[11]	/	/	$O(nm_{max}^2)$	$O(n^2m_{max}^2)$
[2]	$O(m_1)$	/	$O(km_{max})$	$O(knm_{max})$
Our Protocol 4.2	$O(t\kappa)$	$O(t\kappa)$	/	$O(t^2\kappa)$
Computational Complexity (Number of Symmetric Key Operations)				
MPSI-CA Scheme	Primary Leader	Secondary Leader	Client	Total
Our Protocol 4.2	$O(tm_1\log(m_1))$	$O((n-t)m + tm_1\log(m_1))$	$O(tm)$	$O((n-t)tm + t^2m_1\log(m_1))$
Communication Complexity (Bits)				
MPSI-CA Scheme	Primary Leader	Secondary Leader	Client	Total
[11]	/	/	$O(nm_{max})$	$O(n^2m_{max})$
[2]	$O(m_1)$	/	$O(km_{max})$	$O(knm_{max})$
Our Protocol 4.2	$O(tm_1\log(m_1))$	$O(km + tm_1\log(m_1))$	$O(km)$	$O(k(n-1)m + t^2m_1\log(m_1))$

Acknowledgement. We are very grateful to the reviewers for their valuable comments. This work was supported in part by the National Key Research and Development Project 2020YFA0712300.

References

1. Chandran, N., Dasgupta, N., Gupta, D., Obbattu, S.L.B., Sekar, S., Shah, A.: Efficient linear multiparty psi and extensions to circuit/quorum PSI. In: Proceedings of the 2021 ACM SIGSAC Conference on Computer and Communications Security, pp. 1182–1204 (2021)
2. Debnath, S.K., Stănică, P., Kundu, N., Choudhury, T.: Secure and efficient multiparty private set intersection cardinality. Adv. Math. Commun. **15**(2), 365 (2021)
3. Demmler, D., Schneider, T., Zohner, M.: Aby-a framework for efficient mixed-protocol secure two-party computation. In: NDSS (2015)
4. Dong, C., Chen, L., Wen, Z.: When private set intersection meets big data: an efficient and scalable protocol
5. Egert, R., Fischlin, M., Gens, D., Jacob, S., Senker, M., Tillmanns, J.: Privately computing set-union and set-intersection cardinality via bloom filters. In: Foo, E., Stebila, D. (eds.) ACISP 2015. LNCS, vol. 9144, pp. 413–430. Springer, Cham (2015). https://doi.org/10.1007/978-3-319-19962-7_24
6. Evans, D., Kolesnikov, V., Rosulek, M., et al.: A pragmatic introduction to secure multi-party computation. Found. Trends® Priv. Secur. **2**(2–3), 70–246 (2018)
7. Garimella, G., Mohassel, P., Rosulek, M., Sadeghian, S., Singh, J.: Private set operations from oblivious switching. In: Garay, J.A. (ed.) PKC 2021. LNCS, vol. 12711, pp. 591–617. Springer, Cham (2021). https://doi.org/10.1007/978-3-030-75248-4_21
8. Garimella, G., Pinkas, B., Rosulek, M., Trieu, N., Yanai, A.: Oblivious key-value stores and amplification for private set intersection. In: Malkin, T., Peikert, C. (eds.) CRYPTO 2021. LNCS, vol. 12826, pp. 395–425. Springer, Cham (2021). https://doi.org/10.1007/978-3-030-84245-1_14
9. Ion, M., et al.: On deploying secure computing: private intersection-sum-with-cardinality. In: 2020 IEEE European Symposium on Security and Privacy (EuroS&P), pp. 370–389. IEEE (2020)
10. Ion, M., et al.: Private intersection-sum protocol with applications to attributing aggregate ad conversions. Cryptology ePrint Archive (2017)
11. Kissner, L., Song, D.: Private and threshold set-intersection. Carnegie-mellon univ pittsburgh pa dept of computer science. Technical report (2004)
12. Kolesnikov, V., Matania, N., Pinkas, B., Rosulek, M., Trieu, N.: Practical multiparty private set intersection from symmetric-key techniques. In: Proceedings of the 2017 ACM SIGSAC Conference on Computer and Communications Security, pp. 1257–1272 (2017)
13. Lv, S., et al.: Unbalanced private set intersection cardinality protocol with low communication cost. Futur. Gener. Comput. Syst. **102**, 1054–1061 (2020)
14. Mohassel, P., Sadeghian, S.: How to hide circuits in MPC an efficient framework for private function evaluation. In: Johansson, T., Nguyen, P.Q. (eds.) EUROCRYPT 2013. LNCS, vol. 7881, pp. 557–574. Springer, Heidelberg (2013). https://doi.org/10.1007/978-3-642-38348-9_33

15. Nevo, O., Trieu, N., Yanai, A.: Simple, fast malicious multiparty private set intersection. In: Proceedings of the 2021 ACM SIGSAC Conference on Computer and Communications Security, pp. 1151–1165 (2021)
16. Pinkas, B., Schneider, T., Zohner, M.: Scalable private set intersection based on OT extension. ACM Trans. Priv. Secur. (TOPS) **21**(2), 1–35 (2018)
17. Trieu, N., Yanai, A., Gao, J.: Multiparty private set intersection cardinality and its applications. Cryptology ePrint Archive (2022)

Amortizing Division and Exponentiation

Cong Zhang[1,2], Shuaishuai Li[1,2], and Dongdai Lin[1,2](✉)

[1] State Key Laboratory of Information Security, Institute of Information Engineering, Chinese Academy of Sciences, Beijing 100093, China
{zhangcong,lishuaishuai,ddlin}@iie.ac.cn

[2] School of Cyber Security, University of Chinese Academy of Sciences, Beijing 100049, China

Abstract. Multiparty computation (MPC) has developed rapidly in the past three decades. The research on general MPC only considers addition and multiplication in a circuit because they are Turing-complete. However, when we consider other arithmetic operations, such as division and exponentiation, the customed protocols are often more efficient. In this work, we optimize the overhead of computing division and exponentiation. Our main idea is to use vector oblivious linear-function evaluation (VOLE) to generate correlation multiplication triples and use these triples to compute correlation multiplication in division and exponentiation protocols. Our method can reduce the cost of a single division to strictly no more than 2 multiplications. In the batch setting, we reduce the cost of n correlation division to almost the same as that of one division. In addition, we use the same method to reduce the cost of n correlation private exponentiation by about 33%.

Keywords: MPC · Division · Exponentiation

1 Introduction

Multiparty computation (MPC) allows a set of parties to jointly compute a function over their inputs while keeping them private. The feasibility of MPC was demonstrated in the 1980s, where it was shown that any probabilistic polynomial-time functionality can be securely computed [24,43]. In the last decade, MPC has developed from a largely theoretical field to a practical one where many applications have been developed on top of it [19,22]. This is mostly due to the rise of compilers which translate high-level code to secure branching, additions and multiplications on secret data [7,18,29,35,45].

However, in many cases such as privacy-preserving data-mining/statistical learning [8,12,33,34] and distributed generation of cryptographic keys [16], the desired functionality f involves mostly arithmetic operations such as addition, multiplication, division, and exponentiation over the integers and/or the finite fields. More efficient protocols for these basic operations can result in an more efficient protocol for f.

Y. Deng and M. Yung (Eds.): Inscrypt 2022, LNCS 13837, pp. 192–210, 2023.
https://doi.org/10.1007/978-3-031-26553-2_10

In this work, we focus on reducing the amortized cost of secure division and distributed exponentiation over a finite field. Secure division means that the parties have shares of a and b and want to compute the share of $a \cdot b^{-1}$ over a finite field. There are three cases in secure distributed exponentiation: *public base* (the base is public and the exponent is secret shared), *public exponent* (the base is secret shared and the exponent is public) and *private exponentiation* (both the base and the exponent are secret shared). Our focus is private exponentiation, that is, the parties have shares of a and b and want to compute the share of b^a. As we have mentioned, the goal of this paper is to reduce the cost of division and distributed exponentiation. We achieve this goal in the multiple-execution setting, where the parties run many correlated division and exponentiation of the protocol. As we will see, this enables the parties to amortize the cost of the correlated randomness over many executions.

Related Work. As previously mentioned, almost all known general MPC protocols over arithmetic circuit (computation is over a finite field $\mathbb{F}_p$) [5,6,17,24,28] only support addition and multiplication. We remark that arithmetic circuits are Turing complete, and so any function can be represented in this form. However, designing special operation protocols for different operations will significantly improve the efficiency of the protocol. For example, to compute secure division in $\mathbb{F}_p$, a naive method is to first compute $b^{-1} := b^{p-2}$ by Fermat's little theorem, and then compute the multiplication of a and b^{-1}. This naive method need $p-1$ multiplication and can be reduced to $O(\log p)$ by square multiplication algorithm, which is very inefficient when p is large. Bar-Ilan and Beaver [3] proposed the first constant round inverse protocol, which only need one multiplication to compute b^{-1}, thus reducing the cost of division to just two secure multiplications. This seems to be the optimal method to compute division over the three decades.

Private exponentiation was first considered in [15] as an application of their bit-decomposition protocol. They use the number of multiplicative invocations to measure the efficiency of the protocol. The number of multiplications of their protocol is $O(l \log l)$, where l is the bit length of field element. Later, Ning and Xu [38,39] introduced several protocols aiming to remove the necessity of decomposing secret inputs into bit representations. They achieve this by using a series of constructions based on bitwise operations over some randomness. Their work achieves linear invocation of multiplication $O(l)$. Yu et al. [44] proposed two-party exponential protocols, which are based on homomorphic encryption (HE) and oblivious transfer (OT), respectively. Their HE-based protocol is inefficient due to the low efficiency of HE, and their OT-based protocol need to communicate $O(l^2)$ bits. Recently, Aly et al. [1] proposed a new private exponentiation protocol, which only needs to invoke constant number of multiplications, instead of depending on element length.

Our Contribution. Our main idea is to use vector oblivious linear evaluation (VOLE) to generate correlated randomness in a batched manner, and use these correlated randomness to reduce the overhead of division and exponential protocol. Our protocols are considered in semi-honest setting. We remark that our protocols can be made secure against malicious adversaries by standard but rather expensive techniques such as zero-knowledge proofs. The possibility of an efficient security-strengthening transformation is outside our scope. Our main contributions are as follows:

- We reduce the cost of single division from 2 independent multiplication invocations to 2 (more efficient) correlated multiplications.
- We reduce the cost of n correlation division to only more $\log n$ factors than one division.
- We reduce about 33% costs of n correlated private exponentiation.

2 Preliminaries

2.1 Notation

We use κ to denote the computational security parameters. We denote the additive sharing of a value x by $[x]$, that is, $[x] = (x_1, \ldots, x_n)$ s.t. $x_1 + \cdots + x_n = x$. For a bit string v we let v_i denote the i-th bit. We use $\mathbb{F}_{2^\sigma}$ to denote finite field composed of all σ-long bit strings. We say that a function f is negligible in κ if it vanishes faster than the inverse of any polynomial in κ, and write it as $f(\kappa) = \mathsf{negl}(\kappa)$. We use the abbreviation PPT to denote probabilistic polynomial-time. By $a \stackrel{R}{\leftarrow} A$, we denote that a is randomly selected from the set A. $a \leftarrow \mathsf{A}(x)$ denotes that a is the output of the randomized algorithm A on input x, and $a := b$ denotes that a is assigned by b.

2.2 Security Model

Motivated by building more efficient protocols for basic operations, we operate in the *semi-honest model*, where adversaries may try to learn as much information as possible from a given protocol execution but are not able to deviate from the protocol steps. This is in contrast to malicious adversaries which are able to deviate arbitrarily from the protocol. We remark that our protocols can be made secure against malicious adversaries by standard but rather expensive techniques such as zero-knowledge proofs. The possibility of an efficient security-strengthening transformation is outside our scope.

Semi-honest Security. We use the standard security definition for multiparty computation [13,23] in this work. In brief, an n-party protocol π is defined by n interactive PPT Turing machines $P_1, \ldots, P_n$, called parties. The parties hold the security parameter 1^κ as their joint input and each party P_i holds a private input x_i. The computation proceeds in rounds. In each round j of the protocol, each party sends a message to each of the other parties (and receives messages from all other parties). The number of rounds in the protocol is expressed as some function $r(\kappa)$ in the security parameter.

The view of a party in an execution of the protocol contains its private input, its random tape, and the messages it received throughout this execution.

The random variable $\mathsf{view}^{\pi}_{P_i}(\vec{x}, 1^{\kappa})$ describes the view of P_i when executing π on inputs $\vec{x} = (x_1, \ldots, x_n)$ (with security parameter κ). Here, x_i denotes the input of party P_i. The output of an execution of π on $\vec{x}$ is described by the random variable $\mathsf{Output}^{\pi}(\vec{x}, 1^{\kappa}) = (\mathsf{Output}^{\pi}_{P_1}(\vec{x}, 1^{\kappa}), \ldots, \mathsf{Output}^{\pi}_{P_n}(\vec{x}, 1^{\kappa}))$, where $\mathsf{Output}^{\pi}_{P}(\vec{x}, 1^{\kappa})$ is the output of party P in this execution, and is implicit in the view of P. Similarly, for a set of parties with indices $I \in [n]$, we denote by $\vec{x}_I$ the set of their inputs, by $\mathsf{view}^{\pi}_{I}(\vec{x}, 1^{\kappa})$ their joint view, and by $\mathsf{Output}^{\pi}_{I}(\vec{x}, 1^{\kappa})$ their joint output.

Definition 1. *A protocol* π *is said to securely compute functionality* $f : (\{0,1\}^*)^n \to (\{0,1\}^*)^n$ *in the semi-honest model if there exists a PPT simulator* Sim *such that for every* $I \subset [n], |I| < n$ *and every* $\vec{x} \in (\{0,1\}^*)^n$*, it holds that:*

$$\{(\mathsf{view}^{\pi}_{I}(\vec{x}, 1^{\kappa}), \mathsf{output}^{\pi}(\vec{x}, 1^{\kappa}))\} \approx_c \{(\mathsf{Sim}(I, \vec{x}_I, f_I(\vec{x}), 1^{\kappa}), f(\vec{x}))\}$$

2.3 Vector Oblivious Linear-Function Evaluation

Oblivious linear-function evaluation (OLE) can be viewed as a arithmetic generalization of oblivious transfer (OT). The OLE functionality allows a receiver to learn a secret linear combination of two field elements held by a sender. OLE is a common building block for secure computation of arithmetic circuits [20,26,36], analogously to the role of OT for boolean circuits [20,24,25,30].

A useful extension of OLE is vector OLE (VOLE), allowing the receiver to learn a linear combination of two *vectors* held by the sender. In several applications of OLE, one can replace a large number of instances of OLE by a small number of long instances of VOLE [2]. Many recent works on pseudorandom correlation generator (PCG) [9–11,14,40,42] has made it very efficient to generate a large number of VOLEs. As a result, to generate length l VOLE, the communication cost is only $O(\kappa \log l)$. The formal definition of $\mathcal{F}_{\mathsf{vole}}$ is given in Fig. 1.

Parameters: Sender $\mathcal{S}$, Receiver $\mathcal{R}$, a finite field $\mathbb{F}$, the length of vector l
Functionality:

- Wait for input $x \in \mathbb{F}$ from the receiver $\mathcal{R}$.
- Wait for input $\vec{a}, \vec{b} \in \mathbb{F}^l$ from the sender $\mathcal{S}$.
- Give $\vec{a}x + \vec{b} \in \mathbb{F}^l$ to the receiver $\mathcal{R}$.

Fig. 1. Vector oblivious linear-function evaluation functionality $\mathcal{F}_{\mathsf{vole}}$

2.4 Generating Random Shares and Coins

We define the ideal functionality $\mathcal{F}_{\mathsf{rand}}$ to generate an additive sharing of a random value unknown to the parties, and $\mathcal{F}_{\mathsf{coin}}$ to generate a random value to all parties. A formal description appears in Fig. 2 and Fig. 3.

Parameters: Party $P_i, i \in [n]$, a finite field $\mathbb{F}$
Functionality:

- Upon receiving request from the parties, the ideal functionality chooses a random $r \in \mathbb{F}$ and generates a sharing $[r] = (r_1, \ldots, r_n)$ under the constraint that $r_1 + \cdots + r_n = r$. Then, the functionality sends each party P_i its share r_i.

Fig. 2. Generating random shares functionality $\mathcal{F}_{\mathsf{rand}}$

Parameters: Party $P_i, i \in [n]$, a finite field $\mathbb{F}$
Functionality:

- Upon receiving request from the parties, the ideal functionality chooses a random $r \in \mathbb{F}$. Then, the functionality sends r to each party P_i.

Fig. 3. Generating random coins functionality $\mathcal{F}_{\mathsf{coin}}$

We note that the functionality $\mathcal{F}_{\mathsf{rand}}$ can be implemented trivially from that each party select a random value locally, with no communication. And a simple way to compute $\mathcal{F}_{\mathsf{coin}}$ is to use $\mathcal{F}_{\mathsf{rand}}$ to generate a random sharing and then open it. The open procedure can be implemented from that all parties send their shares of r to each other, resulting the communication is $O(n^2\kappa)$.

2.5 Secure Multiplication

We define the multiplication functionality $\mathcal{F}_{\mathsf{mult}}$ that receives shares of two values x, y as input and outputs shares of the product $z = xy$ in Fig. 4.

Parameters: Party $P_i, i \in [n]$, a finite field $\mathbb{F}$
Functionality:

- Upon receiving additive shares $[x], [y]$ from the parties, the ideal functionality reconstructs x, y and computes $z := xy$. Then, the functionality shares $[z] = (z_1, \ldots, z_n)$ and sends z_i to each party P_i.

Fig. 4. Secure multiplication functionality $\mathcal{F}_{\mathsf{mult}}$

This functionality is a basic operation in MPC, and there are many different methods to computes this functionality, e.g. OT, homomorphic encryption (HE). Our work considers to use preprocessing multiplication triple [4] (also called

Beaver triple) to compute this functionality, which is commonly used in many MPC protocols [6,17,21,27,28,31,32,37,41].

A multiplication triple is a triple of shares $([a],[b],[c])$ with the property that $c = ab$. Given shares of $[x],[y]$ and of $[a],[b],[c]$, to compute $[z] = [xy]$, the parties compute and open shares of $\sigma = x - a$ and $\rho = y - b$, these values reveal nothing about x and y since a, b are both random. Then all parties compute $[z] := \sigma[b] + \rho[a] + [c] + \sigma\rho$. The correctness can be easily verified by equation $z = xy = (x - a + a)(y - b + b) = \sigma\rho + \sigma b + \rho a + c$. The advantage of using multiplication triple is that most of the multiplication overhead can be put into the offline stage, which greatly improves the efficiency of the online stage.

To generate a multiplication triple, all distinct parties need to perform an instance of OLE, the total cost is $n(n-1)$ OLE. We note that the communication of single OLE instance is $O(\kappa)$. Since the cost of a multiplication is 2 openings and $n(n-1)$ OLE, the communication is $O(n^2\kappa)$.

2.6 Secure Inversion

In the secure inversion functionality $\mathcal{F}_{\mathsf{inver}}$, the parties input an additive share $[x]$ and want to compute the inversion sharing $[x^{-1}]$. The formal definition is described in Fig. 5.

Parameters: Party $P_i, i \in [n]$, a finite field $\mathbb{F}$
Functionality:

- Upon receiving additive shares $[x]$ from the parties, the ideal functionality reconstructs x and computes x^{-1} over $\mathbb{F}$. Then, the functionality shares $[x^{-1}]$ to the parties.

Fig. 5. Secure inversion functionality $\mathcal{F}_{\mathsf{inver}}$

Now we describe the inversion protocols of Bar-Ilan and Beaver [3], which only uses one multiplication. The parties first invoke $\mathcal{F}_{\mathsf{rand}}$ functionality to generate a random share $[r]$. Then the parties invoke the $\mathcal{F}_{\mathsf{mult}}$ functionality with inputs $[x]$ and $[r]$, and obtain $[xr]$. Now, all parties open the xr and compute $[x^{-1}] := (xr)^{-1}[r]$. The cost of this inversion protocol is 1 multiplication and 1 opening, and the communication is $O(n^2\kappa)$.

2.7 Unbounded Fan-In Multiplication

Bar-Ilan and Beaver [3] also proposed a technique called unbounded fan-in multiplication, which means we can do unbounded fan-in multiplication in constant rounds. The functionality $\mathcal{F}^{l}_{\mathsf{unbounded\text{-}mult}}$ is described in Fig. 6.

The protocol is as follows:

Parameters: Party $P_i, i \in [n]$, a finite field $\mathbb{F}$, the number of multiplication l
Functionality:

- Upon receiving additive shares $[x_1], \ldots, [x_l]$ from the parties, the ideal functionality reconstructs $x_1, \ldots, x_l$ and computes $x := \Pi_{i=1}^{l} x_i$ over $\mathbb{F}$. Then, the functionality shares $[x]$ to the parties.

Fig. 6. Unbounded fan-in multiplication functionality $\mathcal{F}^{l}_{\mathsf{unbounded\text{-}mult}}$

1. The parties invoke $\mathcal{F}_{\mathsf{rand}}$ to generate $l+1$ random shares $[r_0], [r_1], \ldots, [r_l]$.
2. The parties invoke $\mathcal{F}_{\mathsf{inver}}$ with inputs $[r_0], \ldots, [r_l]$ and obtain $[r_0^{-1}], \ldots, [r_l^{-1}]$.
3. For $i = 1, \ldots, l$, the parties invoke 2 $\mathcal{F}_{\mathsf{mult}}$ to compute $[d_i] := [r_{i-1}] \cdot [x_i] \cdot [r_i^{-1}]$. Then the parties open d_i to each other.
4. The parties invoke $\mathcal{F}_{\mathsf{mult}}$ with input $[r_0^{-1}]$ and $[r_l]$, and compute $[x] = \Pi_{i=1}^{l}[x_i] := \Pi_{i=1}^{l} d_i \cdot [r_0^{-1}] \cdot [r_l]$.

The correctness follows from $x = \Pi_{i=1}^{l} d_i \cdot r_0^{-1} \cdot r_l == \Pi_{i=1}^{l} r_{i-1} \cdot x_i \cdot r_i^{-1} \cdot r_0^{-1} \cdot r_l = \Pi_{i=1}^{l} x_i$. There are $l+1$ multiplications and $l+1$ openings in step 2, and there are $2l$ multiplications and l openings in step 3. Only 1 multiplication is used in step 4. The total cost is $3l+2$ multiplications and $2l+1$ openings. The communication is $O(n^2 \kappa l)$.

2.8 Public Base Exponentiation

In the public base exponentiation functionality $\mathcal{F}_{\mathsf{pbexp}}$, the parties input an additive share $[a]$, a public base b, and want to compute the share of $[b^a]$. The formal definition is described in Fig. 7.

Parameters: Party $P_i, i \in [n]$, a finite field $\mathbb{F}$
Functionality:

- Upon receiving additive shares $[a]$ and a public base b from the parties, the ideal functionality reconstructs a and computes b^a over $\mathbb{F}$. Then, the functionality shares $[b^a]$ to the parties.

Fig. 7. Public base exponentiation functionality $\mathcal{F}_{\mathsf{pbexp}}$

Now we describe the public base exponentiation protocols of Aly et al. [1]. Each party P_i locally computes $c_i := b^{a_i}$, where a_i is the share of a. Then P_i shares $[c_i]$ to all parties. Finally, the parties invoke $\mathcal{F}^{n}_{\mathsf{unbounded\text{-}mult}}$ to compute $[\Pi_{i=1}^{n} c_i] = [b^a]$. Note that the cost of share all $[c_i]$'s is equal to one opening. The cost of this public base exponentiation protocol is $3n+2$ multiplications and $2n+2$ openings. The communication is $O(n^3 \kappa)$.

3 Correlated Multiplication

In this section, we describe our core observation, that is, batch correlated multiplication is almost as efficient as single multiplication.

3.1 Correlated Multiplication Triple Generation

We generalize the multiplication triple to the correlated multiplication triples, i.e. $[a_1], \dots, [a_l], [b], [c_1], \dots, [c_l]$, satisfing $a_i b = c_i$ for $i = 1, \dots, l$. The formal definition is given in Fig. 8.

Parameters: Party $P_i, i \in [n]$, a finite field $\mathbb{F}$, the number of triple l
Functionality:

- Upon receiving request from the parties, the ideal functionality selects random $a_1, \dots, a_n, b \xleftarrow{R} \mathbb{F}$ and computes $c_i := a_i b$ for $i = 1, \dots, l$. Then, the functionality shares $[a_1], \dots, [a_l], [b], [c_1], \dots, [c_l]$ to the parties.

Fig. 8. Correlated multiplication triple generation functionality $\mathcal{F}^l_{\mathsf{ctriple}}$

Our main idea is to use VOLE to generate correlated multiplication triples. The protocol is showed in Fig. 9.

Parameters:

- Party $P_i, i \in [n]$, a finite field $\mathbb{F}$, the number of triple l
- Ideal $\mathcal{F}_{\mathsf{vole}}$ primitives specified in Figure 1.
- Ideal $\mathcal{F}_{\mathsf{rand}}$ primitives specified in Figure 2.

Protocol:

1. The parties invoke $\mathcal{F}_{\mathsf{rand}}$ to generate $[a_1], \dots, [a_l], [b]$, where $[a_k] = (a_1^k, \dots, a_n^k), [b] = (b_1, \dots, b_n)$ conditioned on $\sum_{j=1}^n a_j^k = a_k, \sum_{j=1}^n b_j = b$ for $k = 1, \dots, l$.
2. For every distinct $i, j = 1, \dots, n$, P_j picks $v_{i,j}^k \xleftarrow{R} \mathbb{F}$ for $k = 1, \dots, l$ and defines $\vec{a_j} := (a_j^1, \dots, a_j^l) \in \mathbb{F}^l, \vec{v_{i,j}} := (v_{i,j}^1, \dots, v_{i,j}^l)$. Then P_i and P_j invoke $\mathcal{F}_{\mathsf{vole}}$, where P_i acts as receiver with input b_i and P_j acts as sender with input $(\vec{a_j}, -\vec{v}_{i,j})$. As a result, P_i receives $\vec{u_{i,j}} = \vec{a_j} b_i - \vec{v_{i,j}}$.
3. For $i = 1, \dots, n, k = 1, \dots, l$, P_i computes $c_i^k := a_i^k b_i + \sum_{j \neq i} (u_{i,j}^k + v_{j,i}^k)$

Fig. 9. Correlated multiplication triple generation protocol π^l_{ctriple}

Correctness. The correctness of π^l_{ctriple} is as follows:

$$\begin{aligned}
\sum_{i=1}^{n} c_i^k &= \sum_{i=1}^{n}(a_i^k b_i + \sum_{j\neq i}(u_{i,j}^k + v_{j,i}^k)) \\
&= \sum_{i=1}^{n} a_i^k b_i + \sum_{1\le i,j\le n, j\neq i}(u_{i,j}^k + v_{j,i}^k) \\
&= \sum_{i=1}^{n} a_i^k b_i + \sum_{1\le i,j\le n, j\neq i}(u_{i,j}^k + v_{i,j}^k) \\
&= \sum_{i=1}^{n} a_i^k b_i + \sum_{1\le i,j\le n, j\neq i}(a_j^k b_i - v_{i,j}^k + v_{i,j}^k) \\
&= \sum_{i=1}^{n} a_i^k b_i + \sum_{1\le i,j\le n, j\neq i} a_j^k b_i \\
&= (\sum_{i=1}^{n} a_i^k)(\sum_{i=1}^{n} b_i) = c_k
\end{aligned}$$

Security. We prove the security of above protocols as follows:

Theorem 1. *The protocol in Fig. 9 securely computes $\mathcal{F}^l_{\mathsf{ctriple}}$ against semi-honest adversaries in the $(\mathcal{F}_{\mathsf{rand}}, \mathcal{F}_{\mathsf{vole}})$-hybrid model.*

Proof. Assume the set of corrupt parties is I, and let $H := [n] \setminus I$ be the set of honest parties. The simulator obtains input and output shares of adversaries $\{a_i^k\}_{i\in I,k\in[l]}, \{b_i\}_{i\in I}, \{c_i^k\}_{i\in I,k\in[l]}$. To simulate the view of adversaries, the simulator executes as follows:

1. The simulator invokes simulator of $\mathcal{F}_{\mathsf{rand}}$ with input shares $\{a_i^k\}_{i\in I,k\in[l]}$, $\{b_i\}_{i\in I}$ and appends the output to the view.
2. For any $(i,j) \in [n]\times[n]$ and $i \neq j$, there are three cases need to be simulated:
   - If $i \in H, j \in I$, the simulator selects random $v_{i,j}^k \xleftarrow{R} \mathbb{F}$ for $k = 1,\ldots,l$. Then the simulator invokes simulator of $\mathcal{F}_{\mathsf{vole}}$ with input $(\vec{a}_j, -\vec{v}_{i,j})$ and appends the output to the view.
   - If $i,j \in I$, the simulator executes honestly in $\mathcal{F}_{\mathsf{vole}}$ with adversaries' inputs. Note that for any (i,j) pair, two instances of $\mathcal{F}_{\mathsf{vole}}$ need to be simulated: P_i acts as sender and P_i acts as receiver.
   - If $i \in I, j \in H$, the simulator selects random $u_{i,j}^k \xleftarrow{R} \mathbb{F}$ conditioned on $a_i b_i^k + \sum_{j\neq i}(u_{i,j}^k + v_{j,i}^k) = c_i^k$ for $k = 1,\ldots,l$. Then the simulator invokes simulator of $\mathcal{F}_{\mathsf{vole}}$ with input $(b_i, \vec{u}_{i,j})$ and appends the output to the view.

For $i \in H, j \in I$, the simulated input of adversary is the same as real. For $i \in I, j \in H$, since $u_{i,j}^k = a_j^k b_i - v_{i,j}^k$, where $v_{i,j}^k$ was selected randomly by honest party, the distribution of $u_{i,j}^k$ is uniform random. The indistinguishability between simulated view and the real view can be obtained directly from the underlining $\mathcal{F}_{\mathsf{rand}}$ and $\mathcal{F}_{\mathsf{vole}}$ security.

Cost. Recent excellent work on VOLE [9–11,14,40,42] makes it possible to generate length l VOLE only with cost of $O(\log l)$ single OLE. Thus the cost of generating length l correlated multiplication triple is about equal to the cost of generating $O(\log l)$ multiplication triples.

4 Amortizing Division

In this section we describe our amortizing division protocols. Our construction includes two aspects: single division case and batch division case.

4.1 Single Division Case

We define the secure division functionality $\mathcal{F}_{\mathsf{div}}$ in Fig. 10.

Parameters: Party $P_i, i \in [n]$, a finite field $\mathbb{F}$
Functionality:

- Upon receiving additive shares $[x]$ and $[y]$ from the parties, the ideal functionality reconstructs x, y and computes $x^{-1}y$ over $\mathbb{F}$. Then, the functionality shares $[x^{-1}y]$ to the parties.

Fig. 10. Secure division functionality $\mathcal{F}_{\mathsf{div}}$

As we introduced in Sect. 2.6, a simple method to implement $\mathcal{F}_{\mathsf{div}}$ is executing $\mathcal{F}_{\mathsf{inver}}$ first to obtain $[x^{-1}]$. Then the parties invoke $\mathcal{F}_{\mathsf{mult}}$ with input $[x^{-1}], [y]$ to compute $[x^{-1}y]$.

However, the above method need two indenpendent multiplication invocations. Can we do better? Our observation is that since $[x^{-1}]$ and $[x^{-1}y]$ only has difference in y, we can compute the multiplication of $[x^{-1}]$ and $[y]$ inner inversion protocol! Let us room in the inversion protocol: to compute $[x^{-1}]$, the parties generate a random $[a]$ and compute $[a \cdot x]$, then open the ax and compute $(ax)^{-1}[a]$. If we compute $[ax]$ and $[ay]$ *at the same time*, then open ax as before, the division $[x^{-1}y]$ can be obtained directly from $(ax)^{-1}[ay]$. Note that the cost of computing $[ax]$ and $[ay]$ is strictly less than two multiplications as we shown in Sect. 3. We obtain a division protocol with better efficiency.

We describe our division protocol in Fig. 11.

Correctness. The correctness of π_{div} follows from:
$$r^{-1}s = (\rho b + c_1)^{-1}(\sigma b + c_2) = ((x - a_1)b + c_1)^{-1}((y - a_2)b + c_2) = x^{-1}y.$$

Security. We prove the security of above protocols as follows:

Theorem 2. *The protocol in Fig. 11 securely computes $\mathcal{F}_{\mathsf{div}}$ against semi-honest adversaries in the $\mathcal{F}^{l}_{\mathsf{ctriple}}$-hybrid model.*

Parameters:

- Party $P_i, i \in [n]$, a finite field $\mathbb{F}$.
- Ideal $\mathcal{F}^l_{\mathsf{ctriple}}$ primitives specified in Figure 8.

Protocol:

1. The parties invoke $\mathcal{F}^2_{\mathsf{ctriple}}$ to generate $[a_1], [a_2], [b], [c_1], [c_2]$, where $a_1 b = c_1, a_2 b = c_2$.
2. The parties compute $[\rho] := [x - a_1], [\sigma] := [y - a_2]$ locally and open them.
3. The parties compute $[r] = [bx] := \rho[b] + [c_1]$ and $[s] = [by] := \sigma[b] + [c_2]$.
4. The parties open r and compute $[x^{-1}y] := r^{-1}[s]$.

Fig. 11. Single division protocol π_{div}

Proof. Assume the set of corrupt parties is I, and let $H := [n] \setminus I$ be the set of honest parties. The simulator obtains input and output shares of adversaries $\{x_i\}_{i\in I}, \{y_i\}_{i\in I}, \{z_i\}_{i\in I}$, where $z = x^{-1}y$ and $[z] = (z_1, \ldots, z_n)$. The main idea of simulation is that conditioned on the output shares of the adversary are $\{z_i\}_{i\in I}$, all intermediate values are selected randomly. To simulate the view of adversary, the simulator executes as follows:

1. The simulator selects random shares of $a^1_i, a^2_i, b_i \xleftarrow{R} \mathbb{F}$ for $i \in I$ and computes $\rho_i := x_i - a^1_i, \sigma_i := y_i - a^2_i$ for $i \in I$.
2. For $i \in H$, the simulator selects random $\rho_i, \sigma_i \xleftarrow{R} \mathbb{F}$ and computes $\rho := \sum_{i=1}^n \rho_i, \sigma := \sum_{i=1}^n \sigma_i$.
3. The simulator selects a random $r \xleftarrow{R} \mathbb{F}$ and computes a random share of $[r]$.
4. The simulator computes $s_i := rz_i$ for $i \in I$.
5. The simulator computes $c^1_i := r_i - \rho b_i$ and $c^2_i := s_i - \sigma b_i$ for $i \in I$.
6. The simulator invokes simulator of $\mathcal{F}^l_{\mathsf{ctriple}}$ with input $\{a^1_i\}_{i\in I}, \{a^2_i\}_{i\in I}, \{b_i\}_{i\in I}, \{c^1_i\}_{i\in I}, \{c^2_i\}_{i\in I}$ and appends the output to the view.
7. The simulator appends honest parties' shares of ρ, σ, r to the view, that is, $\{\rho_i\}_{i\in H}, \{\sigma_i\}_{i\in H}, \{r_i\}_{i\in H}$.

The distinguishability follows from two facts: 1. the selection of a_1, a_2 are uniform random, which infers $\rho = x - a_1$ and $\sigma = y - a_2$ are also uniform random and honest party's sharing of ρ and σ is random. 2. b is randomly selected, which means $r = bx$ is also random distribution over $\mathbb{F}$, thus the hones party's sharing of r is random. As a result, the distribution of simulator's output is identical to the real view.

Cost. The cost of π_{div} is 3 openings and one instance of length 2 correlated multiplication triple generation. We note that the cost of a length 2 correlated multiplication triple generation is strictly less than 2 independent multiplication triple generation.

4.2 Batch Division Case

Since it often happens that many correlated divisions are computed at the same time, we define the secure division functionality in batch setting $\mathcal{F}_{\mathsf{bdiv}}$ in Fig. 12.

Parameters: Party $P_i, i \in [n]$, a finite field $\mathbb{F}$, the number of division l
Functionality:

- Upon receiving additive shares $[x]$ and $[y_1], \ldots, [y_l]$ from the parties, the ideal functionality reconstructs $x, y_1, \ldots, y_l$ and computes $x^{-1}y_i$ over $\mathbb{F}$ for $i = 1, \ldots, l$. Then, the functionality shares $[x^{-1}y_i]$ to the parties.

Fig. 12. Batch division functionality $\mathcal{F}_{\mathsf{bdiv}}$

We describe our batch division protocol in Fig. 13.

Parameters:

- Party $P_i, i \in [n]$, a finite field $\mathbb{F}$.
- Ideal $\mathcal{F}^{l}_{\mathsf{ctriple}}$ primitives specified in Figure 8.

Protocol:

1. The parties invoke $\mathcal{F}^{l+1}_{\mathsf{ctriple}}$ to generate $[a_0], [a_1], \ldots, [a_l], [b], [c_0], [c_1], \ldots, [c_l]$, where $a_i b = c_i$ for $i = 0, 1, \ldots, l$.
2. The parties compute $[\rho] := [x - a_0], [\sigma_i] := [y_i - a_i]$ locally for $i = 1, \ldots, l$ and open them.
3. The parties compute $[r] = [bx] := \rho[b] + [c_0]$ and $[s_i] = [by_i] := \sigma_i[b] + [c_i]$ for $i = 1, \ldots, l$.
4. The parties open r and compute $[x^{-1}y_i] := r^{-1}[s_i]$ for $i = 1, \ldots, l$.

Fig. 13. Batch division protocol π_{bdiv}

Correctness. The correctness of π_{bdiv} is similar to that of π_{div}.

Security. The security of π_{bdiv} is similar to that of π_{div} and we omit here.

Cost. The cost of π_{bdiv} is $l+2$ openings and one instance of length $l+1$ correlated multiplication triple generation. Since the open step does not need computation, and the cost of $l + 1$ correlated multiplication triple generation is only about $O(\log l)$ multiplication triple generation. The cost of our protocol is almost the same as a single division instance (except a logarithmic factor).

5 Amortizing Exponentition

In this section, we consider the batch execution of private exponentition, that is, the parties input $[y], [x_1], \ldots, [x_l]$ and want to compute $[y^{x_1}], \ldots, [y^{x_l}]$. The formal definition is described in Fig. 14.

Parameters: Party $P_i, i \in [n]$, a finite field $\mathbb{F}$, the number of exponentition l
Functionality:

- Upon receiving additive shares $[y], [x_1], \ldots, [x_l]$ from the parties, the ideal functionality reconstructs $y, x_1, \ldots, x_l$ and computes $y^{x_1}, \ldots, y^{x_l}$ over $\mathbb{F}$. Then, the functionality shares $[y^{x_1}], \ldots, [y^{x_l}]$ to the parties.

Fig. 14. Batch private exponentiation functionality $\mathcal{F}_{\mathsf{bexp}}$

We improve the state-of-the-art private exponentiation protocol of [1] in single-instance setting so that the protocol supports batching. The main idea is also to use correlated multiplication triple to recude the cost of batch exponentition. We describe our protocol in Fig. 15. We note that if change the step 2 in our protocol to generating a single multiplication triple and change the step 6–9 of our protocol to a single execution, the protocol in Fig. 15 is exactly the same as [1].

Correctness. The correctness of π_{bexp} follows from:

$$\begin{aligned} q_i s_i &= p^{x_i} \cdot g^{r_i} \\ &= (t \cdot y)^{x_i} \cdot g^{-\sigma_i b - c_i} \\ &= g^{b x_i} y^{x_i} \cdot g^{-b x_i} = y^{x_i} \end{aligned}$$

Security. We prove the security of above protocols as follows:

Theorem 3. *The protocol in Fig. 15 securely computes $\mathcal{F}_{\mathsf{bexp}}$ against semi-honest adversaries in the $(\mathcal{F}^l_{\mathsf{ctriple}}, \mathcal{F}_{\mathsf{coin}}, \mathcal{F}_{\mathsf{rand}}, \mathcal{F}_{\mathsf{pbexp}}, \mathcal{F}_{\mathsf{mult}})$-hybrid model.*

Proof. Assume the set of corrupt parties is I, and let $H := [n] \setminus I$ be the set of honest parties. The simulator obtains input and output shares of adversaries $\{x_i^1, \ldots, x_i^l\}_{i \in I}, \{y_i\}_{i \in I}, \{z_i^1, \ldots, z_i^l\}_{i \in I}$, where $z_j = x_j^{-1} y$ and $[z_j] = (z_1^j, \ldots, z_n^j)$ for $j = 1, \ldots, l$. To simulate the view of adversary, the simulator executes as follows:

1. In step 1, the simulator picks a random generator $g \xleftarrow{\mathrm{R}} \mathbb{F}$. Then the simulator invokes simulator of $\mathcal{F}_{\mathsf{coin}}$ with input g and appends the output to the view.

Parameters:

- Party $P_i, i \in [n]$, a finite field $\mathbb{F}$, the number of exponentition l
- Ideal $\mathcal{F}^l_{\mathsf{ctriple}}$ primitives specified in Figure 8.
- Ideal $\mathcal{F}_{\mathsf{rand}}$ primitives specified in Figure 2.
- Ideal $\mathcal{F}_{\mathsf{coin}}$ primitives specified in Figure 3.
- Ideal $\mathcal{F}_{\mathsf{pbexp}}$ primitives specified in Figure 7.
- Ideal $\mathcal{F}_{\mathsf{mult}}$ primitives specified in Figure 4.

Protocol:

1. The parties invoke $\mathcal{F}_{\mathsf{coin}}$ to generate a random generator $g \in \mathbb{F}$.
2. The parties invoke $\mathcal{F}^l_{\mathsf{ctriple}}$ to generate $[a_1], \ldots, [a_l], [b], [c_1], \ldots, [c_l]$.
3. The parties invoke $\mathcal{F}_{\mathsf{pbexp}}$ with inputs $g, [b]$ to obtain $[t] = [g^b]$.
4. The parties invoke $\mathcal{F}_{\mathsf{mult}}$ with inputs $[y], [t]$ to obtain $[p] = [t \cdot y]$.
5. The parties open p.
6. For $i = 1, \ldots, l$, the parties invoke $\mathcal{F}_{\mathsf{pbexp}}$ with inputs $p, [x_i]$ to obtain $[q_i] = [p^{x_i}]$.
7. For $i = 1, \ldots, l$, the parties compute $[\sigma_i] := [x_i - a_i]$ locally and open σ_i. Then the parties compute $[r_i] := -\sigma_i[b] - [c_i]$.
8. For $i = 1, \ldots, l$, the parties invoke $\mathcal{F}_{\mathsf{pbexp}}$ with input $g, [r_i]$ to obtain $[s_i] = [g^{r_i}]$.
9. For $i = 1, \ldots, l$, the parties invoke $\mathcal{F}_{\mathsf{mult}}$ with input $[q_i]$ and $[s_i]$ to obtain $[y^{x_i}] := [q_i s_i]$.

Fig. 15. Batch private exponentition protocol π_{bexp}

2. In step 2, the simulator selects random shares of $a_i^1, \ldots, a_i^l, b_i, c_i^1, \ldots, c_i^l \xleftarrow{R} \mathbb{F}$ for $i \in I$. Then the simulator invokes simulator of $\mathcal{F}^l_{\mathsf{ctriple}}$ with above shares as input and appends the output to the view.
3. In step 3, the simulator selects random shares of $\{t_i\}_{i \in I}$. Then the simulator invokes simulator of $\mathcal{F}_{\mathsf{pbexp}}$ with input $g, \{b_i\}_{i \in I}, \{t_i\}_{i \in I}$ and appends the output to the view.
4. In step 4, the simulator selects random shares of $\{p_i\}_{i \in I}$. Then the simulator invokes the simulator of $\mathcal{F}_{\mathsf{mult}}$ with input $\{y_i\}_{i \in I}, \{t_i\}_{i \in I}, \{p_i\}_{i \in I}$ and appends the output to the view.
5. In step 5, the simulator picks the random shares of p for honest party, that is, $\{p_i\}_{i \in H}$ and computes $p := \sum_{i=1}^n p_i$. The simulator appends $\{p_i\}_{i \in H}$ to the view.
6. In step 6, for $i = 1, \ldots, l$ the simulator selects random shares of q_i, that is, $\{q_j^i\}_{j \in I}$. Then the simulator invokes the simulator of $\mathcal{F}_{\mathsf{pbexp}}$ with input $p, \{x_j^i\}_{j \in I}, \{q_j^i\}_{j \in I}$ and appends the output to the view.
7. In step 7, for $i = 1, \ldots, l$, the simulator computes $\sigma_j^i := x_j^i - a_j^i$ for $j \in I$ and selects random $\sigma_j^i \xleftarrow{R} \mathbb{F}$ for $j \in H$. The simulator computes $\sigma_i := \sum_{j \in I} \sigma_j^i$ and $r_j^i := -\sigma_i b_j - c_j^i$ for $j \in I$. Then the simulator appends $\{\sigma_j^i\}_{j \in H}$ to the view.

8. In step 8, for $i = 1, \ldots, l$, the simulator selects random shares of s_i, that is, $\{s_j^i\}_{j \in I}$. Then the simulator invokes the simulator of $\mathcal{F}_{\mathsf{pbexp}}$ with input $g, \{r_j^i\}_{j \in I}, \{s_j^i\}_{j \in I}$ and appends the output to the view.
9. In step 9, for $i = 1, \ldots, l$, the simulator invokes the simulator of $\mathcal{F}_{\mathsf{mult}}$ with input $\{q_j^i\}_{j \in I}, \{s_j^i\}_{j \in I}, \{z_j^i\}_{j \in I}$ and appends the output to the view.

In addition to the views of the subprotocols, the simulator only needs to simulate the openings of p and σ_i for $i = 1, \ldots, l$. Since $a_1, \ldots, a_l$ are randomly generated by $\mathcal{F}^l_{\mathsf{ctriple}}$ and $\sigma_i = x_i - a_i$, thus the honest parties' shares of σ_i are also distributed randomly. Since b is also randomly generated by $\mathcal{F}^l_{\mathsf{ctriple}}$, which implies $t = g^b$ is uniform random, we have $p = ty$ is uniform random in $\mathbb{F}$. As a result, the simulator's output is identical to the real view in the open step. In the subprotocol invocation step, the distinguishability follows from the security of underlining functionality directly.

Cost. The cost of π_{bexp} is as follows:

- In step 1, one opening is needed in $\mathcal{F}_{\mathsf{coin}}$.
- In step 2, length l correlated multiplication triple generation.
- In step 3, one public base exponentition is needed, including $3n + 2$ multiplications and $2n + 2$ openings.
- In step 4, one multiplication is needed.
- In step 5, one opening is needed.
- In step 6, l public base exponentition is needed, including $(3n + 2)l$ multiplications and $(2n + 2)l$ openings.
- In step 7, l openings are needed.
- In step 8, l public base exponentitions are needed, including $(3n + 2)l$ multiplications and $(2n + 2)l$ openings.
- In step 9, l multiplications are needed.

The total costs are $2n+4+(4n+5)l$ openings, a length l correlated multiplication triple generation, $3n + 3 + (6n + 5)l$ multiplications. While in the original single instance protocol of [1], the costs are $6n+9$ openings and $9n+9$ multiplications. If we use l instance of [1] to implement the batch private exponentiation, the costs are $(6n + 9)l$ openings and $(9n + 9)l$ multiplications. Since the main costs is multiplication, the costs saved by our protocol is about 33%.

6 Conclusions

In this paper, we use the VOLE protocol to generate correlated multiplication triples, we further use these triples to improve the efficiency of the division in both single and batch settings and private exponentiation in batch setting. Our protocols are simple and easy to follow and offer security against semi-honest adversaries.

The extension of the work runs through several directions. First, our technique can be used to improve any protocol using multiplication triples, so that the protocol can reduce the overhead in the case of batch processing. It is desirable to find more protcols that meet this setting. Second, the malicious security is the ultimate goal, and how to use an efficient method to transform our protocols to satisfing malicious security (instead of general zero knowledge proof) remains to be studied. Third, our protocols only consider a single operation, i.e. the division and exponentiation. In complex circuits, e.g. neural networks and machine learning, how to apply our optimization is also a problem to be studied.

Acknowledgement. We are grateful for the helpful comments from the anonymous reviewers. Our work is supported by the National Key Research and Development Program of China (No. 2020YFB1805402) and the National Natural Science Foundation of China (Grants No. 61872359 and No. 61936008).

References

1. Aly, A., Abidin, A., Nikova, S.: Practically efficient secure distributed exponentiation without bit-decomposition. In: Meiklejohn, S., Sako, K. (eds.) FC 2018. LNCS, vol. 10957, pp. 291–309. Springer, Heidelberg (2018). https://doi.org/10.1007/978-3-662-58387-6_16
2. Applebaum, B., Damgård, I., Ishai, Y., Nielsen, M., Zichron, L.: Secure arithmetic computation with constant computational overhead. In: Katz, J., Shacham, H. (eds.) CRYPTO 2017, Part I. LNCS, vol. 10401, pp. 223–254. Springer, Cham (2017). https://doi.org/10.1007/978-3-319-63688-7_8
3. Bar-Ilan, J., Beaver, D.: Non-cryptographic fault-tolerant computing in constant number of rounds of interaction. In: Proceedings of the Eighth Annual ACM Symposium on Principles of Distributed Computing, Edmonton, Alberta, Canada, 14–16 August 1989, pp. 201–209 (1989)
4. Beaver, D.: Efficient multiparty protocols using circuit randomization. In: Feigenbaum, J. (ed.) CRYPTO 1991. LNCS, vol. 576, pp. 420–432. Springer, Heidelberg (1992). https://doi.org/10.1007/3-540-46766-1_34
5. Ben-Or, M., Goldwasser, S., Wigderson, A.: Completeness theorems for non-cryptographic fault-tolerant distributed computation (extended abstract). In: Proceedings of the 20th Annual ACM Symposium on Theory of Computing, 2–4 May 1988, Chicago, Illinois, USA, pp. 1–10 (1988)
6. Bendlin, R., Damgård, I., Orlandi, C., Zakarias, S.: Semi-homomorphic encryption and multiparty computation. In: Paterson, K.G. (ed.) EUROCRYPT 2011. LNCS, vol. 6632, pp. 169–188. Springer, Heidelberg (2011). https://doi.org/10.1007/978-3-642-20465-4_11
7. Bogdanov, D., Laur, S., Willemson, J.: Sharemind: a framework for fast privacy-preserving computations. In: Jajodia, S., Lopez, J. (eds.) ESORICS 2008. LNCS, vol. 5283, pp. 192–206. Springer, Heidelberg (2008). https://doi.org/10.1007/978-3-540-88313-5_13
8. Bogetoft, P., et al.: Secure multiparty computation goes live. In: Dingledine, R., Golle, P. (eds.) FC 2009. LNCS, vol. 5628, pp. 325–343. Springer, Heidelberg (2009). https://doi.org/10.1007/978-3-642-03549-4_20
9. Boyle, E., Couteau, G., Gilboa, N., Ishai, Y.: Compressing vector OLE. In: Proceedings of the 2018 ACM SIGSAC Conference on Computer and Communications Security, CCS 2018, Toronto, ON, Canada, 15–19 October 2018, pp. 896–912 (2018)

10. Boyle, E., et al.: Efficient two-round OT extension and silent non-interactive secure computation. In: CCS 2019 (2019)
11. Boyle, E., Couteau, G., Gilboa, N., Ishai, Y., Kohl, L., Scholl, P.: Efficient pseudorandom correlation generators: silent OT extension and more. In: Boldyreva, A., Micciancio, D. (eds.) CRYPTO 2019, Part III. LNCS, vol. 11694, pp. 489–518. Springer, Cham (2019). https://doi.org/10.1007/978-3-030-26954-8_16
12. Bunn, P., Ostrovsky, R.: Secure two-party k-means clustering. In: Proceedings of the 2007 ACM Conference on Computer and Communications Security, CCS 2007, Alexandria, Virginia, USA, 28–31 October 2007, pp. 486–497 (2007)
13. Canetti, R.: Universally composable security: a new paradigm for cryptographic protocols. In: FOCS 2001 (2001)
14. Couteau, G., Rindal, P., Raghuraman, S.: Silver: silent VOLE and oblivious transfer from hardness of decoding structured LDPC codes. In: Malkin, T., Peikert, C. (eds.) CRYPTO 2021. LNCS, vol. 12827, pp. 502–534. Springer, Cham (2021). https://doi.org/10.1007/978-3-030-84252-9_17
15. Damgård, I., Fitzi, M., Kiltz, E., Nielsen, J.B., Toft, T.: Unconditionally secure constant-rounds multi-party computation for equality, comparison, bits and exponentiation. In: Halevi, S., Rabin, T. (eds.) TCC 2006. LNCS, vol. 3876, pp. 285–304. Springer, Heidelberg (2006). https://doi.org/10.1007/11681878_15
16. Damgård, I., Mikkelsen, G.L.: Efficient, robust and constant-round distributed RSA key generation. In: Micciancio, D. (ed.) TCC 2010. LNCS, vol. 5978, pp. 183–200. Springer, Heidelberg (2010). https://doi.org/10.1007/978-3-642-11799-2_12
17. Damgård, I., Pastro, V., Smart, N., Zakarias, S.: Multiparty computation from somewhat homomorphic encryption. In: Safavi-Naini, R., Canetti, R. (eds.) CRYPTO 2012. LNCS, vol. 7417, pp. 643–662. Springer, Heidelberg (2012). https://doi.org/10.1007/978-3-642-32009-5_38
18. Demmler, D., Schneider, T., Zohner, M.: ABY - a framework for efficient mixed-protocol secure two-party computation. In: 22nd Annual Network and Distributed System Security Symposium, NDSS 2015, San Diego, California, USA, 8–11 February 2015 (2015)
19. Doerner, J., Evans, D., Shelat, A.: Secure stable matching at scale. In: Proceedings of the 2016 ACM SIGSAC Conference on Computer and Communications Security, Vienna, Austria, 24–28 October 2016, pp. 1602–1613 (2016)
20. Döttling, N., Ghosh, S., Nielsen, J. B., Nilges, T., Trifiletti, R.: TinyOLE: efficient actively secure two-party computation from oblivious linear function evaluation. In: Proceedings of the 2017 ACM SIGSAC Conference on Computer and Communications Security, CCS 2017, Dallas, TX, USA, 30 October–03 November 2017, pp. 2263–2276 (2017)
21. Furukawa, J., Lindell, Y., Nof, A., Weinstein, O.: High-throughput secure three-party computation for malicious adversaries and an honest majority. In: Coron, J.-S., Nielsen, J.B. (eds.) EUROCRYPT 2017, Part II. LNCS, vol. 10211, pp. 225–255. Springer, Cham (2017). https://doi.org/10.1007/978-3-319-56614-6_8
22. Gascón, A., et al.: Privacy-preserving distributed linear regression on high-dimensional data. Proc. Priv. Enhancing Technol. **2017**(4), 345–364 (2017)
23. Goldreich, O.: The Foundations of Cryptography - Volume 2: Basic Applications. Cambridge University Press, Cambridge (2004)
24. Goldreich, O., Micali, S., Wigderson, A.: How to play any mental game or a completeness theorem for protocols with honest majority. In: STOC 1987 (1987)

25. Ishai, Y., Prabhakaran, M., Sahai, A.: Founding cryptography on oblivious transfer – efficiently. In: Wagner, D. (ed.) CRYPTO 2008. LNCS, vol. 5157, pp. 572–591. Springer, Heidelberg (2008). https://doi.org/10.1007/978-3-540-85174-5_32
26. Ishai, Y., Prabhakaran, M., Sahai, A.: Secure arithmetic computation with no honest majority. In: Reingold, O. (ed.) TCC 2009. LNCS, vol. 5444, pp. 294–314. Springer, Heidelberg (2009). https://doi.org/10.1007/978-3-642-00457-5_18
27. Keller, M., Orsini, E., Scholl, P.: MASCOT: faster malicious arithmetic secure computation with oblivious transfer. In: Proceedings of the 2016 ACM SIGSAC Conference on Computer and Communications Security, Vienna, Austria, 24–28 October 2016, pp. 830–842 (2016)
28. Keller, M., Pastro, V., Rotaru, D.: Overdrive: making SPDZ great again. In: Nielsen, J.B., Rijmen, V. (eds.) EUROCRYPT 2018, Part III. LNCS, vol. 10822, pp. 158–189. Springer, Cham (2018). https://doi.org/10.1007/978-3-319-78372-7_6
29. Keller, M., Scholl, P., Smart, N.P.: An architecture for practical actively secure MPC with dishonest majority. In: 2013 ACM SIGSAC Conference on Computer and Communications Security, CCS 2013, Berlin, Germany, 4–8 November 2013, pp. 549–560 (2013)
30. Kilian, J.: Founding cryptography on oblivious transfer. In: Proceedings of the 20th Annual ACM Symposium on Theory of Computing, 2–4 May 1988, Chicago, Illinois, USA, pp. 20–31 (1988)
31. Larraia, E., Orsini, E., Smart, N.P.: Dishonest majority multi-party computation for binary circuits. In: Garay, J.A., Gennaro, R. (eds.) CRYPTO 2014, Part II. LNCS, vol. 8617, pp. 495–512. Springer, Heidelberg (2014). https://doi.org/10.1007/978-3-662-44381-1_28
32. Lindell, Y., Nof, A.: A framework for constructing fast MPC over arithmetic circuits with malicious adversaries and an honest-majority. In: Proceedings of the 2017 ACM SIGSAC Conference on Computer and Communications Security, CCS 2017, Dallas, TX, USA, 30 October–03 November 2017, pp. 259–276 (2017)
33. Lindell, Y., Pinkas, B.: Privacy preserving data mining. J. Cryptol. **15**(3), 177–206 (2002)
34. Lindell, Y., Pinkas, B.: Secure multiparty computation for privacy-preserving data mining. J. Priv. Confidentiality **1**(1) (2009)
35. Mohassel, P., Rindal, P.: ABY^3: a mixed protocol framework for machine learning. In: Proceedings of the 2018 ACM SIGSAC Conference on Computer and Communications Security, CCS 2018, Toronto, ON, Canada, 15–19 October 2018, pp. 35–52 (2018)
36. Naor, M., Pinkas, B.: Oblivious polynomial evaluation. SIAM J. Comput. **35**(5), 1254–1281 (2006)
37. Nielsen, J.B., Nordholt, P.S., Orlandi, C., Burra, S.S.: A new approach to practical active-secure two-party computation. In: Safavi-Naini, R., Canetti, R. (eds.) CRYPTO 2012. LNCS, vol. 7417, pp. 681–700. Springer, Heidelberg (2012). https://doi.org/10.1007/978-3-642-32009-5_40
38. Ning, C., Xu, Q.: Multiparty computation for modulo reduction without bit-decomposition and a generalization to bit-decomposition. In: Abe, M. (ed.) ASIACRYPT 2010. LNCS, vol. 6477, pp. 483–500. Springer, Heidelberg (2010). https://doi.org/10.1007/978-3-642-17373-8_28
39. Ning, C., Xu, Q.: Constant-rounds, linear multi-party computation for exponentiation and modulo reduction with perfect security. In: Lee, D.H., Wang, X. (eds.) ASIACRYPT 2011. LNCS, vol. 7073, pp. 572–589. Springer, Heidelberg (2011). https://doi.org/10.1007/978-3-642-25385-0_31

40. Schoppmann, P., Gascón, A., Reichert, L., Raykova, M.: Distributed vector-ole: improved constructions and implementation. In: CCS 2019, pp. 1055–1072 (2019)
41. Wang, X., Ranellucci, S., Katz, J.: Global-scale secure multiparty computation. In: Proceedings of the 2017 ACM SIGSAC Conference on Computer and Communications Security, CCS 2017, Dallas, TX, USA, 30 October–03 November 2017, pp. 39–56 (2017)
42. Weng, C., Yang, K., Katz, J., Wang, X.: Wolverine: fast, scalable, and communication-efficient zero-knowledge proofs for boolean and arithmetic circuits. In: 42nd IEEE Symposium on Security and Privacy, SP 2021, San Francisco, CA, USA, 24–27 May 2021, pp. 1074–1091 (2021)
43. Yao, A.C.-C.: How to generate and exchange secrets (extended abstract). In: FOCS (1986)
44. Yu, C.-H., Chow, S.S.M., Chung, K.-M., Liu, F.-H.: Efficient secure two-party exponentiation. In: Kiayias, A. (ed.) CT-RSA 2011. LNCS, vol. 6558, pp. 17–32. Springer, Heidelberg (2011). https://doi.org/10.1007/978-3-642-19074-2_2
45. Zahur, S., Evans, D.: Obliv-C: a language for extensible data-oblivious computation. IACR Cryptology ePrint Archive, p. 1153 (2015)

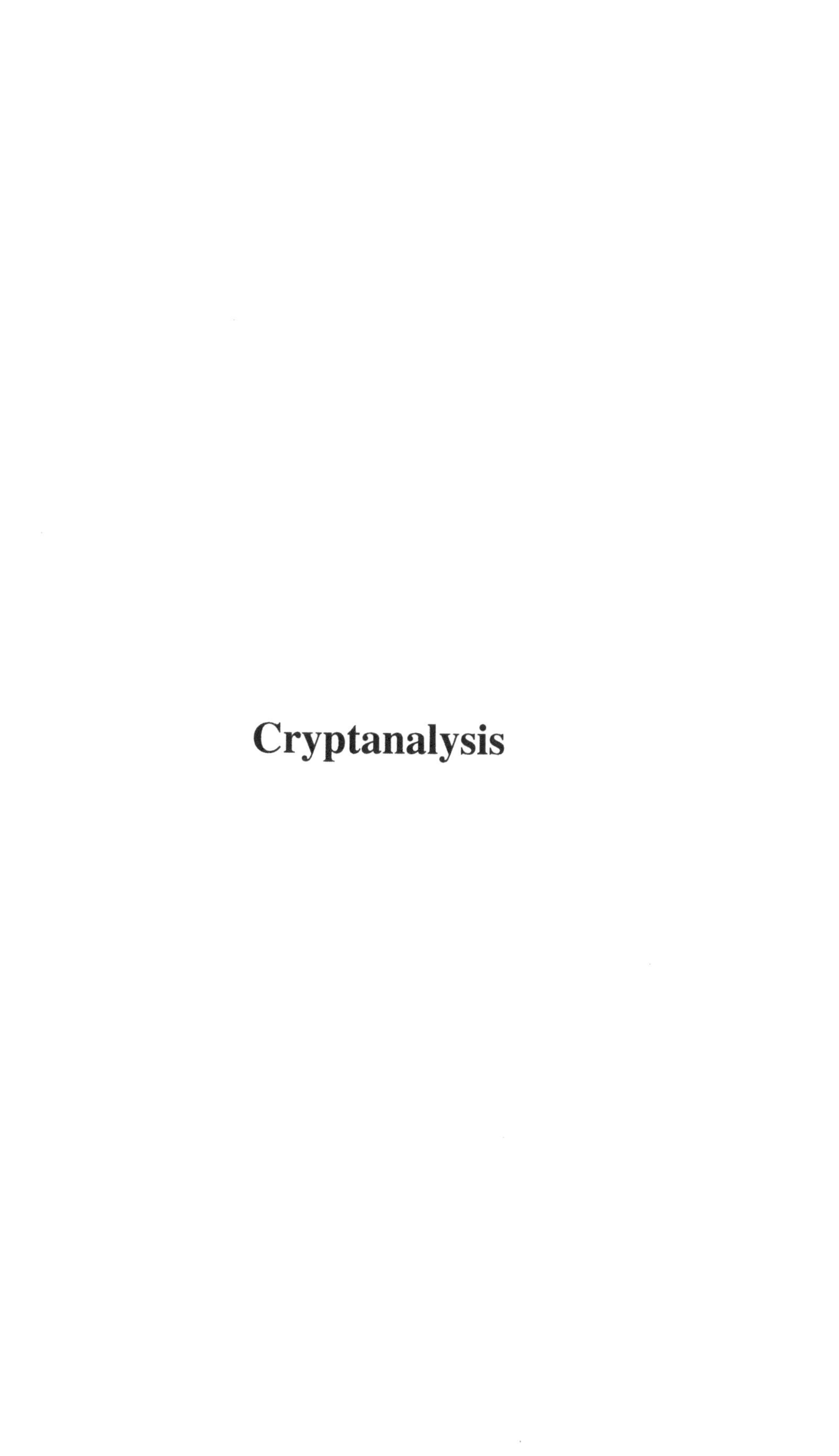

Cryptanalysis

Generalized Boomerang Connectivity Table and Improved Cryptanalysis of GIFT

Chenmeng Li[1,2], Baofeng Wu[1,2(✉)], and Dongdai Lin[1,2]

[1] State Key Laboratory of Information Security, Institute of Information Engineering, Chinese Academy of Sciences, Beijing 100093, China
{lichenmeng,wubaofeng,ddlin}@iie.ac.cn

[2] School of Cyber Security, University of Chinese Academy of Sciences, Beijing 100049, China

Abstract. Boomerang connectivity table (BCT), an essential tool in boomerang attack, gives a unified description of the probability in the middle round of a boomerang distinguisher. However, it suffers the drawback that the asymmetric relationship between the upper and lower differentials in the middle round is ignored. To make up for this deficiency, we propose the generalized boomerang connectivity table (GBCT), which characterizes all combinations of upper and lower differentials to provide a more precise probability in the middle round. We first study the cryptographic properties of GBCT and introduce its variants applied in multiple rounds and Feistel structure. Then, we provide an automatic search algorithm to increase the probability of the boomerang distinguisher by adding thorough considerations that more trails can be included, which is applicable to all S-box based ciphers. Finally, we increase the probabilities of the 20-round GIFT-64 distinguisher from $2^{-58.557}$ to $2^{-57.43}$ and the 19-round GIFT-128 distinguisher from $2^{-109.626}$ to $2^{-108.349}$, both of which are the highest so far. Applying the key recovery attack proposed by Dong et al. at Eurocrypt 2022 on the new distinguisher, we achieve the lowest complexities of the attack on GIFT-64 and the best rectangle attack on GIFT-128.

Keywords: Rectangle attack · Automatic search algorithm · BCT · GIFT

1 Introduction

Differential cryptanalysis, proposed by Biham and Shamir [4] in 1990, is one of the most effective and widely used methods to attack many cryptographic primitives. However, it is often hard to find differential characteristics with high probabilities as the rounds of a cipher increase. In 1999, Wagner [21] proposed boomerang attack to replace one bad long differential trail with two good short

Y. Deng and M. Yung (Eds.): Inscrypt 2022, LNCS 13837, pp. 213–233, 2023.
https://doi.org/10.1007/978-3-031-26553-2_11

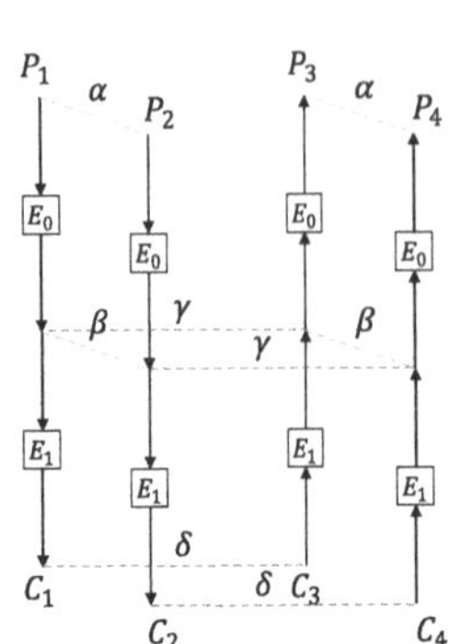

Fig. 1. The boomerang attack

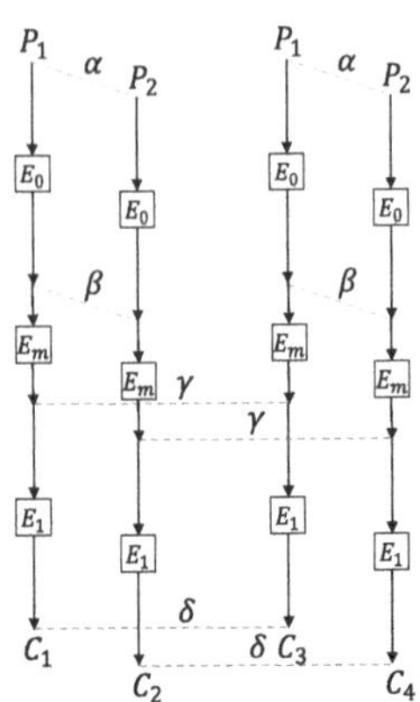

Fig. 2. The sandwich attack

differential trails. This attack makes it possible to conquer more rounds, and indicates that the security of a cipher cannot be guaranteed only by the non-existence of differentials with high probability.

In a boomerang attack, the target cipher E is decomposed into two parts as $E = E_1 \circ E_0$, where E_0 has a differential trail $\alpha \to \beta$ and E_1 has a differential trail $\gamma \to \delta$. Compositing the two sub-ciphers in a swerving way admits a boomerang distinguisher as long as $\beta \neq \gamma$, see Fig. 1. Under the independence assumption of E_0 and E_1, the probability of this distinguisher should be p^2q^2. However, it requires an adaptive chosen-plaintext/ciphertext scenario, which is not applicable to most key recovery settings. Then, the rectangle attack [3], a chosen-plaintext attack, is proposed to not only overcome this issue but also increase the probability of the distinguisher. It actually covers all possible differential trails $\alpha \to \beta_i$ for E_0 and $\gamma_j \to \delta$ for E_1 in the framework of a boomerang attack, thus increases the probability of the distinguisher to $2^{-n}\hat{p}^2\hat{q}^2$, where $\hat{p} = \sqrt{\sum_i \Pr^2(\alpha \to \beta_i)}$ and $\hat{q} = \sqrt{\sum_j \Pr^2(\gamma_j \to \delta)}$. To perform a rectangle attack, one needs to sieve right quarters (x, y, z, w) with $x \oplus y = z \oplus w = \alpha$ according to this probability.

It was noticed later that the independence assumption was invalid. To reveal this phenomenon, Biryukov and Khovratovich [5] proposed the boomerang switch to connect two differentials with a strong dependency. The observations were depicted in the framework of sandwich attack [13], which decomposes the cipher as $E = E_1 \circ E_m \circ E_0$, where the middle part E_m is the connection of the upper trail $\alpha \to \beta$ and the lower trail $\gamma \to \delta$, see Fig. 2. Then, E_m can be regarded as a small boomerang distinguisher with probability r, where

$$r = \Pr[E_m^{-1}(E_m(x) \oplus \gamma) \oplus E_m^{-1}(E(x \oplus \beta) \oplus \gamma) = \beta].$$

Thus, the probability of the whole boomerang distinguisher is $\hat{p}^2\hat{q}^2r$. Besides, Murphy [18] has pointed out that there may be incompatibility when connecting two independently chosen differential trails, which will result in an invalid boomerang distinguisher. Since the dependency between these two differential trails has a great impact on the probability of a boomerang distinguisher, at Eurocrypt 2018, Cid et al. [10] captured the above observations in a unified table called boomerang connectivity table (BCT) when E_m is a single S-box layer. A new switch method named generalized switch was also depicted by the BCT.

As automatic tools has been widely used in searching for cryptographic distinguishers, it is natural to consider integrating BCTs with automatic tools to search for good distinguishers. There are mainly three automatic search tools in cryptanalysis, namely MILP (mixed integer linear programming), SAT/SMT (satisfiabality module theory) and Matsui's algorithm. Liu and Sasaki [17] gave the first generic model of BCT to search for related-key boomerang distinguishers with SMT. Later, Ji et al. [16] proposed an automatic search algorithm by improving Matsui's algorithm to search for the clustering of related-key differential trails utilized in the related-key boomerang distinguisher for GIFT-64 and GIFT-128, obtaining the best result up to now.

GIFT [2] is a lightweight block cipher with SPN structure. Because of its excellent performance in both hardware and software implementations, GIFT has been chosen as primitives in the design of many ciphers, such as GIFT-COFB [1], HYENA [8], LOCTUS-AEAD and LOCUS-AEAD [7], all of which are submitted to NIST's Lightweight Cryptography Project, with GIFT-COFB being selected as one of the ten finalists. Studying the security of GIFT is therefore crucial and imperative.

Our Contributions. The main contributions of this paper are summarized below.

1. **We propose a generalized boomerang connectivity table (GBCT).** The GBCT, which can be viewed as a generalized version of BCT, receives four distinct differences as input to determine the number of quartets that meet these four differences. Additionally, we study the cryptographic properties of GBCT and give some variants of GBCT applied in multiple rounds and Feistel structure.
2. **We provide a new search algorithm for boomerang distinguishers with considerations that more trails can be included, and increase the probability of distinguishers for GIFT.** By adding three additional factors to the algorithm in [16], a better automatic search algorithm for boomerang distinguishers is obtained. Firstly, we relax the condition of input/output differences from optimal to suboptimal to get a better clustering effect. Secondly, we modify their method of searching for differential trails to search for differentials within a probability range. Lastly, we incorporate GBCT to ensure the compatibility of E_0 and E_1. Using the new algorithm, we improved the probabilities of distinguishers for GIFT-64 and GIFT-128, which increase from $2^{-58.557}$ to $2^{-57.43}$ and from $2^{-109.626}$ to $2^{-108.349}$ respectively.

Table 1. Summary of the cryptanalytic results on GIFT

Rounds	Approach	Setting	Time	Data	Memory	Ref.
GIFT-64						
23	Boomerang	RK	$2^{126.60}$	$2^{63.3}$	–	[17]
25	Rectangle	RK	$2^{120.92}$	$2^{63.78}$	$2^{64.10}$	[16]
26	Differential	RK	$2^{123.23}$	$2^{60.96}$	$2^{120.86}$	[20]
26	Rectangle	RK	$2^{122.78}$	$2^{63.78}$	$2^{63.78}$	[12]
26	Rectangle	RK	$2^{121.75}$	$2^{62.715}$	$2^{62.715}$	Section 5
GIFT-128						
22	Boomerang	RK	$2^{112.63}$	$2^{112.63}$	2^{52}	[16]
23	Rectangle	RK	$2^{126.89}$	$2^{121.31}$	$2^{121.63}$	[16]
23	Rectangle	RK	$2^{125.175}$	$2^{120.175}$	$2^{120.175}$	Section 5
23	Differential	SK	2^{120}	2^{120}	2^{86}	[23]
26	Differential	SK	$2^{125.75}$	$2^{120.25}$	$2^{120.25}$	[16]

3. **We decrease the complexity of the attack on GIFT-64/GIFT-128 under the key recovery framework proposed by Dong et al.**
   We apply the key recovery attack proposed by Dong et al. on the distinguishers and achieve a lower complexity than previous attacks. The data and time complexity drop from $2^{63.78}$ to $2^{62.72}$ and from $2^{122.78}$ to $2^{121.75}$ when attacking the 26-round GIFT-64. When attacking 23-round GIFT-128, the data and time complexity decrease from $2^{121.31}$ to $2^{120.175}$ and from $2^{126.89}$ to $2^{124.25}$ respectively. The current cryptanalytic results on GIFT are summarized in Table 1.

Outline. The rest of the paper is organized as follows. In Sect. 2, we give a brief overview of some previous work. In Sect. 3, we introduce the generalized boomerang connectivity table and study properties and variants of it. In Sect. 4, we outline the strategies for searching for a rectangle distinguisher, and give a new search algorithm. In Sect. 5, we provide the complexity analysis of the 26/23-round attacks on GIFT-64/GIFT-128. Section 6 concludes the paper.

2 Background and Previous Work

In this section, we give some preliminaries. First, we introduce some tables used to connect two sub-ciphers, such as BCT, BDT, EBCT (Figs. 3 and 4). Secondly, we give a brief introduction of some concepts necessary to search for a rectangle distinguisher, including the automatic search tool and the clustering effect. Finally, we recall the latest advances in key recovery attacks given in [12].

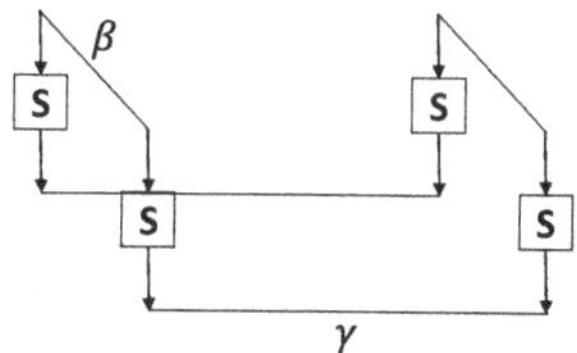

Fig. 3. Structure of BCT

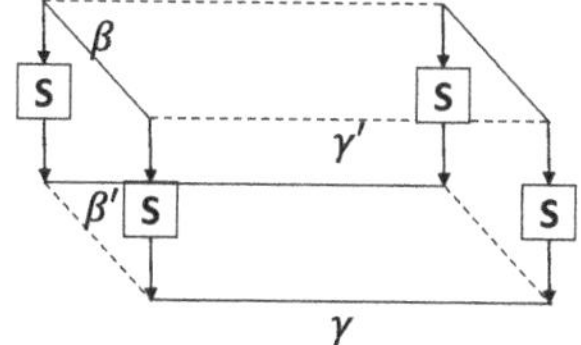

Fig. 4. Structures of BDT and EBCT

2.1 BCT, BDT, EBCT

BCT is the first unified tool for evaluating dependencies between E_0 and E_1, but only applicable when E_m is a single S-box layer. For $\beta,\ \gamma \in \mathbb{F}_2^n$, define

$$BCT(\beta,\gamma) = \#\{x \in \mathbb{F}_2^n \mid S^{-1}(S(x)\oplus\gamma)\oplus S^{-1}(S(x\oplus\beta)\oplus\gamma)=\beta\}.$$

Song et al. [19] noticed that dependencies could affect more rounds. Meanwhile, some practical experiments [9,17] showed that a higher probability could be achieved when E_m contained two rounds. It is reasonable to believe that the more rounds E_m contains, the more accurate the probability will be. Then, how to employ BCT in more rounds received much attention in the following research. Wang et al. [22] proposed a systematic analysis of the boomerang switching effect in multiple rounds and gave the boomerang difference table (BDT), renamed as UBCT in [11]. And its variant called BDT' is also denoted by D_{BCT} in [19] and renamed as LBCT in [11]. Its entry for $(\beta,\beta',\gamma)\in(\mathbb{F}_2^n)^3$ is computed by

$$BDT(\beta,\beta',\gamma) = \#\left\{x \in \mathbb{F}_2^n \;\middle|\; \begin{array}{l} S(x)\oplus S(x\oplus\beta)=\beta', \\ S^{-1}(S(x)\oplus\gamma)\oplus S^{-1}(S(x\oplus\beta)\oplus\gamma)=\beta \end{array}\right\}.$$

After that, Delaune et al. [11] provided a new table to connect two differentials in more than two rounds, called extended boomerang connectivity table (EBCT), where for $(\beta,\beta',\gamma,\gamma')\in(\mathbb{F}_2^n)^4$,

$$EBCT(\beta,\beta',\gamma',\gamma) = \#\left\{x \in \mathbb{F}_2^n \;\middle|\; \begin{array}{l} S(x)\oplus S(x\oplus\beta)=\beta',\ S(x)\oplus S(x\oplus\gamma')=\gamma, \\ S^{-1}(S(x)\oplus\gamma)\oplus S^{-1}(S(x\oplus\beta)\oplus\gamma)=\beta \end{array}\right\}.$$

Besides, Hadipour et al. [14] introduced a new tool to model the dependency in more rounds called double boomerang connectivity table (DBCT) and used it for automatic searching for boomerang distinguishers.

2.2 Automatic Tools Modeling BCT

Because of its efficiency and simplicity, automatic tools have become crucial techniques for cryptanalysis in recent years. The effect of many commonly used attacks can be improved with the help of automatic tools, not only in searching for distinguishers but also in key recovery attacks. In this paper, we propose an algorithm to search for boomerang distinguishers with the automatic tool SMT. Here we give a brief introduction to it.

SMT is refereed to the problem of determining whether a mathematical formula is satisfiable. In cryptanalysis, one can use languages (e.g., SMTLIB2, CVC or BTOR) to model the property of components of a cipher, such as propagation of a differential and its probability, as an SMT problem, and obtain a desired solution (e.g., a differential trail with high probability) by SMT solvers. For example, in [17] the authors modelled the DDT and BCT with boolean constraints of an S-box. Following is an example of the description of BCT.

Example 1. Given boomerang propagations ($2 \rightarrow 5$) and ($2 \rightarrow 6$) of a 4×4 S-box with $BCT(2,5) = BCT(2,6) = 4$, we can model them with the logic expression $(x = 2) \wedge ((y = 5) \vee (y = 6))$. It is true when $x = 2$ and $y = 5$ or 6. Meanwhile, the probability is depicted by $w_4 = ((x = 2) \wedge (y = 5) \vee (x = 2) \wedge (y = 6))$, which means $w_4 = 1$ when the expression in the RHS is true, and the probability is obviously $4 \cdot w_4/16$.

2.3 Clustering Effect in Boomerang Distinguishers

When utilizing a boomerang distinguisher, two essential factors are the input and output differences and the probability of the boomerang trail. Except for the input and output differences, the specific value of the differentials in the middle rounds is no longer important. We use $\hat{r}$ to denote the probability of getting a right quartet that follows an exact boomerang trail. The actual probability r is composed of the probabilities $\hat{r}$ corresponding to all possible intermediate differences and hence r is always greater than or equal to any single $\hat{r}$. Ji et al. gave a definition of the clustering of the related-key differential trails utilized in an R-round related-key boomerang distinguisher and proposed an automatic search algorithm for boomerang distinguishers, which exploits the concept of clustering effect to make the probability improved [16].

2.4 Key-Recovery Algorithms for Rectangle Attacks

Much research has been done on the key recovery algorithm for the rectangle attacks. The first rectangle attack [3] was proposed by Biham et al. in 2001, and was applied to Serpent in the single-key setting. Later, numerous research have been done to reduce the complexity of the attacks. For ciphers with linear key schedules, Dong et al. recently built a new key recovery attack model, with which the ratio of right quartets greatly soared. They found the right quartets must satisfy some nonlinear relations, which could be exploited to filter the wrong ones, so as to increase the proportion of the right quartets and decrease the attack complexity. The key recovery attack on GIFT-64 with their algorithm is the best so far. Afterwards, Dong et al. [12] made some modifications on their algorithm to give a unified and generic key recovery algorithm, which achieved the optimal complexity by selecting different parameters. In order to better illustrate the advantage of the new distinguisher, we use the same attack in [12]

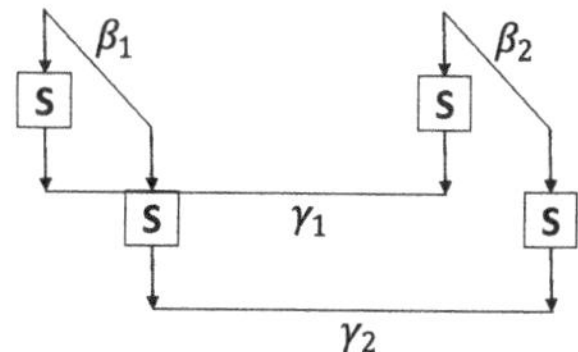

Fig. 5. Structure of GBCT

to launch on GIFT. Symbols used in the complexity analysis in Sect. 5 of our attack are the same to theirs as well.

3 Generalized Boomerang Connectivity Table

In this section, we give a generalized boomerang connectivity table (GBCT), which looses the limitation of the symmetric connections to be arbitrary. After that, some cryptographic properties of GBCT are exhibited. In addition, we present some variants of GBCT for multiple rounds and Feistel structure. Finally, the benefits of GBCT are illustrated by some applications.

3.1 Introduction to GBCT

The idea for generalizing the BCT is natural, that is, instead of considering symmetric differences in two directions of the connection part of two sub-ciphers, we take all possible values in four directions in to consideration, see Fig. 5. When loosing the limitation of the symmetric input and output differences to be arbitrary, all possible connections of two sub-ciphers E_0 and E_1 are covered. Thus, a more precise probability of a boomerang distinguisher can be obtained with GBCT. This idea was mentioned in the [14] with no formal description given.

Definition 1. *Let S be a permutation over $\mathbb{F}_2^n$ and $\beta_1, \beta_2, \gamma_1, \gamma_2 \in \mathbb{F}_2^n$. The generalized boomerang connectivity table of S is a four-dimensional table, in which the entry for $(\beta_1, \beta_2; \gamma_1, \gamma_2)$ is computed by*

$$GBCT(\beta_1, \beta_2; \gamma_1, \gamma_2) = \#\{x \in \mathbb{F}_2^n | S^{-1}(S(x) \oplus \gamma_1) \oplus S^{-1}(S(x \oplus \beta_1) \oplus \gamma_2) = \beta_2\}.$$

It is easy to see that GBCT can also be represented as

$$GBCT(\beta_1, \beta_2; \gamma_1, \gamma_2) = \#\left\{(x, y) \in \mathbb{F}_2^n \times \mathbb{F}_2^n \;\middle|\; \begin{array}{l} S(x) \oplus S(y) = \gamma_1, \\ S(x \oplus \beta_1) \oplus S(y \oplus \beta_2) = \gamma_2 \end{array}\right\}.$$

The probability for an S-box with a given quarter of differences $(\beta_1, \beta_2; \gamma_1, \gamma_2)$ is $p = \frac{1}{2^n} \times GBCT(\beta_1, \beta_2; \gamma_1, \gamma_2)$. The time complexity for generating the GBCT for an n-bit S-box is $O(2^{4n})$.

In the following, we explain why GBCT can gain more solutions than BCT with the S-box of GIFT as an example.

Example 2. Given an input difference $\beta = 8$, and two output differences $\gamma_1 = 8$, $\gamma_2 = c$, the value of GBCT, DDT, and BCT are $GBCT(8, 8; 8, c) = 16$, $DDT(8, 8) = DDT(8, c) = 0$, $BCT(8, 8) = BCT(8, c) = 0$, respectively.

By looking up the DDT, we can find $\{\gamma_1' : DDT(\gamma_1', 8) = 2\} = \{\gamma_2' : DDT(\gamma_2', c) = 2\} = \{1, 3, 5, 7, 9, b, c, e\}$, and the solution for each input difference is shown in the following table.

γ_1'	1	3	5	7	9	b	c	e
(x_1, x_1')	$(2,3)$	(d,e)	$(9,c)$	$(0,7)$	$(1,8)$	$(4,f)$	$(6,a)$	$(5,b)$
γ_2'	1	3	5	7	9	b	c	e
(x_2, x_2')	(a,b)	$(5,6)$	$(1,4)$	$(8,f)$	$(9,0)$	$(c,7)$	$(2,e)$	$(3,d)$

It is clear that $(x_1, x_1') \oplus (x_2, x_2') = (8, 8)$ always holds when $\gamma_1' = \gamma_2'$. That means if (x_1, x_1') and (x_2, x_2') are the solutions of two faces of a boomerang structure, we can use a difference $\beta_1 = \beta_2 = 8$ to connect the differential trails on both sides to get a boomerang trail. Due to the symmetry of solutions, we can obtain 16 solutions in total.

Example 3. Given two input differences $\beta_1 = 1$, $\beta_2 = 7$ and an output difference $\gamma = 5$, the value of GBCT, DDT, and BCT are $GBCT(1, 7; 5, 5) = 10$, $DDT(1, 5) = DDT(7, 5) = 2$, $BCT(1, 5) = BCT(7, 5) = 2$, respectively. By looking up the DDT, we can find $\{\gamma' : DDT(\gamma', 5) = 2 \text{ or } 4\} = \{1, 2, 3, 4, 5, 7\}$. Solutions of $DDT(\gamma', 5) > 0$ are given below.

γ'	1	2	3	4	5	7
(x, x')	(c,d)	$(0,2)$	$(8,b)$	$(1,5)$	(a,f)	$(9,e)$
		(4,6)		(3,7)		

Let $\beta_1 = 1$ and $\beta_2 = 7$, we can get $(x \oplus \beta_1, x' \oplus \beta_2)$ as follows.

(x, x')	$(c,d)(d,c)$	$(0,2)(2,0)$	$(4,6)(6,4)$	$(8,b)(b,8)$	$(1,5)(5,1)$	$(3,7)(7,3)$	$(a,f)(f,a)$	$(9,e)(e,9)$
$(x \oplus \beta_1, x' \oplus \beta_2)$	$(d,a)(c,b)$	$(1,5)(3,7)$	$(5,1)(7,3)$	$(9,c)(a,f)$	$(0,2)(4,6)$	$(2,0)(6,4)$	$(b,8)(e,d)$	$(8,9)(f,e)$

When x and x' are shifted by $\beta_1 = 1$ and $\beta_2 = 7$ respectively, there are 10 solutions whose output differences are 5. A boomerang trail can be obtained by connecting the differential trails on both sides of a boomerang structure with differences $\beta_1 = 1$ and $\beta_2 = 7$.

It can be concluded from the above examples that for a boomerang structure, (x_1, x_1') and (x_2, x_2') are solutions to differential trails $\gamma_1' \to \gamma_1$ and $\gamma_2' \to \gamma_2$ respectively on both sides of the structure, then $GBCT(\beta_1, \beta_2; \gamma_1, \gamma_2) > 0$ as long as there exists two differences β_1 and β_2 such that $(x_2 \oplus \beta_1, x_2' \oplus \beta_2) = (x_1, x_1')$.

3.2 Properties of GBCT

In the following we give some basic properties of GBCT and its links with other tables, most of which can be deduced directly from the definition, so some proofs are omitted here.

Proposition 1. *(Symmetry of GBCT)*

$$\begin{aligned} &GBCT(\beta_1, \beta_2; \gamma_1, \gamma_2) \\ &= GBCT(\beta_2, \beta_1; \gamma_1, \gamma_2) = GBCT(\beta_1, \beta_2; \gamma_2, \gamma_1) = GBCT(\beta_2, \beta_1; \gamma_2, \gamma_1). \end{aligned}$$

Proposition 2. *(Telations with DDT and BCT)*

$$\begin{aligned} &GBCT(\beta, \beta; \gamma, \gamma) = BCT(\beta; \gamma), \quad GBCT(\beta_2, \beta_1; 0, \gamma_2) = DDT(\beta_1 \oplus \beta_2; \gamma_2), \\ &GBCT(0, \beta_2; \gamma_1, \gamma_2) = DDT(\beta_2; \gamma_1 \oplus \gamma_2). \end{aligned}$$

Proposition 3. *(Summation formula I)*

$$\begin{aligned} \sum_{\beta_1} GBCT(\beta_1, \beta_2; \gamma_1, \gamma_2) &= \sum_{\beta_2} GBCT(\beta_1, \beta_2; \gamma_1, \gamma_2) = 2^n, \\ \sum_{\gamma_1} GBCT(\beta_1, \beta_2; \gamma_1, \gamma_2) &= \sum_{\gamma_2} GBCT(\beta_1, \beta_2; \gamma_1, \gamma_2) = 2^n. \end{aligned}$$

Proposition 4. *(Summation formula II)*

$$\sum_{\beta_1, \beta_2} GBCT(\beta_1, \beta_2; \gamma_1, \gamma_2) = \sum_{\gamma_1, \gamma_2} GBCT(\beta_1, \beta_2; \gamma_1, \gamma_2) = 2^{2n}.$$

Proposition 5.

$$GBCT_{S^{-1}}(\gamma_1, \gamma_2; \beta_1, \beta_2) = GBCT_S(\beta_1, \beta_2; \gamma_1, \gamma_2).$$

Proposition 6.

$$\begin{aligned} &GBCT(\beta_1, \beta_2; \gamma_1, \gamma_2) \\ &= CDDT(\beta_1, \gamma_2; \beta_2, \gamma_1) + \sum_{\alpha \neq 0, \beta_2} \# \left(\bigcup_{\alpha, \gamma_1} \cap \left(\bigcup_{\alpha \oplus \gamma_1 \oplus \gamma_2, \gamma_2} \oplus \beta_1 \right) \right), \end{aligned}$$

where $\bigcup_{a,b} := \{x \in \mathbb{F}_2^n | S(x) \oplus S(x \oplus a) = b\}$ *and the cross-DDT of* S *is*

$$CDDT(\beta_1, \gamma_2; \beta_2, \gamma_1) = \# \left\{ x \in \mathbb{F}_2^n \;\middle|\; \begin{array}{l} S(x) \oplus S(x \oplus \beta_1) = \gamma_2, \\ S(x) \oplus S(x \oplus \beta_2) = \gamma_1 \end{array} \right\}.$$

Proposition 7.

$$GBCT(\beta_1, \beta_2; \gamma_1, \gamma_2) = \frac{1}{2^{4n}} \cdot \sum_{a,b,c,d} (-1)^{a\cdot\gamma_1 \oplus b\cdot\gamma_2 \oplus c\cdot\beta_1 \oplus d\cdot\beta_2} \cdot W_F(c,a) \cdot W_F(c,b) \cdot W_F(d,a) \cdot W_F(d,b).$$

where $W_F(u,v) := \sum_x (-1)^{ux \oplus vF(x)}$.

Proof. We have

$$\begin{aligned}
&GBCT(\beta_1, \beta_2; \gamma_1, \gamma_2)\\
&= \#\{(x,y) \in \mathbb{F}_2^n \times \mathbb{F}_2^n | F(x) \oplus F(y) = \gamma_1,\ F(x \oplus \beta_1) \oplus F(y \oplus \beta_2) = \gamma_2\}\\
&= \frac{1}{2^{2n}} \sum_{x,y} \sum_{a,b} (-1)^{a(F(x)\oplus F(y)\oplus\gamma_1)} (-1)^{b(F(x\oplus\beta_1)\oplus F(y\oplus\beta_2)\oplus\gamma_2)}\\
&= \frac{1}{2^{2n}} \sum_{a,b} (-1)^{a\gamma_1 \oplus b\gamma_2} \sum_{x,y} (-1)^{a\cdot F(x) \oplus b\cdot F(x\oplus\beta_1)} (-1)^{a\cdot F(y) \oplus b\cdot F(y\oplus\beta_2)}\\
&= \frac{1}{2^{2n}} \sum_{a,b} (-1)^{a\gamma_1 \oplus b\gamma_2} C_{\beta_1}(a,b) C_{\beta_2}(a,b),
\end{aligned}$$

where

$$\begin{aligned}
C_\beta(a,b) &= \sum_x (-1)^{a\cdot F(x) \oplus b\cdot F(x\oplus\beta)}\\
&= \frac{1}{2^n} \sum_w (-1)^{w(x\oplus y)} \sum_{x,y} (-1)^{a\cdot F(x) \oplus F(y\oplus\beta)}\\
&= \frac{1}{2^n} \sum_w (-1)^{w\cdot z} \sum_{x,z} (-1)^{a\cdot F(x) \oplus b\cdot F(x\oplus z\oplus\beta)}\\
&= \frac{1}{2^n} \sum_{w,x,z} (-1)^{[a\cdot F(x) \oplus w\cdot x] \oplus [b\cdot F(x\oplus z\oplus\beta) \oplus w(x\oplus z\oplus\beta)] \oplus w\cdot\beta}\\
&= \frac{1}{2^n} \sum_w (-1)^{w\cdot\beta} W_F(w,a) \cdot W_F(w,b).
\end{aligned}$$

Proposition 8. *Let F, G be two permutations of $\mathbb{F}_2^n$ with $G = F \circ L$ for an invertible affine transformation L of $\mathbb{F}_2^n$. Then we have*

$$g_G(a_1, a_2; b_1, b_2) = g_F(L_1(a_1), L_1(a_2), L_2^{-1}(b_1), L_2^{-1}(b_2)).$$

for all $a, b \in \mathbb{F}_2^n$, where $g_F(a_1, a_2; b_1, b_2) = GBCT(a_1, a_2; b_1, b_2)$ for F.

3.3 Variants of GBCT

GBCT in Multi-rounds. Just as how Wang et al. extend BCT to be used in two-round E_m, GBCT can also be converted with the same idea to be applied in two rounds. We introduce the generalized boomerang differential table (GBDT) (Fig. 6).

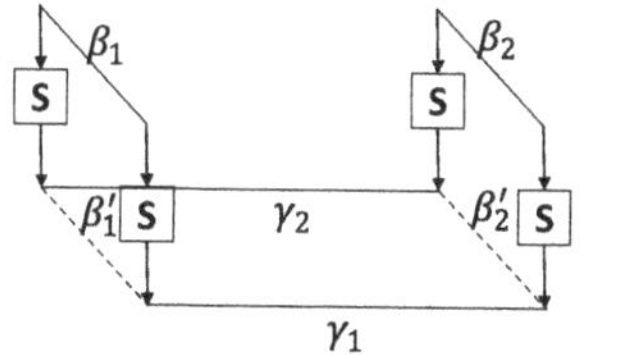

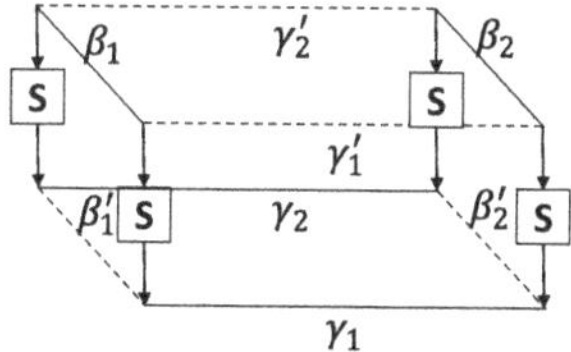

Fig. 6. Structures of GBDT (left) and GBET (right)

Definition 2. *Let S be a permutation over $\mathbb{F}_2^n$ and $\beta_1, \beta_2, \gamma_1, \gamma_2, \beta_1', \beta_2' \in \mathbb{F}_2^n$. The generalized boomerang differential table (GBDT) of S is a 6-dimensional table, in which the entry for $(\beta_1, \beta_2; \gamma_1, \gamma_2; \beta_1', \beta_2')$ is computed by*

$$\begin{aligned} & GBDT(\beta_1, \beta_2; \gamma_1, \gamma_2; \beta_1', \beta_2') \\ & = \# \left\{ (x,y) \in \mathbb{F}_2^n \times \mathbb{F}_2^n \;\middle|\; \begin{array}{l} S(x) \oplus S(y) = \gamma_1, S(x \oplus \beta_1) \oplus S(y \oplus \beta_2) = \gamma_2, \\ S(x) \oplus S(x \oplus \beta_1) = \beta_1', S(x) \oplus S(x \oplus \beta_2) = \beta_2' \end{array} \right\}. \end{aligned}$$

GBDT and BDT shares some properties, most of which can be easily obtained from the definition, so it is not proved here. Refer interested readers to [22] for more details.

Next, we use the same notations as in [22] to show how to calculate the probability with GBDT. The probability of a two-round E_m is the product of the two probabilities $r = p_1 p_2$, where

$$p_1 = \prod_{(\Delta_1, \Delta_2; \nabla_1'', \nabla_2''; \Delta_1', \Delta_2') \in L_1} GBDT(\Delta_1, \Delta_2; \nabla_1'', \nabla_2''; \Delta_1', \Delta_2')/2^n,$$

$$p_2 = \prod_{(\nabla_1, \nabla_2; \Delta_1'', \Delta_2''; \nabla_1', \nabla_2') \in L_2} GBDT(\nabla_1, \nabla_2; \Delta_1'', \Delta_2''; \nabla_1', \nabla_2')/2^n.$$

When E_m covers more rounds, we can borrow the idea of EBCT [11] to give the definition of GBET.

Definition 3. *Let S be a permutation over $\mathbb{F}_2^n$ and $\beta_1, \beta_2, \gamma_1, \gamma_2, \beta_1', \beta_2', \gamma_1', \gamma_2' \in \mathbb{F}_2^n$. The generalized boomerang extended table (GBET) of S is a 8-dimensional table, in which the entry for $(\beta_1, \beta_2; \gamma_1, \gamma_2; \beta_1', \beta_2'; \gamma_1', \gamma_2')$ is computed by*

$$\begin{aligned} & GBET(\beta_1, \beta_2; \gamma_1, \gamma_2; \beta_1', \beta_2'; \gamma_1', \gamma_2') \\ & = \# \left\{ (x,y) \in \mathbb{F}_2^n \times \mathbb{F}_2^n \;\middle|\; \begin{array}{l} x \oplus y = \gamma_1', (x \oplus \beta_1) \oplus (y \oplus \beta_2) = \gamma_2', \\ S(x) \oplus S(x \oplus \beta_1) = \beta_1', S(y) \oplus S(y \oplus \beta_2) = \beta_2', \\ S(x) \oplus S(y) = \gamma_1, S(x \oplus \beta_1) \oplus S(y \oplus \beta_2) = \gamma_2 \end{array} \right\}. \end{aligned}$$

When E_m covers more rounds, the probability is $r = \prod_i p_i$, where

$$p_i = \prod_{(\Delta_1, \Delta_2; \nabla_1, \nabla_2; \nabla_1', \nabla_2'; \Delta_1', \Delta_2') \in L_i} GBDT(\Delta_1, \Delta_2; \nabla_1, \nabla_2; \nabla_1', \nabla_2'; \Delta_1', \Delta_2')/2^n,$$

and L_i has the same meaning as the previous one.

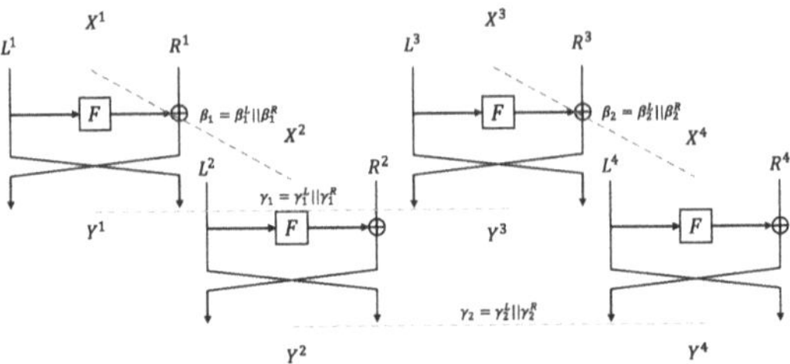

Fig. 7. The GBCT in a Feistel structure

Put GBCT into a Feistel Structure. The FBCT was proposed as a counterpart of BCT for Feistel structures and its properties have also been studied in [6,15]. Similar to BCT, GBCT is also applicable into Feistel structures. Here we take a generic Feistel structure as example, as shown in Fig. 7. Denote the output after one round of $X^i = L^i||R^i, i = 1, ..., 4$ as $Y^i = G^i||L^i, i = 1, ..., 4$. Assume that $X^1 \oplus X^2 = \beta_1 = \beta_1^L||\beta_1^R$, $Y^1 \oplus Y^3 = \gamma_1 = \gamma_1^L||\gamma_1^R$ and $Y^2 \oplus Y^4 = \gamma_2 = \gamma_2^L||\gamma_2^R$. Now, we check whether $X^3 \oplus X^4 = \beta_2 = \beta_2^L||\beta_2^R$:

$$
\begin{aligned}
\beta_2^L &= L^3 \oplus L^4 = L^1 \oplus \gamma_1^R \oplus L^2 \oplus \gamma_2^R = \beta_1^L \oplus \gamma_1^R \oplus \gamma_2^R,\\
\beta_2^R &= R^3 \oplus R^4 = F(L^3) \oplus G^3 \oplus F(L^4) \oplus G^4\\
&= R^1 \oplus R^2 \oplus \gamma_1^L \oplus \gamma_2^L \oplus F(L^1) \oplus F(L^1 \oplus \gamma_1^R) \oplus F(L^2) \oplus F(L^2 \oplus \gamma_2^R)\\
&= \beta_1^R \oplus \gamma_1^L \oplus \gamma_2^L \oplus F(L^1) \oplus F(L^1 \oplus \gamma_1^R) \oplus F(L^1 \oplus \beta_1^L) \oplus F(L^1 \oplus \beta_1^L \oplus \gamma_2^R).
\end{aligned}
$$

If $X^3 \oplus X^4 = \beta_2$, then β_2 should satisfy $\beta_2^L = \beta_1^L \oplus \gamma_1^R \oplus \gamma_2^R$ and $\beta_2^R = \beta_1^R \oplus \gamma_1^L \oplus \gamma_2^L \oplus F(L^1) \oplus F(L^1 \oplus \gamma_1^R) \oplus F(L^1 \oplus \beta_1^L) \oplus F(L^1 \oplus \beta_1^L \oplus \gamma_2^R)$.

We degenerate the F function to the S-box layer. For each S-box, the input difference deduced from $\beta_i^L, i = 1, 2$ and $\gamma_i^R, i = 1, 2$ are denoted as $\Delta_i^L, i = 1, 2$ and $\Delta_i^R, i = 1, 2$. The output differences are denoted as $\nabla_i, i = 1, 2$ which are deduced from $\beta_i^R \oplus \gamma_i^L$. Then, the definition of FGBCT for each S-box is given below:

Definition 4. *Let $S : \mathbb{F}_2^n \rightarrow \mathbb{F}_2^m$, $\Delta_1^L, \Delta_1^R, \Delta_2^L, \Delta_2^R, \nabla_1, \nabla_2 \in \mathbb{F}_2^n$. The FGBCT of S is given by a 6-dimensional table, in which the entry for the $(\Delta_1^L, \Delta_1^R; \Delta_2^L, \Delta_2^R; \nabla_1, \nabla_2)$ position is given by*

$$
\begin{aligned}
&FGBCT(\Delta_1^L, \Delta_1^R; \Delta_2^L, \Delta_2^R; \nabla_1, \nabla_2)\\
&= \# \left\{ x \in \mathbb{F}_2^n \;\middle|\; \begin{array}{l} S(x) \oplus S(x \oplus \Delta_1^L) \oplus S(x \oplus \Delta_1^R) \oplus S(x \oplus \Delta_1^L \oplus \Delta_2^R) \oplus \nabla_1 \oplus \nabla_2 = 0, \\ \Delta_1^L \oplus \Delta_2^L \oplus \Delta_1^R \oplus \Delta_2^R = 0 \end{array} \right\}.
\end{aligned}
$$

Then, the probability of a boomerang for a Feistel structure with an S-box is given by $2^{-n} \cdot FGBCT(\Delta_1^L, \Delta_1^R; \Delta_2^L, \Delta_2^R; \nabla_1, \nabla_2)$.

Similarly, we give the definition of FGBDT and FGBET used in multi-round E_m. Symbols in the definitions are shown in the Fig. 8.

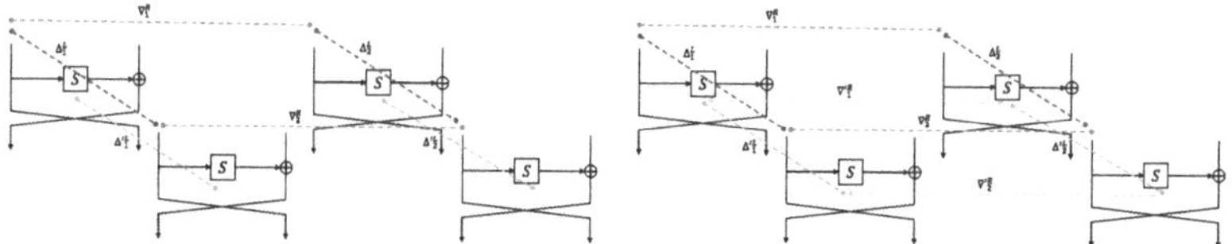

Fig. 8. Structures of FGBDT and FGBET

Definition 5. *Let $S : \mathbb{F}_2^n \rightarrow \mathbb{F}_2^m$, and the differences $\Delta_1^L, \Delta_1^R, \Delta_2^L, \Delta_2^R, \nabla_1, \nabla_2, {\Delta_1'}^L, {\Delta_2'}^L \in \mathbb{F}_2^n$. The FGBDT of S is given by a 8-dimensional table, in which the entry for the $(\Delta_1^L, \Delta_1^R; \Delta_2^L, \Delta_2^R; \nabla_1, \nabla_2; {\Delta_1'}^L, {\Delta_2'}^L)$ position is given by*

$$FGBDT(\Delta_1^L, \Delta_1^R; \Delta_2^L, \Delta_2^R; \nabla_1, \nabla_2; {\Delta_1'}^L, {\Delta_2'}^L)$$
$$= \# \left\{ x \in \mathbb{F}_2^n \;\middle|\; \begin{array}{l} S(x) \oplus S(x \oplus \Delta_1^L) \oplus S(x \oplus \Delta_1^R) \oplus S(x \oplus \Delta_1^L \oplus \Delta_2^R) \oplus \nabla_1 \oplus \nabla_2 = 0, \\ \Delta_1^L \oplus \Delta_2^L \oplus \Delta_1^R \oplus \Delta_2^R = 0, \\ S(x) \oplus S(x \oplus \Delta_1^L) = {\Delta_1'}^L, S(x) \oplus S(x \oplus \Delta_2^L) = {\Delta_2'}^L \end{array} \right\}.$$

Definition 6. *Let $S : \mathbb{F}_2^n \rightarrow \mathbb{F}_2^m$, and the differences $\Delta_1^L, \Delta_1^R, \Delta_2^L, \Delta_2^R, \nabla_1, \nabla_2, {\Delta_1'}^L, {\Delta_2'}^L, {\Delta_1'}^R, {\Delta_2'}^R \in \mathbb{F}_2^n$. The FGBET of S is given by a 10-dimensional table, in which the entry for the $(\Delta_1^L, \Delta_1^R; \Delta_2^L, \Delta_2^R; \nabla_1, \nabla_2; {\Delta_1'}^L, {\Delta_2'}^L; {\Delta_1'}^R, {\Delta_2'}^R)$ position is given by*

$$FGBET(\Delta_1^L, \Delta_1^R; \Delta_2^L, \Delta_2^R; \nabla_1, \nabla_2; {\Delta_1'}^L, {\Delta_2'}^L; {\Delta_1'}^R, {\Delta_2'}^R)$$
$$= \# \left\{ x \in \mathbb{F}_2^n \;\middle|\; \begin{array}{l} S(x) \oplus S(x \oplus \Delta_1^L) \oplus S(x \oplus \Delta_1^R) \oplus S(x \oplus \Delta_1^L \oplus \Delta_2^R) \oplus \nabla_1 \oplus \nabla_2 = 0, \\ \Delta_1^L \oplus \Delta_2^L \oplus \Delta_1^R \oplus \Delta_2^R = 0, \\ S(x) \oplus S(x \oplus \Delta_1^L) = {\Delta_1'}^L, S(x) \oplus S(x \oplus \Delta_2^L) = {\Delta_2'}^L, \\ S(x) \oplus S(x \oplus \nabla_1^R) = {\nabla_1'}^R, S(x) \oplus S(x \oplus \nabla_2^R) = {\nabla_2'}^R \end{array} \right\}.$$

3.4 The Advantages of GBCT

The probability of a boomerang distinguisher with BCT in one-round E_m is calculated in [16] as

$$\hat{p}^2 \hat{q}^2 = \frac{1}{2^n} \sum_{i,j} p_i^2 \cdot q_j^2 \cdot BCT(\beta_i, \gamma_j).$$

For each boomerang trail $\alpha \rightarrow \beta_i \rightarrow \gamma_j \rightarrow \delta$, if the value of $BCT(\beta_i, \gamma_j)$ is 0, even if the value of $p_i^2 \cdot q_j^2$ is high enough, the trail is still in vain. Yet, BCT is limited to connecting β and γ that are symmetric in two faces of E_m, leaving out a large number of asymmetric combinations, which can be completed by GBCT.

In order to illustrate that GBCT can completely describe all combinations of β and γ, we list the distribution of GBCTs of some 4-bit S-boxes used in cryptographic primitives in Table 2, where the blue font represents the corresponding value of BCT. It turns out that GBCT can provide some probabilities that BCT cannot. The following example illustrates a boomerang trail that is incompatible when connecting E_0 and E_1 via BCT but effective with GBCT.

Table 2. GBCTs of 4-bit S-boxes from Sage's **Cryptography** package; see https://doc.sagemath.org/html/en/reference/cryptography/sage/crypto/sboxes.html

S-boxs	Prob.									
	1	0.63	0.5	0.44	0.38	0.31	0.25	0.19	0.13	0.06
GIFT	34(32)	6(2)	48(12)	0	278(6)	24	2426(30)	0	16212(72)	15424
PRESENT	33(33)	0	108(8)	0	60(12)	40	2856(36)	0	16172(60)	16096
SKINNY_4	37(33)	0	116(16)	0	64(0)	96	3028(32)	0	16040(72)	16440
Elephant	35(33)	0	112(12)	0	64(8)	64	2900(32)	0	16140(64)	16184
KNOT	33(33)	0	108(8)	0	60(6)	40	2856(36)	1240	16172(60)	16096
Spook	37(33)	0	116(16)	0	64(0)	96	3028(32)	840	16040(72)	16440
GOST_1	34(32)	6(2)	48(12)	0	278(6)	24	2426(30)	1736	16212(72)	15424
LBlock_0	37(33)	10(0)	116(16)	0	64(0)	96	3028(32)	840	16040(72)	16440
SERPENT_S0	35(33)	0	112(12)	0	64(8)	64	2900(32)	1128	16104(64)	16184
KLEIN	31(31)	4(4)	0	16	62(14)	0	1807(23)	2512	16184(72)	17384
Midori_Sb0	33(33)	0	108(8)	0	60(12)	40	2856(36)	1240	16172(60)	16096
Piccolo	37(33)	0	116(16)	0	64(0)	96	3028(32)	840	16040(72)	16440
Pride	37(33)	0	116(16)	0	64(0)	96	3028(32)	840	16040(72)	16440
PRINCE	31(31)	1(1)	2(2)	0	75(11)	60	1824(28)	2380	15970(78)	17888
Rectangle	33(33)	0	108(8)	0	60(12)	40	2856(36)	1240	16172(60)	16096
TWINE	31(31)	0	0	0	30(30)	0	1455(15)	2280	17940(60)	16320
BLAKE_1	31(31)	0	75(7)	4	90(14)	114	2056(40)	2756	14990(66)	16680
Iceberg_S0	31(31)	4(4)	0	16	62(14)	0	1807(23)	2512	16184(72)	17384
Kuznyechik_nu0	31(31)	0	0	0	166(14)	80	1275(27)	2608	16732(84)	17256
Serpent_type_S0	33(33)	0	108(8)	0	60(12)	40	2856(36)	1240	16172(60)	16096
Golden_S0	31(31)	1(1)	13(5)	0	58(14)	148	1980(28)	2508	15525(69)	17344

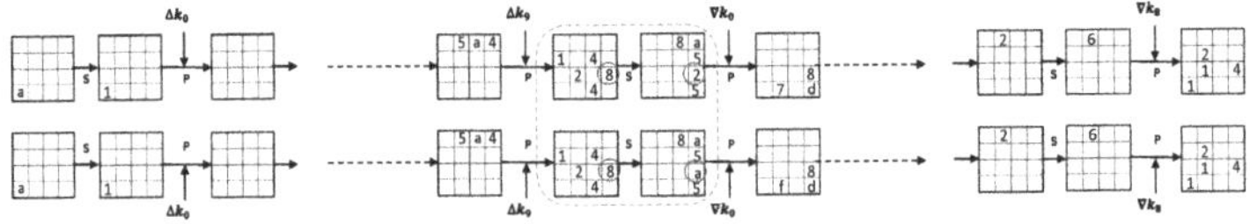

Fig. 9. 20-round boomerang trail with GBCT

Example 4. A 20-round boomerang trail of GIFT-64 with GBCT is shown in Fig. 9. The trail is obtained by connecting two 10-round related-key differential trails in E_0 and two 9-round related-key differential trails in E_1 with GBCT. And two key differences are

$$\Delta iniK = 0x00040000000000800000000000000010,$$
$$\nabla iniK = 0x20000000000000000800000002000800$$

The probability of this distinguisher is $p^2q^2r = 2^{-21\cdot 2} \cdot 2^{-15\cdot 2} \cdot 2^{-1} = 2^{-73}$ when connected with GBCT, but 0 when connected with BCT.

4 New Search Algorithm for a Boomerang Distinguisher

The instance in Example 4 illustrates the effectiveness of using GBCT as the connection in a boomerang trail. Then, we consider to construct a generic model of the GBCT with automatic the search tool SMT, and search for boomerang distinguishers.

4.1 Strategies in the Search Algorithm

In [16], Ji et al. proposed an automatic search algorithm to boost the probability of a related-key boomerang distinguisher by taking the cluster effect into account, which has the best performance in searching for boomerang distinguishers. Making some improvements on the base of the algorithm, we obtain a new search algorithm performing better. With the new algorithm, we get boomerang distinguishers with higher probabilities for GIFT-64 and GIFT-128. The details of the distinguishers will be given in the next subsection.

Here gives the strategy to search for a rectangle distinguisher. Firstly, we find that when searching for the 10-round differential trails the optimal probability is $2^{-19.83}$, rather than $2^{-20.415}$ searched in [16]. The details of the optimal differentials are listed in Table 6 in Appendix A. Taking the probability range $bw = 4$, and choosing the optimal α, we discover that it has only 263 output differences β_i and a total of 308 trails can be obtained, which is smaller than the quantity of that with the suboptimal α, who has 2944 distinct β_i and a total of 5728 trails. Thus, to get a better cluster effect, we should select α and δ with more β and γ in the first phase. In addition, replacing the probability of each differential trail with the probability of differential is a better way to approximate the real probability. Thirdly, the completeness of the connections in E_m should be ensured to form more valid boomerang trails. Finally, an improved boomerang distinguisher search Algorithm 1 is proposed in light of the aforementioned factors. And the search algorithm in single-key setting can be obtained likewise. Symbols used in Algorithm 1 is explained in Table 3.

Table 3. Symbols in Algorithm 1

$P(\cdot)$, $K(\cdot)$	PermBits operation, AddRoundKey operation
ΔX_i, ΔY_i	the differential value of X_i, Y_i in round i
$\Delta iniK_i$, $\nabla iniK_j$	the master key difference of differential trails in E_0, E_1
$W(l)$	the weight of the differential trail l
B_R, $\bar{B}_R$	the weight of the R-round optimal, sub-optimal trails
B_{c_R}	the upper bound of B_R
bw, $\bar{bw}$	$bw = B_{c_R} - B_R$, $\bar{bw} \geq bw$

Algorithm 1: The search algorithm for related-key boomerang distinguishers

Input: R_0, R_1; bw, $\bar{bw}$
Output: Pd; ΔY_1^i, $\Delta iniK_i$; $\Delta X_{R_1-1}^j$, $\nabla iniK_j$

Phase 1: Determine all the distinct $\Delta Y_1^i, \Delta iniK_i$ and $\Delta X_{R_1-1}^j, \nabla iniK_j$ with minimal and sub minimal weight
Search for the R_0-round related-key differential trails with B_{R_0} and $\bar{B}_{R_0}$ for E_0 with SMT.
$\Delta Y_1^i, \Delta iniK_i$ and $B_{R_0}^i$, $1 \leq i \leq m \leftarrow$ first-round output difference, the master key difference and weight of each R_0-round trail.
Search for the R_1-round related-key differential trails with B_{R_1} and $\bar{B}_{R_1}$ for E_1 with SMT.
$\Delta X_{R_1-1}^j, \nabla iniK_j$ and $B_{R_1}^j$, $1 \leq j \leq n \leftarrow$ last-round input difference, the master key difference and weight of each R_1-round trail.
Phase 2: Search for all the clusters in E_0 and E_1
for *each* $\Delta Y_1^i, \Delta iniK_i, B_{R_0}^i, 1 \leq i \leq m$ **do**
  $\beta_i^u = K \circ P(\Delta Y_{R_0}^i), 1 \leq u \leq s \leftarrow$ all distinct output differences of E_0 within the probability range $(B_{R_0}^i + bw)$ searched with SMT.
  for *each* $\beta_i^u, 1 \leq u \leq s$ **do**
    $l_i^{u_1}, ..., l_i^{u_g} \leftarrow$ all the trails under the probability range $(B_{R_0}^i + \bar{bw})$ searched with SMT.
    $B_{R_0}^{iu_d} \leftarrow W(l_i^{u_d}), 1 \leq d \leq g$
    $p_i^u = \sum_{1 \leq d \leq g} 2^{-B_{R_0}^{iu_d}} \leftarrow$ the approximate probability of $(\Delta Y_1^i, \beta_i^u)$.
  end
end
for *each* $\Delta X_{R_1-1}^j, \nabla iniK_j, \bar{B}_{R_1}, 1 \leq j \leq n$ **do**
  $\gamma_j^v = P^{-1} \circ K^{-1}(\Delta X_1), 1 \leq v \leq t \leftarrow$ all distinct input differences of E_1 within the probability range $(B_{R_1}^j + bw)$ searched with SMT.
  for *each* $\gamma_j^v, 1 \leq v \leq t$ **do**
    $l_j^{v_1}, ..., l_j^{v_h} \leftarrow$ all the trails under the probability range $(B_{R_1}^j + \bar{bw})$.
    $B_{R_1}^{iv_e} \leftarrow W(l_j^{v_e}), 1 \leq e \leq h$
    $q_j^v = \sum_{1 \leq h \leq e} 2^{-B_{R_1}^{iv_e}} \leftarrow$ the approximate probability of $(\gamma_j^v, \Delta X_{R_1-1}^j)$.
  end
end
Phase 3: Determine the boomerang distinguisher with highest probability
for *each* $(\Delta Y_1^i, \Delta X_{R_1-1}^j)$, *and all* $\beta_i^u, \beta_i^{u'}, 1 \leq u, u' \leq s$, $\gamma_j^v, \gamma_j^{v'}, 1 \leq v, v' \leq t$ **do**
  $r(\beta_i^u, \beta_i^{u'}, \gamma_j^v, \gamma_j^{v'}) = \frac{1}{2^n} GBCT(\beta_i^u, \beta_i^{u'}, \gamma_j^v, \gamma_j^{v'})$
  $P_{i,j} \leftarrow \sum_{u,u',v,v'} p_i^u \cdot p_i^{u'} \cdot q_j^v \cdot q_j^{v'} \cdot r(\beta_i^u, \beta_i^{u'}, \gamma_j^v, \gamma_j^{v'})$
end
$Pd \leftarrow \max_{i,j}\{P_{i,j}\}$

4.2 The Improved Distinguisher with GBCT for GIFT

Here, we give the details of the new distinguisher of GIFT-64 and GIFT-128.

Choosing $R_0 = 10$ for E_0, $R_1 = 9$ for E_1, $R_m = 1$ for E_m and $bw = \bar{bw} = 4$ to search for a 20-round GIFT-64 distinguisher. The experimental result indicates that the probability of the new distinguisher is optimal with the α and δ used in [16]. But, in Phase 2, we get 376 differentials trails with 376 distinct γ_j more than 312 differentials trails searched in [16]. In phase 3, we found a total of 5520 boomerang trails that were left out as BCT could not connect. Finally, the probability of the 20-round distinguisher found in [16] is increased to $2^{-57.43}$.

For GIFT-128, we chose R_0= 9 for E_0, R_1 =9 for E_1, $R_m = 1$ for E_m and $bw = \bar{bw} = 4$. In phase 1, we got 10184 distinct β. All the β and γ can form $(10184 \times 2944)^2$ possible boomerang trails, which leads to an excessive calculating complexity. So we select the top 200 β and 450 γ with high probability to connect by GBCT$(\beta^i, \beta^j; \gamma^s, \gamma^t)$, and the remaining are still connected by BCT(β, γ). Finally, 2782 trails ignored under BCT connection are obtained, and the probabilities of these trails are accumulated to obtain the probability of the distinguisher of $2^{-108.349}$.

All the parameters of the 20/19-round related-key rectangle distinguisher for GIFT-64/128 are shown in Table 4 and Table 5.

Table 4. The specifications of the 20-round related-key rectangle distinguisher for GIFT-64

$R_0 = 10, R_m = 1, R_1 = 9; B_{c_{R0}} = 24.415, B_{c_{R1}} = 17.415; \hat{p}^2\hat{q}^2 = 2^{-57.43}$		
E_0	α_1	$\Delta iniK_0$
	0000 0000 0000 a000	0004 0000 0000 0800 0000 0000 0000 0010
E_1	δ_1	$\nabla iniK_1$
	0400 0000 0120 1000	2000 0000 0000 0000 0800 0000 0200 0800

Table 5. The specifications of the 19-round related-key rectangle distinguisher for GIFT-128

$R_0 = 9, R_m = 1, R_1 = 9; B_{c_{R0}} = 34, B_{c_{R1}} = 34; \hat{p}^2\hat{q}^2 = 2^{108.349}$		
E_0	α_1	$\Delta iniK_0$
	0000 0000 0000 00a0 0000 0000 6000 0000;	8000 0000 0000 0000 0000 0000 0002 0000
E_1	δ_1	$\nabla iniK_1$
	0020 0000 0000 0000 0000 0040 0000 2020;	000 0000 0000 0000 0002 0000 0002 0000

5 Rectangle Attacks on GIFT-64 and GIFT-128 with Reduced Complexities

Since the new distinguishers for GIFT-64 and GIFT-128 improve only the probability while using the same input-output differences as in [16], Dong's key recovery algorithm can be directly applied with it. Here, we only give the complexity analysis of the attack and will not dwell on the details of the key recovery process. Interested readers are referred to [12,16].

Complexity Analysis of Key-Recovery Attack on GIFT-64

The target key bits are 68 with 30 bits in E_b and 38 bits in E_f. We first guess $m_b + m'_f = 60$ bits subkey to construct quartet candidates. Then eliminate the wrong quartets in a guess and filter procedure to determine the remaining 8 bits. Finally, guess the remaining $128 - h$ bit keys to check the full key.

- **Data complexity:** we need to prepare $4 \cdot D = 4 \cdot y \cdot 2^{r_b} = \sqrt{s} \cdot 2^{n/2+2}/\hat{p}\hat{q} = \sqrt{s} \cdot 2^{62.715}$ data.
- **Memory complexity:** we need $4 \cdot D + 2^{68-x} = \sqrt{s} \cdot 2^{62.715} + 2^{68-x}$ memory to store the data and key counters.
- **Time complexity:** Firstly, we need $T_1 = \sqrt{s} \cdot 2^{m_b+m'_f+n/2+1}/\hat{p}\hat{q} = \sqrt{s} \cdot 2^{121.715}$ to generate quartet candidates. Then, the time complexity of filtering wrong quartets is $T_2 = (s \cdot 2^{m_b+m'_f-n+2r_f-2h_f}/\hat{p}^2\hat{q}^2) \cdot \varepsilon = s \cdot 2^{83.43} \cdot \varepsilon$. Finally, we need $T_3 = 2^{128-h}$ for an exhaustive search.

To balance the above complexity, we choose $x = 8$, $h = 20$ and $s = 1$ in order to achieve a success probability of 69.45%. At last, we have a time complexity of $2^{121.715}$ for 26-round encryptions, a data complexity of $2^{62.715}$ and a memory complexity of $2^{62.715}$.

Complexity Analysis of Key-Recovery Attack on GIFT-128

The target key bits is 39 with 6 bits in E_b and 33 bits in E_f. We repeat the same process as the attack on GIFT-64 for GIFT-128 with $m_b + m'_f = 6 + 0 = 6$.

- **Data complexity:** we need to prepare $4 \cdot D = \sqrt{s} \cdot 2^{120.175}$ data.
- **Memory complexity:** we need $4 \cdot D + 2^{68-x} = \sqrt{s} \cdot 2^{120.175} + 2^{39}$ memory to store the data and key counters.
- **Time complexity:** Firstly, we need $T_1 = \sqrt{s} \cdot 2^{m_b+m'_f+n/2+1}/\hat{p}\hat{q} = \sqrt{s} \cdot 2^{125.175}$ to generate quartet candidates. Then, the time complexity of filtering wrong quartets is $T_2 = (s \cdot 2^{m_b+m'_f-n+2r_f-2h_f}/\hat{p}^2\hat{q}^2) \cdot \varepsilon = s \cdot 2^{90.5} \cdot \varepsilon$. Finally, we need $T_3 = 2^{128-h}$ for an exhaustive search.

To balance the above complexity, We choose $h = 20$ and $s = 1$ in order to achieve a good success probability of 84.00%. At last, we have a time complexity of $2^{125.175}$ 23-round encryptions, a data complexity of $2^{120.175}$ and a memory complexity of $2^{120.175}$.

6 Conclusion and Future Discussion

In this paper, we propose the GBCT to complement the leaky part that can not be evaluated by BCT, so as to obtain a more accurate distinguisher probability. Then, an automatic search algorithm applicable to all S-box-based block ciphers is provided to obtain a rectangle distinguisher with higher probability. Utilizing the algorithm, we achieve the optimal probability of distinguishers for 20/19-round GIFT-64/128, and therefore the lowest data and time complexities of the related-key rectangle attacks on GIFT-64/128 up to now.

There are still some unfinished work to be investigated in the future. More variables introduced by GBCT are very constrained for the MILP model when $E_m > 1$. In addition, the search algorithm is only applicable to ciphers with S-boxes as the nonlinear layers. In the future, we will extend the research to fully assess the probability in E_m, not only when $E_m > 1$, but also for ciphers with nonlinear components like modular additions or bit-wise AND operations.

Acknowledgement. This work was supported by the National Natural Science Foundation of China (Grant No. 61872359, No. 61936008 and No. 61972393) and the Climbing Program from Institute of Information Engineering CAS (Grant No. E1Z0041112).

A 10-Round Optimal (Related-Key) Differentials for GIFT-64

Table 6. Input and Output differences of 10-round related-key differential trails with weight 19.8 of GIFT-64

i	input differences α_i	master key differences $\Delta iniK$
1	0000 0000 0000 6002 0000 0000 0000 6004	000C 0000 0000 0000 0040 0000 0000 0011
2	0000 0000 6002 0000 0000 0000 6004 0000	00C0 0000 0000 0000 0004 0000 0000 0022
3	0000 6002 0000 0000 0000 6004 0000 0000	0C00 0000 0000 0000 4000 0000 0000 0044
4	6002 0000 0000 0000 6004 0000 0000 0000	C000 0000 0000 0000 0400 0000 0000 0088

i	output differences δ_i	master key differences $\nabla iniK$
1	0800 0400 0220 0310	000C 0000 0000 0000 0040 0000 0000 0011
2	0310 0800 0400 0220	00C0 0000 0000 0000 0004 0000 0000 0022
3	0220 0310 0800 0400	0C00 0000 0000 0000 4000 0000 0000 0044
4	0400 0220 0310 0800	C000 0000 0000 0000 0400 0000 0000 0088

References

1. Banik, S., et al.: GIFT-COFB. Cryptology ePrint Archive, Paper 2020/738 (2020)
2. Banik, S., Pandey, S.K., Peyrin, T., Sasaki, Yu., Sim, S.M., Todo, Y.: GIFT: a small present - towards reaching the limit of lightweight encryption. In: Fischer, W., Homma, N. (eds.) CHES 2017. LNCS, vol. 10529, pp. 321–345. Springer, Cham (2017). https://doi.org/10.1007/978-3-319-66787-4_16
3. Biham, E., Dunkelman, O., Keller, N.: The rectangle attack—rectangling the serpent. In: Pfitzmann, B. (ed.) EUROCRYPT 2001. LNCS, vol. 2045, pp. 340–357. Springer, Heidelberg (2001). https://doi.org/10.1007/3-540-44987-6_21
4. Biham, E., Shamir, A.: Differential cryptanalysis of DES-like cryptosystems. J. Cryptol. **4**(1), 3–72 (1991)
5. Biryukov, A., Khovratovich, D.: Related-key cryptanalysis of the full AES-192 and AES-256. In: Matsui, M. (ed.) ASIACRYPT 2009. LNCS, vol. 5912, pp. 1–18. Springer, Heidelberg (2009). https://doi.org/10.1007/978-3-642-10366-7_1
6. Boukerrou, H., Huynh, P., Lallemand, V., Mandal, B., Minier, M.: On the feistel counterpart of the boomerang connectivity table: introduction and analysis of the FBCT. IACR Trans. Symmetric Cryptol. **2020**(1), 331–362 (2020)
7. Chakraborti, A., Datta, N., Jha, A., Lopez, C.M., CINVESTAV, Sasaki, Y.: LOTUS-AEAD and LOCUS-AEAD. Submission to the NIST Lightweight Cryptography project (2019)
8. Chakraborti, A., Datta, N., Jha, A., Nandi, M.: HYENA. Submission to the NIST Lightweight Cryptography project (2019)
9. Cid, C., Huang, T., Peyrin, T., Sasaki, Y., Song, L.: A Security Analysis of Deoxys and its Internal Tweakable Block Ciphers. IACR Trans. Symmetric Cryptol. **3**, 73–107 (2017)
10. Cid, C., Huang, T., Peyrin, T., Sasaki, Yu., Song, L.: Boomerang connectivity table: a new cryptanalysis tool. In: Nielsen, J.B., Rijmen, V. (eds.) EUROCRYPT 2018. LNCS, vol. 10821, pp. 683–714. Springer, Cham (2018). https://doi.org/10.1007/978-3-319-78375-8_22
11. Delaune, S., Derbez, P., Vavrille, M.: Catching the fastest boomerangs application to SKINNY. IACR Trans. Symmetric Cryptol. **2020**(4), 104–129 (2020)
12. Dong, X., Qin, L., Sun, S., Wang, X.: Key guessing strategies for linear key-schedule algorithms in rectangle attacks. IACR Cryptol. ePrint Arch., p. 856 (2021)
13. Dunkelman, O., Keller, N., Shamir, A.: A practical-time related-key attack on the Kasumi cryptosystem used in GSM and 3G telephony. In: Rabin, T. (ed.) CRYPTO 2010. LNCS, vol. 6223, pp. 393–410. Springer, Heidelberg (2010). https://doi.org/10.1007/978-3-642-14623-7_21
14. Hadipour, H., Bagheri, N., Song, L.: Improved rectangle attacks on SKINNY and CRAFT. IACR Trans. Symmetric Cryptol. **2021**(2), 140–198 (2021)
15. Hadipour, H., Nageler, M., Eichlseder, M.: Throwing boomerangs into feistel structures: application to CLEFIA, WARP, LBlock, LBlock-s and TWINE. Cryptology ePrint Archive, Paper 2022/745 (2022)
16. Ji, F., Zhang, W., Zhou, C., Ding, T.: Improved (related-key) differential cryptanalysis on GIFT. In: Dunkelman, O., Jacobson, Jr., M.J., O'Flynn, C. (eds.) SAC 2020. LNCS, vol. 12804, pp. 198–228. Springer, Cham (2021). https://doi.org/10.1007/978-3-030-81652-0_8
17. Liu, Y., Sasaki, Yu.: Related-key boomerang attacks on GIFT with automated trail search including BCT Effect. In: Jang-Jaccard, J., Guo, F. (eds.) ACISP 2019. LNCS, vol. 11547, pp. 555–572. Springer, Cham (2019). https://doi.org/10.1007/978-3-030-21548-4_30

18. Murphy, S.: The return of the cryptographic boomerang. IEEE Trans. Inf. Theory **57**(4), 2517–2521 (2011)
19. Song, L., Qin, X., Hu, L.: Boomerang connectivity table revisited. Application to SKINNY and AES. IACR Trans. Symmetric Cryptol. **2019**(1), 118–141 (2019)
20. Su, L., Wang, W., Wang, M.: Accelerating the search of differential and linear characteristics with the SAT method. IACR Trans. Symmetric Cryptol. **2021**(1), 269–315 (2021)
21. Wagner, D.: The boomerang attack. In: Knudsen, L. (ed.) FSE 1999. LNCS, vol. 1636, pp. 156–170. Springer, Heidelberg (1999). https://doi.org/10.1007/3-540-48519-8_12
22. Wang, H., Peyrin, T.: Boomerang switch in multiple rounds. Application to AES variants and deoxys. IACR Trans. Symmetric Cryptol. **2019**(1), 142–169 (2019)
23. Zhu, B., Dong, X., Yu, H.: MILP-based differential attack on round-reduced GIFT. IACR Cryptol. ePrint Arch. **2018**, 390 (2018)

Cryptanalysis of Ciminion

Lulu Zhang[1,2], Meicheng Liu[1,2(✉)], Shuaishuai Li[1,2], and Dongdai Lin[1,2(✉)]

[1] State Key Laboratory of Information Security, Institute of Information Engineering, Chinese Academy of Sciences, Beijing, China
{liumeicheng,lishuaishuai,ddlin}@iie.ac.cn

[2] School of Cyber Security, University of Chinese Academy of Sciences, Beijing, China

Abstract. Ciminion is a symmetric cryptographic algorithm proposed by Dobraunig et al. in EUROCRYPT 2021, which is based on Toffoli-Gates over $\mathbb{F}_{2^n}$ or $\mathbb{F}_p$. This cipher is a multiparty computation (MPC), fully-homomorphic encryption (FHE) and zero-knowledge (ZK) friendly symmetric-key primitive due to its low multiplicative complexity. There is currently no published third-party cryptanalysis of this algorithm. In this paper, we give the first analysis on Ciminion based on higher order differential cryptanalysis and integral cryptanalysis. We consider the three sets of instances, i.e., "standard" set, "conservative" set and the instances used in MPC application, and construct the corresponding reduced-round distinguishers over $\mathbb{F}_{2^n}$ and $\mathbb{F}_p$, respectively. On the other hand, we observe a linear relation between the input and output of the round function and conclude a new set of weak random numbers based on this observation. For an aggressive evolution of Ciminion called Aiminion, we recover the subkeys under these weak random numbers. Although we cannot recover the master key, the information disclosure of the subkeys also poses certain potential threats to the cryptographic algorithm. Our results can provide guidance for designers to choose round random numbers.

Keywords: Ciminion · Aiminion · Higher order differential cryptanalysis · Integral cryptanalysis · Distinguisher · Weak random numbers

1 Introduction

Recently, many symmetric cryptographic schemes have been proposed to realize low multiplicative complexity motivated by the implementations of ciphers in the context of multiparty computation (MPC), fully-homomorphic encryption (FHE) and zero-knowledge (ZK) schemes. In these situations, linear operations come almost for free, since they only incur local computation (resp. do not increase the noise much), whereas the bottleneck are nonlinear operations that involve symmetric cryptographic operations and communication between parties (resp. increase the noise considerably). According to the underlying field on which the operation is based, these cryptographic algorithms can be roughly divided into two categories. For instance, Flip [23], Keyvrium [10], LowMC [4]

Y. Deng and M. Yung (Eds.): Inscrypt 2022, LNCS 13837, pp. 234–251, 2023.
https://doi.org/10.1007/978-3-031-26553-2_12

and Rasta [14] are the ciphers that use the multiplications in $\mathbb{F}_2$. The other category contains the ciphers having a natural description in large fields, which are mostly binary extension fields $\mathbb{F}_{2^n}$ and prime fields with odd characteristic $\mathbb{F}_p$, for example, MiMC [3], GMiMC [2], Jarvis [6], Hades [18], Poseidon [17], Vision [5], Rescue [5] and Ciminion [15].

The cryptanalysis of these ciphers have been receiving widespread attention. The many potentially devastating attacks on recently published designs imply that the design of schemes with low multiplicative complexity has not reached a mature state yet. For example, there exist Gröbner bases attacks on Jarvis [1] and higher order differential attacks on MiMC [16]. To resist common attacks, most primitives operating in large fields have a variant of powering field elements, e.g., x^3 or x^{-1}. These mappings become popular to guard against linear and differential cryptanalysis, and they often have an inverse of high degree, which provides protection against algebraic attacks. However, they impose some restrictions, e.g., the map $x \rightarrow x^\alpha$ for integer $\alpha \geq 2$ is a bijection in $\mathbb{F}_q$ ($q = 2^n$ or $q = p$) if and only if $\gcd(q-1, \alpha) = 1$. Hence, one has to consider several power values α in order for x^α to stay a permutation for any field. Ciminion [15] proposed by Dobraunig et al. in EUROCRYPT 2021 adopts the Toffoli gate [25] as the nonlinear element which is a permutation for any field, instead of a power mapping and chooses to multiply two elements of the state, instead of operating on a single state element, in order to increase the nonlinear diffusion. With respect to the linear layer, the authors learned from ciphers like LowMC [4] that very heavy linear layers can have a considerably negative impact on the performance of applications [13]. So they decided to pair the Toffoli gate with a relatively lightweight linear layer to construct a cryptographic permutation on triples of field elements. Due to that the nonlinear transformation has a low degree, attacks with algebraic techniques seem to be the potential threats to Ciminion. Note that no nontrivial third-party attack has been published so far[1]. In this paper, we propose the first third-party cryptanalysis for Ciminion.

Contributions. In this paper, we give the cryptanalysis of Ciminion over binary extension fields and prime fields with odd characteristic, and show that there are still potentially threats. Our attacks are based on the higher order differential cryptanalysis [19,22] and integral cryptanalysis [9,21]. Our results are detailed as follows:

1. For the "standard" instance of Ciminion where the data available to the attacker is limited to 2^s, we give $(s+3)$-round and $(s+2)$-round distinguishers over $\mathbb{F}_{2^n}$ and $\mathbb{F}_p$, respectively, where s is the security level. We firstly utilize the higher order differential cryptanalysis and integral cryptanalysis to construct a forward $(s+1)$-round distinguisher for the permutation. Then we consider the output of the first block of the cipher, and the first two branches

[1] Recently, the work [7] in Tosc 2022 gave an analysis on Ciminion. They constructed a new polynomial system to recover the full internal state. The idea is different from ours in this paper, so it will not be described carefully here. Interested readers can refer to [7].

of the output can be computed by the corresponding plaintexts and ciphertexts while the third branch is unknown, so we introduce a new variable to represent it. In binary extension fields, we use the vectorial Boolean function instead of the univariate representation to represent the round function. We consider the middle state after inverting two rounds from the output of the first block of the cipher, and find that the algebraic degrees on the introduced variables of the first two branches of this middle state are low, which results in that the number of equations we collected is sufficient to eliminate all the introduced variables. This means that some linear combinations of the bits of the first two branches of the middle state depend only on the first two branches of the output of the cipher. As a result, we can extend the $(s+1)$-round distinguisher to the distinguisher of $(s+3)$-round Ciminion by inverting 2 rounds from the output of the first block of the cipher. In prime fields with odd characteristic, we also can concatenate the last one round of the cipher by inverting 1 round and eliminating the new introduced variable to obtain the integral property of $(s+2)$-round Ciminion. In addition, We also consider the "conservative" instance of Ciminion and the instances used in MPC application and give the corresponding results using similar methods. The detailed results can be seen in Tables 5 and 6.
2. We observe a linear relation between the input and output of Ciminion's round function and conclude that this linear relation can be transmitted to the following round when the adjacent round random numbers satisfy $t_i \cdot t_{i+1} = -1$. This condition gives a new set of weak random numbers and improves the constraint $t_i \notin \{0,1\}$ in [15].
3. Under the weak random numbers, we present an analysis to Aiminion which is an aggressive evolution of Ciminion. We can recover the subkeys $K_3, \ldots, K_{2\frac{s}{2}}$ when all the round random numbers t_i of P_E satisfy the conditions $t_i \cdot t_{i+1} = -1$ and can recover K_1 when the all round random numbers t_i of P_C also satisfy the conditions. Note that we cannot directly recover the master key because the key schedule is so complicated. It evidences that the security of Ciminion relies on the key schedule.

Organization. Next, we describe some preliminaries. Algebraic distinguishers of reduced-round Ciminion are built in Sect. 3. Then we give a subkey recovery attacks of Aiminion under weak random numbers in Sect. 4. Finally, we conclude this paper in Sect. 5.

2 Preliminaries

2.1 Description of Ciminion

Ciminion is a nonce-based stream-encryption scheme proposed by Dobraunig et al. [15] in EUROCRYPT 2021, which minimizes the number of field multiplications in large binary or prime fields. In contrast to other schemes that aim to minimize field multiplications in $\mathbb{F}_2^n$ or $\mathbb{F}_p$, Ciminion relies on the Toffoli gate to improve the nonlinear diffusion and uses a very lightweight linear layer. In this section, we give the specific description of Ciminion.

As shown in Fig. 1, the scheme takes a nonce $\mathcal{N}$ along with two subkey elements K_1 and K_2 as input, and processes the input with a permutation P_C to output an intermediate state. Then this intermediate state is used as the input of a permutation P_E. The output state is truncated to two elements, which are used to encrypt two plaintext elements P_1 and P_2. If more elements need to be encrypted, the intermediate state can be expanded by repeatedly performing an addition of two subkey elements, then followed by a call to the rolling function *rol*. After each call to the rolling function rol, the output state is used as the input of the corresponding permutation P_E. In this way, two more plaintext elements P_{2i-1} and P_{2i} are encrypted by the truncated elements of the resulting state.

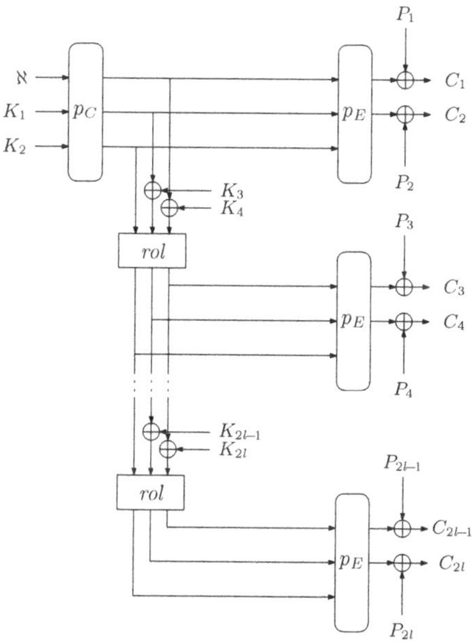

Fig. 1. Encryption with Ciminion over $\mathbb{F}_2^n$. The construction is similar over $\mathbb{F}_p$ ($\oplus$ is replaced by $+$, the addition modulo p)

Next, we describe the two permutations P_C and P_E used in Ciminion. They act on a state of triples $(a, b, c) \in \mathbb{F}_q^3$ where $q = 2^n$ (over binary extension field) or $q = p \approx 2^n$ (over prime field). Both permutations are the result of the repeated application of a round function. P_C and P_E have N and L rounds, respectively. The round function is shown in Fig. 2. Denote the i-th round function by f_i with $i = 0, \cdots, N-1$. The i-th round functions of P_C and P_E are f_i and f_{i+N-L}, respectively. The round function f_i uses four round constants (u_i, v_i, w_i, t_i) which are generated with Shake-256 [8,24]. Note that Ciminion requires $t_i \notin \{0, 1\}$. We formally state the round function f_i as follows:

$$\begin{bmatrix} a_{i+1} \\ b_{i+1} \\ c_{i+1} \end{bmatrix} := \begin{bmatrix} 0 & 0 & 1 \\ 1 & t_i & t_i \\ 0 & 1 & 1 \end{bmatrix} \cdot \begin{bmatrix} a_i \\ b_i \\ c_i + a_i \cdot b_i \end{bmatrix} + \begin{bmatrix} u_i \\ v_i \\ w_i \end{bmatrix}.$$

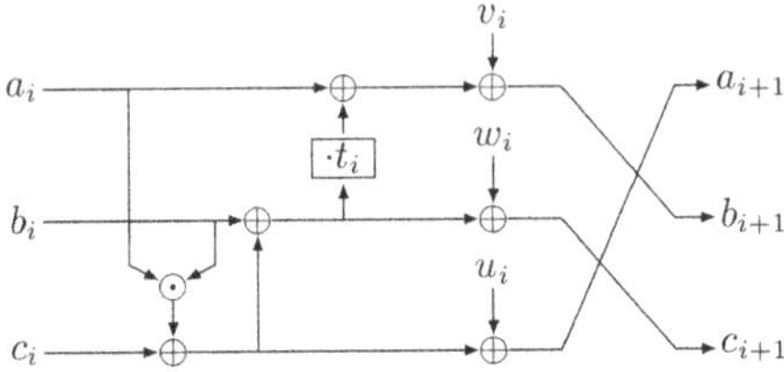

Fig. 2. Round function f_i

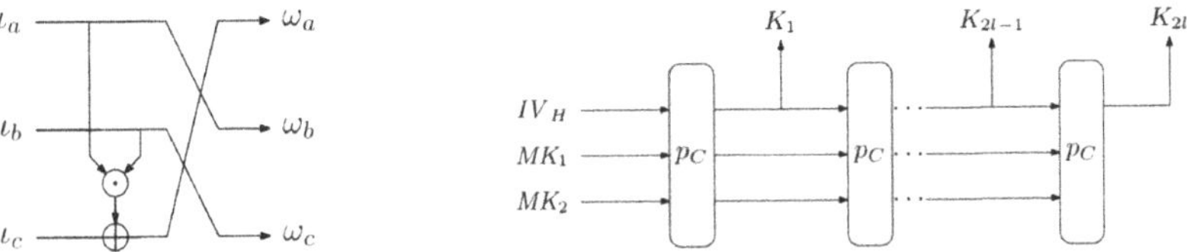

Fig. 3. Rolling function.

Fig. 4. Key generation.

The rolling function *rol* is a simple NLFSR, as depicted in Fig. 3. It takes three field elements ι_a, ι_b and ι_c as the input. It outputs three field elements: $\omega_a := \iota_c + \iota_a$, $\omega_b := \iota_a$ and $\omega_c := \iota_b$. The subkey K_i is derived from two master keys MK_1 and MK_2. As shown in Fig. 4, to expand the key, the authors used the sponge construction instantiated with the permutation P_C. The value IV_H can be made publicly available, and is typically set to 1.

The designers defined three sets of round numbers for each permutation in the encryption scheme, as seen in Table 1. We assume throughout that the security level of s bits satisfies the condition $64 \leq s \leq \lfloor \log_2(q) \rfloor$. The "standard" set guarantees s bit of security. For MPC application, the data available to the attackers is limited to $2^{\frac{s}{2}}$. The "conservative" number of rounds is obtained by arbitrarily increasing the number of rounds by 50% of the standard instance.

Aiminion. It is an aggressive evolution of Ciminion the authors presented in [15] for further analysis. Compared to Ciminion, Aiminion uses the identity mapping as the rolling function *rol*, and fixes the number of rounds to 9 for the permutation P_E. The parameters of Aiminion can be seen in Table 2.

Table 1. Proposed number of rounds based on f for three encryption instances.

Instance	P_C	P_E (two output words per block)
Standard	$s+6$	$\max\{\lceil \frac{s+37}{12} \rceil, 6\}$
Data limit $2^{\frac{s}{2}}$ elements	$\frac{2(s+6)}{3}$	$\max\{\lceil \frac{s+37}{12} \rceil, 6\}$
Conservative	$s+6$	$\max\{\lceil \frac{3}{2} \cdot \frac{s+37}{12} \rceil, 9\}$

Table 2. Proposed number of rounds for Aiminion.

Instance	P_C	P_E (two output words per block)
Data limit $2^{\frac{s}{2}}$ elements	$\frac{2(s+6)}{3}$	9

2.2 Polynomial Representations over Binary Extension Fields

Every function $E : \mathbb{F}_{2^n} \rightarrow \mathbb{F}_{2^n}$ can be uniquely represented by a polynomial over $\mathbb{F}_{2^n}$ in variable X with maximum degree $2^n - 1$, i.e., $E(X) = \sum_{i=0}^{2^n-1} \phi_i \cdot X^i$ for $\phi_i \in \mathbb{F}_{2^n}$. We refer to this representation as the *word-level representation*, the degree of a single variable in E as the *univariate degree*. On the other hand, the function E admits a unique representation as an n-tuple $E_0, E_1, \ldots, E_{n-1}$ of polynomials over $\mathbb{F}_2$ in variables $X_0, \ldots, X_{n-1}$, where $E_j : \mathbb{F}_2^n \rightarrow \mathbb{F}_2$ is a Boolean function:

$$E_j(X_0, \ldots, X_{n-1}) = \bigoplus_{\mu=(\mu_0,\ldots,\mu_{n-1})\in\{0,1\}^n} \phi_{j,\mu} \cdot \prod_{k=0}^{n-1} X_k^{\mu_k},$$

where the coefficients $\phi_{j,\mu} \in \mathbb{F}_2$. Denote $E : \mathbb{F}_2^n \rightarrow \mathbb{F}_2^n$ as vectorial Boolean functions, the degree of E as the *algebraic degree*. We call this description the *vectorial Boolean function representation* of E. The link between the algebraic degree and the univariate degree of a vectorial Boolean function is established in [11, Section 2.2]. Lemma 1 in [12] makes this link explicit.

Lemma 1 [11,12]. *Let $E : \mathbb{F}_{2^n} \rightarrow \mathbb{F}_{2^n}$ be a function over $\mathbb{F}_{2^n}$ and let $E(X) = \sum_{i=0}^{2^n-1} \phi_i \cdot X^i$ denote the corresponding univariate polynomial description over $\mathbb{F}_{2^n}$. The algebraic degree $\delta(E)$ of E as a vectorial Boolean function is the maximum over all Hamming weight of exponents of non-vanishing monomials, that is*

$$\delta(E) = \max_{0 \leq i \leq 2^n-1} \{HW(i) | \phi_i \neq 0\}.$$

3 Algebraic Distinguishers of Reduced-Round Ciminion

In this section, we give the cryptanalyses of reduced-round Cinimion using the higher order differentials over binary extension fields and integral cryptanalysis over prime fields with odd characteristic. Specially, we consider the two cases that the branch b of the input to P_C is fixed to 0 or not, as the authors considered when proposing the rounds number of the permutation P_C. Denote the attack rounds by $R = R_c + R_e$, where R_c and R_e are the numbers of rounds of P_C and P_E, respectively. We describe our attack process with the special cases of $R_e = 1$ or 2 and $R_c = R - R_e$.

3.1 Higher Order Differential Distinguisher over Binary Extension Fields

One of the most powerful cryptanalytic methods for symmetric primitives over $\mathbb{F}_2^n$ with low-degree round function is higher order differential cryptanalysis. This method allows distinguishing a given Boolean function from a random one. The idea was introduced by Lai [19,22]. If the algebraic degree of a vectorial Boolean function $E : \mathbb{F}_2^n \to \mathbb{F}_2^n$ (like a permutation) is d, then the sum over the outputs of the function applied to all elements of a vector space of dimension $\geq d+1$ is 0, i.e., for any vector subspace $V \subseteq \mathbb{F}_2^n$ with dimension strictly greater than the algebraic degree of E and for any $c \in \mathbb{F}_2^n$

$$\bigoplus_{x \in V} E(x + c) = 0. \tag{1}$$

In Ciminion, we can only directly manipulate a single element (nonce $\mathcal{N}$). The other two elements are secret subkeys (K_1 and K_2). We therefore operate with $\mathcal{N}$ (as variable x) to input value set, while keeping K_1 and K_2 fixed. Each output element is the result of a nonlinear function depending on the input elements x, K_1 and K_2. For simplicity, we consider the "standard" set encryption scheme as an example to describe our cryptanalysis, which guarantees s bit of security under the assumption that the data available to the attacker is limited to 2^s. By Lemma 1 and Eq. (1), if we choose 2^s nonces forming a subspace V of $\mathbb{F}_2^n$, then we can construct a distinguisher for the permutation P_C when the algebraic degree denoted of permutation P_C is less than s.

Forward Distinguisher of R_c-Round Permutation P_C. We study the evolution of the algebraic degree of the permutation P_C where the round function f (see Fig. 2) is iterated N times. We only consider the degrees of the first two branches, since the degree of the third branch is higher than them. Furthermore, we conclude that the upper bounds on the degree of the first two branches is as Table 3. The univariate degree is obtained obviously from the expression of round function over $\mathbb{F}_{2^n}$ because the maximal univariate degree of the function can be doubled per round in the best case. The corresponding algebraic degree can be obtained from Lemma 1.

According to the table, we can build a distinguisher for R_c-round permutation P_C, where $R_c = s$, because the algebraic degree of the function is at most $s - 1$ and the dimension of the available subspace is s. The first two outputs of s-round P_C can be expressed as $F_j(x, K_1, K_2)$ for $j = 0, 1$. Then, for any fixed basis of $\mathbb{F}_2^n$

Table 3. Upper bounds on the degree of the first two branches of P_C.

Number of rounds	1	2	3	4	$\cdots$	i	$\cdots$	s	s+1
Univariate degree	1	2	4	8	$\cdots$	2^{i-1}	$\cdots$	2^{s-1}	2^s
Algebraic degree	1	1	2	3	$\cdots$	$i-1$	$\cdots$	$s-1$	s

over $\mathbb{F}_2$ defining an isomorphism between $\mathbb{F}_{2^n}$ and $\mathbb{F}_2^n$, each element in $\mathbb{F}_{2^n}$ can be uniquely represented as an n-dimension vector in $\mathbb{F}_2^n$. Therefore, the above outputs can be rewritten by the following form under the fixed basis:

$$F_j^i(x_0, x_1, \ldots, x_{n-1}),$$

for $i = 0, \cdots, n-1$ and $j = 0, 1$, where $(x_0, x_1, \ldots, x_{n-1})$ is the vectorial representation of x. We omit the notation of the corresponding vector representations of subkeys K_1, K_2 in the equations for simplicity. So we have $2n$ equations over $\mathbb{F}_2$ as follows:

$$\bigoplus_{\vec{x} \in V} F_j^i(x_0, x_1, \ldots, x_{n-1}) = 0, \tag{2}$$

where $(x_0, x_1, \ldots, x_{n-1})$ is denoted by $\vec{x}$ and V is a set of nonces input which is a subspace of $\mathbb{F}_2^n$ (i.e., $V \subseteq \mathbb{F}_2^n$). So a distinguisher for P_C with s-round iterations is built.

We also consider the case where the input of permutation P_C at branch b is 0. Then the degree of the first two branches of P_C remains unchanged for two rounds. Its increasing trend is as Table 4. Similarly, we can construct an $(s+1)$-round distinguisher for P_C.

Table 4. Upper bounds on the degree of the first two branches of P_C when the branch b is zero.

Number of rounds	1	2	3	4	$\cdots$	i	$\cdots$	s+1	s+2
Univariate degree	1	1	2	4	$\cdots$	2^{i-2}	$\cdots$	2^{s-1}	2^s
Algebraic degree	1	1	1	2	$\cdots$	$i-2$	$\cdots$	$s-1$	s

Note that for the "conservative" set, there are the same results because they have the same limitation in data available to attackers. For the MPC application, if the data available to the attacker is limited to $2^{\frac{s}{2}}$, then there are $\frac{s}{2}$-round distinguisher and $(\frac{s}{2}+1)$-round distinguisher for the above two cases.

The Distinguisher of Reduced-Round Ciminion. Based on the above forward distinguishers, we concatenate the reduced-round permutation P_E to extend the distinguishers. We denote the matrix of linear layer by H. The inverse matrix of the transformation is H^{-1}:

$$H = \begin{bmatrix} 0 & 0 & 1 \\ 1 & t_i & t_i \\ 0 & 1 & 1 \end{bmatrix}, H^{-1} = \begin{bmatrix} 0 & 1 & -t_i \\ -1 & 0 & 1 \\ 1 & 0 & 0 \end{bmatrix}.$$

As depicted in Fig. 1, the output of the first call to P_E is truncated to two elements as the first two stream keys, while the output of the third branch is unknown. Let the output at the third branch of permutation P_E be y, the first and the second branches be M_1 and M_2. So $M_1 \oplus P_1 = C_1$, $M_2 \oplus P_2 = C_2$[2], and M_1, M_2 are the first two stream keys where P_1 and P_2 are the plaintexts, C_1 and C_2 are the corresponding ciphertexts. Now we deduce expressions of the intermediate state reversely from the output of permutation P_E, i.e., M_1, M_2 and y. Recall that the number of rounds of P_E is R_e. The expressions by inverting one round are as follows:

$$\begin{bmatrix} a_{R_e-1} \\ b_{R_e-1} \\ c_{R_e-1} + a_{R_e-1} \cdot b_{R_e-1} \end{bmatrix} = \begin{bmatrix} 0 & 1 & -t_{R_e-1} \\ -1 & 0 & 1 \\ 1 & 0 & 0 \end{bmatrix} \cdot \begin{bmatrix} M_1 - u_{R_e-1} \\ M_2 - v_{R_e-1} \\ y - w_{R_e-1} \end{bmatrix},$$

then denoted the state by

$$\begin{bmatrix} a_{R_e-1} \\ b_{R_e-1} \\ c_{R_e-1} \end{bmatrix} := \begin{bmatrix} g_0(M_1, M_2, y) \\ g_1(M_1, M_2, y) \\ g_2(M_1, M_2, y) \end{bmatrix}, \tag{3}$$

where g_i is a polynomial over $\mathbb{F}_{2^n}$ for $i = 0, 1, 2$. We conclude that the univariate degree of g_i in variable y is 1 for $i = 0, 1$ and the univariate degree of g_2 is 2. Similarly, we can deduce the expressions by inverting two rounds as follows:

$$\begin{bmatrix} a_{R_e-2} \\ b_{R_e-2} \\ c_{R_e-2} \end{bmatrix} := \begin{bmatrix} g'_0(M_1, M_2, y) \\ g'_1(M_1, M_2, y) \\ g'_2(M_1, M_2, y) \end{bmatrix},$$

where g'_i is a polynomial over $\mathbb{F}_{2^n}$ for $i = 0, 1, 2$. We conclude that the univariate degree of g'_i in variable y is 2 for $i = 0, 1$ and the univariate degree of g'_2 is 4.

According to Lemma 1, the algebraic degree of a vectorial Boolean function can be computed from its univariate representation. So, the algebraic degrees of g_i and g'_i are 1 for $i = 0, 1$ when they are seen as the vectorial Boolean function over $\mathbb{F}_2^n$. We can collect $2n$ Boolean expressions after inverting two rounds as follows:

$$G_j^i(y_0, y_1, \dots, y_{n-1}, \vec{M}_1, \vec{M}_2),$$

for $i = 0, \cdots, n-1$ and $j = 0, 1$, where $(y_0, y_1, \dots, y_{n-1})$, $\vec{M}_1$ and $\vec{M}_2$ are the vectorial representations of y, M_1 and M_2, respectively.

When we assume that $R_e = 2$, then for $i = 0, \cdots, n-1$ and $j = 0, 1$, we have

$$F_j^i(x_0, x_1, \dots, x_{n-1}) = G_j^i(y_0, y_1, \dots, y_{n-1}, \vec{M}_1, \vec{M}_2).$$

This system includes $2n$ linear equations in terms of variables x_0, x_1, $\dots$, x_{n-1}, y_0, y_1, $\dots$, y_{n-1}, $\vec{M}_1$, $\vec{M}_2$. Our aim is to get a reduced set of equations by somehow eliminating $y_0, y_1, \dots, y_{n-1}$ from the variable set. There remains around n

[2] $\oplus$ is replaced by $+$, the addition modulo p on $\mathbb{F}_p$.

expressions on the right side denoted by $G' := (G'_0, \dots, G'_{n-1})$, which are only on variables $\vec{M}_1$, $\vec{M}_2$. The left side needs to be manipulated by the same transformation, and the result is denoted by $F' := (F'_0, \dots, F'_{n-1})$. This process can be seen as a linear transformation denoted by $\mathcal{L} = (\mathcal{L}_0, \dots, \mathcal{L}_{n-1})$. Then we have

$$\begin{aligned} F' &= G', \\ F' &:= \mathcal{L}(F_0^0, \dots, F_0^{n-1}, F_1^0, \dots, F_1^{n-1}), \\ G' &:= \mathcal{L}(G_0^0, \dots, G_0^{n-1}, G_1^0, \dots, G_1^{n-1}). \end{aligned} \tag{4}$$

From the Eqs. (2) and (4), for $j = 0, \cdots, n-1$, we have

$$\begin{aligned} \bigoplus_{(\vec{M}_1, \vec{M}_2) \in W} G'_j &= \bigoplus_{\vec{x} \in V} F'_j \\ &= \bigoplus_{\vec{x} \in V} \mathcal{L}_j(F_0^0, \dots, F_0^{n-1}, F_1^0, \dots, F_1^{n-1}) \\ &= \mathcal{L}_j(\bigoplus_{\vec{x} \in V} F_0^0, \dots, \bigoplus_{\vec{x} \in V} F_0^{n-1}, \bigoplus_{\vec{x} \in V} F_1^0, \dots, \bigoplus_{\vec{x} \in V} F_1^{n-1}) \qquad (5) \\ &= 0, \qquad (6) \end{aligned}$$

where W is the set of pair of $(\vec{M}_1, \vec{M}_2)$ corresponding to the set V of nonces while $(\vec{M}_1, \vec{M}_2)$ can be represented by the corresponding plaintexts P_1, P_2 and ciphertexts C_1, C_2. So far, we have obtained a distinguisher of the corresponding plaintexts and ciphertexts under these 2^s nonces.

Specially, a distinguisher of $(s + 1 + 2)$-round Ciminion is built if the branch b is 0 and a distinguisher of $(s + 2)$-round Ciminion is built if the branch b is not 0. Similarly, for "conservative" set and MPC application, the number of rounds of the distinguisher can also be extended two more rounds. Note that the time complexity of this cryptanalysis is of around the same order of magnitude as the data complexity. Table 5 gives these results.

Table 5. The distinguishers over $\mathbb{F}_{2^n}$.

	Standard (or conservative)	MPC application
Data limitation	2^s	$2^{\frac{s}{2}}$
Rounds ($b = 0$)	(s+1)+2	$(\frac{s}{2}+1)+2$
Rounds ($b \neq 0$)	s+2	$\frac{s}{2}+2$
Complexity	2^s	$2^{\frac{s}{2}}$

Remark 1. The representations of the penultimate third round of P_E from the output have higher algebraic degree on variables $y_0, y_1, \dots, y_{n-1}$. The equations we collected are not enough to eliminate these variables.

3.2 Integral Property over Prime Fields with Odd Characteristic

The above cryptanalysis utilizes the higher order differential technique, which can be seen as a variant of *integral attacks* [21]. This comes from the fact that the sum of the images by E of all inputs in V corresponds to a value of a derivative of E of order (dim V) [19,22]. But this fact does not hold anymore in odd characteristic, and the same technique cannot be applied directly. In CRYPTO 2020 Beyne et al. presented a similar result for the prime case in odd characteristic in [9, Proposition 2]. We rewrite the property as follows:

Proposition 1 [9]. *Let V be a multiplicative subgroup of $\mathbb{F}_p^\times$, where p is an odd prime. For any $E : \mathbb{F}_p \to \mathbb{F}_p$ such that the $deg(E) < |V|$,*

$$\sum_{x \in V} E(x) - E(0) \cdot |V| = 0. \tag{7}$$

Next, we can find an integral property for the permutation P_C base on this proposition.

Forward Integral Property of R_c-Round Permutation P_C. Similarly, we still can only directly manipulate a single element, i.e., nonce $\mathcal{N}$ (as variable x). From Table 3, we can conclude that the univariate degree on variable x of the first two branches of P_C over $\mathbb{F}_p$ also can be doubled per round in the best case. The first two outputs of s-round P_C can be expressed as $F_j(x, K_1, K_2)$ for $j = 0, 1$ and for simplicity we sometimes denote it as F_j. Then we have $deg(F_j) \leq 2^{s-1}$ for $j = 0, 1$. Consider the case that the attackers only have access to at most 2^s nonces for "standard" set. Denote a subgroup of $\mathbb{F}_p^\times$ by T such that $deg(F_j) < |T| \leq 2^s$ for $j = 0, 1$. Then we have for $j = 0, 1$

$$\sum_{x \in T} F_j(x) = F_j(0) \cdot |T|. \tag{8}$$

In other words, the sum of images by F_j of all inputs in the subgroup[3] T is $F_j(0) \cdot |T|$, which is a multiple of $|T|$. The value of $F_j(0)$ is related to the subkeys K_1 and K_2. So there is an integral property of R_c-round permutation P_C, where $R_c = s$. For "conservation" set, there is a same result because they have the same limited data. For the instances used in the MPC application, there is an integral property of $\frac{s}{2}$-round permutation P_C.

When the branch b is 0, i.e., the subkey K_1 is always 0, then the upper bounds on the univariate degree of the first two branches of P_C is as Table 4. We can obtain similar results (see Table 6).

The Integral Property of Reduced-Round Ciminion. Like the description over binary extension fields, we use the same notations. The expressions of the state obtained by inverting one round from the output of permutation P_E can be seen in Eq. (3). So for $j = 0, 1$, the equations hold:

[3] Note that this analysis only holds for certain large prime numbers, That is, when the subspace T that satisfies the condition must exist.

$$F_j(x) = g_j(M_1, M_2, y).$$

We only consider the univariate degrees on variable y of g_0 and g_1, where $deg(g_0) = deg(g_1) = 1$. So the variable y can be eliminated from these two equations, and denote this linear transformation by $\mathcal{L}'$ and the remaining equation by G' including around only one equation. Let F' be the item of F corresponding to G' after performing the transformation. Then

$$\begin{aligned} G'(M_1, M_2) &= F'(x), \\ G'(M_1, M_2) &:= \mathcal{L}'(g_0, g_1, g_2), \\ F'(x) &:= \mathcal{L}'(F_0, F_1, F_2). \end{aligned}$$

By Eq. (8), we know that

$$\begin{aligned} \sum_{(M_1,M_2)\in W} G'(M_1, M_2) &= \sum_{x\in T} F_0'(x) \\ &= \sum_{x\in T} \mathcal{L}'(F_0, F_1, F_2) \\ &= \mathcal{L}'(\sum_{x\in T} F_0, \sum_{x\in T} F_1, \sum_{x\in T} F_2) \\ &= \mathcal{L}'(F_0(0)\cdot |T|, F_1(0)\cdot |T|, F_2(0)\cdot |T|) \\ &= |T| \cdot \mathcal{L}'(F_0(0), F_1(0), F_2(0)), \end{aligned} \tag{9}$$

where W is the set of pair of (M_1, M_2) corresponding to the set T of nonces while (M_1, M_2) can be represented by the corresponding plaintexts P_1,P_2 and ciphertexts C_1, C_2. So the sum of the images by G' of all $(M_1, M_2) \in W$ is a multiple of $|T|$. So for "standard" set, we build an $(s+1)$-round integral property. For "conservation" set, there is a same result because they have the same limited data. For the instances used in MPC application, there is an $(\frac{s}{2}+1)$-round integral property. When the branch b is 0, we can obtain similar results. We summarize the results for all cases as Table 6.

Remark 2. In the known-key setting [20], we assume that the subkeys have known values. The attack goal is to find non-random properties of the resulting permutation. $F_0(0), F_1(0), F_2(0)$ can be computed from the known subkeys K_1 and K_2. In this way, Eq. (9) shows that the sum of the images by G' is a constant.

3.3 General Cases

In the above, we present our cryptanalysis for R-round Ciminion where $R = R_c + R_e$ with $R_e = 2$ over $\mathbb{F}_2^n$ and $R_e = 1$ over $\mathbb{F}_p$. In fact, we do not need to limit the number of rounds for P_E to 1 (or 2). We allow that the number of rounds for P_E is greater than 1 (or 2), i.e., $R_e \geq 2$ over $\mathbb{F}_2^n$ (or $R_e \geq 1$ over $\mathbb{F}_p$), then the corresponding number of rounds for P_C is $R_c = R - R_e$.

Table 6. Integral property over $\mathbb{F}_p$.

	Standard (or conservative)	MPC application
Data limitation	2^s	$2^{\frac{s}{2}}$
Rounds ($b = 0$)	(s+1)+1	$(\frac{s}{2}+1)+1$
Rounds ($b \neq 0$)	s+1	$\frac{s}{2}+1$
Complexity	2^s	$2^{\frac{s}{2}}$

4 Subkey Recovery Under Weak Random Numbers

4.1 Observations on the Round Function

The round function includes nonlinear transformation, linear transformation and round constant addition, which uses four random numbers (u_i, v_i, w_i, t_i). According to the Fig. 2, we can rewrite the output of the i-th round iteration as follows:

$$\begin{aligned} a_{i+1} &= c_i + a_i \cdot b_i + u_i, \\ b_{i+1} &= a_i + t_i \cdot b_i + t_i \cdot c_i + t_i \cdot a_i \cdot b_i + v_i, \\ c_{i+1} &= b_i + c_i + a_i \cdot b_i + w_i, \end{aligned}$$

where $i = 0, \cdots, N-1$.

Observation 1. *Consider the round function of Ciminion. We denote the input of the i-th round iteration by (a_i, b_i, c_i) and denote the i-th round constants by (u_i, v_i, w_i, t_i), for $t_i \notin \{0, 1\}$. The relation*

$$b_{i+1} - t_i \cdot a_{i+1} = a_i + t_i \cdot b_i + v_i - t_i \cdot u_i \quad (10)$$

holds for $i = 0, \cdots, N-1$.

Specially, for permutation P_C, $a_0 = \mathcal{N}$, $b_0 = K_1$ and $c_0 = K_2$. For example

$$\begin{aligned} i = 0: \quad & b_1 - t_0 \cdot a_1 = a_0 + t_0 \cdot b_0 + v_0 - t_0 \cdot u_0 \\ & \qquad\qquad\; = \mathcal{N} + t_0 \cdot K_1 + v_0 - t_0 \cdot u_0, \\ i = 1: \quad & b_2 - t_1 \cdot a_2 = a_1 + t_1 \cdot b_1 + v_1 - t_1 \cdot u_1, \\ i = 2: \quad & b_3 - t_2 \cdot a_3 = a_2 + t_2 \cdot b_2 + v_2 - t_2 \cdot u_2, \\ & \vdots \end{aligned}$$

From the above expressions, if $a_1+t_1 \cdot b_1$ is always a multiple of $b_1-t_0 \cdot a_1$, then $b_2 - t_1 \cdot a_2$ can be represented linearly by $\mathcal{N}$ and K_1. Assume that $a_1 + t_1 \cdot b_1 = \lambda \cdot (b_1 - t_0 \cdot a_1)$, then $b_2 - t_1 \cdot a_2 = \lambda \cdot (\mathcal{N} + t_0 \cdot K_1 + v_0 - t_0 \cdot u_0) + v_1 - t_1 \cdot u_1$ where λ is some constant. For this we need t_0, t_1 to satisfy the equation $t_0 \cdot t_1 = -1$. Next, we can conclude that

Observation 2. *Consider the round function of Ciminion. We denote the input of the i-th round iteration by* (a_i, b_i, c_i) *and denote the i-th round constants by* (u_i, v_i, w_i, t_i)*, for* $t_i \notin \{0, 1\}$. *For each* $i = 0, \cdots, N-2$*, if* $t_i \cdot t_{i+1} = -1$*, then there is a linear relation between the output of the* $(i+1)$*-round* a_{i+2}, b_{i+2} *and the input of the i-round* a_i, b_i.

Proof. By Observation 1, we have

$$b_{i+1} - t_i \cdot a_{i+1} = a_i + t_i \cdot b_i + v_i - t_i \cdot u_i,$$
$$b_{i+2} - t_{i+1} \cdot a_{i+2} = a_{i+1} + t_{i+1} \cdot b_{i+1} + v_{i+1} - t_{i+1} \cdot u_{i+1}.$$

If $t_i \cdot t_{i+1} = -1$, then we have

$$\begin{aligned} b_{i+2} - t_{i+1} \cdot a_{i+2} &= a_{i+1} + t_{i+1} \cdot b_{i+1} + v_{i+1} - t_{i+1} \cdot u_{i+1} \\ &= t_{i+1} \cdot \left(\frac{1}{t_{i+1}} \cdot a_{i+1} + b_{i+1} \right) + v_{i+1} - t_{i+1} \cdot u_{i+1} \\ &= t_{i+1} \cdot (b_{i+1} - t_i \cdot a_{i+1}) + v_{i+1} - t_{i+1} \cdot u_{i+1} \\ &= t_{i+1} \cdot (a_i + t_i \cdot b_i + v_i - t_i \cdot u_i) + v_{i+1} - t_{i+1} \cdot u_{i+1} \\ &= t_{i+1} \cdot a_i - b_i + \delta_i, \end{aligned}$$

where $\delta_i = t_{i+1} \cdot v_i + u_i + v_{i+1} - t_{i+1} \cdot u_{i+1}$ is a known constant after the instance is fixed. □

Remark 3. Specially, the condition becomes $t_i \cdot t_{i+1} = 1$ over binary extension fields, which means that the random numbers t of the adjacent rounds cannot be inverse of each other. The designers only limited that $t_i \notin \{0, 1\}$ [15]. So we give a new set of weak random numbers.

Corollary 1. *Consider the round function of Ciminion. We denote the input of the i-th round iteration by* (a_i, b_i, c_i) *and denote the i-th round constants by* (u_i, v_i, w_i, t_i)*, for* $t_i \notin \{0, 1\}$. (a_r, b_r, c_r) *is the output of the permutation* P_C *with r-round iteration, where* $2 \leq r \leq R_c$. *If* $t_i \cdot t_{i+1} = -1$ *for* $i = 0, \cdots, r-2$*, then there is a linear relation on* a_r, b_r, $\mathcal{N}$ *and* K_1*, i.e.,* $b_r - t_{r-1} \cdot a_r = \alpha_r \cdot (\mathcal{N} + t_0 \cdot K_1) + \delta$*, where* $\alpha_r = t_{r-1} t_{r-2} \cdots t_1$, δ *is related to the round random numbers.*

Remark 4. In fact, $\alpha_r = 0$ when $(r-1) \mod 4 = 0$; $\alpha_r = t_1$ when $(r-1) \mod 4 = 1$; $\alpha_r = -1$ when $(r-1) \mod 4 = 2$; $\alpha_r = -t_1$ when $(r-1) \mod 4 = 3$. For example, if $r = 8$, $\alpha_r = -t_1$.

When the conditions in Corollary 1 are met, if the attackers obtain the intermediate state after r-round P_C, then they can recover the subkey K_1 from the linear relation. Next, we give an analysis for Aiminion under these weak random numbers.

4.2 Subkey Recovery of Aiminion Under Weak Random Numbers

Based on the observations as above, we present a cryptanalysis strategy on Aiminion under weak random numbers. Aiminion [15] is an aggressive evolution of Ciminion. Compared to Ciminion, it uses the identity mapping as the rolling function rol, and fixes the number of rounds to 9 for P_E. In this strategy, we assume that the random numbers[4] of P_E satisfy $t_i \cdot t_{i+1} = -1$ for $i = 0, \cdots, 7$.

By Fig. 1, several outputs are generated from the same unknown middle state by permutation P_E. For a given nonce $\mathcal{N}$, let $(s_0^{\mathcal{N}}, s_1^{\mathcal{N}}, s_2^{\mathcal{N}}) \in (\mathbb{F}_q)^3$ be the corresponding middle state. Let the first two elements in the output of the t-th call of P_E be M_{2t-1} and M_{2t} assuming[5] that $1 \le t \le 2^{\frac{s}{2}-1}$.

According to Observations 1 and 2, there is a linear relation in terms of $s_0^{\mathcal{N}}$, $s_1^{\mathcal{N}}$, M_1 and M_2 from the first call of P_E. The relation can be rewritten as follows:

$$M_1 - t_8 \cdot M_2 = -t_1 \cdot (s_0^{\mathcal{N}} + t_0 \cdot s_1^{\mathcal{N}}) + \delta', \tag{11}$$

where δ' is related to the round random numbers since $\alpha_8 = -t_1$. Similarly, for the second and third calls of P_E, the equations are

$$M_3 - t_8 \cdot M_4 = -t_1 \cdot (s_0^{\mathcal{N}} + K_4) - t_1 \cdot t_0 \cdot (s_1^{\mathcal{N}} + K_3) + \delta', \tag{12}$$

$$M_5 - t_8 \cdot M_6 = -t_1 \cdot (s_0^{\mathcal{N}} + K_4 + K_6) - t_1 \cdot t_0 \cdot (s_1^{\mathcal{N}} + K_3 + K_5) + \delta'. \tag{13}$$

By subtracting (12) from (11) and (13) from (12), we have

$$M_1 - M_3 - t_8 \cdot (M_2 - M_4) = t_1 \cdot (K_4 + t_0 \cdot K_3), \tag{14}$$

$$M_3 - M_5 - t_8 \cdot (M_4 - M_6) = t_1 \cdot (K_6 + t_0 \cdot K_5). \tag{15}$$

If we choose another nonce $\mathcal{N}'$ ($\mathcal{N}' \neq \mathcal{N}$, the corresponding round random numbers are t'_i satisfying $t'_i \cdot t'_{i+1} = -1$ for $i = 0, \cdots, 7$), the corresponding equations are

$$M'_1 - M'_3 - t'_8 \cdot (M'_2 - M'_4) = t'_1 \cdot (K_4 + t'_0 \cdot K_3), \tag{16}$$

$$M'_3 - M'_5 - t'_8 \cdot (M'_4 - M'_6) = t'_1 \cdot (K_6 + t'_0 \cdot K_5). \tag{17}$$

Then, from Eqs. (14)–(17), K_3, K_4, K_5 and K_6 can be solved. Note that we can collect $2^{(\frac{s}{2}-2)}$ equations for each nonce when we have access to $2^{\frac{s}{2}}$ stream keys, so we can solve K_i for $i = 3, \cdots, 2^{\frac{s}{2}-1}$ by a similar discussion.

Furthermore, if all the round random numbers of P_C also satisfy the conditions in Corollary 1, then we can solve the subkey K_1.

The subkeys K_i are generated by the two master keys MK_1 and MK_2 as shown in Fig. 4. Since the key schedule is complicated and the security of the algorithm relies on the key schedule, the master keys can not be recovered directly. But the information disclosure of the subkeys also poses a certain potential threat to the cryptographic algorithm. Our analysis can provide guidance for designers to choose round random numbers.

[4] From Sect. 2.1, we know that the random numbers used in P_E are the round random numbers from the last 9 rounds of P_C.

[5] For Aiminion, the data limit is $2^{\frac{s}{2}}$ elements. So the number of stream keys we used is at most $2^{\frac{s}{2}}$.

5 Conclusion

In this paper, we focus on the symmetric-key primitive Ciminion and its aggressive evolution called Aiminion. We give the distinguishers of Ciminion over binary extension fields and prime fields with odd characteristic, respectively, utilizing higher order differential cryptanalysis and integral cryptanalysis. We also consider the security of three instances of Ciminion, i.e., "standard" set, "conservative" set and the instances used in MPC application. On the other hand, we observe a linear relation between the input and output of the round function and give a set of weak random numbers. We propose attacks based on these observations to recover the subkeys under weak random numbers. Our attacks pose certain potential threats to this algorithm. This can provide some references for the design of Ciminion.

Acknowledgement. This work was supported by the National Natural Science Foundation of China (Grant No. 61872359, 62122085 and 61936008), the National Key R&D Program of China (Grant No. 2020YFB1805402), and the Youth Innovation Promotion Association of Chinese Academy of Sciences.

References

1. Albrecht, M.R., Cid, C., Grassi, L., Khovratovich, D., Lüftenegger, R., Rechberger, C., Schofnegger, M.: Algebraic cryptanalysis of stark-friendly designs: application to MARVELLOUS and MiMC. In: Galbraith, S.D., Moriai, S. (eds.) ASIACRYPT 2019, Part III. LNCS, vol. 11923, pp. 371–397. Springer, Cham (2019). https://doi.org/10.1007/978-3-030-34618-8_13
2. Albrecht, M.R., et al.: Feistel structures for MPC, and more. In: Sako, K., Schneider, S., Ryan, P.Y.A. (eds.) ESORICS 2019, Part II. LNCS, vol. 11736, pp. 151–171. Springer, Cham (2019). https://doi.org/10.1007/978-3-030-29962-0_8
3. Albrecht, M., Grassi, L., Rechberger, C., Roy, A., Tiessen, T.: MiMC: efficient encryption and cryptographic hashing with minimal multiplicative complexity. In: Cheon, J.H., Takagi, T. (eds.) ASIACRYPT 2016, Part I. LNCS, vol. 10031, pp. 191–219. Springer, Heidelberg (2016). https://doi.org/10.1007/978-3-662-53887-6_7
4. Albrecht, M.R., Rechberger, C., Schneider, T., Tiessen, T., Zohner, M.: Ciphers for MPC and FHE. In: Oswald, E., Fischlin, M. (eds.) EUROCRYPT 2015, Part I. LNCS, vol. 9056, pp. 430–454. Springer, Heidelberg (2015). https://doi.org/10.1007/978-3-662-46800-5_17
5. Aly, A., Ashur, T., Ben-Sasson, E., Dhooghe, S., Szepieniec, A.: Design of symmetric-key primitives for advanced cryptographic protocols. IACR Trans. Symmetric Cryptol. **2020**(3), 1–45 (2020). https://doi.org/10.13154/tosc.v2020.i3.1-45
6. Ashur, T., Dhooghe, S.: Marvellous: a stark-friendly family of cryptographic primitives. IACR Cryptol. ePrint Arch., p. 1098 (2018). https://eprint.iacr.org/2018/1098
7. Bariant, A., Bouvier, C., Leurent, G., Perrin, L.: Algebraic attacks against some arithmetization-oriented primitives. IACR Trans. Symmetric Cryptol. **2022**(3), 73–101 (2022). https://doi.org/10.46586/tosc.v2022.i3.73-101

8. Bertoni, G., Daemen, J., Peeters, M., Assche, G.V.: The Keccak SHA-3 submission (version 3.0) (2011)
9. Beyne, T., et al.: Out of Oddity – New Cryptanalytic Techniques Against Symmetric Primitives Optimized for Integrity Proof Systems. In: Micciancio, D., Ristenpart, T. (eds.) CRYPTO 2020, Part III. LNCS, vol. 12172, pp. 299–328. Springer, Cham (2020). https://doi.org/10.1007/978-3-030-56877-1_11
10. Canteaut, A., et al.: Stream ciphers: a practical solution for efficient homomorphic-ciphertext compression. J. Cryptol. **31**(3), 885–916 (2018). https://doi.org/10.1007/s00145-017-9273-9
11. Carlet, C., Charpin, P., Zinoviev, V.: Codes, bent functions and permutations suitable for des-like cryptosystem (1998)
12. Cid, C., Grassi, L., Gunsing, A., Lüftenegger, R., Rechberger, C., Schofnegger, M.: Influence of the linear layer on the algebraic degree in SP-networks. Cryptology ePrint Archive, Paper 2020/536 (2020)
13. Dinur, I., Kales, D., Promitzer, A., Ramacher, S., Rechberger, C.: Linear equivalence of block ciphers with partial non-linear layers: application to LowMC. In: Ishai, Y., Rijmen, V. (eds.) EUROCRYPT 2019, Part I. LNCS, vol. 11476, pp. 343–372. Springer, Cham (2019). https://doi.org/10.1007/978-3-030-17653-2_12
14. Dobraunig, C., et al.: Rasta: a cipher with low ANDdepth and few ANDs per bit. In: Shacham, H., Boldyreva, A. (eds.) CRYPTO 2018, Part I. LNCS, vol. 10991, pp. 662–692. Springer, Cham (2018). https://doi.org/10.1007/978-3-319-96884-1_22
15. Dobraunig, C., Grassi, L., Guinet, A., Kuijsters, D.: Ciminion: symmetric encryption based on Toffoli-gates over large finite fields. In: Canteaut, A., Standaert, F.-X. (eds.) EUROCRYPT 2021, Part II. LNCS, vol. 12697, pp. 3–34. Springer, Cham (2021). https://doi.org/10.1007/978-3-030-77886-6_1
16. Eichlseder, M., et al.: An algebraic attack on ciphers with low-degree round functions: application to full MiMC. In: Moriai, S., Wang, H. (eds.) ASIACRYPT 2020, Part I. LNCS, vol. 12491, pp. 477–506. Springer, Cham (2020). https://doi.org/10.1007/978-3-030-64837-4_16
17. Grassi, L., Khovratovich, D., Rechberger, C., Roy, A., Schofnegger, M.: Poseidon: a new hash function for zero-knowledge proof systems. In: Bailey, M., Greenstadt, R. (eds.) 30th USENIX Security Symposium, USENIX Security 2021, 11–13 August 2021, pp. 519–535. USENIX Association (2021). https://www.usenix.org/conference/usenixsecurity21/presentation/grassi
18. Grassi, L., Lüftenegger, R., Rechberger, C., Rotaru, D., Schofnegger, M.: On a generalization of substitution-permutation networks: the HADES design strategy. In: Canteaut, A., Ishai, Y. (eds.) EUROCRYPT 2020, Part II. LNCS, vol. 12106, pp. 674–704. Springer, Cham (2020). https://doi.org/10.1007/978-3-030-45724-2_23
19. Knudsen, L.R.: Truncated and higher order differentials. In: Preneel, B. (ed.) FSE 1994. LNCS, vol. 1008, pp. 196–211. Springer, Heidelberg (1995). https://doi.org/10.1007/3-540-60590-8_16
20. Knudsen, L.R., Rijmen, V.: Known-key distinguishers for some block ciphers. In: Kurosawa, K. (ed.) ASIACRYPT 2007. LNCS, vol. 4833, pp. 315–324. Springer, Heidelberg (2007). https://doi.org/10.1007/978-3-540-76900-2_19
21. Knudsen, L., Wagner, D.: Integral cryptanalysis. In: Daemen, J., Rijmen, V. (eds.) FSE 2002. LNCS, vol. 2365, pp. 112–127. Springer, Heidelberg (2002). https://doi.org/10.1007/3-540-45661-9_9
22. Lai, X.: Higher order derivatives and differential cryptanalysis. In: Blahut, R.E., Costello, D.J., Maurer, U., Mittelholzer, T. (eds.) Communications and Cryptography. The Springer International Series in Engineering and Computer Science, vol.

276, pp. 227–233. Springer, Boston (1994). https://doi.org/10.1007/978-1-4615-2694-0_23
23. Méaux, P., Journault, A., Standaert, F.-X., Carlet, C.: Towards stream ciphers for efficient FHE with low-noise ciphertexts. In: Fischlin, M., Coron, J.-S. (eds.) EUROCRYPT 2016, Part I. LNCS, vol. 9665, pp. 311–343. Springer, Heidelberg (2016). https://doi.org/10.1007/978-3-662-49890-3_13
24. NIST: SHA-3 standard: permutation-based hash and extendable-output functions (2015)
25. Toffoli, T.: Reversible computing. In: de Bakker, J., van Leeuwen, J. (eds.) ICALP 1980. LNCS, vol. 85, pp. 632–644. Springer, Heidelberg (1980). https://doi.org/10.1007/3-540-10003-2_104

Clustering Effect of Iterative Differential and Linear Trails

Tianyou Ding[1,2], Wentao Zhang[1,2](✉), and Chunning Zhou[1,2]

[1] State Key Laboratory of Information Security, Institute of Information Engineering, Chinese Academy of Sciences, Beijing, China
{dingtianyou,zhangwentao,zhouchunning}@iie.ac.cn

[2] School of Cyber Security, University of Chinese Academy of Sciences, Beijing, China

Abstract. Differential and linear cryptanalysis are two of the most important kinds of cryptanalysis for symmetric-key primitives. In this paper, we propose a graph-based method of evaluating the clustering effect of iterative differential and linear trails. We also exploit the iterative trails to find exploitable difference and linear propagations. We apply our method to four lightweight SPN primitives including PRESENT, GIFT-64, RECTANGLE and KNOT-256. For KNOT-256, we improve the best difference and linear propagations by 5 and 9 rounds respectively. For RECTANGLE, we improve the best 14-round linear propagation. Our other results are consistent with the best known results. We illustrate the dominance of iterative trails by showing the proportion of trails that are incorporated in our method in a difference or linear propagation. Additionally, for the primary version of KNOT, we find difference and linear propagations leading to different differential and linear attacks. We stress here that our results do not threaten the security of KNOT.

Keywords: Lightweight cryptography · Differential cryptanalysis · Linear cryptanalysis · Iterative trails · Clustering effect · Graph theory

1 Introduction

Differential cryptanalysis [4] and linear cryptanalysis [10] are two of the most powerful attacks against modern symmetric-key cryptographic primitives. The maximum expected differential probability (EDP) of difference propagations and the maximum expected linear potential (ELP) of linear propagations are used to evaluate the security of a primitive against differential and linear cryptanalysis. The maximum EDP and ELP are usually estimated by the maximum differential probability of differential trails and the maximum correlation square of linear trails. The two main kinds of automated search tools for differential and linear trails are dedicated depth-first search algorithms, e.g. Matsui's branch-and-bound algorithm [11] and methods based on mathematical solvers, e.g. the modelling method using Mixed Integer Linear Programming (MILP) [12,15–17,23].

Y. Deng and M. Yung (Eds.): Inscrypt 2022, LNCS 13837, pp. 252–271, 2023.
https://doi.org/10.1007/978-3-031-26553-2_13

The clustering effect is that a set of trails with the same number of rounds share the same input and output differences (masks) but propagate along different intermediate differences (masks). This effect was already recognized for differential cryptanalysis in [9] and linear cryptanalysis in [13]. By considering a large number of trails, we may obtain a more accurate estimation on EDP (ELP) for difference (linear) propagations. To find multiple trails, one approach is to enumerate as many trails as possible using a method of searching trails. One of these works is [2], where multiple trails are found for lightweight primitives using an SAT/SMT modelling method. Another breadth-first approach is to conduct the computation round by round, which scales well with the number of trails but has high memory requirements. Two examples of this breadth-first approach are to use partial, sparse transition matrices [1] and to use a multistage graph combined with memory reservation techniques [7].

In experiments, using Matsui's algorithm or the solver-based methods, we find it costly to find the best differential and linear trails of KNOT-256 when the number of rounds is large and to enumerate trails to investigate the clustering effect for RECTANGLE and KNOT-256. Observing that the best long differential and linear trails of RECTANGLE and KNOT-256 always contain rotational iterative trails, we conceive a method of finding iterative trails and then exploiting them to effectively and efficiently construct difference and linear propagations considering the clustering effect.

Our Contributions

1. We introduce a new concept called the *average weight growth* as an indicator of the advantage of an iterative difference or linear propagation. Based on available algorithms in graph theory, we propose a new method of quantificationally evaluating the clustering effect of iterative trails. We apply this method to PRESENT [5], RECTANGLE [21], GIFT-64 [3] and KNOT-256 [22]. Our results are shown in Table 1.
2. We propose a method of finding exploitable difference and linear propagations contributed by trails containing iterative ones. We apply this method to PRESENT, RECTANGLE, GIFT-64 and KNOT-256 and the main results are shown in Table 2. For KNOT-256, we find the best difference and linear propagations so far, which are respectively improved by 5 and 9 rounds compared to the designers' results. For RECTANGLE, we improve the linear potential of the best 14-round linear propagation from $2^{-62.98}$ [7] to $2^{-62.05}$. Our other results are consistent with the best previous results.
3. For the primary version of KNOT, a round 2 candidate of the NIST lightweight cryptography standardization process, we find difference and linear propagations leading to various differential and linear attacks. Our results are shown in Table 3. We stress that our results do not threaten the security of KNOT.
4. Taking RECTANGLE and KNOT-256 as examples, we illustrate the dominance of trails containing iterative ones in a difference or linear propagation by showing the proportion of such trails from all trails.

Table 1. Summary of results on evaluating the clustering effect of iterative trails for PRESENT, RECTANGLE, GIFT-64 and KNOT-256. awg_t is the minimum average weight growth of iterative trails. awg_c is the minimum average weight growth of iterative difference or linear propagations. The smaller the average weight growth is, the more advantageous an iterative trail or propagation is. $\frac{awg_c}{awg_t}$ shows the clustering effect of iterative trails.

Cipher	Differential			Linear		
	awg_t	awg_c	$\frac{awg_c}{awg_t}$	awg_t	awg_c	$\frac{awg_c}{awg_t}$
PRESENT	4.50	4.11	0.913	4.00	2.76	0.690
RECTANGLE	5.00	5.00	1.000	6.00	5.46	0.910
GIFT-64	5.00	4.88	0.976	6.00	6.00	1.000
KNOT-256	5.33	4.86	0.912	6.00	4.91	0.818

Table 2. Summary of results on finding the best difference and linear propagations for PRESENT, RECTANGLE, GIFT-64 and KNOT-256. The results in bold refresh the published best ones.

Cipher	Differential			Linear		
	#Rounds	Weight	Reference	#Rounds	Weight	Reference
PRESENT	16	61.80	[7]	24	63.61	[7]
	16	61.81	Section 4.2	24	63.61	Section 4.2
RECTANGLE	14	60.63	[2]	14	62.98	[7]
	14	60.64	Section 4.2	14	**62.05**	Section 4.2
GIFT-64	13	60.42	[7]	12	64.00	[7]
	13	60.42	Section 4.2	12	64.00	Section 4.2
KNOT-256	48	252	[22]	44	250	[22]
	53	**253.63**	Section 4.2	**53**	**255.89**	Section 4.2

Organization. The paper is organized as follows. In Sect. 2, we introduce notations and concepts. In Sect. 3, we present a new graph-based method of evaluating the clustering effect of iterative trails and exploiting iterative trails to find exploitable difference and linear propagations. In Sect. 4, We apply our methods to four SPN symmetric-key primitives and show the results. In Sect. 5, we conclude our paper.

2 Preliminaries

A block cipher is a function $\mathcal{E} : \mathbb{F}_2^k \times \mathbb{F}_2^n \rightarrow \mathbb{F}_2^n$ with $C = \mathcal{E}(K, P)$ where K, P and C are the k-bit master key, n-bit plaintext and n-bit ciphertext. A permutation is a bijective function $\mathcal{P} : \mathbb{F}_2^n \rightarrow \mathbb{F}_2^n$ with $SO = \mathcal{P}(SI)$ where SI and SO are the n-bit input and output state. For a fixed key K, $\mathcal{E}_K = \mathcal{E}(K, \cdot)$ is a permutation. In this paper, we focus on iterated key-alternating primitives based on SPN permutations. The state of such a primitive can be separated into m words of s bits and it holds that $n = s \times m$. The round function of the i-th round consists of three layers and is denoted by $\mathcal{R}_i = \mathcal{L} \circ \mathcal{S} \circ \mathcal{A}_{W_i}$ where the three layers are:

Table 3. Summary of previous and new results on the various differential and linear attacks for the primary versions of KNOT.

Scheme	Target phase	Type of attack	Cryptanalysis	#Rounds	Reference
KNOT-AEAD	Initialization	Distinguisher	Differential	14	Section 4.3
		Key recovery	Linear	13	Section 4.3
		Key recovery	Diff-linear	15	[20]
	Encryption	Distinguisher	Linear	12	Section 4.3
		Forgery	Differential	12	Section 4.3
	Finalization	Forgery	Differential	13	Section 4.3
KNOT-Hash	Absorbing	Collision	Differential	12	Section 4.3
	Squeezing	Collision	Differential	13	Section 4.3

- Addition layer $\mathcal{A}_{W_i}$: xor the i-th n-bit round key or constant W_i to the state;
- Non-linear layer $\mathcal{S}$: apply m parallel s-bit bijective S-boxes to the words, i.e.

$$\mathcal{S} = \mathcal{S}_0 || \cdots || \mathcal{S}_{m-1};$$

- Linear layer $\mathcal{L}$: multiply an invertible matrix to the state.

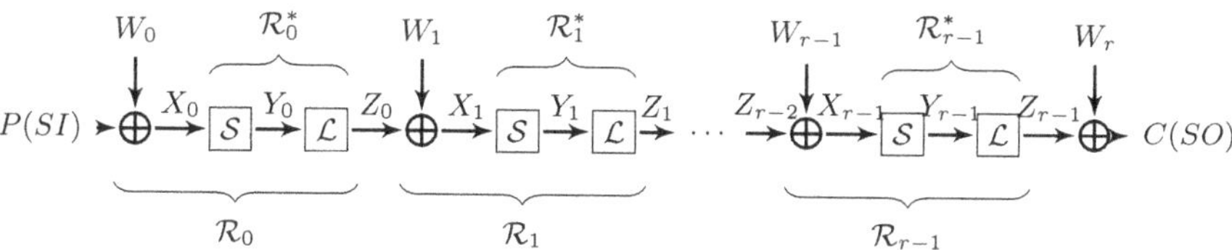

Fig. 1. Structure of an SPN block cipher or permutation

We show the structure of an SPN primitive in Fig. 1. We use W_i to denote the i-th round key for a block cipher or round constant for a permutation. We denote the states before the non-linear layer, before the linear layer and after the linear layer of the i-th round function by X_i, Y_i and Z_i. $X_i[j]$ denotes the j-th word of X_i. The primitive iterates the round function r times. We denote the i-th round function excluding the addition layer by $\mathcal{R}_i^* = \mathcal{L} \circ \mathcal{S}$.

2.1 Differential Cryptanalysis

In differential cryptanalysis, an attacker tries to find an exploitable *difference propagation*, which is a difference pair, with high probability that the differences of the input and output values have a strong relation. For a permutation $\mathcal{P}$: $\mathbb{F}_2^n \rightarrow \mathbb{F}_2^n$, the *differential probability* of a difference propagation (α, β) is

$$\mathbb{P}(\alpha \xrightarrow{\mathcal{P}} \beta) = 2^{-n} \cdot \left| \{x \in \mathbb{F}_2^n | \mathcal{P}(x) \oplus \mathcal{P}(x \oplus \alpha) = \beta\} \right|.$$

An r-round differential trail is a sequence of $r+1$ differences $(\Delta X_0, \cdots, \Delta X_r)$ with probability computed based one the Markov assumption [9],

$$\mathbb{P}(\Delta X_0 \xrightarrow{\mathcal{R}_0} \cdots \xrightarrow{\mathcal{R}_{r-1}} \Delta X_r) \approx \prod_{i=0}^{r-1} \prod_{j=0}^{m-1} \mathbb{P}(\Delta X_i[j] \xrightarrow{\mathcal{S}_i} \Delta Y_i[j]),$$

where $\Delta X_{i+1} = \mathcal{L}(\Delta Y_i), 0 \leq i < r$. Considering the clustering effect, the Expected Differential Probability (EDP) of a difference propagation (α, β) is better estimated by summing the probabilities of all differential trails sharing the same input and output differences:

$$\mathrm{EDP}(\alpha \xrightarrow{\mathcal{E}} \beta) \approx \sum_{\substack{\Delta X_0 = \alpha, \Delta X_r = \beta \\ \Delta X_1, \cdots, \Delta X_{r-1}}} \prod_{i=0}^{r-1} \prod_{j=0}^{m-1} \mathbb{P}(\Delta X_i[j] \xrightarrow{\mathcal{S}_i} \Delta Y_i[j]).$$

Truncated Difference Propagation. Let λ be a linear function corresponding to an $n \times l$ binary matrix M. The probability of a *truncated* difference propagation of $\lambda \circ \mathcal{P}$ is given by [6]:

$$\mathbb{P}(\alpha \xrightarrow{\lambda \circ \mathcal{P}} \beta) = \sum_{\omega | \beta = M\omega} \mathbb{P}(\alpha \xrightarrow{\mathcal{P}} \omega).$$

2.2 Linear Cryptanalysis

In linear cryptanalysis, an attacker tries to find an exploitable *linear propagation*, which is a mask pair, revealing an approximate linear relation between the input and output values. The correlation of a boolean function $f : \mathbb{F}_2^n \to \mathbb{F}_2$ is

$$c_f = 2^{-n} \cdot \left(\left| \{x \in \mathbb{F}_2^n | f(x) = 0\} \right| - \left| \{x \in \mathbb{F}_2^n | f(x) = 1\} \right| \right).$$

For a permutation $\mathcal{P} : \mathbb{F}_2^n \to \mathbb{F}_2^n$, the correlation of a linear propagation (α, β) is

$$\mathrm{Cor}(\alpha \xrightarrow{\mathcal{P}} \beta) = c_{\alpha \cdot x \oplus \beta \cdot \mathcal{P}(x)}.$$

An r-round linear trail is a sequence of $r+1$ masks $(\Gamma X_0, \cdots, \Gamma X_r)$ with correlation

$$\mathrm{Cor}(\Gamma X_0 \xrightarrow{\mathcal{R}_0} \cdots \xrightarrow{\mathcal{R}_{r-1}} \Gamma X_r) = (-1)^{\oplus_{i=0}^{r} \Gamma X_i \cdot W_i} \prod_{i=0}^{r-1} \prod_{j=0}^{m-1} \mathrm{Cor}(\Gamma X_i[j] \xrightarrow{\mathcal{S}_i} \Gamma Y_i[j]),$$

where $\Gamma Y_i = \mathcal{L}^T(\Gamma X_{i+1}), 0 \leq i < r$. Considering the clustering effect, for a permutation, the correlation of a linear propagation (α, β) is the signed sum of correlations of all linear trails sharing the same input and output masks:

$$\mathrm{Cor}(\alpha \xrightarrow{\mathcal{P}} \beta) = \sum_{\substack{\Gamma X_0 = \alpha, \Gamma X_r = \beta \\ \Gamma X_1, \cdots, \Gamma X_{r-1}}} (-1)^{\oplus_{i=0}^{r} \Gamma X_i \cdot W_i} \prod_{i=0}^{r-1} \prod_{j=0}^{m-1} \mathrm{Cor}(\Gamma X_i[j] \xrightarrow{\mathcal{S}_i} \Gamma Y_i[j]).$$

For a key-alternating block cipher, the Expected Linear Potential (ELP) of a linear propagation (α, β) is calculated by summing the correlation squares of all linear trails sharing the same input and output masks according to Theorem 7.9.1 in [6]:

$$\mathrm{ELP}(\alpha \xrightarrow{\mathcal{E}} \beta) = \sum_{\substack{\Gamma X_0=\alpha, \Gamma X_r=\beta \\ \Gamma X_1, \cdots, \Gamma X_{r-1}}} \prod_{i=0}^{r-1} \prod_{j=0}^{m-1} \mathrm{Cor}^2(\Gamma X_i[j] \xrightarrow{\mathcal{S}_i} \Gamma Y_i[j]).$$

2.3 Iterative Trails

Iterative differential trails were exploited in the differential cryptanalysis against DES [4]. We restate the definition of an iterative differential (linear) trail for an SPN symmetric-key primitive as follow:

Definition 1 (Iterative trail). *A differential (linear) trail with its difference (mask) sequence* $(\alpha_0, \cdots, \alpha_r)$ *is iterative if* $\alpha_0 = \alpha_r$.

2.4 Concepts in Graph Theory

A *directed graph* $G = (V, E)$ consists of a set of *vertices* V and a set E of ordered pairs of distinct vertices called *edges*. We denote a directed edge from a vertex u to a vertex v by $u \to v$. We denote the *cost* of the edge $u \to v$ by $c(u \to v)$. A *path* $p_{u,v}$ is a sequence of vertices $(u = v_0, v_1, \cdots, v_{k-1}, v = v_k)$ such that $v_i \to v_{i+1} \in E, 0 \leq i < k$. The *length* of the path is $l(p_{u,v}) = k$. the *cost* of the path is $c(p_{u,v}) = \prod_{i=1}^{k} c(v_{i-1} \to v_i)$. A *hull* of (u, v) is defined as the set of all paths $p_{u,v}$ leading from u to v. More specifically, we define a k-length hull of (u, v), denoted by $h_{u,v}^k$, as the set of all paths $p_{u,v}$ satisfying $l(p_{u,v}) = k$. The cost of $h_{u,v}^k$ is $c(h_{u,v}^k) = \sum_{l(p_{u,v})=k} c(p_{u,v})$. A path $p_{u,u}$ is called a *circuit*. A circuit is *elementary* if no vertex but the first and last appears twice. Two circuits are distinct if one is not a cyclic permutation of the other. An induced subgraph $G' = (V', E')$ is a *strong component* of G, if for all $u, v \in V'$, there exist paths p_{uv} and p_{vu} and this property holds for no subgraph of G induced by a vertex set $\overline{V'}$ such that $V' \subset \overline{V'} \subseteq V$. Tarjan's algorithm [18] is based on a depth-first traversal and outputs the strong components with space and time complexity $\mathcal{O}(|V| + |E|)$. Johnson's algorithm [8], which is based on Tarjan's algorithm, enumerates all the elementary circuits with space complexity $\mathcal{O}(|V| + |E|)$ and time complexity $\mathcal{O}((|V| + |E|)(n_c + 1))$ where n_c is the number of elementary circuits in G.

Viewing the trail search problem as a graph problem, we associate the concepts in graph theory with the concepts in searching differential and linear trails as shown in the following:

Concepts in graph theory	Concepts in searching differential/linear trails
A vertex	A difference or mask
An edge	A 1-round trail
The cost of an edge	Differential probability or correlation square
A k-length path	A k-round trail
A circuit	An iterative trail
A k-length hull	A k-round difference or linear propagation

3 Method of Finding and Exploiting Iterative Trails

In this section, first we extend the definition of iterative trails so that we can deal with ciphers having the rotational symmetry. Next, we present our method of evaluating the clustering effect of iterative trails and exploiting iterative trails to find exploitable difference and linear propagations. To facilitate the narrative, we present our methods in the case of differential cryptanalysis. The situation is analogous in the case of linear cryptanalysis and we will state the difference when there is one.

3.1 Extending the Definition of Iterative Trails

Definition 1 is not suitable for primitives having the rotational symmetry like RECTANGLE and KNOT-256. Defining $\mathrm{rotl}_j(\alpha) = \alpha[j]||\alpha[j+1]||\cdots||\alpha[m-1]||\alpha[0]||\cdots||\alpha[j-1]$ and $\mathrm{rotr}_j(\cdot)$ as its inverse, we give a 1-round differential trail of RECTANGLE in Example 1. To adapt Example 1 to Definition 1, we extend Definition 1 by considering the rotational equivalence relation as in Definition 2. We call an iterative trail based on the rotational equivalence relation as a rotational iterative trail.

Example 1. Let α be $0x6000000000020000$, a 1-round differential trail of RECTANGLE [21] with differential probability 2^{-5} is $(\alpha, \mathrm{rotl}_1(\alpha))$. Then we can construct a long-round differential trail as $(\alpha, \mathrm{rotl}_1(\alpha), \mathrm{rotl}_2(\alpha), \cdots)$.

Definition 2 (Rotational equivalence relation). *For $\alpha = \alpha[0]||\cdots||\alpha[m-1]$ and $\beta = \beta[0]||\cdots||\beta[m-1]$ where $\alpha[i], \beta[i] \in \mathbb{F}_2^s, \forall i \in [0, m-1]$, α and β are rotational equivalent, if there exists a $j \in [0, m-1]$ such that $\beta = rotl_j(\alpha)$, where $rotl_j(\alpha) = \alpha[j]||\alpha[j+1]||\cdots||\alpha[m-1]||\alpha[0]||\cdots||\alpha[j-1]$.*

We define the *representative* of a rotational equivalence class as the maximum difference value in lexicographical order and the *distance* between a difference a and its representative $\mathrm{rep}(a)$ as the j such that $\mathrm{rotl}_j(a) = \mathrm{rep}(a)$. We use $\alpha \xrightarrow{15} \alpha$ to denote the class of 16 rotational iterative trails in Example 1 where each of them is $\mathrm{rotr}_i(\alpha) \to \mathrm{rotr}_{(i+15) \bmod 16}(\alpha), \forall i = 0, \cdots, 15$. For primitives that don't have the rotational symmetry, the distance from a difference to its representative will always be zero.

3.2 Graph Generating

Viewing finding iterative trails as finding circuits in a graph, we can utilize currently available graph algorithms. The first step is to generate an interesting graph, since the graph will be exceedingly huge if we consider all 2^n differences given the block size n. Thus we only consider differences with no more than A active S-boxes in each round, where A is a parameter for us to set. The larger A is, the more accurate the results will be and the more memory and runtime is needed.

We first enumerate input differences activating no more than A S-boxes. Additionally, we filter out any input difference u such that $\mathrm{Asn}(\mathcal{L}^{-1}(u)) > A$ ($\mathrm{Asn}(\mathcal{L}^T(u)) > A$ for finding iterative linear trails) where $\mathrm{Asn}(\cdot)$ returns the number of active S-boxes. Because such a difference will not appear in any circuit in the generated graph. Then we enumerate output differences v such that the probability p of the 1-round trail $u \to v$ is not zero and $\mathrm{Asn}(v) \leq A$. For each $u \to v$, we insert edge $\mathrm{rep}(u) \xrightarrow{d} \mathrm{rep}(v)$, where $d = (j_v - j_u) \mod m, rotl_{j_u}(u) = \mathrm{rep}(u), rotl_{j_v}(v) = \mathrm{rep}(v)$, into the graph and set the cost of the edge $c(\mathrm{rep}(u) \xrightarrow{d} \mathrm{rep}(v))$ to be p. It is worth mentioning that multiple edges can exist between $\mathrm{rep}(u)$ and $\mathrm{rep}(v)$, each labelled by a different d. We use a three-layer hash table $\mathcal{H}$ to restore the graph, i.e. $\mathcal{H}[\mathrm{rep}(u)][\mathrm{rep}(v)][d] = p$.

After the graph is generated, we reduce it by removing vertices that don't have at least one incoming and one outgoing edge until no more vertices can be removed. The remaining graph, which we call an *iterative structure*, will contain the strong components and paths linking two different strong components. When finding iterative differential trails and iterative difference propagations, only the strong components are useful (Sect. 3.3 and 3.4). Paths linking two different strong components are useful in finding difference propagations contributed by trails containing iterative ones (Sect. 3.5), for we can concatenate two iterative trails from two different strong components by such paths. Given the parameter A, we generate the iterative structure IS as shown in Algorithm 1.

3.3 Finding the Best Iterative Differential Trail

Given the iterative structure, we can apply Johnson's algorithm for enumerating all elementary (rotational) iterative differential trails. For a differential trail with probability 2^{-w}, we call w the weight of it. For an r-round iterative differential trail with weight w, we define its *average weight growth* as w/r and use it as an indicator of the advantage of an iterative trail. We refer the best iterative differential trail to the one with the minimum average weight growth.

Theorem 1. *One of the best iterative trails must be elementary.*

Proof. Suppose that none of the best iterative trails is elementary. We choose one best iterative trail it_0 with r_0 rounds and weight w_0. Since it is not elementary, we can divide it into two iterative trails it_1, it_2 with r_1, r_2 rounds and w_1, w_2 as weights respectively and we have $r_1 + r_2 = r_0, w_1 + w_2 = w_0$. If $\frac{w_1}{r_1} < \frac{w_2}{r_2}$, then

Algorithm 1. Generate the iterative structure given the maximum number of active S-boxes

Input: A: the maximum number of active S-boxes in each round
Output: IS: the iterative structure

procedure
  Create an empty hash table IS.
  for each $u \in \mathbb{F}_2^n$ satisfying $\text{Asn}(u) \leq A$ and $\text{Asn}(\mathcal{L}^{-1}(u)) > A$ **do**
    $j_u \leftarrow$ the j such that $\text{rotl}_j(u) = \text{rep}(u)$
    for each $v \in \mathbb{F}_2^n$ satisfying $\text{Asn}(v) \leq A$ and $u \rightarrow v$ is valid **do**
      $j_v \leftarrow$ the j such that $\text{rotl}_j(v) = \text{rep}(v)$
      $IS[r_u][r_v][j_v - j_u \mod m] \leftarrow \mathbb{P}(u \rightarrow v)$
    end for
  end for
  Find a vertex in IS that has no incoming or outgoing edge and delete the vertex and its corresponding edges, until no such vertex can be found.
  return IS
end procedure

$\frac{w_1}{r_1} < \frac{w_0}{r_0} < \frac{w_2}{r_2}$, which contradicts to that $\frac{w_0}{r_0}$ is the minimum. Else if $\frac{w_1}{r_1} = \frac{w_2}{r_2}$, then it_1, it_2 are not elementary since they are also the best. Thus the above steps can be continuously conducted on it_1 and it_2. However, the division can't be conducted infinite times. it_1 or it_2 will be elementary at some time and then we will get a contradiction.

According to Theorem 1, the best average weight growth of iterative trails equals that of elementary ones. Thus it is enough to investigate only elementary circuits applying Johnson's algorithm. We obtain the average weight growth for each of the elementary circuits and find the best one. The procedure is given as shown in Algorithm 2.

Algorithm 2. Find the best iterative trail in IS

Input: IS: the iterative structure
Output: The best average weight growth of an iterative trail

procedure
  $bawg \leftarrow \infty$
  for each elementary circuit $(\alpha_0, \cdots, \alpha_r = \alpha_0)$ in IS **do**
    $w_i \leftarrow \min_d - \log_2 IS[\alpha_i][\alpha_{i+1}][d], \forall 0 \leq i < r$
    $bawg \leftarrow \min\{\sum_{i=0}^{r-1} \frac{w_i}{r}, bawg\}$
  end for
  return $bawg$
end procedure

3.4 Finding the Best Iterative Difference Propagation

If two iterative differential trails have any common difference, we observe that a better iterative difference propagation can be constructed. Suppose that we find two elementary iterative differential trail $it_0 = (\alpha_0, \alpha_1, \alpha_0)$ with average weight growth awg_0 and $it_1 = (\alpha_0, \alpha_1, \alpha_2, \alpha_0)$ with average weight growth awg_1. Then the average weight growth of the 6-round difference propagation (α_0, α_0) is $-\log_2(2^{-awg_0} + 2^{-awg_1})$, which is better than either of that of the two single iterative trails.

In order to investigate the clustering effect of iterative trails, we search for the best iterative difference propagation in the iterative structure IS, that is, to compute $\min_{r,u \in IS}(-\log_2 c(h^r_{u,u}))/r$. For an r-round difference propagation with weight w, we also use its average weight growth w/r to evaluate its strength. We expect the gap between the average weight growth of the best single iterative differential trail and that of the best iterative difference propagation reflects the strength of the clustering effect of iterative trails.

We obtain the strong components SC of the iterative structure by applying Tarjan's algorithm. If a difference reaches out of the strong component it lies in, it will never reach itself once again. Thus we first reduce the iterative structure IS to its strong components SC and then we compute $\min_{u \in SC,r}(-\log_2 c(h^r_{u,u}))/r$. The procedure is shown in Algorithm 3. As the number of round increases, the clustering effect will be no weaker if it exists. We cease increasing the number of rounds r when $\min -\log_2 c(h^r_{u,u})$ exceeds the block size n.

3.5 Finding the Best Difference Propagation Contributed by Trails Containing Iterative Ones

An iterative trail can be exploited to form a long trail in two phases. Firstly, it is concatenated to itself several times. Secondly, the resulting trail is extended both forward and backward by several rounds. Following this idea, we conceive a method of exploiting the iterative structure in order to find a exploitable difference propagation. In the following, for a graph G, we denote its vertex set as $G.V$.

We first build three graphs: backward, middle and forward graph denoted by G^b, G^m and G^f. G^m is set to be the iterative structure IS and G^b, G^f is initialized to be IS. For each vertex in the IS, we extend it both backward and forward by r^e rounds to obtain short-round trails using a depth-first traversal. We collect as many such extended trails as possible while keeping memory usage acceptable. We use an extra parameter w^e to limit the scope of extended trails. That is, we collect k-round backward (or forward) extended trails $(\alpha_0, \cdots, \alpha_k)$ with weight w satisfying: (1) $\alpha_k \in IS.V$ (or $\alpha_0 \in IS.V$); (2) $k \leq r^e$; (3) $w \leq w^e - w^{min}(r^e - k)$, where w^{min} is the minimum weight of one-round trails. These trails are inserted into G^b and G^f respectively.

To find the best difference propagation, we can directly conduct a round-by-round breadth-first traversal, of which the memory complexity of the breadth-first traversal is $\mathcal{O}(|G^b.V| \cdot |G^f.V|)$. Note that $|G^b.V|$ and $|G^f.V|$ is far larger

Algorithm 3. Find the best iterative difference propagation in IS

Input: IS: the iterative structure
Output: The best average weight growth of iterative difference propagations

procedure
    $bawg \leftarrow \infty$, $r \leftarrow 1$, $SC, \mathcal{H} \leftarrow$ the strong components of IS
    do
        $w \leftarrow \min_{u,d} - \log_2 \mathcal{H}[u][u][d]$, $bawg \leftarrow \min\{w/r, bawg\}$,
        $\text{ADD}(\mathcal{H}, SC)$, $r \leftarrow r + 1$
    while $w > n$
    return $bawg$
end procedure
procedure $\text{ADD}(\mathcal{H},\mathcal{H}')$
    $\mathcal{H}_{tmp} \leftarrow \emptyset$
    for each key (u, v, d_1) of $\mathcal{H}$ **do**
        for each key (v, w, d_2) of $\mathcal{H}'$ **do**
            $d \leftarrow d_1 + d_2 \mod m$
            if (u, w, d) exists in $\mathcal{H}_{tmp}$ **then**
                $\mathcal{H}_{tmp}[u][w][d] \leftarrow \mathcal{H}_{tmp}[u][w][d] + \mathcal{H}[u][v][d_1] \cdot \mathcal{H}'[v][w][d_2]$
            else
                $\mathcal{H}_{tmp}[u][w][d] \leftarrow \mathcal{H}[u][v][d_1] \cdot \mathcal{H}'[v][w][d_2]$
            end if
        end for
    end for
    $\mathcal{H} \leftarrow \mathcal{H}_{tmp}$
end procedure

than $|IS.V|$ and $|G^b.V| \cdot |G^f.V|$ will be too large. Instead, we first conduct a breadth-first traversal on the three graphs G^b, G^m and G^f separately, of which the memory complexity is $\mathcal{O}(|G^b.V| \cdot |IS.V| + |IS.V| \cdot |IS.V| + |IS.V| \cdot |G^f.V|)$. And then we traverse the three graphs by considering each vertex in $G^b.V$ separately, where the memory complexity can be reduced from $\mathcal{O}(|G^b.V| \cdot |G^f.V|)$ to $\mathcal{O}(|G^f.V|)$ in the cost of increasing the time complexity by $|G^b.V|$ times. Compared to [7], taking advantage of the limited size of the iterative structure, our time-memory tradeoff avoids duplicate computations by increasing the memory complexity while keeping it acceptable. The procedure is shown in Algorithm 4.

4 Experimental Results

We apply our methods to 4 SPN symmetric-key primitives including PRESENT, RECTANGLE, GIFT-64 and KNOT-256. All the experiments are conducted on a PC with Intel(R) Core(TM) i7-4720HQ CPU @ 2.60 GHz and 8 GB memory.

4.1 Evaluation of the Clustering Effect of Iterative Differential and Linear Trails

To have a direct understanding of an iterative structure, we first visualize some of the iterative structures as shown in Fig. 2. Then we evaluate the clustering

Algorithm 4. Find the best difference propagation contributed by trails containing iterative ones

Input: IS: the iterative structure; r: the number of rounds; r^e: the maximum number of rounds to be extended; w^e: the weight limiting the scope of extended trails.
Output: The weight of the best difference propagation contributed by trails containing iterative ones

procedure
  $G^b \leftarrow IS, G^f \leftarrow IS$
  for each vertex u in IS **do**
    for each trail $(\alpha_0, \cdots, \alpha_k)$ with weight w satisfying $k \leq r^e$, $w \leq w^{min}(r^e - k) + w^e$ and $\alpha_0 = u$ or $\alpha_k = u$ **do**
      $j_i \leftarrow$ the j such that $\text{rotl}_j(\alpha_i) = \text{rep}(\alpha_i), \forall 0 \leq i \leq k$
      if the trail is starting from $\alpha_k = u$ **then**
        $G^b[\text{rep}(\alpha_i)][\text{rep}(\alpha_{i+1})][j_{i+1} - j_i \mod m] \leftarrow c(\alpha_i \rightarrow \alpha_{i+1}), \forall 0 \leq i < k$
      else if the trail is starting from $\alpha_0 = u$ **then**
        $G^f[\text{rep}(\alpha_i)][\text{rep}(\alpha_{i+1})][j_{i+1} - j_i \mod m] \leftarrow c(\alpha_i \rightarrow \alpha_{i+1}), \forall 0 \leq i < k$
      end if
    end for
  end for
  $\mathcal{H}^b \leftarrow G^b, \mathcal{H}^f \leftarrow G^f, \mathcal{H}^m \leftarrow IS$, $bw \leftarrow \infty$
  Conduct $\text{ADD}(\mathcal{H}^b, G^b)$ and $\text{ADD}(\mathcal{H}^f, G^f)$ $(r^e - 1)$ times.
  Conduct $\text{ADD}(\mathcal{H}^m, IS)$ $(r - 2r^e - 1)$ times.
  for each first key u of $\mathcal{H}^b$ **do**
    $\mathcal{H}[u] \leftarrow \mathcal{H}^b[u]$, $\text{ADD}(\mathcal{H}, \mathcal{H}^m)$, $\text{ADD}(\mathcal{H}, \mathcal{H}^f)$
    $bw \leftarrow \min\{\min_{v,d} - \log_2 \mathcal{H}[u][v][d], bw\}$
  end for
  return bw
end procedure

effect of iterative trails by giving the average weight growth of the best iterative differential (linear) trails and that of the best iterative difference (linear) propagation as shown in Fig. 3.

For PRESENT, the best iterative differential trail has 4 rounds and average weight growth 4.50, which is exactly the one given in [19]. From Fig. 3(a), we can observe a clustering effect of iterative differential trails. Our results in Fig. 3(b) also shows a strong clustering effect of iterative linear trails with one active S-box in each round (which are also 1-bit trails), which is in compliance with the work in [14]. For GIFT-64, we observe a clustering effect of iterative differential trails where the average weight growth decreases from 5.00 to 4.88 (Fig. 3(c)). It is noteworthy that we observe no clustering effect of iterative linear trails as shown in Fig. 3(d) while the four iterative linear trails are all disconnected with each other in Fig. 2(c). For RECTANGLE, we observe no clustering effect of rotational iterative differential trails (Fig. 3(e)) and a clustering effect of rotational iterative linear trails where the average weight growth decreases from 6.00 to 5.46 (Fig. 3(f)). For KNOT-256, of which the design inherits that of RECTANGLE, we observe both clustering effect or rotational iterative differ-

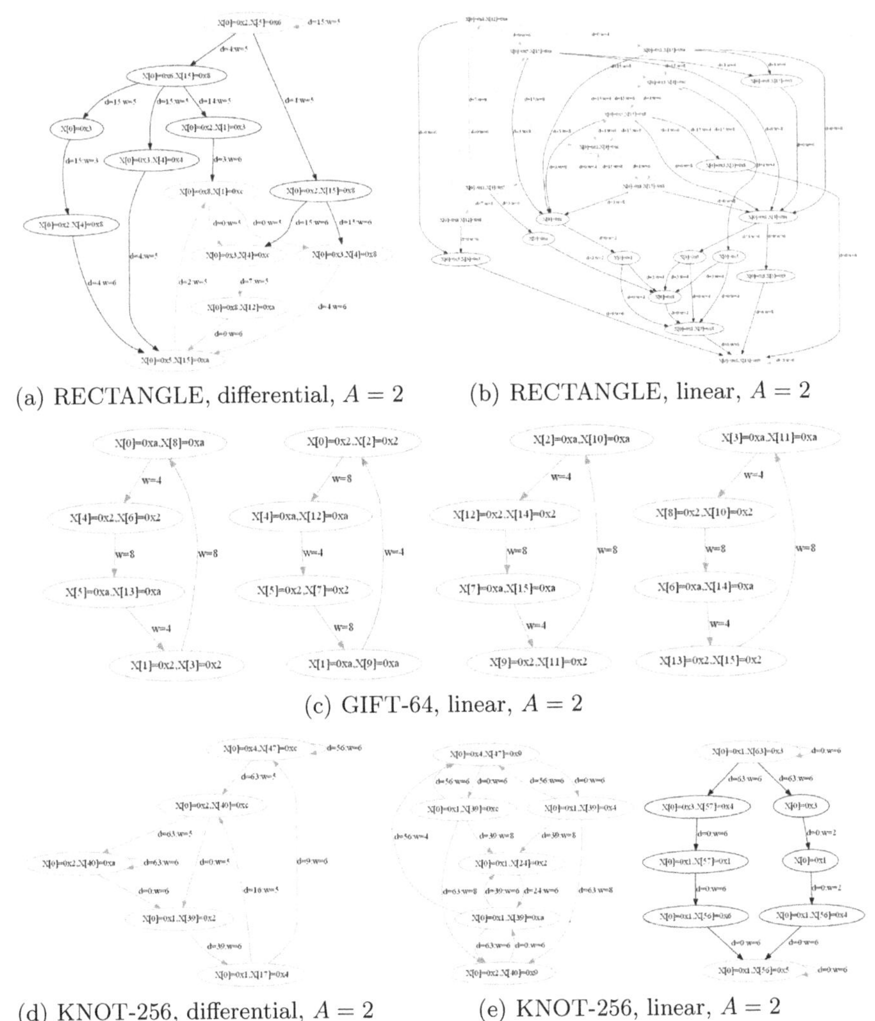

(a) RECTANGLE, differential, $A = 2$ (b) RECTANGLE, linear, $A = 2$

(c) GIFT-64, linear, $A = 2$

(d) KNOT-256, differential, $A = 2$ (e) KNOT-256, linear, $A = 2$

Fig. 2. The differential iterative structures of RECTANGLE and KNOT-256 and the linear iterative structures of RECTANGLE, GIFT-64 and KNOT-256. To clarify, edge $X[0] = 0x2, X[5] = 0x6 \xrightarrow{d=15:w=5} X[0] = 0x2, X[5] = 0x6$ in Figure (a) indicates a 1-round differential trail 0x6000000000020000 → 0x 0600000000002000 has probability 2^{-5}. The red part is the strong components computed by Tarjan's algorithm. One circuit always lies in one strong component. The remaining blue part contains one-way paths linking disconnecte d strong components.

ential and linear trails where the average weight growth decreases from 5.33 to 4.86 (Fig. 3(g)) and from 6.00 to 4.91 (Fig. 3(h)).

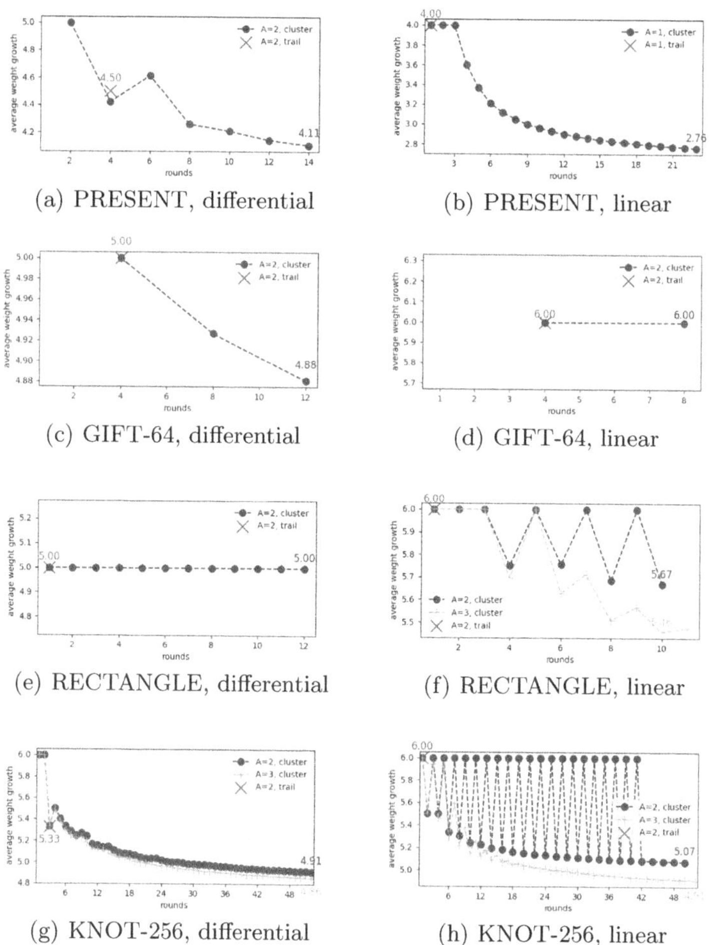

(a) PRESENT, differential (b) PRESENT, linear

(c) GIFT-64, differential (d) GIFT-64, linear

(e) RECTANGLE, differential (f) RECTANGLE, linear

(g) KNOT-256, differential (h) KNOT-256, linear

Fig. 3. Comparison of the best average weight growth of iterative trails and that of iterative difference and linear propagations. The red cross marks the average weight growth of the best iterative trail with the minimum number of rounds. The blue plot is the average weight growth of the best iterative difference or linear propagation w.r.t. the number of rounds. Additionally, we increment A by 1 and recompute the best average weight growth. If there is an improvement, we show the results as the orange plot. (Color figure online)

4.2 Results on Finding the Best Difference and Linear Propagations Contributed by Trails Containing Iterative Ones

Since we observe clustering effects of iterative trails in most circumstances. Thus we expect to find exploitable difference and linear propagation utilizing this clustering effect. Applying Algorithm 4, we search for the best difference and linear propagations contributed by trails containing iterative ones. The parameters and experimental results are shown in Table 4.

For PRESENT and GIFT-64, our results are consistent with the best known results [7]. For RECTANGLE, we find the best 14-round linear propagation so far of which the correlation potential is $2^{-62.05}$. The previous best weight is $2^{-62.98}$ [7]. For KNOT-256, the designers find the best 48-round differential trail with differential probability 2^{-252} and the best 40-round linear trail with correlation potential 2^{-226} and deduce that the best 44-round linear trail has correlation potential 2^{-250} [22]. We find a 53-round exploitable difference propagation with differential probability $2^{-253.63}$ and a 53-round exploitable linear propagation with correlation potential $2^{-255.89}$, improving the designers' results by 5 and 9 rounds respectively.

Table 4. Results on finding the best difference and linear propagations contributed by trails containing iterative ones. r is the number of rounds. A is the maximum number of active S-boxes. r^e is the maximum number of rounds of the extended trails. w^e bounds the weights of the extended trails. (r^e, w^e) determines the scope of extended trails we consider. wt_t and wt_c is the weight of the best trail and cluster we find. wt^{prev} is the weight of the best previous result. Time is the runtime of Algorithm 4.

Cryptanalysis	Cipher	r	A	(r^e, w^e)	wt_t	wt_c	wt^{prev}	Time
Differential	KNOT-256	53	3	(3, 12)	279	253.63	279 [22]	13.4 h
	RECTANGLE	14	2	(6, 23)	61	60.64	60.63 [2]	20.0 h
	GIFT-64	13	2	(3, 12)	62	60.42	60.42 [7]	2 s
	PRESENT	16	3	(2, 6)	70	61.81	61.80 [7]	112 s
Linear	KNOT-256	53	3	(2, 6)	306	255.89	306 [22]	118 s
	RECTANGLE	14	3	(3, 10)	68	62.05	62.98 [7]	8.0 h
	GIFT-64	12	3	(3, 12)	64	64.00	64.00 [7]	3.0 h
	PRESENT	24	2	(3, 8)	92	63.61	63.61 [7]	0.5 h

4.3 Results on the Security of KNOT-AEAD and KNOT-Hash Against Differential and Linear Attacks

For KNOT, the distinguishers found in Sect. 4.2 are oriented towards the inner permutation and can't be used to attack the AEAD and hash scheme of KNOT. We need to further consider that: (1) the input and output differences or masks are restricted to zero according to the attacks towards the sponge construction; (2) the output difference in the capacity or non-tag part is not required, leading to a truncated difference propagation.

For the primary version of KNOT-AEAD, the block, rate, capacity, key and nonce size b, r, c, k, n are $256, 64, 192, 128, 128$. For an inner state S, we can separate it by the nonce and key part denoted by $(S_N, S_K), |S_N| = n, |S_K| = k$, by the rate and capacity part denoted by $(S_R, S_C), |S_R| = r, |S_C| = c$ or by the tag and non-tag part denoted by $(S_T, S_{nT}), |S_T| = k, |S_{nT}| = b - k$. For the primary version of KNOT-Hash, the block, rate, capacity and tag size b, r, c, r' are $256, 32, 224, 128$. For an inner state S, we can separate it by the rate and capacity part denoted by $(S_R, S_C), |S_R| = r, |S_C| = c$ or by the tag and non-tag part denoted by $(S_T, S_{nT}), |S_T| = r', |S_{nT}| = b - r'$.

In Table 5, we list differential and linear attacks targeting different phases, each demanding specific restrictions and truncated conditions on the distinguishers. The attacks proposed are general for cryptographic schemes based on the sponge construction. For each attack, we give the largest differential probability or absolute linear correlation of the longest distinguisher of the primary version of KNOT.

Table 5. Results on the best differential and linear distinguishers for the primary version of KNOT

Cryptanalysis	Phase	Type	Restrictions and truncations	r	A	(r^e, w^e)	wt
Differential	Initialization	Distinguisher	$\Delta SI_K = 0$, truncated in ΔSO_C	14	3	(5,20)	61.08
Linear	Initialization	Key recovery	$\Gamma SO_C = 0$	13	3	(3,8)	31.28
Linear	Encryption	Distinguisher	$\Gamma SI_C = 0$, $\Gamma SO_C = 0$	12	3	(3,10)	30.52
Differential	Encryption	Forgery	$\Delta SI_C = 0$, $\Delta SO_C = 0$	12	3	(5,20)	62.05
Differential	Finalization	Forgery	$\Delta SI_C = 0$, truncated in ΔSO_{nT}	13	3	(5,20)	60.67
Differential	Absorbing	Collision	$\Delta SI_C = 0$, $\Delta SO_C = 0$	12	3	(5,20)	62.30
Differential	Squeezing	Collision	$\Delta SI_C = 0$, truncated in ΔSO_{nT}	13	3	(5,20)	60.67

According to Table 5, it's suggested that the best differential or linear propagations for the initialization, encryption and finalization phase of KNOT-AEAD reach 14, 12 and 13 rounds respectively., while the number of rounds of the three phases are 52, 28 and 32 respectively. The best differential or linear propagations for the absorbing and squeezing phase of KNOT-Hash reach 12 and 13 round resp., while the number of rounds of the two phases are 68 and 68 resp. We stress that our results do not threaten the security of KNOT.

4.4 Verification of the Dominance of Trails Containing Iterative Ones in a Difference or Linear Propagation

To verify the accuracy of our method, we need to know whether trails containing iterative ones account for the majority of all the trails in an exploitable difference or linear propagation. On one hand, we list the number of trails that are considered in our method grouped by the weight of one trail. On the other hand, for comparison, we enumerate all the trails of which the weight is below a certain threshold fixing the input and output difference or mask using the MILP method.

For the 14-round difference propagation of RECTANGLE with input difference 0x1000060000000000 and output difference 0x8610000000000100, we enumerate all trails with weight between 61 and 71. For the 15-round linear propagation of RECTANGLE with input mask 0x5000000600000000 and output mask 0x0002000060000400, we enumerate all trails with weight between 37 and 40. For the 10-round difference propagation of KNOT-256 with input difference $\Delta X[32] = 0x1, \Delta X[49] = 0x1$ and output difference $\Delta X[39] = 0x1, \Delta X[63] = 0x1$, we enumerate all trails with weight between 56 and 74. For the 10-round linear propagation of KNOT-256 with input mask $\Gamma X[0] = 0x1, \Gamma X[25] = 0x1$ and output mask $\Gamma X[24] = 0x1, \Gamma X[41] = 0x1$, we enumerate all trails with weight between 30 and 48. For these four difference and linear propagations, we also output the number of trails considered in our method. The comparison results are shown in Fig. 4.

Table 6. Results of the accumulative differential probabilities (linear potentials) of the four difference (linear) propagations corresponding to Fig. 4. $[a, b]$ is the weight range within which we enumerate trails for the propagation. $wt^g_{[a,b]}$ is the accumulative weight of the enumerated trails within weight range $[a, b]$. A and (r^e, w^e) are the parameters of our method. $wt^{ite}_{[a,b]}$ is the accumulative weight of the trails containing iterative ones considered in our method within weight range $[a, b]$. wt^{ite} is the accumulative weight of all trails containing iterative ones considered in our method.

Cipher	Propagation	$[a, b]$	$wt^g_{[a,b]}$	A	(r^e, w^e)	$wt^{ite}_{[a,b]}$	wt^{ite}
RECTANGLE	Difference	[61,71]	60.66	3	(6,22)	60.66	60.63
	Linear	[37,40]	69.14	3	(4,16)	69.15	67.89
KNOT-256	Difference	[56,74]	53.49	4	(3,20)	53.49	53.49
				3		53.53	53.53
	Linear	[30,48]	56.21	4		56.21	56.21
				3		56.22	56.22

For RECTANGLE, from Fig. 4(a), 4(b) and Table 6, trails containing iterative ones almost cover the trails enumerated with weights within the weight range. Beyond the weight range, a large number of more trails containing iterative ones are incorporated, while enumerating trails beyond the weight range will be too costly. And these extra trails improve the accumulative differential probability and linear potential.

For KNOT-256, from Fig. 4(c), 4(d) and Table 6, when $A = 4$, trails considered in our method account for the vast majority. we can also see that, though we can incorporate more trails setting $A = 4$, the accumulative differential probability or linear potential increases little compared to that setting $A = 3$, implying that trails containing iterative trails with no more than 3 active S-boxes in each round dominates the contribution to the accumulative differential probability or linear potential.

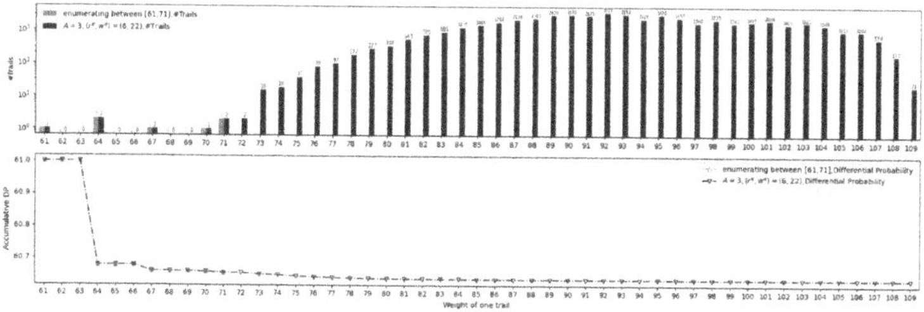

(a) RECTANGLE, $r = 14$, input difference: 0x1000060000000000, output difference: 0x8610000000000100.

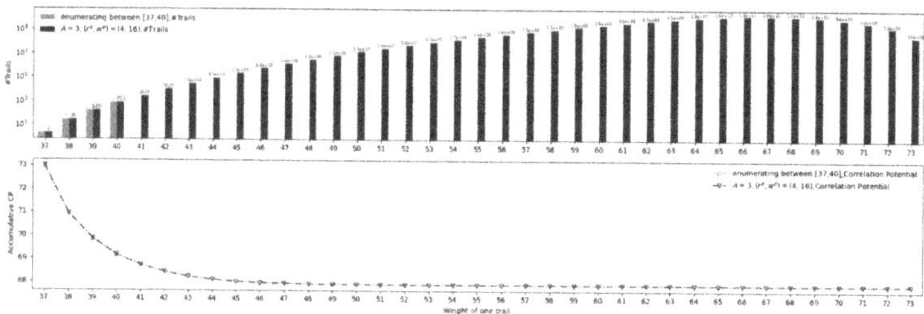

(b) RECTANGLE, $r = 15$, input mask: 0x5000000600000000, output mask: 0x0002000060000400.

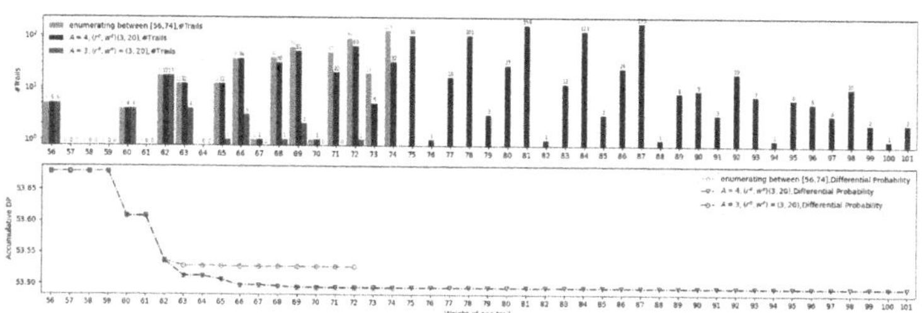

(c) KNOT-256, $r = 10$, input difference: $X_{32} = 0x1, X_{49} = 0x1$, output difference: $X_{39} = 0x1, X_{63} = 0x1$.

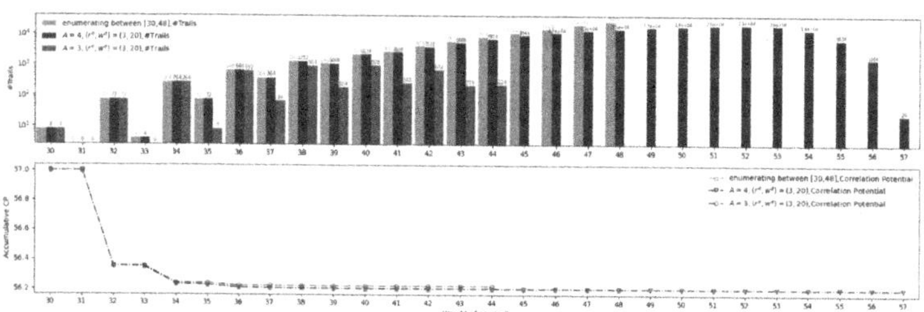

(d) KNOT-256, $r = 10$, input mask: $X_0 = 0x1, X_{25} = 0x1$, output mask: $X_{24} = 0x1, X_{41} = 0x1$.

Fig. 4. Results of the number of trails considered in the four difference and linear propagations grouped by the weight of one trail.

5 Conclusion

In this paper, for four SPN symmetric-key primitives, using a graph approach, we evaluated the clustering effect of (rotational) iterative trails and exploited (rotational) iterative trails to find exploitable difference and linear propagations. We improved the best linear propagation of RECTANGLE and improved both the best difference and linear propagation of KNOT-256. For the primary version of KNOT, we find the best difference and linear propagations suitable for differential and linear attacks on the sponge construction. Moreover, we gave RECTANGLE and KNOT-256 as examples to illustrate how trails containing iterative ones dominate the contribution to the differential probability of a difference propagation or the linear potential of a linear propagation. We leave the studies on the other three version of KNOT and other primitives including ASCON, Xoodyak and ARX ciphers for future work.

Acknowledgements. The authors thank the anonymous reviewers of Inscrypt and ToSC for their valuable comments and suggestions to improve the quality of the paper. This work was supported by the National Natural Science Foundation of China (Grant No. 61379138).

References

1. Abdelraheem, M.A.: Estimating the probabilities of low-weight differential and linear approximations on PRESENT-like ciphers. In: Kwon, T., Lee, M.-K., Kwon, D. (eds.) ICISC 2012. LNCS, vol. 7839, pp. 368–382. Springer, Heidelberg (2013). https://doi.org/10.1007/978-3-642-37682-5_26
2. Ankele, R., Kölbl, S.: Mind the gap-a closer look at the security of block ciphers against differential cryptanalysis. In: Cid, C., Jacobson, M., Jr. (eds.) SAC 2018. LNCS, vol. 11349, pp. 163–190. Springer, Cham (2018). https://doi.org/10.1007/978-3-030-10970-7_8
3. Banik, S., Pandey, S.K., Peyrin, T., Sasaki, Y., Sim, S.M., Todo, Y.: GIFT: a small present. In: Fischer, W., Homma, N. (eds.) CHES 2017. LNCS, vol. 10529, pp. 321–345. Springer, Cham (2017). https://doi.org/10.1007/978-3-319-66787-4_16
4. Biham, E., Shamir, A.: Differential cryptanalysis of des-like cryptosystems. J. Cryptol. **4**(1), 3–72 (1991)
5. Bogdanov, A., et al.: PRESENT: an ultra-lightweight block cipher. In: Paillier, P., Verbauwhede, I. (eds.) CHES 2007. LNCS, vol. 4727, pp. 450–466. Springer, Heidelberg (2007). https://doi.org/10.1007/978-3-540-74735-2_31
6. Daemen, J., Rijmen, V.: The Design of Rijndael, vol. 2. Springer, Heidelberg (2002)
7. Hall-Andersen, M., Vejre, P.S.: Generating graphs packed with paths estimation of linear approximations and differentials. IACR Trans. Symmetric Cryptol. **2018**(3), 265–289 (2018). https://doi.org/10.13154/tosc.v2018.i3.265-289
8. Johnson, D.B.: Finding all the elementary circuits of a directed graph. SIAM J. Comput. **4**(1), 77–84 (1975)
9. Lai, X., Massey, J.L., Murphy, S.: Markov ciphers and differential cryptanalysis. In: Davies, D.W. (ed.) EUROCRYPT 1991. LNCS, vol. 547, pp. 17–38. Springer, Heidelberg (1991). https://doi.org/10.1007/3-540-46416-6_2

10. Matsui, M.: Linear cryptanalysis method for DES cipher. In: Helleseth, T. (ed.) EUROCRYPT 1993. LNCS, vol. 765, pp. 386–397. Springer, Heidelberg (1994). https://doi.org/10.1007/3-540-48285-7_33
11. Matsui, M.: On correlation between the order of S-boxes and the strength of DES. In: De Santis, A. (ed.) EUROCRYPT 1994. LNCS, vol. 950, pp. 366–375. Springer, Heidelberg (1995). https://doi.org/10.1007/BFb0053451
12. Mouha, N., Wang, Q., Gu, D., Preneel, B.: Differential and linear cryptanalysis using mixed-integer linear programming. In: Wu, C.-K., Yung, M., Lin, D. (eds.) Inscrypt 2011. LNCS, vol. 7537, pp. 57–76. Springer, Heidelberg (2012). https://doi.org/10.1007/978-3-642-34704-7_5
13. Nyberg, K.: Linear approximation of block ciphers. In: De Santis, A. (ed.) EUROCRYPT 1994. LNCS, vol. 950, pp. 439–444. Springer, Heidelberg (1995). https://doi.org/10.1007/BFb0053460
14. Ohkuma, K.: Weak keys of reduced-round PRESENT for linear cryptanalysis. In: Jacobson, M.J., Rijmen, V., Safavi-Naini, R. (eds.) SAC 2009. LNCS, vol. 5867, pp. 249–265. Springer, Heidelberg (2009). https://doi.org/10.1007/978-3-642-05445-7_16
15. Sun, S., Hu, L., Song, L., Xie, Y., Wang, P.: Automatic security evaluation of block ciphers with S-bP structures against related-key differential attacks. In: Lin, D., Xu, S., Yung, M. (eds.) Inscrypt 2013. LNCS, vol. 8567, pp. 39–51. Springer, Cham (2014). https://doi.org/10.1007/978-3-319-12087-4_3
16. Sun, S., et al.: Towards finding the best characteristics of some bit-oriented block ciphers and automatic enumeration of (related-key) differential and linear characteristics with predefined properties. IACRCryptology ePrint Archive **747**, 2014 (2014)
17. Sun, S., Hu, L., Wang, P., Qiao, K., Ma, X., Song, L.: Automatic security evaluation and (related-key) differential characteristic search: application to SIMON, PRESENT, LBlock, DES(L) and other bit-oriented block ciphers. In: Sarkar, P., Iwata, T. (eds.) ASIACRYPT 2014. LNCS, vol. 8873, pp. 158–178. Springer, Heidelberg (2014). https://doi.org/10.1007/978-3-662-45611-8_9
18. Tarjan, R.: Depth-first search and linear graph algorithms. SIAM J. Comput. **1**(2), 146–160 (1972)
19. Wang, M.: Differential cryptanalysis of reduced-round PRESENT. In: Vaudenay, S. (ed.) AFRICACRYPT 2008. LNCS, vol. 5023, pp. 40–49. Springer, Heidelberg (2008). https://doi.org/10.1007/978-3-540-68164-9_4
20. Wang, S., Hou, S., Liu, M., Lin, D.: Differential-linear cryptanalysis of the lightweight cryptographic algorithm KNOT. In: Yu, Yu., Yung, M. (eds.) Inscrypt 2021. LNCS, vol. 13007, pp. 171–190. Springer, Cham (2021). https://doi.org/10.1007/978-3-030-88323-2_9
21. Zhang, W., Bao, Z., Lin, D., Rijmen, V., Yang, B., Verbauwhede, I.: RECTANGLE: a bit-slice lightweight block cipher suitable for multiple platforms. Sci. China Inf. Sci. **58**(12), 1–15 (2015)
22. Zhang, W., et al.: KNOT: algorithm specifications and supporting document (2019). https://csrc.nist.gov/CSRC/media/Projects/lightweight-cryptography/documents/round-2/spec-doc-rnd2/knot-spec-round.pdf
23. Zhou, C., Zhang, W., Ding, T., Xiang, Z.: Improving the MILP-based security evaluation algorithm against differential/linear cryptanalysis using a divide-and-conquer approach. IACR Trans. Symmetric Cryptol. **4**, 438–469 (2019)

Differential Cryptanalysis of Round-Reduced SPEEDY Family

Qingyuan Yu[1,4], Keting Jia[2,5(✉)], Guangnan Zou[3], and Guoyan Zhang[1,4,6]

[1] School of Cyber Science and Technology, Shandong University, Qingdao 266237, Shandong, China
yuqy@mail.sdu.edu.cn, guoyanzhang@sdu.edu.cn

[2] Institute for Network Sciences and Cyberspace, BNRist, Tsinghua University, Beijing 10084, China
ktjia@tsinghua.edu.cn

[3] Department of Computer Sciences and Technology, Tsinghua University, Beijing 10084, China

[4] Key Laboratory of Cryptologic Technology and Information Security, Ministry of Education, Shandong University, Qingdao 266237, Shandong, China

[5] Zhongguancun Laboratory, Beijing, China

[6] Shandong Institute of Blockchain, Jinan, Shandong, China

Abstract. SPEEDY is a family of ultra low latency block ciphers proposed at TCHES 2021 by Leander *et al.*. The standard version, SPEEDY-6-192 offers 128-bit security with high encryption speed in hardware. Differential cryptanalysis proposed in 1990 by Biham and Shamir is one of the most popular methods of cryptanalysis of block ciphers. It is usually the first choice to evaluate the security for designers when designing a new block cipher. The automatic search for various distinguishers based on SAT and MILP models etc. boosts the cryptanalysis of block ciphers. However, the performance of the automatic search is not always satisfactory, especially for searching long differential trails of block ciphers with large state sizes. Hence, we endeavor to accelerate the SAT-based automatic search model for differentials of SPEEDY. In this paper, we give a 3.5-round differential characteristic with the probability of $2^{-104.83}$ and a 4.5-round differential characteristic with the probability of $2^{-150.15}$. Furthermore, by balancing the key recovery and the differential distinguisher, we adjust the distinguisher to speed up filtering wrong pairs with some tricks. Finally we launch a valid 6-round attack for SPEEDY-7-192 with a complexity of $2^{158.06}$. We also propose a 5-round attack utilizing a 3.5-round differential distinguisher with the time complexity of $2^{108.95}$.

Keywords: SPEEDY · Differential cryptanalysis · Automatic search · SAT model

1 Introduction

SPEEDY [9], proposed by Leander *et al.* at TCHES'21, is a family of ultra low latency block ciphers which is designed to be fast in CMOS hardware. The ultra

Y. Deng and M. Yung (Eds.): Inscrypt 2022, LNCS 13837, pp. 272–291, 2023.
https://doi.org/10.1007/978-3-031-26553-2_14

low-latency 6-bit S-box with a two-level NAND gates tree was introduced to provide confusion, and the linear layer with the depth of 3 XOR was applied to provide strong diffusion with branch number 8.

Differential cryptanalysis [3] is one of the most fundamental techniques for cryptanalysis of block ciphers, which was proposed by Biham and Shamir in 1990 to break the Data Encryption Standard (DES). Differential cryptanalysis is essential to evaluate the security of block ciphers. And many generalizations are proposed like truncated differentials [7], impossible differential attack [1,6], the boomerang attack [19] and the rectangle attack [2] etc.

Searching for a good differential characteristic is one of the most important parts to carry out a differential attack. In [11], Matsui proposed a depth-first branch-and-bound searching algorithm to identify the optimal differentials with the maximum probability of block ciphers. The advantage of this algorithm is enhanced by taking in the customized optimization for the specific cipher. In recent years, tools for solving the basic mathematical method have been used to search distinguishers in cryptanalysis. The Boolean satisfiability problem (SAT) is one of the important basic problems on which the automatic search models are based, it is NP-complete.

The efficiency of the automatic search model is one of the important problems we have to face, although some works aimed at improving the efficiency of the automatic search model proposed, it is still a disturbing problem. The runtime of solving the automatic search model mainly depends on the solvers. It has been experimentally shown that minimizing the number of inequalities in a MILP model did not always minimize the runtime [14], as well there are a few works considering the acceleration of the automatic search based on SAT method. The automatic search for bit-oriented block ciphers is more difficult for both methods, because more variables are introduced for each state and the linear layer mixes the variables fastly. It is challenging that building an efficient automatic search model for SPEEDY family, on account of 192-bit suggested block size.

Our Contributions. In this paper, we deliberate on the security of SPEEDY-r -192 with reduced rounds using differential attack. We unveil some new distinguishers, their structural properties, and key recovery attacks on SPEEDY-r-192 which were not reported before. Table 1 gives a summary of attacks on SPEEDY till date.

Firstly, we proposed an accelerated automatic search model for SPEEDY-r-192 based on SAT method. Due to a large internal state of 192 bit and the fast diffusion property, it is hard to exhaust all the values of the bit-level state for long rounds. Thus it seems difficult to build an effective automatic search model for SPEEDY-r-192. In this paper, we revisit the constraints of the upper bound, which is called the Sequential Encoding Method [15], and reduce the number of auxiliary variables introduced in the clauses by utilizing the properties of the weight of the probability in differentials for SPEEDY-r-192. In this way, we build an effective automatic model for searching the differential trails of SPEEDY-r-192. To evaluate the probability of the differential distinguisher more precisely, we search for the clustering of differentials with the same input and output differences. We get the longest differential distinguishers for SPEEDY-r-192, and the runtime is practical and much lower than the previous method.

Secondly, We make a balance in the probability of the differential distinguisher and the non-active bits in the plaintext state that can be used to filter the wrong pairs. The balance strategy speeds up filtering the pairs that do not satisfy the differential distinguisher for SPEEDY. Since the differential distinguisher with maximum probability does not necessarily lead to the most effective key recovery attack, the truncated differentials in the extended rounds also impact the complexity of the differential cryptanalysis. This case has been discussed in some rectangle attacks [5,12,20]. Therefore, we adjust the input difference of the distinguisher and add some conditions to control the difference propagation in the extended rounds to make there are some bits with zero difference in the plaintext. The zero difference in the plaintext can filter the wrong pairs in advance in the data collection phase, which greatly reduces the time complexity in key recovery phase.

With these techniques, we launch a 6-round key-recovery attack for SPEEDY-7-192 within the claimed security, which is the longest attack on SPEEDY-r-192 as far as we know. We also proposed a 5-round attack with lower complexity. The results are shown in Table 1.

Table 1. Summary of cryptanalytic results on SPEEDY.

Distinguishers					
Method	Round	Data	Time	Memory	Ref.
Differential and linear	2	2^{39}	2^{39}	–	[9]
	3	2^{69}	2^{69}	–	[9]
Cube	2	2^{14}	2^{14}	–	[13]
Cube	3	2^{13}	2^{13}	–	[13]
Differential	4.5	$2^{150.15}$	$2^{150.15}$	–	Sect. 4.1
Differential	3.5	$2^{104.83}$	$2^{104.83}$	–	Sect. 5.1
Key recovery					
Integral	3	$2^{17.6}$	$2^{52.5}$	$2^{25.2}$	[13]
Differential	5	$2^{108.91}$	$2^{108.95}$	$2^{108.91}$	Sect. 4
Differential	6	$2^{158.04}$	$2^{158.06}$	$2^{158.04}$	Sect. 5

2 Preliminary

2.1 Description of SPEEDY

SPEEDY [9] is a family of ultra-low latency block ciphers designed by Leander *et al.* at TCHES 2021, the designers use SPEEDY-r-6ℓ to differentiate all the variants, where $6l$ denotes the block and key size, and r indicates the number of iterated rounds.

The internal state is viewed as an $\ell \times 6$ binary matrix, and we use $x_{[i,j]}$ to denote the bit located at row i, column j of the state x, where $0 \leq i < \ell$ and $0 \leq j < 6$.

The default block and key size for SPEEDY is 192, *i.e.* $\ell = 32$. And this is the only block size we considered in this paper, the designers claimed the security for this instance with iterated rounds 5, 6 and 7. The 5-round version SPEEDY-5-192 has a security level of 2^{128} time complexity with 2^{64} data complexity as restriction, SPEEDY-6-192 and SPEEDY-7-192 can achieve 128-bit and 192-bit security levels, respectively. We pay attention to the differential cryptanalysis of the default version SPEEDY-r-192.

We review the details of the round function for encryption of SPEEDY-r-192. The round function consists of the following five different operations: **SubSbox(SB)**, **ShiftColumns (SC)**, **MixColumns (MC)**, **AddRoundConstant** (A_{C_i}) and **AddRoundKey** (A_{k_i}). For encryption, the iterated round function except the last is defined as

$$\mathcal{R}_i = A_{C_i} \circ \mathbf{MC} \circ \mathbf{SC} \circ \mathbf{SB} \circ \mathbf{SC} \circ \mathbf{SB} \circ A_{k_i}, \text{ with } 0 \leq i \leq r-2.$$

The round function in the last round is

$$\mathcal{R}_{r-1} = A_{k_r} \circ \mathbf{SB} \circ \mathbf{SC} \circ \mathbf{SB} \circ A_{k_{r-1}}.$$

The last round omit the linear layer and constant addition, and append an extra key addition. Here, we introduce the round operations in the following.

SubSbox (SB): The 6-bit S-box S (seen Table 2) is applied to each row of the state, *i.e.* for $0 \leq i < 32$,

$$(y_{[i,0]}, y_{[i,1]}, y_{[i,2]}, y_{[i,3]}, y_{[i,4]}, y_{[i,5]}) = S(x_{[i,0]}, x_{[i,1]}, x_{[i,2]}, x_{[i,3]}, x_{[i,4]}, x_{[i,5]}).$$

Table 2. The S-box S *in SPEEDY*

s_0s_1	$s_2s_3s_4s_5$															
	.0	.1	.2	.3	.4	.5	.6	.7	.8	.9	.a	.b	.c	.d	.e	.f
0	08	00	09	03	38	10	29	13	0c	0d	04	07	30	01	20	23
1	1a	12	18	32	3e	16	2c	36	1c	1d	14	37	34	05	24	27
2	02	06	0b	0f	33	17	21	15	0a	1b	0e	1f	31	11	25	35
3	22	26	2a	2e	3a	1e	28	3c	2b	3b	2f	3f	39	19	2d	3d

ShiftColumns (SC): The j-th column of the state is rotated upside by j bits.

$$y_{[i,j]} = x_{[i+j,j]}, \ 0 \leq i < 32, \ 0 \leq j < 6.$$

MixColumns (MC): For SPEEDY-r-192, a cyclic binary matrix $M(32 \times 32)$ is multiplied to each column of the state. Use $\boldsymbol{x}_{[j]}$ to denote the input of the j-th column, and use $\boldsymbol{y}_{[j]}$ to denote the output of the column transform. The column transform $\boldsymbol{y}_{[j]} = M \cdot \boldsymbol{x}_{[j]}$ is

$$\begin{aligned}\boldsymbol{y}_{[j]} &= \boldsymbol{x}_{[j]} \oplus (\boldsymbol{x}_{[j]} \lll 1)\\ &\oplus (\boldsymbol{x}_{[j]} \lll 5) \oplus (\boldsymbol{x}_{[j]} \lll 9) \oplus (\boldsymbol{x}_{[j]} \lll 15) \oplus (\boldsymbol{x}_{[j]} \lll 21) \oplus (\boldsymbol{x}_{[j]} \lll 26),\end{aligned}$$

where $\boldsymbol{x}_{[j]} \lll t$ means the column $\boldsymbol{x}_{[j]}$ rotated upside by t bits, i.e., $x_{[i,j]} = x_{[i+t,j]}$, $\forall\, 0 \leq i < 32$.

AddRoundKey(A_{k_r}): The 192-bit round key k_r is XORed to the internal state, as:

$$y_{[i,j]} = x_{[i,j]} \oplus k_{r_{[i,j]}},\ 0 \leq i < 32,\ 0 \leq j < 6.$$

AddRoundConstant(A_{c_r}): The 192-bit constant c_r is XORed to the whole of the state.

$$y_{[i,j]} = x_{[i,j]} \oplus c_{r_{[i,j]}},\ 0 \leq i < 32,\ 0 \leq j < 6.$$

Since AddRoundConstant does not alter the validities of attacks in this paper, the constants $c_{r_{[i,j]}}$ are not introduced.

Key Schedule: The algorithm receives a 192-bit master key and initializes it as the subkey k_0. Then a bit permutation PB is used to compute the next round subkey, *i.e.*

$$k_{r+1} = PB(k_r).$$

For more details of SPEEDY, please refer to [9].

2.2 Observations on Differential Properties of SPEEDY

For the **SB** operation with the input difference α and the output difference β, and differential pair (α, β) satisfies the Eq. 1. We have the following observations according to the Differential Distribution Table.

$$S(x) \oplus S(x \oplus \alpha) = \beta. \tag{1}$$

Observation 1. *For given α = 100000 and β = *****0($\beta \neq 0$), the probability of the propagation $\Pr\{\alpha \xrightarrow{SB} \beta\} = 3/4 \approx 2^{-0.42}$, and the number of β is 15, where '*' means the unknown bit value. Each differential pair (α, β) satisfies the Eq. 1.*

Observation 2. *For given α = 001000 and β = 0*****($\beta \neq 0$), the probability $\Pr\{\alpha \xrightarrow{SB} \beta\} = 15/16 \approx 2^{-0.09}$, and the number of β is 17, where '*' means the unknown bit value. The differential pair (α, β) satisfies Eq. (1).*

Observation 3. *For given α = **0***($\alpha \neq 0$) and β = 010000, the probability $\Pr\{\alpha \xrightarrow{SB} \beta\} \approx 2^{-0.54}$, where '*' means the unknown bit value, and the differential pair (α, β) satisfies equation (1). Given β = 010000, when α = 0***** or α = *****0, the probability becomes 2^{-1} or $2^{-0.67}$.*

For each column of **MC** operation, we have the following observation:

Observation 4. *Let $\boldsymbol{y}$ be a column of the input of the inverse of* **MC** *and the corresponding output be $\boldsymbol{x}$, i.e. $\boldsymbol{y} = M \cdot \boldsymbol{x}$. We simply consider the output form $\boldsymbol{x}$, where $\boldsymbol{y}$ has the form $\boldsymbol{y}_t \neq 0$ $(t = i, j)$ and $\boldsymbol{y}_t = 0$ $(t \notin \{i, j\})$, $\boldsymbol{y}_t$ denotes the t-th bit of $\boldsymbol{y}$.*

- $j = i + 1$, *the Hamming weight $H(\boldsymbol{x})$ is 14, when $i = 0$, $\boldsymbol{x}$ = 0x4CD019F4;*
- $j = i + 2$, *the Hamming weight $H(\boldsymbol{x})$ is 14, when $i = 0$, $\boldsymbol{x}$ = 0x6AB8150E;*
- $j = i + 3$, *the Hamming weight $H(\boldsymbol{x})$ is 16, when $i = 0$, $\boldsymbol{x}$ = 0x798C1373;*
- $j = i + 4$, *the Hamming weight $H(\boldsymbol{x})$ is 12, when $i = 0$, $\boldsymbol{x}$ = 0xF016104D;*
- $j = i + 5$, *the Hamming weight $H(\boldsymbol{x})$ is 15, when $i = 0$, $\boldsymbol{x}$ = 0xB4DB11D2.*

2.3 Complexity Analysis of the Differential Attack

Let $\Delta_{in} \to \Delta_{out}$ be a r-round differential characteristic of an algorithm $E(x, k)$, which is a $\mathbb{F}_2^n \times \mathbb{F}_2^m \to \mathbb{F}_2^n$ mapping, the couple of $(\Delta_{in}, \Delta_{out})$ should satisfy

$$Pr\{E(x, k) \oplus E(x \oplus \Delta_{in}, k) = \Delta_{out}\} > 2^{-n}$$

for $x \in \mathbb{F}_2^n$ and any fixed $k \in \mathbb{F}_2^m$.

The probability is calculated as the sum of probabilities regarding all trails sharing the same input and output differences with the differential [8]. Denote the probability of the r-round differential distinguisher as p_0 and the number of plaintext (or ciphertext) pairs utilized in the attack as N_D. Then under the right key guess, the counter memorizing the number of pairs satisfying the differential distinguisher follows a binomial distribution of parameters (N_D, p_0). On the other side, suppose that the probability of a pair fulfilling the differential under a wrong key guess is p_1. Consequently, the counter follows a binomial distribution of parameters (N_D, p_1). We set a threshold τ_D for the attack, if the counter of the right pairs is no less than τ_D, the key guess will be accepted.

There are two types of errors which are always need to face in the hypothesis test, which are denoted by α, the non-detection error probability, and β, the false alarm error probability. α and β can be got from the formulas in [4].

Then the total time complexity of the differential cryptanalysis T can be departed into three parts, denoted by $T = T_1 + T_2 + T_3$. T_1 is the number of encryptions to prepare the necessary plaintext and ciphertext pairs which lead to the right pairs passing the distinguisher. We can estimate T_1 by N times of encryption, where N is the number of plaintexts (ciphertexts) we chose, which corresponds to the data complexity.

Time complexity T_2 denotes the average complexity needed to decide whether a pair satisfy the distinguisher under our key guess. For the N_D pairs we utilized in the attack, use T_E to denote the time for one encryption, if we need time T_F to determine whether a pair satisfy the distinguisher or not on average. Then the time complexity can be estimated by

$$T_2 = \frac{T_F}{T_E} \cdot N_D.$$

After the key recovery phase, there will be $2^m \cdot \beta$ keys remaining in the theory. Therefore, we expected

$$T_3 = 2^m \cdot \beta \cdot (1 - 2^{-n})$$

encryptions to recover the entire master key. And the success probability of the attack is equal to $1 - \alpha$.

2.4 Automatic Searching Model Based on SAT Problem

The Boolean Satisfiability (SAT) problem studies the satisfiability of a given Boolean formula, it is said satisfiable if there exists an assignment of Boolean values to variables so that the formula is evaluated to be True.

Conjunctive Normal Form (CNF) is a generic representation of SAT problem. The formula is expressed as conjunction ($\wedge$) of one or more clauses, where a clause is a disjunction ($\vee$) of many Boolean variables (possibly negated). The CNF encodings for basic operations in cryptographic primitives are introduced. In this section, we use $\alpha_i (0 \leq i < n)$ to denote the i-th element of the n-bit vector α, α_0 stands for the most significant bit.

- **Building constraints for non-probabilistic models.** For the linear operations in cryptographic primitives, we can also build the clauses of the SAT model by the same method of building clauses for S-boxes without introducing auxiliary variables, in this section, we just list the clauses for some basic operations.
  Clauses for XOR operation. For a n-bit XOR operation with two input differences α and β, and the output difference is denoted by γ. The differential $\alpha \oplus \beta = \gamma$ holds if and only if the values of α, β and γ validate all the assertions in the following.

$$\left.\begin{array}{l} \overline{\alpha_i} \vee \overline{\beta_i} \vee \overline{\gamma_i} = 1 \\ \overline{\alpha_i} \vee \beta_i \vee \gamma_i = 1 \\ \alpha_i \vee \overline{\beta_i} \vee \overline{\gamma_i} = 1 \\ \alpha_i \vee \beta_i \vee \overline{\gamma_i} = 1 \end{array}\right\} 0 \leq i \leq n-1$$

  Clauses for COPY operation. For the n-bit COPY operation with input difference α and output difference β. The differential $\beta = \alpha$ holds if and only if the values of α and β validate all the assertions in the following.

$$\left.\begin{array}{l} \alpha_i \vee \overline{\beta_i} = 1 \\ \overline{\alpha_i} \vee \beta_i = 1 \end{array}\right\} 0 \leq i \leq n-1$$

  For differentials, the clauses of COPY operation $\alpha = \beta$ can be also applied to shifting operations.
- **Building constraints for S-box.** The propagations of differences and linear masks for S-box operations are probabilistic. Use an s-bit S-box for example, according to the method in [17], let $(I_0, I_1, \ldots, I_{s-1})$ denote

the variables which indicate the input difference, and $(O_0, O_1, \dots, O_{s-1})$ denote the output difference, introduce several variables $\rho_0, \rho_1, \dots, \rho_{h-1}$ to denote the weight of the opposite number of the binary logarithm of the probability. Because the SAT problem is oriented to binary variables, the number of auxiliary variables depends on the weight of the probability. With these variables, we can define a $(2s+h)$-bit Boolean function $f(\boldsymbol{z})$, where $\boldsymbol{z} = (I_0, I_1, \dots, I_{s-1}, O_0, \dots, O_{s-1}, \rho_0, \dots, \rho_{h-1})$, if $(I_0, \dots, I_{s-1}) \rightarrow (O_0, \dots, O_{s-1})$ is a possible propagation with the probability weight $w_0 \cdot \rho_0 + w_1 \cdot \rho_1 + \cdots + w_{h-1} \cdot \rho_{h-1}$, then $f(\boldsymbol{z}) = 1$, else $f(\boldsymbol{z}) = 0$. Then we can get a set of Boolean equations by reformulating the $f(\boldsymbol{z})$ as the product-of-sum representation

$$f(\boldsymbol{z}) = \bigwedge_{\boldsymbol{c} \in \mathbb{F}_2^{2s+h}} \Big(f(\boldsymbol{c}) \vee \bigvee_{i=0}^{2s+h-1} (\boldsymbol{z}_i \oplus \boldsymbol{c}_i) \Big),$$

where $\boldsymbol{c} = (\boldsymbol{c}_0, \boldsymbol{c}_1, \dots, \boldsymbol{c}_{2s+h-1})$, after getting the Boolean equations, we can simplify the expression utilizing some openly available programs like Logical Friday[1], and yield a smaller set of clauses.

- **Sequential encoding method for constraining the upper bound.** When we aim at r-round differential trails, denote the auxiliary variables stand for the probability for the j-th S-box in the i-th round as $\rho_l^{(i,j)}$, where $0 \le i \le r-1$, $0 \le j \le n-1$ and $0 \le l \le h-1$. The weight equals to the opposite number of the binary logarithm of the probability of the differential trail should be $\sum_{i=0}^{r-1} \sum_{j=0}^{n-1} \sum_{l=0}^{h-1} w_l \cdot \rho_l^{(i,j)}$. In theory, if we want to constrain the solution range with the prospective value ω as the weight of the trail, our model should add the additional constraint

$$\sum_{i=0}^{r-1} \sum_{j=0}^{n-1} \sum_{l=0}^{h-1} w_l \cdot \rho_l^{(i,j)} \le \omega.$$

However, all the variables in the SAT are binary, it is unfeasible to handle the decimal and the integer part at the same time. So we convert the bound into several parts with different decimal weights and handle the part with different weights separately. For example, let the $\rho_{h-1}^{(i,j)}$ denote the part with decimal weight for each S-box, and the other variables denote the part with integer weight. Then the constraints for the upper bound can be rewritten as $\sum_{i=0}^{r-1} \sum_{j=0}^{n-1} \sum_{l=0}^{h-2} \rho_l^{(i,j)} + w_{h-1} \cdot \sum_{i=0}^{r-1} \sum_{j=0}^{n-1} \rho_{h-1}^{(i,j)}$. The objective function of the SAT problem consists of the following two inequalities.

$$\sum_{i=0}^{r-1} \sum_{j=0}^{n-1} \sum_{l=0}^{h-2} \rho_l^{(i,j)} \le \omega_I, \ \sum_{i=0}^{r-1} \sum_{j=0}^{n-1} \rho_{h-1}^{(i,j)} \le \omega_D \tag{2}$$

where ω_I and ω_D are two non-negative integers, and $\omega = \omega_I + w_{h-1} \cdot \omega_D$.

[1] https://web.archive.org/web/20131022021257/http://www.sontrak.com/.

These two restrictions in 2 meet the form $\sum_{i=0}^{n-1} u_i \leq k$, where k is a non-negative integer. If $k = 0$, this constraint is equivalent to the following n Boolean expressions:

$$\bar{u_i} = 1, 0 \leq i \leq n-1.$$

Else if $k > 0$, according to the method in [10], which is called **sequential encoding method**. we introduce $(n-1) \cdot k$ auxiliary Boolean variables $v_{i,j}(0 \leq i \leq n-2, 0 \leq j \leq k-1)$, and use the following clauses to build the constraints for $\sum_{i=0}^{n-1} u_i \leq k$:

$$\begin{array}{l}
\overline{u_0} \vee v_{0,0} = 1 \\
\overline{v_{0,j}} = 1, 1 \leq j \leq k-1 \\
\left.\begin{array}{l}
\overline{u_i} \vee v_{i,0} = 1 \\
\overline{v_{i,0}} \vee v_{i,0} = 1 \\
\left.\begin{array}{l}
\overline{u_i} \vee \overline{v_{i-1,j-1}} \vee v_{i,j} = 1 \\
\overline{v_{i-1,j}} \vee v_{i,j} = 1
\end{array}\right\} 1 \leq j \leq k-1 \\
\overline{u_i} \vee \overline{v_{i-1,k-1}} = 1
\end{array}\right\} 1 \leq i \leq n-2 \\
\overline{u_{n-1}} \vee \overline{v_{n-2,k-1}} = 1
\end{array}$$

Using the model shown above, we build the constraints of the SAT problem for searching differential characteristics, and we utilize CryptoMinisat5 [16] as the solver with parameters set as shown in Sect. 3.

3 Searching for Good Differential Trails for SPEEDY

It requires searching a space of exponential size in the number of Boolean variables to solve the SAT problem. We believe that the size of the problem needed to be solved is one of the most important factors affecting the runtime of the SAT based automatic search model. In this section, we try to build the automatic search model for the differential trails of `SPEEDY-r-192` with as few variables as possible based on the SAT model and discuss how to solve the model with as few as possible running times.

3.1 Improved Automatic Searching Model for SPEEDY

For **SubSbox** operation of `SPEEDY-r-192`, the entries in the DDT of S-box have six possible evaluations, which are 0, 2, 4, 6, 8, and 16, with corresponding differential probabilities in the set $\{0, 2^{-5}, 2^{-4}, 2^{-3.415}, 2^{-3}, 1\}$. When we use the automatic search model proposed in [17,18], six auxiliary Boolean variables are required for each S-box, and $O((n-1) \cdot k)$ auxiliary Boolean variables are also needed according to the sequential encoding method in Sect. 2.4 to build the constraints for the upper bound of the probability for the distinguishers, where n is the number of variables which denote the probability for each S-box and k is the upper bound for the probability of the whole distinguisher. In order to descend the scale of the auxiliary variables, we introduce four Boolean variables

$\rho_0, \rho_1, \rho_2, \rho_3$, let p denote the probability of the possible differential propagation, then we build the constraints for the variables as follows:

$$\rho_0||\rho_1||\rho_2||\rho_3 = \begin{cases} 1110, & if\ p = 2^{-5} \\ 0110, & if\ p = 2^{-4} \\ 0011, & if\ p = 2^{-3.415} \\ 0010, & if\ p = 2^{-3} \\ 0000, & if\ p = 1 \end{cases}$$

In order to build the constraints for the upper bound of the probability of the whole distinguisher with as few auxiliary variables as possible, we depart the objective function of the SAT problem into three parts, which are:

$$\sum_{i=0}^{r-1}\sum_{j=0}^{31}\sum_{l=0}^{2}\rho_l^{(i,j)} \leq \omega_I,\ \sum_{i=0}^{r-1}\sum_{j=0}^{31}\rho_2^{(i,j)} \leq \omega_S \text{ and } \sum_{i=0}^{r-1}\sum_{j=0}^{31}\rho_3^{(i,j)} \leq \omega_D.$$

where ω_I, ω_S and ω_D are non-negative integers, and $0 \leq i \leq r-1, 0 \leq j \leq 31$. The prospective value for the weight of the trail ω can be represented by $\omega = \sum_{i=0}^{r-1}\sum_{j=0}^{31}\sum_{k=0}^{2}\rho_l^{(i,j)} + 2 \cdot \sum_{i=0}^{r-1}\sum_{j=0}^{31}\rho_2^{(i,j)} + 0.415 \cdot \sum_{i=0}^{r-1}\sum_{j=0}^{31}\rho_3^{(i,j)}$. It is obvious that the number of S-boxes in the trail can be represented as $\sum_{i=0}^{r-1}\sum_{j=0}^{31}\rho_2^{(i,j)}$, so we can follow the steps in Sect. 3.2 to solve the model.

The constraints for **ShiftRows**, **MixColumns** and **AddRoundKey** have nothing to do with the probability of the trail, so we do not need to make addtional constraints on these operations.

3.2 Process of Solving the Model

$p_1 = \sum_{i=0}^{r-1}\sum_{j=0}^{31}\sum_{k=0}^{2}\rho_k^{(i,j)}$, $p_2 = \sum_{i=0}^{r-1}\sum_{j=0}^{31}\rho_2^{(i,j)}$ and $p_3 = \sum_{i=0}^{r-1}\sum_{j=0}^{31}\rho_3^{(i,j)}$ denote the summation of partial weights respectively. Suppose the optimal trail we found has the prospective value for the weight of the probability $\omega = a + 2 \cdot b + 0.415 \cdot c$, *i.e.* $p_1 = a$, $p_2 = b$ and $p_3 = c$, if the number of active S-boxes is not less than this trail, the trails with higher probability must satisfy the conditions of the parameters as shown below, the trivial cases $p_1 \leq a$ and $p_3 \leq c$ are ruled out.

Table 3. Possible value combinations of p_1, p_2 and p_3

	p_1	p_2	p_3
1	$a+n$	b	$c - \lceil \frac{n}{0.415} \rceil$
2	$a-n$	b	$c + \lfloor \frac{n}{0.415} \rfloor$
3	$\leq a-k+n$	$b+1$	$\leq c - \lceil \frac{n-k+2}{0.415} \rceil$
4	$\leq a-k-n$	$b+1$	$\leq c + \lfloor \frac{n+k-2}{0.415} \rfloor$

The case where the number of active S-boxes is greater than $b+1$ can be dealt with inductively. And we notice that although there are many possible scenarios theoretically, we need not test all of them, because the parameter p_1 usually increases with the number of active S-boxes. So we proposed a heuristic method to search for the differential trail with optimal probability. Firstly we search for the minimized number of active S-boxes, *i.e.* we set the objective function to minimize the parameter p_2, suppose the obtained minimum is b. Secondly, we run the solver again with the objective function to minimize the parameter p_1 with the constraint $p_2 = b$ and suppose the minimize objective function is a, then with the constraints $p_1 = a$ and $p_2 = b$, we set the objective function to minimize the parameter p_3, and denote the value is c. Finally, we test the possible value combinations of p_1, p_2 and p_3 in Table 3 to ensure the probability of the trail we found is optimal, if it is not, repeat the test.

The minimum of the parameter p_1, p_2 and p_3 have already constrained the candidate of the test, so we just need to repeat the test few times to ensure the trail is optimal. The size of the auxiliary variables we introduced is $O(r \cdot (3\omega_I + \omega_S + \omega_D))$, which is several times less than the size of the problem that we build constraints with 6 auxiliary variables for each S-box. The improvement of the runtime is significant, the average time of solving our model to search for the 4.5-round distinguisher once is about 3 h, as well the time for solving the model normally once to search for the 4.5-round distinguisher is over 24 h.

4 Differential Cryptanalysis on 6-Round SPEEDY

In this section, we give differential cryptanalysis of SPEEDY-7-192 to achieve the rounds as long as possible. According to the round function of SPEEDY, we first select the differential distinguisher with $N + 0.5$ rounds which are suitable for the key-recovering phase with the optimal probability and mount a $1 + N + 1$ key-recovery attack under chosen-ciphertext ability. In this section, we show that we can achieve a 6-round attack for SPEEDY-7-192 with the time complexity of $2^{158.06}$ and data complexity of $2^{158.04}$.

4.1 The 4.5-Round Differential Distinguisher

Because of the rapid propagation of the truncated differential trails of SPEEDY, it will cost lots of time complexity on filtering out the wrong pairs which do not conform with the differential trail in the key recovery phase. However, there is just one **ShiftColumns (SC)** operation in the last round of round-reduced SPEEDY-7-192, the truncated propagation of the second **SubBox (SB)** operation can be easily handled because the 6-bit non-zero difference of each S-box only leads to 6 active bits in the state of ciphertexts. So we search for an optimal 4.5-round differential trail as the distinguisher and launch a 6-round key recovery attack on SPEEDY-7-192 under chosen-ciphertext ability.

According to the method in Sect. 3.2, firstly we find out that the minimum number of active S-boxes of 4.5-round differential trails for SPEEDY is 43, and then we search for the optimal differential distinguishers with 43 active S-boxes and get the maximum probability of 4.5-round differential path is $2^{-150.15}$. Finally we resolve the automatic model several times with the constraints for adjusted parameters to ensure that there are no trails with 44 or 45 active S-boxes have probability higher than $2^{-150.15}$. The 4.5-round differential path we got from the SAT solver is shown in Fig. 1.

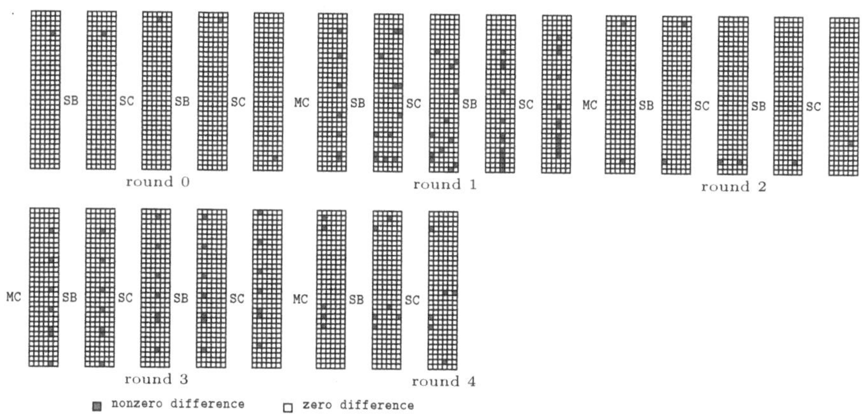

Fig. 1. The 4.5-round differential distinguisher for SPEEDY-r-192

4.2 Speed Up Filtering Wrong Pairs by Optimizing the Distinguisher

We launch a 6-round key recovery attack based on the 4.5-round differential path by extending 1 round at the beginning and 0.5 round at the end.

The chosen-ciphertext attack with data structure is applied to reduce the time complexity. We choose 2^s structures of size 2^t (t denotes the number of active bits in the differences of ciphertext). There are about 2^{2t-1} pairs for each structure. Let p be the probability of the differential distinguisher we found. We choose enough ciphertexts such that there are about $2^{s+2t-1-t} \times p \geq 1$ pairs satisfying the output of the differential distinguisher. Hence, the data complexity is 2^{s+t}. We need to guess the subkeys for the 2^{s+2t-1} pairs, which plays a dominant role in the time complexity of the key recovery phase. Therefore, we adjust the input difference of the distinguisher and add some conditions to control the difference propagation in the extend round to make some bits in the plaintext with zero difference. The zero difference in the plaintext can remove some pairs not satisfying the truncated differential in the data collection phase, which reduces the time complexity of the key recovery phase.

Here, we describe the methods to make the differences of some bits of plaintext pairs become zero. The differential distinguisher with the maximum probability does not necessarily lead to the most effective key recovery attack, the truncated differentials in the extended rounds also impact the complexity of the differential cryptanalysis. For partial decryption, the operation $\mathbf{MC}^{-1}$ can spread one active S-box at the beginning of the distinguisher to 19 active S-boxes, which can diffuse to the whole plaintext state (all the 32 S-boxes are active) after partial decryption through $\mathbf{SC}^{-1} \circ \mathbf{SB}^{-1}$. But according to the Observation 4, two active S-boxes at the beginning of the distinguisher can lead to less active S-boxes after propagation through $\mathbf{MC}^{-1}$, which make there are some bits with zero-difference can be used to filter wrong pairs in the data collection phase. Hence we proposed the trade-off strategy to balance the time complexity.

As shown in Fig. 3, we adjust the differential propagation in round 1, such that the two active S-boxes at the beginning of the differential distinguisher can lead to 12 active S-boxes after propagation through $\mathbf{MC}^{-1}$. The probability of the altered differential characteristic is $2^{-155.735}$. And the probability of the differential distinguisher is $2^{-155.2}$, which is recalculated by multi differential trials. The altered distinguisher can generate 2 rows with zero difference in the state of plaintext, which are row 8 and row 9.

Meanwhile, considering the differences in rows 19 to 26 of the plaintexts, although these rows may be active after propagating through $\mathbf{SC}^{-1} \circ \mathbf{SB}^{-1}$, the actual number of active S-boxes of the first $\mathbf{SB}$ operation the rows 19 to 26 of round 0 depends on the output difference of the rows 18 and 24 of the second $\mathbf{SB}$ layer in round 0. So we exhaust all the possible differences of these active S-boxes propagating backward through the $\mathbf{SB}^{-1} \circ \mathbf{SC}^{-1} \circ \mathbf{SB}^{-1}$ operation, and find that the probability of the situations that the differences in rows 21 to 23 of the plaintext state are all zero is $2^{-1.415}$, which can be viewed as a part of the truncated differential.

Up to now, we get the altered distinguisher with zero difference in rows 8, 9, 21, 22 and 23 in plaintexts and zero difference in position 3 of the 6-th column in ciphertexts. The 4.5-round differential can generate plaintexts by partial decryption with zero differences in rows 9 to 10 and 21 to 23 of the plaintext state with the probability $2^{-155.2-1.415-0.42} = 2^{-157.04}$. And this distinguisher leads to 30-bit filter in the data collection phase (Fig. 2).

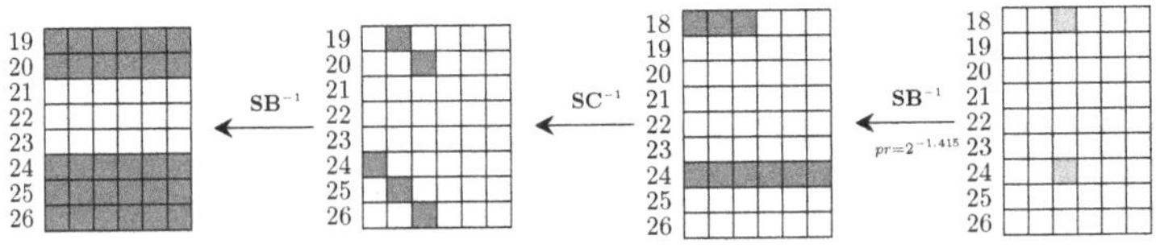

Fig. 2. Improved pre-filtering phase for the head of the distinguisher.

According to the truncated differential structure, we choose 2^s structures, each including 2^{29} ciphertexts by traversing the active bits with fixed random values for non-active bits and query the corresponding plaintexts. Let the bits with the zero-difference of the plaintext as the index to obtain the pairs. There are about $2^{s+29\times 2-1-30} = 2^{s+27}$ pairs remaining.

4.3 Key Recovery of 6-Round SPEEDY-192

Some precomputation tables are used to reduce the time complexity in the key recovery phase. Use the notations with the meaning in equation (1), we build a hash table H indexed by (α, β) to store the values $(x, SB(x))$. For given $\alpha = 4, 5, \texttt{0x20}$, there are about 21, 27 and 23 values of β, respectively. For each active row of the ciphertext pairs, we compute the output difference β of each pair, and removing the pairing which can not generate the given input difference α. There are about $2^{s+27} \times 2^{22.1-29} = 2^{s+20.1}$ pairs remaining. Then look up the table H to get the value $S(x)$ by the index, and deduce the key bits involved in this row. So in the last key addition, we deduce the key bits involved in rows 3, 16, 21, 23 and 30 of the state of ciphertexts by looking up tables. And we get $2^{s+20.1}$ pairs each corresponding to $2^{7.48}$ 30-bit keys.

As the key schedule used in SPEEDY family is linear, use the key bit in the set 0 to 191 of the zero-th round key k_0 to denote the obtained 30-bit key in the last round, seen in Table 4.

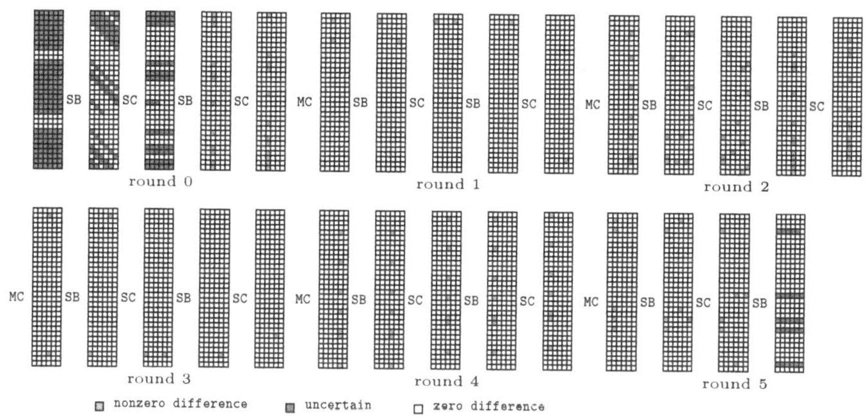

Fig. 3. 6-round attack for SPEEDY-7-192.

Then we deduce the key bits involved in row 18 after $\mathbf{SC} \circ \mathbf{SB}$ operation of round 0. We first deduce the key bits involved in row 20 in the plaintext state, because the key bit of position 120 is known, there are about $2^{s+20.1}$ pairs each corresponding to $2^{7.48}$ 35-bit keys after looking up the hash table H to deduce the 5 key bits left. Then compute the key bits involved in row 19 by looking up the hash table, we get $2^{s+20.1}$ pairs, which correspond to $2^{7.48}$ 40-bit keys. Deduce the key bits involved in the 18-th row by table lookups to obtain $2^{s+20.1}$ pairs, which are corresponding to $2^{8.48}$ 45-bit keys. Then we guess the unknown 3 bits values in row 18 of the state after the first **SC** and check the known output difference. Up to now we obtain $2^{s+20.1}$ pairs, which are corresponding to $2^{5.48}$ 46-bit key.

Table 4. The deduced key bits involved in the last key addition

Row	Key guess					
3	138	91	44	189	142	95
16	120	73	26	171	124	77
21	54	7	152	105	58	11
23	66	19	164	117	70	23
30	12	157	110	63	16	161

For the other rows, we just need to calculate the key bits that are not involved in the positions that we have obtained, the time complexity is much lower than computing the key bits involved in the first three rows as shown above. For example, we only need to guess the key bits involved in rows 13 to 17 when filtering with row 13 after the second **SB** layer. The time complexity of each looking up hash table is approximate to the looking up S-box. The time complexity is about $(2^{s+27} + 2^{s+20.1} \times (8 + 2^6)) \times 1/32 \times 1/12 \approx 2^{s+19}$.

Each guess determines a 168-bit key, and we exhaust the remaining key bits. By the complexity cryptanalysis in Sect. 2.3, we set $s = 129.04$. Under the right key guess, $2^{s+2\times29-1-29} \times 2^{-157.04} = 1$ pair is expected in content with the 4.5-round differential. About $2^{s+27-29-162} = 2^{-35.38}$ pairs will validate the input and output differences of the 4.5-round distinguisher under a wrong 168-bit key guess. According to the formulas, we have $\alpha < 0.2$ and $\beta < 2^{-40}$, hence the success probability is $P_S = 1 - \alpha > 80\%$ and the total time complexity of the 6-round attack is given by

$$2^{129.04+29} + 2^{129.04+19} + 2^{192} \cdot 2^{-40} \cdot (1 - 2^{-192}) = 2^{158.06}.$$

The data complexity of the 6-round attack is $2^{s+29} = 2^{158.04}$.

5 Differential Cryptanalysis of 5-Round SPEEDY

5.1 Speed up Filtering Wrong Pairs with a 3.5-Round Differential Distinguisher

In this section, we give an improved 3.5-round differential for SPEEDY-r-192 and mount a 5-round differential attack.

The searching method of a 3.5-round differential is the same as that used for searching the 4.5-round differential distinguisher of SPEEDY-r-192. Firstly we search for the differential characteristic with the minimum number of active S-boxes. Then we alter the constraints for other parameters and find the optimal differential trails with the maximum probability. We find out that the minimum number of active S-boxes of the 3.5-round is 31, and the optimal 3.5-round differential trail with the probability of $2^{-104.83}$ got from the solver is shown in Fig. 4.

The differential 000010 $\xrightarrow{SB}$ 000100 and 000010 $\xrightarrow{SB}$ 001000 for S-boxes of SPEEDY both has probability 2^{-3}. So we reduce the number of active S-boxes in the last **AK** operation from 8 to 5 without changing the probability. And following the idea in Sect 4.2, we just alter the differential propagation in the first round to get a distinguisher with two non-active S-boxes in rows 9 and 10 of the plaintexts. The detail of the altered differential distinguisher is shown in Fig. 5, and the probability of the trail is $2^{-106.66}$. After searching for all the differential characteristics with the same input and output difference as well as no more than 35 active S-boxes, the probability of the differential trail is adjusted to $2^{-105.7}$.

In order to increase the number of zero-difference bits in the plaintexts which are used to remove more wrong pairs in the data collection, we made a few adjustments to the above distinguisher. Because the active bits in rows 8, 11 and 27 after the first **SB** layer originate from three different S-boxes in the second **SB** layer. According to Observation 3, the differential probability Pr{**0*** $\xrightarrow{SB}$ 010000} $= 2^{-0.54}$, Pr{0***** $\xrightarrow{SB}$ 010000} $= 2^{-1}$, and Pr{*****0 $\rightarrow$ 010000} $= 2^{-0.67}$. And these three S-boxes are disjoint in the truncated differential. Such that the probability of the truncated differential that the difference in rows 8, 11 and 27 of plaintext state are all zero is $2^{-0.54-1-0.67} = 2^{-2.21}$.

The 3.5-round differential can generate plaintexts by partial decryption with zero differences in rows 8 to 11 and 27 of the plaintexts, having the probability $2^{-105.7-2.21} = 2^{-107.91}$.

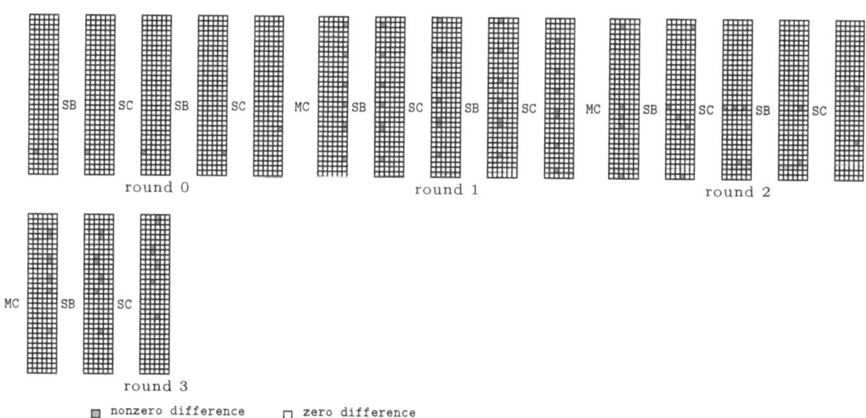

Fig. 4. The 3.5-round differential distinguisher for SPEEDY-r-192.

5.2 Key Recovery of 5-Round SPEEDY-r-192

We launch a 5-round differential attack by extending 1 round at the beginning of the 3.5-round differential and appending 0.5 round. According to Observation 2, we choose the ciphertexts with output differences in the form `0*****` instead of `******` at rows 13 and 21, which can generate the input difference 001000 effectively. There are 28 active bits seen in Fig. 5.

Use the same method in Sect. 4.3, we build a hash table indexed by input and output differences (α, β) to store the values $(x, SB(x))$ for S-box. For given $\alpha = 8, 12$, there are about 17, 27 values of β, respectively.

We choose 2^s structures, each including 2^{28} ciphertexts by traversing the active bits with fixed random values for non-active bits and query the corresponding plaintexts. Let the bits with the zero-difference of the plaintext as the index obtain the pairs. There are about $2^{s+28\times2-1-30} = 2^{s+25}$ pairs remaining. For each active row of the ciphertext pairs, we compute the output difference β of each pair, and remove the pairing which can not generate the given input difference α. There are about $2^{s+25} \times 2^{22.44-28} = 2^{s+19.44}$ pairs remaining. Then look up the table H to get the value $S(x)$ by the index, and deduce the key bits involved in these rows. Hence, we deduce the key bits of k_6 involved in rows 1, 6, 10, 13 and 21. There are about $2^{s+19.44}$ pairs each corresponding to $2^{5.56}$ 30-bit keys.

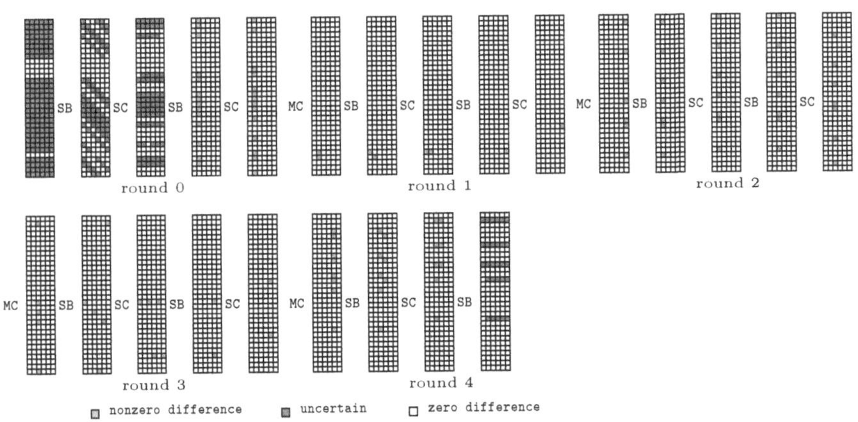

Fig. 5. 5-round attack for `SPEEDY-r-192`.

For the first key addition, we first deduce the key bits involved in row 25 of the state after the **SC** ∘ **SB** in round 0. According to the linear key schedule of `SPEEDY-r-192`, the key bits in positions 155, 163, 169, 173, 183, 185 and 177 have been guessed. First, we deduce the key bits involved in row 28 of the plaintext state, because the key bits in positions 169 and 173 are known, there are about $2^{s+19.44}$ pairs each corresponding to $2^{5.56}$ 34-bit keys after looking up the hash table to deduce the 4 key bits left. Then compute the key bits involved in row 30 by looking up the hash table, because the key bits in positions 183 and 183 are known, we get $2^{s+19.44}$ pairs each corresponding to $2^{6.56}$ 38-bit keys. Deduce the key bits involved in row 25 and get $2^{s+19.44}$ pairs with $2^{7.56}$ 43-bit keys remaining with the known key bit 155, and deduce the key bits involved in row 29 and get $2^{19.44}$ pairs with $2^{9.56}$ 48-bit keys with the known key bits 177. Finally, we guess the key bits involved in row 26, get $2^{19.44}$ pairs with $2^{11.56}$ 54-bit keys remaining, and guess the unknown key bits in row 25 of the state after the first **SC**, check the output difference to get a 6-bit filter. Up to now, we obtain $2^{s+19.44}$ pairs each corresponding to $2^{6.56}$ 55-bit keys.

For the other rows, we just need to compute the unknown key bits involved in the row, the complexity is much lower than the process we stated above. The time complexity of guessing the key bits involved in the first key addition is about $(2^{s+25} + 2^{19.44} \times (11 + 2^6)) \times 1/32 \times 1/10 \approx 2^{s+18}$.

Each guess determines a 166-bit key, and we exhaust the remaining key bits. In order to get one right pair under the right key guess, we expect $2^{s+2\times 28-1-28} \times 2^{-107.91} \geq 1$, and set $s = 80.91$. For the wrong key guess, about $2^{108.91-28-162} = 2^{-81.09}$ pairs will validate the input and output differences of the 3.5-round distinguisher. According to the formulas in [4], $\alpha < 0.15$ and $\beta < 2^{-100}$, hence the success probability of the attack is $P_S > 85\%$ and the total time complexity of the 5-round attack is given by

$$2^{80.91+28} + 2^{80.91+18} + 2^{192} \cdot 2^{-100} \cdot (1 - 2^{-192}) \approx 2^{108.95}.$$

The data used in the attack is about $2^{80.91+28} = 2^{108.91}$.

6 Conclusion

In this paper, an accelerated automatic search model for SPEEDY-r-192 based on SAT method is proposed, the automatic search model is practical to give the optimal probability of the differential trail for SPEEDY. A 4.5-round differential characteristic with the probability of $2^{-150.15}$ and a 3.5-round differential characteristic with the probability of $2^{-104.83}$ are found by the solver. Furthermore, we propose a 5-round and a 6-round key-recovery attack for SPEEDY-r-192 utilizing the modified differential distinguisher. These are the attacks that covered the longest rounds for SPEEDY-r-192 in our knowledge. Our 6-round attack, with $2^{158.06}$ time complexity and $2^{158.04}$ data complexity, can be viewed as a valid attack under the security claim for the round-reduced version of SPEEDY-7-192, which covers 6/7 rounds of the block cipher. And our 5-round attack with $2^{108.91}$ data complexity and $2^{108.95}$ time complexity can be viewed as a valid attack for the round-reduced version of SPEEDY-6-192.

Acknowledgements. We would like to thank the anonymous reviewers for their valuable comments to improve the quality of this paper. This paper is supported by the National Key Research and Development Program of China (Grant Nos. 2018YFA0704701), the National Natural Science Foundation of China (Grant Nos. 62072270), Shandong Province Key Research and Development Project (Grant Nos. 2020ZLYS09 and 2019JZZY010133).

References

1. Biham, E., Biryukov, A., Shamir, A.: Cryptanalysis of skipjack reduced to 31 rounds using impossible differentials. In: Stern, J. (ed.) EUROCRYPT 1999. LNCS, vol. 1592, pp. 12–23. Springer, Heidelberg (1999). https://doi.org/10.1007/3-540-48910-X_2
2. Biham, E., Dunkelman, O., Keller, N.: The rectangle attack—rectangling the serpent. In: Pfitzmann, B. (ed.) EUROCRYPT 2001. LNCS, vol. 2045, pp. 340–357. Springer, Heidelberg (2001). https://doi.org/10.1007/3-540-44987-6_21
3. Biham, E., Shamir, A.: Differential cryptanalysis of DES-like cryptosystems. In: Menezes, A.J., Vanstone, S.A. (eds.) CRYPTO 1990. LNCS, vol. 537, pp. 2–21. Springer, Heidelberg (1991). https://doi.org/10.1007/3-540-38424-3_1
4. Blondeau, C., Gérard, B., Tillich, J.: Accurate estimates of the data complexity and success probability for various cryptanalyses. Des. Codes Cryptogr. **59**(1–3), 3–34 (2011). https://doi.org/10.1007/s10623-010-9452-2
5. Dong, X., Qin, L., Sun, S., Wang, X.: Key guessing strategies for linear key-schedule algorithms in rectangle attacks. In: Dunkelman, O., Dziembowski, S. (eds.) EUROCRYPT 2022, Part III. LNCS, vol. 13277, pp. 3–33. Springer, Cham (2022). https://doi.org/10.1007/978-3-031-07082-2_1
6. Knudsen, L.: Deal - a 128-bit block cipher. In: NIST AES Proposal (1998)
7. Knudsen, L.R.: Truncated and higher order differentials. In: Preneel, B. (ed.) FSE 1994. LNCS, vol. 1008, pp. 196–211. Springer, Heidelberg (1995). https://doi.org/10.1007/3-540-60590-8_16
8. Lai, X., Massey, J.L., Murphy, S.: Markov ciphers and differential cryptanalysis. In: Davies, D.W. (ed.) EUROCRYPT 1991. LNCS, vol. 547, pp. 17–38. Springer, Heidelberg (1991). https://doi.org/10.1007/3-540-46416-6_2
9. Leander, G., Moos, T., Moradi, A., Rasoolzadeh, S.: The SPEEDY family of block ciphers engineering an ultra low-latency cipher from gate level for secure processor architectures. IACR Trans. Cryptogr. Hardw. Embed. Syst. **2021**(4), 510–545 (2021). https://doi.org/10.46586/tches.v2021.i4.510-545
10. Liu, Y., Wang, Q., Rijmen, V.: Automatic search of linear trails in ARX with applications to SPECK and chaskey. In: Manulis, M., Sadeghi, A.-R., Schneider, S. (eds.) ACNS 2016. LNCS, vol. 9696, pp. 485–499. Springer, Cham (2016). https://doi.org/10.1007/978-3-319-39555-5_26
11. Matsui, M.: On correlation between the order of S-boxes and the strength of DES. In: De Santis, A. (ed.) EUROCRYPT 1994. LNCS, vol. 950, pp. 366–375. Springer, Heidelberg (1995). https://doi.org/10.1007/BFb0053451
12. Qin, L., Dong, X., Wang, X., Jia, K., Liu, Y.: Automated search oriented to key recovery on ciphers with linear key schedule applications to boomerangs in SKINNY and forkskinny. IACR Trans. Symmetric Cryptol. **2021**(2), 249–291 (2021). https://doi.org/10.46586/tosc.v2021.i2.249-291
13. Rohit, R., Sarkar, S.: Cryptanalysis of reduced round SPEEDY. IACR Cryptol. ePrint Arch., p. 612 (2022). https://eprint.iacr.org/2022/612
14. Sasaki, Yu., Todo, Y.: New algorithm for modeling S-box in MILP based differential and division trail search. In: Farshim, P., Simion, E. (eds.) SecITC 2017. LNCS, vol. 10543, pp. 150–165. Springer, Cham (2017). https://doi.org/10.1007/978-3-319-69284-5_11
15. Sinz, C.: Towards an optimal CNF encoding of Boolean cardinality constraints. In: van Beek, P. (ed.) CP 2005. LNCS, vol. 3709, pp. 827–831. Springer, Heidelberg (2005). https://doi.org/10.1007/11564751_73

16. Soos, M., Nohl, K., Castelluccia, C.: Extending SAT solvers to cryptographic problems. In: Kullmann, O. (ed.) SAT 2009. LNCS, vol. 5584, pp. 244–257. Springer, Heidelberg (2009). https://doi.org/10.1007/978-3-642-02777-2_24
17. Sun, L., Wang, W., Wang, M.: Accelerating the search of differential and linear characteristics with the SAT method. IACR Trans. Symmetric Cryptol. **2021**(1), 269–315 (2021). https://doi.org/10.46586/tosc.v2021.i1.269-315
18. Sun, L., Wang, W., Wang, M.: Improved attacks on GIFT-64. In: AlTawy, R., Hülsing, A. (eds.) SAC 2021. LNCS, vol. 13203, pp. 246–265. Springer, Cham (2022). https://doi.org/10.1007/978-3-030-99277-4_12
19. Wagner, D.: The boomerang attack. In: Knudsen, L. (ed.) FSE 1999. LNCS, vol. 1636, pp. 156–170. Springer, Heidelberg (1999). https://doi.org/10.1007/3-540-48519-8_12
20. Zhao, B., Dong, X., Jia, K.: New related-tweakey boomerang and rectangle attacks on deoxys-bc including BDT effect. IACR Trans. Symmetric Cryptol. **2019**(3), 121–151 (2019). https://doi.org/10.13154/tosc.v2019.i3.121-151

Mathematical Aspects of Crypto

A Note on Inverted Twisted Edwards Curve

Luying Li[1,2] and Wei Yu[1,2](✉)

[1] State Key Laboratory of Information Security, Institute of Information Engineering, Chinese Academy of Sciences, Beijing, China
yuwei_1_yw@163.com

[2] School of Cyber Security, University of Chinese Academy of Sciences, Beijing, China

Abstract. This paper is a complementary work to the Edwards curve family. In this paper, we study the inverted Edwards coordinates on twisted Edwards curves (denoted by inverted twisted Edwards curves). We provide explicit addition, doubling, and tripling formulae on inverted twisted Edwards curves with projective coordinates and extended projective coordinates. Using the extended projective coordinates, the new explicit unified addition formulas cost 9**M**.

Keywords: Elliptic curve · Scalar multiplication · Addition · Doubling · Tripling · Explicit formulas

1 Introduction

Elliptic curve cryptography (ECC) is one of the most well-known cryptosystems, widely employed into reality since 2005. For instance, a research in 2017 sampled 100 major websites and found that 69 of them employing ECC for key exchange [12], Apple employs elliptic curve digital signature algorithm (ECDSA) as the signature of iMessage [10].

Compared with other elliptic curves, Edwards curve does not have a long history in cryptography, even though its mathematical studies could date back to the days of Gauss and Euler. For a long time afterward, this form of elliptic curve seemed to vanish from the sea of literature. It was not until 2007 that Edwards brought this curve back into the public eye and proved that it is a normal elliptic curve model [7]. The beautiful addition law of the Edwards curve rapidly caught the attention of cryptographers. In the same year that Edwards discovered this curve, Bernstein and Lange introduced the Edwards curve into the elliptic curve cryptosystem [2].

The importance of Edwards curves and their generalized forms, especially the twisted Edwards curves, is indisputable. Ever since the Edwards form was introduced to ECC, there has been a rapid development of it in elliptic curve cryptosystems. It can also be stated that the Edwards curve form is one of the most significant elliptic curve forms over finite fields with large characteristics,

Y. Deng and M. Yung (Eds.): Inscrypt 2022, LNCS 13837, pp. 295–304, 2023.
https://doi.org/10.1007/978-3-031-26553-2_15

and one of the most favored forms by current standards. The standards that employed Edwards curves include the Transport Layer Security (TLS) Protocol Version 1.3 [15], Internet Engineering Task Force Request for Comments(IETF RFC) 8079 [14], and the National Institute of Standards and Technology (NIST) draft FIPS 800-186 [5].

The significance of twisted Edwards curves comes from the fact that there is state-of-the-art scalar multiplication on them. Scalar multiplication is a procedure that repeatedly adds the same point on itself, which is one of the most essential parts of ECC. It is also the costliest section of some broadly applied ECC protocols, e.g., ECDSA. Different forms of elliptic curves have been utilized to achieve better scalar multiplication efficiency. The improvement of scalar multiplications has always been a hot research topic in elliptic curve cryptography [1,13,16].

In scalar multiplication, the most noteworthy two operations are point addition and doubling. In recent years, the efficient calculations of points tripling have also aroused interest [16]. Not only the family of Edwards curves provides efficient point addition and doubling formulas, but also offers *strongly unified* point addition formulas, which are highly efficient and easily implemented. When the parameters of the Edwards curve satisfy certain conditions, a better *complete* addition formula can be obtained. If a point addition formula works for point doubling, it is called strongly unified, and if it is valid for all inputs, it is called complete.

In this paper, we study the point operations on inverted twisted Edwards curve, which is also one of the Edwards forms. The inverted twisted Edwards curve is the curve corresponding to the inverted Edwards coordinates on twisted Edwards curves. The inverted Edwards coordinates were introduced to accelerate the addition formulae in scalar multiplication computation of Edwards curves by Bernstein and Lange [3]. Galbraith employed one of the twisted inverted Edwards curves as an example curve in his study [9]. In this study, we provide the addition, doubling, and tripling formulae on inverted twisted Edwards curves. Each formula is based on projective and extended projective coordinates. The addition, doubling, and tripling explicit formulas on the inverted twisted Edwards curve are almost as fast as those on twisted Edwards curve.

The rest of this paper is organized as follows: in Sect. 2, we recall the background of the family of Edwards curves. In Sect. 3, we provide the arithmetic on inverted twisted Edwards curves. In Sect. 4, we provide our new readdition formula and tripling formula on inverted twisted Edwards curves. Compared with previous works [3], the readdition formula saves 2 multiplication with constants and the tripling formula saves one multiplication. In Sect. 5, we present addition, doubling, and tripling on extended projective coordinates, which are almost as faster as the state-of-the-art formulas on twisted Edwards curves. In Sect. 6, we give a time costs comparison. In Sect. 7, we indicate how to compute the single point scalar multiplication efficiently.

2 Background

When looking back to Euler's time, it is the time that elliptic curves were more commonly referred to as elliptic functions. Euler implied that elliptic curves $x^2 + y^2 + x^2y^2 = 1$ had the following addition law [8]:

$$X = \frac{xy' + yx'}{1 - xyx'y'}, \qquad Y = \frac{yy' - xx'}{1 + xyx'y'}.$$

A few decades later, this addition law was explicitly proposed by Gauss when he studied a variant of this curve [11]. Edwards restudied Euler and Gauss's work and generalized the special curve to the form $x^2 + y^2 = a^2 + a^2x^2y^2$ [7]. He indicated that if a satisfies $a^5 \neq a$, then the following addition law holds for the above curve.

$$X = \frac{1}{a} \cdot \frac{xy' + yx'}{1 + xyx'y'}, \qquad Y = \frac{1}{a} \cdot \frac{yy' - xx'}{1 - xyx'y'}.$$

Meanwhile, the form $x^2 + y^2 = a^2 + a^2x^2y^2$ is a normal form. The "normal" means that every elliptic curve over a non-binary field can employ a birational map to a relative Edwards curve in an appropriate extension field.

Bernstein and Lange added a new parameter to the Edwards curves [2] to make the Edwards curve more applicable in cryptography. They generalized the Edwards curves to the form $x^2+y^2 = a^2(1+dx^2y^2)$, showing that the well-known curve25519 is birational equivalent to the curve $x^2+y^2 = 1+121665/121666x^2y^2$, and presented $3\mathbf{M}+4\mathbf{S}$, i.e., 3 field multiplications and 4 field squarings doubling formulae and $10\mathbf{M}+1\mathbf{S}$ addition formulae under the assumption $c = 1$. Bernstein and Lange pointed out that this assumption is easy to achieve. The doubling and addition formulae broke the speed record of multi-scalar multiplication at that time.

To further lower the cost, Bernstein and Lange introduced inverted Edwards coordinates on Edwards curves [3]. Employing the inverted Edwards coordinates, the doubling, tripling, and addition formulae cost $3\mathbf{M}+4\mathbf{S}$, $9\mathbf{M}+4\mathbf{S}$, and $9\mathbf{M}+1\mathbf{S}$, respectively.

Bernstein et al. introduced twisted Edwards curves, allowing the family of Edwards curves to cover a wider family of elliptic curves in cryptography. Each twisted Edwards curve is a twist of an Edwards curve [1].

So far, the fastest addition formula algorithm in the family of Edwards curves is proposed by Hisil, Wong, Carter, and Dawson with extended twisted Edwards coordinates [13]. Their unified formula costs $9\mathbf{M} + 2\mathbf{M}_a$, and their fast addition formula costs $9\mathbf{M} + \mathbf{M}_a$, where $\mathbf{M}_a$ is a field multiplication with a constant. When a equals -1, one $\mathbf{M}$ and one $\mathbf{M}_a$ will be saved on each formula.

In [9], Galbraith employed elliptic curves of Edwards form to carry out the implementation of their Gallant-Lambert-Vanstone (GLV) method.

3 Arithmetic on Inverted Twisted Edwards Curves

The inverted twisted Edwards curves are the elliptic curves with the following equation:

$$x^2 + ay^2 = d + x^2y^2.$$

∞ is the neutral element, and $(-x, y)$ is the negative of a point (x, y).

The projective form of inverted twisted Edwards curves is

$$(X^2 + aY^2)Z^2 = dZ^4 + X^2Y^2. \tag{1}$$

When $Z \neq 0$, the point with projective coordinates $(X : Y : Z)$ is corresponding to an affine point $(X/Z, Y/Z)$. When $Z = 0$, the point is one of two singularities at infinity. An inverted twisted Edwards curve is isomorphic to a twisted Edwards curve by the map $\phi(X, Y, Z) = (Z/X, Z/Y)$.

If further allowing T to be an auxiliary coordinate satisfying $T = XY/Z$, then the extended twisted Edwards coordinates $(T : X : Y : Z)$ are obtained. However, this representation may cause an error when $Z = 0$. Instead, the inverted twisted Edwards curve with extended twisted Edwards coordinates can be considered as the intersection of the following two surfaces:

$$X^2 + aY^2 = dZ^2 + T^2, \qquad \text{and } XY = ZT.$$

Then, the point is well-defined even if $Z = 0$. By this definition, the point at infinity can be represented as $(1 : 1 : 0 : 0)$. The curve has four points of order 4: $T_1 = (\sqrt{a} : 0 : 1 : 0)$, $T_2 = (0 : \sqrt{d} : 0 : 1)$, $T_3 = (-\sqrt{a} : 0 : 1 : 0)$, $T_4 = (0 : -\sqrt{d} : 0 : 1)$ and three points of order 2: $T_1 + T_2 = (0 : 0 : -\sqrt{d} : \sqrt{a})$, $T_1 - T_2 = (0 : 0 : \sqrt{d} : \sqrt{a})$, $2T_1 = 2T_2 = (1 : -1 : 0 : 0)$ in the extension field. In the following sections, we will refer to the extended twisted Edwards coordinates simply as extended projective coordinates.

A point on extended projective coordinates can map to a point in projective coordinates by ignoring the coordinates T. A point $(X : Y : Z)$ on projective coordinates with $XYZ \neq 0$ can map to the point $(XY : XZ : YZ : Z^2)$ on extended projective coordinates.

Considering the projective map from extended twisted Edwards coordinates to projective coordinates, the point at infinity $(1 : 1 : 0 : 0)$ and the 2-order point $(1 : -1 : 0 : 0)$ will both map to $(1 : 0 : 0)$ and lose the distinction between them. Similarly, in projective coordinates, the distinction between T_1 and T_3 will be lost. Since the elliptic curve systems always employ the points in prime order subgroups as the inputs of the scalar multiplications, these losings would not require exceptional handles.

According to [1] and [9], the unified addition law for inverted twisted Edwards curves is

$$(x_3, y_3) = (x_1, y_1) + (x_2, y_2) = \left(\frac{x_1x_2y_1y_2 + d}{x_2y_1 + x_1y_2}, \frac{x_1x_2y_1y_2 - d}{x_1x_2 - ay_1y_2}\right). \tag{2}$$

The following theorem reveals the exception inputs of this addition law.

Theorem 1. *Let K be a field of odd characteristic. Assuming that $P = (x_1, y_1)$ is a fixed point on inverted twisted Edwards curve $E : x^2 + ay^2 = d + x^2y^2$ which is defined over K. Let Q be another point on this curve.*

If $x_1y_1 = 0$, then $x_2y_1 + x_1y_2 = 0$ if and only if $Q \in S_x = \{(x_1, -y_1), (-x_1, y_1)\}$; $x_1x_2 - ay_1y_2 = 0$ if and only if $Q \in S_y = \{(\sqrt{a}y_1, x_1/\sqrt{a}), (-\sqrt{a}y_1, -x_1/\sqrt{a})\}$. Otherwise, S_x and S_y are given by

$$S_x = \{(x_1, -y_1), (-x_1, y_1), (\sqrt{d}/y_1, -\sqrt{d}/x_1), (-\sqrt{d}/y_1, \sqrt{d}/x_1)\},$$

$$S_y = \{(\sqrt{a}y_1, x_1/\sqrt{a}), (-\sqrt{a}y_1, -x_1/\sqrt{a}), (\sqrt{ad}/x_1, -\sqrt{d}/\sqrt{a}y_1), (-\sqrt{ad}/x_1, \sqrt{d}/\sqrt{a}y_1)\}.$$

Proof. S_x is given by solving the equations $x_1^2 + ay_1^2 = d + x_1^2y_1^2$, $x_2^2 + ay_2^2 = d + x_2^2y_2^2$ and $x_2y_1 + x_1y_2 = 0$. Similarly, S_y is given by solving the equations $x_1^2 + ay_1^2 = d + x_1^2y_1^2$, $x_2^2 + ay_2^2 = d + x_2^2y_2^2$ and $x_1x_2 - ay_1y_2 = 0$.

By Theorem 1, the addition law (2) is unified. Meanwhile, there is no suitable selection of a and d that can make addition law (2) complete, the exceptions always exist. The following lemma shows that exceptional cases are not required to be handled for scalar multiplication with a prime order point as input.

Lemma 1. *Let K, E, P, Q be defined as in Theorem 1. If $Q \in S_x \cup S_y$, then Q is of even order.*

Proof. The proof of this lemma is similar to the proof of Lemma 1 in [13].

4 Points Operations in Projective Coordinates

4.1 Readdition Formula

The *readdition* can be performed in $9\mathbf{M} + 1\mathbf{S}$ with cached values $R_1 = X_2Y_2$, $T_2 = X_2Y_2/Z_2$, $R_2 = dZ_2$, $R_3 = aR_1$, $R_4 = aY_2$, where the term readdition means one of the inputs of the point addition is fixed and some values of this input have already been cached. The specific algorithm is:

$$A = X_1 \cdot Y_1;\ B = (X_1 + X_2) \cdot (Y_1 + Y_2) - A - R_1;$$
$$C = (X_2 + Y_1) \cdot (X_1 - R_4) + R_3 - A;\ D = Z_1^2;\ E = R_2 \cdot D;\ F = A \cdot T_2;$$
$$X_3 = (E + F) \cdot C;\ Y_3 = (F - E) \cdot B;\ Z_3 = Z_1 \cdot B \cdot C.$$

A $8\mathbf{M}+1\mathbf{S}+1\mathbf{M}_a$ mixed addition formula can be derived by setting $Z_2 = 1$.

4.2 Tripling in Projective Coordinates

By the doubling and addition formulae, the tripling formulae can be obtained as

$$X_3 = X_1(X_1^4 + 2aX_1^2Y_1^2 + a^2Y_1^4 - 4adY_1^2Z_1^2)(X_1^4 - 2aX_1^2Y_1^2 - 3a^2Y_1^4 + 4adY_1^2Z_1^2),$$

$$Y_3 = Y_1(-X_1^4 - 2aX_1^2Y_1^2 - a^2Y_1^4 + 4dX_1^2Z_1^2)(-3X_1^4 - 2aX_1^2Y_1^2 + a^2Y_1^4 + 4dX_1^2Z_1^2),$$
$$Z_3 = Z_1(3X_1^4 + 2A1X_1^2Y_1^2 - a^2Y_1^4 - 4dX_1^2Z_1^2)(X_1^4 - 2aX_1^2Y_1^2 - 3a^2Y_1^4 + 4adY_1^2Z_1^2).$$

The new tripling formula can be computed in $9\mathbf{M}+3\mathbf{S}+2\mathbf{M}_a$ by the following algorithm:

$$A = X_1^2;\ B = aY_1^2;\ C = A + B - dZ_1^2;$$
$$D = (A + B) \cdot (A - B);\ E = 2A \cdot C;\ F = 2B \cdot C;$$
$$X_3 = X_1 \cdot (D+F) \cdot (D-F);\ Y_3 = -Y_1 \cdot (D+E) \cdot (D-E);\ Z_3 = Z_1 \cdot (D-F) \cdot (D-E).$$

5 Points Operations in Extended Projective Coordinates

5.1 Addition in Extended Projective Coordinates

The addition law for extended projective coordinates can be obtained as: $(T_1 : X_1 : Y_1 : Z_1) + (T_2 : X_2 : Y_2 : Z_2) = (T_3 : X_3 : Y_3 : Z_3)$, where

$$T_3 = (T_1T_2 + dZ_1Z_2)(T_1T_2 - dZ_1Z_2),$$
$$X_3 = (T_1T_2 + dZ_1Z_2)(X_1X_2 - aY_1Y_2),$$
$$Y_3 = (T_1T_2 - dZ_1Z_2)(X_2Y_1 + X_1Y_2),$$
$$Z_3 = (X_1X_2 - aY_1Y_2)(X_2Y_1 + X_1Y_2).$$

Derived from the addition law, we have the following algorithm to compute the addition formulae with $9\mathbf{M}+2\mathbf{M}_a$.

$$A = dZ_1 \cdot Z_2;\ B = T_1 \cdot T_2;\ C = X_1 \cdot X_2;\ D = Y_1 \cdot Y_2;$$
$$E = (X_1 + Y_1) \cdot (X_2 + Y_2) - C - D;\ H = C - aD;\ X_3 = (A + B) \cdot H;$$
$$Y_3 = (B - A) \cdot E;\ Z_3 = H \cdot E;\ T_3 = (A + B) \cdot (B - A).$$

The readdition costs $9\mathbf{M}$ with the caching of $R_1 = dZ_2$, $R_2 = aY_2$, $R_3 = X_2Y_2$, and $R_4 = aX_2Y_2$.

$$A = Z_1 \cdot R_1;\ B = T_1 \cdot T_2;\ C = X_1 \cdot Y_1;\ D = (X_1 + Y_1) \cdot (X_2 + Y_2) - C - R_3;$$
$$E = (X_2 + Y_1) \cdot (X_1 - R_2) + R_3 - C;\ F = B + A;\ G = B - A;$$
$$T_3 = F \cdot G;\ X_3 = F \cdot E;\ Y_3 = G \cdot D; Z_3 = D \cdot E.$$

For the case $a = -1$, the addition formula can be optimized as

$$A = dZ_1 \cdot Z_2;\ B = T_1 \cdot T_2;\ C = (X_1 + Y_1) \cdot (X_2 + Y_2);\ D = (X_1 - Y_1) \cdot (X_2 - Y_2);$$
$$E = -C - D;\ H = C - D;\ X_3 = 2(A + B) \cdot H;$$
$$Y_3 = 2(B - A) \cdot E;\ Z_3 = H \cdot E;\ T_3 = 4(A + B) \cdot (B - A).$$

This formula costs $8\mathbf{M} + 1\mathbf{M}_a$. The readdition costs $8\mathbf{M}$ with a cached value dZ_2. And the mixed addition costs $7\mathbf{M} + 1\mathbf{M}_a$ by assuming $Z_2 = 1$.

5.2 Doubling in Extended Projective Coordinates

The explicit doubling formulas, in this case, need $4\mathbf{M} + 4\mathbf{S} + 2\mathbf{M}_a$. X_1, Y_1, and Z_1 are required to be the inputs.

$$A = X_1^2;\ B = Y_1^2; C = (X_1 + Y_1)^2 - A - B;\ D = 2dZ_1^2;\ E = a \cdot B;$$
$$X_3 = (A + E) \cdot (A - E);\ Y_3 = C \cdot (A + E - D);$$
$$Z_3 = C \cdot (A - E);\ T_3 = (A + E) \cdot (D - A - E).$$

One $\mathbf{M}$ will be saved if output a point in projective coordinates.

5.3 Tripling in Extended Projective Coordinates

For extended projective coordinates, we present two sets of tripling formulas. The first set needs $11\mathbf{M} + 3\mathbf{S} + 1\mathbf{M}_a$, requiring all of X_1, Y_1, Z_1, and T_1 as inputs. This tripling formula can be performed as

$$A = X_1^2;\ B = aY_1^2;\ C = 2T_1^2 - A - B;$$
$$D = (A + B) \cdot (A - B);\ E = 2A \cdot C;\ F = 2B \cdot C;$$
$$X_3 = X_1 \cdot (D + F) \cdot (D - F);\ Y_3 = -Y_1 \cdot (D + E) \cdot (D - E);$$
$$Z_3 = Z_1 \cdot (D - F) \cdot (D - E);\ T_3 = -T_1 \cdot (D + F) \cdot (D + E).$$

Two $\mathbf{M}$ can be saved if a point in projective coordinates is output by ignoring the computation of T_3.

The second set needs $11\mathbf{M} + 3\mathbf{S} + 2\mathbf{M}_a$, requiring X_1, Y_1, and Z_1 as inputs:

$$A = X_1^2;\ B = aY_1^2;\ C = A + B - 2dZ_1^2;$$
$$D = (A + B) \cdot (A - B);\ E = 2A \cdot C;\ F = 2B \cdot C;$$
$$G = X_1 \cdot (D + F);\ H = -Y_1 \cdot (D + E);\ I = Z_1 \cdot (D - F);\ J = Z_1 \cdot (D - E);$$
$$X_3 = G \cdot I;\ Y_3 = H \cdot J;\ Z_3 = I \cdot J;\ T_3 = G \cdot H.$$

6 Comparison

In Sect. 4 and Sect. 5, we introduce the point operations in projective coordinates and extended projective coordinates. In the following table, we compare the explicit formulae on twisted Edwards curves and inverted twisted Edwards curves.

As in Table 1, on the projective coordinates, the new readdition formula saves $2\mathbf{M}_a$ and the new tripling formula saves $1\mathbf{M}$. The new addition formula ($a = -1$) on extended coordinates saves $1\mathbf{M} + 1\mathbf{S} + 1\mathbf{M}_a$ while doubling require $1\mathbf{M}$ more. The extra cost in the doubling formula can be eliminated by using a mixture of projective and extended coordinates. For details, please refer to Sect. 7.

Table 1. Time costs for points operations on inverted twisted Edwards curves

Curve	Coordinates	ADD			reADD			Doubling			Tripling		
		M	S	M_a	M	S	M_a	M	S	M_a	M	S	M_a
Twisted Edwards [3]	inv-inv	9	1	2	9	1	2	3	4	2	9	4	2
Inverted twisted Edwards (This work)	proj-proj	/			9	1	0	/			9	3	2
Inverted twisted Edwards ($a = -1$, this work)	ext-ext	8	0	1	8	0	0	4	4	1	11	3	1
Inverted twisted Edwards ($a = -1$, this work)	ext-proj	7	0	1	7	0	0	3	4	1	9	3	1
Inverted twisted Edwards (this work)	ext-ext	9	0	2	9	0	0	4	4	2	11	3	2
Inverted twisted Edwards (this work)	ext-proj	8	0	2	8	0	0	3	4	2	9	3	1

7 Fast Scalar Multiplication

In order to obtain better efficiency, Cohen, Miyaji, and Ono proposed a strategy of carefully mixing different coordinates on short Weierstrass curves [6] combined the best doubling and addition system. Hisil et al. introduced this strategy on twisted Edwards curves, combing the projective and extended twisted Edwards coordinates to achieve better efficiency. We follow a similar approach.

Recall that given $(X : Y : Z)$ in projective coordinates passing to extended projective coordinates requires $3\mathbf{M} + 1\mathbf{S}$ by computing $(XY : XZ : YZ : Z^2)$. Given $(T : X : Y : Z)$ in passing to projective coordinates is cost-free by simply ignoring T.

On inverted twisted Edwards curves, combining extended projective coordinates with projective coordinates speeds up scalar multiplications. When performing a scalar multiplication, some suggestions are provided in the following:

(1) If a point doubling or tripling is followed by another point doubling or tripling, the corresponding formula on projective coordinates is recommended to be employed.
(2) After each addition, the tripling scalar multiplication *should* be performed as early as possible.
(3) If a point doubling or tripling is followed by a point addition, please use the doubling or tripling on extended projective coordinates the addition with input points on extended projective coordinates and output projective coordinates point for the point doubling or tripling and the point addition.
(4) If suggestion (2) is followed and a point addition after tripling still needs to be calculated, then using projective coordinates is faster than using extended Edwards coordinates as the coordinates of the midpoint.

In order to achieve better efficiency, the doubling and tripling operations should be performed under the projective coordinates as much as possible. Since the inputs values in doubling and tripling formulas on extended projective coordinates do not contain T-coordinates, these formulas can be regarded as the doubling and tripling formulas passing the input points on projective coordinates to the output points on extended projective coordinates. Compared to the doubling and tripling formulas on projective coordinates, the doubling and tripling formulas on projective coordinates cost additional **M** and 2**M** respectively. Therefore, the tripling points operation should be performed as early as possible to lower the costs. If the point addition after tripling is inevitable, then they require 18**M** + 4**S** on projective coordinates and 19**M** + 3**S** if the output point of tripling is a point on extended projective coordinates. **M** always takes more time than **S**. In Bernstein and Lange Explicit-Formulas Database [4], **S** is assumed to be 0.67**M** to 1**M**. Employing the projective coordinates to perform this procedure will be more efficient.

8 Conclusion

We investigate point arithmetic formulas on inverted twisted Edwards curves for the cases with the curve parameter $a = -1$ and the cases without restrictions on curve parameters. These formulas could be applied to elliptic curve cryptosystems in the future.

Acknowledgment. The authors would like to thank the anonymous reviewers for many helpful comments. This work is supported by the National Natural Science Foundation of China (No. 62272453, U1936209, 61872442, and 61502487).

References

1. Bernstein, D.J., Birkner, P., Joye, M., Lange, T., Peters, C.: Twisted Edwards curves. In: Vaudenay, S. (ed.) AFRICACRYPT 2008. LNCS, vol. 5023, pp. 389–405. Springer, Heidelberg (2008). https://doi.org/10.1007/978-3-540-68164-9_26
2. Bernstein, D.J., Lange, T.: Faster addition and doubling on elliptic curves. In: Kurosawa, K. (ed.) ASIACRYPT 2007. LNCS, vol. 4833, pp. 29–50. Springer, Heidelberg (2007). https://doi.org/10.1007/978-3-540-76900-2_3
3. Bernstein, D.J., Lange, T.: Inverted Edwards coordinates. In: Boztaş, S., Lu, H.-F.F. (eds.) AAECC 2007. LNCS, vol. 4851, pp. 20–27. Springer, Heidelberg (2007). https://doi.org/10.1007/978-3-540-77224-8_4
4. Bernstein, D.J., Lange, T.: Explicit-formulas database (2020). http://hyperelliptic.org/EFD/
5. Chen, L., Moody, D., Regenscheid, A., Randall, K.: Draft NIST special publication 800-186 recommendations for discrete logarithm-based cryptography: elliptic curve domain parameters. Technical report, National Institute of Standards and Technology (2019)
6. Cohen, H., Miyaji, A., Ono, T.: Efficient elliptic curve exponentiation using mixed coordinates. In: Ohta, K., Pei, D. (eds.) ASIACRYPT 1998. LNCS, vol. 1514, pp. 51–65. Springer, Heidelberg (1998). https://doi.org/10.1007/3-540-49649-1_6
7. Edwards, H.M.: A normal form for elliptic curves. In: Bulletin of the American Mathematical Society, pp. 393–422 (2007)

8. Euler, L.: Observationes de comparatione arcuum curvarum irrectificibilium. Novi commentarii academiae scientiarum Petropolitanae, pp. 58–84 (1761)
9. Galbraith, S.D., Lin, X., Scott, M.: Endomorphisms for faster elliptic curve cryptography on a large class of curves. J. Cryptol. **24**, 446–469 (2011)
10. Garman, C., Green, M., Kaptchuk, G., Miers, I., Rushanan, M.: Dancing on the lip of the volcano: chosen ciphertext attacks on apple iMessage. In: 25th USENIX Security Symposium (USENIX Security 2016), Austin, TX, pp. 655–672. USENIX Association (2016)
11. Gauss, C.F.: Carl Friedrich Gauss Werke, vol. 3
12. Harkanson, R., Kim, Y.: Applications of elliptic curve cryptography: a light introduction to elliptic curves and a survey of their applications. In: Proceedings of the 12th Annual Conference on Cyber and Information Security Research (2017)
13. Hisil, H., Wong, K.K.-H., Carter, G., Dawson, E.: Twisted Edwards curves revisited. In: Pieprzyk, J. (ed.) ASIACRYPT 2008. LNCS, vol. 5350, pp. 326–343. Springer, Heidelberg (2008). https://doi.org/10.1007/978-3-540-89255-7_20
14. Miniero, L., Murillo, S.G., Pascual, V.: Guidelines for End-to-End Support of the RTP Control Protocol (RTCP) in Back-to-Back User Agents (B2BUAs). RFC 8079 (2017)
15. Rescorla, E.: The Transport Layer Security (TLS) Protocol Version 1.3. RFC 8446 (2018)
16. Yu, W., Musa, S.A., Li, B.: Double-base chains for scalar multiplications on elliptic curves. In: Canteaut, A., Ishai, Y. (eds.) EUROCRYPT 2020. LNCS, vol. 12107, pp. 538–565. Springer, Cham (2020). https://doi.org/10.1007/978-3-030-45727-3_18

Efficiently Computable Complex Multiplication of Elliptic Curves

Xiao Li[1,2], Wei Yu[1(✉)], Yuqing Zhu[3,4], and Zhizhong Pan[5]

[1] State Key Laboratory of Information Security, Institute of Information Engineering, Chinese Academy of Sciences, Beijing 100195, China
{lixiao,yuwei}@iie.ac.cn

[2] School of Cyber Security, University of Chinese Academy of Sciences, Beijing 100049, China

[3] Beijing Key Laboratory of Security and Privacy in Intelligent Transportation, Beijing Jiaotong University, Beijing 100044, China
zhuyuqing@bjtu.edu.cn

[4] School of Computer and Information technology, Beijing Jiaotong University, Beijing 100044, China

[5] Huawei Technologies Co., Ltd., Shenzhen, China

Abstract. After the GLV and GLS methods were proposed, a great deal of attention was devoted to the efficiently computable complex multiplication of elliptic curves. In this paper, we mainly compute the rational expressions of complex multiplications of elliptic curves. Our contribution involves two aspects. We propose a new algorithm to effectively compute the rational expression of a complex multiplication over finite field. We also present a method to construct an elliptic curve with efficiently computable complex multiplication by a given quadratic imaginary field. Specifically, we show all 13 classes of elliptic curves with complex multiplication over quadratic imaginary fields. This is the first systematic study of the expression of complex multiplication.

Keywords: Elliptic curves · Complex multiplication · Explicit expression · GLV method

1 Introduction

In elliptic curve cryptography, the additive group structure of the elliptic curve is widely used. Examples include the elliptic curve Diffie-Hellman key exchange and the elliptic curve digital signature algorithm. The calculation of the scalar multiplication of points on elliptic curves is a basic and important task. Scalar multiplication acceleration has received much attention for a long time, and has been extensively studied by the cryptography community.

This work is supported by the National Natural Science Foundation of China (No. 62272453, U1936209, 62002015, 61872442, and 61502487) and the Fundamental Research Funds for the Central Universities (No. 2021RC259).

Y. Deng and M. Yung (Eds.): Inscrypt 2022, LNCS 13837, pp. 305–317, 2023.
https://doi.org/10.1007/978-3-031-26553-2_16

In 2001, a groundbreaking algorithm named the Gallant-Lambert-Vanstone (GLV) method [1] was proposed to achieve the accelerated computation of scalar multiplication. Specifically, the GLV method works as follows. Suppose E is an elliptic curve over finite field and P is a point of prime order n. If there is an efficiently computable endomorphism $\phi \in \text{End}(E)$, then we can compute kP for $k \in [1, n-1]$ via the decomposition

$$kP = k_1P + k_2\phi(P), \quad k_1, k_2 \approx \sqrt{n}.$$

We call the vector $(k_1, k_2) \in \mathbb{Z} \times \mathbb{Z}$ a short vector if it satisfies $k_1, k_2 \approx \sqrt{n}$. When the computational cost of ϕ is small and $k_1P + k_2Q$ can be computed simultaneously, such as using Shamir's trick, the calculation of scalar multiplication can be accelerated.

An important and basic assumption of the GLV method is the existence of efficiently computable complex multiplications. Most elliptic curves have only the multiplication-by-integer endomorphisms. An elliptic curve that possesses extra endomorphisms is said to have complex multiplication (CM). Frobenius morphism, which is a trivial complex multiplication, can be used for Koblitz curves over binary fields. Thus, the Koblitz curves enable very fast scalar multiplication. However, the safety of the Koblitz curve has been questioned. Therefore, we consider the complex multiplication of elliptic curves over finite field $\mathbb{F}_p$. Some existing complex multiplications, such as $\pm\sqrt{-1}$, $\frac{-1\pm\sqrt{-3}}{2}$, are often used. The paper [1] provides 4 examples. We list one of them here.

$E_{7,1}$ is an elliptic curve over $\mathbb{F}_p$ defined by

$$y^2 = x^3 - \frac{3}{4}x^2 - 2x - 1, \tag{1}$$

where $p > 3$ is a prime such that -7 is a quadratic residue modulo p. There is a map Φ defined by

$$\Phi(x, y) = (\frac{x^2 - \xi}{\xi^2(x-a)}, \frac{y(x^2 - 2ax + \xi)}{\xi^3(x-a)^2})$$

as an endomorphism of $E_{7,1}$, where $\xi = (1+\sqrt{-7})/2$ and $a = (\xi - 3)/4$. Moreover, Φ satisfies the equation

$$\Phi^2 - \Phi + 2 = 0,$$

and $\mathbb{Z}[\Phi] = \mathbb{Z}[\frac{1+\sqrt{-7}}{2}] \subseteq \mathbb{Q}(\sqrt{-7})$.

The endomorphism ring of an ordinary elliptic curve E with complex multiplication is an order in a quadratic imaginary field K [6]. In the 4 examples in [1], all of the class numbers of the relevant quadratic imaginary fields are equal to 1, and the complex multiplications are exactly defined over quadratic imaginary fields. Actually, there are only 13 quadratic imaginary fields of class number 1 (9 fundamental, 4 non-fundamental), four of which were presented in the above examples. These examples have been widely used. For instance, secp256k1 (one case of elliptic curve E_2) is the key mechanism for the implementations of Bitcoin and Ethereum [3]. As a well-known cryptocurrency, Bitcoin's market capitalization has exceeded one trillion US dollars. However, we have been unable to find more examples of elliptic curves with useful endomorphisms in the literature. Therefore, one of our goals is to find a way to calculate the efficiently computable complex multiplication.

In this paper, we are concerned with 2 aspects of complex multiplication: If a complex multiplication differs from the Frobenius morphism, how can we determine its explicit expression; and what are the elliptic curves whose endomorphism rings are contained in the other 9 quadratic imaginary fields of class numbers 1.

Firstly, we present a new algorithm to calculate the explicit expression of a complex multiplication of any given elliptic curve over $\mathbb{F}_p$. Stark [8] once proposed a method of continuous fraction expansion to calculate the rational expressions of complex multiplications. Our algorithm is a brand new method, completely different from Stark's. We prove Theorem 4, which states that the degree of a complex multiplication is equal to its norm. In Theorem 5, we introduce our algorithm for calculating the rational expression of a complex multiplication. This algorithm uses the method of undetermined coefficients, and is in time polynomial in the degree of complex multiplication.

Secondly, for the remaining 9 quadratic imaginary fields of class number 1, we obtain 9 classes of elliptic curves with complex multiplications. We propose a new method to compute the explicit expressions over quadratic imaginary fields for complex multiplications of these elliptic curves. This result is convenient for us to provide the rational expression of the complex multiplication over any finite field $\mathbb{F}_p$. The details of these elliptic curves and their complex multiplications are at the end of Sect. 4.

Paper Organization. The rest of the paper is organized as follows. In Sect. 2, we briefly describe the properties of the endomorphism rings of elliptic curves over finite field and introduce the Kohel's algorithm for calculating endomorphism rings. In Sect. 3, we restrict the complex multiplication to finite field, and propose an algorithm for calculating the rational expression of complex multiplication. Finally in Sect. 4, for a class of special elliptic curves, we give a method to obtain explicit expressions of the complex multiplications.

2 Preliminary

We briefly introduce endomorphism ring and complex multiplication of elliptic curve.

By an endomorphism of an elliptic curve E/k, we mean a homomorphism $\alpha : E(\bar{k}) \to E(\bar{k})$ that is given by rational functions. If the Weierstrass equation of E is written as $y^2 = x^3 + ax + b$, then there are polynomials $f(x), g(x)$ and rational function $r(x, y)$ with coefficients in $\bar{k}$ such that

$$\alpha(x, y) = (\frac{f(x)}{g(x)}, r(x, y))$$

for all $(x, y) \in E(\bar{k})$. We define the degree of α as

$$\deg(\alpha) = \mathrm{Max}\{\deg f(x), \deg g(x)\}.$$

All the endomorphisms of E form a ring, called the endomorphism ring of E, which is denoted as $\mathrm{End}(E)$.

The multiplication by arbitrary integers is always included in $\mathrm{End}(E)$. We say that E has complex multiplication if $\mathrm{End}(E)$ is strictly larger than $\mathbb{Z}$. Each complex multiplication can be represented as a complex number.

It is known that an elliptic curve E over finite field $\mathbb{F}_p$ always has complex multiplication. The p-Frobenius endomorphism, denoted by π, has characteristic polynomial

$$X^2 - tX + p = 0,$$

where $|t| \le 2\sqrt{p}$. It is obvious that this function has no root in $\mathbb{Z}$. That is,

$$\mathbb{Z} \ne \mathbb{Z}[\pi] \subseteq \mathrm{End}(E).$$

Proposition 1 ([9, Theorem 10.6]). Let E be an elliptic curve over finite field of characteristic p.

1) If E is ordinary, then $\mathrm{End}(E)$ is an order in a quadratic imaginary field.
2) If E is supersingular, then $\mathrm{End}(E)$ is a maximal order in a definite quaternion algebra that is ramified at p and ∞ and is split at the other primes.

We only consider the ordinary cases in this paper, which means E satisfies any of the following equivalent conditions.

1) $E[p] \cong \mathbb{Z}/p\mathbb{Z}$.
2) The trace t of π is prime to p.
3) E has a Hasse invariant of 1.

Since $\mathbb{Z}[\pi] \subseteq \mathrm{End}(E) \subset K$ for some quadratic imaginary field K, it is clear that K is equal to the fractional field $\mathbb{Z}[\pi] \otimes \mathbb{Q} = \mathbb{Q}[\pi]$. Let $\mathcal{O}_K$ be the maximal order of K, then we have

$$\mathbb{Z}[\pi] \subseteq \mathrm{End}(E) \subseteq \mathcal{O}_K. \tag{2}$$

For the quadratic imaginary field, the following basic conclusions in algebraic number theory exist.

Lemma 2 ([9, p. 314]). Let K be the quadratic imaginary field $\mathbb{Q}(\sqrt{-N})$, where N is a square-free positive integer.

1) The integer ring of K is $\mathcal{O}_K = [1, \omega]$, where $\omega = \sqrt{-N}$ when $N \equiv 1, 2 \mod 4$, and $\omega = \frac{1+\sqrt{-N}}{2}$ when $N \equiv 3 \mod 4$.
2) Suppose $\mathcal{O}$ is an order of the quadratic imaginary field K. It can be represented as $[1, m\omega]$, where $m = [\mathcal{O}_K : \mathcal{O}]$ is called the conductor of $\mathcal{O}$.

3) If an order $\mathcal{O}$ can be written as $[\alpha, \beta]$, define its discriminant D as

$$D = \left(\det\begin{pmatrix} \alpha & \beta \\ \bar{\alpha} & \bar{\beta} \end{pmatrix}\right)^2,$$

where $\bar{\cdot}$ is the complex conjugate.

4) Moreover, take the discriminant of $\mathcal{O}_K$ as the discriminant D_K of number field K, then

$$D = m^2 D_K.$$

For a given elliptic curve E and chosen prime p, SEA algorithm [4] can be used to calculate the trace t of π on $E(\mathbb{F}_p)$ in the polynomial time of $O(p^{5+\epsilon})$; therefore, we may know the ring $\mathbb{Z}[\pi]$ and the field K. Assume the discriminant of K is D_K, and the conductor of $\mathbb{Z}[\pi]$ is $m = [\mathcal{O}_K : \mathbb{Z}[\pi]]$. Then

$$D = \mathrm{disc}(\mathbb{Z}[\pi]) = t^2 - 4p = m^2 D_K.$$

It can be verified that

$$\mathcal{O}_K = \mathbb{Z}\left[\frac{\pi - a}{m}\right]$$

for $a = t/2$ if $D_K \equiv 0 \mod 4$, and $a = (t+m)/2$ if $D_K \equiv 1 \mod 4$.

To compute $\mathrm{End}(E)$, denoted later by $\mathcal{O}$, one actually needs to determine $[\mathcal{O}_K : \mathcal{O}]$ or $[\mathcal{O} : \mathbb{Z}[\pi]]$. Note that $[\mathcal{O}_K : \mathbb{Z}[\pi]] = m$ and

$$\pi - a \equiv 0 \mod m\mathcal{O}_K.$$

If $[\mathcal{O} : \mathbb{Z}[\pi]] = n_0$, then,

$$\pi - a \equiv 0 \mod n_0\mathcal{O},$$
$$\pi - a \not\equiv 0 \mod kn_0\mathcal{O}$$

with positive integers $n_0 | m,\ k > 1$.

3 Explicit Expression of Complex Multiplication over $\mathbb{F}_p$

The endomorphism ring of a given elliptic curve can be computed by Kohel's algorithm [2], and in this section we focus on specific complex multiplication. Our goal is to find an efficiently computable complex multiplication, and propose an algorithm to calculate its expression.

In this paper, we denote the isomorphism of an endomorphism ring and an order by

$$[\cdot] : \mathbb{C} \xrightarrow{\sim} \mathrm{End}(E).$$
$$\lambda \mapsto [\lambda]$$

λ always represents a complex number, and $[\lambda]$ always represents an endomorphism.

3.1 Complex Multiplication Restricted to a Finite Field

For a given complex multiplication $[\lambda] \in \mathrm{End}(E)$, where λ has the characteristic polynomial $x^2 + rx + s = 0$, we consider the morphism $[\lambda]$ restricted to $\mathbb{F}_p$.

Recall that π denotes the Frobenius endomorphism over $\mathbb{F}_p$. For any point $P \in E(\mathbb{F}_p)$,

$$\pi([\lambda]P) = [\lambda](\pi(P)) = [\lambda]P,$$

so $[\lambda]P \in E(\mathbb{F}_p)$.

The following conclusion is trivial, and there are many different proofs. For the needs of the following calculation, we give a computational proof.

Lemma 3. Let E be an ordinary elliptic curve over finite field $\mathbb{F}_p$. The point $P \in E(\mathbb{F}_p)$ such that $\mathrm{order}(P) = n$ is a prime and $n^2 \nmid \#E(\mathbb{F}_p)$. Then, the action of a complex multiplication $[\lambda] \in \mathrm{End}(E)$ on the group $\langle P \rangle$ is equal to the action of some scalar multiplication.

The conclusion is obvious. It is worth noting that the scalar multiplication is actually a root of the characteristic polynomial of the complex multiplication modulo n.

For a given complex multiplication $[\lambda] \in \mathrm{End}(E)$, there is always an integer k such that $[\lambda]P = kP$ for $P \in E(\mathbb{F}_p)$. When $[\lambda] = \pi$, the relevant k is obviously 1. When $[\lambda] \notin \mathbb{Z}[\pi]$, we may calculate $[\lambda]P$ instead of kP. If Kohel's algorithm shows that $\mathrm{End}(E)$ is greater than $\mathbb{Z}[\pi]$, then there is a complex multiplication that might be used for computational optimization.

3.2 Computing the Rational Expression of CM over $\mathbb{F}_p$

To achieve the scalar multiplication of elliptic curve using complex multiplication, we would like to provide an algorithm to compute the rational expression of a given $[\lambda]$, and find the condition to determine whether the expression can be effectively computed.

Suppose $E/\mathbb{F}_p$ is an ordinary elliptic curve with Weierstrass function $y^2 = x^3 + ax + b$, $\mathrm{End}(E) \subseteq K$ where $K = \mathbb{Q}(\sqrt{-N})$ is an quadratic imaginary field with discriminant D_K. Define $\omega = \sqrt{-N}$ if $N \equiv 1, 2 \mod 4$, and $\omega = \frac{1+\sqrt{-N}}{2}$ if $N \equiv 3 \mod 4$. Then, the integer ring $\mathcal{O}_K = \mathbb{Z}[\omega]$. Note that $\mathrm{Norm}(\omega) = -D_K/4$ or $(1 - D_K)/4$ and $\mathrm{tr}(\omega) = 0$ or 1. Thus for any $\lambda = i\omega + j \in \mathrm{End}(E) \backslash \mathbb{Z} \subseteq \mathbb{Z}[\omega]$ with characteristic polynomial

$$x^2 + rx + s = 0,$$

we may have a lower bound estimate for s

$$\begin{aligned} s =& \mathrm{Norm}(\lambda) \\ =& i^2 \cdot \mathrm{Norm}(\omega) + ij \cdot \mathrm{tr}(\omega) + j^2 \\ =& i^2(\mathrm{Norm}(\omega) + j/i \cdot \mathrm{tr}(\omega) + j^2/i^2) \\ \geq& \mathrm{Norm}(\omega) + j/i \cdot \mathrm{tr}(\omega) + j^2/i^2 \\ \geq& -D_K/4. \end{aligned}$$

We wish to bound the degree of $[\lambda]$ by the norm s. Actually, we have the following theorem.

Theorem 4. Suppose the elliptic curve $E/\mathbb{F}_p$ is an ordinary elliptic curve, and $[\lambda] \in \mathrm{End}(E)$ is a complex multiplication of E. If $\mathrm{Norm}(\lambda) = s, \deg([\lambda]) = m$, then $s = m$.

Proof. Denote the dual to $[\lambda]$ by $[\lambda']$, the conjugate of λ by $\overline{\lambda}$ and the conjugate of λ' by $\overline{\lambda'}$.

Since $\deg([\lambda]) = m$, we have

$$\lambda \cdot \lambda' = m.$$

Considering the norm on both sides of the equation, we easily know that $\mathrm{Norm}(\lambda') = \frac{m^2}{s}$, which means

$$\lambda' \cdot \overline{\lambda'} = \frac{m^2}{s}.$$

Note that both $[\lambda']$ and $[\overline{\lambda'}]$ are the endomorphisms of E, and the norm of λ' is an integer because $\lambda' \in \mathrm{End}(E) \subseteq \mathcal{O}_K$. Furthermore, we consider both sides of the equation as endomorphisms of E and determine their degrees. Combining the fact that $\deg([\lambda']) = \deg([\lambda]) = m$, we have

$$\deg([\overline{\lambda'}]) = \frac{(m^2/s)^2}{\deg([\lambda'])} = \frac{m^3}{s^2}.$$

Therefore, in general, starting with the conditions $\mathrm{Norm}(\lambda) = s$ and $\deg([\lambda]) = m$, we have

$$\mathrm{Norm}(\overline{\lambda'}) = \mathrm{Norm}(\lambda') = m^2/s, \deg([\overline{\lambda'}]) = m^3/s^2.$$

Now, define a sequence of endomorphisms $\{[\gamma_i]\}_{i \geq 0}$. Let

$$\gamma_0 = \lambda, \quad \gamma_{i+1} = \overline{\gamma_i'}, i \geq 0.$$

From the above process, we can obtain $\mathrm{Norm}(\gamma_i) = m^{2i}/s^{2i-1}$ and $\deg([\gamma_i]) = m^{2i+1}/s^{2i}$ for all $i \geq 0$. Since $\gamma_i \in \mathcal{O}_K$ is integral algebraic and $[\gamma_i]$ is an endomorphism, norm and degree should be integers for all i. So s must be a factor of m.

On the other hand, denote the dual to $[\overline{\lambda}]$ by $[\overline{\lambda}']$, and consider the norm and degree. Similarly, we can get that

$$\mathrm{Norm}(\overline{\lambda}') = s^3/m^2, \deg([\overline{\lambda}']) = s^2/m.$$

Define a sequence $\{[\tau_i]\}_{i \geq 0}$ such that $\tau_0 = \lambda$ and $\tau_{i+1} = \overline{\tau_i}'$ for all $i \geq 0$. In the same way, m must be a factor of s.

In summary, it is clear that $s = m$. □

Now consider the expression of complex multiplication. The endomorphism $[\lambda]$ is rational. Therefore, we set

$$x([\lambda](X,Y)) = f(X)/g(X)$$

for some polynomial $f, g \in \mathbb{F}_p[X]$, where x represents the x-coordinate. According to Theorem 4,

$$s = \deg([\lambda]) = \max\{\deg(f), \deg(g)\}.$$

Based on the maximum of $\deg(f)$ and $\deg(g)$, we can use the method of undetermined coefficients to calculate the formulas of f and g.

Theorem 5. There is an algorithm to calculate the rational expression of f and g relevant to the complex multiplication $[\lambda]$ in time polynomial in $\log p$ and $s = \mathrm{Norm}(\lambda)$.

Proof. Suppose $f(X) = a_s X^s + \cdots + a_1 X + a_0, g(X) = b_s X^s + \cdots + b_1 X + b_0 \in \mathbb{F}_p(X)$. For any point $P(X,Y) \in E(\mathbb{F}_p)$, denote $X' = x([\lambda]P)$. Then, we have $f(X)/g(X) = X'$. That is,

$$X^s a_s + X^{s-1} a_{s-1} + \cdots + X a_1 + a_0 - X' X^s b_s - \cdots - X' X b_1 - X' b_0 = 0.$$

If we compute the corresponding X_i' for enough X_i, we can obtain a system of linear equations for $\{a_s, \cdots, a_0, b_s, \cdots, b_0\}$. Linear algebra tells us that the coefficients can be solved when the number of equations is at least $2s+2$. In general, when we pick equations that are much more than $2s+2$, the solution space of the linear system should be one dimensional.

Therefore, we choose N random points $P_1, \cdots, P_N$ where $N \geq 2s+2$, and define the matrix

$$A_{N\times(2s+2)} = \begin{pmatrix} X_1^s & \cdots 1 & -X_1' X_1^s & \cdots & -X_1' \\ \vdots & \vdots \ \vdots & \vdots & \vdots & \vdots \\ X_N^s & \cdots 1 & -X_N' X_N^s & \cdots & -X_N' \end{pmatrix}.$$

Solve the equation $Ax = 0$ and obtain a vector v. Then, $(a_s, \cdots, a_0, b_s, \cdots, b_0) = v$ up to a constant multiple.

The computation of this algorithm is concentrated in two parts. The time complexity of computing kP for N times is $O(s \log^{2+\epsilon} p)$. The time complexity of solving a matrix equation of order $2s+2$ is $O(s^3 \log^{1+\epsilon} p)$. Therefore, the time complexity of our algorithm is $O(s \log^{2+\epsilon} p) + O(s^3 \log^{1+\epsilon} p)$. □

Specifically, considering that the group of the elliptic curve used practically in cryptography is usually a cyclic group of prime order, there is the following algorithm for such a case.

Algorithm 1. Computation of the rational expression of CM

Input: Finite field $\mathbb{F}_p$; elliptic curve E; $P(x_P, y_P)$ and its prime order n; characteristic polynomial $x^2 + rx + s = 0$ of λ

Output: $h(x)$

1: $k \longleftarrow (-r + \sqrt{r^2 - 4s})/2 \mod n$

2: deg $\longleftarrow s, N \longleftarrow 2s + 2$. If p is small, N could be larger to ensure that matrix A is sufficiently random.

3: **for** $i = 1$ to N **do**

4: Randomly select $P_i(X_i, Y_i) \in \langle P \rangle$

5: $X_i' \longleftarrow x(kP_i)$

6: **end for**

7: $A_{N\times(2\deg+2)} \longleftarrow \begin{pmatrix} X_1^{\deg} & \cdots & 1 & -X_1'X_1^{\deg} & \cdots & -X_1' \\ \vdots & & \vdots & \vdots & & \vdots \\ X_N^{\deg} & \cdots & 1 & -X_N'X_N^{\deg} & \cdots & -X_N' \end{pmatrix}$

8: **if** $\mathrm{rank}(A) < 2\deg+1$ **then**

9: Go to 3

10: **else**

11: $(a_{\deg}, \cdots, a_0, b_{\deg}, \cdots, b_0) \longleftarrow \mathrm{Solve}(Ax = 0)$

12: $f(x) \longleftarrow a_{\deg}x^{\deg} + \cdots + a_0$, $g(x) \longleftarrow b_{\deg}x^{\deg} + \cdots + b_0$

13: $h \longleftarrow f/g$

14: **end if**

15: **return** $h(x)$

Remark 1. The above discussion ensures that $\mathrm{rank}(A) \leq 2\deg+1$. If $\mathrm{rank}(A) < 2\deg+1$, one possible reason is that the selected points are still not random enough, especially when p is small. Therefore, it is necessary to repeat the calculation several times.

Applying this algorithm to a given elliptic curve E over finite field $\mathbb{F}_p$, the calculation is efficient only if s is $O(\log p)$. Based on previous discussion, s has a lower bound $-D_K/4$. For the elliptic curve E, the discriminant of $\mathbb{Z}[\pi]$ is a certain value $D = t^2 - 4p$. Therefore, if we want D_K to be small, $D = m^2 D_K$ must have a large square part and a small square-free part. More specifically, consider

$$t^2 - 4p = m^2 D_K$$

as a factorization. Here, $|D_K|$ needs to be small enough to be approximately $\log p$. This is exactly the condition under which the rational expression of the complex multiplication can be efficiently computed. Therefore, although P-224 and W-448 have complex multiplications, their rational expressions cannot yet be computed efficiently.

4 $\mathbb{Q}$-Elliptic Curves and Their Complex Multiplications

In this section, for a class of special elliptic curves, which are defined over $\mathbb{Q}$ and have nontrival complex multiplications (hereafter refered to as $\mathbb{Q}$-elliptic curves), we give a method to compute the explicit expressions of their complex multiplications. All 13 $\mathbb{Q}$-elliptic curves as well as explicit expressions of their complex multiplications will be stated at the end of this section.

If a quadratic imaginary complex number has a class number of 1, then the corresponding generated elliptic curve can be naturally defined over $\mathbb{Q}$. In this subsection, with the help of Algorithm 1 to calculate the expression over $\mathbb{F}_p$ of a complex multiplication, we give a method to obtain the explicit expressions of the complex multiplications of the $\mathbb{Q}$-elliptic curves.

Proposition 6. ([5, Theorem 2.2])

1) Let $E/\mathbb{C}$ be an elliptic curve with complex multiplication by ring $R \subset \mathbb{C}$. Then,
$$[\alpha]_E^\delta = [\alpha^\delta]_{E^\delta} \quad \text{for all } \alpha \in R \text{ and all } \delta \in \mathrm{Aut}(\mathbb{C}),$$
where $[\cdot]_E$ represents the isomorphism $R \xrightarrow{\sim} \mathrm{End}(E)$.
2) Let E be an elliptic curve over a field $L \subset \mathbb{C}$ and with complex multiplication by the quadratic imaginary field $K \subset \mathbb{C}$. Then, every endomorphism of E is defined over the compositum LK.

For an elliptic curve $E/\mathbb{Q}$ with endomorphism ring $R \subset K = \mathbb{Q}(\sqrt{-N})$, its complex multiplication, if it exists, is defined over K according to Proposition 6.2. This means that we can take a rational expression for the complex multiplication with coefficients in K. The elliptic curve E is defined over $\mathbb{Q}$, which leads to the fact that $j(E) \in \mathbb{Q}$. This case is satisfied only when the class number of the endomorphism ring R is 1. Smith [7] showed that there are totally 13 quadratic imaginary discriminants of class number 1:

$$\mathrm{Disc}(\mathrm{R}_{1,1}) = -4,\ \mathrm{Disc}(\mathrm{R}_{1,2}) = -16,\ \mathrm{Disc}(\mathrm{R}_{2,1}) = -8,$$
$$\mathrm{Disc}(\mathrm{R}_{3,1}) = -3,\ \mathrm{Disc}(\mathrm{R}_{3,2}) = -12,\ \mathrm{Disc}(\mathrm{R}_{3,3}) = -27,$$
$$\mathrm{Disc}(\mathrm{R}_{7,1}) = -7,\ \mathrm{Disc}(\mathrm{R}_{7,2}) = -28,$$
$$\mathrm{Disc}(\mathrm{R}_{11,1}) = -11,\ \mathrm{Disc}(\mathrm{R}_{19,1}) = -19,\ \mathrm{Disc}(\mathrm{R}_{43,1}) = -43,$$
$$\mathrm{Disc}(\mathrm{R}_{67,1}) = -67,\ \mathrm{Disc}(\mathrm{R}_{163,1}) = -163.$$

$R_{N,i}$ is an order of $\mathbb{Q}(\sqrt{-N})$ with conductor i. Denote the elliptic curve associated with $R_{N,i}$ as $E_{N,i}$. The j-invariants of these elliptic curves, also stated by Smith, are all rational numbers, thus the equations are given. Now we calculate the explicit expressions of the complex multiplications of these elliptic curves.

For a complex multiplication $[\lambda]$ of $E_{N,i}$ that satisfies the equation $x^2 + rx + s = 0$, $r, s \in \mathbb{Z}$, we set
$$x([\lambda](X, Y)) = f(X)/g(X)$$

for some polynomials $f(X), g(X) \in K[X]$. Suppose

$$f(X) = (c_s + d_s\sqrt{-N})X^s + \cdots + (c_0 + d_0\sqrt{-N}), \tag{3}$$

$$g(X) = (e_s + f_s\sqrt{-N})X^s + \cdots + (e_0 + f_0\sqrt{-N}), \tag{4}$$

where $s = \text{Norm}(\lambda)$, $c_i, d_i, e_i, f_i \in \mathbb{Q}$ for $i = 0, 1, \cdots, s$. Choose a large prime p such that $-N$ is a quadratic residue modulo p. Since $E_{N,i}$ is defined over $\mathbb{Q}$, we can take an equation for $E_{N,i}$ with coefficients in $\mathbb{Q}$, and reduce the equation to $\mathbb{F}_p$ to obtain the equation of $E_{N,i}/\mathbb{F}_p$. We can also obtain a complex multiplication $[\lambda]_{E_{N,i}/\mathbb{F}_p}$, denoted by $[\lambda]_p$, whose definition equation is still $x^2 + rx+s = 0$. The complex multiplication $[\lambda]_p$ of $E_{N,i}/\mathbb{F}_p$ has the rational expression

$$x([\lambda]_p(X,Y)) = \frac{a_s X^s + \cdots + a_0}{b_s X^s + \cdots + b_0},$$

where $a_i \equiv c_i + d_i N_p \mod p$, $b_i \equiv e_i + f_i N_p \mod p$ for $i = 0, 1, \cdots, s$, and $N_p \in \mathbb{F}_p$ is a root of the function $X^2 \equiv -N \mod p$. We can use Algorithm 1 to calculate a_i and b_i. Additionally, let δ be the complex conjugate. Then, according to Proposition 6.1 as well as the fact that $E/\mathbb{Q}$ is fixed by action of δ, we have

$$[\lambda^\delta] = [\lambda]^\delta.$$

This indicates that $[\bar{\lambda}]$ has rational expression $x([\bar{\lambda}](X,Y)) = \bar{f}(X)/\bar{g}(X)$. Therefore, we have

$$x([\bar{\lambda}]_p(X,Y)) = \frac{a'_s X^s + \cdots + a'_0}{b'_s X^s + \cdots + b'_0},$$

where $a'_i \equiv c_i - d_i N_p \mod p$, $b'_i \equiv e_i - f_i N_p \mod p$ for $i = 0, 1, \cdots, s$. Once again, we can calculate a'_i and b'_i. In summary, we have the following equations:

$$\begin{cases} c_i + d_i N_p \equiv a_i \mod p \\ c_i - d_i N_p = a'_i \mod p \end{cases} \tag{5}$$

and

$$\begin{cases} e_i + f_i N_p \equiv b_i \mod p \\ e_i - f_i N_p \equiv b'_i \mod p \end{cases}. \tag{6}$$

Therefore, we obtain c_i, d_i, e_i, f_i modulo p.

Now, we want to reconstruct $c_i, d_i, e_i, f_i \in \mathbb{Q}$. For a given complex multiplication $[\lambda]$, its coefficients are deterministic. The numerator and denominator of the coefficients have a specific upper bound, called height and denoted by H. When p is large enough so that it is greater than $2H^2$ (or select many primes and use CRT), we can reconstruct the rational fraction c_i, d_i, e_i, f_i even though we do not know the value of H. Specifically, we have the following conclusion.

Lemma 7. $R = \mathbb{Z}/m\mathbb{Z}$ is a ring of m elements, and u is an element of R. There is at most one rational number v such that for the representation $v = n/d$ in minimal terms, it holds that $n \cdot d^{-1} \equiv u \mod m, |n| < \sqrt{m/2}$ and $0 < d < \sqrt{m/2}$.

Proof. If there are two rational numbers $v = n/d$ and $v' = n'/d'$ that satisfy the conditions, then

$$n \cdot d^{-1} \equiv n' \cdot d'^{-1} \equiv u \mod m.$$

This is equivalent to $n \cdot d' - n' \cdot d \equiv 0 \mod m$. However, we have

$$|n \cdot d' - n' \cdot d| \leq |n| \cdot |d'| + |n'| \cdot |d| < m,$$

so it must hold that $n \cdot d' - n' \cdot d = 0$. Thus, $v = v'$. □

The math package Magma has a function 'RationalReconstruction(s)' to complete this process. If a response of false is given, it holds that $H > \sqrt{p/2}$. We need to change a larger prime p. When the reconstruction succeeds, we obtain the explicit expression of complex multiplication $[\lambda]$. The correctness is guaranteed by uniqueness.

We compute all 13 elliptic curve over $\mathbb{Q}$ with complex multiplications and explicit expressions of their complex multiplications. The classic four cases have been given in Sect. 1. The remaining 9 elliptic curves and their complex multiplications are shown at https://github.com/moyuyi/CM.git.

5 Conclusions

Our contributions are summarized in 2 parts: Firstly, we describe a method to determine whether a given elliptic curve over finite field has efficiently computable complex multiplications, and propose a new algorithm to calculate the rational expression of a chosen complex multiplication. Secondly, we construct all 13 classes of elliptic curves over $\mathbb{Q}$ with complex multiplications defined over quadratic imaginary fields. We develop a method to compute the explicit expressions of these complex multiplications. For elliptic curve cryptography, our results provide more useful complex multiplications of elliptic curves.

References

1. Gallant, R.P., Lambert, R.J., Vanstone, S.A.: Faster point multiplication on elliptic curves with efficient endomorphisms. In: Kilian, J. (ed.) CRYPTO 2001. LNCS, vol. 2139, pp. 190–200. Springer, Heidelberg (2001). https://doi.org/10.1007/3-540-44647-8_11
2. Kohel, D.: Endomorphism rings of elliptic curves over finite fields. Math Comp. (1996)
3. Mayer, H.: ECDSA security in bitcoin and ethereum: a research survey. CoinFaabrik **28**(126), 50 (2016)
4. Schoof, R.: Counting points on elliptic curves over finite fields. J. de Theorie des Nombres de Bordeaux **7**, 219–254 (1995)
5. Silverman, J.H.: Advanced Topics in the Arithmetic of Elliptic Curves, vol. 151. Springer, Heidelberg (1994). https://doi.org/10.1007/978-1-4612-0851-8

6. Silverman, J.H.: The Arithmetic of Elliptic Curves, vol. 106. Springer, Heidelberg (2009). https://doi.org/10.1007/978-0-387-09494-6
7. Smith, B.: The $\mathbb{Q}$-curve construction for endomorphism-accelerated elliptic curves. J. Cryptol. **29**(4), 806–832 (2016)
8. Stark, H.M.: Class-numbers of complex quadratic fields. In: Kuijk, W. (ed.) Modular Functions of One Variable I, pp. 153–174. Springer, Heidelberg (1973). https://doi.org/10.1007/978-3-540-38509-7_5
9. Washington, L.C.: Elliptic Curves: Number Theory and Cryptography. Chapman and Hall/CRC, Boca Raton (2008)

Several Classes of Niho Type Boolean Functions with Few Walsh Transform Values

Yanan Wu[1], Nian Li[2(✉)], Xiangyong Zeng[1], and Yuhua Cai[1]

[1] Hubei Key Laboratory of Applied Mathematics, Faculty of Mathematics and Statistics, Hubei University, Wuhan 430062, China
yanan.wu@aliyun.com, xzeng@hubu.edu.cn

[2] Hubei Key Laboratory of Applied Mathematics, School of Cyber Science and Technology, Hubei University, Wuhan 430062, China
nian.li@hubu.edu.cn

Abstract. Boolean functions with n variables are functions from $\mathbb{F}_{2^n}$ to $\mathbb{F}_2$. They play an important role in both cryptographic and error correcting coding activities. The important information about the cryptographic properties of Boolean functions can be obtained from the study of the Walsh transform. Generally speaking, it is difficult to construct functions with few Walsh transform values and determine the Walsh transform value completely due to the difficulty in solving equations. In this paper, we study the Walsh transform of the Niho type Boolean function with the form

$$f(x) = \sum_{i=l}^{k} \mathrm{Tr}_1^n(ax^{s_i(2^m-1)+1}),$$

where k, l, m, n are positive integers satisfying $1 \le l \le k < 2^m$, $n = 2m$ and $a + a^{2^m} \neq 0$. By choosing s_i properly, three classes of such functions with at most 5-valued Walsh transform are obtained. Besides, by using particular techniques in solving equations over finite fields, the value distributions of the Walsh transform for these functions are also completely determined.

Keywords: Boolean function · Walsh transform · Niho exponent · Value distribution

1 Introduction

Let n, m be two positive integers and $\mathbb{F}_{p^n}$ be a finite field with p^n elements, where p is a prime. An S-box is a vectorial Boolean function from $\mathbb{F}_{2^n}$ to $\mathbb{F}_{2^m}$, also called an (n, m)-function. The security of most modern block ciphers importantly relies on cryptographic properties of their S-boxes since S-boxes usually are the only nonlinear components of these cryptosystems. It is therefore significant to investigate the cryptographic properties of functions applied in S-boxes.

Walsh transform is a basic tool in studying the cryptographic properties of cryptographic functions. Let $f(x)$ be a function from $\mathbb{F}_{p^n}$ to $\mathbb{F}_p$. The Walsh transform of $f(x)$ is defined by

Y. Deng and M. Yung (Eds.): Inscrypt 2022, LNCS 13837, pp. 318–333, 2023.
https://doi.org/10.1007/978-3-031-26553-2_17

$$\widehat{f}(\lambda) = \sum_{x \in \mathbb{F}_{p^n}} \omega^{f(x) - \mathrm{Tr}_1^n(\lambda x)}, \ \lambda \in \mathbb{F}_{p^n},$$

where ω is the complex primitive p-th root of unity and $\mathrm{Tr}_1^n(\cdot)$ is the absolute trace function from $\mathbb{F}_{p^n}$ to $\mathbb{F}_p$. The multiset $\{\{\widehat{f}(w) : w \in \mathbb{F}_{p^n}\}\}$ is called the Walsh spectrum of $f(x)$. It is a long-studied problem to construct functions with few Walsh transform values and determine its distributions completely. Some relevant literatures can be found in [8,13–15,20,21].

Walsh transform is also closely related to Gauss periods and the weight distributions of cyclic codes. It can be immediately recognizable that if $f(x) = \mathrm{Tr}_1^n(x^d)$ whose univariate representation consists of exactly one monomial, then the Walsh spectrum of $f(x)$ gives the distribution of cross-correlation values of an m-sequence and its d-decimation, as well as the weight distribution of the cyclic codes of length $p^n - 1$ with two zeros α and α^d, where α is the primitive element of $\mathbb{F}_{p^n}$. In particular, if d is a Niho type exponent over the finite field $\mathbb{F}_{p^n}$ $(n = 2m)$, namely, x^d is linear restricted to $\mathbb{F}_{p^m}$ or in other words,

$$d \equiv p^i \,(\mathrm{mod}\ p^m - 1)\,,$$

it was proven in [3,9] that for any prime p, the cross correlation of m-sequences is at least 4-valued. Moreover, it should be noted that for $p = 2$, all the known d-decimations with 4-valued cross correlation are Niho type exponents. The reader is referred to [4,5,9,16] for more details.

Besides, if considering $f(x)$ is a trace function of a linear combination of power functions with the form

$$f(x) = \sum_{i=1}^{k} \mathrm{Tr}_1^n(a_i x^{d_i}), \tag{1}$$

where $n = 2m$ and d_i is Niho type for $1 \leq i \leq k$, then some new functions with good cryptographic properties can also be produced. The pioneering work in this direction is due to Dobbertin, Leander, Canteaut et al. in [6]. They investigated the bent property of the Boolean function $f(x)$ as defined in (1) when $k = 2$ and $a_1, a_2 \in \mathbb{F}_{2^n}^*$ satisfying $\left(a_1 + a_1^{2^m}\right)^2 = a_2^{2^m+1}$. Based on a classical theorem of Niho [16] and new methods to handle Walsh transforms of Niho power functions, they proposed three pairs of (d_1, d_2) under which $f(x)$ are bent functions. By using the same approach, the authors in [10] generalized one of the constructions in [6] from a linear combination of 2 Niho exponents to that of 2^r Niho exponents. Afterwards, Li, Helleseth, Kholosha and Tang tried to investigate the Walsh spectrum of $f(x)$ in (1), where $k = p^r - 1$ for some interger $r < m$, $d_i = (ip^{m-r} + 1)(p^m - 1) + 1$ and $a_i = a$ satisfying $a^{p^m} + a \neq 0$ for all $1 \leq i \leq k$ [12]. By using the theory of quadratic forms over finite fields and some basic discussions on certain equations, they proved that the Walsh transform of $f(x)$ takes on at most four values and they determined its distributions completely for any prime p. As a special case, they found that $f(x)$ is a bent function when $p = 2$ and $\gcd(m, r) = 1$.

In General, it is not a easy task to construct functions with few Walsh transform values and determine the Walsh transform value completely. Motivated by the previous works, in this paper, we aim to seek functions of the form (1) which have several Walsh transform values. More precisely, we consider Boolean functions $f(x) \in \mathbb{F}_{2^n}[x]$ as

$$f(x) = \sum_{i=l}^{k} \mathrm{Tr}_1^n(ax^{s_i(2^m-1)+1}), \tag{2}$$

where k, l, m, n are positive integers satisfying $1 \leq l \leq k < 2^m$, $n = 2m$ and $a + a^{2^m} \neq 0$. We mainly consider three kinds of parameters (k, l, s_i) of $f(x)$ in (2) as follows: (i) $(k, l, s_i) = (2^{m-1}, 1, 2i)$; (ii) $(k, l, s_i) = (2^{m-2} + 1, 2, 6 - 4i)$ and (iii) $(k, l, s_i) = (2^{m-1}, 1, 4i - 2)$. By employing the method to treat the Walsh transform from [10], the Walsh transform value of $f(x)$ in (2) is related to the number of solutions in unit circle of a high degree equation. Because of the particularity of the parameters we choose, we can further transform this problem into solving equations with low degree over finite fields. Based to the known results on the quadratic equation, cubic equation and the quartic equation, we explicitly characterize the Walsh transform value distributions of $f(x)$ in (2) for the cases (i)-(iii). Notably, all of these functions lead to at most 5-valued Walsh transform, and thus, we provide three other classes of available functions with few Walsh transform values.

2 Preliminaries

In this section, we state some basic notations and results which will be mainly used in the sequel.

2.1 The Walsh Transform

For a given function $f(x)$, its Walsh transform has the following well-known properties.

Lemma 1 ([2]). *Let $f : \mathbb{F}_{p^n} \to \mathbb{F}_p$ be a function in n variables, then its Walsh transform satisfies*

(1) $\sum_{\lambda \in \mathbb{F}_{p^n}} \widehat{f}(\lambda) = p^n w^{f(0)}$;
(2) $\sum_{\lambda \in \mathbb{F}_{p^n}} |\widehat{f}(\lambda)|^2 = p^{2n}$ (Parseval's relation).

Let $n = 2m$ and p be a prime, then x^{p^m} is called the conjugate of $x \in \mathbb{F}_{p^n}$. For simplify, we denote it by $\overline{x}$, i.e., $\overline{x} = x^{p^m}$. The unit circle of $\mathbb{F}_{p^n}$ is the set

$$U = \{x \in \mathbb{F}_{p^n} : x\overline{x} = 1\}.$$

An equivalent characterization on the Walsh spectrum of $f(x)$ with the form (1) for any prime p has been stated in [10,17] as below.

Lemma 2. *Let $n = 2m$, $q = p^m$, k be a positive integer and $d_i = (q-1)s_i + 1$ for $i = 1, 2, \cdots, k$. The Walsh transform value of $\sum_{i=1}^{k} \mathrm{Tr}_1^n\left(a_i x^{d_i}\right)$ is given by*

$$(N(\lambda) - 1)q,\ \lambda \in \mathbb{F}_{q^2}$$

where $N(\lambda)$ is the number of $z \in U$ such that

$$\sum_{i=1}^{k}\left(a_i z^{s_i} + \overline{a}_i z^{1-s_i}\right) - \overline{\lambda} z - \lambda = 0.$$

2.2 The Roots of Low-Degree Equations

In this subsection, we are going to review the relevant results for solutions of low-degree equations over $\mathbb{F}_{2^n}$ including the quadratic equation, cubic equation and the quartic equation. The following lemma describes the root distributions in U of a quadratic equation.

Lemma 3 ([1,7,18]). *Let $n = 2m$ be an even positive integer and $a, b \in \mathbb{F}_{2^n}^*$. Then the quadratic equation $x^2 + ax + b = 0$ has solutions in $\mathbb{F}_{2^n}$ if and only if $\mathrm{Tr}_1^n\left(\frac{b}{a^2}\right) = 0$. Furthermore,*

(1) *both solutions in the unit circle if and only if*

$$b = \frac{a}{\overline{a}} \text{ and } \mathrm{Tr}_1^m\left(\frac{b}{a^2}\right) = \mathrm{Tr}_1^m\left(\frac{1}{a\overline{a}}\right) = 1;$$

(2) *exactly one solution in the unit circle, if and only if*

$$b \neq \frac{a}{\overline{a}} \text{ and } (1 + b\overline{b})(1 + a\overline{b} + b\overline{b}) + a^2\overline{b} + \overline{a}^2 b = 0.$$

In the following, descriptions on the factorizations of cubic polynomials and quatric polynomials over the finite field $\mathbb{F}_{2^n}$ will be presented. Given a cubic polynomial $f(x) = x^3 + a_1 x + a_0$ with $a_0 \neq 0$. Let t_1, t_2 denote the roots of $t^2 + a_0 t + a_1^3 = 0$. For simplify, if $f(x)$ factors into a product of three linear factors, we write $f = (1, 1, 1)$. If $f(x)$ factors as a product of a linear factor and an irreducible quadratic factor, we write $f = (1, 2)$. Otherwise, we will write $f = (3)$.

Lemma 4 ([19]). *Let $f(x) = x^3 + a_1 x + a_0 \in \mathbb{F}_{2^n}[x]$ and $a_0 \neq 0$. Then the factorization of $f(x)$ over $\mathbb{F}_{2^n}$ can be characterized as*

(1) $f = (1, 1, 1) \Leftrightarrow \mathrm{Tr}_1^n\left(a_1^3/a_0^2\right) = \mathrm{Tr}_1^n(1)$, *$t_1$, t_2 are cubes in* $\mathbb{F}_{2^n}$ (n even), $\mathbb{F}_{2^{2n}}$ (n odd);
(2) $f = (1, 2) \Leftrightarrow \mathrm{Tr}_1^n\left(a_1^3/a_0^2\right) \neq \mathrm{Tr}_1^n(1)$;
(3) $f = (3) \Leftrightarrow \mathrm{Tr}_1^n\left(a_1^3/a_0^2\right) = \mathrm{Tr}_1^n(1)$, *$t_1$, t_2 are not cubes in* $\mathbb{F}_{2^n}$ (n even), $\mathbb{F}_{2^{2n}}$ (n odd).

Similarly as cubic polynomials, the factorization of a quartic polynomial over finite field $\mathbb{F}_{2^n}$ can be given in terms of the roots of a related cubic equation. Let $f(x) = x^4 + a_2x^2 + a_1x + a_0$ with $a_0a_1 \neq 0$ and $g(y) = y^3 + a_2y + a_1$ with the roots r_1, r_2, r_3. When the roots exist in $\mathbb{F}_{2^n}$, we set $w_i = a_0r_i^2/a_1^2$.

Lemma 5 ([11]). *Let $f(x) = x^4 + a_2x^2 + a_1x + a_0 \in \mathbb{F}_{2^n}[x]$ with $a_0a_1 \neq 0$. The factorization of $f(x)$ over $\mathbb{F}_{2^n}$ are characterized as follows:*

(1) $f = (1, 1, 1, 1) \Leftrightarrow g = (1, 1, 1)$ *and* $\mathrm{Tr}_1^n(w_1) = \mathrm{Tr}_1^n(w_2) = \mathrm{Tr}_1^n(w_3) = 0$;
(2) $f = (2, 2) \Leftrightarrow g = (1, 1, 1)$ *and* $\mathrm{Tr}_1^n(w_1) = 0, \mathrm{Tr}_1^n(w_2) = \mathrm{Tr}_1^n(w_3) = 1$;
(3) $f = (1, 3) \Leftrightarrow g = (3)$;
(4) $f = (1, 1, 2) \Leftrightarrow g = (1, 2)$ *and* $\mathrm{Tr}_1^n(w_1) = 0$;
(5) $f = (4) \Leftrightarrow g = (1, 2)$ *and* $\mathrm{Tr}_1^n(w_1) = 1$.

Next, we will present our main results of this paper and give the corresponding proofs.

3 The Value Distributions of Niho-type Functions

From now on, we always assume $q = 2^m$ and observe the functions $f(x)$ with the form (2). By selecting s_i properly which is actually linear on i, namely, $s_i = \mu + \nu i$ for some integers μ and ν, we propose three classes of functions whose Walsh transforms take on at most five values and the value distributions are completely determined.

According to Lemma 2, in order to investigate the Walsh transform values of $f(x)$, we need to calculate $N(\lambda)$, i.e., the number of roots $z \in U$ of

$$\sum_{i=l}^{k} \left(az^{s_i} + \overline{a}z^{1-s_i}\right) + \overline{\lambda}z + \lambda = 0. \tag{3}$$

Since $s_i = \mu + \nu i$ and μ, ν are integers, we can obtain that if $z \neq 1$, then

$$\begin{aligned}\sum_{i=l}^{k} z^{s_i} = z^{\mu}\sum_{i=l}^{k} z^{\nu i} &= z^{\mu}\frac{z^{\nu l}\left(1 + (z^{\nu})^{k-l+1}\right)}{1 + z^{\nu}} \\ &= \frac{z^{\mu}\left(z^{\nu l} + z^{\nu(k+1)}\right)}{1 + z^{\nu}}\end{aligned}$$

and

$$\begin{aligned}\sum_{i=l}^{k} z^{1-s_i} = z^{1-\mu}\sum_{i=l}^{k} z^{-\nu i} &= z^{1-\mu}\frac{z^{-\nu l}\left(1 + (z^{-\nu})^{k-l+1}\right)}{1 + z^{-\nu}} \\ &= \frac{z^{1-\mu}\left(z^{\nu(1-l)} + z^{-\nu k}\right)}{1 + z^{\nu}}.\end{aligned}$$

Therefore, when considering the solution $z \in U\backslash\{1\}$ of (3), it is equivalent to consider the following equation

$$az^{\mu}\left(z^{\nu l}+z^{\nu(k+1)}\right)+\overline{a}z^{1-\mu}\left(z^{\nu(1-l)}+z^{-\nu k}\right)+\left(\overline{\lambda}z+\lambda\right)\left(1+z^{\nu}\right)=0. \quad (4)$$

Moreover, one should note that $z=1$ is a solution of (3) if and only if

$$\sum_{i=l}^{k}(a+\overline{a})+\overline{\lambda}+\lambda=0. \quad (5)$$

3.1 Niho-type Function with $s_i = 2i$

In this subsection, we mainly study the Walsh transform of

$$f(x)=\sum_{i=1}^{2^{m-1}}\mathrm{Tr}_1^n(ax^{s_i(q-1)+1}),\ s_i=2i. \quad (6)$$

Note that $k=2^{m-1}$, $l=1$, $\mu=0$ and $\nu=2$ in this case. Therefore, based on the discussion above, $z=1$ is a solution of (3) if and only if $\overline{\lambda}+\lambda=0$, i.e., $\lambda \in \mathbb{F}_q$, due to (5). Furthermore, from (4), when $z \in U\backslash\{1\}$, (3) can be written as

$$\overline{\lambda}z^3+(a+\overline{a}+\lambda)z^2+\left(a+\overline{a}+\overline{\lambda}\right)z+\lambda=0.$$

By dividing $z+1$, it can be further reduced to

$$\overline{\lambda}z^2+\left(a+\overline{a}+\lambda+\overline{\lambda}\right)z+\lambda=0. \quad (7)$$

One can see that (7) has at most 2 solutions in $U\backslash\{1\}$ due to $a+\overline{a}\neq 0$. Hence, when $\lambda \notin \mathbb{F}_q$, $N(\lambda)$ takes values from $\{0, 1, 2\}$. Otherwise, when $\lambda \in \mathbb{F}_q$, $N(\lambda)$ takes values from $\{1, 2, 3\}$ since $z=1$ is always a solution to (3) in this case. Furthermore, we claim that the Walsh transform of $f(x)$ is at most 4-valued.

Lemma 6. *Let $f(x)$ be defined in (6) and $N(\lambda)$ be defined in Lemma 2. Then $N(\lambda)=3$ occurs $\frac{q}{2}$ times when λ runs over $\mathbb{F}_{q^2}$.*

Proof. From above analysis, $N(\lambda)=3$ can happen only when $\lambda \in \mathbb{F}_q$. Therefore, to prove this lemma, it is sufficient to determine the number of $\lambda \in \mathbb{F}_q$ such that

$$\lambda z^2+(a+\overline{a})z+\lambda=0 \quad (8)$$

has exactly 2 solutions in $U\backslash\{1\}$ from (7). Firstly, we have $\lambda\neq 0$. Otherwise, if $\lambda=0$, then (8) has no solution in $U\backslash\{1\}$ due to $a+\overline{a}\neq 0$. Now assume that $\lambda \in \mathbb{F}_q^*$. Then by using Lemma 3, (8) has 2 solutions in $U\backslash\{1\}$ if and only if

$$\mathrm{Tr}_1^m\left(\frac{1}{\left(\frac{a+\overline{a}}{\lambda}\right)^2}\right)=\mathrm{Tr}_1^m\left(\frac{\lambda}{a+\overline{a}}\right)=1.$$

Then the result follows. This completes the proof. □

From Lemmas 1, 2 and Lemma 6, we can determine the Walsh spectrum of $f(x)$ in (6) as below.

Theorem 1. *Let m and n be positive integers with $n = 2m$. The Walsh transform of $f(x)$ defined as (6) with $a + \overline{a} \neq 0$ takes values from $\{-q, 0, q, 2q\}$. Furthermore, the value distributions is given by*

$$\widehat{f}(\lambda) = \begin{cases} -q, \text{ occurs } \frac{q(q-2)}{2} \text{ times;} \\ 0, \quad \text{occurs } \frac{3q}{2} \text{ times;} \\ q, \quad \text{occurs } \frac{q(q-2)}{2} \text{ times;} \\ 2q, \text{ occurs } \frac{q}{2} \text{ times.} \end{cases}$$

Proof. From the analysis above, we can obtain that $N(\lambda)$ takes values from the set $\{0, 1, 2, 3\}$ when λ runs through $\mathbb{F}_{q^2}$ and therefore, the first assertion follows. Assume that

$$A_i = |\{\lambda \in \mathbb{F}_{q^2} : N(\lambda) = i\}|, \ 0 \leq i \leq 3.$$

According to Lemma 2, $\widehat{f}(\lambda)$ takes values $(i-1)q$ exactly A_i $(0 \leq i \leq 3)$ times, respectively. Note that $A_3 = \frac{q}{2}$ from Lemma 6. Besides, Lemma 1 gives that

$$\begin{cases} \sum_{i=0}^{3} A_i = q^2; \\ \sum_{i=0}^{3} A_i(i-1)q = q^2; \\ \sum_{i=0}^{3} A_i((i-1)q)^2 = q^4 \end{cases}$$

due to $f(0) = 0$. The proof is completed by solving the above system of linear equations. □

Example 1. Let $m = 3$, ω be a primitive element of $\mathbb{F}_{2^6}$ and $a = \omega$. Magma experiment shows that the Walsh transform of $f(x)$ defined as (6) is 4-valued and its value distribution is

$$\widehat{f}(\lambda) = \begin{cases} -8, \text{ occurs } 24 \text{ times;} \\ 0, \quad \text{occurs } 12 \text{ times;} \\ 8, \quad \text{occurs } 24 \text{ times;} \\ 16, \text{ occurs } 4 \text{ times} \end{cases}$$

which is consistent with the result given in Theorem 1.

3.2 Niho-type Function with $s_i = 6 - 4i$

In this subsection, we are going to consider the function as

$$f(x) = \sum_{i=2}^{2^{m-2}+1} \mathrm{Tr}_1^n(ax^{s_i(q-1)+1}), \ s_i = 6 - 4i. \tag{9}$$

By taking $k = 2^{m-2}+1$, $l = 2$, $\mu = 6$ and $\nu = -4$, we can get that $z = 1$ is a solution to (3) if and only if $\lambda + \overline{\lambda} = 0$, i.e., $\lambda \in \mathbb{F}_q$. Besides, when $z \in U\backslash\{1\}$, (3) can be reduced to

$$\overline{\lambda}z^5 + \lambda z^4 + (a+\overline{a})z^3 + (a+\overline{a})z^2 + \overline{\lambda}z + \lambda = 0$$

by (4), which is equivalent to

$$\overline{\lambda}z^4 + (\lambda+\overline{\lambda})z^3 + (a+\overline{a}+\lambda+\overline{\lambda})z^2 + (\lambda+\overline{\lambda})z + \lambda = 0 \tag{10}$$

due to $z \neq 1$. Let $u \in \mathbb{F}_q$, $r \in \mathbb{F}_{q^2}\backslash\mathbb{F}_q$. It is clear that the mapping $u \mapsto \frac{u+r}{u+\overline{r}}$ is a bijective and $\frac{u+r}{u+\overline{r}} \in U\backslash\{1\}$. Without loss of generality, selecting $r \in \mathbb{F}_{q^2}\backslash\mathbb{F}_q$ such that $r + \overline{r} = 1$. By substituting z with $\frac{u+r}{u+\overline{r}}$ in (10), the number of solutions $z \in U\backslash\{1\}$ to (10) is equal to the number of solutions $u \in \mathbb{F}_q$ to

$$\overline{\lambda}\left(\frac{u+r}{u+\overline{r}}\right)^4 + (\lambda+\overline{\lambda})\left(\frac{u+r}{u+\overline{r}}\right)^3 + (a+\overline{a}+\lambda+\overline{\lambda})\left(\frac{u+r}{u+\overline{r}}\right)^2 + (\overline{\lambda}+\lambda)\left(\frac{u+r}{u+\overline{r}}\right) + \lambda = 0.$$

Multiplying both sides of above equation by $(u+\overline{r})^4$ gives

$$c_0u^4 + c_1u^2 + c_2u + c_3 = 0, \tag{11}$$

where $c_0 = a+\overline{a}$, $c_1 = a+\overline{a}$, $c_2 = \lambda+\overline{\lambda}$ and $c_3 = \lambda\overline{r} + \overline{\lambda}r + (a+\overline{a})r^2\overline{r}^2$. Note that $c_i \in \mathbb{F}_q$ for all $0 \leq i \leq 3$ and $c_0 \neq 0$ due to $a + \overline{a} \neq 0$. Thus, (11) becomes

$$u^4 + u^2 + \frac{c_2}{c_0}u + \frac{c_3}{c_0} = 0. \tag{12}$$

In order to determine the Walsh transform value distributions of $f(x)$ defined in (9), it is necessary to calculate the number of solutions $u \in \mathbb{F}_q$ of (12) when λ runs over $\mathbb{F}_{q^2}$. For the case that $\lambda \in \mathbb{F}_q$ and $\lambda \in \mathbb{F}_{q^2}\backslash\mathbb{F}_q$, we have the following results, respectively.

Lemma 7. *Let $f(x)$ be defined in (9) and $N(\lambda)$ be defined in Lemma 2. If $\lambda \in \mathbb{F}_q$, then $N(\lambda)$ takes values from the set $\{1, 3\}$. Moreover, both $N(\lambda) = 1$ and $N(\lambda) = 3$ occur $\frac{q}{2}$ times.*

Proof. One should note that $\lambda \in \mathbb{F}_q$ if and only if $z = 1$ is a solution to (3). For $z \in U\backslash\{1\}$, (3) is reduced to $u^4 + u^2 + \frac{c_3}{c_0} = 0$ due to (12) and $\lambda + \overline{\lambda} = 0$. Let $v = u^2$, then the above equation is equal to

$$v^2 + v + \frac{\lambda}{a+\overline{a}} + r^2\overline{r}^2 = 0. \tag{13}$$

From Lemma 3, one can see that (13) has either 2 solutions or no solution, depending on whether the value of $\mathrm{Tr}_1^m\left(\frac{\lambda}{a+\overline{a}} + r^2\overline{r}^2\right)$ equals 0 or not, which implies that the number of solutions to (12) is 2 or 0. Therefore, $N(\lambda) = 1$ or $N(\lambda) = 3$ and both cases occur 2^{m-1} times when λ runs through $\mathbb{F}_q$ since the balance of trace function. This completes the proof. $\square$

Lemma 8. *Let $f(x)$ be defined in (9) and $N(\lambda)$ be defined in Lemma 2. If $\lambda \in \mathbb{F}_{q^2} \backslash \mathbb{F}_q$, then $N(\lambda)$ takes values from the set $\{0, 1, 2, 4\}$. Moreover, $N(\lambda) = 1$ occurs $\frac{q(q-1)}{3}$ times when m is even and $\frac{q(q+1)}{3}$ times when m is odd.*

Proof. One can see that (12) has at most four solutions in $\mathbb{F}_q$. Suppose it has three solutions in $\mathbb{F}_q$, then two of them have multiplicity 1 and one of them has multiplicity 2. On the other hand, if (12) has repeated roots, then its derivative have a common solution with it which implies that $c_2 = 0$, a contradiction with $\lambda \in \mathbb{F}_{q^2} \backslash \mathbb{F}_q$. Therefore, (12) has 0, 1, 2 or 4 solutions when λ runs through $\mathbb{F}_{q^2} \backslash \mathbb{F}_q$. This implies $N(\lambda)$ takes values from the set $\{0, 1, 2, 4\}$.

According to Lemma 5(3), (12) has one solution indicates that the polynomial $g(y) = y^3 + y + \frac{\lambda + \overline{\lambda}}{a + \overline{a}} = (3)$. Considering the corresponding quadratic polynomial

$$H(t) = t^2 + \theta t + 1, \ \theta = \frac{\lambda + \overline{\lambda}}{a + \overline{a}}.$$

Let t_1, t_2 be the zeros of $H(t)$. Clearly, $t_1 t_2 = 1$ and $t_1 + t_2 = \theta$. By Lemma 4(c), $g = (3)$ if and only if $\mathrm{Tr}_1^m\left(\frac{1}{\theta}\right) = \mathrm{Tr}_1^m(1)$ and t_1, t_2 not cubes in $\mathbb{F}_q$ when m is even, or $\mathbb{F}_{q^2}$ when m is odd. As $t_1 t_2 = 1$, t_1, t_2 are both cubes or both not cubes in $\mathbb{F}_q$ if $\mathrm{Tr}_1^m\left(\frac{1}{\theta}\right) = 0$, or $\mathbb{F}_{q^2}$ if $\mathrm{Tr}_1^m\left(\frac{1}{\theta}\right) = 1$.

If m is even, $g = (3)$ if and only if $\mathrm{Tr}_1^m\left(\frac{1}{\theta}\right) = 0$ and t_1 is not a cube in $\mathbb{F}_q^*$ since $t_1 \neq 0$. Let

$$T_1 = \{t_1 \in \mathbb{F}_q^* : t_1^{\frac{q-1}{3}} \neq 1\}.$$

It can be easily verified that $\#T_1 = \frac{2}{3}(q-1)$. On the other hand, for any $t_1 \in T_1$, we have $\mathrm{Tr}_1^m(\frac{1}{\theta}) = 0$ since $t_1, t_2 \in \mathbb{F}_q$ are the roots of $H(t) = 0$. Review that $t_1 t_2 = 1$ and $t_1 + t_2 = \theta$, the relation between t_1 and θ is 2-to-1. Therefore, one have

$$E_1 = |\{\theta \in \mathbb{F}_q : g = (3)\}| = \frac{q-1}{3}.$$

It induces that $N(\lambda) = 1$ occurs $\frac{q}{3}(q-1)$ times when λ runs through $\mathbb{F}_{q^2} \backslash \mathbb{F}_q$ due to $\theta = \frac{\lambda + \overline{\lambda}}{a + \overline{a}}$.

If m is odd, then $g = (3)$ if and only if $\mathrm{Tr}_1^m\left(\frac{1}{\theta}\right) = 1$ and t_1 is not a cube in $\mathbb{F}_{q^2}^*$. By Lemma 3, one has $t_1 \in U$. Similarly as m is even, considering the set $\{t_1 \in U : t_1^{\frac{q+1}{3}} \neq 1\}$ which has cardinality $\frac{2}{3}(q+1)$. One can conclude that the corresponding number of λ satisfying $N(\lambda) = 1$ is $\frac{q}{3}(q+1)$ and we omit the proof here. This completes the proof. □

From Lemmas 7 and 8, we can see that the Walsh transform of $f(x)$ defined by (9) takes at most five possible values. With the help of Lemmas 1, 7 and 8, we determine the Walsh transform value distribution as stated in Theorem 2.

Theorem 2. *Let m be a positive integer, $n = 2m$ and $q = 2^m$. The Walsh transform of $f(x)$ defined as*

$$f(x) = \sum_{i=2}^{2^{m-2}+1} \mathrm{Tr}_1^n(a x^{s_i(q-1)+1}), \ s_i = 6 - 4i$$

for $a \in \mathbb{F}_{q^2}$ and $a + \overline{a} \neq 0$ takes values from $\{-q, 0, q, 2q, 3q\}$. Further, when λ runs through $\mathbb{F}_{q^2}$, the value distributions is given by

$$\widehat{f}(\lambda) = \begin{cases} -q, \text{ occurs } \frac{q(3q-4)}{8} \text{ times;} \\ 0, \text{ occurs } \frac{q(2q+1)}{6} \text{ times;} \\ q, \text{ occurs } \frac{q^2}{4} \text{ times;} \\ 2q, \text{ occurs } \frac{q}{2} \text{ times;} \\ 3q, \text{ occurs } \frac{q(q-4)}{24} \text{ times} \end{cases}$$

when m is even, and

$$\widehat{f}(\lambda) = \begin{cases} -q, \text{ occurs } \frac{3q(q-2)}{8} \text{ times;} \\ 0, \text{ occurs } \frac{q(2q+5)}{6} \text{ times;} \\ q, \text{ occurs } \frac{q(q-2)}{4} \text{ times;} \\ 2q, \text{ occurs } \frac{q}{2} \text{ times;} \\ 3q, \text{ occurs } \frac{q(q-2)}{24} \text{ times} \end{cases}$$

when m is odd.

Proof. The first assertion is due to Lemmas 2, 7 and 8. Assume that

$$A_i = |\{\lambda \in \mathbb{F}_{q^2} : N(\lambda) = i\}|, \ 0 \leq i \leq 4.$$

Then $\widehat{f}(\lambda)$ takes values $(i-1)q$ exactly A_i $(0 \leq i \leq 4)$ times, respectively. Again by Lemmas 7 and 8, one has $A_3 = \frac{q}{2}$ and $A_1 = \frac{q}{2} + \frac{q}{3}(q-1) = \frac{q(2q+1)}{6}$ if m is even and otherwise, $A_1 = \frac{q}{2} + \frac{q}{3}(q+1) = \frac{q(2q+5)}{6}$. Besides, Lemma 1 gives that

$$\begin{cases} \sum_{i=0}^{4} A_i = q^2; \\ \sum_{i=0}^{4} A_i(i-1)q = q^2; \\ \sum_{i=0}^{4} A_i((i-1)q)^2 = q^4 \end{cases}$$

due to $f(0) = 0$. The proof is completed by solving the above system of linear equations. □

Example 2. Let $m = 4$, $a = \omega$, where ω is a primitive element of $\mathbb{F}_{2^8}$. Then one has $a + \overline{a} \neq 0$. By a Magma program, it shows that the Walsh transform of $f(x)$ defined as (9) is 5-valued and its value distribution is given by

$$\widehat{f}(\lambda) = \begin{cases} -16, \text{ occurs } 88 \text{ times;} \\ 0, \text{ occurs } 88 \text{ times;} \\ 16, \text{ occurs } 64 \text{ times;} \\ 32, \text{ occurs } 8 \text{ times;} \\ 48, \text{ occurs } 8 \text{ times} \end{cases}$$

which is consistent with the result given in Theorem 2.

Example 3. Let $m = 5$, $a = \omega$, where ω is a primitive element of $\mathbb{F}_{2^{10}}$. By a Magma program, it shows that $a + \overline{a} \neq 0$ and the Walsh transform of $f(x)$ defined as (9) is 5-valued whose value distribution is given by

$$\widehat{f}(\lambda) = \begin{cases} -32, \text{ occurs } 360 \text{ times;} \\ 0, \quad \text{ occurs } 368 \text{ times;} \\ 32, \quad \text{occurs } 240 \text{ times;} \\ 64, \quad \text{occurs } 16 \text{ times;} \\ 96, \quad \text{occurs } 40 \text{ times.} \end{cases}$$

It is also consistent with the result given in Theorem 2.

3.3 Niho-type Function with $s_i = 4i - 2$

In this subsection, we continue to discuss the other kind of Niho-type functions of the form

$$f(x) = \sum_{i=1}^{2^{m-1}} \mathrm{Tr}_1^n \left(a x^{s_i(q-1)+1} \right), \; s_i = 4i - 2. \tag{14}$$

Similarly as before, it is sufficient to calculate the number of roots $z \in U$ of

$$\sum_{i=1}^{2^{m-1}} \left(a z^{4i-2} + \overline{a} z^{1-(4i-2)} \right) + \overline{\lambda} z + \lambda = 0 \tag{15}$$

Note that $z = 1$ is a solution to (15) if and only if $\lambda \in \mathbb{F}_q$. For any $z \in U \backslash \{1\}$, (15) is equivalent to

$$(\overline{a} + \overline{\lambda}) z^3 + \lambda z^2 + \overline{\lambda} z + \lambda + a = 0$$

by (4). Substituting z with $\frac{u+r}{u+\overline{r}}$, where $u \in \mathbb{F}_q$ and $r = a$ for some $a \in \mathbb{F}_{q^2} \backslash \mathbb{F}_q$, then the number of solutions to (15) in $z \in U \backslash \{1\}$ is reduced to calculate the number of solutions $u \in \mathbb{F}_q$ to

$$\tau_0 u^3 + \tau_1 u + \tau_2 = 0,$$

where $\tau_0 = a + \overline{a}$, $\tau_1 = \left(a\overline{a} + (\lambda + \overline{\lambda})(a + \overline{a}) \right)(a + \overline{a})$ and $\tau_2 = \left(a\overline{a} + \overline{\lambda} a + \lambda \overline{a} \right)(a + \overline{a})^2$. Therefore, the above equation is equivalent to

$$u^3 + \frac{\tau_1}{\tau_0} u + \frac{\tau_2}{\tau_0} = 0 \tag{16}$$

due to $\tau_0 = a + \overline{a} \neq 0$.

In order to solve the distribution of the Walsh transform of $f(x)$ defined in (14), we firstly present the values of $N(\lambda)$ for $\lambda \in \mathbb{F}_q$ and $\lambda \in \mathbb{F}_{q^2} \backslash \mathbb{F}_q$, respectively.

Lemma 9. *Let $f(x)$ be defined in (14) and $N(\lambda)$ be defined in Lemma 2. When $\lambda \in \mathbb{F}_q$ runs through $\mathbb{F}_q$, then $N(\lambda)$ takes values from the set $\{1, 2, 3, 4\}$. Moreover, $N(\lambda)$ takes value 2 or 4 exactly $\frac{q}{2}$ times or $\frac{q-4}{6}$ times if m is even; otherwise, exactly $\frac{q}{2} - 1$ times or $\frac{q-2}{6}$ times if m is odd.*

Proof. Since $\lambda \in \mathbb{F}_q$, $z = 1$ must be a solution to (15). For $z \in U\backslash\{1\}$, the number of solutions to (15) is equal to the number of solutions to (16), which is reduced to

$$u^3 + a\overline{a}u + (a\overline{a} + a\lambda + \overline{a}\lambda)(a + \overline{a}) = 0 \tag{17}$$

due to $\lambda + \overline{\lambda} = 0$. If $a\overline{a} + a\lambda + \overline{a}\lambda = 0$, then $\lambda = \frac{a\overline{a}}{a+\overline{a}} \in \mathbb{F}_q$ and it induces that (17) has solutions $u_1 = 0$ and $u_2 = (a\overline{a})^{\frac{1}{2}}$. Since (17) is a cubic equation, $N(\lambda)$ takes values $\{1, 2, 3, 4\}$ when $\lambda \in \mathbb{F}_q$. Hereafter, we will always assume that $\lambda \neq \frac{a\overline{a}}{a+\overline{a}}$. Notice that $N(\lambda)$ takes value 2 or 4 only if (17) has exactly one solution or three solutions.

(i) From Lemma 4, one can easily check that (17) has only one solution if and only if $\mathrm{Tr}_1^m\left(\frac{(a\overline{a})^3}{(a+\overline{a})^2(a\overline{a}+\lambda(a+\overline{a}))^2}\right) \neq \mathrm{Tr}_1^m(1)$. Therefore, $N(\lambda) = 2$ occurs $\frac{q}{2}$ times or $\frac{q}{2} - 1$ times for even m and odd m respectively, since $(a\overline{a} + \lambda(a + \overline{a}))(a + \overline{a})$ is a permutation over $\mathbb{F}_q$ when λ ranges over $\mathbb{F}_q$.

(ii) (17) has three solutions. Again by Lemma 4, this case happens if and only if $\mathrm{Tr}_1^m\left(\frac{(a\overline{a})^3}{(a+\overline{a})^2(a\overline{a}+\lambda(a+\overline{a}))^2}\right) = \mathrm{Tr}_1^m(1)$ and t_1, t_2 cubes in $\mathbb{F}_q$ (m even), $\mathbb{F}_{q^2}$ (m odd), where t_1, t_2 are the roots of

$$t^2 + (a\overline{a} + a\lambda + \overline{a}\lambda)(a + \overline{a})t + (a\overline{a})^3 = 0. \tag{18}$$

One can see that $t_1 + t_2 = (a\overline{a} + a\lambda + \overline{a}\lambda)(a + \overline{a})$, $t_1 t_2 = (a\overline{a})^3$.

When m is even, $\mathrm{Tr}_1^m\left(\frac{(a\overline{a})^3}{(a+\overline{a})^2(a\overline{a}+\lambda(a+\overline{a}))^2}\right) = 0$ for any $t_1 \in \mathbb{F}_q$ and $t_1^{\frac{q-1}{3}} = 1$ since t_1 is the root of (18). On the other hand, if $t_1 = (a\overline{a})^{\frac{3}{2}}$ which is also a cube, then $a\overline{a} + a\lambda + \overline{a}\lambda = 0$ due to $t_1 = t_2 = (a\overline{a})^{\frac{3}{2}}$, which contradicts the assumption $\lambda \neq \frac{a\overline{a}}{a+\overline{a}}$. Thus, one has

$$|\{\lambda \in \mathbb{F}_q : N(\lambda) = 4\}| = \frac{1}{2}|\{t_1 \in \mathbb{F}_q : t_1^{\frac{q-1}{3}} = 1 \text{ and } t_1 \neq (a\overline{a})^{\frac{3}{2}}\}| = \frac{q-4}{6}.$$

When m is odd, t_1 must belong to the extension field of $\mathbb{F}_q$ due to $\mathrm{Tr}_1^m(1) = 1$. Denote

$$S_1 = \{t_1 \in \mathbb{F}_{q^2}\backslash\mathbb{F}_q : t_1^{\frac{q^2-1}{3}} = 1\}$$

and

$$S_2 = \cup_{j=1}^{\frac{q-2}{3}} \mathbb{F}_q^* \cdot \alpha^{3j},\ \alpha \text{ is a primitive element of } \mathbb{F}_{q^2}.$$

Then we have the following facts.

Fact 1: $|S_1| = |\{t_1 \in \mathbb{F}_{q^2} : t_1^{\frac{q^2-1}{3}} = 1\}| - |\{t_1 \in \mathbb{F}_q : t_1^{\frac{q^2-1}{3}} = 1\}| = \frac{(q-1)(q-2)}{3}$ due to $3\,|\,(q+1)$.

Fact 2: $\mathbb{F}_q^* \cdot \alpha^{3j_1} \cap \mathbb{F}_q^* \cdot \alpha^{3j_2} = \emptyset$ for any $1 \leq j_1, j_2 \leq \frac{q-2}{3}$ and $j_1 \neq j_2$. Suppose $b \in \mathbb{F}_q^* \cdot \alpha^{3j_1} \cap \mathbb{F}_q^* \cdot \alpha^{3j_2}$, then there exists $b_1, b_2 \in \mathbb{F}_q^*$ satisfying $b = b_1\alpha^{3j_1} = b_2\alpha^{3j_2}$. It implies that $\alpha^{3(j_1-j_2)} = \frac{b_2}{b_1} \in \mathbb{F}_q^*$. Therefore, $3(j_1 - j_2) \equiv 0 \pmod{q+1}$. This holds only if $j_1 = j_2$ due to $|j_1 - j_2| < \frac{q+1}{3}$.

From Facts 1 and 2, we can see that $S_1 = S_2$. Besides, one can conclude that there is exactly one $t_1 \in \mathbb{F}_q^* \cdot \alpha^{3j}$ such that $\mathrm{Tr}_1^m\left(\frac{(a\overline{a})^3}{(a+\overline{a})^2(a\overline{a}+\lambda(a+\overline{a}))^2}\right) = 1$ for every $1 \le j \le \frac{q-2}{3}$. Let $b \in \mathbb{F}_q^*$ and $t_1 = b\alpha^{3j}$. Review that t_1, t_2 are the roots of (18). It gives that

$$t_2 = \frac{(a\overline{a})^3}{t_1},\ t_1 + t_2 = t_1 + \frac{(a\overline{a})^3}{t_1} = (a\overline{a} + a\lambda + \overline{a}\lambda)(a + \overline{a}) \in \mathbb{F}_q.$$

Hence, $\left(t_1 + \frac{(a\overline{a})^3}{t_1}\right)^q = t_1 + \frac{(a\overline{a})^3}{t_1}$ which induces that $b = \left(\frac{a\overline{a}}{(\alpha\overline{\alpha})^j}\right)^{\frac{3}{2}}$. Therefore, one can conclude that

$$|\{\lambda \in \mathbb{F}_q : N(\lambda) = 4\}| = \frac{1}{2}|\{t_1 \in \mathbb{F}_{q^2}\backslash\mathbb{F}_q : t_1^{\frac{q^2-1}{3}} = 1 \,\text{and}\, t_1 + \frac{(a\overline{a})^3}{t_1} \in \mathbb{F}_q\}| = \frac{q-2}{6}.$$

This completes the proof. $\square$

Lemma 10. *Let $f(x)$ be defined in (14) and $N(\lambda)$ be defined in Lemma 2. When λ runs through $\mathbb{F}_{q^2}\backslash\mathbb{F}_q$, then $N(\lambda)$ takes values from the set $\{0, 1, 2, 3\}$ and it takes value 2 exactly $q - 2$ times.*

Proof. Since $\overline{\lambda} + \lambda \neq 0$, then equation (16) is equivalent to

$$u^3 + \left((\lambda + \overline{\lambda})(a + \overline{a}) + a\overline{a}\right) u + (a\overline{a} + a\overline{\lambda} + \overline{a}\lambda)(a + \overline{a}) = 0, \tag{19}$$

which has at most three solutions in $\mathbb{F}_q$. Suppose it has two solutions in $\mathbb{F}_q$, then one of them have multiplicity 1 and the other has multiplicity 2. It implies that $(a\overline{a}+a\overline{\lambda}+\overline{a}\lambda)(a+\overline{a}) = 0$. On the other hand, from the previous analysis, we can see that $N(\lambda) = 2$ means (19) has two different solutions. Therefore, $N(\lambda)$ can take value 2 only when $a\overline{a} + a\overline{\lambda} + \overline{a}\lambda = 0$ due to $a + \overline{a} \neq 0$. Let (19) have two different roots u_1, u_2, then we have $u_1 = 0$, $u_2 = (\lambda a + \overline{\lambda}\overline{a})^{\frac{1}{2}}$ and $u_1 \neq u_2$. It gives that

$$|\{\lambda \in \mathbb{F}_{q^2}\backslash\mathbb{F}_q : N(\lambda) = 2\}| = |\{\lambda \in \mathbb{F}_{q^2}\backslash\mathbb{F}_q : a\overline{a} + a\overline{\lambda} + \overline{a}\lambda = 0 \text{ and } \lambda a \neq \overline{\lambda}\overline{a}\}|.$$

Denote

$$M_1 = |\{\lambda \in \mathbb{F}_{q^2}\backslash\mathbb{F}_q : a\overline{a} + a\overline{\lambda} + \overline{a}\lambda = 0\}|,$$
$$M_2 = |\{\lambda \in \mathbb{F}_{q^2}\backslash\mathbb{F}_q : a\overline{a} + a\overline{\lambda} + \overline{a}\lambda = 0 \text{ and } \lambda a = \overline{\lambda}\overline{a}\}|.$$

We then have

$$M_1 = |\{\lambda \in \mathbb{F}_{q^2} : \mathrm{Tr}_m^n(\lambda/a) = 1\}| - |\{\lambda \in \mathbb{F}_q : \mathrm{Tr}_m^n(\lambda/a) = 1\}| = 2^m - 1$$

and

$$M_2 = |\{\lambda \in a^{-1}\mathbb{F}_q : a\overline{a} + a\overline{\lambda} + \overline{a}\lambda = 0\}| = 1.$$

Hence, $|\{\lambda \in \mathbb{F}_{q^2}\backslash\mathbb{F}_q : N(\lambda) = 2\}| = M_1 - M_2 = 2^m - 2$. The proof is completed. $\square$

Combining Lemmas 9, 10 and Lemma 1, we can immediately present our main result of this subsection as follows.

Theorem 3. *Let m be a positive integer, $n = 2m$ and $q = 2^m$. The Walsh transform of $f(x)$ defined as*

$$f(x) = \sum_{i=1}^{2^{m-1}} \mathrm{Tr}_1^n \left(a x^{s_i(q-1)+1} \right), \ s_i = 4i - 2$$

for $a \in \mathbb{F}_{q^2}$ and $a + \overline{a} \neq 0$ takes values from $\{-q, 0, q, 2q, 3q\}$. Further, when λ runs through $\mathbb{F}_{q^2}$, the value distribution is given by

$$\widehat{f}(\lambda) = \begin{cases} -q, \text{ occurs } \frac{q^2-q}{3} \text{ times;} \\ 0, \quad \text{occurs } \frac{3q^2-4q+4}{6} \text{ times;} \\ q, \quad \text{occurs } \frac{3q-4}{2} \text{ times;} \\ 2q, \ \text{occurs } \frac{q^2-4q+12}{6} \text{ times;} \\ 3q, \ \text{occurs } \frac{q-4}{6} \text{ times} \end{cases}$$

when m is even, and

$$\widehat{f}(\lambda) = \begin{cases} -q, \text{ occurs } \frac{q^2-q-2}{3} \text{ times;} \\ 0, \quad \text{occurs } \frac{3q^2-4q+14}{6} \text{ times;} \\ q, \quad \text{occurs } \frac{3q-6}{2} \text{ times;} \\ 2q, \ \text{occurs } \frac{q^2-4q+10}{6} \text{ times;} \\ 3q, \ \text{occurs } \frac{q-2}{6} \text{ times} \end{cases}$$

when m is odd.

Example 4. Let $m = 4$, ω be a primitive element of $\mathbb{F}_{2^8}$ and $a = \omega$. Then one has $a + \overline{a} \neq 0$. Magma experiment shows that the Walsh transform of $f(x)$ defined as (14) is 5-valued and its value distribution is given by

$$\widehat{f}(\lambda) = \begin{cases} -16, \text{ occurs } 80 \text{ times;} \\ 0, \quad \text{occurs } 118 \text{ times;} \\ 16, \ \text{occurs } 22 \text{ times;} \\ 32, \ \text{occurs } 34 \text{ times;} \\ 48, \ \text{occurs } 2 \text{ times} \end{cases}$$

which is consistent with the result given in Theorem 3.

Example 5. Let $m = 5$, ω be a primitive element of $\mathbb{F}_{2^{10}}$ and $a = \omega$. Then one has $a + \overline{a} \neq 0$. Magma experiment shows that the Walsh transform of $f(x)$ defined as (14) is 5-valued and its value distribution is given by

$$\widehat{f}(\lambda) = \begin{cases} -32, \text{ occurs } 330 \text{ times;} \\ 0, \quad \text{occurs } 493 \text{ times;} \\ 32, \ \text{occurs } 45 \text{ times;} \\ 64, \ \text{occurs } 151 \text{ times;} \\ 96, \ \text{occurs } 5 \text{ times} \end{cases}$$

which is also consistent with the result given in Theorem 3.

4 Conclusions

Because of the importance of the Walsh spectrum in studying the properties of cryptographic functions, it is a valuable problem to find functions with few Walsh transform values and determine their value distributions explicitly. In this paper, by considering the Boolean function which is a linear combination of power functions with Niho type exponents as in (2) and selecting proper parameters, a class of multinomials with 4-valued Walsh spectrum and two classes of multinomials with 5-valued Walsh spectrum are obtained. Moreover, we give the value distributions of all of them by treating certain equations. The numerical experimental data suggests that other parameters can also be considered to construct functions of the form (2) with few Walsh transform and therefore, it is a problem worthy to be further investigated in the future.

Acknowledgements. This work was supported by the National Natural Science Foundation of China (No. 62072162), the Natural Science Foundation of Hubei Province of China (No. 2021CFA079), the Knowledge Innovation Program of Wuhan-Basic Research (No. 2022010801010319), the National Key Research and Development Program of China (No. 2021YFA1000600) and the China Scholarship Council (No. 202108420195).

References

1. Alahmadi, A., Akhazmi, H., Helleseth, T., Hijazi, R., Muthana, N. M., Solé, P.: On the lifted Zetterberg code. Des. Codes, Cryptogr. **80**(3), 561–576 (2016)
2. Carlet, C., Ding, C.: Highly nonlinear mappings. J. Complexity **20**(2–3), 205–244 (2004)
3. Charpin, P.: Cyclic codes with few weights and Niho exponents. J. Comb. Theory **108**(2), 247–259 (2004)
4. Dobbertin, H.: One-to-one highly nonlinear power functions on GF(2^n). Appl. Algebra Eng. Commun. Comput. **9**, 139–15 (1998)
5. Dobbertin, H., Felke, P., Helleseth, T., Rosendahl, P.: Niho type cross-correlation functions via Dickson polynomials and Kloosterman sums. IEEE Trans. Inf. Theory **52**(2), 613–627 (2006)
6. Dobbertin, H., Leander, G., Canteaut, A., Carlet, C., Gaborit, P.: Construction of bent functions via Niho power functions. J. Comb. Theory **113**(5), 779–798 (2006)
7. Dodunekov, S.M., Nilsson, J.E.M.: Algebraic decoding of the Zetterberg codes. IEEE Trans. Inf. Theory **38**(5), 1570–1573 (1992)
8. Helleseth, T., Kholosha, A.: Cross correlation of m-sequences, exponential sums, bent functions and Jacobsthal sums. Cryptogr. Commun. **3**(4), 281–291 (2011)
9. Helleseth, T., Rosendahl, P.: New pairs of m-sequences with 4-level cross-correlation. Finite Fields Appl. **11**(4), 674–683 (2005)
10. Leander, G., Kholosha, A.: Bent functions with 2^r Niho exponents. IEEE Trans. Inf. Theory **52**(12), 5529–5532 (2006)
11. Leonard, P.A., Williams, K.S.: Quartics over GF(2^n). Proc. Amer. Math. Soc. **36**(2), 347–350 (1972)
12. Li, N., Helleseth, T., Kholosha, A., Tang, X.: On the Walsh transform of a class of functions from Niho exponents. IEEE Trans. Inf. Theory **59**(7), 4662–4667 (2013)

13. Luo, J., Feng, K.: On the weight distribution of two classes of cyclic codes. IEEE Trans. Inf. Theory **54**(12), 5332–5344 (2008)
14. Luo, J., Feng, K.: Cyclic codes and sequences from generalized Coulter-Matthews funtion. IEEE Trans. Inf. Theory **54**(12), 5345–5353 (2008)
15. Ness, G.J., Helleseth, T., Kholosha, A.: On the correlation distribution of the Coulter-Matthews decimation. IEEE Trans. Inf. Theory **52**(5), 2241–2247 (2006)
16. Niho, Y.: Multivalued cross-correlation functions between two maximal linear recursive sequences, Ph.D. Thesis, Univ. Southern, California, Los Angeles (1972)
17. Rosendahl, P.: A generalization of Niho's theorem. Des. Codes Cryptogr. **38**(3), 331–336 (2006)
18. Tu, Z., Zeng, X., Li, C., Helleseth, T.: A class of new permutation trinomials. Finite Fields Appl. **50**, 178–195 (2018)
19. Williams, K.S.: Note on cubics over GF(2^n) and GF(3^n). J. Number Theory **7**(4), 361–365 (1975)
20. Wu, Y., Yue, Q., Li, F.: Three families of monomial functions with three-valued Walsh spectrum. IEEE Trans. Inf. Theory **65**(5), 3304–3314 (2019)
21. Zeng, X., Liu, J., Hu, L.: Generalized Kasami sequences: the large set. IEEE Trans. Inf. Theory **53**(7), 2587–2598 (2007)

Stream Ciphers

Higher-Order Masking Scheme for Trivium Hardware Implementation

Bohan Li[1,2], Hailong Zhang[1,2](✉), and Dongdai Lin[1,2]

[1] State Key Laboratory of Information Security, Institute of Information Engineering, Chinese Academy of Sciences, Beijing, China

[2] School of Cyber Security, University of Chinese Academy of Sciences, Beijing, China

{libohan,zhanghailong,ddlin}@iie.ac.cn

Abstract. Trivium as a representative stream cipher has been adopted by ISO/IEC in 2012. It can be foreseen that Trivium will be widely used to achieve the goal of information security. In practice, probing attacks can be used to recover key bits used by an implementation of Trivium under the (glitch-extended) probing model. In light of this, higher-order masking scheme secure under the glitch-extended probing model should be proposed for Trivium. Inspired by the ideas of the DOM masking scheme proposed by Gross *et al.* and the CHES 2021 masking scheme proposed by Shahmirzadi *et al.*, we propose two versions of higher-order masking scheme for Trivium. We analyze the security of two versions of higher-order masking scheme under the glitch-extended probing model. Then, the performance of two versions of higher-order masking scheme is evaluated on ASIC and FPGA with or without the pipeline technique, and meaningful observations are obtained. Overall, higher-order masking schemes that are secure under the glitch-extended probing model are proposed for Trivium and their performances are evaluated on typical hardware platforms.

Keywords: Trivium · Higher-order masking scheme · Side-channel attacks · Glitch-extended probing model · Performance evaluation

1 Introduction

In practice, stream ciphers are used to guarantee the privacy and confidentiality in many high-performance applications and constrained hardware systems. In 2004, the European Network of Excellence in Cryptology launched a four-year eSTREAM project [6] to call for proposals of new stream ciphers. After three rounds of evaluation, two portfolios of stream ciphers were finally confirmed. Since then, stream ciphers contained in these two portfolios have received great attentions. Especially, Trivium [5] as a synchronous stream cipher listed in Portfolio 2 (hardware-oriented) has been chosen as one of the keystream generators for lightweight stream ciphers in ISO/IEC 29192-3 [14].

Y. Deng and M. Yung (Eds.): Inscrypt 2022, LNCS 13837, pp. 337–356, 2023.
https://doi.org/10.1007/978-3-031-26553-2_18

In light of this, the security of Trivium has attracted great attentions from cryptanalysts in recent years. For example, Fu *et al.* [9] have proposed a key-recovery attack on 855-round Trivium with a novel nullification technique of the Boolean polynomial where only three equivalent key bits can be recovered, while Ye *et al.* [30] have shown a conditional differential cryptanalysis on 978-round Trivium where only one key bit can be recovered. Although published works have shown that Trivium is secure against classical cryptanalyses, implementations of Trivium may be threatened by side-channel attacks. Indeed, published works [8,15] have given differential power analysis (DPA) [16] and correlation power analysis (CPA) [1] against Trivium implementations.

In order to secure a cryptographic implementation against different styles of side-channel attacks, different styles of countermeasures are proposed. Typical ones are masking [3,13], shuffling [27], random delay [4], and so on. Among them, masking as a provably secure countermeasure can be the most famous one. Since the idea of masking was first proposed at CRYPTO 1999 [2], masking schemes for software implementations and hardware implementations have been proposed over the past two decades. Compared with software implementations, hardware implementations may face the security problems related to glitch. In order to analyze the security of masking schemes, adversary models that fit with practical scenarios should be proposed. Ishai *et al.* for the first time proposed *d-probing model* at CRYPTO 2003 [13] where the adversary is assumed to have the ability of obtaining d bits with d probes. However, the security of the hardware implementation of a cryptographic algorithm under the d-probing model can be not enough since the leakage related to *glitch* is not considered [17]. For example, [18,19] applied side-channel attacks on masked AES hardware implementations, and they lead to the conclusion that glitch can pose a serious threat on the security of masked AES hardware implementations. In order to consider the security problems related to glitch, the idea of *glitch-extended probing model* was first proposed at CRYPTO 2015 [22]. Then, its formal version was proposed at CHES 2018 [7].

The first glitch-resistant masking scheme, i.e. *Threshold Implementation (TI)*, was proposed by Nikova et al. at ICISC 2006 [21]. Three conditions, i.e. correctness, non-completeness and uniformity should be satisfied in TI. In order to achieve the non-completeness condition, at least $td+1$ shares should be used in TI where t denotes the degree of a non-linear function and d denotes the security order. Therefore, the number of shares needed in TI can be large. Then, in order to decrease the number of shares needed in TI, Reparaz *et al.* proposed *Consolidating Masking Schemes (CMS)* at CRYPTO 2015 [22] by using fresh randomness. After that, many glitch-resistant masking schemes, such as *Domain-Oriented Masking (DOM)* [12] and *Unified Masking Approach (UMA)* [11] were proposed to reduce the number of fresh randomness.

The overhead of masking schemes depends on two factors, i.e. the number of shares and the number of fresh randomness. Theoretically, d^{th} order masking schemes cannot counteract $(d+1)^{th}$ order attacks [20]. Therefore, at least d masks should be used to achieve d^{th} order security. Recently proposed masking schemes focus on reducing the number of fresh randomness. In detail, DOM proposed by Gross *et al.* [12] can reduce the number of fresh randomness to $d(d+1)/2$. Then, UMA proposed by Gross *et al.* at CHES 2017 can reduce the number of fresh randomness from $d(d+1)/2$ to $d(d+1)/4$. At CHES 2021, Shahmirzadi *et al.* proposed 1st order [24] and 2nd order [25] masking schemes that are glitch-resistant with (almost) no fresh randomness.

In this paper, we show that the naive implementation of Trivium can be insecure under $d-$probing attacks. In detail, three types of side-channel attacks are proposed to recover key bits used by an implementation of Trivium. Among them, Type 1 and Type 2 attacks can work under the $d-$probing model, while Type 3 attack can work under the glitch-extended probing model. In light of this, masking schemes that are secure under the glitch-extended probing model should be proposed for Trivium. In practice, the price of d-probing attack increases significantly with the number of probes [13]. In this paper, in order to secure the hardware implementation of Trivium, higher-order masking schemes with order up to 3 are proposed for Trivium. Inspired by the ideas of the DOM masking scheme and the CHES 2021 masking scheme, two versions of higher-order masking schemes are proposed for Trivium. In detail, 1st order, 2nd order and 3rd order cases are considered in version-1 masking scheme, while 1st order and 2nd order cases are considered in version-2 masking scheme. We theoretically analyze the security of two versions of higher-order masking scheme under the glitch-extended probing model.

Then, the performance of two versions of higher-order masking schemes for hardware implementation of Trivium is evaluated on ASIC and FPGA in two scenarios. The overhead of fresh randomness is not considered in scenario-1, while it is considered in scenario-2. Then, three meaningful observations can be obtained. First, the performance of version-1 masking scheme can be better than that of version-2 masking scheme with or without pipeline technique on both ASIC and FPGA in scenario-1, even though the advantage is not obvious. Second, the performance of version-2 masking scheme can be better than that of version-1 masking scheme with or without pipeline technique on both ASIC and FPGA in scenario-2 with an obvious advantage. Third, the pipeline technique can optimize the throughput of two versions of higher-order masking schemes for hardware implementation of Trivium with the price of a little extra consumed area. Overall, higher-order masking schemes that are secure under the glitch-extended probing model are proposed for Trivium and their performances are evaluated on typical hardware platforms.

The rest of the paper is organized as follows. Preliminaries are presented in Sect. 2. Then, three types of probing attacks are proposed to recover key bits of a Trivium implementation in Sect. 3. In Sect. 4, two versions of higher-order masking schemes secure under the glitch-extended probing model are proposed for Trivium. In Sect. 5, the performance of two versions of higher-order masking schemes is evaluated on ASIC and FPGA. In Sect. 6, T-Test is used to evaluate the security of the masked hardware implementation of Trivium in the simulated scenario. Finally, conclusions are drawn in Sect. 7.

2 Background

Firstly, the details of Trivium is presented; then, the glitch-extended probing model is presented; third, the higher-order masking schemes proposed by Gross *et al.* at TIS@CCS 2016 and Shahmirzadi *et al.* at CHES 2021 are presented.

2.1 Trivium

Trivium is a hardware and bit oriented synchronous stream cipher with two inputs: an 80-bit secret key and an 80-bit initialization vector (IV). Trivium is composed of three shift registers with feeding back into one another making up an integrated *internal state* denoted as $S = (s_1, \cdots, s_{288})$. The internal state is initially loaded with the key and IV as well as some padding 0s and 1s. The setup loading is listed in (1) as follows.

$$
\begin{aligned}
(s_1, s_2, \ldots, s_{93}) &\leftarrow (k_{80}, \ldots, k_1, 0, \ldots, 0), \\
(s_{94}, s_{95}, \ldots, s_{177}) &\leftarrow (iv_{80}, \ldots, iv_1, 0, \ldots, 0), \\
(s_{178}, s_{179}, \ldots, s_{288}) &\leftarrow (0, \ldots, 0, 1, 1, 1).
\end{aligned} \tag{1}
$$

Trivium is consisted of two phases: an initialization phase and a keystream generation phase. During both phases, the internal state is repeatedly updated according to the *update functions* shown in (2).

$$
\begin{aligned}
t_1 &\leftarrow s_{66} \oplus s_{93} \oplus s_{91} \odot s_{92} \oplus s_{171}, \\
t_2 &\leftarrow s_{162} \oplus s_{177} \oplus s_{175} \odot s_{176} \oplus s_{264}, \\
t_3 &\leftarrow s_{243} \oplus s_{288} \oplus s_{286} \odot s_{287} \oplus s_{69}.
\end{aligned} \tag{2}
$$

The update process of Trivium is shown in (3), where the internal state rotates clock-wisely one bit per clock cycle, with s_1, s_{94}, s_{178} updated by t_3, t_1, t_2 respectively.

$$
\begin{aligned}
(s_1, s_2, \ldots, s_{93}) &\leftarrow (t_3, s_1, \ldots, s_{92}), \\
(s_{94}, s_{95}, \ldots, s_{177}) &\leftarrow (t_1, s_{94}, \ldots, s_{176}), \\
(s_{178}, s_{179}, \ldots, s_{288}) &\leftarrow (t_2, s_{178}, \ldots, s_{287}).
\end{aligned} \tag{3}
$$

During the initialization phase the state rotates 4 full cycles ($288 \times 4 = 1152$ clocks) without generating any keystream bits. Then, during the keystream generation phase, one bit keystream z is generated per clock cycle according to the keystream generation function (4).

$$
z \leftarrow s_{66} \oplus s_{93} \oplus s_{162} \oplus s_{177} \oplus s_{243} \oplus s_{288}. \tag{4}
$$

2.2 Glitch-Extended Probing Model

Security of masking schemes is commonly evaluated under $d-$probing model [13], where the adversary can put up to d probes on intermediate variables of the implementation of a masking scheme. The $d-$probing model is formally defined in Definition 1.

Definition 1 (d–Probing Model [13]). *Given a combinational logic circuit G, an adversary with d probes can observe up to d internal wires of G.*

However, glitch exists in hardware implementations. It means that by putting a probe on the output of G, one may obtain the input of G. Consequently, the security of hardware implementations should be considered under the glitch-extended probing model. The glitch-extended probing model is formally defined in Definition 2.

Definition 2 (Glitch-Extended Probing Model [7]). *Given a combinational logic circuit G, an adversary with glitch-extended probes can observe all the inputs of G up to the latest synchronization point by probing any output of G.*

Example. Given a combinational logic circuit G which can implement function $g = G(x_1, \cdots, x_n)$, the inputs of G can be represented as x_i where $0 < i < n$ while the output of G can be represented by g. Under the glitch-extended probing model, one may obtain the inputs of G *i.e.* x_i by probing g. Note that G can be some operations in a cryptographic algorithm, and the input and the output of G are not necessarily the input and the output of the whole cryptographic algorithm.

2.3 Higher-Order Masking Scheme

The main idea of a higher-order masking scheme with order d is to split every sensitive intermediate value v into $d+1$ shares. Each of the $d+1$ shares and more generally each collection of d or less shares should be statistically independent of v. The operation can then be performed safely by hiding the value of v in $d+1$ shares. For a sensitive binary variable a, we denote the shares of a with a_i, where $0 \leq i \leq d$, and the equation $a = \sum_{i=0}^{d} a_i$ should be satisfied. Then, the exclusive OR between a and b can be denoted as $c = a \oplus b$ while the AND between a and b can be denoted as $c = a \odot b$.

At TIS@CCS 2016, Gross *et al.* [12] proposed the DOM masking scheme to reduce the number of fresh randomness to $d(d+1)/2$. For a non-linear function $x = f(a, b) = ab$, (5) shows how the DOM scheme can be used to achieve 1st order, 2nd order and 3rd order security under the glitch-extended probing model [12]. Note that all $\oplus$ in the brackets can be computed parallel. Then, the $\oplus$ out of the brackets can be computed in any order. Therefore, two register stages are required in the DOM masking scheme.

$$\begin{cases} x_0 = (a_0 \odot b_0) \oplus (a_0 \odot b_1 \oplus r_0) \oplus (a_0 \odot b_2 \oplus r_1) \oplus (a_0 \odot b_3 \oplus r_3) \oplus \cdots \\ x_1 = (a_1 \odot b_0 \oplus r_0) \oplus (a_1 \odot b_1) \oplus (a_1 \odot b_2 \oplus r_2) \oplus (a_1 \odot b_3 \oplus r_4) \oplus \cdots \\ x_2 = (a_2 \odot b_0 \oplus r_1) \oplus (a_2 \odot b_1 \oplus r_2) \oplus (a_2 \odot b_2) \oplus (a_2 \odot b_3 \oplus r_5) \oplus \cdots \\ x_3 = (a_3 \odot b_0 \oplus r_3) \oplus (a_3 \odot b_1 \oplus r_4) \oplus (a_3 \odot b_2 \oplus r_5) \oplus (a_3 \odot b_3) \oplus \cdots \\ \quad \vdots \qquad\qquad \vdots \qquad\qquad \vdots \qquad\qquad \vdots \end{cases} \tag{5}$$

At CHES 2021, Shahmirzadi *et al.* proposed a search algorithm to find 1st order masking scheme [24] without any fresh randomness and 2nd order [25] masking scheme with almost no fresh randomness. The CHES 2021 masking scheme satisfies three conditions proposed by Nikova *et al.* [21] *i.e.* correctness, non-completeness and uniformity. Therefore, the CHES 2021 masking scheme can be secure under the glitch-extended probing model [24]. For a particular function $x = f(a, b, c) = ab + c$, (6) and (7) can reach the 1st order and 2nd order security under the glitch-extended probing model [24,25]. One can see that there are no fresh randomness in (6) and (7). Note that each x'_i represents one register to counteract glitch. Overall, it can be seen from (6) and (7) that two register stages are required in version-2 masking scheme.

$$\begin{cases} (a_0 \odot b_0) \oplus c_0 = x'_0 \\ (a_0 \odot b_1) \qquad\quad = x'_1 \\ (a_1 \odot b_0) \qquad\quad = x'_2 \\ (a_1 \odot b_1) \oplus c_1 = x'_3 \end{cases} \qquad \begin{matrix} x'_0 \oplus x'_1 = x_0 \\ x'_2 \oplus x'_3 = x_1 \end{matrix} \tag{6}$$

$$\begin{cases} (a_0 \odot b_0) \oplus b_0 = x'_0 \\ (a_0 \odot b_1) = x'_1 \\ (a_0 \odot b_2) \oplus c_0 = x'_2 \\ (a_1 \odot b_0) \oplus b_0 = x'_3 \\ (a_1 \odot b_1) = x'_4 \\ (a_1 \odot b_2) \oplus b_2 \oplus c_1 = x'_5 \\ (a_2 \odot b_0) \oplus a_2 \oplus c_2 = x'_6 \\ (a_2 \odot b_1) = x'_7 \\ (a_2 \odot b_2) \oplus a_2 \oplus b_2 = x'_8 \end{cases} \qquad \begin{matrix} x'_0 \oplus x'_1 \oplus x'_2 = x_0 \\ x'_3 \oplus x'_4 \oplus x'_5 = x_1 \\ x'_6 \oplus x'_7 \oplus x'_8 = x_2 \end{matrix} \tag{7}$$

3 Security Analysis of Trivium Implementation

In this part, we propose three types of attacks against Trivium implementation. Type 1 attack and Type 2 attack can work under the $d-$probing model, while Type 3 attack can work under the glitch-extended probing model. There are three *update stages* (s_1, s_{94}, s_{178}) which are updated by t_3, t_1, t_2 respectively. t_p^q denotes the update value of t_p at round q where $p \in \{1, 2, 3\}$ and $q \geq 1$. Then, we present the process of three attack styles in detail. Note that three types of attacks are of theoretical interest. In practice, it is very difficult to obtain the exact bit value or even glitch with probes.

3.1 Type 1 Attack

The update functions shown in (2) do not use the update bits (t_p^q) until the 67th round. Inspired by this fact, we note that the entire 80-bit key can be completely recovered by analyzing the update equations if the leakages related to s_1 (t_3) and s_{94} (t_1) in the first 66 rounds can be measured. In general, the leakages related to s_1 (t_3) can be used to recover $k_{12} - k_{77}$, and the leakages related to

s_{94} (t_1) can be used to recover $k_1 - k_{11}$ and $k_{78} - k_{80}$. The detailed key-recovery process is described as follows.

According to the loading rule of Trivium, in the first 66 rounds (s_{162}, s_{177}, $s_{175}, s_{176}, s_{264}$) in (2) are loaded with padding 0s and known IV bits. Therefore, the value of t_2 is known and we do not need to recover the value of t_2.

According to (1), s_{69} is loaded with $k_{77} - k_{12}$ in the first 66 rounds while $s_{243}, s_{288}, s_{286}, s_{287}$ are loaded with padding 0/1s. By substituting $s_{243}, s_{288}, s_{286}$, s_{287} with padding 0/1s, t_2 in (2) can be written as (8). In (8), the only non-deterministic terms are $k_{77} - k_{12}$. We assume that the values of $t_3^1 - t_3^{66}$ can be obtained by analyzing the leakages related to the processing of $t_3^1 - t_3^{66}$. Consequently, the values of $k_{77} - k_{12}$ can be recovered.

$$\begin{cases} t_3^1 \leftarrow 0 \oplus 1 \oplus 1 \odot 1 \oplus k_{12}, \\ \vdots \\ t_3^{66} \leftarrow 0 \oplus 0 \oplus 0 \odot 0 \oplus k_{77}. \end{cases} \tag{8}$$

Now, 66 bits of the secret key are recovered. The remaining 14 bits can be recovered with the leakages of s_{94} (t_1). According to (1), $s_{66}, s_{93}, s_{91}, s_{92}$ are loaded with padding 0s or $k_{80} - k_1$ in the first 66 rounds while s_{171} is loaded with $IV_3 - IV_{68}$. So, it is necessary to divide the update progress of t_1 into two parts according to the values loaded.

The first part contains the 14th to the 24th rounds. According to (1), s_{66} is loaded with $k_{28} - k_{38}$; s_{93} is loaded with $k_1 - k_{11}$; s_{91} is loaded with $k_3 - k_{13}$; s_{92} is loaded with $k_2 - k_{12}$ and s_{171} is loaded with $IV_{16} - IV_{26}$. Then, t_1 in (2) can be written as (9).

$$\begin{cases} t_1^{14} \leftarrow k_{28} \oplus k_1 \oplus k_3 \odot k_2 \oplus IV_{16}, \\ \vdots \\ t_1^{24} \leftarrow k_{38} \oplus k_{11} \oplus k_{13} \odot k_{12} \oplus IV_{26}. \end{cases} \tag{9}$$

In (9), $k_1 - k_{11}$ can be recovered with Algorithm 1:

Algorithm 1: Compute $k_1 - k_{11}$

Input: $[t_1^{14}, t_1^{15}, \ldots, t_1^{24}]$
Output: $[k_1, k_2, \ldots, k_{11}]$

for $j = 10 \rightarrow 0$ **do**
  $T \leftarrow t_1^{14+j}$;
  $PK_1 \leftarrow k_{28+j}$;
  $PK_2 \leftarrow k_{3+j}$;
  $PK_3 \leftarrow k_{2+j}$;
  $IV \leftarrow IV_{16+j}$;
  compute k_{1+j} by $k_{1+j} \leftarrow T \oplus PK_1 \oplus PK_2 \odot PK_3 \oplus IV$;
end
return $[k_1, k_2, \ldots, k_{11}]$.

In Algorithm 1, t_1^{14+j} can be recovered with the leakages related to the processing of t_1^{14+j}; k_{28+j} is already recovered and therefore is known; k_{3+j} and k_{2+j} are either known or computed in the previous loop; finally, IV_{16+j} is a public value. Therefore, k_{1+j} can be recovered.

The second part contains the 64th to the 66th rounds. According to (1), s_{66} is loaded with $k_{78} - k_{80}$; s_{93} is loaded with $k_{51} - k_{53}$; s_{91} is loaded with $k_{53} - k_{55}$; s_{92} is loaded with $k_{52} - k_{54}$ and s_{171} is loaded with $IV_{66} - IV_{68}$. Then, t_1 in (2) can be written as (10).

$$\begin{cases} t_1^{64} \leftarrow k_{78} \oplus k_{51} \oplus k_{53} \odot k_{52} \oplus IV_{66}, \\ t_1^{65} \leftarrow k_{79} \oplus k_{52} \oplus k_{54} \odot k_{53} \oplus IV_{67}, \\ t_1^{66} \leftarrow k_{80} \oplus k_{53} \oplus k_{55} \odot k_{54} \oplus IV_{68}. \end{cases} \tag{10}$$

By analyzing the leakages related to the processing of t_1^{64}, t_1^{65} and t_1^{66}, we can recover the values of t_1^{64}, t_1^{65} and t_1^{66}. First, the values of k_{51}, k_{52} and k_{53} are known while the value of IV_{66} is public. Therefore, the value of k_{78} can be computed. Second, the values of k_{52}, k_{53} and k_{54} are known while the value of IV_{67} is public. Therefore, the value of k_{79} can be computed. Third, the values of k_{53}, k_{54} and k_{55} are known while the value of IV_{68} is public. Therefore, the value of k_{80} can be computed.

Overall, 80 bits of the secret key can be recovered with Type 1 attack. In practice, measuring the leakages related to two registers at the same time *i.e.* 2nd order attack may significantly increase the attack price. In light of this, Type 2 attack which is 1st order attack is proposed.

3.2 Type 2 Attack

In Type 2 attack, we measure the leakages related to the processing of s_1 (i.e. t_3) in the first 69 rounds; then, we measure the leakages related to the processing of s_{178} (i.e. t_2) from the 83rd to the 93rd rounds. In general, the leakages related to s_1 (t_3) can be used to recover $k_{12} - k_{77}$ and $k_{78} - k_{80}$, and the leakages related to s_{178} (i.e. t_2) can be used to recover $k_1 - k_{11}$. The detailed key-recovery process is described as follows.

As in Type 1 attack, $k_{77} - k_{12}$ can be recovered with the leakages related to the processing of s_1 in the first 66 rounds.

According to (1), during the 67th to the 69th rounds, s_{243} is loaded with $t_2^1 - t_2^3$; $s_{286} - s_{288}$ are loaded with padding 0s and s_{69} is loaded with $k_{78} - k_{80}$. Then, t_3 in (2) can be written as (11).

$$\begin{cases} t_3^{67} \leftarrow t_2^1 \oplus 0 \oplus 0 \odot 0 \oplus k_{78}, \\ t_3^{68} \leftarrow t_2^2 \oplus 0 \oplus 0 \odot 0 \oplus k_{79}, \\ t_3^{69} \leftarrow t_2^3 \oplus 0 \oplus 0 \odot 0 \oplus k_{80}. \end{cases} \tag{11}$$

As the same with Type 1 attack, $t_2^1 - t_2^3$ can be computed with public values and are therefore known. By analyzing the leakages related to the processing of $t_3^{67} - t_3^{69}$, the values of $t_3^{67} - t_3^{69}$ can be recovered. Then, with the values of $t_2^1 - t_2^3$, the values of $k_{78} - k_{80}$ can be recovered.

According to (1), during the 83rd to the 93rd rounds, s_{162} is loaded with $t_1^{14} - t_1^{24}$; $s_{175} - s_{177}$ are loaded with IV bits or $t_1^1 - t_1^{11}$ and s_{264} is loaded with padding 0s or $t_2^1 - t_2^6$. So, it is necessary to divide the update progress of t_2 into four parts according to the values loaded.

The first part contains the 83rd round. According to (1), s_{162} is loaded with t_1^{14}; s_{177} is loaded with IV_{79}; s_{175} is loaded with t_1^1; s_{176} is loaded with IV_{80} and s_{264} is loaded with padding 0. Then, t_2 in (2) can be written as (12).

$$t_2^{83} \leftarrow t_1^{14} \oplus IV_{79} \oplus t_1^1 \odot IV_{80} \oplus 0. \tag{12}$$

The second part contains the 84th round. According to (1), s_{162} is loaded with t_1^{15}; s_{177} is loaded with IV_{80}; s_{175} is loaded with t_1^2; s_{176} is loaded with t_1^1 and s_{264} is loaded with padding 0. Then, t_2 in (2) can be written as (13).

$$t_2^{84} \leftarrow t_1^{15} \oplus IV_{80} \oplus t_1^2 \odot t_1^1 \oplus 0. \tag{13}$$

The third part contains the $85^{th} - 87^{th}$ rounds. According to (1), s_{162} is loaded with $t_1^{16} - t_1^{18}$; s_{177} is loaded with $t_1^1 - t_1^3$; s_{175} is loaded with $t_1^3 - t_1^5$; s_{176} is loaded with $t_1^2 - t_1^4$ and s_{264} is loaded with padding 0. Then, t_2 in (2) can be written as (14).

$$\begin{cases} t_2^{85} \leftarrow t_1^{16} \oplus t_1^1 \oplus t_1^3 \odot t_1^2 \oplus 0, \\ \vdots \\ t_2^{87} \leftarrow t_1^{18} \oplus t_1^3 \oplus t_1^5 \odot t_1^4 \oplus 0. \end{cases} \tag{14}$$

The fourth part contains the $88^{th} - 93^{rd}$ rounds. According to (1), s_{162} is loaded with $t_1^{19} - t_1^{24}$; s_{177} is loaded with $t_1^4 - t_1^9$; s_{175} is loaded with $t_1^6 - t_1^{11}$; s_{176} is loaded with $t_1^5 - t_1^{10}$ and s_{264} is loaded with $t_2^1 - t_2^6$. Then, t_2 in (2) can be written as (15).

$$\begin{cases} t_2^{88} \leftarrow t_1^{19} \oplus t_1^4 \oplus t_1^6 \odot t_1^5 \oplus t_2^1, \\ \vdots \\ t_2^{93} \leftarrow t_1^{24} \oplus t_1^9 \oplus t_1^{11} \odot t_1^{10} \oplus t_2^6. \end{cases} \tag{15}$$

According to (1), $t_1^1 - t_1^{11}$ can be computed with $k_{15} - k_{25}$ (already known) and public values. In (12)–(15), the only unknown terms are $t_1^1 - t_1^{24}$. We assume that the values of $t_2^{83} - t_2^{93}$ can be recovered with the leakages related to the processing of $t_2^{83} - t_2^{93}$. Then, the values of $t_1^{14} - t_1^{24}$ can be obtained. With the values of $t_1^{14} - t_1^{24}$, the values of $k_{11} - k_1$ can be recovered with Algorithm 1.

According to the definition of d-probing model [13], a probe can be switched to another cell between clock cycles. Thus, Type 2 attack fulfills such requirement and can be a really 1-probe attack. However, in practice, such switch may be hard to be applied between clock cycles. In light of this, two methods can be used. First, for a fully controlled device, one can suspend the running of Trivium after 69 rounds, and run it after the probe is switched. Second, one can run the Trivium twice with different runs focusing on different cells.

3.3 Type 3 Attack

Under the glitch-extended probing model, all the input of one function can be obtained by probing its output. In light of this, the key-recovery process can be much easy. According to (1), from the 14th to the 66th rounds, s_{66} is loaded with $k_{28} - k_{80}$; s_{93} is loaded with $k_1 - k_{53}$; s_{91} is loaded with $k_3 - k_{55}$; s_{92} is loaded with $k_2 - k_{54}$ and s_{171} is loaded with $IV_{16} - IV_{68}$. Then, t_1 in (2) can be written as (16).

$$\begin{cases} t_1^{14} \leftarrow k_{28} \oplus k_1 \oplus k_3 \odot k_2 \oplus IV_{16}, \\ t_1^{15} \leftarrow k_{29} \oplus k_2 \oplus k_4 \odot k_3 \oplus IV_{17}, \\ \vdots \\ t_1^{65} \leftarrow k_{79} \oplus k_{52} \oplus k_{54} \odot k_{53} \oplus IV_{67}, \\ t_1^{66} \leftarrow k_{80} \oplus k_{53} \oplus k_{55} \odot k_{54} \oplus IV_{68}. \end{cases} \tag{16}$$

If the values of $t_1^{14} - t_1^{66}$ can be obtained with probe, glitch can leak all the inputs in (16) *i.e.* $k_1 - k_{80}$ and $IV_{16} - IV_{68}$ in the right hand of (16). Consequently, 80 bits of the secret key $k_1 - k_{80}$ can be recovered. Note that such glitch-extended probing model is too strong to be satisfied. In practice, even if a small number of the input of the combinational logic circuit can be hardly recovered with glitch. In this case, 80 bits of the secret key may not be easy to be recovered.

4 Glitch-Resistant Higher-Order Masking Schemes for Trivium

In this section, under the idea of DOM masking scheme, glitch-resistant 1st order, 2nd order and 3rd order masking schemes are proposed for Trivium while under the idea of CHES 2021 masking scheme, glitch-resistant 1st order and 2nd order masking schemes are proposed for Trivium. All three update functions of Trivium have the same form. Therefore, we use (17) to represent three update functions.

$$y = Y(a, b, c, d, e) = a \odot b \oplus c \oplus d \oplus e. \tag{17}$$

In order to achieve the d order security under the glitch-extended probing model, each variable in (17) is split into $d+1$ shares. For example, $a = a_0 \oplus \cdots a_d$. Besides, Y is split into n *component functions* Y_i with $0 \leq i \leq n-1$ which are used to compute shares of y. Then, the sum of component functions gives the value of y as is shown in (18).

$$y = Y(a, b, c, d, e) = Y_0 \oplus Y_1 \oplus \cdots \oplus Y_{n-1}. \tag{18}$$

4.1 Version-1 Masking Scheme

Here, 1st order, 2nd order and 3rd order cases are considered in version-1 masking scheme, which can be shown in (19), (20) and (21). Note that r_i represents a fresh randomness bit and each y_i' represents one register. Therefore, one can see from (19)–(21) that version-1 masking scheme requires two register stages in all three cases.

$$\begin{cases} (a_0 \odot b_1) \oplus c_0 \oplus d_0 \oplus e_0 \oplus r = y'_0 \\ (a_1 \odot b_0) \oplus c_1 \oplus d_1 \oplus e_1 \oplus r = y'_1 \end{cases} \quad \begin{array}{l} y'_0 \oplus (a_0 \odot b_0) = y_0 \\ y'_1 \oplus (a_1 \odot b_1) = y_1 \end{array} \tag{19}$$

$$\begin{cases} (a_0 \odot b_1) \oplus r_0 \oplus c_0 \oplus d_0 = y'_0 \\ (a_0 \odot b_2) \oplus r_1 \oplus e_0 \qquad = y'_1 \\ (a_1 \odot b_0) \oplus r_0 \oplus c_1 \oplus d_1 = y'_2 \\ (a_1 \odot b_2) \oplus r_2 \oplus e_1 \qquad = y'_3 \\ (a_2 \odot b_0) \oplus r_1 \oplus c_2 \oplus d_2 = y'_4 \\ (a_2 \odot b_1) \oplus r_2 \oplus e_2 \qquad = y'_5 \end{cases} \quad \begin{array}{l} y'_0 \oplus y'_1 \oplus (a_0 \odot b_0) = y_0 \\ y'_2 \oplus y'_3 \oplus (a_1 \odot b_1) = y_1 \\ y'_4 \oplus y'_5 \oplus (a_2 \odot b_2) = y_2 \end{array} \tag{20}$$

$$\begin{cases} (a_0 \odot b_1) \oplus r_0 \oplus c_0 = y'_0 \\ (a_0 \odot b_2) \oplus r_1 \oplus d_0 = y'_1 \\ (a_0 \odot b_3) \oplus r_3 \oplus e_0 = y'_2 \\ (a_1 \odot b_0) \oplus r_0 \oplus c_1 = y'_3 \\ (a_1 \odot b_2) \oplus r_2 \oplus d_1 = y'_4 \\ (a_1 \odot b_3) \oplus r_4 \oplus e_1 = y'_5 \\ (a_2 \odot b_0) \oplus r_1 \oplus c_2 = y'_6 \\ (a_2 \odot b_1) \oplus r_2 \oplus d_2 = y'_7 \\ (a_2 \odot b_3) \oplus r_5 \oplus e_2 = y'_8 \\ (a_3 \odot b_0) \oplus r_3 \oplus c_3 = y'_9 \\ (a_3 \odot b_1) \oplus r_4 \oplus d_3 = y'_{10} \\ (a_3 \odot b_2) \oplus r_5 \oplus e_3 = y'_{11} \end{cases} \quad \begin{array}{l} y'_0 \oplus y'_1 \oplus y'_2 \oplus (a_0 \odot b_0) \quad = y_0 \\ y'_3 \oplus y'_4 \oplus y'_5 \oplus (a_1 \odot b_1) \quad = y_1 \\ y'_6 \oplus y'_7 \oplus y'_8 \oplus (a_2 \odot b_2) \quad = y_2 \\ y'_9 \oplus y'_{10} \oplus y'_{11} \oplus (a_3 \odot b_3) = y_3 \end{array} \tag{21}$$

Security Analysis. Three conditions, *i.e.* correctness, non-completeness and uniformity should be satisfied in version-1 masking scheme to ensure that it is secure under the glitch-extended probing model. First, correctness requires that the sum of the output shares gives the desired output. Indeed, the correctness of version-1 masking scheme can be verified by summing up all component functions in (19), (20) or (21). Second, non-completeness requires every component function is independent of at least one share of each of the input variables. In version-1 masking scheme, registers should be inserted into the computation of component functions to satisfy the non-completeness condition under the glitch-extended probing model. Indeed, with the inserted registers, each probe at most leak one share of each variable even under the glitch-extended probing model. For example, the masking scheme in (20) should be secure with upto 2 glitch-extended probes, which means one cannot obtain any secret value with even 2 glitch-extended probes. In order to obtain as much information as possible, the glitch-extended probe should be located on y'_* or y_*, which can be classified into three cases, *i.e.*, (y'_*, y'_*), (y'_*, y_*) and (y_*, y_*). When probing (y'_0, y'_1), one can only obtain a_0, b_0, b_1, c_0, d_0 and e_0, which will not leak values of a, b, c, d and e. Similarly, when probing (y'_*, y_*) or (y_*, y_*), the values of a, b, c, d and e cannot be obtained. Third, uniformity requires any values obtained under the glitch-extended probing model be independent of the inputs of an update function. In version-1 masking scheme, all shares are independent of the inputs of an update function; fresh randomness bits are obviously independent of the inputs of an update function; finally, y_i' is independent of the inputs of an update function because a fresh randomness bit is added in the computation of y_i'.

Therefore, uniformity is satisfied in version-1 masking scheme. Overall, all three conditions are satisfied in version-1 masking scheme. Therefore, version-1 masking scheme can be secure under the glitch-extended probing model.

4.2 Version-2 Masking Scheme

Here, 1st order and 2nd order cases are considered in version-2 masking scheme, which can be shown in (22) and (23). Note that each y_i' represents one register. Therefore, version-2 masking scheme requires two register stages in both 1st order and 2nd order case.

$$\begin{cases} (a_0 \odot b_0) \oplus c_0 \oplus e_0 = y_0' \\ (a_0 \odot b_1) \oplus d_0 = y_1' \\ (a_1 \odot b_0) \oplus d_1 = y_2' \\ (a_1 \odot b_1) \oplus c_1 \oplus e_1 = y_3' \end{cases} \qquad \begin{matrix} y_0' \oplus y_1' = y_0 \\ y_2' \oplus y_3' = y_1 \end{matrix} \tag{22}$$

$$\begin{cases} (a_0 \odot b_0) \oplus b_0 \oplus c_0 = y_0' \\ (a_0 \odot b_1) \oplus e_0 = y_1' \\ (a_0 \odot b_2) \oplus b_2 \oplus d_0 = y_2' \\ (a_1 \odot b_0) \oplus b_0 \oplus c_1 = y_3' \\ (a_1 \odot b_1) \oplus e_1 = y_4' \\ (a_1 \odot b_2) \oplus d_1 = y_5' \\ (a_2 \odot b_0) \oplus d_2 \oplus c_2 = y_6' \\ (a_2 \odot b_1) \oplus e_2 = y_7' \\ (a_2 \odot b_2) \oplus b_2 = y_8' \end{cases} \qquad \begin{matrix} y_0' \oplus y_1' \oplus y_2' = y_0 \\ y_3' \oplus y_4' \oplus y_5' = y_1 \\ y_6' \oplus y_7' \oplus y_8' = y_2 \end{matrix} \tag{23}$$

Security Analysis. First, the correctness of version-2 masking scheme can be satisfied by summing up all component functions in (22) or (23). Second, under glitch-extended probing model, one can not obtain all shares of a variable with d probes. Therefore, the non-completeness condition is satisfied. For example, in (22), when probing y_0' under the glitch-extended probing model, one can only obtain a_0, b_0, c_0 and e_0, which will not leak values of a, b, c and e. Similarly, in (23), when probing arbitrary two registers under the glitch-extended probing model, one can not obtain full shares of a, b, c, d and e. Third, we evaluate the statistical relationship between a group of intermediate variables (*e.g.* shares and/or y_i') and the inputs of an update function, and obtain the result that these two are statistically independent. For example, when probing y_0 and y_0' under the glitch-extended probing model, one can obtain $a_0, b_0, c_0, y_0', y_1'$ and y_2'. Then, by traversing the inputs of an update function and estimating the statistical distribution of $(a_0, b_0, c_0, y_0', y_1', y_2')$, we can obtain the result that the statistical distribution of $(a_0, b_0, c_0, y_0', y_1', y_2')$ is independent of values of a, b, c, d and e. Therefore, the uniformity condition can be satisfied in version-2 masking scheme. Overall, the higher-order masking schemes shown in (22) and (23) can be secure under the glitch-extended probing model.

4.3 Hardware Cost

According to (19)–(23), the hardware cost of version-1 and version-2 masking schemes can be summarized in Table 1. In detail, *AND* represents the number of $\odot$ operations needed, *XOR* represents the number of $\oplus$ operations needed, *Rand.* represents the number of fresh randomness bits needed, *Register* represents the number of registers needed and *Stage* represents the number of clock cycles needed in each scheme.

Table 1. Overview of the hardware costs of different masking schemes

Order	AND	XOR	Rand	Register	Stage	Version
Unpro	1	3	0	0	0	–
1st order	4	10	1	2	2	version-1
	4	8	0	4	2	version-2
2nd order	9	21	3	6	2	version-1
	9	19	0	9	2	version-2
3rd order	16	36	6	12	2	version-1

It can be seen from Table 1 that version-1 masking scheme and version-2 masking scheme require the same number of AND operation in the 1st order and 2nd order cases, and they both require 2 clock cycle in all three cases. Comparatively, version-2 masking scheme needs more registers while version-1 masking scheme needs more XOR operations in the 1st order and 2nd order cases. Note that version-2 masking scheme does not require any fresh randomness while version-1 masking scheme require 1, 3 and 6 fresh randomness bits in the 1st order, 2nd order and 3rd order case respectively. Note that the trade-off between the Register and the Stage can be possible. For example, the 1st order version-2 masking scheme can also be implemented with 3 registers in 3 clock cycles. In the first clock cycle, y'_0 and y'_1 can be computed and stored in 2 registers. In the second clock cycle, y_0 can be computed by y'_0 and y'_1 and stored in 1 register. At the same time, y'_2 and y'_3 can be computed and stored in the 2 registers that store y'_0 and y'_1. In the third clock cycle, y_1 can be computed by y'_2 and y'_3.

5 Performance Evaluation

In this part, two versions of masking schemes are implemented on two typical hardware platforms *i.e.* ASIC and FPGA. For the ASIC hardware platform, the TSMC 130nm process with 1V supply voltage and 25°C is adopted. Besides, the implementation of two versions of masking schemes are synthesized with the Synopsys Design Compiler L-2016.03-SP1. The FPGA hardware platform is the Xilinx Spartan7 serial [28]. The Synthesis and the Implementation of two versions of masking schemes are conducted in Vivado 2020.1 [29] which is the standard IDE for Spartan7 serials using the Verilog hardware design language. In order to evaluate the performance more precisely, only the primary component *look up table (LUT)* in FPGA is used and resources like SRL16/SRL32, BRAM and DSP are not applied in our implementations.

Then, the performance of two versions of masking schemes is evaluated in two scenarios. In scenario-1, fresh randomness are assumed to be generated by external Pseudo Random Number Generator (PRNG). Therefore, the overhead of the generation of fresh randomness is not considered in scenario-1. In scenario-2, following the routine of [11], the fresh randomness used are generated with the unprotected parallel implementation of Trivium. Finally, the pipeline technique can be used to achieve the goal of parallelization with the price of some extra consumed area. Overall, the evaluation results of two versions of masking schemes in scenario-1 can be summarized in Table 2.

Table 2. Evaluation results on ASIC and FPGA (scenario-1)

Order	Rand. (Bits/Cyc.)	Stage	ASIC		FPGA				Version
			Area[a] (GE)	Max Thr.[b] (Mbps)	Area[c] LUT	FF	Slice	Max Thr.[b] (Mbps)	
Unpro.	0	1	2658	2273	169	305	48	376	–
1st order	1.5	2	5092	961	444	605	123	182	version-1
	3	1	5152	1923	454	606	127	355	version-1-p[d]
	0	2	5132	909	449	611	124	181	version-2
	0	1	5197	1786	458	612	127	352	version-2-p
2nd order	4.5	2	7502	909	648	911	175	179	version-1
	9	1	7711	1754	666	910	184	352	version-1-p
	0	2	7623	862	644	920	177	179	version-2
	0	1	7739	1613	668	920	190	343	version-2-p
3rd order	9	2	9952	806	858	1227	233	174	version-1
	18	1	10394	1408	881	1233	251	347	version-1-p

[a] Area is obtained under the 1GHz clock.
[b] The throughput is calculated under the max frequency.
[c] Area is obtained under the 200MHz clock.
[d] "-p" represents the pipeline mode.

According to Table 2, the following observations can be obtained. First, the performance of version-1 masking scheme can be better than that of version-2 masking scheme, even though the advantage is not obvious. Second, the pipeline technique can significantly optimize the throughput of two versions of masking schemes with the price of a little extra consumed area. Third, the performance of two versions of masking schemes decreases with the masking order. Fourth, no fresh randomness is needed for version-2 masking scheme while the number of fresh randomness bits that should be used in version-1 masking scheme increases with the masking order. Overall, in practice, when fresh randomness can be obtained through external PRNG, version-1 masking scheme should be used to protect a hardware implementation of Trivium.

Then, the evaluation results of two versions of masking schemes in scenario-2 can be summarized in Table 3. Note that in Table 3, the price to generate fresh randomness is evaluated. Besides, the efficiency of a masking scheme as a metric is computed to evaluate its overall performance.

Table 3. Evaluation results on ASIC and FPGA (scenario-2).

Order	ASIC			FPGA			Version
	Area		Efficiency	Area		Efficiency	
	(GE)	%	(Mbps/GE)	Slice	%	(Mbps/Slice)	
Unpro.	2658	100%	0.377	48	100%	4.17	
1st **order**	7811	100%	0.064	174	100%	0.57	version-1
mask	5092	65.2%		123	70.7%		
PRNG	2719	34.8%		51	29.3%		
1st **order-p**	7871	100%	0.127	178	100%	1.12	version-1
mask	5152	65.5%		127	71.3%		
PRNG	2719	34.5%		51	28.7%		
1st **order**	5132	100%	0.097	124	100%	0.807	version-2
1st **order-p**	5197	100%	0.192	127	100%	1.575	version-2
2nd **order**	10490	100%	0.048	233	100%	0.43	version-1
mask	7580	72.3%		175	75.1%		
PRNG	2910	27.7%		58	24.9%		
2nd **order-p**	10621	100%	0.094	242	100%	0.83	version-1
mask	7711	72.6%		184	76%		
PRNG	2910	27.4%		58	24%		
2nd **order**	7623	100%	0.066	177	100%	0.565	version-2
2nd **order-p**	7739	100%	0.129	190	100%	1.053	version-2
3rd **order**	13902	100%	0.036	301	100%	0.33	version-1
mask	9952	73.2%		233	77.4%		
PRNG	3729	26.8%		68	22.6%		
3rd **order-p**	14123	100%	0.071	319	100%	0.63	version-1
mask	10394	73.6%		251	78.7%		
PRNG	3729	26.4%		68	21.3%		

According to Table 3, the following observations can be obtained. First, when the price of fresh randomness is considered, the performance of version-2 masking scheme can be better than that of version-1 masking scheme, and the advantage can be obvious. Second, the price of fresh randomness can be significant. In fact, an unprotected parallel implementation of Trivium can be used to generate fresh randomness. If an unprotected serial implementation of Trivium is used to generate fresh randomness, the price can be much higher. Third, the ratio of the price of fresh randomness in the overall price of a masking scheme decreases with the mask order. The reason is that compared with the increasing rate of the price of fresh randomness, the increasing rate of the price of a masking scheme can be higher. Fourth, even through the addition of fresh randomness decreases the efficiency of version-1 masking scheme, the advantage of the performances of masking schemes with pipeline technique over the performances of masking schemes without pipeline technique can remain. Overall, in scenarios where the price to generate fresh randomness is high, version-2 masking scheme can be used to protect a hardware implementation of Trivium.

Discussion. When d probes are used to detect variables in two clock cycles shown in (19)–(23), two versions of masking schemes can be secure under the glitch-extended probing model. However, when variables in (19)–(23) beyond two clock cycles are detected by d probes, version-1 masking scheme can still be secure under the glitch-extended probing model, while version-2 masking scheme may be insecure under the glitch-extended probing model. The reason is that, the outputs of component functions in version-1 masking scheme are uniform and random, while the outputs of component functions in version-2 masking scheme can be uniform but not random. In this case, when variables beyond two clock cycles are combined, the inputs of update functions may be recovered. In light of this, version-1 masking scheme should be used in security-critical scenarios.

6 Side-Channel Evaluation

T-Test proposed by Goodwill et al. [10] can be used to evaluate the security of two versions of masked implementations of Trivium in the simulated scenario. More specifically, the *non-specific* T-Test leakage detection methodology is used. Two sets of simulated traces are collected under the *Hamming Distance Model.* For a fixed secret key, set Q_1 collects simulated traces with a fixed IV and set Q_2 collects simulated traces with randomly chosen IVs. If the number of samples contained in one power trace is denoted as N_s, the value v of T-Test at sample $w(1 \leq w \leq N_s)$ can be computed as

$$v_w = \frac{X_{1,w} - X_{2,w}}{\sqrt{\frac{S_{1,w}^2}{N_1} + \frac{S_{2,w}^2}{N_2}}}, \tag{24}$$

where $X_{1,w}$ denotes the mean of the power traces contained in Q_1 at sample w, $X_{2,w}$ denotes the mean of the power traces contained in Q_2 at sample w, $S_{1,w}^2$ denotes the variance of the power traces contained in Q_1 at sample w, $S_{2,w}^2$ denotes the variance of the power traces contained in Q_2 at sample w, N_1 denotes the number of power traces contained in Q_1 and N_2 denotes the number of power traces contained in Q_2. The null-hypothesis is that the means of both trace sets can be equal, which is accepted if the computed T-Test values are between the threshold of ± 4.5. If the T-Test values exceed this threshold then the null-hypothesis is rejected with a confidence larger than 99.999%. In order to evaluate the security of higher-order masked implementations of Trivium, the higher-order T-Test should be used as the evaluation tool. The higher-order T-Test requires one to preprocess the traces. According to [23,26], the dth-order T-Test needs one to remove the means of the traces and raise them to power d. Then, the T-Test values can be computed with the preprocessed traces.

We observe that the variance of the signal under the Hamming Distance Model can be between 20 and 75. In order to simulate the practical hardware environment, at most the signal-to-noise ratio of 0.02 should be adopted, which means the variance of the noise should be between 1000 and 3500. We observe that the leakage for unprotected implementation can be obtained with only 10,000 traces. The number of traces in the simulated scenario is less than that needed in the practical hardware environment. The reason can be as follows. In the simulated scenario, the signal leakage can perfectly follow the Hamming Distance Model, while the practical hardware environment can be much more complicated and the signal leakage can be much harder to simulated. Thus, much more traces can be needed in the practical hardware environment. The evaluation results for two versions of masked implementations of Trivium can be shown in Fig. 1 and Fig. 2 respectively.

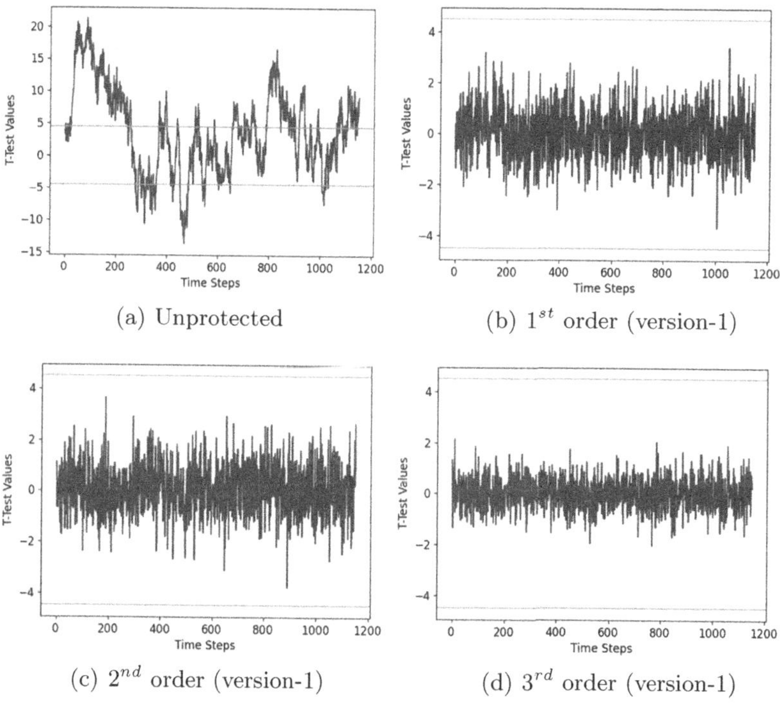

(a) Unprotected

(b) 1st order (version-1)

(c) 2nd order (version-1)

(d) 3rd order (version-1)

Fig. 1. T-Test results on the version-1 masking implementations of Trivium

Figure 1(a) shows the evaluation results of T-Test on the unprotected hardware implementation of Trivium during the initial phase. The large T-Test values

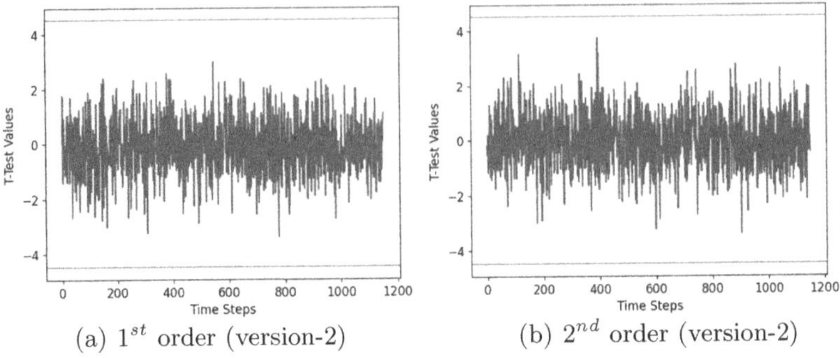

(a) 1st order (version-2)

(b) 2nd order (version-2)

Fig. 2. T-Test results on the version-2 masking implementations of Trivium

give a strong indication of leakage for unprotected hardware implementation of Trivium, which means that the unprotected hardware implementation of Trivium can be vulnerable to side-channel attacks in practice. For version-1 masking scheme, Fig. 1(b) shows the evaluation results of T-Test on the 1st order masked hardware implementation of Trivium. The T-Test values are located between the threshold of ± 4.5, which shows that it can resist the first-order side-channel attack. Figure 1(c) shows the evaluation results of T-Test on the 2nd order masked hardware implementation of Trivium. The T-Test values are located between the threshold of ± 4.5, which shows that it can resist the second-order side-channel attack. Fig 1(d) shows the evaluation results of T-Test on the 3rd order masked hardware implementation of Trivium. The T-Test values are located between the threshold of ± 4.5, which shows that it can resist the third-order side-channel attack. For version-2 masking scheme, Fig. 2(a) and Fig. 2(b) show the evaluation results of T-Test on the 1st and 2nd order masked hardware implementation of Trivium respectively. The T-Test values are located between the threshold of ± 4.5, which shows that it can resist the first-order and the second-order side-channel attack.

7 Conclusion

In this paper, three types of probing attacks are proposed to recover secret key bits used by an implementation of Trivium. Then, inspired by the ideas of the DOM masking scheme proposed by Gross *et al.* and the CHES 2021 masking scheme proposed by Shahmirzadi *et al.*, two versions of higher-order masking schemes are proposed to protect hardware implementations of Trivium. The security of two versions of masking schemes are proved under the glitch-extended probing model. Then, we evaluate the performance of two versions of masking schemes on ASIC and FPGA with or without the pipeline technique. The evaluation results show that, in scenarios where fresh randomness can be obtained through external PRNG, version-1 masking scheme can be used to protect a hardware implementation of Trivium. However, when the price of fresh randomness should be considered, version-2 masking scheme may be used to protect a hardware implementation of Trivium.

Acknowledgments. This work was supported by the National Key Research and Development Program of China [No. 2020YFB1805402], the Open Fund of Advanced Cryptography and System Security Key Laboratory of Sichuan Province [Grant No. SKLACSS-202116] and the National Natural Science Foundation of China [Grants No. 61872359, No. 61936008 and No. 62272451].

References

1. Brier, E., Clavier, C., Olivier, F.: Correlation power analysis with a leakage model. In: Joye, M., Quisquater, J.-J. (eds.) CHES 2004. LNCS, vol. 3156, pp. 16–29. Springer, Heidelberg (2004). https://doi.org/10.1007/978-3-540-28632-5_2
2. Chari, S., Jutla, C.S., Rao, J.R., Rohatgi, P.: Towards sound approaches to counteract power-analysis attacks. In: Wiener, M. (ed.) CRYPTO 1999. LNCS, vol. 1666, pp. 398–412. Springer, Heidelberg (1999). https://doi.org/10.1007/3-540-48405-1_26
3. Coron, J.-S., Goubin, L.: On Boolean and arithmetic masking against differential power analysis. In: Koç, Ç.K., Paar, C. (eds.) CHES 2000. LNCS, vol. 1965, pp. 231–237. Springer, Heidelberg (2000). https://doi.org/10.1007/3-540-44499-8_18
4. Coron, J.-S., Kizhvatov, I.: An efficient method for random delay generation in embedded software. In: Clavier, C., Gaj, K. (eds.) CHES 2009. LNCS, vol. 5747, pp. 156–170. Springer, Heidelberg (2009). https://doi.org/10.1007/978-3-642-04138-9_12
5. De Cannière, C., Preneel, B.: Trivium. In: Robshaw, M., Billet, O. (eds.) New Stream Cipher Designs. LNCS, vol. 4986, pp. 244–266. Springer, Heidelberg (2008). https://doi.org/10.1007/978-3-540-68351-3_18
6. eSTREAM: Ecrypt stream cipher project. http://www.ecrypt.eu.org/stream
7. Faust, S., Grosso, V., Merino Del Pozo, S., Paglialonga, C., Standaert, F.X.: Composable masking schemes in the presence of physical defaults & the robust probing model. IACR Trans. Cryptogr. Hardware Embed. Syst. 89–120 (2018). https://doi.org/10.13154/tches.v2018.i3.89-120
8. Fischer, W., Gammel, B.M., Kniffler, O., Velten, J.: Differential power analysis of stream ciphers. In: Abe, M. (ed.) CT-RSA 2007. LNCS, vol. 4377, pp. 257–270. Springer, Heidelberg (2006). https://doi.org/10.1007/11967668_17
9. Fu, X., Wang, X., Dong, X., Meier, W.: A key-recovery attack on 855-round Trivium. In: Shacham, H., Boldyreva, A. (eds.) CRYPTO 2018. LNCS, vol. 10992, pp. 160–184. Springer, Cham (2018). https://doi.org/10.1007/978-3-319-96881-0_6
10. Gilbert Goodwill, B.J., Jaffe, J., Rohatgi, P., et al.: A testing methodology for side-channel resistance validation. In: NIST Non-invasive Attack Testing Workshop, vol. 7, pp. 115–136 (2011)
11. Gross, H., Mangard, S.: A unified masking approach. J. Cryptogr. Eng. **8**(2), 109–124 (2018). https://doi.org/10.1007/s13389-018-0184-y
12. Groß, H., Mangard, S., Korak, T.: Domain-oriented masking: compact masked hardware implementations with arbitrary protection order. In: TIS@ CCS, p. 3 (2016)
13. Ishai, Y., Sahai, A., Wagner, D.: Private circuits: securing hardware against probing attacks. In: Boneh, D. (ed.) CRYPTO 2003. LNCS, vol. 2729, pp. 463–481. Springer, Heidelberg (2003). https://doi.org/10.1007/978-3-540-45146-4_27

14. ISO/IEC: Information technology - Security techniques - Lightweight cryptography - Part 3: Stream ciphers. Standard, International Organization for Standardization, Geneva, CH (2012)
15. Jia, Y., Hu, Y., Wang, F., Wang, H.: Correlation power analysis of Trivium. Secur. Commun. Netw. **5**(5), 479–484 (2012)
16. Kocher, P., Jaffe, J., Jun, B.: Differential power analysis. In: Wiener, M. (ed.) CRYPTO 1999. LNCS, vol. 1666, pp. 388–397. Springer, Heidelberg (1999). https://doi.org/10.1007/3-540-48405-1_25
17. Mangard, S., Popp, T., Gammel, B.M.: Side-channel leakage of masked CMOS gates. In: Menezes, A. (ed.) CT-RSA 2005. LNCS, vol. 3376, pp. 351–365. Springer, Heidelberg (2005). https://doi.org/10.1007/978-3-540-30574-3_24
18. Mangard, S., Pramstaller, N., Oswald, E.: Successfully attacking masked AES hardware implementations. In: Rao, J.R., Sunar, B. (eds.) CHES 2005. LNCS, vol. 3659, pp. 157–171. Springer, Heidelberg (2005). https://doi.org/10.1007/11545262_12
19. Mangard, S., Schramm, K.: Pinpointing the side-channel leakage of masked AES hardware implementations. In: Goubin, L., Matsui, M. (eds.) CHES 2006. LNCS, vol. 4249, pp. 76–90. Springer, Heidelberg (2006). https://doi.org/10.1007/11894063_7
20. Messerges, T.S.: Using second-order power analysis to attack DPA resistant software. In: Koç, Ç.K., Paar, C. (eds.) CHES 2000. LNCS, vol. 1965, pp. 238–251. Springer, Heidelberg (2000). https://doi.org/10.1007/3-540-44499-8_19
21. Nikova, S., Rechberger, C., Rijmen, V.: Threshold implementations against side-channel attacks and glitches. In: Ning, P., Qing, S., Li, N. (eds.) ICICS 2006. LNCS, vol. 4307, pp. 529–545. Springer, Heidelberg (2006). https://doi.org/10.1007/11935308_38
22. Reparaz, O., Bilgin, B., Nikova, S., Gierlichs, B., Verbauwhede, I.: Consolidating masking schemes. In: Gennaro, R., Robshaw, M. (eds.) CRYPTO 2015. LNCS, vol. 9215, pp. 764–783. Springer, Heidelberg (2015). https://doi.org/10.1007/978-3-662-47989-6_37
23. Schneider, T., Moradi, A.: Leakage assessment methodology. In: Güneysu, T., Handschuh, H. (eds.) CHES 2015. LNCS, vol. 9293, pp. 495–513. Springer, Heidelberg (2015). https://doi.org/10.1007/978-3-662-48324-4_25
24. Shahmirzadi, A.R., Moradi, A.: Re-consolidating first-order masking schemes: nullifying fresh randomness. IACR Trans. Cryptogr. Hardware Embed. Syst. 305–342 (2021)
25. Shahmirzadi, A.R., Moradi, A.: Second-order SCA security with almost no fresh randomness. IACR Trans. Cryptogr. Hardw. Embed. Syst. 708–755 (2021)
26. Standaert, F.-X.: How (not) to use Welch's T-test in side-channel security evaluations. In: Bilgin, B., Fischer, J.-B. (eds.) CARDIS 2018. LNCS, vol. 11389, pp. 65–79. Springer, Cham (2019). https://doi.org/10.1007/978-3-030-15462-2_5
27. Veyrat-Charvillon, N., Medwed, M., Kerckhof, S., Standaert, F.-X.: Shuffling against side-channel attacks: a comprehensive study with cautionary note. In: Wang, X., Sako, K. (eds.) ASIACRYPT 2012. LNCS, vol. 7658, pp. 740–757. Springer, Heidelberg (2012). https://doi.org/10.1007/978-3-642-34961-4_44
28. Xilinx: 7 series FPGAs data sheet: Overview. https://www.xilinx.com
29. Xilinx: Vivado design suite - HLx editions. https://www.xilinx.com/products/design-tools/vivado.html
30. Ye, C.D., Tian, T., Zeng, F.Y.: The MILP-aided conditional differential attack and its application to Trivium. Des. Codes Crypt. **89**(2), 317–339 (2021)

An Experimentally Verified Attack on 820-Round Trivium

Cheng Che and Tian Tian(✉)

PLA Strategic Support Force Information Engineering University, Zhengzhou 450001, China
tiantian_d@126.com

Abstract. The cube attack is one of the most important cryptanalytic techniques against Trivium. As the method of recovering superpolies becomes more and more effective, another problem of cube attacks, i.e., how to select cubes that can effectively attack, is attracting more and more attention. In this paper, we present a novel framework to search for valuable cubes whose superpolies have an independent secret variable each, i.e., a linear variable not appearing in any nonlinear term. To control online complexity, valuable cubes are selected from very few large cubes. New ideas are given on the large cube construction and the subcube sieve. As illustrations, we apply the new algorithm to the stream cipher Trivium. For 815-round Trivium, the complexity of full key-recovery attack is $2^{47.32}$. For 820-round Trivium, the complexity of full key-recovery attack is $2^{53.17}$. Strong experimental evidence shows that the full key-recovery attacks on 815- and 820-round Trivium could be completed within six hours and two weeks on a PC with two RTX3090 GPUs, respectively.

Keywords: Cube attacks · Key-recovery attacks · Division property · Trivium

1 Introduction

Cube Attack: The cube attack is a new method of analyzing symmetric-key cryptosystems proposed by Dinur and Shamir in [1]. The output bit of a stream cipher can be regarded as a tweakable polynomial in the secret variables $\boldsymbol{k}$ and the public IV variables $\boldsymbol{v}$, expressed as $f(\boldsymbol{k}, \boldsymbol{v})$. In cube attacks, some IV variables are set as active, that is, all possible combinations of 0/1 are taken, and the rest of the IV variables are inactive and set to constants. The set of these values is called a cube. By taking the values of $f(\boldsymbol{k}, \boldsymbol{v})$ over all values in the cube, the sum leads to a relation of secret variables. This relation is called the superpoly of the cube, and it is much simpler than $f(\boldsymbol{k}, \boldsymbol{v})$. Based on these superpolys, information about the secret variables can be obtained.

In [1,2], $f(\boldsymbol{k}, \boldsymbol{v})$ is regarded as a blackbox polynomial and analyzed experimentally. In [3], the division property was first introduced to cube attacks on stream ciphers, and it could be used to identify the secret variables not involved

Y. Deng and M. Yung (Eds.): Inscrypt 2022, LNCS 13837, pp. 357–369, 2023.
https://doi.org/10.1007/978-3-031-26553-2_19

in the superpoly efficiently. To improve the effectiveness of cube attacks based on division property, some new techniques were given in [4,5]. However, the traditional division property only confirms that a specific monomial does not appear in the superpoly if the division property cannot propagate to the output bit. This inaccuracy of the traditional division property makes many previous key-recovery attacks, e.g., [4,6], degenerate to distinguishing attacks [5,7]. This was finally resolved by Hao et al. in [8], where the model for three-subset division property without unknown subset was proposed.

Trivium: Trivium [9] is a bit-oriented synchronous stream cipher designed by De Cannière and Preneel, which is one of the eSTREAM hardware-oriented finalists. When the cube attack was first proposed, a key-recovery attack on 767-round Trivium was given, in which 35 linear superpolies were recovered [1]. Next, key-recovery attacks on 784- and 799-round of Trivium were given in [2]. Recently, an effective method to construct cubes for linear superpolies was proposed in [10], and a practical attack against 805-round Trivium was given. On the other hand, cube attacks based on division property theoretically evaluate the security of Trivium by targeting a very high round number. In [8], Hao et al. accurately recovered the superpolies of 840-, 841-, and 842-round Trivium by using three-subset division property without unknown subset. Meanwhile, Hu et al. in [11] described the propagation of monomials from a pure algebraic perspective and proposed monomial prediction technique. Recently, Hu et al. [12] combined the monomial prediction technique with the backtracking method in [7] and presented a new framework for recovering the exact ANFs of massive superpolies, recovering the superpolies for 843-, 844- and 845-round Trivium. At FSE 2021, Sun proposed a new heuristic method in [13] to reject cubes without independent secret variables from a preset of candidate cubes. Using the heuristic algorithm, they recovered a balanced superpoly for 843-round Trivium and presented practical attacks against 806- and 808-round Trivium.

Motivation: Our work aims to enhance the ability of a practical key-recovery attack on Trivium. Firstly, we use a special class of balanced superpolies. For a superpoly p, if p could be decomposed into $p(\boldsymbol{k}) = p'(\boldsymbol{k}) \oplus k_i$, where k_i does not appear in p', then we say that p has an **independent variable** k_i. If we obtain many such superpolies, it is easy to select n superpolies to provide n-bit key information. We say a cube is **valuable** if its superpoly has at least one independent secret variable. Secondly, to reduce the complexity of the online phase, the existing practical attacks [10,13] all selected a large cube I and searched the subcubes of I. So, the attacker only needs $2^{|I|}$ times to query the encryption oracle. In the following paper, a desirable large cube is called a **mother cube**. Therefore, a good mother cube and a method of searching for valuable subcubes are critical for practical attacks.

Our work is motivated by the heuristic method of rejecting useless cubes in [13]. There are two obvious drawbacks of this search algorithm. On one hand, both rejection and acceptance of this method may be wrong, and it is difficult for practical attacks to control the size of cube if some valuable cubes are rejected. On the other hand, when there are many subcubes in the test, it cannot terminate within an acceptable period of time. Instead of rejecting useless cubes, we consider choosing cubes that are more likely to be valuable. Firstly, we observe that low-degree superpolies are easier to recover and more likely to contain independent variables. Moreover, for many low-degree balanced superpolies, it is easy to select n superpolies to provide n-bits of key information. For simplicity, **the degree of a cube** refers to the degree of the superpoly corresponding to the cube. Secondly, we note that the existence of linear terms is necessary for a superpoly to have independent secret variables. We find that many superpolies do not have linear terms in experimental tests. It is obvious that these superpolies without linear terms cannot contain independent secret variables.

Our Contribution: We present a novel framework to search for valuable subcubes from a mother cube, which is experimentally verified to be quite effective. It consists of the following three aspects.

1. We modify the algorithm for constructing cubes targeting linear superpolies presented in [10]. We aim to construct a mother cube with many low-degree subcubes rather than several low-degree cubes unrelated to each other. Therefore, we modify the end of the first stage in order to construct a potentially good mother cube.
2. We propose an efficient method to search for low-degree subcubes. The deep-first-search strategy is used. We first enumerate the degrees of all the subcubes with one less variable for a given mother cube. Then, for the subcubes with degree less than 5, we continually enumerate the subcubes with one less variable until there is no subcube with degree less than 5. As a result, we can identify most of the low-degree subcubes efficiently.
3. We propose a method for searching for valuable subcubes. We note that the existence of linear terms is necessary for a superpoly to have independent secret variables. Moreover, since linear terms account for only a small part of the superpoly, it is efficient to recover all linear terms of a cube. Therefore, we recover the linear terms of the low-degree subcubes and reject the subcubes without linear terms, or all the linear terms have been covered by some simple superpolies. Experimental data on 820-Trivium show that only about 20% of the superpolies are left after the rejection.

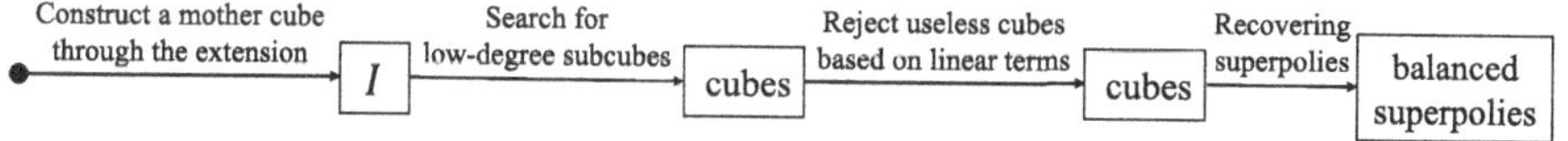

Fig. 1. The sketch of our idea

As an illustration, we apply our methods, whose sketch is shown in Fig. 1, to the well-known stream cipher Trivium. Practical attacks on 815- and 820-round Trivium are given. For 815-round Trivium, we could obtain 35-bit key information at 2^{47} online computation complexity. Hence, the total online complexity is

$2^{47}+2^{45}$. For 820-round Trivium, we could obtain 30-bit key information at 2^{53} online computation complexity. Hence, the total online complexity is $2^{53}+2^{50}$. This attack on 820-round Trivium improves the previous best practical cube attacks by 12 more rounds. As a comparison, we summarize full key-recovery attacks against the round-reduced Trivium in Table 1.[1]

Table 1. A summary of key-recovery attacks on Trivium

Attack type	# of rounds	Off-line phase		On-line phase	Total time	Ref.
		Cube size	# of key bits			
Practical	672	12	63	2^{17}	$2^{18.56}$	[1]
	767	28–31	35	2^{45}	$2^{45.00}$	[1]
	784	30–33	42	2^{38}	$2^{39.00}$	[2]
	805	32–38	42	2^{38}	$2^{41.40}$	[10]
	806	33–37	45	2^{35}	$2^{39.88}$	[13]
	808	39–41	37	2^{43}	$2^{44.58}$	[13]
	815	44–46	35	2^{45}	$2^{47.32}$	Sect. 4.1
	820	48–51	30	2^{50}	$2^{53.17}$	Sect. 4.2
Theoretical	799	32–37	18	2^{62}	$2^{62.00}$	[2]
	802	34–37	8	2^{72}	$2^{72.00}$	[14]
	805	28	7	2^{73}	$2^{73.00}$	[15]
	832	72	1	2^{79}	$2^{79.01}$	[3, 5]
	835	35	5	2^{75}	$2^{75.00}$	[15]
	840	75	3	2^{77}	$2^{77.32}$	[11]
	840	78	1	2^{79}	$2^{79.58}$	[8]
	841	78	1	2^{79}	$2^{79.58}$	[8]
	841	76	2	2^{78}	$2^{78.58}$	[11]
	842	76	2	2^{79}	$2^{78.58}$	[11]
	842	78	1	2^{79}	$2^{79.58}$	[8]
	843	54–57,76	5	2^{75}	$2^{76.58}$	[12]
	843	78	1	2^{79}	$2^{79.58}$	[13]
	844	54–55	2	2^{78}	$2^{78.00}$	[12]
	845	54–55	2	2^{78}	$2^{78.00}$	[12]

2 Preliminaries

2.1 Boolean Functions and Algebraic Degree

A Boolean function on n variables is a mapping from $\mathbb{F}_2^n$ to $\mathbb{F}_2$, where $\mathbb{F}_2$ is the binary field and $\mathbb{F}_2^n$ is an n-dimensional vector space over $\mathbb{F}_2$. A Boolean function f can be uniquely represented as a multivariable polynomial over $\mathbb{F}_2$,

$$f(x_1, x_2, \ldots, x_n) = \bigoplus_{c=(c_1,c_2,\ldots,c_n)\in\{0,1\}^n} a_c \prod_{i=1}^{n} x_i^{c_i},\ a_c \in \mathbb{F}_2,$$

[1] All the related codes and results could be found on https://github.com/LLuckyRabbit/search-for-valuables-cubes.

which is called the algebraic normal form (ANF) of f. In the following paper, $\prod_{i=1}^{n} x_i^{c_i}$ is called a term of f. One important feature of a Boolean function is its algebraic degree which is denoted by $\deg(f)$ and defined as

$$\deg(f) = \max\{wt(\boldsymbol{c}) | a_{\boldsymbol{c}} \neq 0\},$$

where $wt(\boldsymbol{c})$ is the Hamming Weight of $\boldsymbol{c}$, i.e., $wt(\boldsymbol{c}) = \sum_{i=1}^{n} c_i$.

2.2 Trivium

Trivium is a bit-oriented synchronous stream cipher that was one of the eSTREAM hardware-oriented finalists. The main building block of Trivium is a Galois nonlinear feedback shift register, and its internal states are 288 bits in total. For every clock cycle, three bits of the internal state are updated by quadratic feedback functions, and all the remaining bits of the internal state are updated by shifting. In the initialization phase, an 80-bit secret key and an 80-bit IV are loaded in the internal state of Trivium. After updating the internal state iteratively for 1152 rounds, Trivium starts to output keystream bits. For more details, please refer to [9].

2.3 Cube Attacks

The cube attack was first proposed by Dinur and Shamir in [1]. In cube attacks, the output bit of a stream cipher can be regarded as a tweakable polynomial $f(\boldsymbol{k}, \boldsymbol{v})$, where $\boldsymbol{k} = (k_1, k_2, ..., k_n)$ are secret key variables and $\boldsymbol{v} = (v_1, v_2, ..., v_m)$ are public IV variables. For a randomly chosen set $I = \{v_{i_1}, v_{i_2}, \ldots, v_{i_d}\}$, $f(\boldsymbol{k}, \boldsymbol{v})$ can be represented uniquely as

$$f(\boldsymbol{k}, \boldsymbol{v}) = t_I \cdot p_I(\boldsymbol{k}, \boldsymbol{v}) \oplus q_I(\boldsymbol{k}, \boldsymbol{v}),$$

where $t_I = v_{i_1} \cdots v_{i_d}$, and q_I misses at least one variable in I. The IV variables in I are called **cube variables**. These cube variables are set as active, that is, all possible combinations of 0/1 are taken, and the rest of the IV variables are inactive and set to constants. The set of these values is denoted as a **cube**, and the polynomial p_I is called the **superpoly** of I in f. It can be seen that the summation of the 2^d functions derived from f by assigning all the possible values to d variables in I equals p_I. Therefore, in the online phase, it takes 2^d queries the cipher oracle to get the value of the superpoly $p_I(\boldsymbol{k}, \boldsymbol{v})$.

Obviously, $p_I(\boldsymbol{k}, \boldsymbol{v})$ is much simpler than $f(\boldsymbol{k}, \boldsymbol{v})$. Once an attacker recovers a certain number of superpolies, he could build a system of equations on secret key variables $\boldsymbol{k}$ by inquiring the values of all the superpolies. Then some information about the secret variables can be achieved. In particular, if a superpoly is balanced, namely $|\{\boldsymbol{k} \in \mathbb{F}_2^n \mid f(\boldsymbol{k}) = 0\}| = |\{\boldsymbol{k} \in \mathbb{F}_2^n \mid f(\boldsymbol{k}) = 1\}| = 2^{n-1}$, then 2^{n-1} illegal keys will be filtered out. However, in a key recovery attack, it is difficult to obtain ℓ-bits of information about the key even if there are ℓ balanced superpolies. Moreover, when ℓ is large, it is almost impossible.

2.4 A Heuristic Algorithm of Constructing Cubes Targeting Linear Superpolies

In [10], Ye et al. combined the division property based degree evaluation method with some greedy strategies to construct cubes targeting linear superpolies. The author heuristically gave a small set of cube variables and then extended it iteratively. In order to construct cubes targeting linear superpolies, the extension phase is subdivided into two stages.

- In the first stage, we select a steep IV variable which could decrease the degrees of the superpolies as fast as possible in each iteration.
- In the second stage, we select a gentle IV variable which decrease the degrees of the superpolies as slowly as possible in each iteration.

It may fail to construct cubes with linear superpolies by only adding steep IV variables. The goal of the second stage is to ensure that the degree of the superpoly could be close to 1 rather than suddenly dropping to 0.

3 A Search Algorithm for Valuable Cubes

To mount key-recovery attacks, enough valuable cubes need to be collected. A modified algorithm for constructing mother cubes and an efficient method for searching low-degree subcubes are introduced in Sects. 3.1 and 3.2, respectively. In Sect. 3.3, we present a method for rejecting useless cubes. Combining the new methods given in these three sections, we present a novel general framework for making key-recovery attacks.

3.1 A Modified Algorithm of Constructing Mother Cubes

In [10], Ye et al. completed a practical key-recovery attack on 805-round Trivium using linear superpolies. As the number of rounds increases, recovering linear superpolies is not enough to mount a practical attack. We aim to extend linear superpolies to low-degree superpolies in a practical attack. To reduce the number of requests in the online phase, we construct a mother cube and then search its subcubes. When constructing the mother cube, we want a cube that has many low-degree subcubes and is as small as possible. Therefore, we do not need to add some gentle IV variables that make the degree of cube approach 1, and we only need the first stage of the algorithm in Sect. 2.4.

We modify the beginning and the end of the first stage. In [10], the authors gave a method for determining starting cube sets. In fact, many starting cubes meet the criteria. We consider selecting the cube with the smallest degree as a starting set. In the end, because the iteration only adds a steep IV variable, the degree of the cube drops to 0 quickly. Then, in the last iteration, the resulting cubes with a non-zero degree are low-degree cubes. However, we want a mother cube that contains many low-degree subcubes, not some cubes whose last variable is different. Therefore, for the results of the last iteration, we select several

IV variables to add to the cube to get a large cube. Then, how many IV variables to choose and which IV variables to choose is a matter for us to consider.

We focus on IV variables that reduce the cube to a lower degree, such as IV variables with a cube degree less than five after being added. For example, assuming there are five such IV variables, we will get ten new large cubes if we combine the three and add them to the original cube. The algebraic degrees of all subcubes with one less variable are evaluated for the ten large cubes. The large cube is selected as the mother cube if it has the most subcubes of degree less than 5. In particular, if the degrees of all subcubes are not small, for example, greater than 4, it is considered that more IV variables are needed to reduce the degree of the whole.

3.2 A Method for Searching Low-Degree Subcubes

For the mother cube obtained in Sect. 3.1, the next step is to search for valuable subcubes. In [13], Sun directly dealt with candidate subcubes to select the cube that is more likely to have independent variable k_i. However, when attacking 820-round Trivium, a mother cube of size 52 has many subcubes. If we deal with them together and then judge, the time is unacceptable.

Among all subcubes, there will be some complicated cubes, which occupy most of the solving time. Naturally, we tend to choose subcubes that are more likely to be valuable and solve faster. The algebraic degree is the most common way to measure the complexity of a cube. It is generally agreed that low-degree superpolies are easier to recover. In particular, low-degree superpolies are also more likely to have independent variables. Therefore, we first evaluate the degree of a subcube and then judge whether the subcube is valuable. Since the subcubes are contained in a large cube, we can strategically evaluate algebraic degrees. Our strategy is based on the following observation.

Observation 1. *For a given cube I, the degree of most subcubes is higher than the degree of I.*

We do an experiment where we choose ten large cubes. In all the subcubes with one variable less, about 90% of the subcubes have higher degrees than the original cube. Therefore, we use a deep-first-search strategy to evaluate degrees.

Taking 815-round Trivium as an example, for a 47-dimensional cube, we first enumerate the degrees of 46-dimensional subcubes. Then enumerate the subcubes with one less variable for the cubes whose degrees are less than 5 in the 46-dimensional subcubes. Because of Observation 1, it is difficult to get some low-degree subcubes in a cube whose degree is greater than 5. Therefore, we always enumerate subcubes with one less variable for low-degree cubes until there is no cube whose degree is less than 5. Using this strategy, we can enumerate a small number of subcubes and obtain the vast majority of low-degree subcubes, effectively speeding up the search for low-degree subcubes.

3.3 A Method for Searching Valuable Subcubes

A large number of low-degree subcubes can be obtained using the method in Sect. 3.2. The problem to be solved here is how to search for valuable cubes among many low-degree subcubes. The natural idea is to test whether a specific secret variable k_i is independent. This method only needs to compute the monomials that involve the variable k_i and is more efficient. However, Trivium, for example, has 80 secret variables. If each secret variable is tested, it can be more complicated than recovering the superpolies directly, so verifying all secret variables for a cube is impractical.

Instead of pointlessly verifying all secret variables, we consider which variables need to be verified for a given cube. We note that the independent secret variable is a linear term, and the existence of linear terms is necessary for a superpoly to have independent secret variables. Therefore, if a superpoly does not contain linear terms, we can reject it without error. If a superpoly contains linear terms, we only need to verify that these variables are independent. Based on this consideration, we give the criteria for the primary filtration of candidate cubes.

The Primary Filtration. *If the superpoly corresponding to a cube has no linear term, then we can reject the cube.*

Linear terms account for only a small part of the superpoly, so it is efficient to recover all the linear terms of a cube. We make simple statistics on the low-degree cubes of 820-round Trivium, and the cube with linear terms accounts for about 40%. The specific data are listed in Table 2.

Table 2. Statistics the remaining cubes after filtering for 820-round Trivium

Dim	#Cubes	#Cubes with linear terms	#Remaining cubes
51	31	7	3
50	78	30	17
49	364	157	77
48	195	96	54
Total	668	290	151

After we recover the superpolies of many subcubes, we find that these superpolies have complex algebraic relations, that is, one superpoly may be generated by the combination of other superpolies. Therefore, some linear terms occur frequently in superpolies. We only need one superpoly containing the independent secret variable for a linear term that occurs frequently. Therefore, we can also do secondary filtering for cubes that contain the same linear term.

The Secondary Filtration. *If the linear terms of the superpoly corresponding to a cube have been recovered in linear or quadratic balanced superpolies, then we can reject the cube.*

For independent variables appearing in balanced superpolies of degree three or more, we expect to obtain simpler superpolies. Therefore, we reject only the independent variables previously obtained in linear or quadratic balanced superpolies. In particular, to perform the secondary filtration more efficiently, we first recover the cube with the lowest degree for all cubes with the same linear term. In the fourth column of Table 2, we also list the remaining cubes filtered twice during the practical recovery process. The details of our idea are described in Algorithm 1.

When recovering the remaining cubes, we can use the observation given in [13] that the higher-degree terms obtained by the subsystem will appear in the superpoly with high probability. Therefore, we divide the whole system into several subsystems to solve the superpoly. If the high-degree term related to the linear term is obtained in a subsystem, then we can reject the cube. In the practical recovery, the superpolies that we fully recover are all balanced.

Algorithm 1. The algorithm of searching valuable cubes based on linear terms

Require: a set of low-degree cubes $B = \{I_1, \ldots, I_c\}$ and the target round r
$K \leftarrow \emptyset$;
for $I \in B$ **do**
  Recover the linear terms of the superpoly corresponding to cube I;
  $L \leftarrow$ linear terms variables;
  /* Primary filtration and secondary filtration */
  if $L \neq \emptyset$ and $L \not\subset K$ **then**
    Recover the superpoly p corresponding to cube I;
    if superpoly p is balanced **then**
      Record cube I and superpoly p;
      /* The independent secret variables corresponding to the simple superpoly is updated, which can be used for secondary filtering. */
      if $\deg(p) \leq 2$ **then**
        $K \leftarrow K \cup \{$independent secret variables$\}$;
      end if
    end if
  end if
end for

4 Applications

In this section, we apply the new framework to Trivium. Practical attacks on 815- and 820-round Trivium are given. Due to the page limits, more details are provided in our full version [16].

4.1 A Practical Key-Recovery Attack on 815-Round Trivium

To attack 815-round Trivium, we construct the mother cube I_1 of size 47, and found 35 valuable cubes, as shown in Table 3. Next, we need a linearization method to deal with nonlinear balanced superpolies. Consistent with the method in [13], we first enumerate the values of 45 variables: $\{k_0, k_1, k_2, k_3, k_8, k_9, k_{10}, k_{11}, k_{13}, k_{14}, k_{15}, k_{16}, k_{17}, k_{19}, k_{21}, k_{27}, k_{28}, k_{32}, k_{36}, k_{37}, k_{39}, k_{40}, k_{41}, k_{45}, k_{50}, k_{52}, k_{54},$

k_{57}, k_{59}, $k_{61}, k_{63}, k_{64}, k_{65}, k_{66}, k_{67}, k_{68}$, k_{69}, k_{70}, k_{71}, k_{72}, k_{73}, k_{76}, $k_{77}, k_{78}, k_{79}\}$, and the complexity is 2^{45}. For each enumeration, the values of the remaining 35 variables can be deduced iteratively in the order: (k_{23}, k_{35}, k_{48}, k_{49}, k_{56}, k_{58}, k_{60}, k_{62}, k_{43}, k_{47}, k_{24}, $k_{51}, k_{44}, k_6, k_7, k_{33}, k_{55}, k_{34}, k_{42}, k_{38}$, k_4, k_{12}, k_{31}, $k_5, k_{25}, k_{53}, k_{46}, k_{20}$, $k_{26}, k_{29}, k_{18}, k_{22}, k_{74}, k_{30}, k_{75}$), and this deduction only costs constant time. The total attack complexity is $2^{47} + 2^{45}$. On a PC with two RTX3090 GPUs, we mount a practical key-recovery attack within six hours. Specifically, we use two GPUs to obtain the corresponding values of all cubes in 3.2 h and then use one GPU to guess and enumerate all possible keys in about 2 h. Finally, we successfully obtain the 80-bit key. Comparing 808-round Trivium attack in [13], we increase the number of attacked rounds by seven by adding only three IV variables. This also shows that our search algorithm is more efficient.

Table 3. Valuable cubes for attacking 815-round Trivium

Cube indices	Independent bits	Cube indices	Independent bits
$I_1\backslash\{58,67\}$	k_{23}	$I_1\backslash\{44,71\}$	$k_{33}, k_{42}, k_{51}, k_{62}$
$I_1\backslash\{43,67\}$	k_{35}	$I_1\backslash\{41,44\}$	$k_{33}, k_{38}, k_{42}, k_{49}, k_{60}, k_{65}$
$I_1\backslash\{19,58,67\}$	k_{48}	$I_1\backslash\{2,42,44\}$	k_4, k_{54}
$I_1\backslash\{2,44,60\}$	k_{35}, k_{49}	$I_1\backslash\{33,67\}$	k_{12}, k_{39}
$I_1\backslash\{35,43\}$	k_{35}, k_{56}	$I_1\backslash\{19,67\}$	$k_{12}, k_{31}, k_{39}, k_{40}, k_{47}, k_{67}$
$I_1\backslash\{2\}$	k_{58}	$I_1\backslash\{14,41\}$	$k_5, k_{14}, k_{41}, k_{42}$
$I_1\backslash\{41,44,67\}$	k_{60}	$I_1\backslash\{56,58,67\}$	k_{25}
$I_1\backslash\{58,59\}$	k_{62}	$I_1\backslash\{58,67,71\}$	k_{44}, k_{53}
$I_1\backslash\{3,18\}$	k_{43}, k_{70}	$I_1\backslash\{19,44\}$	$k_{10}, k_{19}, k_{28}, k_{37}, k_{46}, k_{55}$
$I_1\backslash\{3,60\}$	k_{43}, k_{47}, k_{70}	$I_1\backslash\{33,44,66\}$	$k_6, k_{10}, k_{11}, k_{19}, k_{20}, k_{28}, k_{38}, k_{47}, k_{55}, k_{72}$
$I_1\backslash\{0,15,41\}$	k_{24}, k_{37}, k_{56}	$I_1\backslash\{19,33,44\}$	$k_8, k_{17}, k_{26}, k_{57}, k_{59}$
$I_1\backslash\{42,44,46\}$	k_{50}, k_{51}	$I_1\backslash\{44,53,67\}$	$k_{11}, k_{20}, k_{29}, k_{47}$
$I_1\backslash\{3,19,44\}$	k_{44}, k_{56}, k_{71}	$I_1\backslash\{3,29\}$	k_{18}
$I_1\backslash\{34,41,44\}$	k_6, k_{49}	$I_1\backslash\{3,14,41\}$	k_{22}
$I_1\backslash\{36,58\}$	k_7, k_{48}	$I_1\backslash\{31\}$	$k_2, k_{24}, k_{29}, k_{47}, k_{49}, k_{53}, k_{56}, k_{74}$
$I_1\backslash\{36,43\}$	k_{33}	$I_1\backslash\{14,33,44\}$	k_3, k_6, k_{30}
$I_1\backslash\{43,62,67\}$	k_{55}	$I_1\backslash\{31,67\}$	$k_3, k_{10}, k_{12}, k_{19}, k_{21}, k_{27}, k_{28}, k_{66}, k_{75}$
$I_1\backslash\{0,2\}$	k_{34}, k_{47}		

I_1 = {0, 1, 2, 3, 4, 6, 8, 10, 12, 14, 15, 16, 18, 19, 20, 23, 25, 27, 29, 31, 33, 34, 35, 36, 37, 40, 41, 42, 43, 44, 46, 51, 53, 55, 56, 58, 59, 60, 61, 62, 66, 67, 69, 71, 73, 77, 79}

4.2 A Practical Key-Recovery Attack on 820-Round Trivium

To attack 820-round Trivium, we construct two mother cubes I_2 and I_3 of size 52, and found 30 valuable cubes, as shown in Table 4. Next, we need to enumerate the values of 50 variables: $\{k_0, k_1, k_4, k_5, k_6, k_7, k_9, k_{11}, k_{12}$, $k_{15}, k_{16}, k_{17}, k_{18}, k_{19}, k_{21}$,

k_{22}, k_{23}, k_{24}, k_{28}, k_{30}, k_{31}, k_{32}, k_{33}, k_{34}, k_{35}, k_{37}, k_{38}, k_{40}, k_{41}, k_{42}, k_{44}, k_{45}, k_{46}, k_{47}, k_{48}, k_{49}, k_{50}, k_{52}, k_{57}, k_{59}, k_{62}, k_{64}, k_{67}, k_{68}, k_{69}, $k_{71}, k_{73}, k_{76}, k_{77}, k_{78}\}$, and the complexity is 2^{50}. For each enumeration, the values of the remaining 30 variables can be deduced iteratively in the order: (k_{55}, k_{61}, k_{63}, k_{51}, k_{43}, k_{27}, k_{56}, k_{58}, k_{79}, k_{25}, k_{53}, k_{54}, k_{70}, k_{39}, k_{29}, k_{2}, k_{36}, k_{10}, k_{72}, k_{26}, k_{13}, k_{14}, k_{60}, k_{65}, k_{74}, k_{3}, k_{75}, k_{8}, k_{20}, k_{66}), and this deduction only costs constant time. The total attack complexity is $2^{53} + 2^{50}$. Because this calculation is the same as that in Sect. 4.1, we estimate that the attack on 820-round Trivium could be completed in two weeks on the same computer.

Table 4. Valuable cubes for attacking 820-round Trivium

Cube indices	Independent bits	Cube indices	Independent bits
$I_2\backslash\{66\}$	k_{55}	$I_3\backslash\{2,14\}$	$k_2, \mathbf{k_{29}}$
$I_2\backslash\{4,7,62\}$	k_{61}	$I_3\backslash\{38,54\}$	k_{36}
$I_2\backslash\{3,13\}$	k_{63}	$I_2\backslash\{4,20,44\}$	$k_{10}, \mathbf{k_{37}}$
$I_2\backslash\{3,26\}$	$k_{51}, \mathbf{k_{78}}$	$I_3\backslash\{51\}$	$\mathbf{k_{45}}, k_{72}$
$I_2\backslash\{3,62,66\}$	$k_{43}, \mathbf{k_{51}}, \mathbf{k_{78}}$	$I_2\backslash\{17,53,62,68\}$	$\mathbf{k_{12}}, k_{26}, \mathbf{k_{27}}, \mathbf{k_{39}}, \mathbf{k_{54}}$
$I_3\backslash\{6,42,52\}$	k_{27}	$I_3\backslash\{18,31\}$	$k_{13}, \mathbf{k_{40}}$
$I_3\backslash\{7,9\}$	k_{56}	$I_3\backslash\{18,24,31\}$	$k_{14}, \mathbf{k_{41}}, \mathbf{k_{68}}$
$I_3\backslash\{7,58\}$	k_{58}	$I_2\backslash\{1,31\}$	$\mathbf{k_{33}}, k_{60}$
$I_3\backslash\{3,7,17\}$	$\mathbf{k_{52}}, k_{79}$	$I_2\backslash\{5,62,66\}$	$\mathbf{k_{38}}, k_{65}$
$I_3\backslash\{1,3,32\}$	$k_{25}, \mathbf{k_{52}}$	$I_3\backslash\{23,38\}$	$\mathbf{k_{27}}, \mathbf{k_{47}}, k_{74}$
$I_2\backslash\{6,29\}$	k_{53}	$I_3\backslash\{23,52\}$	$k_3, \mathbf{k_{63}}$
$I_3\backslash\{18,54\}$	$\mathbf{k_{27}}, k_{54}$	$I_3\backslash\{13,63\}$	$\mathbf{k_{48}}, k_{75}$
$I_3\backslash\{27,53\}$	$\mathbf{k_{43}}, \mathbf{k_{58}}, k_{70}$	$I_3\backslash\{21,29,55,68\}$	k_8
$I_2\backslash\{53,68\}$	$\mathbf{k_{12}}, k_{39}, \mathbf{k_{63}}$	$I_2\backslash\{14,29,37,68\}$	k_{20}
$I_3\backslash\{6,18,29\}$	k_{29}	$I_2\backslash\{6,21,29\}$	k_{66}

$I_2 = \{0, 1, 2, 3, 4, 5, 6, 7, 8, 9, 10, 11, 12, 13, 14, 15, 16, 17, 18, 19, 20, 21, 23, 25, 26, 28, 29, 30, 31, 32, 34, 36, 37, 41, 43, 44, 46, 49, 52, 53, 55, 56, 59, 61, 62, 64, 66, 68, 72, 74, 76, 79\}$

$I_3 = \{0, 1, 2, 3, 4, 6, 7, 8, 9, 10, 11, 12, 13, 14, 15, 17, 18, 19, 21, 23, 24, 25, 26, 27, 28, 29, 30, 31, 32, 34, 36, 38, 39, 40, 41, 42, 46, 49, 51, 52, 53, 54, 55, 58, 61, 63, 66, 69, 72, 74, 76, 78\}$

5 Conclusion

In this paper, we focus on full key-recovery attacks on Trivium. A cube leading to a special kind of balanced superpoly is called a valuable cube. We present a novel framework to efficiently search for valuable cubes in cube attacks so that many balanced superpolies can be collected. As applications, two attacks on 815- and

820-round Trivium are given with time complexity $2^{47.32}$ and $2^{53.17}$, respectively. It is experimentally verified that the two attacks could be completed in six hours and two weeks on a PC with two RTX3090 GPUs, respectively. Although the key recovery process is practical, it seems unpractical to collect so many keystream bits required in our attacks during online communication. Hence, we call our attacks on 815- and 820-round Trivium experimentally verified attacks. Since the idea of this new framework to search for valuable cubes is generic in cube attacks, we believe that it is also helpful in cube attacks on other NFSR-based cryptosystems.

When analyzing Trivium with some large number of rounds, e.g., 845, recovering only a linear term of a superpoly is already time-consuming because of the large round number and large cube size. In this case, it is infeasible to sieve several subcubes. Hence, targeting Trivium with more than 845 rounds is worthy of working on in the future.

References

1. Dinur, I., Shamir, A.: Cube attacks on tweakable black box polynomials. In: Joux, A. (ed.) EUROCRYPT 2009. LNCS, vol. 5479, pp. 278–299. Springer, Heidelberg (2009). https://doi.org/10.1007/978-3-642-01001-9_16
2. Fouque, P.-A., Vannet, T.: Improving key recovery to 784 and 799 rounds of Trivium using optimized cube attacks. In: Moriai, S. (ed.) FSE 2013. LNCS, vol. 8424, pp. 502–517. Springer, Heidelberg (2014). https://doi.org/10.1007/978-3-662-43933-3_26
3. Todo, Y., Isobe, T., Hao, Y., Meier, W.: Cube attacks on non-blackbox polynomials based on division property. In: Katz, J., Shacham, H. (eds.) CRYPTO 2017. LNCS, vol. 10403, pp. 250–279. Springer, Cham (2017). https://doi.org/10.1007/978-3-319-63697-9_9
4. Wang, Q., Hao, Y., Todo, Y., Li, C., Isobe, T., Meier, W.: Improved division property based cube attacks exploiting algebraic properties of superpoly. In: Shacham, H., Boldyreva, A. (eds.) CRYPTO 2018. LNCS, vol. 10991, pp. 275–305. Springer, Cham (2018). https://doi.org/10.1007/978-3-319-96884-1_10
5. Wang, S., Hu, B., Guan, J., Zhang, K., Shi, T.: MILP-aided method of searching division property using three subsets and applications. In: Galbraith, S.D., Moriai, S. (eds.) ASIACRYPT 2019. LNCS, vol. 11923, pp. 398–427. Springer, Cham (2019). https://doi.org/10.1007/978-3-030-34618-8_14
6. Fu, X., Wang, X., Dong, X., Meier, W.: A key-recovery attack on 855-round Trivium. In: Shacham, H., Boldyreva, A. (eds.) CRYPTO 2018. LNCS, vol. 10992, pp. 160–184. Springer, Cham (2018). https://doi.org/10.1007/978-3-319-96881-0_6
7. Ye, C., Tian, T.: Revisit division property based cube attacks: key-recovery or distinguishing attacks? IACR Trans. Symmetric Cryptol. **2019**(3), 81–102 (2019)
8. Hao, Y., Leander, G., Meier, W., Todo, Y., Wang, Q.: Modeling for three-subset division property without unknown subset. In: Canteaut, A., Ishai, Y. (eds.) EUROCRYPT 2020. LNCS, vol. 12105, pp. 466–495. Springer, Cham (2020). https://doi.org/10.1007/978-3-030-45721-1_17
9. Cannière, C.D., Preneel, B.: Trivium specifications. eSTREAM portfolio, Profile 2 (HW) (2006)

10. Ye, C.-D., Tian, T.: A practical key-recovery attack on 805-round Trivium. In: Tibouchi, M., Wang, H. (eds.) ASIACRYPT 2021. LNCS, vol. 13090, pp. 187–213. Springer, Cham (2021). https://doi.org/10.1007/978-3-030-92062-3_7
11. Hu, K., Sun, S., Wang, M., Wang, Q.: An algebraic formulation of the division property: revisiting degree evaluations, cube attacks, and key-independent sums. In: Moriai, S., Wang, H. (eds.) ASIACRYPT 2020. LNCS, vol. 12491, pp. 446–476. Springer, Cham (2020). https://doi.org/10.1007/978-3-030-64837-4_15
12. Hu, K., Sun, S., Todo, Y., Wang, M., Wang, Q.: Massive superpoly recovery with nested monomial predictions. In: Tibouchi, M., Wang, H. (eds.) ASIACRYPT 2021. LNCS, vol. 13090, pp. 392–421. Springer, Cham (2021). https://doi.org/10.1007/978-3-030-92062-3_14
13. Sun, Y.: Automatic search of cubes for attacking stream ciphers. IACR Trans. Symmetric Cryptol. **2021**(4), 100–123 (2021)
14. Ye, C., Tian, T.: A new framework for finding nonlinear superpolies in cube attacks against trivium-like ciphers. In: Susilo, W., Yang, G. (eds.) ACISP 2018. LNCS, vol. 10946, pp. 172–187. Springer, Cham (2018). https://doi.org/10.1007/978-3-319-93638-3_11
15. Liu, M., Yang, J., Wang, W., Lin, D.: Correlation cube attacks: from weak-key distinguisher to key recovery. In: Nielsen, J.B., Rijmen, V. (eds.) EUROCRYPT 2018. LNCS, vol. 10821, pp. 715–744. Springer, Cham (2018). https://doi.org/10.1007/978-3-319-78375-8_23
16. Che, C., Tian, T.: An experimentally verified attack on 820-round Trivium (full version). IACR Cryptol. ePrint Arch. **2022**, 1518 (2022)

Malware

HinPage: Illegal and Harmful Webpage Identification Using Transductive Classification

Yunfan Li[1,2,3], Lingjing Yu[1,2(✉)], and Qingyun Liu[1,2]

[1] Institute of Information Engineering, Chinese Academy of Sciences, Beijing, China
{liyunfan,yulingjing,liuqingyun}@iie.ac.cn

[2] National Engineering Laboratory for Information Security Technologies, Beijing, China

[3] School of Cyber Security, University of Chinese Academy of Sciences, Beijing, China

Abstract. With the growing popularity of the Internet, websites could make significant profit by hosting illegal and harmful content, such as violence, sexual, illegal gambling, drug abuse, etc. They are serious threats to a safe and secure Internet, and they are especially harmful to the underage population. Government agencies, ISPs, network administrators at various levels, and parents have been seeking for accurate and robust solutions to block such illegal and harmful webpages. Existing solutions detect inappropriate pages based on content, e.g., using keyword matching or content-based image classification. They could be easily escaped by altering the internal format of texts or images, e.g., mixing different alphabets. In this paper, we propose to utilize relatively stable features extracted from the relationships between the targeted illegal/harmful webpages to discover and identify illegal webpages. We introduce a new mechanism, namely HinPage, that utilizes such features for the robust identification of PG (pornographic and gambling) pages. HinPage models the candidate PG pages and the resources on the pages with a heterogeneous information network (HIN). A transductive classification algorithm is then applied to the HIN to identify PG pages.

Through experiments on 10,033 candidate PG pages, we demonstrate that HinPage achieves an accuracy of 83.5% on PG page identification. In particular, it is able to identify illegal/harmful PG pages that cannot be recognized by SOTA commercial products.

Keywords: Illegal and harmful webpages · Webpage classification · Heterogeneous information network · Transductive classification

1 Introduction

In the past several decades, with the rapid development of the Internet, websites play a vital role in people's daily life. While most websites are supposed to be benign and bring positive/useful information, however, some websites provide illegal and harmful content such as gambling, drug abuse, sexual, violence,

Y. Deng and M. Yung (Eds.): Inscrypt 2022, LNCS 13837, pp. 373–390, 2023.
https://doi.org/10.1007/978-3-031-26553-2_20

crime, or political misinformation [14]. These websites not only bring dreadful online experiences but also threaten the safety of people, especially underage individuals, and even society. To prevent the spread of illegal/harmful content over the Internet, governments, ISPs (Internet Service Providers), cooperate IT, and parents often monitor websites and block illegal/harmful ones.

Previous work on detecting illegal/harmful webpages is mainly based on identifying certain keywords, pictures or source code on the content of webpages [2–4,15–20]. For instance, the content of webpages could be directly matched with pre-selected keywords at the network gateways. [5–7,11,12] integrate visual and textual features to provide better precision and recall. However, as encryption techniques are widely adopted by all websites to protect content in transmission, it is significantly harder to identify illegal/harmful websites through passive traffic filtering. To tackle this problem, new solutions have been proposed to actively probe for illegal webpages rather than waiting for them passively. For instance, Yang et al. [8] search for high-frequency keywords in search engines to find illegal webpages and use the XGboost model to improve the accuracy. Starov et al. [9] discover malicious campaigns iteratively through IDs, which are given by third parties and are used in the source code of known malicious webpages. These approaches were shown to be effective in the active detection of illegal/harmful content on the Internet, while commercial products, such as Google's SafeSearch and Baidu security, have been introduced to the market as well. However, they could be easily evaded by manipulation of the content, e.g., deformation of keywords, using a different but visually similar alphabet [30], or adversarial explicit content [31]. To improve the performance of active illegal/harmful content detection, new solutions with better accuracy and *robustness* are expected.

By analyzing a large amount of known illegal/harmful webpages, we have two important observations: (1) illegal/harmful webpages from different sources often contain similar third-party content, such as advertisements, pictures, text, and JavaScript. (2) In the web graph, known illegal/harmful pages are often strongly associated with other illegal/harmful pages. Based on these observations, we argue that connectivity information in the web graph and shared third-party content could be used as reliable features in the identification of illegal/harmful pages on the Internet. In particular, we propose a novel mechanism named HinPage to discover and identify pornographic and gambling webpages, denoted as PG webpages in this paper. We pick these types of pages because: (1) while the porn and gambling pages are especially harmful to underage individuals, they could be legal in many countries, so that they are not prosecuted by law enforcement; (2) many known webpage filtering and parental control tools (e.g., Symantec) often provide low accuracy in identifying such pages, especially when the pages do not contain malware (Trojan); (3) these two types of websites are often interconnected on the Internet, i.e., pornographic websites often contain links to illegal gambling websites; and (4) they often share advertising platforms with malicious advertisers or involve in malvertising. Therefore, we consider them inappropriate content in our HinPage solution.

HinPage consists of three main steps: data collection, HIN construction, and classification. In the data collection process, HinPage first searches for potentially PG webpages using keywords on search engines and manually confirms a small set of the discovered PG webpages (the *root set*). Next, a snowball crawling approach is developed to collect a *candidate set* of PG sites based on network connections or shared HTML elements (e.g., images and JavaScript code segments). Although PG webpages could modify text or pictures to evade content-based detection, the connections between sites and the associations with their advertising agents or certain service providers (e.g., Search Engine Optimization) could not be changed easily. Therefore, in the identification process, HinPage first models webpages, images, JavaScript code segments, iframes, and IP addresses using a heterogeneous information network (HIN). HinPage then applies a transductive classification algorithm HetPathMine [1] that utilizes the relationships among HIN nodes to identify PG webpages from the candidate set.

The main contributions of this paper are three-fold: (1) We have identified the disadvantages of the content-based identification of illegal/harmful pages, and propose to utilize the more robust graph-based page-relationship features for illegal/harmful page identification. (2) We present a novel approach, HinPage, for PG page identification, as a complementary mechanism to the existing methods. HinPage models candidate PG pages using a heterogeneous information network (HIN), and implements a transductive classification algorithm HetPathMine to identify PG pages through mining the relationships among web resources from the candidate pages. (3) We evaluate the performance of HinPage on 5 different datasets. For larger datasets with more nodes/edges and complex relationships among nodes in HIN, HinPage achieves better performance. Through experiments on the merged dataset, which has 10,033 candidate PG pages, we demonstrate that HinPage could identify PG pages, with an 83.05% accuracy, 89.96% precision, 86.57% recall, and 88.24% F1 score. (4) In particular, HinPage recognizes 954 and 536 illegal/harmful webpages out of the 10,033 candidate PG pages that are determined as benign by Symantec's WebPulse Site Review [25] and Baidu AI [26] respectively.

The rest of this paper is organized as follows. The related work is introduced in Sect. 2, followed by the theoretical foundation of the HinPage approach in Sect. 3. The details of the implementation of HinPage are presented in Sect. 4 and the experimental results are presented in Sect. 5. Finally, we conclude the paper and future plans in Sect. 6.

2 Related Work

In this section, we review the research in the literature that is related to PG webpages discovery and identification. Existing methods are broadly classified into three types: text-based, vision-based, and combined methods.

Text-based methods rely on keywords or tags in HTML for classification. Early work [10,13] removed tags and JavaScript from the source code of webpages, and transformed webpage detection tasks into document classification tasks. Later work focused on keywords in texts. Yang et al. [8] searched for keywords in search engines to discover illegal webpages. Then the XGboost algorithm was applied to features, which were extracted from keywords, domain, and HTML, to classify webpages. Starov et al. [9] took advantage of IDs in known malicious webpages provided by third parties to discover malicious campaigns. Yang et al. [2] extracted texts included by HTML tags, such as <*title*>, <*meta*>, <*li*>, <*a*>, <*h*>, and applied TF-IDF algorithm on these texts to generate features vectors, which was utilized to identify gambling webpages by support vector machine(SVM) algorithm. Lee et al. [19] designed a bilingual pornographic webpage recognition engine based on the frequency of keywords on webpages. Farman et al. [3] proposed a system applying fuzzy ontology/SVM on keywords collected from webpages to identify pornographic content. Some work also extracted hyperlinks in webpages [15] or headers and cookies from HTTP post requests [32] to identify pornographic and gambling sites. While these text-based methods could achieve high accuracy in recognizing ordinary PG webpages, they often go to fail on some dedicated webpages. For example, webpages could escape from inspection through keyword deformation. In addition, this type of approach presents the problem of hypervigilance. For example, some benign medical websites and law popularization websites might be blocked.

With the development of technology in image recognition, vision-based methods have received more attention. Li et al. [4] explored the Bag of Words model on images in webpages to identify pornographic and gambling webpages. Moustafa et al. [33] extracted features of images by a multi-layer convolutional neural network to detect pornographic webpages. [16,17] detected bare skin in images to identify pornographic webpages. [20] implemented a child pornography detection system based on distinguishing features of the face and skin color.

To improve detection accuracy, some researchers [5–7,11] integrated textual and visual features for webpage classification. Chen et al. [7] improved the Bag-of-Visual-Words model to generate embeddings of webpage screenshots and then applied a logistic regression algorithm on the embeddings and text features to identify pornographic and gambling pages. Huang et al. [6] extracted texts from screenshots of webpages and learned text features for classification. Wang et al. [11] proposed a multi-level fusion system employing a multi-modal deep network on videos and texts to identify pages with live porn videos.

While the combined methods have achieved high accuracy, some tricks, such as keyword deformation, image/pixel modification, and sensitive content occlusion, could be employed to escape from such methods. As we have observed that the webpages' relationships, which are measured by shared content, are relatively stable, HinPage could be employed as a complementary mechanism for PG webpage discovery and identification to the existing methods.

3 Theoretical Foundation for HinPage

In this section, we present the theoretical foundation for the HinPage approach. HinPage first models images, scripts, iframes, IP addresses, and their relationships from collected webpages as a heterogeneous information network (HIN), and then applies a transductive classification algorithm to the HIN.

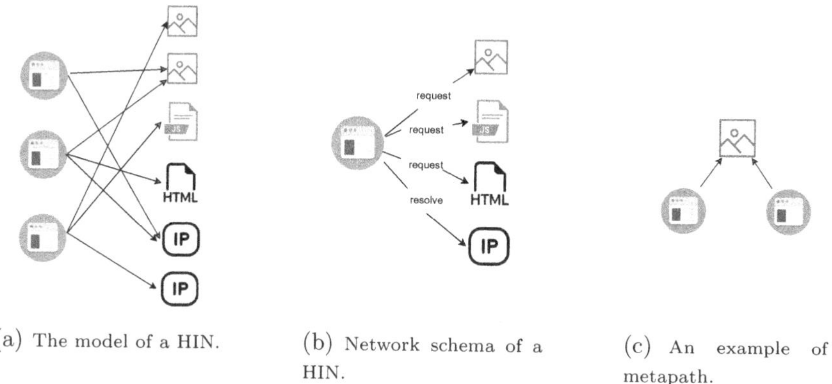

(a) The model of a HIN. (b) Network schema of a HIN. (c) An example of metapath.

Fig. 1. HinPage and its network schema, and an example of metapath.

3.1 Heterogeneous Information Network

Heterogeneous Information Network. Resources of webpages and their relationships of resources are defined as a graph $\boldsymbol{G} = (V, E)$, where the set of nodes V represents resources of webpages and the set of edges E indicate relationships of resources. As both the number of resource types and the number of edge types are more than one, G is a heterogeneous information network.

Figure 1(a) shows a simple model of HIN in HinPage. The HIN includes five types of nodes: webpage($\boldsymbol{w}$), image ($\boldsymbol{img}$), script ($\boldsymbol{js}$), iframe ($\boldsymbol{e}$), IP address ($\boldsymbol{ip}$), as well as two types of edges: resources requesting of webpages and IP addresses resolving of domains.

Network Schema. $\boldsymbol{T_G} = (A, R)$ is the network schema of a HIN $\boldsymbol{G}(V, E)$, where A is node types and R is edge types. $\boldsymbol{T_G}$ focuses on the relationship between node types rather than each node. Both ψ: $V \to A$ and ϕ: $E \to R$ are mapping functions, where A is the set of node types and R is the set of edge types.

Figure 1(b) is the network schema of HIN in Fig. 1(a). For example, the relationship between a webpage and an image on the webpage can be formalized as: $\boldsymbol{w} \xrightarrow{request} \boldsymbol{img}$.

Metapath. A metapath is a path connecting at least two types of nodes on a network schema $\boldsymbol{T_G}$. Its formal definition is $A_0 \xrightarrow{R_1} A_1 \xrightarrow{R_2} \dots \xrightarrow{R_L} A_L$, where L is the length of the metapath. The metapath in Fig. 1(c) indicates that two webpages have requested the same image.

3.2 Transductive Classification on HIN

Transductive Classification (TC). Given a HIN $\boldsymbol{G} = (V, E)$, $V_w \subseteq V$ represents nodes of webpages, and $V_w' \subseteq V_w$ is a set of labeled pages. Transductive classification predicts labels for nodes in $V_w - V_w'$.

LLGC [21] is the first transductive classification method based on homogeneous networks. HetPathMine [1] algorithm extends LLGC from homogeneous networks to heterogeneous networks. HinPage explores HetPathMine to identify PG webpages, which are nodes in the HIN.

Based on the network schema of HinPage, we design a set of metapaths $P = [p_1, p_2, ..., p_6]$, which are described in detail in Sect. 4.3. Based on each metapath, HetPathMine calculates the similarity of two webpages using the PathSim algorithm [24] as follows:

$$PathSim(k_{x,y}) = \frac{2 * |p_{x \to y} : p_{x \to y} \in \boldsymbol{p}_k|}{|p_{x \to x} : p_{x \to x} \in \boldsymbol{p}_k| + |p_{y \to y} : p_{y \to y} \in \boldsymbol{p}_k|} \quad (1)$$

$p_k \in P$ is a metapath, and $p_{i \to j}$ represents the metapath from node i to node j. As the contribution of each metapath to the classification effect of webpages is different, HinPage combines metapaths and the weight vector $B = [\beta_1, \beta_2, ..., \beta_6]$, where β_k represents the weight of metapath p_k, to obtain the webpage similarity matrix M.

$$M = \sum_{k=1}^{6} \beta_k \cdot PathSim(k) \quad (2)$$

The loss function $L(B)$ is designed to narrow the gap between the similarity matrix M and the relationship matrix R.

$$L(B) = \| \sum_{i,j}^{n} R(i,j) - M \| + \mu \| \sum_{k=1}^{6} \beta_k \| \quad (3)$$

$$R(i,j) = \begin{cases} 1 & label(page_i) == label(page_j) \\ 0 & \text{otherwise} \end{cases} \quad (4)$$

where n is the number of labeled webpages, and μ is used to smooth the result.

$Q(F)$ is the cost function for transductive classification. The first term is the smoothness constraint, which indicates that closely related nodes should have the same label. The second term is the fitting constraint, which states that the predictions of the nodes should be as consistent as possible with the initial labels. λ is used to balance the weight of the two terms.

$$Q(F) = \frac{1}{2} \sum_{i,j=1}^{n} M \| \frac{F_i}{\sqrt{D_{ii}}} - \frac{F_j}{\sqrt{D_{jj}}} \|^2 + \lambda \sum_{i=1}^{n} \|F_i - Y_i\|^2 \quad (5)$$

where F is a probability matrix recording the probability of each node corresponding to each category with n rows and 2 columns. n is the number of webpages. Y is the initial label matrix of nodes. D is a diagonal matrix, and the value of row i in D is equal to the sum of all values of row i in M.

HinPage's goal is to minimize the function $Q(F)$ and find the best result for F. Therefore, we take the derivative of F on Q. The theoretical minimum value F^* of F can be calculated as follows.

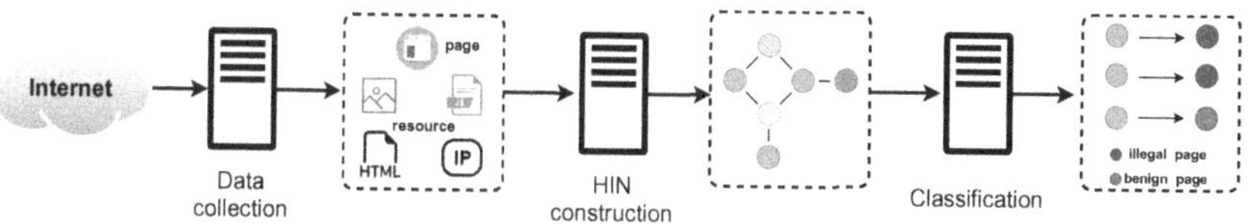

Fig. 2. Overview of the proposed HinPage framework.

$$\frac{dQ}{dF} = F^* - F^*S + \mu(F^* - Y) = 0 \tag{6}$$

$$F^* = \beta(I - \alpha S)^{-1}Y \tag{7}$$

where $\alpha = \frac{1}{1+\mu}$, $\beta = \frac{\mu}{1+\mu}$ and $S = D^{-1/2}MD^{-1/2}$.

After the probability matrix F is calculated, the predicted label of the webpage i can be obtained by the following function.

$$label(i) = \boldsymbol{max}(F(i,0), F(i,1)) \tag{8}$$

4 The Implementation of the HinPage Approach

In this section, we present the implementation of the HinPage approach, and the technical details of each HinPage component.

4.1 Overview of HinPage

Figure 2 illustrates the logical components of the HinPage approach and how they are assembled. HinPage consists of three main components: data collection, HIN construction, and classification. In data collection, HinPage collects a candidate set of suspicious PG webpages and extracts resources such as HTML source code, images, scripts, iframes, and IP addresses from these webpages. Then, HinPage models these resources and their relationships into a heterogeneous information network (HIN). Finally, HinPage applies the transductive classification algorithm on six metapaths we selected to predict unlabeled webpages based on the known labels. In the following subsections, we will present the details of each component.

4.2 Data Collection

In this subsection, we elaborate on the detail of the data collection process. Figure 3 shows the overall framework of the data collection module.

In HinPage, we have designed a standard snowball crawling process for data collection. Initially, we crawl a set of known PG webpages as the *root set*. Existing research in the literature, e.g., [8], has shown that some keywords could be used

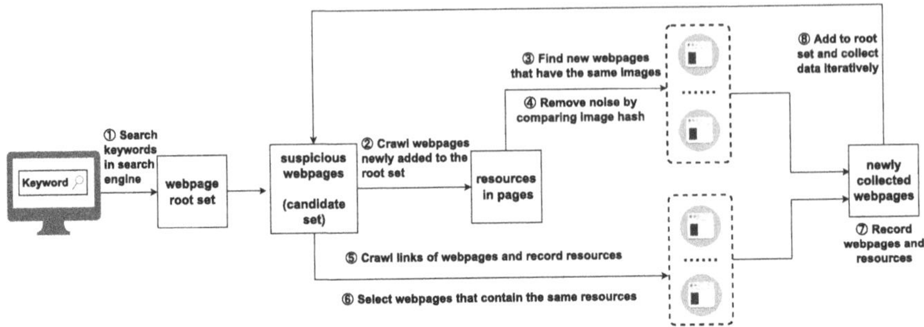

Fig. 3. The data collection process.

to effectively identify webpages in the PG category. For example, some gambling webpages may contain keywords such as *Mark Six Lottery* or *Grand Lisboa*. Hence, we collect a list of keywords from the literature and added additional terms that frequently appeared on PG webpages from our own exploration. We search with these keywords in search engines to discover potential PG webpages. Note that this approach does not provide satisfactory precision and recall, hence, we only use it as a starting point. We manually examined the crawled initial set of webpages to construct the *root set* of PG webpages. We will further expand the root set to construct the *candidate set* of PG sites.

One of the approaches that we utilized to grow the root set is to identify and crawl the sibling pages. A sibling page is a page that shares a significant visual component of the seed PG page, e.g., a webpage that contains the same image, iframe, or referral script of the seed page. HinPage discovers sibling pages using two approaches. The first is to utilize reverse search engines, such as *TinEye*, to search for pages that contain the shared images. The other is to identify shared resources from pages crawled through link-based propagation. Intuitively, a PG page contains a large number of outgoing links, many of which could be benign pages. However, if a page that is referred to by the PG page also shares significant visual components with other PG page(s), this page is more likely to be PG. From these two methods, we are able to grow the candidate PG set and identify the sibling page relationships among all the crawled pages.

To automate the design that is described above, we have developed a webpage crawler named HinCrawl based on Chrome Devtools API [22]. HinCrawl downloads the source code of a webpage, and extracts all HTTP(S) requests/resources on the page. With HinCrawl, we get images and scripts from discovered webpages. To reduce noise, for each crawled image, we performed an image hash comparison [23] with the target image as follows: (1) To normalize the image, we re-scale the image size to 8×8, and then obtain a total of 64 pixels. (2) we convert the image to a 256-level grayscale image. (3) we calculate the mean value of all pixels in the grayscale image. (4) For each pixel, if it is greater than the mean value, it is binarized to 1, otherwise 0. Finally, we get the hash value of the image by flattening the 8×8 binary matrix into a 64-dimensional vector. (5) Any pair of images are considered to be the same when they have the same

Table 1. Description of relationship matrices.

Matrix	Element	Description
P	P_{ij}	If page i contains image j, then $P_{ij} = 1$, otherwise, $P_{ij} = 0$
J	J_{ij}	If page i contains script j, then $J_{ij} = 1$, otherwise, $J_{ij} = 0$
E	E_{ij}	If page i contains iframe j, then $E_{ij} = 1$, otherwise, $E_{ij} = 0$
I	I_{ij}	If the domain of page i resolves to IP Address j, then $I_{ij} = 1$, otherwise, $I_{ij} = 0$

hash value. If an image being compared is in gif format, we split the gif file into frames and compare the hash value of each frame. We consider two gif images to be the same when every frame-wise comparison turned out to be identical. Finally, we invoke the snowball crawling process to collect any potentially PG website, and iteratively add the sibling pages of known candidate PG pages into the candidate set.

4.3 Construction of Heterogeneous Information Network (HIN)

As shown in Figs. 1(a) and 1(b), we extract images, scripts, iframes, and IP addresses from candidate PG pages, and model the pages, resources, and their relationships using a HIN. The relationship between resources is represented by four adjacency matrices, where each element indicate whether two resources are related. They are defined as follows:

- Matrix **P** models the relationships between pages and images.
- Matrix **J** models the relationships between pages and JavaScript snippets.
- Matrix **E** models the relationships between pages and iframes.
- Matrix **I** models the relationships between pages and IP addresses.

The definitions of the elements in these matrices are discussed in Table 1.

The multiple relationships in a HIN can be represented by metapaths. We construct six metapaths (PID1 to PID6) based on the above four relations, as shown in Table 2. We choose these metapaths for the following reasons: (1) Webpages with the same images or iframes, i.e., sibling pages, partially share the same appearance. (2) Webpages may load resources through scripts. Webpages using the same script may share the same resource. (3) If two webpages resolve to the same IP address, they are on the same network segment and they may be managed by the same operator. (4) We further attempt to connect more webpages through resources. Therefore, in PID5 and PID6, we extend PID1 and PID3, respectively, from one hop (page-resource-page) to two hops (page-resource-page-resource-page). In this way, two webpages can also establish a connection through images/iframes and a shared sibling page. Meanwhile, from our observations, it is rare to have multiple IPs corresponding to the same PG page at a specific time, hence, we have not observed any page-IP1-page-IP2-page relationship. Therefore, we do not expand PID4. (5) The main function

Table 2. Description of metapaths.

PID	Metapath	Description
1	$w_a \xrightarrow{P} img \xrightarrow{P^T} w_b$	webpages request the same image
2	$w_a \xrightarrow{J} js \xrightarrow{J^T} w_b$	webpages request the same script
3	$w_a \xrightarrow{E} e \xrightarrow{E^T} w_b$	webpages request the same iframe
4	$w_a \xrightarrow{I} ip \xrightarrow{I^T} w_b$	webpages resolve to the same IP address
5	$w_a \xrightarrow{P} img_a \xrightarrow{P^T} w_b \xrightarrow{P} img_b \xrightarrow{P^T} w_c$	w_a request the same image with w_b, and w_c request the same image with w_b
6	$w_a \xrightarrow{E} e_a \xrightarrow{E^T} w_b \xrightarrow{E} e_b \xrightarrow{E^T} w_c$	w_a request the same iframe with w_b, and w_c request the same iframe with w_b

of the JavaScript snippets is to load multiple or dynamic resources. Therefore, the sibling pages connected through JavaScript demonstrate weaker relevance, hence, we did not make further extensions to PID2.

4.4 Classification

When the candidate PG pages are crawled and modeled with HIN, and a set of known PG and benign sites/pages are manually annotated, the problem of PG page identification becomes a classification problem for graph data. In HinPage, we explore the transductive classification algorithm HetPathMine [1] to the HIN that is constructed in the previous subsection. In particular, we first compute the page similarity matrix through a set of metapaths. Then based on the page similarity matrix, relation matrix, and loss function in Eq. 3, we train the metapath weight vector. Finally, by minimizing the value of the cost function in Eq. 5, we calculate the probability matrix and obtain the predicted label of webpages.

5 Experiments

In this section, we first introduce our collected dataset. Then we present experimental results and analysis.

5.1 Dataset

In order to evaluate the performance of HinPage, we need a manageable set of labeled webpages that have been annotated as *benign* or *PG* webpages. Meanwhile, to investigate how different root sets affect the classification performance, we manually construct 5 non-overlapping root sets. Through the method described in Sect. 4.2, we expand these root sets with four iterations, and extract resources (images, iframes, etc.) from these expanded sets. Although the root subsets are non-overlapping, duplicate webpages would be found when they are

Table 3. The number of nodes in each types in datasets.

Dataset ID	webpage	image	script	iframe	IP
1	3230	6172	2944	172	482
2	1962	5005	2601	107	323
3	2559	4692	2148	123	421
4	1100	342	623	16	200
5	1841	2709	1354	64	367
combined	10033	11027	4381	239	1100

Table 4. The number of edges in each types in datasets.

Dataset ID	webpage-image	webpage-script	webpage-iframe	webpage-IP
1	27267	13161	1041	1493
2	10342	7304	287	575
3	21229	11452	813	1109
4	2135	1842	94	327
5	9146	5876	123	979
combined	55167	25043	1492	3731

iteratively added to each subset. With all the dataset combined, we have collected 10,033 unique webpages. We invite 15 volunteers, who are all graduate students, to annotate the dataset. Volunteers are asked to manually visit each webpage, evaluate the content of the page, and label whether the webpage is PG. We divide all webpages into 5 groups, and each volunteer needs to assign labels to webpages in one group. Hence, each webpage receives three labels from 3 different volunteers. We use a majority voting mechanism to determine the final label of each webpages.

Finally, 5611 webpages are labeled as PG webpages and 4422 webpages are labeled as benign. Table 3 lists the number of all resources, e.g., images, JavaScript snippets, iframes, and IP addresses, extracted from webpages in each dataset. Table 4 lists the edges established from these resources.

5.2 Performance Evaluation

Evaluation Metrics. To evaluate the performance of each model, we consider four evaluation metrics: *Accuracy*, *Precision*, *Recall* and *F1-score*. They are defined as follows, where TP denotes number of true positive pages (illegal/harmful pages labeled as illegal/harmful), FP denotes false positive (benign pages labeled as illegal/harmful), TN denotes true negative (benign pages labeled as benign), and FN denotes false negative (illegal/harmful pages labeled as benign).

$$Accuracy = \frac{TP + TN}{TP + FP + TN + FN} \tag{9}$$

$$Precision = \frac{TP}{TP + FP} \tag{10}$$

$$Recall = \frac{TP}{TP + FN} \tag{11}$$

$$F1\text{-}score\ (F1) = 2 \times \frac{R \times P}{R + P} \tag{12}$$

Performance of HinPage. First, we examine the contribution of different types of resources to webpage classification, using the weight vectors of the metapath. Table 5 shows the result. Images get the highest contribution rate, which may be caused by the fact that images in a distinct category of webpages tend to be different and images in the same category of webpages tend to be similar. Surprisingly, the script makes smaller contributions to webpage classification than the other types of resources. This might be explained by the fact that the same script may be shared by different types of pages, e.g., a script could be employed to load/render different types of resources appearing on different categories of webpages.

Table 5. Contribution ranking of different types of resources to webpage classification.

image	script	iframe	IP address
1	4	3	2

To evaluate the effectiveness of the transductive classification (TC) algorithm employed in HinPage on different sizes of training datasets, we conduct a series of experiments under the condition that 40%, 50%, 60%, or 70% of the randomly selected webpages are labeled and used for training.

As shown in Fig. 4, when the proportion of the training dataset increases, HinPage obtains better performance. Note that when the labeling ratio is 40%, HinPage achieves high recall ($Recall = 88.75\%$) with lower accuracy and precision. In this case, the transductive classifier tends to predict all the webpages towards the PG side. As the proportion of labeled samples increases, the recall rate of TC decreases gradually and remains at around 86.5%, while the accuracy and precision rates increase steadily.

Next, we evaluate the performance of HinPage on each dataset generated from different root sets. We randomly select 70% of each dataset for training and use the rest for testing. We compare the performance of datasets on each evaluation metric.

In general, HinPage's performance on five different datasets are mostly consistent, while the slight differences in classification performance may be explained by the differences in the characteristics of the datasets. For instance, among all

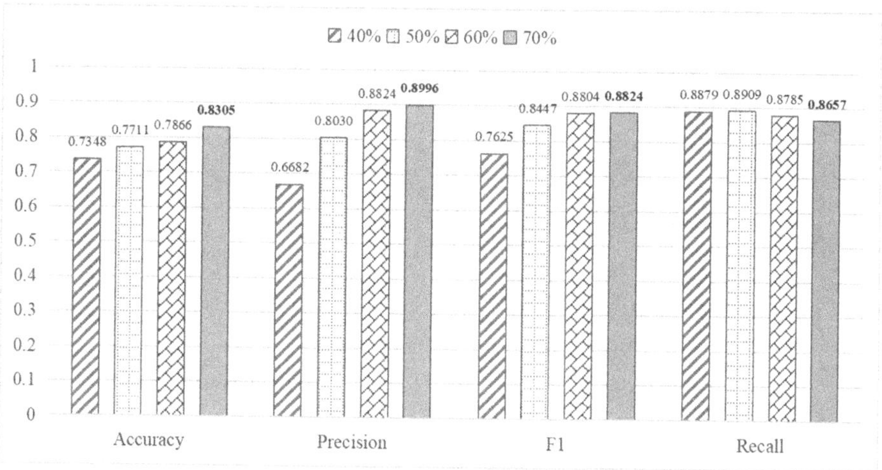

Fig. 4. HinPage's performance with different fractions of training data.

subsets, subset-1 has the best performance with 84.44% accuracy, 86.95% precision, 81.18% recall and 83.97% F1 score, which may be explained by the fact that subset-1 has more nodes and edges in each type. Based on metapaths generated from more nodes and edges, the transductive classification algorithm could achieve better performance in generating the page similarity matrix. For the smaller datasets, we have noticed a 6% decrease in HinPage's performance, e.g., in subset-2, subset-3, and subset-5. Note that subset-4 has the highest recall, but its accuracy and precision are not exceptional. We notice that the edges among nodes in subset-4 are relatively sparse, which may lead to poorer classification ability of HinPage, and some benign webpages would be classified into PG webpages.

Finally, the combined dataset produces the best performance with 83.05% accuracy, 89.96% precision, 86.57% recall, and 88.24% F1 score, which proves that the more complicated the relationships among nodes in HIN are, the better performance the transductive classification algorithm could achieve.

Performance Comparison with Other Algorithms. We compare the transductive classifier used in HinPage with two classic graph-based modeling/ranking algorithms, i.e. HITS [28] and Metapath2vec [29] (Fig. 5).

With HITS, we consider both webpages and resources as nodes of the HIN graph, and the direction of each edge goes from a webpage to a resource. In this way, a directed graph is constructed. Then, an adjacency matrix is generated according to the degree of nodes. The initial labels of webpages are used as the initial node authority. We continuously update the hub values and authority values of nodes according to the iterative operation of the matrix. Finally, we treat the hub values of webpages as the prediction scores. Based on the proportion of illegal/harmful pages in our dataset, we annotate nodes with the top 56% of the scores as illegal.

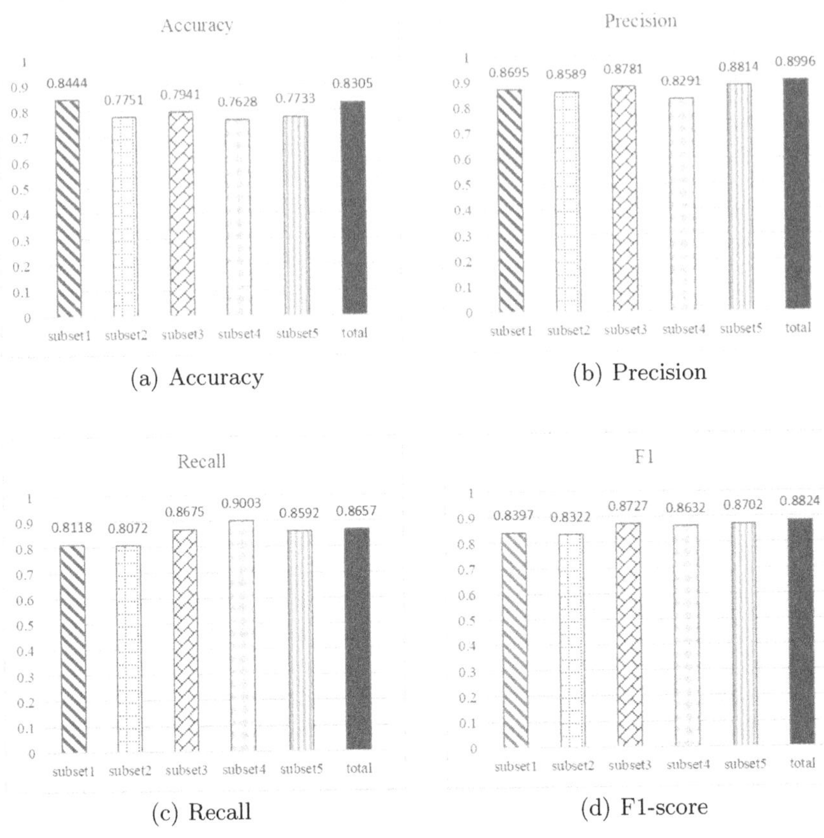

(a) Accuracy (b) Precision

(c) Recall (d) F1-score

Fig. 5. Performance of datasets on each evaluation metric.

With Metapath2vec, we train a 128-dimensional node embedding for each metapath. Then we concatenate node embeddings of six metapaths we choose to get the node embeddings of webpages. A support vector machine approach was used to perform downstream classification.

To test the performance of the above algorithms, we randomly select 70% of our dataset for training and the rest for testing. As shown in Fig. 6, TC achieves the best performance, with 83.05% accuracy, 89.96% precision, 86.57% recall, and 88.24% F1 score. Meanwhile, the performance of HITS is approximately 7% to 15% lower than TC. Note that Metapath2vec outperforms TC in recall. This is because Metapath2vec tends to classify all the samples towards illegal/harmful, which results in poor precision (55%) but relatively high recall.

Compared with HITS, TC improves classification accuracy by 15%. The reason might be that HITS ignores the impact of different node types in classification, while TC properly considers the contribution of different types of resources. Compared to Metapath2vec, TC provides 29% better accuracy. Metapath2vec

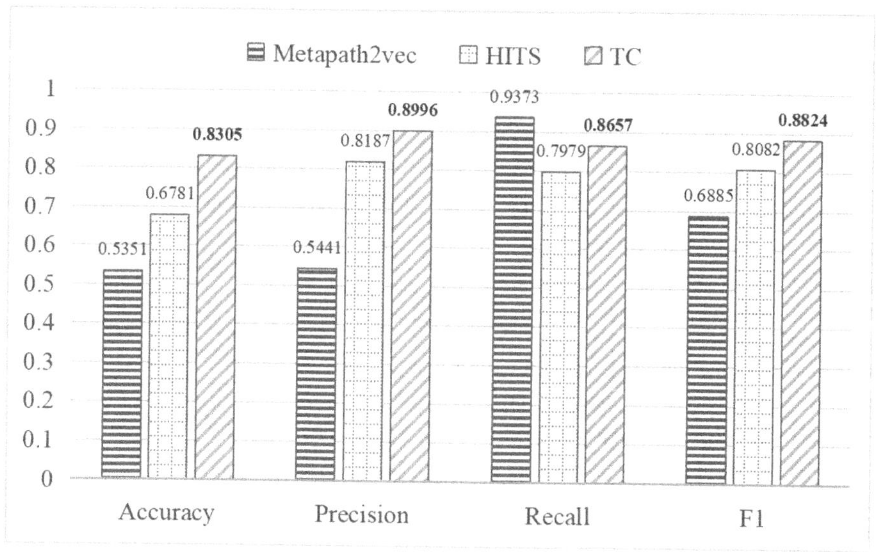

Fig. 6. Performance of Metapath2vec, HITS and TC algorithm.

Table 6. Number of PG pages that fail to be identified by Symantec WebPulse Site Review and Baidu Security Platform.

	Symantec	Baidu security platform
Misclassification	101	4
No results returned	853	532
Total	954	536

has poor precision and high recall, implying that it tends to classify a good portion of benign pages as illegal pages.

Performance Comparison with SOTA Commercial Products. Finally, we compare HinPage with state-of-the-art commercially off-the-shelf (COTS) products for illegal/harmful page detection. We employ Symantec WebPulse Site Review [25] and Baidu Security Platform [26] to evaluate webpages that are correctly identified as PG pages by HinPage. As shown in Table 6, 536 PG webpages are recognized as risk-free by Baidu Security Platform and 954 PG webpages are recognized as benign webpages or fail to be classified by Symantec. We manually examine webpages that are incorrectly classified by Symantec and Baidu Security Platform and observe that some webpages deform sensitive texts and images in them. To our best knowledge, Baidu Security Platform identifies illegal/harmful webpages by distinguishing illegal/harmful content such as keywords, images or scripts [27]. Meanwhile, the reason why Symantec fails to classify some webpages is that they are not on the blacklist of Symantec. This experiment demonstrates that HinPage could discover and identify PG webpages that escape the detection of SOTA commercial products that only utilize content analysis for PG page detection.

6 Conclusion and Future Works

In this paper, we present HinPage, a novel approach for illegal/harmful webpage discovery and identification. We start with a root set of manually validated PG webpages, and iteratively discover new pages that share the same resources. Through four iterations, we have collected 10,033 potential PG webpages. We model the candidate PG pages using a heterogeneous information network (HIN), where the candidate PG pages and resources are associated by metapaths. We further develop a transductive classification algorithm to predict the labels of webpages. As we have demonstrated in the experiments, HinPage could effectively identify illegal/harmful webpages that are mostly missed by Symantec's WebPulse Site Review and the Baidu Security Platform.

In our future work, we plan to improve HinPage in two aspects: scalability and detection accuracy. First, HinPage utilizes the complete graph information in classification. When new nodes are added to the graph, we need to repeat the prediction process. When the size of data is large, HinPage requires large memory and a long computation time. In particular, it could be expensive to inverse the relationship matrices when the matrices are huge. In future work, we plan to use parallel computing to improve HinPage efficiency. For the second aspect, HinPage detects illegal webpages based on the relationships of resources. For isolated webpages that have not established connections with other webpages, HinPage cannot evaluate them. In future work, we plan to supplement HinPage with content-based attributes extracted from the webpages to provide a comprehensive solution.

Acknowledgment. This work is supported by the Strategic Priority Research Program of the Chinese Academy of Sciences with No. XDC02030000, the National Key Research and Development Program of China No. 2021YFB3101403 and National Key R&D Program 2021 (Grant No. 2021YFB3101001).

References

1. Luo, C., Guan, R., Wang, Z., Lin, C.: HetPathMine: a novel transductive classification algorithm on heterogeneous information networks. In: de Rijke, M., et al. (eds.) ECIR 2014. LNCS, vol. 8416, pp. 210–221. Springer, Cham (2014). https://doi.org/10.1007/978-3-319-06028-6_18
2. Yang, H., Du, K., Zhang, Y., et al.: Casino Royale: a deep exploration of illegal online gambling. In: Proceedings of the 35th Annual Computer Security Applications Conference, pp. 500–513 (2019)
3. Farman, A., Pervez, K., Kashif, R., et al.: A fuzzy ontology and SVM-based Web content classification system. IEEE Access 25781–25797 (2017)

4. Li, L., Gou, G., Xiong, G., Cao, Z., Li, Z.: Identifying gambling and porn websites with image recognition. In: Zeng, B., Huang, Q., El Saddik, A., Li, H., Jiang, S., Fan, X. (eds.) PCM 2017. LNCS, vol. 10736, pp. 488–497. Springer, Cham (2018). https://doi.org/10.1007/978-3-319-77383-4_48
5. Hu, W., Wu, O., Chen, Z., et al.: Recognition of pornographic web pages by classifying texts and images. IEEE Trans. Pattern Anal. 1019–1034 (2007)
6. Huang, Y., Liu, D., Yan, Z., et al.: An abused webpage detection method based on screenshots text recognition. In: Proceedings of the 2021 ACM International Conference on Intelligent Computing and its Emerging Applications, pp. 106–110 (2021)
7. Chen, Y., Zheng, R., Zhou, A., et al.: Automatic detection of pornographic and gambling websites based on visual and textual content using a decision mechanism. Sensors (2020)
8. Yang, R., Liu, J., Gu, L., et al.: Search & catch: detecting promotion infection in the underground through search engines. In: IEEE TrustCom, pp. 1566–1571 (2020)
9. Starov, O., Zhou, Y., Zhang, X., et al.: Betrayed by your dashboard: discovering malicious campaigns via web analytics. In: Proceedings of the World Wide Web Conference, pp. 227–236 (2018)
10. Salam, H., Maarof, M.A., Zainal, A.: Design consideration for improved term weighting scheme for pornographic web sites. In: Abraham, A., Muda, A.K., Choo, Y.-H. (eds.) Pattern Analysis, Intelligent Security and the Internet of Things. AISC, vol. 355, pp. 275–285. Springer, Cham (2015). https://doi.org/10.1007/978-3-319-17398-6_25
11. Wang, L., Zhang, J., Wang, M., Tian, J., Zhuo, L.: Multilevel fusion of multimodal deep features for porn streamer recognition in live video. Pattern Recogn. Lett. **140**, 150–157 (2020)
12. Ahmadi, A., Fotouhi, M., Khaleghi, M.: Intelligent classification of webpages using contextual and visual features. Appl. Soft Comput. **11**, 1638–1647 (2011)
13. Maktabar, M., Zainal, A., Maarof, M.A., Kassim, M.N.: Content based fraudulent website detection using supervised machine learning techniques. In: Abraham, A., Muhuri, P.K., Muda, A.K., Gandhi, N. (eds.) HIS 2017. AISC, vol. 734, pp. 294–304. Springer, Cham (2018). https://doi.org/10.1007/978-3-319-76351-4_30
14. European Commission. Illegal and Harmful Content on the Internet COM(96)487final (1996)
15. Shin, J., Lee, S., Wang, T.: Semantic approach for identifying harmful sites using the link relations. In: Proceedings of the 2014 IEEE International Conference on Semantic Computing, pp. 16–18 (2014)
16. Farooq, M.S., Khan, M.A., Abbas, S., et al.: Skin detection based pornography filtering using adaptive back propagation neural network. In: 8th International Conference on Information and Communication Technologies, pp. 106–112 (2019)
17. Yaqub, W., Mohanty, M., et al.: Encrypted domain skin tone detection for pornographic image filtering. In: 15th IEEE International Conference on Advanced Video and Signal Based Surveillance, pp. 1–5 (2018)
18. Granizo, S.L., Caraguay, Á.L., López, L.I., Hernández-Álvarez, M.: Detection of possible illicit messages using natural language processing and computer vision on twitter and linked websites. IEEE Access (2020)
19. Lee, P.Y., Hui, S.C., Fong, A.C.M.: An intelligent categorization engine for bilingual web content filtering. IEEE Trans. Multimed. 1183–1190 (2005)

20. Sae-Bae, N., Sun, X., et al.: Towards automatic detection of child pornography. In: 2014 IEEE International Conference on Image Processing (ICIP), pp. 5332–5336 (2014)
21. Zhou, D., Bousquet, O., Lal, T.N., Weston, J., Schölkopf, B.: Learning with local and global consistency. In: Advances in Neural Information Processing Systems, pp. 321–328 (2004)
22. Chrome DevTools. https://chromedevtools.github.io/devtools-protocol/1-3/Page/
23. OpenCV. https://opencv.org/
24. Sun, Y., Han, J., Yan, X., et al.: PathSim: meta path-based top-k similarity search in heterogeneous information networks. Proc. VLDB Endow. **4**, 992–1003 (2011)
25. Symantec sitereview. https://sitereview.bluecoat.com/
26. Baidu Security Platform. https://bsb.baidu.com/
27. Evaluation Standard of Baidu Security Platform. https://bsb.baidu.com/standard
28. Nomura, S., Oyama, S., Hayamizu, T., et al.: Analysis and improvement of HITS algorithm for detecting web communities. Syst. Comput. **35**, 32–42 (2004)
29. Dong, Y., Chawla, N.V., Swami, A.: metapath2vec: scalable representation learning for heterogeneous networks. In: Proceedings of the 23rd ACM SIGKDD International Conference on Knowledge Discovery and Data Mining, pp. 135–144 (2017)
30. Sokolov, M., Olufowobi, K., Herndon, N.: Visual spoofing in content-based spam detection. In: 13th International Conference on Security of Information and Networks (2020)
31. Yuan, K., et al.: Stealthy porn: understanding real-world adversarial images for illicit online promotion. In: IEEE Symposium on Security and Privacy (SP) (2019)
32. Tong, S., Zhang, H, Shen, B., et al.: Detecting gambling sites from post behaviors. In: IEEE 11th Conference on Industrial Electronics and Applications, pp. 2495–2500 (2016)
33. Moustafa, M., et al.: Applying deep learning to classify pornographic images and videos. arXiv Preprint arxiv:1511.08899 (2015)

Detecting API Missing-Check Bugs Through Complete Cross Checking of Erroneous Returns

Qintao Shen[1,2](✉), Hongyu Sun[3,4](✉), Guozhu Meng[1,2], Kai Chen[1,2], and Yuqing Zhang[3,4]

[1] SKLOIS, Institute of Information Engineering, Chinese Academy of Sciences, Beijing, China
{shenqintao,mengguozhu,chenkai}@iie.ac.cn
[2] School of Cyber Security, University of Chinese Academy of Sciences, Beijing, China
[3] National Computer Network Instrusion Protection Center, University of Chinese Academy of Sciences, Beijing, China
{sunhy,zhangyq}@nipc.org.cn
[4] School of Cyber Engineering, Xidian University, Beijing, China

Abstract. Missing-check of erroneous execution states may cause critical security problems, such as null pointer dereference bugs or logic errors, which could even crash the systems. It's still a challenge to decide automatically whether an erroneous state should be validated or not because of the difficulty in understanding API semantics. Cross-checking is a sound method to resolve the problem. However, recent cross-checking studies suffer from poor accuracy due to inaccurate data-flow analysis, leading to the imprecise analysis of many error states and false positives.

In this paper, we present ERSAnalyzer (Erroneous Return Status Analyzer), a new static analysis method to improve existing tools to completely detect inter-procedural missing-check bugs of return values in the Linux kernel. At first, our approach identifies the functions which may generate error return status. After that, we propose a new method to find out the pointer parameter variables carrying error semantics except for the return values. Then a complete missing-check analysis on these critical variables is performed to confirm if they are validated before or after functions return. By utilizing cross-checking, ERSAnalyzer achieves higher precision of 71.3% in deciding whether a critical variable is checked. ERSAnalyzer reports 335 cases; 239 of those are potential bugs, 25 are manually proved to be actual missing-check bugs. Limited by the understanding of the code logic and some bugs that have been fixed in the latest version. We finally submitted 12 new bugs to the Linux Kernel, and six of our patches have been accepted up to now. The results show the effectiveness of ERSAnalyzer.

Keywords: Missing-check bugs · Static analysis · Cross-checking

Y. Deng and M. Yung (Eds.): Inscrypt 2022, LNCS 13837, pp. 391–407, 2023.
https://doi.org/10.1007/978-3-031-26553-2_21

1 Introduction

Missing-check bugs are common in system software, and those bugs may consequence in unsafe states or even critical security vulnerabilities, especially in large-scale programs such as the Linux kernel. The problem is hard to resolve for many reasons. The most important one is that low-level programming languages like C and assembly, which have poor design for error management, are chosen to implement complex OS kernel modules for better performance and easier direct interaction with hardware. In the Linux kernel, the erroneous states are presented as integer error codes or meaningful pointers which are used to indicate some error semantic, and then returned to their callers. In the developers' view, these erroneous states are desired to be checked and then do something to handle corresponding errors. Recently, static analysis works [1,2,5,8,11,14] have tried to resolve this problem with cross checking. By utilizing cross-checking, the usages of an API function are collected and compared to each other to decide whether the status should be validated after the API function is returned.

Generally, to enforce cross-checking on the API execution status, error-return API functions that may generate error status should be analyzed and recognized at the first. And then, the data-flow analysis will be performed on each callsite of the target API functions to confirm if the possible return error status has been checked. Lastly, after the difference analysis, the cases with inconsistent usage are regarded as bugs. Cross-checking makes the code analysis semantic-aware since most of the usages of critical variables are concerned to be the ground truth. Although existing cross-checking works are effective and some have already been applied to detect inconsistent bugs for over ten years, they are still suffering from low precision and high false positives for many reasons.

(1) Imprecise data-flow analysis. On the one hand, existing studies, like LRScan [11] recognize the functions which return error codes as the API functions may need security checks. However, not all of the error-return functions can be found in existing tools. On the other hand, inaccurate alias analysis results can lead to many cross-check mistakes. For example, CRIX [14] performed their points-to analysis for each pointer to a memory location, relying on LLVM's AliasAnalysis infrastructure. They have improved the points-to analysis to refine the alias results. But based on the analysis of the bug report given by CRIX, there are still more false positives than expected.
(2) The security states are validated in various ways. It is very common that a function could return multiple error states in the Linux kernel. Those error states may be checked and handled immediately or far away along the call chain. Otherwise, based on our investigation, when the execution states should be checked, the developers can check the return values and some other relative pointer variables carrying the same or similar error semantics. In previous papers, these return values are mainly focused on and regarded as critical variables, but the checks for pointer variables mentioned above are ignored.

There are still challenges to enforce cross-checking depending on more accurate and complete analysis. To help this situation, we present our ERSAnalyzer (Erroneous Return Status Analyzer), a new method to improve existing cross-checking precision. The key idea of ERSAnalyzer is to get a better result in error-return function identification and returned-value validation analysis with higher completeness.

ERSAnalyzer starts with a better error-return function identification. With more precise identification of error-return functions, we can perform our analysis on more target functions to reduce possible false negatives. Then we focus on the return values of identified API functions for a complete data-flow analysis to confirm whether they are checked or not. We make the following contributions in this paper:

- **A complete analysis of missing-check erroneous returns.** We propose a new approach, ERSAnalyzer, to enforce a complete analysis based on existing missing-check works and address limitations in current cross-checking works. The main problems contributing to the low precision and high false positives are inaccurate alias analysis, ignoring the various kinds of validation, and poor inter-procedural analysis. We employ multiple new methods to resolve these problems.
- **Improvement methods for a complete analysis of error-return functions and critical pointer variables.** The identification of error-return functions is very important to cross-checking. We improve the existing method used in CRIX to find out more error-return functions as their return values are used for cross-checking. We focus on the real code in the Linux kernel and find that 1) some of the pointer arguments or global variables may also carry error semantics and be checked after the called API is returned, 2) the critical variables may be checked in uncertain ways. To address those problems, we improve the methods for the identification of more critical variables and complete data-flow analysis to confirm the particular states of these critical variables.
- **Finding numerous new bugs in the linux kernel.** ERSAnalyzer generates 335 reports, 239 of which are potential bugs in the Linux kernel. We analyzed all of the reported bugs manually and confirmed 25 of them are actually missing-check bugs; some of them have already been fixed by the other analysts. Finally, 12 new bugs are submitted to the Linux kernel, and 6 of them have been accepted by the kernel maintainers up to today.

2 Background and Related Work

2.1 Security Check

Security checks are essential and necessary in software programs, they are designed to protect sensitive variables from illegal reading/writing, or a null pointer dereference. The bugs caused by missing security checks pose a severe

```
     kfree(iio_dev_opaque);
     return NULL;
     }
-  dev_set_name(&indio_dev->dev, "iio:device%d", iio_dev_opaque->id);
+
+  if (dev_set_name(&indio_dev->dev, "iio:device%d", iio_dev_opaque->id)) {
+     ida_simple_remove(&iio_ida, iio_dev_opaque->id);
+     kfree(iio_dev_opaque);
+     return NULL;
+  }
+
    INIT_LIST_HEAD(&iio_dev_opaque->buffer_list);
    INIT_LIST_HEAD(&iio_dev_opaque->ioctl_handlers);
```

Fig. 1. Example of missing-check bugs from the Linux kernel patch.

security threat to the system. In the 2021 CWE (Common Weakness Enumeration) [15] Top 25, missing-check bugs may carry **CWE-787**, **CWE-125**, **CWE-20**, **CWE-22**, **CWE-476** risks, some of them are presenting an increasing trend comparing to the passed year.

In the Linux kernel, almost all of the modules are written in low-level C programming language. Some of them contain assembly codes for direct interaction with the hardware. So most of the execution status of specific API functions have to be validated to ensure the system's security and reliability. But the missing-check bugs are still common in the Linux kernel, and some may cause serious security problems.

As the real code patch shown in the Fig. 1, missing-check of the API function *dev_set_name* may lead to a system crash because of a null pointer dereference. In fact, we find more than 400 security patches by searching the keyword *dev_set_name* in the kernel commits; Most are adding checks on the function returns, which roughly show that the API function *dev_set_name* is often misused because of missing-check the return value by the kernel developers. In addition, the usages of API functions such as *kstrdup*, *kmalloc*, are suffering similar problems.

2.2 Related Work

Missing-Check Bugs. The missing-check bugs have already attracted the attention of researchers. But it's a challenge to find out all of the bugs with high precision using static analysis, since there are still existing difficulties in program analysis. Earlier works [1,6,7,9,10] researched the problem using manual specific API functions, which would consume most of the time to analyze the target API functions and build a suitable model for future analysis. However, with the rapid development of software programs, it's becoming more and more complex. The manual work may take so much time to understand the error

```
pcpu_sum = kvmalloc_array(num_possible_cpus(),
                          sizeof(struct netvsc_ethtool_pcpu_stats),
                          GFP_KERNEL);
+   if (!pcpu_sum)
+       return;
+
    netvsc_get_pcpu_stats(dev, pcpu_sum);
    for_each_present_cpu(cpu) {
        struct netvsc_ethtool_pcpu_stats *this_sum = &pcpu_sum[cpu];
```

Fig. 2. Check for return value.

semantics and build one or more complex patterns to identify the bugs. There are millions of functions waiting for security analysis in the Linux kernel, and it seems impossible to be completed with fully manual efforts.

Fortunately, recent works proposed new methods to select target API functions automatically. APISan [12] infers security semantic briefs from existing API usages with symbolic execution techniques, bugs are reported after comparing API usages. PeX [13] infers to find security specifications automatically and targets to detect capability permission check errors. CRIX [14] presents the methods of critical variables identification and builds the *peer-slice* by collecting the sources and uses of critical variables and performs cross-checks upon those slices to find bugs.

Cross-checking which takes the more one based on statistics as the ground truth is a sound method to resolve the problem. However, it also suffers from low precision and high false positives due to inaccuracy in the data-flow analysis of the handling of return codes and constraints. On the one hand, mistakes may generate during target API function selection, critical variable analysis, and error handling according to our investigation. On the other hand, developers may realize the code for security checks in various ways since the semantics of variables are flexible, and some excluding return variables may also carry security information.

Error-Handling Analysis. Recently, studies have focused on how to automatically detect the bugs in the error-status handling indicated by the error code returned from critical API functions. EeCatch [17] is used to detect Exaggerated Error Handling (EEH) bugs. It accurately identifies errors, extracts their contexts (spatial and temporal), and automatically infers the appropriate severity level for error handling. HERO [18] precisely pairs both common and custom functions based on the unique error-handling structures and then analyze and identifiers the Disordered Error Handling (DiEH) bugs. Earlier work EIO [1] detects missing-check bugs in file systems by analysis on error-propagation.

```
u64 nfp_rtsym_read_le(..., int *error)
{
    ...
    *error = err;
}
static int nfp_pcie_sriov_read_nfd_limit(...)
{
    ...
    pf->limit_vfs = nfp_rtsym_read_le(pf->rtbl,
    "nfd_vf_cfg_max_vfs", &err);
    if (err)
    ...
}
```

Fig. 3. Argument pointers can carry out error information to the caller functions.

APEx [9], ErrDoc [20], and EPEx [10] reason about the error-code propagation in open-source SSL implementations, either automatically or via user definitions. EESI [21] is a static analysis tool that infers function error specifications for C programs by returning code idioms.

The code for error-handling is meaningful to learn to get more error semantics. It can help to detect more error-return API functions automatically.

2.3 Analysis of Error Returns in Linux Kernel

Without the high-level support of exception mechanisms in high-level programming languages such as Java [3] and C++ [4], the error states are mostly defined as macros mnemonic using simple integers, which are also called error codes. For more convenient use, even the returned pointers would be converted to special long integer error codes to carry more error message to the callers in the Linux kernel. The 3 special inline functions *IS_ERR*, *IS_ERR_OR_NULL*, *PTR_ERR_OR_ZERO* are used to simply check if a pointer infers error or not.

The example in Fig. 2 is the most common method to validate the API execution status in the Linux kernel. The called API functions return their status using error codes or pointers. Then they can be validated directly by comparing to **0** or **NULL** or using inline function **ERR_PTR**. For checks of the return value, most of the existing works focus on this situation.

On the one hand, the called API functions may infer the security information by not only the return error values, but also pointers referenced in arguments or global variables, as the example shown in Fig. 3. The pointer ***error** is assigned with the same semantic with the generated error code ***err***, for carrying out more error message when returning target pointer values.

On the other hand, the developers may validate the return values at an uncertain position like the example in Fig. 4. Not all return values are checked immediately. Some of them are checked just before their use. In the Fig. 4, the

```
static int intel_lpss_acpi_probe(...)
{
  ...
  info->mem = platform_get_resource(...);
  return intel_lpss_probe(&pdev->dev, info);
}
int intel_lpss_probe(struct device *dev,
    const struct intel_lpss_platform_info *info)
{
    ...
    if (!info || !info->mem || info->irq <= 0)
      return -EINVAL;
}
```

Fig. 4. Erroneous Status can be validated in the following called functions.

pointer ***info*** is not checked and directly used as a parameter. But the passed argument ***info*** is validated before use in the API function **intel_lpss_probe**. So it is believed a secure usage.

Not all situations above are considered by existing works, which contribute to many false positives. For cross-checking, precise and complete analysis results are the most important factors as the semantic security belief and ground truth. In other words, better analysis of those steps can lead to better results.

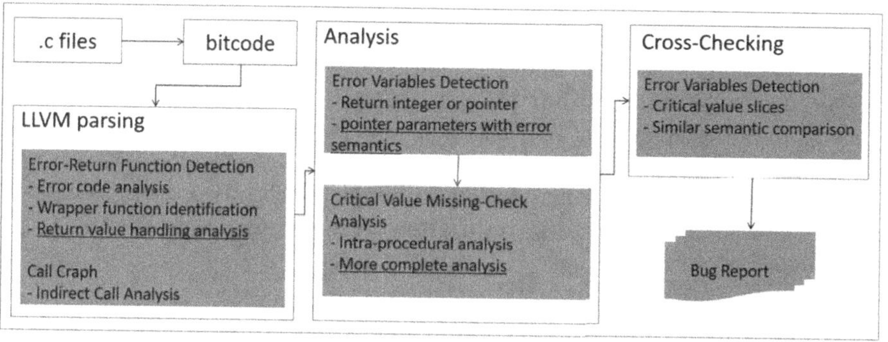

Fig. 5. Overview of ESAlalyzer.

3 Method

3.1 Overview

The key idea of ERSAnalyzer is to improve existing cross-checking works by enforcing more precise and complete analysis. The overview of ERSAnalyzer is shown in Fig. 5. We mainly focus on the improvement for parts of the work during parsing and analysis, which are underlined in the Fig. 5.

The source files are processed as follows. Firstly, the C files of the source code of the Linux kernel are compiled into bitcode files*(.bc format)* by *Clang* compiler. And then we build LLVM passes to analyse the bitcode files. An *error-return function* means that the function may return an error code or pointer to its' callers. Upon the **IR** code, we improve the existing method to identify more error-return functions, which does more analysis on wrapper function identification and the return value analysis, excluding analysis of the return code of the function. The analysis of the call graph focuses on the indirect call by employing the existing method **MLTA** [16].

The second part of ERSAnalyzer is to mark more pointers with error semantic assigned except for these return integers or pointers during error variable analysis. Analysis in Sect. 2.3 infers that many pointers can also carry error semantics for developers to validate in reality. And the analysis of these pointers is still ignored by existing studies up to now.

Then we enforce our missing-check analysis based on all of the critical variables mentioned above. Besides the intra-procedural analysis, which has been performed in most works, we do more improvement to realize a complete missing-check analysis pertinently for the Linux kernel.

Lastly, we implement cross-checking to compare the differences and report bugs with the collected return value operation slices on the target API functions, just like what many other cross-checking tools do.

3.2 Design

The goal of **ERSAnalyzer** is to detect missing-check bugs by improving existing works to get higher accuracy and lower false positives. There are two tasks to achieve this goal according to our analysis in Sect. 2.2 and 2.3. The first one is to detect more potential critical API functions and variables, and the other one is to implement more complete analysis on missing-check analysis. We make several improvements based on existing studies to complete those two tasks. What we do firstly is to identify more error-return functions, and then is to identify more error semantic pointers.

Identifying More Error-Return Functions. Existing work CRIX [14] identifies critical security checks using the approach proposed in LRSan [11]. LRSan can identify the functions returning error codes, and CRIX extends the idea by supporting error-handling functions. We find that the existing methods to identify error-return functions used by LRSan and CRIX mainly focus on the analysis of return codes so that some functions which directly return their callees' results cannot be decided as error-return functions. To address this problem, we extend the existing methods by adding a forward analysis of the handling of the return value of the target API.

Our method is developed as shown in Algorithm 1. Functions returning pointers or integers are selected for the error-return analysis. The variable *isReturnErr*

Algorithm 1. Error-Return Function Analysis

Require: Func: An integer- or pointer-return function
Ensure: *isReturnError*

```
1: function IS_ERROR_RETURN_FUNC(Func)
2:     isReturnErr = False;
3:     for each ReturnInst in Func do
4:         RetVal ← ReturnInst;
5:         if isErrorValue(RetVal) then
6:             isReturnErr ← True
7:             break
8:         if isFromCall(RetVal) then
9:             CalledFunc ← getFunctionFromInstruction(RetVal)
10:            isReturnErr ← IS_ERROR_RETURN_FUNC(CalledFunction)
11:            if isReturnErr is True then
12:                break
13:    if isReturnErr is False then
14:        for each Callsite in CallSites do
15:            RetVariable ← CallInst
16:            if isCheckErr(RetVariable) then
17:                isReturnErr ← True
18:                break
       return isReturnErr
```

is a boolean value which indicates that whether the target API functions is an error-return function, initialized with a false value. The function **isErrorValue** is used to find out whether the given value would be a constant negative integer value, which is used as an error code in the Linux kernel according to the error's macro definition. Firstly, we use a loop to find out whether any *ReturnInst* in the Function returns an error integer code or possibly null pointer. If so, the function is marked as a **error-return function**. This is same to the other works. Sometimes the *ReturnInst* refers a value from *CallInst*, meaning a function call, in LLVM IR the *RetVal* is actually a *CallInst* at this situation, a recursion analysis would be performed to decide the *CalledFunction* may return an error. The function **isFromCall** is realized to determine if the analyzed return-value is from another API function.

And if we still cannot get a result exactly, we would search each of the callsites of the target API function. The function **isCheckErr** used in line 16 takes a forward dataflow analysis on the return values of the analyzed functions to decide whether the return values are used in error-checking statements as the macro described in Sect. 2.3 or the other known specific error-handling functions. If the return values are used to check if they are error codes or null pointers, the functions are also marked as error-return functions.

Identifying More Error Semantic Pointers. Based on the study in Sect. 2.3, pointer arguments of a function can also carry the error messages when the function frames switching. The developers may check the return values and pointer

Algorithm 2. Error Semantic Pointers Analysis.

```
Require: Function: function may return error
Ensure: Collection of EPSet
1: function ERROR_SEMANTIC_POINTER_ANALYSIS(Function)
2:     EPSet ← new Set();
3:     PointerArgs ← getArgs(Function)
4:     for each RetVal in Function do
5:         Constraints ← BackwardInstrFlow(RetVal)
6:         RetConditon ← Constraints
7:         if RetCondition != NULL then
8:             conditionVar ← RetCondition
9:             if conditionVar in PointerArgs then
10:                EPSet.insert(conditionVar)
11:            if isErrorHandling(RetCondition) then
12:                for each PointerArg in PointerArgs do
13:                    if isAssigendErrCode(PointerArg) then
14:                        EPSet.insert(PointerArg)
       return EPSet
```

arguments to decide the execution states. Existing works ignore this situation. To address this problem, we design a new method to mark the error-semantic pointer variables for future missing-check analysis to avoid possible false positives.

According to our observation, the target pointer variables are always used when a function returns after a condition comparison. As shown in Algorithm 2, we perform a backward analysis on each of the *ReturnInst* instruction in the given error-return function. *EPSet* is initialized as a set to store target pointers. The *PointerArgs* is the collection of the pointer parameters of the target function. In the function **BackwardInstrFlow**, line 5, we collect the instructions from the *ReturnInst* to their incoming source blocks. We analyze the constraints from the instruction-flow and try to extract the *RetCondition*, which means the direct conditions of return statements. We get the critical variable *conditionVar* from the *RetCondition* statements.

There are two possible situations pointer arguments may carry out the error information when the *RetCondition* is not NULL. The first one is that the pointer arguments are used as one of the conditions which would return *-EINVAL* if checked failed, which described as line 9 in Algorithm 2. Another one is the pointer arguments assigned the value of the error code or string message before return, such as the example in Fig. 3. We use the function **isErrorHandling**, which is mainly implemented to analyze the *CmpInst* to find the error-handling path, to determine whether the *RetCondition* is placed in the error-handling statements, which indicates the pointers may be assigned values with error-semantic. Then a loop is performed on *PointerArg* to decide each of the *PointerArg* is actually assigned an error code, by using the function **isAssignedErrCode**. Both of the two situations above are marked as critical variables.

More Complete Missing-Check Analysis. Not only the limitations of dataflow analysis technique, but also the flexible programming statements contribute to the inaccurate missing-check analysis results. To improve this situation, we mainly focus on enforcing a more complete analysis on critical variables. This is resolved empirically by optimizing the alias analysis, point-to analysis and specific error-handling analysis, target to eliminate the wrong results as much as possible.

4 Implementation

The ERSAnalyzer is implemented in C++ on top of LLVM, including the building of a global call graph, identification of error-return functions, missing-check analysis, and cross-check analysis.

The Linux kernel code is compiled with *wllvm* [22], using the default configuration of the Linux kernel, and gets 19,063 bitcode files in total. We build the global call graph using the same method with MLTA [11,14]. With the results from MLTA, we can query the callsites of the target API functions or the actually called function at indirect callsites. Then all of the analyses are realized upon the LLVM IR.

For a complete analysis of missing-check analysis, we also do more to improve the results of critical variables' alias analysis and missing-check analysis based on our experiences.

- **Alias analysis of critical variables.** CRIX enforces its' analysis by relying on LLVM's AliasAnalysis infrastructure. Additional field-sensitive analysis has been performed for each pointer used in memory load/store or function calls as parameters. But we find that the inaccurate pointer analysis still causes many false positives. So we fix the problems we found in practice to raise the precision mainly by carefully analyzing the **GetElementPtr** instruction similar to Dr.Checker [23].
- **Complete analysis of missing-check.** To confirm the validation of the target API functions' execution status, existing works focus on finding the **CmpInst** or **SwitchInst** instructions before the critical uses of critical variables. As we study in Sect. 2.3, the developers may check the return values in different ways at uncertain positions. We extend existing methods used by CRIX by a forward analysis on return not only values but also the error semantic pointer arguments. Those critical variables are often checked at the position just after they are generated or propagated to their callers. We notice that some of the critical variables are used as arguments in the called functions, and they would be checked before reading or writing to keep secure execution states. If any of these critical variables are validated at any position before critical uses by the developers, the execution flow is considered safe. To reduce the false positives, we extend the forward analysis to find out all of the situations above.
- **Cross checking for bug detection.** The key idea of cross checking is simple and direct. More usage cases of the target API are believed the correct ones. We employ cross-checking only to compare the return values of critical

functions, which are part of the work done by CRIX. After the usage collection of the same critical API functions, it's easy to decide whether the return values of the critical functions should be checked according to statistics.

5 Evaluation

We evaluate the effectiveness of ERSAnalyzer using the Linux kernel. The experiments were performed on an Ubuntu Server with 128 GB RAM and Intel(R) Xeon(R) Silver 4110 CPU (2.10 GHz) with 32 cores. We test the bug detection efficiency on the Linux kernel version 5.15.6 using LLVM 12.0.1 on the Ubuntu 18.04, and the option *-inline* is disabled for a precise bug position report. For the Linux Kernel, we used clang and wllvm to compile and generate 39,408 Bitcode files. And the bitcode files under directories *drivers/* and *lib/* are chosen to run as our test.

5.1 Overall Analysis of Bug Detection

We perform ERSAnalyzer's analysis on a total of 19,063 bitcode files. In those bitcode files, we parsed out more than 374k functions. More than 169k functions are identified as error-return functions, around 205k functions may not generate errors, and more than 514k callsites are analyzed. ERSAnalyzer reports 335 cases, of which 239 are considered potential bugs, 25 are considered actual missing-check bugs, and 12 of the 25 new bugs have been submitted to the kernel maintainers.

Not all of the reported bugs can be analyzed easily with manual work due to the difficulty of understanding the code logic and data flow. After careful analysis, 25 of them are confirmed to be actual bugs. We finally submit 12 patches to the Linux kernel maintainers, as the rest have already been patched in the latest kernel code. The detail of the bugs we submitted is shown in Table 1.

Most of our submits in Table 1 are **NULL pointer dereference** bugs. Those **NULL pointer dereference** bugs are caused by memory allocation API functions as they are much easier to be understood. The critical variables in rows 8–11 in Table 1 are all members of complex structures. It shows that our tool is effective in alias analysis for structure fields.

Figure 6 shows the detail of the bug at row 12 in Table 1. The variable *ret* keeps the return value of API function **fwnode_property_read_u32**. The previous two return values at line 518 and line 522 are checked immediately, but at line 526 the return value of **fwnode_property_read_u32** is not saved and missing-check. So that the $st{-}{>}channel\_offstate[reg]$ may be assigned to wrong value and bring out logic errors.

5.2 Analysis of Critical Variables and Missing-Checks

Identification of Error-Return Functions. We extend the existing methods used in CRIX to identify more error-return functions, and then compare our

Table 1. Missing-check bugs found by ERSAnalyzer.

#	Position	Critical variable	Vulnerablity type
1	drivers/gpu/drm/msm/disp/msm_dis p_snapshot_util.c:171	new_blk	NULL pointer dereference
2	drivers/md/bcache/request.c:1109	ddip	NULL pointer dereference
3	drivers/misc/lkdtm/fortify.c:43	src	NULL pointer dereference
4	drivers/soc/bcm/bcm63xx/bcm-pmb.c:315	pd	NULL pointer dereference
5	drivers/gpu/drm/omapdrm/ omap_crtc.c:166	wait	NULL pointer dereference
6	drivers/gpu/drm/amd/amdkfd/ kfd_events.c:531	event_waiters	NULL pointer dereference
7	lib/mpi/mpi-mod.c:42	ctx	NULL pointer dereference
8	drivers/crypto/stm32/stm32-hash.c:970	rctx->hw_context	NULL pointer dereference
9	drivers/soc/ti/ti_sci_pm_domains.c: 182	pd_provider-> data.domains	NULL pointer dereference
10	drivers/phy/tegra/xusb.c:668	port->dev.driver	NULL pointer dereference
11	drivers/pinctrl/ralink/pinctrl-rt2880.c:265	p->func[i]->pins	NULL pointer dereference
12	drivers/iio/dac/ad5592r-base.c:526	ret	Logic Error

Table 2. Identification of error-return functions.

Number of bitcode files	Number of total analyzed functions	ERSAnalyzer	CRIX
1,000	31,370	14,701	14,137
3,000	83,660	36,926	35,600
5,000	153,518	70,183	67,981
7,000	254,178	115,911	112,461
9,000	346,788	156,765	151,735

results with CRIX. To evaluate the effectiveness of error-function identification, we test on the different number of bitcode files.

Table 2 shows that the number of identified error-return functions by the two methods. ERSAnalyzer identifies more error-return functions than CRIX, at an average of 3.46%.

```
ret = fwnode_property_read_u32(child, "reg", &reg);
if (ret || reg >= ARRAY_SIZE(st->channel_modes))
    continue;

ret = fwnode_property_read_u32(child, "adi,mode", &tmp);
if (!ret)
    st->channel_modes[reg] = tmp;

fwnode_property_read_u32(child, "adi,off-state", &tmp);
if (!ret)
    st->channel_offstate[reg] = tmp;
```

Fig. 6. Logic bug found by ERSAnalyzer.

One of the main difficulties in error-function identification is that the entire call graph cannot be built exactly and efficiently with existing techniques and tools, even all of the bitcode files are given, to both our tools and CRIX. So we have to divide the files into parts in proportion.

More Critical Pointers and Complete Missing Check Analysis. We improve the existing works mainly by enforcing a complete data-flow analysis for critical variables, including analysis of error-semantic pointers and careful analysis to confirm whether the critical variables are missing-check or not. To evaluate the effects of our complete data-flow analysis, we focus on validating the ERSAnalyzer's reports.

In the reported 335 cases, there are 239 cases that are actually missing-check cases, accounting for 71.3% of the total. We evaluate the improvement by comparing to CRIX, which reports thousands of cases and manually confirms 278 new bugs upon its' top 804 cases (34.58%). CRIX blames the inaccuracy on imprecise points-to analysis (48%), inconsequential checks (25%), implicit checks (8%) and other causes (19%). Almost all of the reasons could result in failures when doing missing-check analysis. Those inaccurate analyses lead to either statistical gaps in cross-checking or mistakes in reporting missing-check cases. Our method resolves this problem pertinently. The accuracy is improved to be higher and the total number of reported cases is less. This reduces the work of manual audit a lot.

5.3 False Positives and False Negatives

There are still false positives and false negatives in the reports of ERSAnalyzer. This is due to the following reasons.

- **Imperfect implementation of data-flow analysis.** The points-to analysis applied in ERSAnalyzer improves a lot upon our experience. It is practically enough, but still not as precise as expected. Almost all of the false positives in the missing-check analysis is attributed to the inaccurate data-flow analysis.

- **Dependence of incomplete call graphs.** We only analyze parts of the kernel files because of the high consumption of memory and time due to our poor code experiences. So we have to perform our analysis on only the kernel drivers and suffer from incomplete call graphs. Due to the incomplete call graphs, only 39.9k error-return functions whose callers can be found are analyzed, and the total number of error-return functions is 203k. It is the main reason for false negatives.

5.4 Bug Confirmation

It's not easy work to confirm a bug according to the reports generated by crossing-check analysis manually. Even though crossing-check checks for the return values of target API functions in most usages. Without complete and accurate data-flow analysis, the fewer missing-check cases can also not be identified as bugs directly. But because of the difficulty in understanding the kernel context, the bug confirmation work is hard and complex. That is why ERS-Analyzer's submits are mostly **NULL pointer dereference** generated from memory allocation API functions.

6 Conclusion

In this paper, we present a new static analysis tool, ERSAnalyzer, for detecting missing-check errors of return values in the Linux kernel. ERSAnalyzer enforces a complete analysis algorithm to confirm whether a critical variable is being checked for better completeness. We implement ERSAnalyzer on top of LLVM 12.0.1 and evaluate it on Linux Kernel version 5.15.6. ERSAnalyzer reports 335 cases, 239 of which are potential bugs. After our manual confirmation, 25 of them are proved as actual missing-check bugs. Among the 25 bugs, 12 newly discovered bugs have been submitted and accepted into the Linux kernel, and the other bugs have been fixed in the latest version. The results demonstrate that ERSAnalyzer can effectively identify missing check bugs.

Acknowledgments. We thank all the anonymous reviewers for their constructive feedback. IIE authors are supported in part by NSFC (U1836211, 61872386, 61902395) and Beijing Nova Program, the other authors are supported in part by NSFC (U183620050).

References

1. Gunawi, H.S., Rubio-González, C., Arpaci-Dusseau, A.C., Arpaci-Dusseau, R.H., Liblit, B.: EIO: error handling is occasionally correct. In: FAST, vol. 8, pp. 1–16 (2008)

2. Min, C., Kashyap, S., Lee, B., et al.: Cross-checking semantic correctness: the case of finding file system bugs. In: Proceedings of the 25th Symposium on Operating Systems Principles, pp. 361–377 (2015)
3. Nanda, M.G., Sinha, S.: Accurate interprocedural null-dereference analysis for Java. In: 2009 IEEE 31st International Conference on Software Engineering, pp. 133–143. IEEE (2009)
4. Rubio-González, C., Gunawi, H.S., Liblit, B., Arpaci-Dusseau, R.H., Arpaci-Dusseau, A.C.: Error propagation analysis for file systems. In: Proceedings of the 30th ACM SIGPLAN Conference on Programming Language Design and Implementation, pp. 270–280 (2009)
5. Mao, J., Chen, Y., Xiao, Q., et al.: RID: finding reference count bugs with inconsistent path pair checking. In: Proceedings of the Twenty-First International Conference on Architectural Support for Programming Languages and Operating Systems, pp. 531–544 (2016)
6. Acharya, M., Xie, T.: Mining API error-handling specifications from source code. In: Chechik, M., Wirsing, M. (eds.) FASE 2009. LNCS, vol. 5503, pp. 370–384. Springer, Heidelberg (2009). https://doi.org/10.1007/978-3-642-00593-0_25
7. Zhong, H., Zhang, L., Xie, T., Mei, H.: Inferring resource specifications from natural language API documentation. In: 2009 IEEE/ACM International Conference on Automated Software Engineering, pp. 307–318. IEEE (2009)
8. Min, C., Kashyap, S., Lee, B., Song, C., Kim, T.: Cross-checking semantic correctness: the case of finding file system bugs. In: Proceedings of the 25th Symposium on Operating Systems Principles. pp. 361–377 (2015)
9. Kang, Y., Ray, B., Jana, S.: APEx: automated inference of error specifications for C APIs. In: Proceedings of the 31st IEEE/ACM International Conference on Automated Software Engineering, pp. 472–482 (2016)
10. Jana, S., Kang, Y.J., Roth, S., Ray, B.: Automatically detecting error handling bugs using error specifications. In: 25th USENIX Security Symposium (USENIX Security 2016), pp. 345–362 (2016)
11. Wang, W., Lu, K., Yew, P.C.: Check it again: detecting lacking-recheck bugs in OS kernels. In: Proceedings of the 2018 ACM SIGSAC Conference on Computer and Communications Security, pp. 1899–1913 (2018)
12. Yun, I., Min, C., Si, X., Jang, Y., Kim, T., Naik, M.: APISan: sanitizing API usages through semantic cross-checking. In: 25th USENIX Security Symposium (USENIX Security 2016), pp. 363–378 (2016)
13. Zhang, T., Shen, W., Lee, D., Jung, C., Azab, A.M., Wang, R.: PeX: a permission check analysis framework for Linux kernel. In: 28th USENIX Security Symposium (USENIX Security 2019), pp. 1205–1220 (2019)
14. Lu, K., Pakki, A., Wu, Q.: Detecting missing-check bugs via semantic-and context-aware criticalness and constraints inferences. In: 28th USENIX Security Symposium (USENIX Security 2019), pp. 1769–1786 (2019)
15. https://cwe.mitre.org/top25/archive/2021/2021_cwe_top25.html
16. Lu, K., Hu, H.: Where does it go? Refining indirect-call targets with multi-layer type analysis. In: Proceedings of the 2019 ACM SIGSAC Conference on Computer and Communications Security, pp. 1867–1881 (2019)
17. Pakki, A., Lu, K.: Exaggerated error handling hurts! an in-depth study and context-aware detection. In: Proceedings of the 2020 ACM SIGSAC Conference on Computer and Communications Security, pp. 1203–1218 (2020)
18. Wu, Q., Pakki, A., Emamdoost, N., McCamant, S., Lu, K.: Understanding and detecting disordered error handling with precise function pairing. In: 30th USENIX Security Symposium (USENIX Security 2021), pp. 2041–2058 (2021)

19. Jiang, Z.M., Bai, J.J., Lu, K., Hu, S.M.: Fuzzing error handling code using context-sensitive software fault injection. In: 29th USENIX Security Symposium (USENIX Security 2020), pp. 2595–2612 (2020)
20. Tian, Y., Ray, B.: Automatically diagnosing and repairing error handling bugs in C. In: Proceedings of the 2017 11th Joint Meeting on Foundations of Software Engineering, pp. 752–762 (2017)
21. DeFreez, D., Baldwin, H.M., Rubio-González, C., Thakur, A.V.: Effective error-specification inference via domain-knowledge expansion. In: Proceedings of the 2019 27th ACM Joint Meeting on European Software Engineering Conference and Symposium on the Foundations of Software Engineering, pp. 466–476 (2019)
22. https://github.com/travitch/whole-program-llvm
23. Machiry, A., Spensky, C., Corina, J., Stephens, N., Kruegel, C., Vigna, G.: DR.CHECKER: a soundy analysis for Linux kernel drivers. In: 26th USENIX Security Symposium (USENIX Security 2017), pp. 1007–1024 (2017)
24. Deng, Z., Chen, K., Meng, G., Zhang, X., Xu, K., Cheng, Y.: Understanding real-world threats to deep learning models in Android apps. In: Proceedings of the 2022 ACM SIGSAC Conference on Computer and Communications Security, pp. 785–799 (2022)

Efficient DNN Backdoor Detection Guided by Static Weight Analysis

Qi Wang, Wenxin Li, Kang Yang, Yiru Zhao(✉), Lei Zhao(✉), and Lina Wang

Key Laboratory of Aerospace Information Security and Trusted Computing, Ministry of Education, School of Cyber Science and Engineering, Wuhan University, Wuhan, China

{zhaoyiru,leizhao}@whu.edu.cn

Abstract. Despite the great progress of deep neural networks (DNNs), they are vulnerable to backdoor attacks. To detect and provide concrete proof for the existence of backdoors, existing techniques generally adopt the reverse engineering approach. However, most of them suffer from high computational complexity and weak scalability. In this paper, we make a key observation that the weights connected to the backdoor target labels in trojaned DNNs tend to have abnormal distributions, including dissimilarity to other labels and anomalously large magnitude. Based on this observation, we propose an efficient and scalable backdoor detection framework guided by static weight analysis. Our approach first detects the outlier existing in weight distributions and identifies suspicious backdoor target/victim label pairs. Then we conduct reverse engineering to recover the triggers, including a newly designed reverse engineering approach for global transformation attacks and one existing approach for local patch attacks. Finally, we analyze the characteristics of the recovered triggers to suppress false positives. Experimental results show that our approach has state-of-the-art performance on MNIST, CIFAR-10, ImageNet, and TrojAI. In particular, it outperforms NC, ABS, and K-Arm by 31%, 8.7%, and 5% on the public detection benchmark TrojAI in terms of detection accuracy while maintaining the highest efficiency.

Keywords: Deep neural network · Backdoor detection · Static weight analysis · Reverse engineering

1 Introduction

Deep neural networks (DNNs) have achieved impressive performance in various domains, including computer vision [16], malware detection [25], autonomous driving [3], etc. As constructing and deploying a well-performed DNN requires a lot of expertise and resources, developers may outsource the training process to cloud vendors (e.g., Amazon) and then retrieve the trained model. Besides, developers can also download pre-trained models directly from the internet repositories, such as Torchvision [29] and TensorFlow Model Garden [35].

Y. Deng and M. Yung (Eds.): Inscrypt 2022, LNCS 13837, pp. 408–428, 2023.
https://doi.org/10.1007/978-3-031-26553-2_22

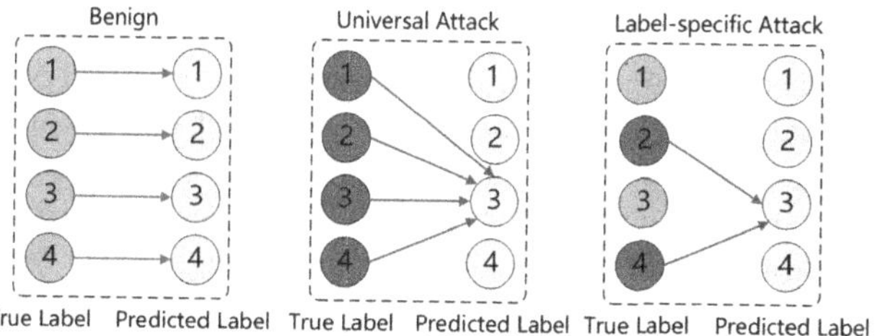

Fig. 1. Illustration of universal attack and label-specific attack. Samples from victim labels (red nodes) are misclassified to the target label. (Color figure online)

However, recent studies have shown that DNNs are prone to backdoor attacks [8,18,20,23], which leads to the critical problem of trustworthiness for a pre-trained DNN from third parties. In the backdoor attack, an adversary typically defines a backdoor *trigger* and then implants a backdoor into the model by poisoning the training dataset [8,21,23]. The *trojaned* model performs normally on benign samples, but will misclassify a sample to a *target label* specified by the adversary when the sample contains the trigger.

Backdoor attacks can be divided into *universal attack* and *label-specific attack*, as shown in Fig. 1. For universal attacks, all samples with the trigger will be misclassified to the target label. As for label-specific attacks, the misclassification only occurs from specific *victim labels* to the target label.

Backdoor detection is determining whether a DNN contains a secret backdoor. To produce a trustworthy and interpretable result, backdoor detection is supposed to achieve two goals. The first is to disclose the target and victim labels specified by the adversary. And the second is to recover the trigger to reveal how the malicious behavior is actually launched. In practice, the defender has zero knowledge about the training process and trigger pattern. To achieve these goals, existing techniques [19,26,31] generally adopt a *reverse engineering* approach. They start with a small collection of validation data and solve an optimization problem to recover the backdoor trigger that causes the model prediction to be overturned from the victim label to the target label.

Although existing reverse engineering based backdoor detection techniques are capable of achieving these goals, there remain two limitations. First, most of them [9,31,32] suffer from high computation complexity due to the inefficient identification of target/victim label pairs. For universal attacks, they treat all output labels as potential target labels and conduct reverse engineering, leading to a tedious scanning time for models with many labels. As for label-specific attacks, blindly enumerating all target/victim label pairs incurs quadratic complexity. Second, most existing techniques [9,26,31] only focus on backdoor attacks with local patch triggers. It is noteworthy that the triggers specified by the adversary are no longer limited to local patches, but also the global transformations, such as Instagram filters [1,19]. Filter triggers can be utilized to launch backdoor attacks as well by adding artistic effects to the original images. Reconstructing global transformation triggers is more challenging because they modify every pixel and vary from one image to another.

To address the aforementioned limitations, we propose an efficient and scalable backdoor detection framework guided by static weight analysis. We make a key observation that the weights connected to the target labels tend to be abnormal, including dissimilarity to weight distributions of other labels and anomalously large values. Based on this observation, we first design a pre-selection algorithm for searching potential target/victim pairs through static weight analysis. Second, we reverse engineer a trigger for each target/victim pair. To counter the challenge of recovering global transformation triggers, we design a new reverse engineering approach and integrate it into our framework in addition to the approach for patch triggers. Finally, we note that reverse engineering for local patch triggers is prone to two types of false positives, namely adversarial perturbations and natural features. These false positives can be considered natural faults of models, which are distinguished from maliciously implanted backdoors. We further suppress those false positives by analyzing the attributes of triggers and activated neuron distributions of models.

Compared with existing detection techniques, our detection framework has the following advantages. First, static weight analysis can precisely identify suspicious target/victim pairs, eliminating optimization for unpromising triggers and benefiting our framework with high efficiency. Second, the abnormal weight distributions are prevailing in trojaned models and are agnostic to model architectures and trigger types. Thus static weight analysis remains effective for various backdoor attacks, which makes our framework scalable to integrate reverse engineering approaches and detect patch and global transformation triggers. Third, our framework with trigger analysis can assist end-users in determining if the reversed triggers are malicious implants or natural faults in DNNs, allowing them to take necessary countermeasures.

To demonstrate the effectiveness of our detection framework, we conduct comprehensive experiments across various model architectures and attack types on MNIST [17], CIFAR-10 [15], ImageNet [6], and a public backdoor detection benchmark TrojAI [12]. Results show that our approach has state-of-the-art (SOTA) performance. For example, our detection accuracy outperforms NC [31], ABS [19], and K-Arm [26] by 31%, 8.7%, and 5% on TrojAI respectively. Meanwhile, the static weight analysis significantly improves the efficiency of large-scale model detection tasks. Specifically, our approach is 23.5, 5.8, and 1.2 times faster than the above techniques. Besides, our approach can detect global transformation attacks as well, with an accuracy of 81%, 95%, and 95% for filter attacks on TrojAI, CIFAR-10, and WaNet [21] attack on CIFAR-10 respectively.

Our contributions are summarized as follows.

- We propose an efficient target/victim pairs identification approach for backdoor detection based on static weight analysis. It is agnostic to model structures and trigger types and thus can significantly improve the efficiency of backdoor detection for local patch attacks and global transformation attacks.
- We propose a backdoor detection framework guided by static weight analysis. Our framework integrates two trigger reverse engineering approaches (1 existing and 1 new) and two novel backdoor diagnosis strategies to provide reliable and interpretable detection results.

- Experiments on various datasets including MNIST, CIFAR-10, ImageNet, and TrojAI against local patch and global transformation attacks demonstrate the significant performance of our approach. For instance, it outperforms SOTA techniques NC, ABS, and K-Arm by 31%, 8.7%, and 5% in terms of detection accuracy, while maintaining the highest efficiency.

2 Background and Motivation

2.1 Threat Model

We assume that an adversary could implant a hidden backdoor before the DNN is acquired by the defenders and users. The attack types may be universal attacks or label-specific attacks. Consistent with the prior work [9,19,26,31], the defenders have full access to the pre-trained model including its architecture and weights, as well as a small set of benign data for validation, but have zero knowledge about the attack types, target/victim pairs, or real triggers. They need to identify whether the model contains a malicious backdoor. In addition, they are also supposed to disclose the target and victim labels specified by the adversary and the trigger that can activate the backdoor behavior.

2.2 Limitations of Existing Techniques

Low Efficiency. NC [31] proposes gradient descent optimization to reverse engineer backdoor triggers. The optimization searches a minimal local patch so that samples stamped with this patch will be misclassified to the target label. It necessitates complex gradient calculations and is time-consuming. In universal attacks, for a DNN model with N output labels, NC treats each label as a potential target to operate the optimization, and the computation complexity is $O(N)$. As for label-specific attacks, NC needs to blindly enumerate all target/victim label pairs, which incurs $O(N^2)$ complexity. Without identification for target/victim pairs, some other reverse engineering based techniques [9,32] suffer from low efficiency as well.

ABS [19] reveals potential backdoor target labels by operating a stimulation analysis for internal neurons. It assumes that the backdoor can be triggered by elevating the activation value of one compromised neuron and exhaustively searches thousands of inner neurons to identify the compromised neurons, leading to a high-cost process. What's more, the one-neuron assumption may not hold when facing advanced attacks, and analyzing the interaction of multiple neurons requires exponential complexity.

Weak Scalability. A common and important type of backdoor attack is triggered by global transformations [1,19,21]. Unlike traditional patch triggers that only cover a local area, global transformation triggers modify every pixel of the original images. Besides, the modification is no longer a constant but varies from one input image to another. As a result, global transformation triggers are harder to detect and recover than local patch triggers.

Most existing approaches [9,26,31] can only handle patch triggers because they define the optimization objective as finding a minimal local constant modification. For example, a recent work K-Arm [26] formalizes the identification of target labels as a multi-arm bandit problem to improve efficiency. It leverages a scheduler that prioritizes the labels by evaluating the trigger size and its reduction rate, which is not scalable to deal with global transformation triggers.

2.3 Key Intuition and Observation

To address these limitations, we propose to design a backdoor detection approach that satisfies the requirements of efficiency and scalability. The intuition behind our approach is that implanting a backdoor tends to result in abnormal weight distributions in DNN models. Capturing the anomaly existing in the weights is highly efficient and agnostic to trigger types and model architectures, which can serve as a promising clue for backdoor detection.

Given a DNN model F, let $R(x)$ denote the output of the penultimate layer for the input image x, which are often referred to as *representations*. The commonly used DNNs [10,24,27] can be formulated as $y = F(x) = Softmax(R(x) \cdot W)$, where W represents the weight matrix in the last hidden layer, and $R(x) \cdot W$ outputs the predicted scores of input x. The $Softmax(\cdot)$ function normalizes the scores to a final confidence level.

In the training process, W is updated by $W - \triangle W$ in each back-propagation step. For a weight vector w_l that denotes all the weights connecting to label l, the formula for updating w_l is: $w_l = w_l - \alpha(\hat{y} - y_l)^T R$, where $\hat{y}$ is the model's output confidence vector, y_l denotes the one-hot ground-truth vector, and α is the learning rate. R is usually the output of the activation function $Relu$, so R is non-negative. Thus the modification direction of w_l is related to whether the training data belongs to l, and the position of modification is related to the activated neurons on R. Since the model learns to connect the features from victim label v with the target label t during the poison training, w_t will have a larger value in the position of features corresponding to v. But the vectors w_c of clean label c and w_v of victim label v have greater values only at positions that represent their intra-class features. Therefore, the distribution of w_t tends to be furthest away from all weight vectors and has a larger magnitude. In addition, w_v is the most similar one to w_t compared with other weight vectors.

We use Fig. 2 for an abstract illustration. It shows a classification task with 4 output labels, where V_1 and V_2 represent the victim labels, T is the target label, and C is the clean label. We simplify the representations to units that contain the features belonging to each class. The blocks in the weight vectors denote the weights connected to the corresponding units. The darker the colors in the weight vectors, the greater the magnitude of the weights. We simply count the number of blocks with the same colors to calculate the similarity between the weight vectors. The similarity between w_t and w_v is 3, greater than 1 between w_t and w_c, while w_c and w_v share a commonly large similarity of 3 with each other. This leads to the following observations.

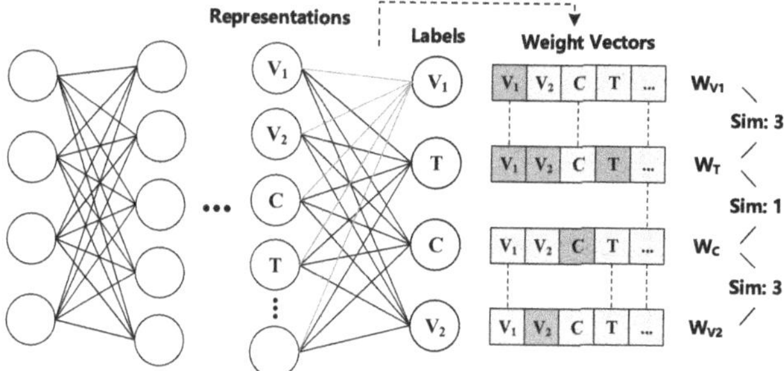

Fig. 2. Illustration of our key intuition. While clean or victim labels only learn their own features, the weight vector of the target label has greater values (denote in a darker color) for features belonging to multiple labels, thus being dissimilar to other labels. (Color figure online)

Observation 1: The weights connected to the backdoor target label show a different distribution from weights connected to other labels, and have a larger magnitude.

During the poison training, the weights connected to the target label receive positive modifications from data belonging to other classes. Thus the target label can be efficiently identified by detecting an outlier among all the weight vectors.

In universal attacks, the weight vectors of all other classes have greater values only at the position corresponding to their intra-class features, while w_t has larger values at all positions, resulting in a greater distance from other weight vectors. For this reason, we can further distinguish universal attacks and label-specific attacks by identifying whether there is an outstanding outlier.

Observation 2: Compared with other labels, the weights connected to the victim labels have a more similar distribution to the weights connected to the target label.

The weights connected to target and victim labels both have greater values at positions that represent the features belonging to the victim class, so they show similar distributions. This can be utilized to construct promising target/victim pairs, which is helpful for the efficient detection of label-specific attacks.

Furthermore, the anomaly in weight distribution is agnostic to trigger types, so the guidance of static weight analysis can assist reverse engineering for different types of triggers. Based on this superiority, we design our framework.

3 Design

3.1 Overview

Figure 3 presents the overview of our detection framework. It consists of 3 components: static weight analysis, trigger reverse engineering, and trigger analysis. First, we design a static weight analysis algorithm that screens out the suspicious target/victim labels. For a given DNN model, we scan the model weights and discover top-k suspicious target labels and corresponding victim labels. Second,

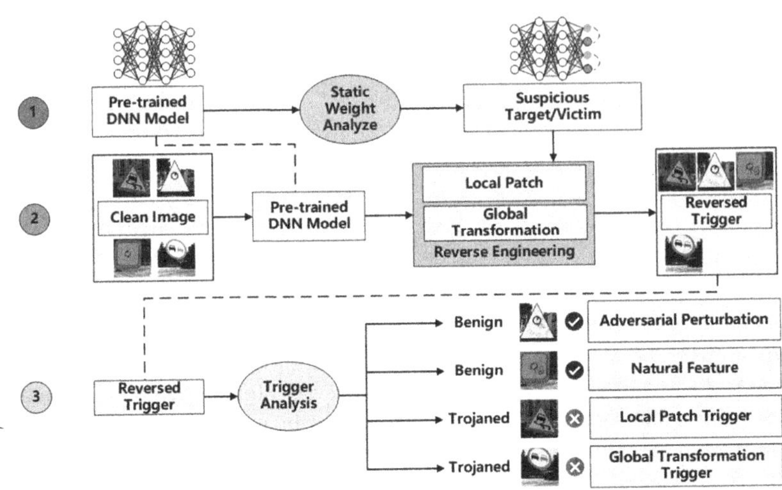

Fig. 3. Overview of our detection framework.

we operate reverse engineering for each suspicious target/victim pair to generate a trigger. We integrate the reverse engineering approach for local patch triggers and our novel reverse engineering approach for global transformation triggers. Finally, we analyze the recovered triggers, exclude adversarial perturbations and natural features that cause false positives, and retain the real backdoor trigger.

3.2 Static Weight Analysis to Identify Suspicious Target and Victim Labels

In static weight analysis, we reveal the suspicious target/victim labels by scanning the weights in pre-trained DNN models. The procedure is described in Algorithm 1.

Identifying Suspicious Target Labels. Recall that in Sect. 2.3, we discover that the weights connected to the backdoor target label tend to have different distributions. So we measure this abnormal weight distribution by calculating the *Divergence* $D(l)$ between labels as:

$$D(l) = -\frac{1}{n-1}\sum_{i=1}^{n}\frac{w_l \cdot w_i}{\|w_l\| \cdot \|w_i\|},\ i \neq l \tag{1}$$

where n is the number of classes, vector w_l denotes the weights connecting to label $l \in \{1, ..., n\}$ in the last fully connected layer. The larger the $D(l)$ is, the less similar the weight vector of label l is to other labels.

What's more, Sect. 2.3 also points out that the weights associated with the target label tend to have a larger magnitude. Thus, we adopt *Summation* $S(l)$ as a statistic to capture this attribute by adding up all the elements in w_l:

$$S(l) = Sum(w_l) \tag{2}$$

Algorithm 1. Static Weight Analysis

Input: F: pre-trained DNN model; k_d: number of *Divergence* candidates; k_s: number of *Summation* candidates; k_v: number of label-specific attack victim candidates; θ: universal attack threshold

Output: T: suspicious backdoor target labels; V: suspicious backdoor victim labels

```
T, V, Divergence, Sum = [];
Extracting the last layer weights W from F;
for label l in F.labels do
    Compute D(l) and S(l);
    Divergence.append(D(l));
    Sum.append(S(l));
end for
D_labels = argsort(−Divergence);
S_labels = argsort(−Sum);
T = D_labels[0 : k_d] ∪ S_labels[0 : k_s];
if Divergence[0] − Divergence[1] > θ then
    V = F.labels;
else
    for label t in T do
        labelSimilarity = [];
        for label l in F.labels, l ≠ t do
            labelSimilarity.append(CosSim(w_t, w_l));
        end for
        V_labels = argsort(−labelSimilarity);
        V[t] = V_labels[0 : k_v];
    end for
end if
return T, V
```

Then we sort the labels according to $D(l_i)$ and $S(l_i)$ and select the top k_d and k_s labels as suspicious target labels that have the largest $D(l_i)$ and $S(l_i)$ respectively. To reduce the overlap between the two sets, we calculate their union to get the final set of suspicious target labels.

Identifying Corresponding Victim Labels. After exposing the suspicious target labels, we identify the victim labels corresponding to each candidate target label. As discussed in **Observation 1**, though both universal and label-specific attacks contribute to the large *Divergence* of target labels, the universal attacks will lead to an outstanding value.

Therefore, we compute the difference between the largest *Divergence* value and the second-largest value. If the difference is larger than a threshold θ, we consider the model as universally trojaned, and the victim labels will be all of the output labels in model F. Otherwise, we consider it as label-specifically trojaned and find its victim labels as follows. For each suspicious target label t, we compute the *cosine similarity* between w_t and other $n-1$ weight vectors, then choose the top-k_v labels as corresponding victim labels. As described in **Observation 2**, the reason behind this approach is that the weight vectors of victim labels are most similar to the target label among all weight vectors, because the trojaned models are forced to make a connection between the benign features of the victim classes and the target label.

3.3 Reverse Engineering of Backdoor Triggers

After exposing suspicious target/victim pairs through static weight analysis, we apply reverse engineering to recover the trigger for each pair.

Handling Local Patch Triggers. Patch trigger can be regarded as a specific pattern added to an image. We formulate the generic function that applies a patch trigger (P, M) to a benign image x as follows.

$$\tilde{x} = x \circ (1 - M) + P \circ M \tag{3}$$

where $\tilde{x}$ is the image stamped with the trigger. Operator $\circ$ stands for Hadamard product. Pattern P is a color matrix that determines the input values of the trigger, and mask M controls the position and transparency of the trigger. Assuming the size of an input image x is $[C, H, W]$. P has the same dimensions as x, while the dimensions of M are $[1, H, W]$, representing each channel shares the same trigger region. Then we generate a reversed trigger for target label y_t by minimizing the objective function:

$$\min_{M,P} \mathcal{L}(y_t, f(\tilde{x})) + \beta \|M\|_1, \ \forall x \in X \tag{4}$$

where $f(\tilde{x})$ outputs the probabilities for $\tilde{x}$. $\mathcal{L}$ is the cross-entropy loss. For label-specific attacks, X contains benign images from one victim class. For universal attacks, X contains benign images from all the classes other than y_t. $\|M\|_1$ measures the size of mask M, and β controls the constraint degree of mask size.

We define the attack success rate (ASR) of a trigger as the percentage of classification results that are successfully flipped from the victim label to the target label. If the generated trigger (M, P) achieves an ASR higher than 99% and the size of M reaches convergence, we stop the optimization process.

Handling Global Transformation Triggers. We devise a novel reverse engineering approach for global transformation triggers. The global transformation trigger modifies all pixels in the image, which is hard to recover through the traditional approach. Actually, the applying process of such triggers can be simplified as a linear transformation to the image that modifies the values of the image's four channels $[R, G, B, A]$ and adds offsets. Thus, we utilize matrix multiplication to implement the linear transformation of the image as follows.

$$\tilde{x} = rgba2rgb(\Gamma \cdot concatenate([x, 1, 1])) \tag{5}$$

where the *concatenate* function adds two channels on x, namely *alpha* and *bias*. Channel *alpha* stands for opacity parameters and *bias* denotes the offsets. Trigger Γ is a 2D matrix of size $[4, 5]$ which modifies the pixel values of five channels

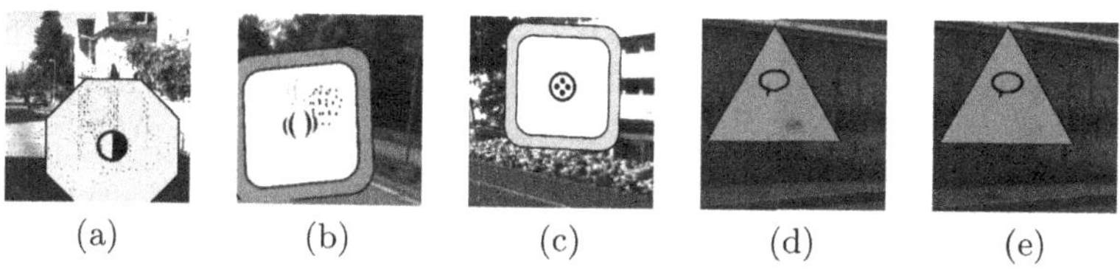

Fig. 4. The optimization results of local patch triggers. (a) and (b) are reversed from clean models. (a) is an adversarial perturbation that is scattered throughout the image; (b) is a natural feature belonging to image (c) from the target class; (d) is the reversed trigger from a trojaned model, and (e) is the ground truth trigger.

and the output is a four-channel $RGBA$ image. The $rgba2rgb$ function converts the transformed $RGBA$ image to an RGB image.

Observing that triggered images still visually look like the original ones, we impose *Structural Similarity (SSIM)* [33] constrain on $\mathcal{F}$ to make sure that $\tilde{x}$ is not seriously distorted. We reverse engineer global transformation triggers by solving the following optimization task:

$$\min_{\Gamma} \mathcal{L}(y_t, f(\tilde{x})) - \gamma SSIM(x, \tilde{x}),\ \forall\ x \in X \tag{6}$$

where hyper-parameter γ balances the constraint of *SSIM*. We discover that in label-specific attacks, the optimization could also generate a trigger for benign labels with a high success rate, but clean models do not have this property. We conjecture that the feature space inside the model poisoned by global transformation triggers is corrupted, and a path to the decision domain of the target label can be created for most labels through a linear transformation. So we optimize from each label to y_t and use an average success rate threshold of 90% to determine whether the model is trojaned.

3.4 Trigger Analysis to Suppress False Positives

After reverse engineering, we compare the L_1 norms of the masks with threshold σ to filter out local patch triggers with very large sizes. However, reverse engineering for local patch triggers is prone to two types of false positives, namely adversarial perturbations and natural features belonging to the benign target label (see Fig. 4). So we further analyze the generated triggers to suppress those false positives.

Excluding Adversarial Perturbations. Previous studies have shown that DNNs are easily fooled by adversarial perturbations [22]. For a clean model, we may also obtain a trigger with a small L_1 norm by reverse engineering, but the reversed trigger is actually an adversarial perturbation as shown in Fig. 4(a). Such small and sparse perturbations make it difficult to successfully implement backdoor attacks in the physical world, thus they are considered as natural faults of models instead of maliciously implanted backdoors.

For this reason, we measure the compactness of the trigger to rule out possible adversarial perturbations. We first divide the whole image evenly into small grids, then we count the number of grids covered by the reversed triggers. Finally, we exclude triggers that cover more than 10% of the grids, since adversarial perturbations are more sparse than real triggers and cover more grids.

Excluding Natural features. Natural features refer to benign features of the images that can cause misclassification like backdoors. They are as compact as real backdoor triggers (see Fig. 4(b)), and thus cannot be ruled out by L_1 norm or compactness. To distinguish natural features from real backdoor triggers, we further analyze the neuron behavior differences based on explainable artificial intelligence (XAI) [2]. According to XAI, different neurons in higher layers can only be activated by specific semantic features. Therefore, images patched with natural features are likely to activate neurons belonging to the target class. However, images stamped with real triggers would activate neurons corresponding to features of the victim class rather than the target class. So we utilize the activated neurons in the penultimate layer to discriminate natural features from real backdoor triggers.

We first use clean validation images from the target label to construct a set N_c of the most activated neurons in the penultimate layer. Next, for each $\tilde{x}$ pasted with the reversed trigger, we also build a set $N_{\tilde{x}}$ of the most activated neurons. Then we calculate the *Neuron Behavior Similarity (NBS)* as follows.

$$NBS = \frac{\sum \mid N_c \cap N_{\tilde{x}} \mid / \mid N_c \cup N_{\tilde{x}} \mid}{\mid \tilde{X} \mid}, \; \forall \tilde{x} \in \tilde{X} \tag{7}$$

The value of *NBS* ranges from 0 to 1. A larger *NBS* indicates that the most activated neurons by images with the generated trigger are more similar to those activated by clean images. If *NBS* is larger than 0.5, we consider the generated trigger to be a natural feature.

4 Experiments

4.1 Experimental Setup

Datasets. The experiment settings are elaborated in Table 1, including trigger types, attack types, number of output labels, number of clean and trojaned models, and model architectures. Datasets details are clarified as follows.

TrojAI. TrojAI [12] is a public benchmark supported by IARPA to combat backdoor attacks. The datasets are released in rounds. Each round consists of trained models with half of them trojaned. We evaluate our approach on Rounds 1–3 test sets including 532 DNN models with various architectures. The trigger types in Rounds 2–3 could be polygon patches or Instagram Filters.[1]

MNIST. We train 100 multi-target models on MNIST [17], which are universally trojaned by BadNets [8]. Each model has 0–3 target labels randomly. The trigger

[1] Datasets details can be found in https://pages.nist.gov/trojai/docs/data.html.

Table 1. Details of experiment settings.

Dataset		Trigger	Attack	#Labels	#Clean	#Trojaned	Architecture
MNIST		Patch	Universal	10	34	66	CCNN [36]
CIFAR-10		Filter	Specific	10	10	10	GoogLeNet, DenseNet-{121,161,169,201}
		WaNet [21]	Universal	10	10	10	ResNet-{18,50}
ImageNet		Hidden [23]	Specific	10	10	10	AlexNet
		Patch	Universal	1000	10	10	DenseNet-{121,161,201}
							ResNet-{18,50,152}
							VGG-{11,13}, VGGbn-{11,16,19}
TrojAI	R1	Patch	Universal	5	50	50	DenseNet-{121,161,169,201} ,GoogLeNet
							ResNet-{18,34,50,101,152}, Inceptionv3
	R2	Patch & Filter	Universal & Specific	5∼25	72	72	ShuffleNet-{1_0,1_5,2_0}
							VGGbn-{11,13,16,19}, MobileNetv2
	R3	Patch & Filter	Universal & Specific	5∼25	144	144	SqueezeNet-{1_0,1_1}
							WideResNet-{50,101}

is a square patch that appears in one or more of the corners. For models with multiple targets, each target label has one corresponding trigger pattern.

CIFAR-10. We train 20 models with different architectures on CIFAR-10 [15]. Half of them are trojaned by *Gotham Filter* or *Nashville Filter* using an open-source TrojAI software framework [13]. In addition, we train 10 models trojaned by WaNet [21], another type of global transformation trigger based on image warping, along with 10 clean models.

ImageNet. Following the settings in Hidden Trigger Attack [23], we train 20 models of 10 labels with different architectures on ImageNet [6]. Half of them are trojaned by this attack. In addition, we download 10 pre-trained clean models with 1000 labels of different architectures and fine-tune them to generate 10 universally trojaned models with polygon patch triggers.

Baseline Techniques. We compare our approach with the state-of-the-art (SOTA) reverse engineering based backdoor detection techniques: NC [31], ABS [19], TABOR [9], DLTND [32], and K-Arm [26]. When testing efficiency, we use the same batch size for all techniques, and the same early stop condition for our approach, NC, and K-Arm to make a fair comparison. Experiments are all conducted on equipment with a single Nvidia TITAN X GPU.

Metrics. We adopt Accuracy and AUC to evaluate the detection effectiveness. We compare the efficiency of our approach with the baseline techniques by calculating the elapsed time. The performance of pre-selection is evaluated by the indicators of Precision, Recall, and F_1 score.

Hyper-parameters. We set $\theta = 0.1$ to determine if the model is universally trojaned, and mask size threshold $\sigma = 350$ to filter out triggers with large L_1 norms. The number of target and victim label candidates $\{k_d, k_s, k_v\}$ are set to $\{3, 2, 2\}$ on TrojAI Rounds 2–3, and $\{1, 1, 2\}$ on ImageNet and CIFAR-10. TrojAI Round 1 only contains universally trojaned models, so we set $\{k_d, k_s\} = \{1, 1\}$. The sensitivity of hyper-parameters is discussed in Sect. 4.5.

Table 2. Experimental results of detecting patch triggers on TrojAI.

Method	TrojAI Round1			TrojAI Round2			TrojAI Round3		
	Acc	AUC	Time(s)	Acc	AUC	Time(s)	Acc	AUC	Time(s)
NC	67%	0.68	2252.2	50%	0.51	6592.4	57%	0.60	6345.8
TABOR	74%	0.76	4195.2	57%	0.61	11455.6	57%	0.56	11459.5
DLTND	78%	0.80	3717.5	–	–	–	–	–	–
ABS	89%	0.93	792.0	75%	0.78	1696.8	77%	0.75	1256.3
K-Arm	83%	0.84	399.0	81%	0.81	166.1	88%	0.89	190.3
Ours (Without TA.)	87%	0.91	–	76%	0.79	–	89%	0.91	–
Ours (With TA.)	**92%**	**0.93**	**326.3**	**83%**	**0.83**	**153.9**	**92%**	**0.92**	**166.5**

"TA." stands for the trigger analysis component.

4.2 Detection Performance on Local Patch Attacks

Detection Effectiveness on TrojAI. Table 2 reports the comparison results of detecting models poisoned by polygon patch triggers on TrojAI Rounds 1–3. For ABS, we run it on TrojAI Round 1 and models in Rounds 2–3 with the same architectures as Round 1, since the authors only published their detection APIs on Round 1 model architectures. For DLTND, it has to enumerate label pairs and spends more than 12 h scanning one model with 15 labels, so we do not run it on Rounds 2–3. And models are all considered universally trojaned on Rounds 2–3 by NC and TABOR for the same reason.

Results in Table 2 show that the detection effectiveness of our approach greatly outperforms NC, TABOR, DLTND, and ABS on all rounds, with 31%, 26.3%, 14%, and 8.7% higher accuracy respectively. While K-Arm has the best performance among the baseline techniques, the detection accuracy of our approach is 9%, 2%, and 4% higher than K-Arm on the three rounds. And we achieve better AUC in the meantime, which is calculated by changing the value of σ. We also report the detection results without the trigger analysis component as an ablation study in Table 2. Note that the trigger analysis benefits our approach with 5%, 7%, 3% higher accuracy and 0.02, 0.04, 0.01 higher AUC on Rounds 1–3. On the whole, our approach achieves SOTA performance in terms of detection accuracy and AUC, indicating the effectiveness of our detection framework and the significance of the trigger analysis component.

Detection Efficiency on TrojAI. We also report the elapsed time of baseline techniques and our approach in Table 2. Without a pre-selection of potential target/victim pairs, NC, TABOR, and DLTND have to reverse engineer for each label. As a result, their inspecting time is 7–74 times as our approach, and can hardly deal with label-specific attacks. As for ABS, it exhaustively searches thousands of inner neurons to identify the compromised neurons, which also leads to a high-cost process, and is 2, 11, and 7.5 times slower than our approach on Rounds 1–3 respectively. K-arm uses a scheduling strategy based on the size convergence rate of patch trigger and utilizes pre-screening to further acceler-

Table 3. Experimental results on ImageNet.

Method	Hidden trigger (10 Labels)			Polygon patch (1000 Labels)			
	Acc	AUC	Time	Acc	AUC	Time	#Samples
ABS	90%	0.90	1707.6	100%	1.00	1038.3	50
K-Arm	90%	0.94	1555.2	90%	0.90	158.9	50
				100%	1.00	178.5	1000
Ours	**100%**	**1.00**	**246.6**	**100%**	**1.00**	**147.6**	–

"#Samples" represents the number of images used for pre-selection. Note that all approaches use the same 50 images for reverse engineering.

ate, so it achieves the highest efficiency among current techniques. However, our approach is still 18%, 7.3%, and 12.5% faster than K-Arm on Rounds 1–3. The results demonstrate that our static weight analysis precisely exposes the target/victim labels, which significantly reduces the detection time.

Detection Results on ImageNet. Table 3 shows the results of detecting Hidden Trigger Attack [23] and polygon patch on ImageNet. NC, TABOR, and DLTND could not finish these detection tasks due to the high computation complexity for label-specific attacks and 1000 labels. For both attacks, we achieve 100% detection accuracy while maintaining the highest efficiency. For Hidden Trigger Attack, K-Arm selects the wrong target labels of 2 poisoned models, and thus fails for detection. ABS mistakes 2 poisoned models as benign due to the wrong selection of compromised neurons. For polygon patch attacks, our approach is 7 times faster than ABS. Besides, our pre-selection needs no input images. K-Arm fails to identify the real target labels with the same clean samples used by ABS during pre-screening, thus could not detect trojaned models correctly sometimes. It needs 20 times the amount of clean samples to achieve a relatively stable detection accuracy. On the whole, the effectiveness of static weight analysis benefits our approach with high accuracy and efficiency.

Visualization of Recovered Local Patch Triggers. Figure 5 presents the original patch triggers used for poisoning and the reversed triggers with our approach. For polygon patch on ImageNet, the trigger locates in a fixed position (bottom right corner), and the reversed triggers for most images mainly concentrate in the same area. As for Hidden Trigger Attack [23] and patch triggers on TrojAI, the original triggers are pasted at random locations. In this scenario, our reversed triggers may appear at any part of the image and have roughly consistent shape and color with the original triggers. In general, the reversed triggers of our approach are visually similar to the original ones.

4.3 Detection Performance on Global Transformation Attacks

Detection Effectiveness and Efficiency. Table 4 shows the detection performance of our approach on global transformation triggers, including Instagram filters and WaNet [21]. We only compare with ABS because other techniques are

Table 4. Global transformation triggers detection results.

Method	TrojAI R2 Filter			TrojAI R3 Filter			CIFAR-10 Filter			CIFAR-10 WaNet		
	Acc	AUC	Time	Acc	AUC	Time	Acc	AUC	Time	Acc	AUC	Time
ABS	67%	0.66	1411.8	64%	0.66	1566.7	75%	0.70	1490.3	85%	0.85	213.1
Ours	**80%**	**0.82**	**766.7**	**81%**	**0.87**	**462.9**	**95%**	**0.92**	**581.3**	**95%**	**0.95**	**136.2**

Fig. 5. Visualization of the reversed triggers.

not applicable for handling global transformation triggers. For Instagram filters, results show that the detection accuracy of our approach outperforms ABS by 13%, 17%, and 20% on Rounds 2–3 and CIFAR-10 respectively. We discover that ABS well identifies trojaned models, but suffers from a high false positive rate. This may be because ABS mistakenly selects the neurons that dominate output results as compromised neurons in clean models. As for WaNet, our approach reaches a detection accuracy of 95%. ABS fails to detect 3 trojaned models, while our approach misses only one trojaned model due to the wrong selection of target label. Besides, the elapsed time of our approach is 1.8, 3.4 times faster than ABS on TrojAI Rounds 2–3, and 2.6, 1.6 times faster on CIFAR-10 Filter and CIFAR-10 WaNet. Results show that our approach has the capability to deal with global transformation triggers.

Visualization of Recovered Global Transformation Triggers. Figure 5 presents the original global transformation triggers and our reversed triggers. For Instagram filter triggers, our reversed triggers are visually consistent with the original ones. WaNet aims to design an imperceptible trigger to escape detection, so the poisoned images are extremely similar to the clean images. Our reversed triggers for trojaned models look similar to the clean images as well while achieving a 100% ASR. In contrast, for benign models, more modification of clean images cannot incur such misclassification. It means that our approach provides an effective defense against the WaNet attack. On the whole, our approach can reconstruct global transformation triggers which are similar to the original ones.

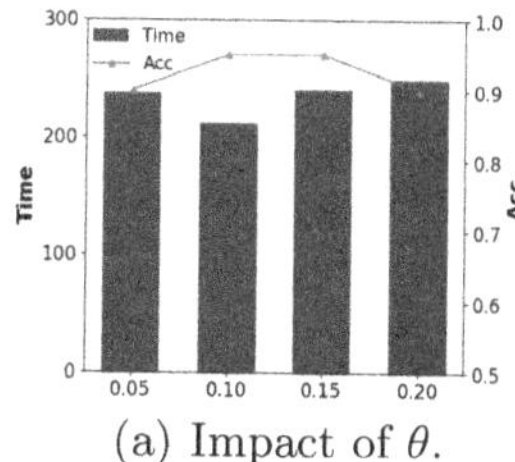

(a) Impact of θ.

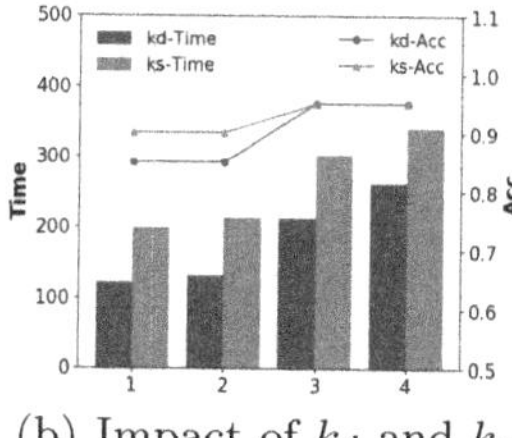

(b) Impact of k_d and k_s.

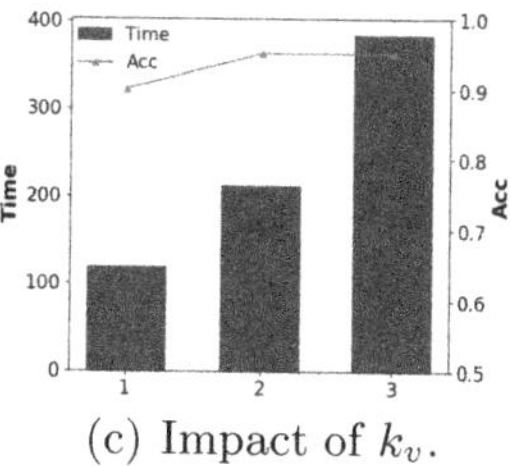

(c) Impact of k_v.

Fig. 6. The impact on detection accuracy and average model inspection time of hyper-parameters θ, k_d, k_s, and k_v.

4.4 Advanced Attack Detection

TrojanNet [28] introduces the attack that implants multiple backdoors into a DNN model. Images are misclassified to different target labels when stamped with different triggers. Existing defenses are all based on the one-target assumption. We experiment to illustrate the possibility of detecting multi-target backdoors. We set the *Divergence* candidate parameter $k_d = 3$. Results show that our approach achieves 100% model-level and 98.1% label-level detection accuracy under the setting of MNIST dataset in Sect. 4.1, indicating the capability of our approach to handling this attack and accurately pinpointing the real targets.

4.5 Hyper-parameter Sensitivity Analysis

We analyze the sensitivity of the following hyper-parameters in this section.

θ is used to distinguish between universal attacks and label-specific attacks. When θ decreases, more models are considered universally trojaned. We measure the detection accuracy and the average model inspection time under different θ on 20 randomly sampled models from TrojAI Round 3. As shown in Fig. 6(a), we achieve a stable accuracy when θ ranges from 0.1 to 0.15. The change of θ has little effect on the average detection time.

k_d and k_s specify the number of target label candidates. And k_v determines the number of suspected victim labels when the model is judged to be label-specifically attacked. Results are measured on the same models as θ. We change k_d and k_s separately while fixing the other one. Figure 6 shows that the detection accuracy will be affected when k_d, k_s, and k_v are small, because our approach may miss the real target or victim labels. As these hyper-parameters increase, the accuracy remains stable, but the average detection time will increase.

The filtering thresholds are used to distinguish adversarial perturbations, natural features, and malicious backdoors. We measure their impact on detection accuracy, False Positive Rate (FPR), and False Negative Rate (FNR) on all models in TrojAI Round 3. Figure 7(a) shows that when the adversarial perturbation threshold is low, it is easy to consider the trojaned models as benign, resulting in high FNR. As the threshold rises, the detection accuracy remains stable in the range of 10% to 15%. Figure 7(b) shows that when the natural

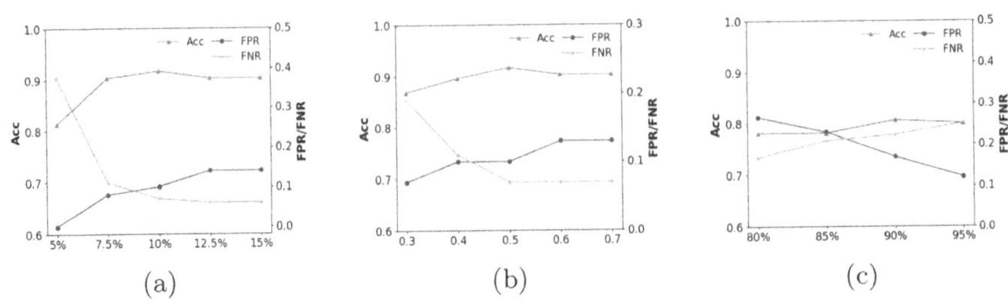

(a) (b) (c)

Fig. 7. The impact on detection accuracy, FPR, and FNR of (a) adversarial perturbation threshold and (b) natural feature filtering threshold for trigger analysis; and (c) attack success rate threshold for global transformation triggers.

Table 5. Experimental results of the adaptive attack.

δ	0	0.01	0.1	1	10	100
Div. Rank	1	6	5	4	6	5
Sum Rank	1	5	4	4	6	6
Clean Acc (%)	85.59	83.57	83.88	83.64	83.56	83.38
ASR (%)	97.51	95.93	95.77	95.73	95.95	95.25

feature filtering threshold increases in the range of 0.3 to 0.5, the FNR will also be reduced and the detection accuracy rises. When it continues to increase from 0.6 to 0.7, the detection accuracy remains stable.

We set different values for the global transformation trigger success rate threshold, and evaluate its impact on all models in TrojAI Round 3. As can be seen from Fig. 7(c), when the success rate threshold rises, the FPR decreases while FNR increases since more models are considered to be clean. On the whole, the accuracy is stable and insensitive to this hyper-parameter.

5 Discussion

In this section, we discuss the possibility of an adaptive attack. The goal is to deliberately evade our static weight analysis by masking the weight anomalies in trojaned DNNs. This is accomplished by introducing weight regularization into the loss in the backdoor training phase. The regularization minimizes the distance between the *Divergence* and *Sum* values of w_t and the average *Divergence* and *Sum* values of the rest weight vectors w as:

$$L_{ada} = L_{troj} + \delta \left\| D(w_t) + S(w_t) - \mathbb{E}(D(w)) - \mathbb{E}(S(w)) \right\|_1 \tag{8}$$

where L_{troj} denotes the cross entropy loss of standard poison training. The regularization strength is controlled by the hyper-parameter δ. For each δ, we train 10 models on CIFAR-10 and report the average results. The clean accuracy and ASR are shown in Table 5. "Div. Rank" and "Sum Rank" represent the

Divergence and *Sum* ranking of w_t across all 10 weight vectors. Results show that the regularization successfully perturbs the weights and suppresses the anomaly existing in w_t. However, the model accuracy on clean data and ASR significantly degrade. Specifically, the accuracy of the model on clean data decreases by 2.02% when $\delta = 0.01$, indicating that the model performs less effectively and might have been trojaned.

6 Related Work

Backdoor Defenses. In addition to the trigger reverse engineering based techniques [9,19,31,32] mentioned above, we further discuss other techniques that defend against backdoor attacks.

Some approaches inspect the poisoned dataset before the DNN training stage. Activation Clustering [4] analyzes the activation values of the training data to determine whether there are maliciously inserted poisonous samples. Spectral Signatures [30] detects the spectrum of feature representations for each input data. These methods require full access to the training set, which is impractical when the training process is outsourced.

SentiNet [5] tries to find triggers by identifying the salient parts of the images. Strip [7] assumes that when the poisoned image is superimposed over a set of random images, the model can still output a confident prediction. These techniques are based on the assumption that the backdoor trigger leads to misclassification for all classes, which may not hold when encountering label-specific attacks. Besides, we focus on the scenario where the real trigger will not be present.

Several advanced defenses detect backdoors by training on a large number of clean and trojaned models. ULP [14] trains a classifier on different output logits for clean and trojaned models when receiving universal litmus patterns. MNTD [34] trains a meta-classifier to predict whether a model is trojaned. Huang et al. [11] characterize the one-pixel signature representation to detect trojaned CNN models. These training-based defenses require high computational costs. Moreover, their generalizability across datasets is questionable.

7 Conclusion

We make a key observation that the weights connected to the backdoor target labels tend to have abnormal distributions and larger magnitudes. Based on this observation, we propose an efficient and scalable DNN backdoor detection framework guided by static weight analysis. The static weight analysis captures abnormal weights to expose potential target/victim pairs, making our approach accurate and efficient. Moreover, the anomaly is prevalent in models trojaned by different attacks, thus our approach is capable of detecting both local patch attacks and global transformation attacks. Finally, we analyze the attributes of recovered triggers and activated neuron distributions of models to suppress false positives. Evaluation results show that the effectiveness and efficiency of our approach outperform state-of-the-art techniques on various widely-used datasets.

Acknowledgement. This work was supported in part by National Natural Science Foundation of China under Grant 62172305 and Key R&D in Hubei Province.

References

1. acoomans (2013). https://github.com/acoomans/instagram-filters
2. Bau, D., Zhu, J.Y., Strobelt, H., Lapedriza, A., Zhou, B., Torralba, A.: Understanding the role of individual units in a deep neural network. Proc. Natl. Acad. Sci. **117**(48), 30071–30078 (2020)
3. Bojarski, M., et al.: End to end learning for self-driving cars. CoRR abs/1604.07316 (2016)
4. Chen, B., et al.: Detecting backdoor attacks on deep neural networks by activation clustering. CoRR abs/1811.03728 (2018)
5. Chou, E., Tramèr, F., Pellegrino, G.: Sentinet: detecting localized universal attacks against deep learning systems. In: 2020 IEEE Security and Privacy Workshops, SP Workshops, San Francisco, 21 May 2020, pp. 48–54. IEEE (2020)
6. Deng, J., Dong, W., Socher, R., Li, L.J., Li, K., Fei-Fei, L.: Imagenet: a large-scale hierarchical image database. In: 2009 IEEE Conference on Computer Vision and Pattern Recognition, pp. 248–255. IEEE (2009)
7. Gao, Y., Xu, C., Wang, D., Chen, S., Ranasinghe, D.C., Nepal, S.: Strip: a defence against trojan attacks on deep neural networks. In: Proceedings of the 35th Annual Computer Security Applications Conference, pp. 113–125 (2019)
8. Gu, T., Dolan-Gavitt, B., Garg, S.: Badnets: Identifying vulnerabilities in the machine learning model supply chain. CoRR abs/1708.06733 (2017)
9. Guo, W., Wang, L., Xing, X., Du, M., Song, D.: Tabor: a highly accurate approach to inspecting and restoring trojan backdoors in AI systems. arXiv preprint arXiv:1908.01763 (2019)
10. He, K., Zhang, X., Ren, S., Sun, J.: Deep residual learning for image recognition. In: Proceedings of the IEEE Conference on Computer Vision and Pattern Recognition, pp. 770–778 (2016)
11. Huang, S., Peng, W., Jia, Z., Tu, Z.: One-pixel signature: characterizing CNN models for backdoor detection. In: Vedaldi, A., Bischof, H., Brox, T., Frahm, J.-M. (eds.) ECCV 2020. LNCS, vol. 12372, pp. 326–341. Springer, Cham (2020). https://doi.org/10.1007/978-3-030-58583-9_20
12. IARPA: Trojai competition (2020). https://pages.nist.gov/trojai/
13. Karra, K., Ashcraft, C., Fendley, N.: The trojai software framework: An open-source tool for embedding trojans into deep learning models. arXiv preprint arXiv:2003.07233 (2020)
14. Kolouri, S., Saha, A., Pirsiavash, H., Hoffmann, H.: Universal litmus patterns: revealing backdoor attacks in CNNs. In: Proceedings of the IEEE/CVF Conference on Computer Vision and Pattern Recognition, pp. 301–310 (2020)
15. Krizhevsky, A., Hinton, G., et al.: Learning multiple layers of features from tiny images. Technical report (2009)
16. Krizhevsky, A., Sutskever, I., Hinton, G.E.: Imagenet classification with deep convolutional neural networks. Adv. Neural. Inf. Process. Syst. **25**, 1097–1105 (2012)
17. LeCun, Y., Bottou, L., Bengio, Y., Haffner, P.: Gradient-based learning applied to document recognition. Proc. IEEE **86**(11), 2278–2324 (1998)
18. Lin, J., Xu, L., Liu, Y., Zhang, X.: Composite backdoor attack for deep neural network by mixing existing benign features. In: Proceedings of the 2020 ACM SIGSAC Conference on Computer and Communications Security, pp. 113–131 (2020)

19. Liu, Y., Lee, W.C., Tao, G., Ma, S., Aafer, Y., Zhang, X.: Abs: scanning neural networks for back-doors by artificial brain stimulation. In: Proceedings of the 2019 ACM SIGSAC Conference on Computer and Communications Security, pp. 1265–1282 (2019)
20. Liu, Y., et al.: Trojaning attack on neural networks. In: 25th Annual Network and Distributed System Security Symposium, NDSS 2018, San Diego, 18–21 February 2018 (2018)
21. Nguyen, A., Tran, A.: Wanet-imperceptible warping-based backdoor attack. arXiv preprint arXiv:2102.10369 (2021)
22. Nguyen, A., Yosinski, J., Clune, J.: Deep neural networks are easily fooled: high confidence predictions for unrecognizable images. In: Proceedings of the IEEE Conference on Computer Vision and Pattern Recognition, pp. 427–436 (2015)
23. Saha, A., Subramanya, A., Pirsiavash, H.: Hidden trigger backdoor attacks. In: The Thirty-Fourth AAAI Conference on Artificial Intelligence, AAAI 2020, pp. 11957–11965. AAAI Press (2020)
24. Sandler, M., Howard, A., Zhu, M., Zhmoginov, A., Chen, L.C.: Mobilenetv 2: inverted residuals and linear bottlenecks. In: Proceedings of the IEEE Conference on Computer Vision and Pattern Recognition, pp. 4510–4520 (2018)
25. Saxe, J., Berlin, K.: Deep neural network based malware detection using two dimensional binary program features. In: 2015 10th International Conference on Malicious and Unwanted Software (MALWARE), pp. 11–20. IEEE (2015)
26. Shen, G., et al.: Backdoor scanning for deep neural networks through k-arm optimization. In: Proceedings of the 38th International Conference on Machine Learning, ICML 2021, Virtual Event, 18–24 July 2021, pp. 9525–9536 (2021)
27. Simonyan, K., Zisserman, A.: Very deep convolutional networks for large-scale image recognition. arXiv preprint arXiv:1409.1556 (2014)
28. Tang, R., Du, M., Liu, N., Yang, F., Hu, X.: An embarrassingly simple approach for trojan attack in deep neural networks. In: KDD 2020: The 26th ACM SIGKDD Conference on Knowledge Discovery and Data Mining, Virtual Event, CA, 23–27 August 2020, pp. 218–228. ACM (2020)
29. Torchvision (2020). https://github.com/pytorch/vision/tree/main/torchvision
30. Tran, B., Li, J., Madry, A.: Spectral signatures in backdoor attacks. In: Advances in Neural Information Processing Systems 31: Annual Conference on Neural Information Processing Systems 2018, NeurIPS 2018, Montréal, 3–8 December 2018, pp. 8011–8021 (2018)
31. Wang, B., et al.: Neural cleanse: identifying and mitigating backdoor attacks in neural networks. In: 2019 IEEE Symposium on Security and Privacy (SP), pp. 707–723. IEEE (2019)
32. Wang, R., Zhang, G., Liu, S., Chen, P., Xiong, J., Wang, M.: Practical detection of trojan neural networks: data-limited and data-free cases. In: Computer Vision - ECCV 2020–16th European Conference, Glasgow, UK, 23–28 August 2020, Proceedings, Part XXIII, pp. 222–238 (2020)
33. Wang, Z., Bovik, A.C., Sheikh, H.R., Simoncelli, E.P.: Image quality assessment: from error visibility to structural similarity. IEEE Trans. Image Process. **13**(4), 600–612 (2004)
34. Xu, X., Wang, Q., Li, H., Borisov, N., Gunter, C.A., Li, B.: Detecting AI trojans using meta neural analysis. In: 2021 IEEE Symposium on Security and Privacy (SP), pp. 103–120. IEEE (2021)

35. Yu, H., et al.: Tensorflow model garden (2020). https://github.com/tensorflow/models
36. Zhang, Y., Liang, P., Wainwright, M.J.: Convexified convolutional neural networks. In: Precup, D., Teh, Y.W. (eds.) Proceedings of the 34th International Conference on Machine Learning, ICML 2017, Sydney, NSW, Australia, 6–11 August 2017. Proceedings of Machine Learning Research, vol. 70, pp. 4044–4053. PMLR (2017)

Mimic Octopus Attack: Dynamic Camouflage Adversarial Examples Using Mimetic Feature for 3D Humans

Jing Li[1,2], Sisi Zhang[1], Xingbin Wang[1], and Rui Hou[1,2](✉)

[1] State Key Laboratory of Information Security, Institute of Information Engineering, CAS, Beijing, China
{lijing6717,zhangsisi,wangxingbin,hourui}@iie.ac.cn

[2] School of Cyber Security, University of Chinese Academy of Sciences, Beijing 100049, China

Abstract. Physical adversarial attacks in object detection have become an attractive topic. Many works have proposed adversarial patches or camouflage to perform successful attacks in the real world, but all of these methods have drawbacks, especially for 3D humans. One is that the camouflage-based method is not dynamic or mimetic enough. That is, the adversarial texture is not rendered in conjunction with the background features of the target, which somehow violates the definition of adversarial examples; the other is that there is no detailing of non-rigid physical surfaces, such that the rendered textures are not robust and very rough in 3D scenarios. In this paper, we propose the Mimic Octopus Attack (MOA) to overcome the above gap, a novel method for generating a mimetic and robust physical adversarial texture to target objects to camouflage them against detectors with Multi-View and Multi-Scene. To achieve joint optimization, it utilizes the combined iterative training of mimetic style loss, adversarial loss, and human eye intuition. Experiments in specific scenarios of CARLA, which is generally recognized as an alternative to physical domains, demonstrate its advanced performance, resulting in a 67.62% decrease in mAP@0.5 for the YOLO-V5 detector compared to normal, an average increase of **4.14%** compared to the state-of-the-art attacks and an average ASR of up to 85.28%. Besides, the robustness in attacking diverse populations and detectors of MOA proves its outstanding transferability.

Keywords: Adversarial attack · Mimetic camouflage · 3D humans

1 Introduction

Deep Neural Networks (DNN) have brought significant advanced changes to human society, especially for computer vision tasks [19,30]. However, Szegedy et al. [36] proposed Adversarial Examples (AE) in 2014 that a tiny and imperceptible adversarial perturbation or noise of the input can make the output of

Y. Deng and M. Yung (Eds.): Inscrypt 2022, LNCS 13837, pp. 429–444, 2023.
https://doi.org/10.1007/978-3-031-26553-2_23

DNN seriously wrong. This leads to untrustworthy DNN and even threaten people's life and property safety. After many fruitful attacks [4,11,26] in the digital domain, attacks in the physical domain also started to rise with the successful experimentation of naïve direct migration attacks by Kurakin et al. [20] in 2016 and the successful patch-like attack on commercial face recognition systems by printing AE onto glasses by Sharif et al. [33]. In this paper, we focus more on the latter as it is a more direct and significant threat to machine learning systems in the real world.

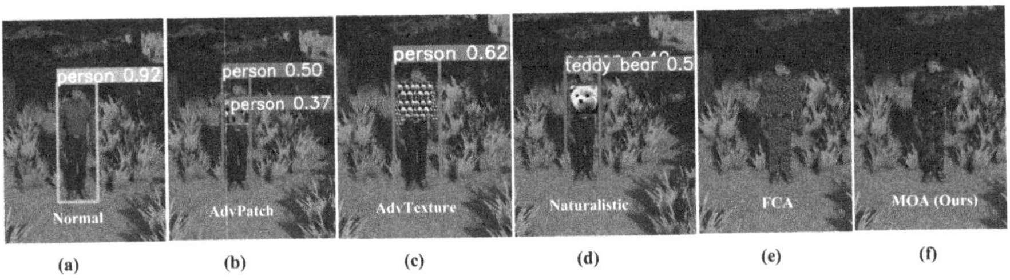

Fig. 1. Attack for 3D humans effect concept demo comparison. (a) Normal without adversarial texture method. (b) Use classic AdvPatch [3] method. (c) Use robust AdvTexture [14] method. (d) Use Naturalistic [13] method. (e) Use FCA [39] method. (f) Use our Mimic Octopus Attack (MOA) method.

The impact of lighting, view, scene, occlusion, and other factors complicates the physical domain attack. To generate AE that is more effective in the real world, recent works [15,35,39–41,43,44,47] based on the 3D attack method EOT [1] and AdvPatch [37], have been done with the help of neural renderer [18] and 3D modeling software (e.g., Unreal Engine, CARLA [6], Blender). Although the existing state-of-the-art methods consider the robustness of the attack in 3D multiple views (Multi-View) or multiple scenes (Multi-Scene), it still has two issues, especially in the subfield of human detection.

The random AdvPatch [37] or robust AdvTexture [14] overly pursues the success rate and almost always generates a conspicuous and fancy adversarial patch, as shown in Fig 1(b)(c), which somehow reduces the tiny and undetectable characteristics of AE. Despite the recent emergence of works on camouflage-based methods [35,39], including the classic patch attack and patch-like attack based on a full-coverage painted called poster attack.

Unfortunately, firstly, they almost all take rigid objects such as vehicles as the primary attack target, which is challenging to apply to 3D humans. Stiff patches do not fit 3D targets well due to folds, posture, and other 3D spatial factors, resulting in significantly lower attack success rates. Secondly, even worse, as shown in Fig 1(d)(e), these camouflage-based AE are still recognizable to the human eye and are not particularly robust. This greatly impairs concealment.

Motivated by the challenge faced in prior works and inspired by the camouflage behavior of animals in nature [29] and Fan et al. [8] camouflaged object detection, we propose a novel poster attack method called Mimic Octopus Attack (MOA), which generates textures similar to the environmental background, making the AE insignificant and thus achieving dynamic mimetic camouflage. Our extensive experiments show that in a given scene, it is difficult to be recognized by humans even if they are concentrating due to visual illusion, and demonstrate its advanced performance on Multi-View, Multi-Scene, diverse populations, and different object detectors. An average increase of 4.14% compared to the state-of-the-art attack. The demo and code of MOA will be availabe at: https://adv-moa.github.io/. In summary, our main contributions can be summarized as follows.

- We present Mimic Octopus Attack (MOA), a method for generating mimetic and robust physical adversarial camouflage for 3D Humans. It combines the advantages of our novel flexible and dynamic textures that mimic the background of the attack target with a realistic 3D rendering engine.
- To the best of our knowledge, a first end-to-end physical adversarial mimetic attack was proposed to generate a robust camouflage to confuse both DNN and humans.
- Extensive experiments show that MOA outperforms existing methods and is robustly applicable to Multi-View, Multi-Scene, diverse populations, and object detectors. Moreover, our camouflage is optimized for non-rigid factors (e.g., folds) and can be more effective in the real world, rendering it unrecognizable to humans.

2 Related Work

2.1 DNN for Human Detection

The DNN-based generic object detectors can be divided into two main types depending on learning high-level features from the data (such as images or 3D object parameters of humans). One class is represented by R-CNN [10] and its variants [12,32]. It is a two-stage process that follows the traditional object detection pipeline, giving a coarse scan of the whole scenario and generating regional proposals first, then classifying each proposal into different object categories. The other class is represented by YOLO [30], its variants [2,17,31,38], and SSD [22]. It is a one-stage process that regards object detection as a regression or classification problem, mapping straightly from image pixels to bounding box coordinates and class probabilities.

2.2 Physical Adversarial Attack

Kurakin et al. [20] first experimentally demonstrated in 2016 that an attack method that directly migrates the digital domain on the classifier to the physical domain can still attack successfully. Lu et al. [24] followed this approach to attack in 2017. The main processes are to print the whole AE and post it onto the stop sign, which is an early patch attack. However, most real-world situations require attacks against detectors mentioned above in Sect. 2.1 and 3D scenes. Moreover, this is also expected to overcome the problem of complex issues (e.g., illumination change, occlusion, distance perspective, different heights, human posture, real-time computation). Athalye et al. proposed EOT [1] and generated Multi-View robust AE by 3D printing. Eykholt et al. [34] performed the first physical adversarial attack on the detector in 2018.

Based on the above work, Thys et al. [37] present a patch attack method in 2019 that successfully hides a person from YOLO-V2 [31]. However, there are two problems with this method. First, the method of using a 2D attack and then printing does not work well in 3D environments with Multi-View and Multi-Scene, as confirmed by an analysis by Lu et al. [25] and another experiment on YouTube [5]. Second, AE is visually very splendid and deviates from the original definition of AE as tiny and imperceptible, whether for local or global perturbations. The above two points have developed methods of attack using 3D rendering (Sect. 2.3) and camouflage-based attack (Sect. 2.4).

2.3 3D Rendering for AE

Xiao et al. [43] first used the neural renderer [18] to generate AE for 3D objects. The neural renderer is a differentiable renderer for 2D images to 3D mesh. By initializing and iteratively training with different Multi-View parameters (i.e., distance, angles, heights), the render could generate the 3D texture mesh to attack. The subsequent works [27,40,44] utilize this method to render adversarial camouflage, especially onto the vehicle surface. Further, Zhang et al. [47], Wu et al. [41], and Wang et al. [39] utilized the CARLA [6] simulator to render an adversarial patch for 3D objects, which is non-differentiable.

2.4 Camouflage-Based AE

Inspired by camouflage clothes, Zhang et al. [47] proposed a camouflage attack to generate AE for vehicles by training a generative adversarial network. Following that, many works [35,39–41,48] presented a more robust attack adversarial camouflage method. However, this camouflage is more of a camouflage clothing effect, which is very weird and still perceptible to the human eye. Hu et al. [13] and Hu et al. [14] proposed an attack method that uses common objects for naturalized camouflage. Yin et al. [45] propose a natural camouflage attack for face recognition with makeup effects. Unfortunately, their camouflage effect does not consider the background of the target; thus, we achieve mimetic camouflage.

3 Method

In this section, we first introduce the threat model and formally defines the problem. Then we describe the proposed end-to-end physical camouflage adversarial attack in detail, including method architecture and the critical loss functions for rendering mimetic textures to tackle the abovementioned issues.

3.1 Threat Model

The attack described in this paper is based on the adversary's inability to control or influence the data processing process in a machine learning system or cyber-physical system (CPS), which differs from the threat model of classical digital domain attacks. It also cannot control or influence the data input side of sensors(e.g., camera, radar) and can only change the target object itself (e.g., human body, face, vehicle) to attack. Thus, methods such as AdvLB [7] that use lasers to perform external attacks at the input are out of the scope of this paper.

3.2 Problem Definition

The ultimate goal of our attack method is to achieve a mimetic attack on generic human detection DNN. It precisely consists of two aspects. One is to make the detector incorrectly or fail to detect the human target, which contains 3D factors such as multi-view, multiple scenes, human pose, and clothing folds. The second is also subjectively imperceptible to the human eye.

We statute the problem as a joint optimization problem and define it formally as follows. Let $\boldsymbol{x}$ as the input (e.g., Multi-View human image) of DNN, $\mathcal{F}$ as the detector function, $\mathcal{R}$ as the 3D render, and $\mathcal{G}$ as the fold generation network. When a perturbation δ is added to $\boldsymbol{x}$ and generates $\boldsymbol{x_{adv}}$, that satisfies $\mathcal{F}(x) \neq y$. The notion $\boldsymbol{y}$ here actually only represents the human label and $T \in \mathbb{R}^{n \times 3}$ as the original 3D object. To generate the mimetic patches, the features are first extracted from the background map of $\boldsymbol{x}$ as the initial value of δ and generate the naïve $\boldsymbol{x_{adv}}$ as $\boldsymbol{x_{init}}$. Suppose $\mathcal{L}(\mathcal{F}(x_{init}), y)$ is a loss function applied to $\mathcal{F}$ that can satisfy the above inequality. Then we can generate the final adversarial mimetic texture $\boldsymbol{x_{adv}^{(n)}}$ by solving Eq. 1.

$$\boldsymbol{x_{adv}^{(n)}} = \arg\max_{\mathbf{x}_{adv}}(\mathcal{F}(\mathcal{R}(\mathcal{G}(\mathbf{T}, HEI(\mathbf{x}_{init}), \theta_{cam}); \theta_{adv}); \theta_f), \mathbf{y}) \tag{1}$$

3.3 MOA Architecture

The overall architecture of MOA is illustrated in Fig. 2. Our goal is to generate a robust and mimetic camouflage texture through the backpropagation of loss and Human Eye Intuition (HEI) (Sect. 4.1). The process of generating AE is divided into three phases: extract Multi-View mimetic features, mesh fold 3D face, and render the final adversarial texture. We first use a generic segmentation network to mask the background of targets, then extract features comprehensively (with the Multi-View (Fig. 3) and Multi-Scene (Fig. 5) overlay). Especially to balance performance by using cross-overlay between images before extracting features on the rendered images as the initialized base texture. Then we optimize the mimetic camouflage by the loss function. Second, we masked the position of AE in the 3D object and folded it through the shape-context matching network. Finally, we render the texture onto the 3D object, then perform the adversarial attack. We control the loss function threshold and the concealment of human eye intuitive

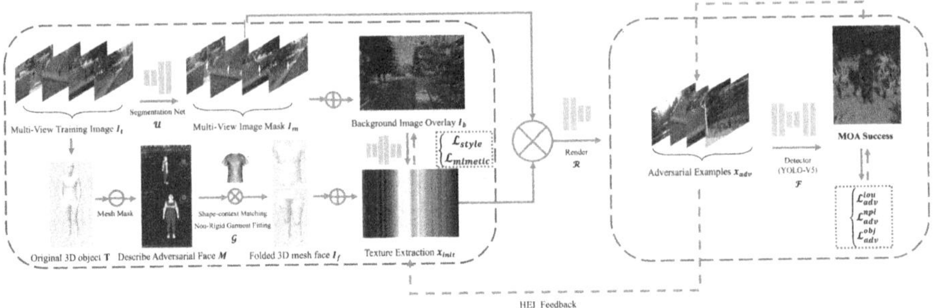

Fig. 2. MOA architecture for generating robust and mimetic adversarial camouflage texture. The area surrounded by the blue and red dashed lines indicate mimetic feature extraction and adversarial texture generation, respectively. The gray dotted line represents the return direction of the gradient descent. (Color figure online)

judgment to update the final AE iteratively. Algorithm 1 also summarizes the overall extract mimetic feature and training scheme.

The loss function here secures the entire attack architecture smoothly. We focus on describing two primary loss functions, the Mimetic Camouflage Loss that makes the AE texture possess the features of the target Multi-View background, and the Adversarial Loss that makes the AE evade the detector.

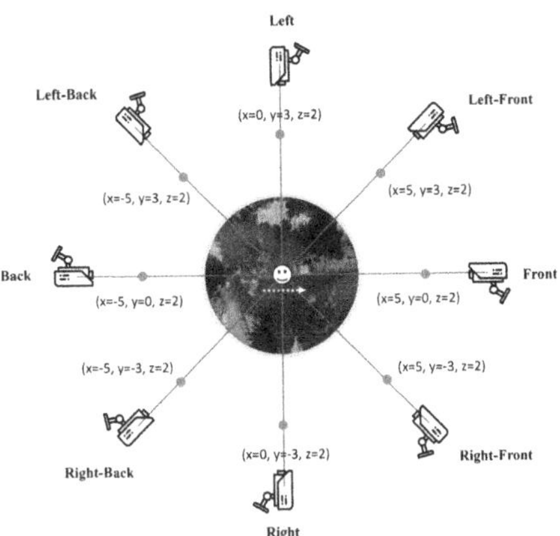

Fig. 3. This top view schematic depicts the camera setup in Multi-View. The ☺ represents a person, the blue dots refer to the camera locations and the yellow dashed line describes the direction of the person's forward movement. The triad $(\mathcal{X}, \mathcal{Y}, \mathcal{Z})$ denotes the horizontal distance, offset, and vertical height respectively.

3.4 Loss Function

As depicted in Fig. 2, we mainly generate mimetic AE by two essential loss functions: Mimetic Camouflage Loss and Adversarial Loss. We split the mimetic camouflage loss into two pieces (Style loss, Mimetic loss). To transfer the style of a reference image onto input to produce the target, we use $\mathcal{L}_{style}$ to coarse-grained reduce the similarity first. Then our intention behind $\mathcal{L}_{mimetic}$ is that fine-grained detail adjustment. Specifically, it includes filling the foreground object regions with the content of the background image to remove features that allow fast perception from feature search. We perform white-box attacks on YOLO-V5 [17], mainly YOLO-V5s. It uses CSPDarknet to optimize the speed of completing classification and regression in a single stage. Therefore, it is necessary to concurrently attack both regression and classification. We split the adversarial loss into three pieces (IoU loss, No-Person loss, and Objectness loss). To make the detector does not detect the person correctly, we first use $\mathcal{L}_{adv}^{iou}$ to minimize the Intersection over Union (IoU) between the prediction and truth *bbox*. Second, we use $\mathcal{L}_{adv}^{npl}$ to reduce the select probability of the target. Then due to reducing the objections (especially for person) score indicates whether the prediction *bbox* contains a person by minimizing its confidence, this loss denotes as $\mathcal{L}_{adv}^{obj}$. To sum up, our final loss is constructed as

$$\mathcal{L}_{total} = \theta_{cam}\mathcal{L}_{cam} + \theta_{iou}\mathcal{L}_{adv}^{iou} + \theta_{npl}\mathcal{L}_{adv}^{npl} + \theta_{obj}\mathcal{L}_{adv}^{obj} \tag{2}$$

where $\theta_{cam}, \theta_{iou}, \theta_{obj}, \theta_{npl}$ are weights for the corresponding losses. Below we describe each loss term in detail.

Mimetic Camouflage Loss. Inspired by the neural style transfer method [9,21,46], we formulate the loss function to generate the desired camouflage texture $\mathbf{x}_{init}$, which rendered from extracts background image overlay $\boldsymbol{I}_b$ features and folded 3D mesh face $\boldsymbol{I}_f$. Formally, the loss function is defined as

$$\mathcal{L}_{cam} = \mathcal{L}_{style} + \mu\mathcal{L}_{mimetic} \tag{3}$$

where $\mathcal{L}_{style}$ and $\mathcal{L}_{mimetic}$ are the style loss and mimetic loss, μ is a weight that balances them, these losses are separately defined as

$$\mathcal{L}_{style} = \sum_{\ell=1}^{L} \frac{\alpha_\ell}{2N_\ell^2} \sum_{i=1}^{N_\ell}\sum_{j=1}^{N_\ell} \left(F_{ij}^{\ell}\left(I_f\right) - F_{ij}^{\ell}\left(I_b\right)\right)^2 \tag{4}$$

$$\mathcal{L}_{\text{mimetic}}^{\ell} = \frac{\beta_\ell}{2N_\ell D_\ell} \sum_{i=1}^{N_\ell}\sum_{j=1}^{D_\ell} \left((1-\mathcal{A}) \odot \left(G_{ij}^{\ell}\left(x_{init}\right) - G_{ij}^{\ell}\left(I_b\right)\right)\right)^2 \tag{5}$$

where L as the total number of convolutional layers in the network and ℓ represents the ℓ-*th* layer. N_ℓ refers to the number of filters, and D_ℓ is the size of vectorized feature map produced by each filter. $F^\ell \in \mathbb{R}^{N_\ell \times N_\ell}$ is a Gram Matrix that describes the feature correlations, where $F_{ij}^{\ell} = \sum_k G_{ik}^{\ell} G_{jk}^{\ell}$ is the inner product between feature maps. $G^\ell \in \mathbb{R}^{N_\ell \times D_\ell}$ is a feature matrix that stores the filter responses, and G^ℓ_{ij} is the activation of the *i-th* filter at position *j*. α_ℓ and β_ℓ are weights controlling the influence of each layer. The $\odot$ denotes the pixel-wise vector and matrix multiplication. $\mathcal{A}$ is a normalized attention map of the target object in $\boldsymbol{I}_t$, which indicates the significance of different regions in identifying the object.

Adversarial Loss

- **IoU loss.** Inspired by FCA [39], we use IoU loss to minimize the area of overlap between each truth *bbox* of Multi-View and the predicted result of the rendered adversarial images to the mean value. In this way, the target object will be missed by the detector because the IoU is below the threshold. The loss is formulated as

$$\mathcal{L}^{iou}_{adv} = \sum_{i=1}^{N}\sum_{j=1}^{M} IoU(y^j_{adv}, y^j_t) \tag{6}$$

  where N denotes the number of perspectives for Multi-View, M denotes the multi-scale parameter set when YOLO-V5 prediction, y^j_{adv} and y^j_t is the *j-th* scale prediction result, and the truth *bbox* of the target.
- **No-Person loss.** We follow the work [39] and choose this loss to reduce the classification probability of the target class. Similarly, we have in the N Multi-View case to select the *j-th* scale probability of the target class which is no a person in the detection result. The loss can be expressed as

$$\mathcal{L}^{npl}_{adv} = \sum_{i=1}^{N}\sum_{j=1}^{M} y^j_{class \neq person} \tag{7}$$

- **Objectness loss.** We follow the classic method [37] and also use the confidence score of the target as this loss, which iteratively determines whether the detection box contains the object.

3.5 Special Optimization for Human

Clothes Folds. Previous works [35,39–41,47] paint the adversarial camouflage on rigid objects (e.g., vehicles) through 2D-to-3D render, which makes it difficult to get convergence and smooth details during training AE for 3D humans. In particular, the final generated texture is so stiff that mesh collision bugs will happen if used directly on a 3D human mask. This AE is unusable for 3D printing and attacks physically. To solve this problem, we refer to 3D pose works [16, 23,28] and introduce a simple but efficient approach that uses shape-context matching to optimize the folds of mimetic textures. As shown in Fig. 2, we make the flods by non-rigid aligning 3D garment fitting to the original 3D object. We use the parametric garment model. Given a garment template $T \in \mathbb{R}^{n\times 3}$ and

Algorithm 1 : Generate camouflage using Mimic Octopus Attack (MOA)

Input: Multi-View training image $\boldsymbol{I}_t$, Original 3D object $\mathbf{T}(\vec{\beta}, \vec{\theta})$, neural renderer $\mathcal{R}$, object detector $\mathcal{F}$, segmentation network $\mathcal{U}$, shape-context matching network $\mathcal{G}$, describe adversarial face M
Output: adversarial mimetic texture $\mathbf{x}_{adv}$
Phase 1: Extract Multi-View feature and Mesh fold face

for the category of people number of $\boldsymbol{I}_t$ **do**
  $\boldsymbol{I}'_m \leftarrow \mathcal{U}(\boldsymbol{I}'_t)$
  $\boldsymbol{I}'_b \leftarrow \prod \boldsymbol{I}'_m$
  $T^G \leftarrow \mathcal{G}(I\ T(\vec{\beta}, \vec{\theta}) + \mathbf{M})$
  $\mathbf{x}'_{init} \leftarrow \mathcal{R}((\mathbf{T}^G, \mathbf{I}'_b); \theta_{cam})$
  if $HEI < 0$ **then**
    return
  end if
  calculate $\mathcal{L}_{cam}$ by Eq. 3
end for
$\mathbf{x}_{init} \leftarrow \sum \mathbf{x}'_{init}$

Phase 2: Render final attack texture

Initial noise texture with $\mathbf{x}_{init}$
for number of training iterations **do**
  $\mathbf{x}_{adv} \leftarrow \mathcal{R}((\mathbf{T}^{\mathbf{G}}, \mathbf{x}_{init}); \theta_{adv})$
  $b \leftarrow \mathcal{F}(\mathbf{x}_{init}; \theta_f)$
  calculate $\mathcal{L}_{total}$ by Eq. 2
  update $\mathbf{x}_{adv}$ with gradient backpropagation
end for

shape $\vec{\beta}$ and pose $\vec{\theta}$ of the original 3D object, then we can articulate a folding garment using SMPL [23] as

$$\boldsymbol{T}^G(\vec{\boldsymbol{\beta}}, \vec{\boldsymbol{\theta}}, \boldsymbol{M}) = \boldsymbol{I}\ \boldsymbol{T}(\vec{\boldsymbol{\beta}}, \vec{\boldsymbol{\theta}}) + \boldsymbol{M} \tag{8}$$

where donates I as a fold deformation mapping matrix described in [16], and $M \in \mathbb{R}^{m \times 3}$ as the mask of original 3D object which we manually set up through modelling software such as 3ds MAX.

Diversity. We also consider the diversity to make the final AE valid in most situations. We intentionally uniformly distributed the datasets when constructing the Multi-View images of the five categories of people, as shown in Fig. 4. This approach makes our AE more robust for different people, and the relevant evaluation results can be obtained in Table 4. Although it is somewhat naïve, it is effective.

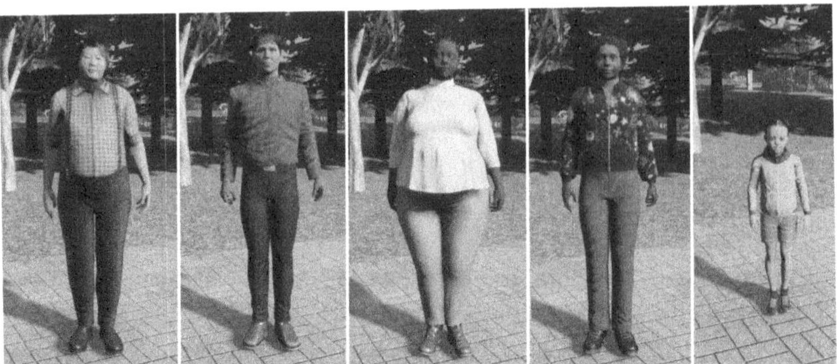

Fig. 4. Multi-View images of five categories of people are uniformly distributed in the training datasets. From left to right are Man (Fat), Man (Thin), Woman (Fat), Woman (Thin), and Kid.

4 Evaluation

4.1 Experimental Setup

Hardware and Datasets. The AE is generated on the server, equipped with two Intel Xeon E5-2678 v3 CPU, NVIDIA A100 PCI-E 40 GB, and 96 GB DDR4 ECC memory, and we utilize PyTorch for implementing MOA. CARLA [6] simulator based on Unreal Engine 4 and relatively mature; previous works mentioned in Sect. 2.3 are based on it for physical emulator experiments. CARLA also supports custom 3D models and textures. We utilize its scenario, pedestrian, and 3D rendering configurations provided in version 0.9.13 to construct the datasets and evaluate the MOA performance in CARLA.

Evaluation Metrics. We want to generate AE that is effective in attacking machine learning systems and human eye intuition. Thus, the evaluation metrics involve false recognition against detectors and imperceptibility evaluation against intuition. The following lists the metrics.

- **Mean Average Precision (mAP).** We use the mAP@0.5, which means when $IOU_{threshold} = 0.5$. It is a commonly used metric for evaluating object detection models.
- **Confidence score (Conf).** Our MOA method can lower the confidence score of the target by mimetic features, so we also introduce the Conf.
- **Attack Success Rate (ASR).** We follow Wu et al. [42] summarize evaluation metric, which is defined as the percentage of the target detected before perturbation and not detected or falsely detected after perturbation.
- **Human Eye Intuition (HEI).** It is important to note that human evaluation is subjective and influenced by psychology, visual illusion, etc. We have performed general, widespread measurements as much as possible. The results in this section are from data from 30 subjects. Furthermore, this evaluation metric is original to this paper.

4.2 Experiments

Comparison of Attacks in Digital Domain. We compare the proposed attacks with several classic and recent advanced adversarial camouflage attacks, including AdvPatch [3], AdvTexture [14], Naturalistic [13], and FCA [39]. The comparison results are listed in Table 1. Note that the target model is all YOLO-V5 [17], and the experiments are conducted in the CARLA simulator. It can be concluded that our MOA significantly outperforms other methods, both in terms of mAP or Conf metrics. In addition, the subjective HEI metric also shows that MOA is more imperceptible than other methods. We got an average increase of **4.14%** compared to the state-of-the-art attacks FCA and compared to earlier methods, an average of 30.38% increased the attack strength. Besides, our approach is imperceptible for the first time in our HEI metric.

Table 1. The comparison result of adversarial attacks in the digital space. The evaluation of HEI can be referred to Fig. 1.

Method	Attack type	mAP@0.5	Conf	HEI
Normal	N/A	95.55	93.04	N/A
AdvPatch [37]	2D patch	74.45	73.84	Conspicuous
AdvTexture [14]	2D patch	51.01	50.69	Conspicuous
Naturalistic [13]	2D poster	49.47	48.94	Recognizable
FCA [39]	3D poster	32.07	30.85	Observable
MOA (Ours)	**3D poster**	**27.93**	**26.10**	**Imperceptible**

Fig. 5. We classify scenes and the weather in constructing of the datasets. Scenes include street, forest park, and near room. Weather includes clean noon and rain sunset. The evaluation of this part is also shown in Table 2.

Multi-scene and Multi-view Adversarial Attack. We perform a comparative experiment on Multi-Scene and Multi-View (8 directions) to evaluate our performance on CARLA simulator instead of in the real world. And every item in Table 2 is conducted on different people mentioned in Sect. 3.5 total of 3600 test images. We obtained an average of 85.28% ASR for the highest mimetic texture in the forest park scene (Fig. 6).

Table 2. The ASR(%) performance of MOA for multi-view of three classic scenes.

Scene	View								
	Front	Right-Front	Right	Right-Back	Back	Left-Back	Left	Left-Front	Average
Street	87.5	85.0	78.2	83.6	87.3	84.8	77.3	82.1	**83.23**
Forest park	90.2	88.9	82.8	89.1	88.6	82.1	79.8	80.7	**85.28**
Near room	83.4	80.1	69.8	82.2	82.9	81.1	70.4	81.7	**78.95**

Fig. 6. Adversarial camouflage of the human Man (Thin) in multi-view (In a forest park at clear noon).

Transferability. To verify the effectiveness of our method on other DNN models, transferable attacks are performed on popular general detectors such as YOLO and its variants, SSD, and R-CNN variants based on the above setup. From the Table 3, we can observe the ability to effectively perform transferability attacks. Moreover, an average of 4%–8% improvement on most detectors compared to FCA. However, we also notice that our MOA is not always better than others. The mAP@0.5 (%) on YOLO-V7, SSD, and Faster R-CNN degrades compared to FCA. We analyzed the score of the normal situation and our mimetic textures themselves. The reason may be attributed to the distinct architectural design of the detectors, some training images are easily identifiable on these models, and they are powerless to improve transferability.

Table 3. The mAP@0.5 (%) comparison of camouflage-based attack strength between detectors in CARLA simulator. The scene and other setup are the same as above.

Detector	Method			
	Normal	Naturalistic [13]	FCA [39]	MOA (ours)
YOLO-V5 [17]	**95.55**	**49.47**	**32.07**	**25.93**
YOLO-V7 [38]	98.31	75.49	54.78	68.04
YOLO-V4 [2]	94.32	22.63	28.91	25.06
SSD [22]	**84.19**	**40.17**	**29.17**	**33.17**
Faster R-CNN [32]	89.42	42.47	24.31	28.02
Mask R-CNN [12]	**92.78**	**43.99**	**35.17**	**31.11**

Table 4. The mAP@0.5 (%) and Conf (%) performance for camouflage objects for different people and weather.

Diversity	Weather	Method	mAP@0.5	Conf
Man (Fat)	Clear noon	Normal	94.41	94.39
		MOA (ours)	**27.32**	**23.98**
	Rain sunset	Normal	92.23	92.18
		MOA (ours)	**22.24**	**18.30**
Man (Thin)	Clear noon	Normal	95.55	93.04
		MOA (ours)	**27.93**	**26.10**
	Rain sunset	Normal	95.04	94.72
		MOA (ours)	**23.22**	**19.87**
Woman (Fat)	Clear noon	Normal	95.02	94.76
		MOA (ours)	**30.12**	**30.10**
	Rain sunset	Normal	93.88	92.99
		MOA (ours)	**28.32**	**27.79**
Woman (Thin)	Clear noon	Normal	94.13	93.81
		MOA (ours)	**25.88**	**24.91**
	Rain sunset	Normal	91.83	91.15
		MOA (ours)	**29.02**	**25.00**
Kid	Clear noon	Normal	95.66	90.32
		MOA (ours)	**29.14**	**27.87**
	Rain sunset	Normal	89.26	83.07
		MOA (ours)	**28.34**	**24.09**
Average	Clear noon	Normal	94.95	93.26
		MOA (ours)	**28.08**	**26.59**
	Rain sunset	Normal	92.45	90.82
		MOA (ours)	**26.23**	**23.01**

Diversity Adversarial Attack. The details of the performance for each diverse situation can be seen in Tab. 4, which implies that our camouflaged textures make the mAP@0.5 score of YOLO-V5 detector much lower, on average by 66.87% and 66.22%, respectively, whether it is clear noon or rain sunset, and in all five types of people. This further highlights the robustness of our method to attack.

5 Conclusion

This paper proposed MOA, an innovative physical adversarial attack method for generating mimetic and robust textures for target objects, especially for 3D humans. In particular, we train AE by jointly optimizing iterations of mimetic loss, adversarial loss, and human eye intuition, further enhancing the dynamic concealment of previous camouflage-based methods. In addition, the gap of attack in human detection is also reduced by non-rigid surface 3D rendering. Extensive experiments included a comparison with previous work in the CARLA simulator, which demonstrated the outstanding performance of MOA in Multi-View and Multi-Scene, and transferability to state-of-the-art detectors. Meanwhile, a better method of using 3D avatar mesh to render virtual humans more closely could further help enhance the quality and realism of the generated textures. This will be explored in future work.

Acknowledgements. We thank the reviewers for their insightful feedback. This work was supported in part by National Natural Science Foundation of China under Grant No. 62272459.

References

1. Athalye, A., Engstrom, L., Ilyas, A., Kwok, K.: Synthesizing robust adversarial examples. In: International Conference on Machine Learning, pp. 284–293. PMLR (2018)
2. Bochkovskiy, A., Wang, C.Y., Liao, H.Y.M.: YOLOv4: optimal speed and accuracy of object detection. arXiv preprint arXiv:2004.10934 (2020)
3. Brown, T.B., Mané, D., Roy, A., Abadi, M., Gilmer, J.: Adversarial patch. arXiv preprint arXiv:1712.09665 (2017)
4. Carlini, N., Wagner, D.: Towards evaluating the robustness of neural networks. In: 2017 IEEE Symposium on Security and Privacy (SP), pp. 39–57. IEEE (2017)
5. CCTVnerd: Can you trick CCTV AI using colorful patterns? (2019). https://youtu.be/fTqhsixhOaM
6. Dosovitskiy, A., Ros, G., Codevilla, F., Lopez, A., Koltun, V.: CARLA: an open urban driving simulator. In: Proceedings of the 1st Annual Conference on Robot Learning, pp. 1–16 (2017)
7. Duan, R., et al.: Adversarial laser beam: Effective physical-world attack to DNNs in a blink. In: Proceedings of the IEEE/CVF Conference on Computer Vision and Pattern Recognition, pp. 16062–16071 (2021)
8. Fan, D.P., Ji, G.P., Cheng, M.M., Shao, L.: Concealed object detection. IEEE Trans. Pattern Anal. Mach. Intell. (2021)
9. Gatys, L.A., Ecker, A.S., Bethge, M.: Image style transfer using convolutional neural networks. In: Proceedings of the IEEE Conference on Computer Vision and Pattern Recognition, pp. 2414–2423 (2016)
10. Girshick, R., Donahue, J., Darrell, T., Malik, J.: Rich feature hierarchies for accurate object detection and semantic segmentation. In: Proceedings of the IEEE Conference on Computer Vision and Pattern Recognition, pp. 580–587 (2014)
11. Goodfellow, I.J., Shlens, J., Szegedy, C.: Explaining and harnessing adversarial examples. arXiv preprint arXiv:1412.6572 (2014)

12. He, K., Gkioxari, G., Dollár, P., Girshick, R.: Mask R-CNN. In: Proceedings of the IEEE International Conference on Computer Vision, pp. 2961–2969 (2017)
13. Hu, Y.C.T., Kung, B.H., Tan, D.S., Chen, J.C., Hua, K.L., Cheng, W.H.: Naturalistic physical adversarial patch for object detectors. In: Proceedings of the IEEE/CVF International Conference on Computer Vision, pp. 7848–7857 (2021)
14. Hu, Z., Huang, S., Zhu, X., Sun, F., Zhang, B., Hu, X.: Adversarial texture for fooling person detectors in the physical world. In: Proceedings of the IEEE/CVF Conference on Computer Vision and Pattern Recognition, pp. 13307–13316 (2022)
15. Huang, L., et al.: Universal physical camouflage attacks on object detectors. In: Proceedings of the IEEE/CVF Conference on Computer Vision and Pattern Recognition, pp. 720–729 (2020)
16. Huang, Z., Xu, Y., Lassner, C., Li, H., Tung, T.: ARCH: animatable reconstruction of clothed humans. In: Proceedings of the IEEE/CVF Conference on Computer Vision and Pattern Recognition, pp. 3093–3102 (2020)
17. Jocher, G., et al.: Ultralytics/YOLOv5: v6.2 - YOLOv5 classification models, Apple M1, reproducibility, ClearML and Deci.ai integrations (2022). https://doi.org/10.5281/zenodo.7002879
18. Kato, H., Ushiku, Y., Harada, T.: Neural 3D mesh renderer. In: Proceedings of the IEEE Conference on Computer Vision and Pattern Recognition, pp. 3907–3916 (2018)
19. Krizhevsky, A., Sutskever, I., Hinton, G.E.: ImageNet classification with deep convolutional neural networks. Commun. ACM **60**(6), 84–90 (2017)
20. Kurakin, A., Goodfellow, I.J., Bengio, S.: Adversarial examples in the physical world. In: Artificial Intelligence Safety and Security, pp. 99–112. Chapman and Hall/CRC (2018)
21. Li, Y., Zhai, W., Cao, Y., Zha, Z.J.: Location-free camouflage generation network. arXiv preprint arXiv:2203.09845 (2022)
22. Liu, W., et al.: SSD: single shot multibox detector. In: Leibe, B., Matas, J., Sebe, N., Welling, M. (eds.) ECCV 2016. LNCS, vol. 9905, pp. 21–37. Springer, Cham (2016). https://doi.org/10.1007/978-3-319-46448-0_2
23. Loper, M., Mahmood, N., Romero, J., Pons-Moll, G., Black, M.J.: SMPL: a skinned multi-person linear model. ACM Trans. Graph. (2015)
24. Lu, J., Sibai, H., Fabry, E.: Adversarial examples that fool detectors. arXiv preprint arXiv:1712.02494 (2017)
25. Lu, J., Sibai, H., Fabry, E., Forsyth, D.: No need to worry about adversarial examples in object detection in autonomous vehicles. arXiv preprint arXiv:1707.03501 (2017)
26. Madry, A., Makelov, A., Schmidt, L., Tsipras, D., Vladu, A.: Towards deep learning models resistant to adversarial attacks. arXiv preprint arXiv:1706.06083 (2017)
27. Maesumi, A., Zhu, M., Wang, Y., Chen, T., Wang, Z., Bajaj, C.: Learning transferable 3D adversarial cloaks for deep trained detectors. arXiv preprint arXiv:2104.11101 (2021)
28. Mir, A., Alldieck, T., Pons-Moll, G.: Learning to transfer texture from clothing images to 3D humans. In: Proceedings of the IEEE/CVF Conference on Computer Vision and Pattern Recognition, pp. 7023–7034 (2020)
29. Poulton, E.: Adaptive coloration in animals. Nature **146**(3692), 144–145 (1940)
30. Redmon, J., Divvala, S., Girshick, R., Farhadi, A.: You only look once: unified, real-time object detection. In: Proceedings of the IEEE Conference on Computer Vision and Pattern Recognition, pp. 779–788 (2016)

31. Redmon, J., Farhadi, A.: YOLO9000: better, faster, stronger. In: Proceedings of the IEEE Conference on Computer Vision and Pattern Recognition, pp. 7263–7271 (2017)
32. Ren, S., He, K., Girshick, R., Sun, J.: Faster R-CNN: towards real-time object detection with region proposal networks. Adv. Neural Inf. Process. Syst. **28** (2015)
33. Sharif, M., Bhagavatula, S., Bauer, L., Reiter, M.K.: Accessorize to a crime: real and stealthy attacks on state-of-the-art face recognition. In: Proceedings of the 2016 ACM SIGSAC Conference on Computer and Communications Security, pp. 1528–1540 (2016)
34. Song, D., et al.: Physical adversarial examples for object detectors. In: 12th USENIX Workshop on Offensive Technologies (WOOT 2018) (2018)
35. Suryanto, N., et al.: DTA: physical camouflage attacks using differentiable transformation network. In: Proceedings of the IEEE/CVF Conference on Computer Vision and Pattern Recognition (CVPR), pp. 15305–15314 (2022)
36. Szegedy, C., et al.: Intriguing properties of neural networks. arXiv preprint arXiv:1312.6199 (2013)
37. Thys, S., Van Ranst, W., Goedemé, T.: Fooling automated surveillance cameras: adversarial patches to attack person detection. In: Proceedings of the IEEE/CVF Conference on Computer Vision and Pattern Recognition Workshops (2019)
38. Wang, C.Y., Bochkovskiy, A., Liao, H.Y.M.: YOLOv7: trainable bag-of-freebies sets new state-of-the-art for real-time object detectors. arXiv preprint arXiv:2207.02696 (2022)
39. Wang, D., et al.: FCA: learning a 3D full-coverage vehicle camouflage for multi-view physical adversarial attack. In: Proceedings of the AAAI Conference on Artificial Intelligence, vol. 36, pp. 2414–2422 (2022)
40. Wang, J., Liu, A., Yin, Z., Liu, S., Tang, S., Liu, X.: Dual attention suppression attack: generate adversarial camouflage in physical world. In: Proceedings of the IEEE/CVF Conference on Computer Vision and Pattern Recognition, pp. 8565–8574 (2021)
41. Wu, T., Ning, X., Li, W., Huang, R., Yang, H., Wang, Y.: Physical adversarial attack on vehicle detector in the Carla simulator. arXiv preprint arXiv:2007.16118 (2020)
42. Wu, Z., Lim, S.-N., Davis, L.S., Goldstein, T.: Making an invisibility cloak: real world adversarial attacks on object detectors. In: Vedaldi, A., Bischof, H., Brox, T., Frahm, J.-M. (eds.) ECCV 2020. LNCS, vol. 12349, pp. 1–17. Springer, Cham (2020). https://doi.org/10.1007/978-3-030-58548-8_1
43. Xiao, C., Yang, D., Li, B., Deng, J., Liu, M.: MeshAdv: adversarial meshes for visual recognition. In: Proceedings of the IEEE/CVF Conference on Computer Vision and Pattern Recognition, pp. 6898–6907 (2019)
44. Yang, K., Lin, X.Y., Sun, Y., Ho, T.Y., Jin, Y.: 3D-Adv: black-box adversarial attacks against deep learning models through 3D sensors. In: 2021 58th ACM/IEEE Design Automation Conference (DAC), pp. 547–552. IEEE (2021)
45. Yin, B., et al.: Adv-makeup: a new imperceptible and transferable attack on face recognition. arXiv preprint arXiv:2105.03162 (2021)
46. Zhang, Q., Yin, G., Nie, Y., Zheng, W.S.: Deep camouflage images. In: Proceedings of the AAAI Conference on Artificial Intelligence, vol. 34, pp. 12845–12852 (2020)
47. Zhang, Y., Foroosh, H., David, P., Gong, B.: CAMOU: learning physical vehicle camouflages to adversarially attack detectors in the wild. In: International Conference on Learning Representations (2018)
48. Zhu, Z., Su, H., Liu, C., Xiang, W., Zheng, S.: You cannot easily catch me: a low-detectable adversarial patch for object detectors. arXiv preprint arXiv:2109.15177 (2021)

Lattices

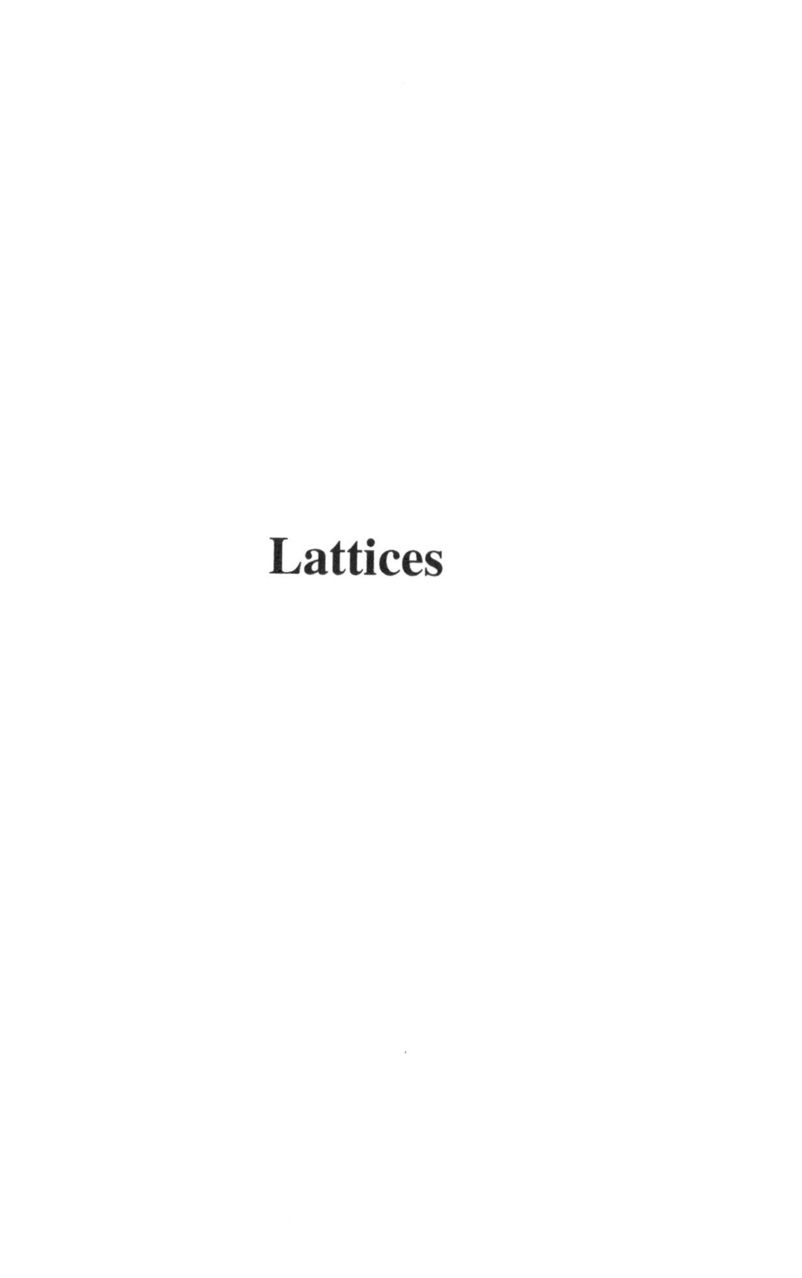

Subfield Attacks on HSVP in Ideal Lattices

Zhili Dong[1,2], Shixin Tian[1,2], Kunpeng Wang[1,2(✉)], and Chang Lv[1]

[1] State Key Laboratory of Information Security, Institute of Information Engineering, Chinese Academy of Sciences, Beijing 100093, People's Republic of China
wangkunpeng@iie.ac.cn

[2] School of Cyber Security, University of Chinese Academy of Science, Beijing 100093, People's Republic of China

Abstract. In this paper, we propose two subfield attacks on HSVP in ideal lattices in number fields (not necessarily Galois fields), both under the canonical embedding and the coefficient embedding. These two attacks use the intersection method and the norm method, respectively. In addition,the reduction steps in our attacks are all in polynomial time. By contrast, the former method reduces HSVP in ideal lattices to HSVP in ideal lattices in subfields with larger approximate factor than the latter one, while the latter method has a wider range of applications. Moreover, in Galois number fields, the intersection method performs better in attacking prime ideals with small decomposition fields, whilst the norm method works better in prime ideals with large decomposition fields. Besides, ideals with small norms are vulnerable by both of these two attacks.

Keywords: Ideal-lattices · Hermite-SVP · Subfield attacks

1 Introduction

In [19], the Learning With Errors problem (LWE) was introduced by Regev. After that, all of lattice-based cryptographic algorithms are designed based on LWE. In 2009, Stehlé, Steinfeld, Tanaka and Xagawa [22] studied Ideal-LWE in power-of-two cyclotomic fields. In the same fields, Lyubashevsky, Peikert and Regev [12] presented a reduction from search Ring-LWE to the decision variant. Ideal-LWE and Ring-LWE improve the efficiency of LWE. To support the security of encryption algorithms based on Ring-LWE, the authors [12,22] gave polynomial-time quantum reductions from the approximate shortest vector problem (ASVP) to Ring-LWE in cyclotomic fields. Later, Peikert, Regev and Stephens-Davidowitz [18] presented a quantum reduction from ASVP to Ring-LWE in all number fields. Moreover, Lyubashevsky et al. [12] proved that, under the assumption that approximating the shortest vector problems (SVP) in the worst-case on ideal lattices are hard for polynomial-time quantum algorithms, then the Ring-LWE distribution is pseudo-random. These results imply that the underlying hard problem of Ring-LWE is ASVP.

Y. Deng and M. Yung (Eds.): Inscrypt 2022, LNCS 13837, pp. 447–462, 2023.
https://doi.org/10.1007/978-3-031-26553-2_24

1.1 Previous Works

With various of lattice-based encryption algorithms [2,7,9,12,16,17,20,22] based on SVP been proposed, SVP becomes more vital. Except for ASVP, the Hermite-SVP (HSVP) is another important variant of SVP. Compared to ASVP and exact SVP, an advantage of HSVP is that one can easily check a solution of it.

There is a naive reduction from HSVP to ASVP. By the definition of the Hermite's constant [8], for an $n-$dimensional lattice $\mathcal{L}$, if one can solve ASVP with factor γ in $\mathcal{L}$, then HSVP with factor $\gamma\sqrt{\gamma_n}$ in $\mathcal{L}$ can also be solved, where γ_n is the Hermite's constant. Oppositely, a non-trivial reduction from ASVP with factor γ^2 to HSVP with factor γ for $\gamma \geq \sqrt{\gamma_n}$ is shown in [10]. Moreover, the best known basis reduction algorithms [1,6,14] showed that an oracle to solve exact SVP in dimension $k \leq n/2$ yielded solutions to HSVP with factor, e.g., $\gamma = \gamma_k^{\frac{n-1}{2(k-1)}}$.

On the other hand, the LLL algorithm [11] solved HSVP with factor $(4/3+\epsilon)^{(d-1)/4}$ in time polynomial in $1/\epsilon$ and the size of the lattice basis. Moreover, with a number of calls to the exact SVP oracle in dimension $\leq k$, Schnorr [21] solved HSVP with factor $(2k)^{d/k}$. Later in [5], Gama et al. improved the factor to $\mathcal{O}(k)^{d/(2k)}$. The best blockwise algorithm is Gama-Nguyen's slide algorithm [6], which approximates HSVP with factor $\sqrt{(1+\epsilon)\gamma_d}^{(d-1)/(k-1)}$, with a polynomial number of calls to a SVP oracle in dimension $\leq k$.

In 2021, Pan et al. [15] proposed a subfield attack on HSVP in prime ideal lattices in the power-of-two cyclotomic fields. They heuristically used the decomposition field of prime ideals. Instead of using the norm of ideals, they used the intersection of ideals. Pan et al.'s work is a connection between algebraic number theory and lattice theory.

1.2 Our Results

In this paper, we exploit subfield attacks on HSVP in ideal lattices in number fields, by improving the results of Pan et al. [15]. Their subfield attack on HSVP in prime ideal lattices in Galois number fields adopting the canonical embedding, and intelligently use the decomposition fields. In our work, we remove the requirement of the Galois extension. Moreover, we change the decomposition fields to any subfields. Since the decomposition fields of prime ideals is difficult to compute in general, our work is more useful in practice.

Firstly, in Subsect. 3.1, we propose two subfield attacks on HSVP in ideal lattices in number fields under the canonical embedding. Let L be a number field with $[L:\mathbb{Q}] = N$, $\mathcal{O}_L$ its integer ring. For any ideal $\mathcal{I}$ of $\mathcal{O}_L$, set $\mathcal{I}_1 = \mathrm{Norm}_{L/K}(\mathcal{I})$ and $\mathcal{I}_2 = \mathcal{I} \cap \mathcal{O}_K$, where K is a subfield of L with $[K:\mathbb{Q}] = n$. Moreover, assume that $\mathcal{I}_2$ has prime ideal decomposition:

$$(*)\ \mathcal{I}_2 = \mathfrak{p}_1\mathfrak{p}_2\cdots\mathfrak{p}_t, \text{satisfying } \mathfrak{p}_i + \mathfrak{p}_j = \mathcal{O}_K \text{ for each } i \neq j.$$

By using the ideal $\mathcal{I}_1$ of $\mathcal{O}_K$, which we call the norm method, we reduce HSVP with factor γ in $\mathcal{I}$ under the canonical embedding to HSVP with factor $\gamma \cdot \frac{|\mathrm{Norm}_{K/\mathbb{Q}}(\mathrm{disc}(L/K))|^{1/2N}}{\sqrt{N/n}\,\mathrm{Norm}_{L/\mathbb{Q}}(\mathcal{I})^{1/n-1/N}}$ in $\mathcal{I}_1$, in polynomial time. Meanwhile, by using the ideal $\mathcal{I}_2$ of $\mathcal{O}_K$, which we call the intersection method, HSVP with factor γ in $\mathcal{I}$ under the canonical embedding is reduced to HSVP with factor $\gamma \cdot |\mathrm{Norm}_{K/\mathbb{Q}}(\mathrm{disc}(L/K))|^{1/2N} \frac{\mathrm{Norm}_{L/\mathbb{Q}}(\mathcal{I})^{1/N}}{\mathrm{Norm}_{K/\mathbb{Q}}(\mathcal{I}_2)^{1/n}\sqrt{N/n}}$ in $\mathcal{I}_2$.

Compared to Pan et al.'s [15] work, there are three improvement in our work. Firstly, we extend their usage of the intersection method on prime ideals to more general ideals, which satisfy the condition $(*)$, by using the Lemma 1. Secondly, we make use of the norm method. By this method, we can deal with ideal lattice without any limits. Thirdly, our work remove the requirement of the decomposition fields. Indeed, we can use any subfields in our attacks. Moreover, in other subfield attacks [3], the approximation factor in previous attacks is greatly affected during lifting, while our lifting cost is not that much.

Next, in Subsect. 3.2, we give two subfield attacks on HSVP in ideal lattices under the coefficient embedding, by using the norm method and the intersection method. Denote $\mathcal{I}, \mathcal{I}_1, \mathcal{I}_2$ as above. Then there is a polynomial time reduction from HSVP in $\mathcal{I}$ with factor γ under the coefficient embedding to HSVP in $\mathcal{I}_1$ with factor $\gamma \cdot \frac{\mathrm{Norm}_{L/\mathbb{Q}}(\mathcal{I})^{1/N}}{\mathrm{Norm}_{L/\mathbb{Q}}(\mathcal{I})^{1/n}}$. In addition, suppose that the ideal $\mathcal{I}$ satisfies the condition $(*)$, then an oracle to solve HSVP in $\mathcal{I}_2$ with factor $\gamma \cdot \frac{\mathrm{Norm}_{L/\mathbb{Q}}(\mathcal{I})^{1/N}}{\mathrm{Norm}_{K/\mathbb{Q}}(\mathcal{I}_2)^{1/n}}$ yields solutions to HSVP with factor γ in $\mathcal{I}$ under the coefficient embedding. We can see that the expressions of factors in sublattices under these two embeddings are quite different. This is because that the volume of $\mathcal{O}_L$ under the coefficient embedding is 1, while under the canonical embedding is not.

Note that $\mathrm{Norm}_{K/\mathbb{Q}}(\mathcal{I}_2)^{1/n}$ is smaller than $\mathrm{Norm}_{K/\mathbb{Q}}(\mathcal{I})^{1/n}$ in general, we conclude that the intersection method induces a larger factor in HSVP in sublattices, which means easier to be attacked. Since the main complexity of our attacks comes from solving HSVP in sublattices, the intersection method gives a more efficient attack on ideals satisfying the condition $(*)$, in general. Now we consider a special case, which is frequently used in practice. Let $L/\mathbb{Q}$ be a Galois extension, and $\mathcal{I} = \mathcal{P}$ be a prime ideal of $\mathcal{O}_L$. Suppose that K is a subfield of L containing the decomposition field of $\mathcal{P}$ in $L/\mathbb{Q}$. Then $\mathrm{Norm}_{K/\mathbb{Q}}(\mathcal{I}_2) = \mathrm{Norm}_{L/\mathbb{Q}}(\mathcal{I})$ and $\mathcal{I}_1 = \mathcal{I}_2$. In this case, HSVP in $\mathcal{I}_1$ and $\mathcal{I}_2$ are the same. However, the reduction steps in the norm method is much simpler than the other one. Hence the norm method performs better than the intersection method in this case. Moreover, for ideal $\mathcal{I}$ with prime ideal decomposition $\mathcal{I} = \mathcal{P}_1 \cdots \mathcal{P}_t$, let L_i be the decomposition field of $\mathcal{P}_i$ in $L/\mathbb{Q}$. Take K to be a subfield of L containing the composite field of L_i. Then the norm method is more efficient than the intersection method in this case.

Also, consider the case where $L/\mathbb{Q}$ is a Galois extension, and $\mathcal{I} = \mathcal{P}$ is an unramified prime ideal of $\mathcal{O}_L$. By the norm method, we need to deal with HSVP in $\mathcal{I}_1$ with factor $\gamma_1 = \gamma \cdot \frac{|\mathrm{Norm}_{K/\mathbb{Q}}(\mathrm{disc}(L/K))|^{1/2N}}{\sqrt{N/n}\,p^{f/n-f/N}}$ (resp., $\gamma_1 = \gamma \cdot p^{f/N-f/n}$) under the canonical embedding (resp., the coefficient embedding), where p is the rational prime under $\mathcal{P}$, and f is the residue degree of $\mathcal{P}$ in $L/\mathbb{Q}$.

Then for a fixed subfield K, γ_1 is a decreasing function of f. Hence, this method performs well in prime ideals with large decomposition fields. While by the intersection method, we have to solve HSVP in $\mathcal{I}_2$ with factor $\gamma_2 = \gamma \cdot |\operatorname{Norm}_{K/\mathbb{Q}}(\operatorname{disc}(L/K))|^{1/2N} \frac{p^{f/N}}{p^{f'/n}\sqrt{N/n}}$ (resp., $\gamma \cdot p^{f/N - f'/n}$) under the canonical embedding (resp., the coefficient embedding), where f' is the residue degree of $\mathcal{P} \cap \mathcal{O}_K$ in $K/\mathbb{Q}$. Note that $f/N - f'/n \leq 0$, and the equivalence holds if and only if $\mathcal{P} \cap \mathcal{O}_K$ is inert in L/K. Therefore, the intersection method works well prime ideals with small decomposition fields.

1.3 Paper Organization

The remainder of the paper was organized as follows. In Sect. 2, we give some preliminaries about lattices and algebraic number theory. In Sect. 3, we propose subfield attacks on HSVP of ideal lattices, both under the canonical embedding and the coefficient embedding. Then in Sect. 4, we give an analysis of our reductions, including the complexity and applications. Finally, conclusions and some open problems are given in Sect. 5.

2 Preliminaries

2.1 Lattice

Lattices are discrete additive subgroups of $\mathbb{R}^D$. Any lattice $\mathcal{L}$ is generated by a finite set of linearly independent vectors $\mathbf{B} = \{\mathbf{b}_1, \cdots, \mathbf{b}_d : \mathbf{b}_i \in \mathbb{R}^D\}$ for some integer $d \leq D$:

$$\mathcal{L} = \left\{ \sum_{i=1}^{d} z_i \mathbf{b}_i \mid z_i \in \mathbb{Z} \right\}.$$

where $\mathbf{B}$ is called a basis of $\mathcal{L}$; d and D are called the rank and dimension of $\mathcal{L}$, respectively. We say that $\mathcal{L}$ is full-rank if $d = D$. Let B be a matrix corresponds to $\mathbf{B}$, then define the determinant of $\mathcal{L}$ to be $\det(\mathcal{L}) = \sqrt{|\det(B^T B)|}$. Clearly, when L is full rank, then $\det(\mathcal{L}) = |\det(B)|$. By the definition, we know that the determinant of $\mathcal{L}$ is exactly the volume of the fundamental domain of it.

The shortest vector problem (SVP) is one of the most hard problems in the lattice theory. There are several important variants of SVP in application. In this article, we describe the Hermite-SVP (HSVP).

HSVP: Given a lattice $\mathcal{L}$ with dimension n, and a constant $\gamma > 0$, find a vector $v \in \mathcal{L}$ such that $\|v\| < \gamma \cdot \det(\mathcal{L})^{1/n}$.

2.2 Algebraic Number Theory

In this subsection, we give some basic concepts and results in algebraic number theory. One can find them in [13].

We say α is an algebraic number if α is a root of a polynomial $f(x)$ in $\mathbb{Z}[x]$. Let L/K be a finite extension of number fields, define the degree of L/K to be the dimension of L as a linear space over K, denoted $[L : K]$. In addition, since $L = K(\alpha)$ for some $\alpha \in L$, we have $[L : K] = \deg f(x)$, where $f(x)$ is the minimal polynomial of α over K. Denote $\mathcal{O}_L$ to be the ring of integers of L, i.e.

$$\mathcal{O}_L = \{x \in L |\ x \text{ is an algebraic number}\}.$$

Definition 1. *Let L/K be a finite extension of number fields with degree n, a basis $(\alpha_1, \cdots, \alpha_n)$ of L over K is called an integral basis if it is a basis of $\mathcal{O}_L$ over $\mathcal{O}_K$.*

An ideal $\mathcal{I}$ of $\mathcal{O}_L$ is an additive subgroup of $\mathcal{O}_L$ such that $x\mathcal{I} \subset \mathcal{I}$, for all $x \in \mathcal{O}_L$. A prime ideal $\mathcal{P}$ of $\mathcal{O}_L$ is an ideal satisfying the following condition:

$$\text{If } xy \in \mathcal{P}, \text{then either } x \in \mathcal{P} \text{ or } y \in \mathcal{P}.$$

For two ideals $\mathcal{I}_1, \mathcal{I}_2$ of $\mathcal{O}_L$, define the addition $\mathcal{I}_1 + \mathcal{I}_2$ to be the set

$$\{x + y | x \in \mathcal{I}_1, y \in \mathcal{I}_2\}.$$

Clearly, $\mathcal{I}_1 + \mathcal{I}_2$ is also an ideal of $\mathcal{O}_L$. In addition, $\mathcal{I}_1$ and $\mathcal{I}_2$ is called coprime if $\mathcal{I}_1 + \mathcal{I}_2 = \mathcal{O}_L$.

The following proposition implies that any ideal in a number field L is a full-rank lattice in $\mathbb{R}^{[L:\mathbb{Q}]}$.

Proposition 1. *Let $L/\mathbb{Q}$ be a finite extension with degree n, then any ideal $\mathcal{I}$ of $\mathcal{O}_L$ is a free module over $\mathbb{Z}$ with rank n.*

Theorem 1. *Let L/K be a finite extension of number fields with degree n.*

(a) For any ideal $\mathcal{I}$ in $\mathcal{O}_L$, there is a unique (up to order) prime ideal decomposition in $\mathcal{O}_L$:

$$\mathcal{I} = \mathcal{P}_1^{e_1} \mathcal{P}_2^{e_2} \cdots \mathcal{P}_g^{e_g},$$

where each $\mathcal{P}_i$ is a prime ideal of $\mathcal{O}_L$;

(b) Let $\mathfrak{p}$ be a prime ideal of $\mathcal{O}_K$, as in (a), we have a prime ideal decomposition

$$\mathfrak{p}\mathcal{O}_L = \mathcal{P}_1^{e_1} \mathcal{P}_2^{e_2} \cdots \mathcal{P}_g^{e_g}.$$

Let $f_i = [\mathcal{O}_L/\mathcal{P}_i : \mathcal{O}_K/\mathfrak{p}]$, then we have

$$n = \sum_{i=1}^{g} f_i e_i.$$

(c) When L/K is a Galois extension, we have

$$e_1 = e_2 = \cdots = e_g = e \text{ and } f_1 = f_2 = \cdots = f_g = f.$$

Moreover, we have

$$n = efg.$$

Definition 2. *Let L/K be a finite extension of number fields. Suppose that $\mathfrak{p}$ is a prime ideal of $\mathcal{O}_K$.*

(a) $\mathfrak{p}$ is unramified in L/K if each e_i in Theorem 1 equals to 1. Otherwise, $\mathfrak{p}$ is ramified in L/K.
(b) f_i is called the residue degree of $\mathcal{P}_i$ in L/K.
(c) $\mathfrak{p}$ is called inert in L/K if $g = 1$ and $e_1 = 1$ in Theorem 1.
(d) Let K'/K be a sub-extension of L/K, then K' is called the decomposition field of $\mathfrak{p}$ in L/K if the split indexes $g_\mathfrak{p}$ satisfies $g_\mathfrak{p}(K'/K) = g_\mathfrak{p}(L/K) = [K' : K]$.

Now, we define the discriminant of an extension L/K of number fields.

Definition 3. *Let L/K be a finite extension of number fields with integral basis $(\alpha_1, \cdots, \alpha_n)$, define the discriminant* $\mathrm{disc}(L/K)$ *of L/K to be*

$$\mathrm{disc}(L/K) = \mathrm{disc}(\alpha_1, \cdots, \alpha_n) = (\det(\sigma_i(\alpha_j)))^2.$$

Remark 1. Proposition 1 implies that an integral basis of number fields L over $K = \mathbb{Q}$ always exists, while for general K does not. However, the discriminant $\mathrm{disc}(L/K)$ of L over K can also be defined, which we will not discuss here.

Lemma 1. *Let L/K be a finite extension of number fields. Suppose that $\mathcal{P}$ is a prime ideal of $\mathcal{O}_L$, then $\mathfrak{p} = \mathcal{P} \cap \mathcal{O}_K$ is a prime ideal of $\mathcal{O}_K$.*

Moreover, let $\mathcal{I}$ be an ideal of $\mathcal{O}_L$ with prime ideal decomposition $\mathcal{I} = \mathcal{P}_1\mathcal{P}_2\cdots\mathcal{P}_t$. Assume that $\mathfrak{p}_i = \mathcal{P}_i \cap \mathcal{O}_K$ are pairwise coprime, then

$$\mathcal{I}' = \mathcal{I} \cap \mathcal{O}_K = \mathfrak{p}_1\mathfrak{p}_2\cdots\mathfrak{p}_t.$$

Proof. The first assertion is clearly. Let $\mathcal{I}_1, \mathcal{I}_2$ be coprime prime ideals in $\mathcal{O}_L$, then $\mathcal{I}_1\mathcal{I}_2 = \mathcal{I}_1 \cap \mathcal{I}_2$. Suppose that $\mathcal{P}_1$ and $\mathcal{P}_2$ are coprime with $\mathcal{P}_3$, then $\mathcal{P}_1\mathcal{P}_2$ is coprime with $\mathcal{P}_3$. Then we have

$$\mathcal{I} \cap \mathcal{O}_K = (\mathcal{P}_1\mathcal{P}_2\cdots\mathcal{P}_t) \cap \mathcal{O}_K = (\bigcap_i \mathcal{P}_i) \cap \mathcal{O}_K = \bigcap_i \mathfrak{p}_i = \mathfrak{p}_1\mathfrak{p}_2\cdots\mathfrak{p}_t.$$

■

□

2.3 Ideal Lattice

Let $L/\mathbb{Q}$ be a finite extension with degree N, $\mathcal{O}_L$ be the integer ring of L. Then any ideal $\mathcal{I}$ of $\mathcal{O}_L$ can be regarded as a lattice in two ways:

1. The canonical embedding: Let $\mathrm{Emb}(L/\mathbb{Q})$ be the set of all embeddings of L into $\mathbb{C}$, i.e.

$$\mathrm{Emb}(L/\mathbb{Q}) = \{\sigma_1, \cdots, \sigma_N\},$$

Define the canonical embedding to be:

$$\begin{aligned} \sigma_L : L &\to \mathbb{R}^{r_1} \times \mathbb{C}^{2r_2} \\ a &\mapsto (\sigma_1(a), \cdots, \sigma_N(a)), \end{aligned}$$

where r_1 is the number of the real embeddings of L, r_2 is the number of complex embedding pairs of L, and $r_1 + 2r_2 = N$.

By Proposition 1, $\sigma_L(\mathcal{I})$ is an N-dimensional lattice. Moreover, the lattice $\sigma_L(\mathcal{I})$ has determinant $\mathrm{Norm}_{L/\mathbb{Q}}(\mathcal{I})\sqrt{\mathrm{disc}(L/\mathbb{Q})}$, where $\mathrm{Norm}_{L/K}$ means the norm map from L to K.

Denote $\|a\|_L$ to be the length of a under the canonical embedding, namely

$$\|a\|_L = \|\sigma_L(a)\|.$$

2. The coefficient embedding: A number field L is monogenic if $L/\mathbb{Q}$ has a power integral basis, i.e. there is an element α in $\mathcal{O}_L$ such that

$$\mathcal{O}_L = \mathbb{Z}[\alpha] = \mathbb{Z} + \alpha\mathbb{Z} + \cdots + \alpha^{N-1}\mathbb{Z}.$$

For a monogenic field L, define the coefficient embedding to be:

$$C_L : L \to \mathbb{R}^N; \quad a = \sum_{i=0}^{N-1} x_i\alpha^i \mapsto (x_0, \cdots x_{N-1}).$$

Obviously, under the coefficient embedding with basis $\{1, \alpha, \cdots, \alpha^{N-1}\}$, $C_L(\mathcal{I})$ is a lattice with dimension N.

Denote $|a|_L$ to be the length of a under the coefficient embedding, namely

$$|a|_L = \|C_L(a)\| = \sqrt{\sum_{i=0}^{N-1} x_i^2}.$$

Remark 2. The coefficient embedding depends on the choice of the basis, whilst the canonical embedding does not. But $|a|_L$ is independent of the choice of power integral basis.

3 Attacks on HSVP of Ideal Lattices

In this section, we propose two subfield attacks on HSVP in ideal lattices in number fields, both under the canonical embedding and the coefficient embedding. We do not require the number fields to be Galois in this section.

Let $L/\mathbb{Q}$ be a finite extension of number fields, $\mathcal{I}$ be an ideal of $\mathcal{O}_L$, we still use $\mathcal{I}$ to represent lattices $\sigma_L(\mathcal{I})$ and $C_L(\mathcal{I})$. For a subfield K of L, denote $\mathcal{I}_1 = \mathrm{Norm}_{L/K}(\mathcal{I}), \mathcal{I}_2 = \mathcal{I} \cap \mathcal{O}_K$ to be ideals of $\mathcal{O}_K$, as well as their corresponding lattices.

3.1 Under the Canonical Embedding

In this subsection, we always consider ideal lattices under the canonical embedding.

Theorem 2 (The Norm Method). *Let $L/\mathbb{Q}$ be a finite extension with degree N, and $\mathcal{I}$ be an ideal of $\mathcal{O}_L$. Suppose that K is an intermediate field of $L/\mathbb{Q}$ with $[K:\mathbb{Q}]=n$. Then the solution to HSVP with factor γ in the sublattice $\mathcal{I}_1$ will also be a solution to HSVP in $\mathcal{I}$ with factor $\frac{\sqrt{N/n}\,\mathrm{Norm}(\mathcal{I})^{1/n-1/N}}{|\mathrm{Norm}_{K/\mathbb{Q}}(\mathrm{disc}(K/\mathbb{Q}))|^{1/2N}}\cdot\gamma$.*

Proof. Consider the following diagram

$$\begin{array}{ccccccc}
\mathcal{I} & \subset & \mathcal{O}_L & \subset & L & \longrightarrow & \mathbb{C}^N \\
| & & | & & | & & | \\
\mathcal{I}_1 & \subset & \mathcal{O}_K & \subset & K & \longrightarrow & \mathbb{C}^n \\
| & & | & & | & & | \\
(m) & \subset & \mathbb{Z} & \subset & \mathbb{Q} & \longrightarrow & \mathbb{C}.
\end{array}$$

For any element $x\in K$, we have

$$\|x\|_L=\sqrt{\frac{N}{n}}\|x\|_K.$$

Then for $x\in K$ satisfying $\|x\|_K<\gamma\cdot(\det\mathcal{I}_1)^{1/n}$, we have

$$\begin{aligned}
\|x\|_L &< \sqrt{\frac{N}{n}}\gamma\cdot(\det\mathcal{I}_1)^{1/n}\\
&= \sqrt{\frac{N}{n}}\gamma\cdot\left(\mathrm{Norm}_{K/\mathbb{Q}}(\mathcal{I}_1)\sqrt{|\operatorname{disc}(K/\mathbb{Q})|}\right)^{1/n}\\
&= \sqrt{\frac{N}{n}}\gamma\cdot\left(\mathrm{Norm}_{L/\mathbb{Q}}(\mathcal{I})\sqrt{\frac{|\operatorname{disc}(L/\mathbb{Q})|^{n/N}}{|\mathrm{Norm}_{K/\mathbb{Q}}(\operatorname{disc}(L/K))|^{n/N}}}\right)^{1/n}\\
&= \sqrt{\frac{N}{n}}\gamma\cdot\frac{(\mathrm{Norm}_{L/\mathbb{Q}}(\mathcal{I}))^{1/n-1/N}}{|\mathrm{Norm}_{K/\mathbb{Q}}(\operatorname{disc}(L/K))|^{1/2N}}\left(\mathrm{Norm}_{L/\mathbb{Q}}(\mathcal{I})\sqrt{|\operatorname{disc}(L/\mathbb{Q})|}\right)^{1/N}\\
&= \sqrt{\frac{N}{n}}\gamma\cdot\frac{(\mathrm{Norm}_{L/\mathbb{Q}}(\mathcal{I}))^{1/n-1/N}}{|\mathrm{Norm}_{K/\mathbb{Q}}(\operatorname{disc}(L/K))|^{1/2N}}(\det(\mathcal{I}))^{1/N}.
\end{aligned}$$

■ □

Theorem 3 (The Intersection Method). *Let $L/\mathbb{Q}$ be a finite extension of number fields with degree N, K be a subfield of L with $[K:\mathbb{Q}]=n$. Suppose that $\mathcal{I}$ is an ideal of $\mathcal{O}_L$ satisfying the condition $(*)$. Then a solution to HSVP with factor γ in the sublattice $\mathcal{I}_2$ yields a solution to HSVP in $\mathcal{I}$ with factor $\gamma\cdot\frac{\mathrm{Norm}_{K/\mathbb{Q}}(\mathcal{I}_2)^{1/n}\sqrt{N/n}}{\mathrm{Norm}_{L/\mathbb{Q}}(\mathcal{I})^{1/N}|\mathrm{Norm}_{K/\mathbb{Q}}(\mathrm{disc}(L/K))|^{1/2N}}$.*

Proof. Similar to the proof of Theorem 2, for $x\in K$ satisfying $\|x\|_K<\gamma\cdot(\det\mathcal{I}_2)^{1/n}$, we have

Algorithm 1: Subfield attack for HSVP under the canonical embedding by the norm method

Input: A number field L with degree N, a subfield K with degree n, an ideal $\mathcal{I}$ of $\mathcal{O}_L$, and a constant γ.

Output: A vector x in $\mathcal{I}$ with $\|x\|_L < \gamma \cdot \det(\mathcal{I})^{1/N}$.

Compute the ideal $\mathcal{I}_1 = \mathrm{Norm}_{L/K}(\mathcal{I})$;

Compute $|\,\mathrm{Norm}_{K/\mathbb{Q}}(\mathrm{disc}(L/K))|$ and $\mathrm{Norm}_{L/\mathbb{Q}}(\mathcal{I})$;

Find a vector x in $\mathcal{I}_1$ such that $\|x\|_K < \gamma \cdot \frac{|\,\mathrm{Norm}_{K/\mathbb{Q}}(\mathrm{disc}(L/K))|^{1/2N}}{\sqrt{N/n}\,\mathrm{Norm}_{L/\mathbb{Q}}(\mathcal{I})^{1/n-1/N}} \det(\mathcal{I}_1)^{1/n}$;

Output x.

$$
\begin{aligned}
\|x\|_L &< \sqrt{\frac{N}{n}}\gamma \cdot (\det \mathcal{I}_2)^{1/n} \\
&= \sqrt{\frac{N}{n}}\gamma \cdot \left(\mathrm{Norm}_{K/\mathbb{Q}}(\mathcal{I}_2)\sqrt{|\,\mathrm{disc}(K/\mathbb{Q})|}\right)^{1/n} \\
&= \sqrt{\frac{N}{n}}\gamma \cdot \left(\prod_{i=1}^{t} \mathrm{Norm}_{L/\mathbb{Q}}(\mathcal{P}_i)^{f_i'/f_i} \sqrt{\frac{|\,\mathrm{disc}(L/\mathbb{Q})|^{n/N}}{|\,\mathrm{Norm}_{K/\mathbb{Q}}(\mathrm{disc}(L/K))|^{n/N}}}\right)^{1/n} \\
&= \sqrt{\frac{N}{n}}\gamma \cdot \frac{\prod_{i=1}^{t} \mathrm{Norm}_{L/\mathbb{Q}}(\mathcal{P}_i)^{f_i'/nf_i - 1/N}}{|\,\mathrm{Norm}_{K/\mathbb{Q}}(\mathrm{disc}(L/K))|^{1/2N}} \left(\mathrm{Norm}_{L/\mathbb{Q}}(\mathcal{I})\sqrt{|\,\mathrm{disc}(L/\mathbb{Q})|}\right)^{1/N} \\
&= \gamma \cdot \frac{\sqrt{N/n} \cdot \mathrm{Norm}_{K/\mathbb{Q}}(\mathcal{I}_2)^{1/n}}{\mathrm{Norm}_{L/\mathbb{Q}}(\mathcal{I})^{1/N} |\,\mathrm{Norm}_{K/\mathbb{Q}}(\mathrm{disc}(L/K))|^{1/2N}} \det(\mathcal{I})^{1/N}.
\end{aligned}
$$

■

□

Algorithm 2: Subfield attack on HSVP under the canonical embedding by the intersection method

Input: A number field L with degree N, a subfield K with degree n, an ideal $\mathcal{I} \subset \mathcal{O}_L$ satisfying the condition $(*)$, and a constant γ.

Output: A vector x in $\mathcal{I}$ with $\|x\|_L < \gamma \cdot \det(\mathcal{I})^{1/N}$.

Compute the ideal $\mathcal{I}_2 = \mathcal{I} \cap \mathcal{O}_K$;

Compute $|\,\mathrm{Norm}_{K/\mathbb{Q}}(\mathrm{disc}(L/K))|$, $\mathrm{Norm}_{K/\mathbb{Q}}(\mathcal{I}_2)$ and $\mathrm{Norm}_{L/\mathbb{Q}}(\mathcal{I})$;

Find a vector x in $\mathcal{I}_2$ such that

$$
\|x\|_K < \gamma \cdot \frac{\mathrm{Norm}_{L/\mathbb{Q}}(\mathcal{I})^{1/N} |\,\mathrm{Norm}_{K/\mathbb{Q}}(\mathrm{disc}(L/K))|^{1/2N}}{\mathrm{Norm}_{K/\mathbb{Q}}(\mathcal{I}_2)^{1/n}\sqrt{N/n}} \det(\mathcal{I}_2)^{1/n};
$$

Output x.

3.2 Under the Coefficient Embedding

In this subsection, we propose two subfield attacks on HSVP of ideal lattices under the coefficient embedding. At the beginning, we compute the determinant of $\mathcal{I}$ under the coefficient embedding.

Lemma 2. *Let $L = \mathbb{Q}(\alpha)$ be a number field with degree N. Suppose that $L/\mathbb{Q}$ has a set of power integral basis. Consider the coefficient embedding C_L of L into $\mathbb{R}^N$, then for each ideal $\mathcal{I}$ in $\mathcal{O}_L$, the determinant of the lattice $C_L(\mathcal{I})$ is $\text{Norm}_{L/\mathbb{Q}}(\mathcal{I})$.*

Proof. By the definition of the coefficient embedding, we have

$$\det(C_L(\mathcal{O}_L)) = 1.$$

Since $[\mathcal{O}_L : \mathcal{I}\mathcal{O}_L] = |\,\text{Norm}_{L/\mathbb{Q}}(\mathcal{I})|$, and C_L is a linear map, we have

$$\det(C_L(\mathcal{I})) = \text{Norm}_{L/\mathbb{Q}}(\mathcal{I}).$$

■ □

From Lemma 2, we can see that although $C_L(a)$ depends on the choice of basis, the determinant of $\mathcal{L}$ is independent of the choice of basis.

In this subsection, we require number fields L, K satisfy the following condition:

(**) Assume that L is a number field with degree N. Let $\{1, \alpha, \alpha^2, \cdots, \alpha^{N-1}\}$ be a power integral basis of $L/\mathbb{Q}$. Moreover, let K be a subfield of L with $[L : K] = t$. Suppose that $K/\mathbb{Q}$ has a power integral basis $\{1, \alpha^t, \alpha^{2t}, \cdots, \alpha^{t(n-1)}\}$, where $n = \frac{N}{t}$.

Remark 3. The condition (**) is not strict in practice, since the cyclotomic fields satisfy this condition.

Theorem 4 (The Norm Method). *Assume that L, K satisfy the condition (**). Let $\mathcal{I}$ be a prime ideal of $\mathcal{O}_L$, and $\mathcal{I}_1 = \text{Norm}_{L/K}(\mathcal{I})$. Then the solution to HSVP with factor γ in the sublattice $\mathcal{I}_1$ will also be a solution to HSVP in $\mathcal{I}$ with factor $\gamma \cdot \text{Norm}(\mathcal{I})^{1/n-1/N}$.*

Proof. For any element $x \in \mathcal{O}_K$, we have $x = \sum_{i=o}^{n-1} (\alpha^t)^i x_i$, then

$$C_K(x) = (x_0, x_1, \cdots, x_{n-1});$$

$$C_L(x) = (x_0, 0, \cdots, 0, x_1, 0, \cdots, 0, \cdots, x_{n-1}, 0, \cdots, 0).$$

Hence

$$|x|_L = |x|_K.$$

Then for $x \in K$ satisfying $|x|_K < \gamma \cdot (\det \mathcal{I}_1)^{1/n}$, we have

$$\begin{aligned}|x|_L &< \gamma \cdot (\det \mathcal{I}_1)^{1/n}\\ &= \gamma \cdot (\mathrm{Norm}_{K/\mathbb{Q}}(\mathcal{I}_1))^{1/n}\\ &= \gamma \cdot (\mathrm{Norm}_{L/\mathbb{Q}}(\mathcal{I}))^{1/n}\\ &= \gamma \cdot \mathrm{Norm}_{L/\mathbb{Q}}(\mathcal{I})^{1/n-1/N}(\det(\mathcal{I}))^{1/N}.\end{aligned}$$

■ □

Algorithm 3: Subfield attack on HSVP under the coefficient embedding by the norm method

---

Input: Number fields L, K satisfying the condition $(**)$, an ideal $\mathcal{I}$ of $\mathcal{O}_L$, and a constant γ.

Output: A vector x in $\mathcal{I}$ with $|x|_L < \gamma \cdot \det(\mathcal{I})^{1/N}$.

Compute the ideal $\mathcal{I}_1 = \mathrm{Norm}_{L/K}(\mathcal{I})$;

Compute $\mathrm{Norm}_{L/\mathbb{Q}}(\mathcal{I})$;

Find a vector x in $\mathcal{I}_1$ such that $|x|_K < \gamma \cdot \frac{\mathrm{Norm}_{L/\mathbb{Q}}(\mathcal{I})^{1/N}}{\mathrm{Norm}_{L/\mathbb{Q}}(\mathcal{I})^{1/n}} \det(\mathcal{I}_1)^{1/n}$;

Output x.

Theorem 5 (The Intersection Method). *Assume that L, K satisfy the condition $(**)$. Let $\mathcal{I}$ be an ideal of $\mathcal{O}_L$ satisfying the condition $(*)$. Then the solution to HSVP with factor γ in the sublattice $\mathcal{I}_2 = \mathcal{I} \cap \mathcal{O}_K$ will also be a solution to HSVP in $\mathcal{I}$ with factor $\gamma \cdot \frac{\mathrm{Norm}_{K/\mathbb{Q}}(\mathcal{I}_2)^{1/n}}{\mathrm{Norm}_{L/\mathbb{Q}}(\mathcal{I})^{1/N}}$.*

Proof. By Lemma 1, we have that

$$\mathcal{I}_2 = \mathfrak{p}_1\mathfrak{p}_2\cdots\mathfrak{p}_t.$$

Then for $x \in K$ satisfying $|x|_K < \gamma \cdot (\det \mathcal{I}_2)^{1/n}$, we have

$$\begin{aligned}|x|_L &< \gamma \cdot (\det \mathcal{I}_2)^{1/n}\\ &= \gamma \cdot (\mathrm{Norm}_{K/\mathbb{Q}}(\mathcal{I}_2))^{1/n}\\ &= \gamma \cdot (\mathrm{Norm}_{L/\mathbb{Q}}(\mathcal{P}_1)^{f_1'/f_1}\,\mathrm{Norm}_{L/\mathbb{Q}}(\mathcal{P}_2)^{f_2'/f_2}\cdots\mathrm{Norm}_{L/\mathbb{Q}}(\mathcal{P}_t)^{f_t'/f_t})^{1/n}\\ &= \gamma \cdot \mathrm{Norm}_{L/\mathbb{Q}}(\mathcal{P}_1)^{f_1'/f_1 n-1/N}\cdots\mathrm{Norm}_{L/\mathbb{Q}}(\mathcal{P}_t)^{f_t'/f_t n-1/N}(\det(\mathcal{I}))^{1/N}\\ &= \gamma \cdot p_1^{f_1'/n-f_1/N}\cdots p_t^{f_t'/n-f_t/N}(\det(\mathcal{I}))^{1/N}\\ &= \gamma \cdot \frac{\mathrm{Norm}_{K/\mathbb{Q}}(\mathcal{I}_2)^{1/n}}{\mathrm{Norm}_{L/\mathbb{Q}}(\mathcal{I})^{1/N}}(\det(\mathcal{I}))^{1/N}.\end{aligned}$$

■ □

Algorithm 4: Subfield attack on HSVP under the coefficient embedding by the intersection method

Input: Number fields L, K satisfying the condition $(**)$, an ideal $\mathcal{I}$ of $\mathcal{O}_L$ satisfying the condition $(*)$, and a constant γ.

Output: A vector x in $\mathcal{I}$ with $|x|_L < \gamma \cdot \det(\mathcal{I})^{1/N}$.

Compute the ideal $\mathcal{I}_2 = \mathcal{I} \cap \mathcal{O}_K$;

Compute $\text{Norm}_{L/\mathbb{Q}}(\mathcal{I})$ and $\text{Norm}_{K/\mathbb{Q}}(\mathcal{I}_2)$;

Find a vector x in $\mathcal{I}_2$ such that $|x|_K < \gamma \cdot \frac{\text{Norm}_{L/\mathbb{Q}}(\mathcal{I})^{1/N}}{\text{Norm}_{K/\mathbb{Q}}(\mathcal{I}_2)^{1/n}} \det(\mathcal{I}_2)^{1/n}$;

Output x.

Remark 4. From the analysis in Sect. 4, we need not to compute the prime ideal decomposition of ideals, which is a hard problem.

4 Analysis

In this section, we give some analysis on complexity, comparison and applications of our algorithms.

4.1 Complexity

Our algorithms reduce HSVP in ideal lattices to sublattices with lower dimensions and smaller approximate factors. Hence, our attacks do not break HSVP in ideal lattices. To express the complexity of our reductions more precisely, we introduce the pseudo-basis.

Definition 4. *Let R be a domain,* Frac(R) *be its fractional field. Suppose that M is a finitely generated, torsion free $R-$module, we say $(\omega_i, \alpha_i)_{1 \le i \le t}$ is a pseudo-basis of M if*

$$M = \alpha_i \omega_i \oplus \cdots \oplus \alpha_t \omega_t.$$

where $\omega_i \in$ Frac$(R)^n$, and α_i is a fractional ideal of R.

By the norm method, the main computational complexity of the reduction steps in Algorithms 1, 3 comes from computing the relative norm $\text{Norm}_{L/K}(\mathcal{I})$. When given an absolute basis of $\mathcal{I}$ and a pseudo-basis of $\mathcal{O}_L$, [4, Algorithm 2.5.2] gives an algorithm in computing $\text{Norm}_{L/K}(\mathcal{I})$. This algorithm is in polynomial time, and performs well in practice.

Similarly, the main technical problem in the reduction steps in Algorithms 2, 4 is to compute $\mathcal{I} \cap \mathcal{O}_K$. An important special case is that an umramified prime ideal $\mathcal{P}$ of $\mathcal{O}_L$ is given by an absolute two-element representation $\mathcal{P} = p\mathcal{O}_L + \alpha\mathcal{O}_L$. Algorithm 2.5.3 in [4] compute $\mathcal{P} \cap \mathcal{O}_K$ in polynomial time. In addition, assume that we have an integral pseudo-basis $(\omega_i, \mathfrak{a}_i)_i$ of $\mathcal{O}_L$ and a pseudo-basis $(\beta_i, \mathfrak{b}_i)_i$ of the ideal $\mathcal{I}$ of $\mathcal{O}_L$, then it is easy to compute $\mathcal{I} \cap \mathcal{O}_K$.

If not already in this form, we can use Algorithm 1.6.1 in [4] to compute the Hermite normal form $(\beta_i, \mathfrak{b}_i)$ of the given pseudo-basis. Hence, $\mathcal{I} \cap \mathcal{O}_K = \mathfrak{b}_1$.

By the above discussion, we can avoid computing the prime ideal decomposition of ideals, which is a hard problem.

4.2 Comparison

In this subsection, we compare the efficiency and applications of the intersection method and the norm method. Let L be a number field with degree N, K be a subfield of L with $[K:\mathbb{Q}] = n$. For any ideal $\mathcal{I}$ of $\mathcal{O}_L$, set $\mathcal{I}_1 = \mathrm{Norm}_{L/K}(\mathcal{I})$ and $\mathcal{I}_2 = \mathcal{I} \cap \mathcal{O}_K$.

Under the canonical embedding (resp. the coefficient embedding), we need to solve HSVP with factor

$$\gamma_{\mathrm{norm}} = \gamma \cdot \frac{|\mathrm{Norm}_{K/\mathbb{Q}}(\mathrm{disc}(L/K))|^{1/2N}}{\sqrt{N/n}\,\mathrm{Norm}_{L/\mathbb{Q}}(\mathcal{I})^{1/n-1/N}} \left(\text{resp., } \gamma \cdot \frac{\mathrm{Norm}_{L/\mathbb{Q}}(\mathcal{I})^{1/N}}{\mathrm{Norm}_{L/\mathbb{Q}}(\mathcal{I})^{1/n}}\right)$$

in an $n-$dimensional sublattice by the norm method. While by the intersection method, we have to deal with HSVP with factor

$$\gamma_{\mathrm{inter}} = \gamma \frac{\mathrm{Norm}_{L/\mathbb{Q}}(\mathcal{I})^{1/N} |\mathrm{Norm}_{K/\mathbb{Q}}(\mathrm{disc}(L/K))|^{1/2N}}{\mathrm{Norm}_{K/\mathbb{Q}}(\mathcal{I}_2)^{1/n}\sqrt{N/n}} \left(\text{resp., } \gamma \frac{\mathrm{Norm}_{L/\mathbb{Q}}(\mathcal{I})^{1/N}}{\mathrm{Norm}_{K/\mathbb{Q}}(\mathcal{I}_2)^{1/n}}\right).$$

Let $\delta = \gamma_{\mathrm{norm}}/\gamma_{\mathrm{inter}}$, then

$$\delta = \frac{\gamma_{\mathrm{norm}}}{\gamma_{\mathrm{inter}}} = \frac{\mathrm{Norm}_{K/\mathbb{Q}}(\mathcal{I}_2)^{1/n}}{\mathrm{Norm}_{L/\mathbb{Q}}(\mathcal{I})^{1/n}} \leq 1.$$

Hence, we have $\gamma_{\mathrm{inter}} \geq \gamma_{\mathrm{norm}}$. As a consequence, by the intersection method, HSVP in sublattices, which we need to deal with, is easier than by the norm method. Since the maximum amount of computational complexity comes from solving HSVP in sublattices, the intersection method is more efficient in general.

Suppose that the ideal $\mathcal{I}$ has prime ideal decomposition $\mathcal{I} = \mathcal{P}_1 \cdots \mathcal{P}_t$. Let L_i be the inertia field corresponding to $\mathcal{P}_i$ in $L/\mathbb{Q}$ for each $i = 1, \cdots, t$, and L' be the composite field of $L_1, \cdots, L_t$. Take K to be a subfield of L containing L', then $\delta = 1$. This means HSVP in sublattices we need to deal with by the two methods are the same. Therefore, the main difference between Algorithms 1 and 2 (resp., Algorithms 3 and 4) is their reduction steps. In [4], we can see that computational complexity of $\mathcal{I}_1$ and $\mathcal{I}_2$ is comparable. But we need to additionally compute $\mathrm{Norm}_{K/\mathbb{Q}}(\mathcal{I}_2)$ in Algorithms 2 and 4. As a result, the norm method performs better in such a case.

Besides the efficiency, we can see that the range of applications of the norm method is wider than the intersection method. More precisely, the formal method can by applied to any ideals, while the latter one can only be used in the ideals satisfying the condition $(*)$. The reason is that we cannot determine the ideal $\mathcal{I} \cap \mathcal{O}_L$ in general, since the intersection operation is not a homomorphism.

4.3 Applications

The discussion of two embeddings is similar, in this subsection, we take the canonical embedding for instance. Moreover, for simplicity, we only consider unramified prime ideals $\mathcal{P}$ of $\mathcal{O}_L$. Set $\mathfrak{p}_1 = \mathrm{Norm}_{L/K}(\mathcal{P})$, and $\mathfrak{p}_2 = \mathcal{P} \cap \mathcal{O}_K$. Denote p to be the rational prime lying under $\mathcal{P}$, and f (resp., f') be the residue degree of $\mathcal{P}$ in $L/\mathbb{Q}$ (resp., $\mathfrak{p}_2$ in $K/\mathbb{Q}$).

In Theorem 2, we can solve HSVP with factor

$$\gamma_1 = \frac{\sqrt{N/n}p^{f/n-f/N}}{|\mathrm{Norm}_{K/\mathbb{Q}}(\mathrm{disc}(K/\mathbb{Q}))|^{1/2N}} \cdot \gamma \left(< \gamma \cdot p^{f/n-f/N}\sqrt{N/n}\right)$$

in the $N-$dimensional prime ideal lattice $\mathcal{P}$ by dealing with HSVP with factor γ in an $n-$dimensional sublattice $\mathfrak{p}_1$. In particular, take $\gamma = \sqrt{n}$, then finding a vector in $\mathfrak{p}_1$ satisfying the Minkowski bound of $\mathfrak{p}_1$ yields a vector in $\mathcal{P}$ satisfying the factor $\sqrt{N}p^{f/n-f/N}$, which is larger than the Minkowski bound of $\mathcal{P}$.

For a fixed subfield K, the factor γ_1 is an increasing function of f. Hence, Algorithm 1 will be efficient when prime ideals has small residue degree f. In particular, in the Galois number fields, primes ideals with large decomposition field can easily to be attacked by the norm method.

In Theorem 3, we give reduction from HSVP with factor

$$\gamma_2 = \frac{p^{f'/n-f/N}\sqrt{N/n}\cdot\gamma}{|\mathrm{Norm}_{K/\mathbb{Q}}(\mathrm{disc}(L/K))|^{1/2N}} \left(< \gamma \cdot p^{f'/n-f/N}\sqrt{N/n}\right)$$

in the $N-$dimensional prime ideal lattice $\mathcal{P}$ to HSVP with factor γ in the $n-$dimensional sublattice $\mathfrak{p}_2$. In particular, take $\gamma = \sqrt{n}$, then finding a vector in $\mathfrak{p}_2$ satisfying the Minkowski bound of $\mathfrak{p}_1$ yields a vector in $\mathcal{P}$ satisfying the Minkowski bound of $\mathcal{P}$.

By some simple computation, we have that $f'/n - f/N \geq 0$. The equivalence hold if and only if $\mathfrak{p}_2$ is inert in L/K. This means Algorithm 2 will work to their greatest advantage in this case. Therefore, the intersection method performs well in prime ideals with small decomposition fields.

Expect for the residue degree, ideals with small norms are also vulnerable in our attacks. Because HSVP in ideals lattices with small norms, namely determinant, will be reduced to sublattices with large factors. This is not secure in practice.

5 Conclusions and Open Problems

In this paper, we made use of the norm method and the intersection method to proposed two subfield attacks on HSVP of ideal lattices in number fields, both under the canonical embedding and the coefficient embedding. By contrast, the norm method can be used in any ideal lattices, and worked better in the ideals with large decomposition fields. While the intersection method can be applied to ideals satisfying the condition (∗), and performed better in ideals with small decomposition fields. Meanwhile, HSVP in ideals with small norm will be vulnerable by both of two methods. Compared with the previous work [15], our work can be used in more general ideal lattices of any number fields and their subfields.

Besides HSVP in ideal lattices, another interesting problem is to study subfield attacks on HSVP of module lattices in number fields. The main obstacle to using our methods in module lattices is the properties of determinant of matrices.

References

1. Aggarwal, D., Li, J., Nguyen, P.Q., Stephens-Davidowitz, N.: Slide reduction, revisited-filling the gaps in SVP approximation. In: Micciancio, D., Ristenpart, T. (eds.) CRYPTO 2020. LNCS, vol. 12171, pp. 274–295. Springer, Cham (2020). https://doi.org/10.1007/978-3-030-56880-1-10
2. Ajtai, M: Generating hard instances of lattice problems. In: Proceedings of the Twenty-Eighth Annual ACM Symposium on Theory of Computing (STOC 1996), pp. 99–108. https://doi.org/10.1145/237814.237838
3. Albrecht, M., Bai, S., Ducas, L.: A subfield lattice attack on overstretched NTRU assumptions. In: Robshaw, M., Katz, J. (eds.) CRYPTO 2016. LNCS, vol. 9814, pp. 153–178. Springer, Heidelberg (2016). https://doi.org/10.1007/978-3-662-53018-4_6
4. Cohen, H.: Advanced Topics in Computational Number Theory. Springer, Cham (1999)
5. Gama, N., Howgrave-Graham, N., Koy, H., Nguyen, P.Q.: Rankin's constant and blockwise lattice reduction. In: Dwork, C. (ed.) CRYPTO 2006. LNCS, vol. 4117, pp. 112–130. Springer, Heidelberg (2006). https://doi.org/10.1007/11818175_7
6. Gama, N., Nguyen, P.Q.: Finding short lattice vectors within mordell's inequality. In STOC (2008)
7. Gentry, C., Peikert, C., Vaikuntanathan, V.: Trapdoors for hard lattices and new cryptographic constructions. In: STOC (2008). https://eprint.iacr.org/2007/432
8. Hermite, C.: Extraits de lettres de M. Hermite à M. Jacobi sur différents objets de la théorie des nombres. J. Reine Angew. Math. **40**, 261–315 (1850)
9. Hoffstein, J., Pipher, J., Silverman, J.H.: NTRU: a ring-based public key cryptosystem. In: Buhler, J.P. (ed.) ANTS 1998. LNCS, vol. 1423, pp. 267–288. Springer, Heidelberg (1998). https://doi.org/10.1007/BFb0054868
10. Lovász, L.: An Algorithmic Theory of Numbers, Graphs and Convexity, vol. 50. SIAM Publications, Philadelphia (1986). CBMS-NSF Regional Conference Series in Applied Mathematics
11. Lenstra, A., Lenstra, H., Lovász, L.: Factoring polynomials with rational coeffiients. Math. Ann. **261**, 513–534 (1982)
12. Lyubashevsky, V., Peikert, C., Regev, O.: On ideal lattices and learning with errors over rings. In: Gilbert, H. (ed.) EUROCRYPT 2010. LNCS, vol. 6110, pp. 1–23. Springer, Heidelberg (2010). https://doi.org/10.1007/978-3-642-13190-5_1
13. Marcus, D.A.: Number Fields: Universitext, 2nd edn. Springer, Cham (2018). https://doi.org/10.1007/978-3-319-90233-3_8
14. Micciancio, D., Walter, M.: Practical, predictable lattice basis reduction. In: Fischlin, M., Coron, J.-S. (eds.) EUROCRYPT 2016. LNCS, vol. 9665, pp. 820–849. Springer, Heidelberg (2016). https://doi.org/10.1007/978-3-662-49890-3_31

15. Pan, Y., Xu, J., Wadleigh, N., Cheng, Q.: On the ideal shortest vector problem over random rational primes. In: Canteaut, A., Standaert, F.-X. (eds.) EUROCRYPT 2021. LNCS, vol. 12696, pp. 559–583. Springer, Cham (2021). https://doi.org/10.1007/978-3-030-77870-5_20
16. Peikert, C.: Public-key cryptosystems from the worst-case shortest vector problem. In: STOC (2009)
17. Peikert, C.: A decade of lattice cryptography. Found. Trends Theor. Comput. Sci. **10**(4), 283–424 (2016)
18. Peikert, C., Regev, O., Stephens-Davidowitz, N.: Pseudorandomness of ring-LWE for any ring and modulus. In: STOC (2017). https://eprint.iacr.org/2017/258
19. Regev, O.: On lattices, learning with errors, random linear codes, and cryptography. In: Gabow H.N., Fagin, R. (eds.) 37th Annual ACM Symposium on Theory of Computing, pp. 84–93. ACM Press (2005)
20. Regev, O.: On lattices, learning with errors, random linear codes, and cryptography. J. ACM **56**(6), 1–40 (2009)
21. Schnorr, C.P.: A hierarchy of polynomial time lattice basis reduction algorithms. Theoret. Comput. Sci. **53**, 201–224 (1987)
22. Stehlé, D., Steinfeld, R., Tanaka, K., Xagawa, K.: Efficient public key encryption based on ideal lattices. In: Matsui, M. (ed.) ASIACRYPT 2009. LNCS, vol. 5912, pp. 617–635. Springer, Heidelberg (2009). https://doi.org/10.1007/978-3-642-10366-7_36

On the Measurement and Simulation of the BKZ Behavior for q-ary Lattices

Zishen Zhao[1,2] and Guangwu Xu[1,2,3(✉)]

[1] School of Cyber Science and Technology, Shandong University, Qingdao 266237, Shandong, China
zhaozs@mail.sdu.edu.cn, gxu4sdq@sdu.edu.cn

[2] Key Laboratory of Cryptologic Technology and Information Security of Ministry of Education, Shandong University, Qingdao 266237, Shandong, China

[3] Quancheng Laboratory, Jinan 250103, China

Abstract. The BKZ algorithm has been one of the most important tools for analyzing and assessing lattice-based cryptosystems. The second order statistical behavior of BKZ algorithm on random lattices has been well measured in the work of Yu and Ducas. Several simulators have been proposed to efficiently and accurately predict the profile shape for random lattices. But for the case q-ary lattices, the situation is much less understood. Recently, Albrecht and Li proposed a simulator that predicts the Z-shape of q-ary lattices a good accuracy. However, we find that this simulator still has its limitations when Z-shape disappears. Our experiments reveal more features for the shape profile of q-ary lattices. Based on some results on the distribution of the length of short vectors and reasonable heuristics, we propose a new simulator for random q-ary lattices with some extensions. Furthermore, the second order statistical behavior of BKZ algorithm on q-ary lattices is characterized, their similarities and differences compared to that for random lattices have been briefly analyzed.

Keywords: BKZ algorithm · q-ary lattice · Cryptanalysis · Simulator

1 Introduction

A lattice $\mathcal{L}$ of dimension n can be spanned by the rows of a rank n matrix $\boldsymbol{B} \in \mathbb{R}^{n\times d}$ via integer combinations: $\mathcal{L}(\boldsymbol{B}) = \{\boldsymbol{x}\boldsymbol{B} : \boldsymbol{x} \in \mathbb{Z}^n\}$. Lattice reduction algorithm aims at finding a good basis made of relatively short and somewhat orthogonal vectors from an arbitrary input basis. A typical attack to a lattice-based cryptosystem is to search short vectors of the involved lattice through some public basis. In [17], Lenstra, Lenstra and Lóvasz proposed a seminal lattice reduction algorithm (LLL) that produces a good reduced basis for the lattice, consisting of short enough and almost orthogonal vectors. After its publication, LLL was immediately recognized as one of the most important algorithmic achievements of the twentieth century, because of its broad applicability

Y. Deng and M. Yung (Eds.): Inscrypt 2022, LNCS 13837, pp. 463–482, 2023.
https://doi.org/10.1007/978-3-031-26553-2_25

and apparent simplicity. Later in [22], Schnorr and Euchner proposed a new lattice reduction algorithm based on LLL algorithm, named the Block Korkine-Zolotarev (BKZ) algorithm. BKZ algorithm can be regarded as a block-size generalization of LLL with potentially super-exponential complexity. The BKZ algorithm uses a block-size parameter $\beta \geq 2$: as the block-size β increases, the running-time increases exponentially and the value of RHF will become smaller. That is because it needs to solve the Shortest Vector Problem (SVP) in β-dimensional lattice inside the BKZ algorithm. LLL algorithm corresponds to the case that $\beta = 2$. By now, several optimizations of BKZ algorithm have been developed, such as BKZ 2.0 algorithm [8] with an early abort technique and pruned enumeration, Progressive BKZ algorithm [4], Self-Dual BKZ algorithm [19]. In [21], Schnorr introduced geometric series assumption (GSA), which heuristically assumes the Gram-Schmidt norms $\|\boldsymbol{b}_i^*\|$ of the BKZ-reduced basis decrease geometrically. More precisely, there exists a quotient r for $i = 1, \ldots, n$ such that the output BKZ-reduced basis satisfies $\|\boldsymbol{b}_i^*\|^2 / \|\boldsymbol{b}_1\|^2 = r^{i-1}$, for some $r \in [3/4, 1)$. We call this r the GSA constant. In [8], it was argued that $r \approx (\frac{\beta}{2\pi e}(\pi\beta)^{\frac{1}{\beta}})^{\frac{1}{\beta-1}}$ when the dimension n is much larger than the block-size β. It was experimentally observed that the GSA approximately fits well with the practical performance of BKZ algorithm. However, in the first few indexes and about the last β indexes, a typical BKZ-reduced basis does not follow GSA closely. In this paper, we use head and tail to denote the first few and about the last β indexes respectively, and use the body for the rest region of indexes.

It is of specific significance to exactly predict the practical performance of BKZ algorithm, and has attracted a series of research work. In [8], Chen and Nguyen firstly proposed a BKZ simulator to predict the Gram-Schimidt lengths $\|\boldsymbol{b}_i^*\|$ on random lattices after the BKZ algorithm. The simulator was based on the assumption that each SVP-solver is able to find a lattice vector whose norm perfectly fits the Gaussian heuristic in the projected local block, except for the tail. The norm of the tail part can be calculated directly by the block-size β and the lattice dimension. Later, Yu and Ducas [26] observed inaccuracies of the previous model for the practical performance of BKZ algorithm and quantified them based on the second order statistical behavior. They proposed two main statistical phenomenons. The first one was that in head and tail regions the behavior of the differences between two consecutive Gram-Schmidt log-norms $r_i := \log\|\boldsymbol{b}_i^*\| - \log\|\boldsymbol{b}_{i+1}^*\|$ can be treated as a function of index. The second was that the covariance between r_i and r_{i+2} is 0 for all i, but r_i and r_{i+1} are inversely correlated. In the body region, the covariance is only influenced by the block-size β, but in the head and tail regions both index i and block-size β influence their covariance.

Building upon [26], the probabilistic BKZ simulator introduced in [5] was based on a probabilistic version of the Gaussian heuristic, or rather, the distribution of shortest non-zero vector in random lattice in [23]. It could better capture the head concavity phenomenon of BKZ algorithm after many tours and display similarly accurate for the body and the tail region. Therefore, the results of [5] match experimental results more precisely. Besides, they also proposed pressed-BKZ (a variant of the BKZ algorithm), intending to exploit this head concavity phenomenon.

Two popular problems proven to be widespread building blocks for lattice-based cryptographic applications [6,13,15,20] are the NTRU problem and Learning with Errors (LWE) problem (with its ring and module variants). Both the NTRU problem and LWE problem are based on q-ary lattices generated by q-ary vectors of the following form (under row-representation):

$$\begin{pmatrix} q\boldsymbol{I}_m & \boldsymbol{0} \\ \boldsymbol{A} & \boldsymbol{I}_n \end{pmatrix} \in \mathbb{Z}^{(m+n)\times(m+n)}.$$

However, even though the behavior of BKZ algorithm on random lattices has been well understood, we are not able to say much about the case for q-ary lattices. There are differences between q-ary lattices and random lattices. For example, a BKZ-reduced basis of q-ary lattices has been observed to exhibit a so-called "Z-shape" in [14,16]. The interesting question of simulating or predicting the behavior of BKZ algorithm on q-ary lattices was proposed as an open problem by Albrecht and Ducas in [2].

1.1 Contributions

Our study strategy about the q-ary lattices is different as the block-size changes: exploring the behavior of the actual experiment for small block-size and analyzing the simulator for large block-size. We investigate the second order statistical behavior of BKZ algorithm for relatively random q-ary lattices and structured q-ary lattices including matrix NTRU lattice and circulant NTRU lattice. To the best of our knowledge, this is a topic that has not been touched on. By exploring r_i, which is the logarithm of the ratio between the i-th and $(i+1)$-st Gram-Schmidt norms in BKZ-reduced basis, we make several observations on the slope and rough shape for Gram-Schmidt norms. Based on our extensive experiments, we confirm that many results (for random lattices) of [26] can also be applied to q-ary lattices. We remark that some observable phenomenon from [26] do not seem to be applicable to q-ary lattices. We further find that when the Gram-Schmidt norms of BKZ-reduced basis remain Z-shape [9,25], the range of the r_i can be divided into five pieces. The ranges of the r_i can be divided into three pieces when the Z-shape is destroyed, just like random lattices. Furthermore, our second part studies the simulation that predicts the behavior of random q-ary lattices. When the Z-shape remained, the experiments from Albrecht and Li's [3] can be reproduced. Its simulator yields a nice prediction. However, we find it fails to capture the head concavity phenomenon when Z-shape is destroyed. To address this problem, we extend Bai-Stehlé-Wen simulator [5] to capture the head concavity phenomenon when Z-shape is destroyed from random lattices to random q-ary lattices.

From the above analysis and motivated by previous related work, we propose a new simulator for q-ary lattices where some features from [3] are extended. More concretely, the excellent first order estimate of ZGSA in [10] is utilized to determine the lower bound for the disappearance of the Z-shape. If Z-shape disappear, treating a shortest non-zero vector of lattice as a random variable and using the distribution described in [23], our simulator provides more accurate predictions of the head region than that by Albrecht-Li simulator [3] and maintains a pretty good approximation on both body and tail regions.

Organization. We arrange the rest of our paper as follows. In Sect. 2, some preliminaries are given. We present the similarity and difference between second order statistical behavior of random lattices and q-ary lattice, and it might cause some quantitative analysis of random lattice can not directly apply to q-ary lattice in Sect. 3. In Sect. 4, we propose a new simulator to predict the behavior of BKZ algorithm for q-ary lattice when Z-shape disappears. Finally, we conclude the paper in Sect. 5.

2 Preliminaries

Notation. In this paper, the notation log stands for the base 2 logarithm. We denote the continuous centered Gaussian (normal) distribution with variance σ^2 as χ_{σ^2}. The chi-square distribution with k degrees of freedom as $\chi^2_{k,\sigma^2} = \sum_{i=1}^{k} X_i^2$, where $X_1, \ldots, X_k$ are independently distributed as χ_{σ^2}. The expectation of chi-square distribution is $k\sigma^2$.

2.1 Lattices

For an $n \times d$ matrix $\boldsymbol{B} \in \mathbb{R}^{n\times d}$ with full rank n, we denote by $\mathcal{L}(\boldsymbol{B}) := \{\boldsymbol{x}\boldsymbol{B} : \boldsymbol{x} \in \mathbb{Z}^n\}$ the n-dimensional lattice spanned by the rows of $\boldsymbol{B}$. The rows of $\boldsymbol{B}$ form a basis of the lattice $\mathcal{L} = \mathcal{L}(\boldsymbol{B})$. For a basis $\boldsymbol{B} = (\boldsymbol{b}_0, \cdots, \boldsymbol{b}_{n-1})^{\mathsf{T}}$ and $i \in \{0, \ldots, n-1\}$, π_i is defined as the orthogonal projection away from $\boldsymbol{b}_0, \ldots, \boldsymbol{b}_{i-1}$, and the Gram-Schmidt vectors as $\boldsymbol{b}_0^*, \ldots, \boldsymbol{b}_{i-1}^*$ where $\boldsymbol{b}_i^* = \pi_i(\boldsymbol{b}_i)$. We use $\boldsymbol{B}_{[l:r)}$ to represent the matrix $[\pi_l(\boldsymbol{b}_l), \cdots, \pi_l(\boldsymbol{b}_{r-1})]^{\mathsf{T}}$. The Euclidean norm of a vector is denoted as $\|\boldsymbol{v}\|$ and the volume of a lattice is denoted as $\mathrm{vol}(\mathcal{L}(\boldsymbol{B}))$, which is given by $\prod_{i=0}^{n-1} \|\boldsymbol{b}_i^*\|$.

Gaussian Heuristic. Let $\mathcal{L}$ be an n-dimensional lattice with volume $\mathrm{vol}(\mathcal{L})$ and $\mathcal{S}$ represents a measurable set in the real span of $\mathcal{L}$. The Gaussian Heuristic states that the number of lattice points $|\mathcal{L} \cap \mathcal{S}|$ approximately equals $\mathrm{vol}(\mathcal{S})/\det(\mathcal{L})$. Furthermore, by applying this to a ball, we can see that the expectation of the first minimum $\lambda_1(\mathcal{L})$ is about

$$\mathrm{gh}(\mathcal{L}) := \frac{\mathrm{vol}(\mathcal{L})^{1/n}}{\mathrm{vol}\left(\mathcal{B}_1\right)^{1/n}} \approx \sqrt{n/(2\pi e)} \cdot \mathrm{vol}(\mathcal{L})^{1/n}$$

The expected first minimum of a n-dimensional lattice with volume 1 is denoted by $\mathrm{gh}(n) \approx \sqrt{n/(2\pi e)}$.

Theorem 1 [7]. The set of all full-rank lattices of dimension n with unit volume is denoted by $\Gamma_n = \{\mathcal{L} \in \mathbb{R}^n \mid \text{vol}(\mathcal{L}) = 1\}$ and the volume of an n-dimensional unit ball is denoted by v_n. Sample $\mathcal{L}$ uniformly in Γ_n. The distribution of $v_n \cdot \lambda_1(\mathcal{L})^n$ converges in distribution to Expo(1/2) as $n \to \infty$.

q-ary Lattice. Let q, m, n and ξ be positive integers, and $\boldsymbol{A} \in \mathbb{Z}^{n\times m}$ be a matrix, $\boldsymbol{I}_n$ denote the $n \times n$ identity matrix. We call the following basis matrix

$$\boldsymbol{B} = \begin{pmatrix} q\boldsymbol{I}_m & \boldsymbol{0} \\ \boldsymbol{A} & \xi\boldsymbol{I}_n \end{pmatrix} \in \mathbb{Z}^{(m+n)\times(m+n)}$$

a (scaled) q-ary basis, which produces a (scaled) q-ary lattice. This q-ary lattice is randomized if each entry of $\boldsymbol{A} \in \mathbb{Z}_q^{n\times m}$ is independently and uniformly sampled form $\mathbb{Z}_q$ [3]. For instance, the NTRU lattice is a q-ary lattice.

2.2 NTRU Lattice

Definition 1 [10]. Let q,n be a positive integer and let $\boldsymbol{f}, \boldsymbol{g} \in (\mathbb{Z}/q\mathbb{Z})[X]$ be polynomials of degree n with small coefficients sampled from some distribution χ under the condition that $\boldsymbol{f}$ is invertible in $\mathcal{R}_q = (\mathbb{Z}/q\mathbb{Z})[X]/(X^n - 1)$. The pair $(\boldsymbol{f}, \boldsymbol{g})$ forms the secret key, and the public key is defined as $\boldsymbol{h} = \boldsymbol{g}/\boldsymbol{f} \pmod{\mathcal{R}_q}$. The NTRU problem is to recover any rotation $(X^i\boldsymbol{f}, X^i\boldsymbol{g})$ of the secret key from public key $\boldsymbol{h}$.

In [27], $\boldsymbol{f}$ and $\boldsymbol{g}$ are chosen to both have ternary coefficients with a constant about $n/3$ of each value in $\{-1, 0, 1\}$. We use exactly the same strategy that each coefficient is sampled from a discrete Gaussian over $\mathbb{Z}$ and the ternary case is regarded as a discrete Gaussian with variance $\sigma = \frac{2}{3}$. Besides, a general matrix description of NTRU where the vectors $\boldsymbol{f}, \boldsymbol{g}, \boldsymbol{h}$ are replaced with matrices $\boldsymbol{F}, \boldsymbol{G}, \boldsymbol{H} \in \mathbb{Z}^{n\times n}$ such that $\boldsymbol{H} = \boldsymbol{G}/\boldsymbol{F} \pmod{q}$ [12]. Same as [10], we consider the original circulant NTRU and the variant, called matrix NTRU. The original circulant NTRU was based on n-dimensional vectors $\boldsymbol{f}, \boldsymbol{g}$ and matrices $\boldsymbol{F}, \boldsymbol{G}$'s associated vectors is $\boldsymbol{f}, \boldsymbol{g}$ respectively. The matrix NTRU whose the matrices $\boldsymbol{F}, \boldsymbol{G}$ have no special structure and the coefficients are independently sampled form a discrete Gaussian.

Definition 2. *Let $(n, q, \boldsymbol{F}, \boldsymbol{G}, \boldsymbol{H})$ be an NTRU case. The NTRU lattice is defined as*

$$\mathcal{L}^{H,q} = \mathbb{Z}^{2n} \cdot \begin{pmatrix} q\boldsymbol{I}_n & \boldsymbol{0} \\ \boldsymbol{H} & \boldsymbol{I}_n \end{pmatrix},$$

and its (secret) dense sublattice of rank n is

$$\mathcal{L}^{G,F} = \mathbb{Z}^n \cdot \boldsymbol{B}^{GF} \subset \mathcal{L}^{H,q}, \boldsymbol{B}^{GF} = (\boldsymbol{G}\ \boldsymbol{F})$$

NTRU problem is to find any rotation $(X^i \boldsymbol{f}, X^i \boldsymbol{g})$ of row vectors $(\boldsymbol{g} \mid \boldsymbol{f})$ in NTRU lattice. These row vectors have length of about $\|(\boldsymbol{g} \mid \boldsymbol{f})\| \approx \sqrt{2n\sigma^2}$, which is much shorter than Gaussian heuristic value $\lambda_1\left(\mathcal{L}^{H,q}\right) \approx \sqrt{nq/(\pi e)}$ of the NTRU lattice $\mathcal{L}^{H,q}$ when $\boldsymbol{H} \in (\mathbb{Z}/q\mathbb{Z})^{n \times n}$ is a truly uniform random lattice. To solve NTRU problem we thus have to resort BKZ algorithm to find these exceptionally short vectors in the NTRU lattice.

2.3 The BKZ Algorithm

Definition 3. *A basis $\boldsymbol{B} = [\boldsymbol{b}_0, \ldots, \boldsymbol{b}_{n-1}]$ is called BKZ-β reduced if*

$$\|\mathbf{b}_\kappa^*\| = \lambda_1\left(\mathcal{L}_{[\kappa:\min(\kappa+\beta,d))}\right) \text{ for all } \kappa = 0, \ldots, d-1$$

The BKZ algorithm outputs a BKZ-reduced basis from any arbitrary basis. It finds a shortest vector in each local block $\boldsymbol{B}_{[\kappa:\min(\kappa+\beta,d))}$ by using an SVP-solver. Applying this once to all positions $k = 1, \cdots, n-2$ is called a BKZ tour. In this process, if $\lambda_1\left(\Lambda_{[k,\min(k+\beta-1,n)]}\right) > \delta \cdot \|\mathbf{b}_k^*\|$, we use LLL to reduce the local block. Otherwise, BKZ algorithm updates the local block by inserting the vector found by SVP-solver between indices $k-1$ and k, then using LLL to reduce the updated block. A complete description of the BKZ algorithm is in Algorithm 1.

Algorithm 1. The BKZ algorithm

Input: A lattice basis $\boldsymbol{B}$, a block-size $\beta \geq 2$ and a constant $\delta < 1$.
Output: A BKZ-β reduced basis of $\mathcal{L}(\boldsymbol{B})$

repeat
  for $k = 1$ to $n-1$ do
    Find any b such that $\|\pi_k(\mathbf{b})\| = \lambda_1\left(\Lambda_{[k,\min(k+\beta-1,n)]}\right.$
    if $\delta \cdot \|\mathbf{b}_k^*\| > \|\mathbf{b}\|$ then
      LLL-reduce $(b_1, \cdots, b_{k-1}, b, b_k, \cdots, b_{min(k+\beta,n)})^{\mathsf{T}}$
    else
      LLL-reduce $(b_1, \cdots, b_{min(k+\beta,n)})^{\mathsf{T}}$
    end if
  end for
until no change occurs.

It has already proved that the output basis of BKZ algorithm would be of sufficiently good quality after $C \cdot \frac{n^2}{\beta^2}\left(\log n + \log\log \max \frac{\|\mathbf{b}_i^*\|}{\mathrm{vol}(\mathcal{L})^{1/n}}\right)$ tours, where C is a small constant. But in practice, the quality of output basis is not much improved after a few dozen tours. To accommodate this, Aono *et al.* [4] proposed a variant of the BKZ algorithm named Progressive BKZ. Instead of running many tours of BKZ-β, Progressive BKZ runs only a few tours using increasingly larger block sizes $\beta' = 2, 3, \ldots, \beta$. Following experimental analysis of BKZ algorithm [7], Albrecht [1] identifies 16 as the number of tours after which few improvements is made to the basis quality for Progressive BKZ.

Definition 4. Geometric Series Assumption(GSA) [21] *After lattice reduction, the norms of the Gram-Schmidt vectors b_i^* satisfy*

$$\|\boldsymbol{b}_i^*\| = \alpha^{i-1} \cdot \|\boldsymbol{b}_1\|, \textit{for some } 0 < \alpha < 1.$$

GSA gives an excellent first order estimate of the basis profile after BKZ-reduction. When a basis is BKZ-β reduced, α can be regarded as a function of β. But for q-ary lattice, things are a bit different. For q-ary lattice, the initial basis has $\|\mathbf{b}_0^*\| = \cdots = \left\|\mathbf{b}_{n-1}^*\right\| = q$ and $\|\mathbf{b}_n^*\| = \cdots = \left\|\mathbf{b}_{d-1}^*\right\| = 1$. The length of b_0 can not increase in the BKZ algorithm if the length of block-size β is much less than half of dimension of lattice. Also, $\mathbf{b_1}$ can not increase in length and the tail region can not drop below 1 for the same reasons. But the BKZ algorithm still can guarantee a sloped part in the middle region, and thus the norms of the Gram-Schmidt vectors exhibit a Z-shape that have been observed in [2,16,25]. It leads to another heuristic: ZGSA.

Heuristic 2. ZGSA. Let $\mathbf{B}$ be a basis of a $2n$-dimensional q-ary lattice $\mathcal{L}$ with n q-vectors. After BKZ-β reduction the profile's shape is as follow:

$$\|\mathbf{b}_i^*\| = \begin{cases} q & \text{if } i \leqslant n-m, \\ \sqrt{q} \cdot \alpha_\beta^{\frac{2n-1-2i}{2}}, & \text{if } n-m < i < n+m-1 \\ 1, & \text{if } i \geqslant n+m-1 \end{cases}$$

where $\alpha_\beta = \mathrm{gh}(\beta)^{2/(\beta-1)}$, and $m = \frac{1}{2} + \frac{\ln(q)}{2\ln(\alpha_\beta)}$.

2.4 The BKZ Simulator

Chen and Nguyen [8] firstly presented a simulator (see Algorithm 2) to predict the practical behavior of BKZ algorithm with a relatively large block size (e.g., $\beta \geq 45$) for random lattices. It aimed to estimate the practical behavior of BKZ for hard instances. In simulator, one tour is divided into two pieces, one part is $[1, n-45]$ and another is $[n-46, n]$. At the beginning, a boolean flag τ is initialized to be true, which records the changes in each index k. In one part, the simulator will find the first minimum for each local block by calculating the Gaussian heuristic value of the local block: $\mathrm{GH}\left(\mathbf{B}_{[k,\min(k+\beta-1,n-45)]}\right)$ in **line 8** of Algorithm 2.

Not only the computed index $\mathbf{k}$ is used to update but also the remaining indices $k' \in [k+1, n-45]$ are all updated one by one to the Gaussian heuristic $\mathbf{GH}\left(\mathbf{B}_{[k',\min(k'+\beta-1,n-45)]}\right)$ in **line 9–16** of Algorithm 2, if it is smaller than the current $\|\mathbf{b}_k^*\|$. In another part indices $k \in [n-46, n]$, it is simulated with the experimental result of 45-dimensional unit-volume lattices in **line 19–21** of Algorithm 2. The length of 45 was chosen due to the extensive experiments [8] that the minimum length obeys Gaussian heuristic quite well when the block-size $\beta \geq 45$. Applying this once to all positions is called a tour. Just like the BKZ algorithm, the simulator can run many tours.

Algorithm 2. The Chen-Nguyen simulator for random lattices

Input: The Gram-Schmidt log-norms $\{\ell_i = \log \|\mathbf{b}_i^*\|\}_{i \le n}$ and an integer $N \ge 1$

Output: A prediction of the Gram-Schmidt log-norms $\left\{\widehat{\ell_i} = \log \|\mathbf{b}_i^*\|\right\}_{i \le n}$ after N tours of BKZ

1: **for** $i = 1$ to 45 **do** $r_i \leftarrow \mathbb{E}\left[\log \|\mathbf{b}_k^*\| : \mathbf{B} \text{ HKZ-reduced basis of } \Lambda \leftarrow \Gamma_{45}\right]$
2: **end for**
3: **for** $j = 1$ to N **do**
4:   $\tau \leftarrow$ **true**
5:   **for** $k = 1$ to $N - 45$ **do**
6:     $d \leftarrow min(\beta, n-k+1)$; $e \leftarrow k+d-1$
7:     $\log \operatorname{vol}\left(\Lambda_{[k,e]}\right) \leftarrow \sum_{i=1}^{e} \ell_i - \sum_{i=1}^{k-1} \widehat{\ell_i}$
8:     $g \leftarrow \left(\log \operatorname{vol}\left(\Lambda_{[k,e]} - \log v_d\right)\right)/d$
9:     **if** $\tau =$ **true then**
10:       **if** $g < l_k$ **then**
11:         $\widehat{\ell_k} \leftarrow g$
12:         $\tau \leftarrow$ **false**
13:       **end if**
14:     **else**
15:       $\widehat{\ell_k} \leftarrow g$
16:     **end if**
17:   **end for**
18:   $\log \operatorname{vol}\left(\Lambda_{[k,e]}\right) \leftarrow \sum_{i=1}^{n} \ell_i - \sum_{i=1}^{n-45} \widehat{\ell_i}$
19:   **for** $k' = n - 44$ **to** n **do**
20:     $\widehat{\ell_{k'}} \leftarrow \frac{\log \operatorname{vol}\left(\Lambda_{[k,e]}\right)}{45} + r_{k'+45-n}$
21:   **end for**
22:   $\{\ell_1, \cdots, \ell_n\} \leftarrow \left\{\widehat{\ell_1}, \cdots, \widehat{\ell_n}\right\}$
23: **end for**

Later, Bai *et al.* refined the Chen-Nguyen simulator and the main difference is the probabilistic nature of the minimum in random lattices. When Bai-Stehlé-Wen simulator find minimum in each local block $\Lambda_{[k,e]} = \Lambda\left(\mathbf{B}_{[k,e]}\right)$ for some $k \le n-45$ and $e = \min(k+\beta-1, n-45)$ with dimension $d = min(\beta, n-45-k+1)$, by Theorem 1, $\lambda_1\left(\Lambda_{[k,e]}\right)$ is distributed as

$$\lambda_1\left(\Lambda_{[k,e]}\right) = \left(\frac{X \cdot \operatorname{vol}\left(\Lambda_{[k,e]}\right)}{v_d}\right)^{1/d}$$

where X is sampled with distribution Expo[1/2], v_d is the volume of n-dimensional unit ball. Thus, in **line 12** of Algorithm 2, it use the logarithm of $\lambda_1\left(\Lambda_{[k,e]}\right)$ to obtain

$$\log \lambda_1\left(\Lambda_{[k,e]}\right) = \frac{\log X + \log \operatorname{vol}\left(\Lambda_{[k,e]}\right) - \log v_d}{d}.$$

Besides, there were several subtle changes in Bai-Stehlé-Wen simulator. When the Gaussian Heuristic value is smaller than the current $\|\mathbf{b}_k^*\|$, Chen-Nguyen simulator updated the remaining indices $k' \in [k+1, n-45]$ but Bai-Stehlé-Wen simulator only update the remaining indices $k' \in [k+1, e]$ in the local block. The update of adjacent index $k' = k+1$ was based on the uniform distribution in every dimension and the update of other indices in $k' \in [k+2, e]$ in the local block gained an average of the difference between the new value and old value in indices $k' = k, k+1$. It is reflected in **line 13–20** of Algorithm 2.

It also set two sequences of a boolean flag $t_0^{(i)}, t_1^{(i)}, i \in [1, n]$ in **line 3, 5**. The sequence of $t_0^{(i)}, i \in [1, n]$ initialized to be true and set of $t_1^{(i)}$ initialized to be false, which can record the changes in each index k and terminate the simulator when no changes happen.

Algorithm 3. The Bai-Stehlé-Wen simulator for random lattice

Input: The Gram-Schmidt log-norms $\{\ell_i = \log \|\mathbf{b}_i^*\|\}_{i \le n}$ and an integer $N \ge 1$
Output: A prediction of the Gram-Schmidt log-norms $\left\{\widehat{\ell}_i = \log \|\mathbf{b}_i^*\|\right\}_{i \le n}$ after N tours of BKZ

1: **for** $i = 1$ to 45 **do** $r_i \leftarrow \mathbb{E}[\log \|\mathbf{b}_k^*\| : \mathbf{B}$ HKZ-reduced basis of $\Lambda \leftarrow \Gamma_{45}]$
2: **end for**
3: $t_0^{(i)} \leftarrow$ **true**, $\forall i \le n$
4: **for** $j = 1$ to N **do**
5: $t_1^{(i)} \leftarrow$ **false**, $\forall i \le n$
6: **for** $k = 1$ to $n - 45$ **do**
7: $d \leftarrow min(\beta, n-k+1)$; $e \leftarrow k + d$; $\tau \leftarrow$ **false**
8: **for** $k' = k$ to e **do** $\tau \leftarrow \tau \| t_0^{(k')}$
9: **end for**
10: $\log \mathrm{vol}\left(\Lambda_{[k,e]}\right) \leftarrow \sum_{i=1}^{e-1} \ell_i - \sum_{i=1}^{k-1} \widehat{\ell}_i$
11: **if** $\tau =$ **true then**
12: $X \hookleftarrow \mathrm{Expo}[1/2]$; $g \leftarrow \left(\log X + \log \mathrm{vol}\left(\Lambda_{[k,e]}\right) - \log v_d\right)/d$
13: **if** $g < l_k$ **then**
14: $\widehat{\ell}_k \leftarrow g$; $\widehat{\ell}_{k+1} \leftarrow \ell_k + \log(\sqrt{1 - 1/d})$
15: $\gamma \leftarrow (\ell_k + \ell_{k+1}) - \left(\widehat{\ell}_k + \widehat{\ell}_{k+1}\right)$
16: **for** $k' = k+2$ to e **do**
17: $\widehat{\ell}_{k'} \leftarrow \ell_{k'} + \gamma/(d-2)$; $t_1^{(k')} \leftarrow$ **true**
18: **end for**
19: $\tau \leftarrow$ **false**
20: **end if**
21: **end if**
22: $\{\ell_k, \cdots, \ell_{e-1}\} \leftarrow \left\{\widehat{\ell}_k, \cdots, \widehat{\ell}_{e-1}\right\}$
23: **end for**
24: $\log \mathrm{vol}\left(\Lambda_{[k,e]}\right) \leftarrow \sum_{i=1}^{n} \ell_i - \sum_{i=1}^{n-45} \widehat{\ell}_i$
25: **for** $k' = n - 44$ **to** n **do**
26: $\widehat{\ell}_{k'} \leftarrow \frac{\log \mathrm{vol}\left(\Lambda_{[k,e]}\right)}{45} + r_{k'+45-n}$; $t_1^{(k')} \leftarrow$ **true**
27: **end for**

$\{\ell_1, \cdots, \ell_n\} \leftarrow \left\{\widehat{\ell}_1, \cdots, \widehat{\ell}_n\right\}$; $\left\{t_0^{(1)}, \cdots, t_0^{(n)}\right\} \leftarrow \left\{t_1^{(1)}, \cdots, t_1^{(n)}\right\}$

end for

3 Second Order Statistical Behavior for q-ary Lattice

The difference between two consecutive Gram-Schmidt log-norms $r_i := \log \|\boldsymbol{b}_i^*\| - \log \|\boldsymbol{b}_{i+1}^*\|$ reflect the slope of the shape of Gram-Schmidt log-norms after BKZ$-\beta$ reduced. For a basis $\boldsymbol{B}$ of an n-dimensional lattice $\mathcal{L}$, the root Hermite factor $\mathrm{rhf}(\boldsymbol{B}) = \left(\frac{\|\boldsymbol{b}_1\|}{\mathrm{vol}(\mathcal{L})^{1/n}}\right)^{1/n}$, as a measure of the quality of a reduced basis in [11], can be represented as $\mathrm{rhf}(\boldsymbol{B}) = \exp\left(\frac{1}{n^2}\sum_{1\leq i\leq n-1}(n-i)r_i(\mathbf{B})\right)$ in terms of r_i. This means that the root Hermite factor can be assessed and analyzed by measuring the r_i. Based on the above reasons, extensive experiments in [26] have been conducted to reveal second order statistical behavior for running BKZ on random lattices.

Motivated by their idea, we consider the issue of exploring the second order statistical behaviors of the BKZ algorithm for q-ary lattices with a lot of experiments and compare it with that of random lattices. From an actual cryptography perspective, we are more interested in three types of $q-$ary lattice. The first family consists of random $q-$ary lattices corresponding to LWE with $\boldsymbol{A}$ being uniform, and the other two families are original circulant NTRU and matrix NTRU as mentioned in Subsect. 2.2. The sampling procedures of random q-ary lattices produced by fpylll [24] and original circulant NTRU and matrix NTRU are sampled according to [10]. In order to achieve a greater rate of convergence, we use a simplified progressive strategy that is to run BKZ algorithm with blocksize $\beta' = 2, 3, 4 \ldots \beta$ progressively. It is noted that for original circulant NTRU and matrix NTRU, we only show the cases for parameters $n = 140, \beta = 5, 10$, in order to avoid the probability of finding short vectors. Meanwhile, in order to avoid the influence of overstretched q described in [10], q is set to be 31. As conclusion, the root Hermite factor can also be quantitatively handled for q-ary lattices. Some analysis is given as well. All the results and verification codes are provided in https://github.com/zzszhao/behavior-and-simulator.

3.1 The Mean and Variance of r_i

From Fig. 1, the curves of the mean and the variance of random variable r_i inside the body are nearly complete overlap and are almost horizontal for the various n but the same β, which implies it seems depends on β only. In [26], it gave a strong claim that the distribution of r_i inside the body doesn't depend on i for random lattices and ran the Kolmogorov-Smirnov test [18] on samples of r_i and r_j for varying i, j to verify this claim. In this paper, we also ran the Kolmogorov-Smirnov test in Fig. 2 to confirm that the strong claim still holds for q-ary lattices. In this figure, a black pixel at coordinate (i, j) represent that the fact that the pair of distributions $\mathbb{D}_i(\beta, 100)$ and $\mathbb{D}_j(\beta, 100)$ passed Kolmogorov-Smirnov Test, *i.e.* two distributions are close.

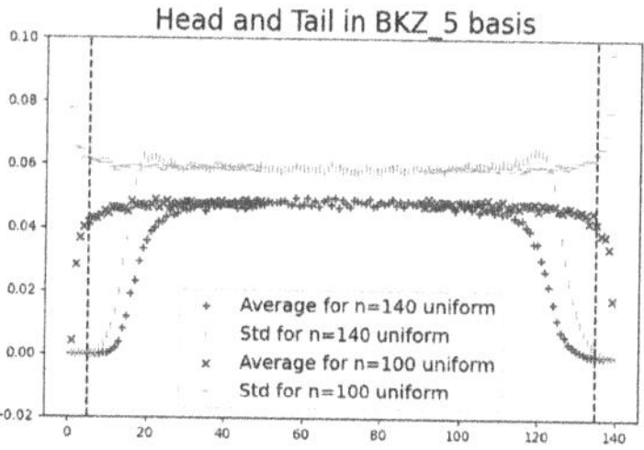

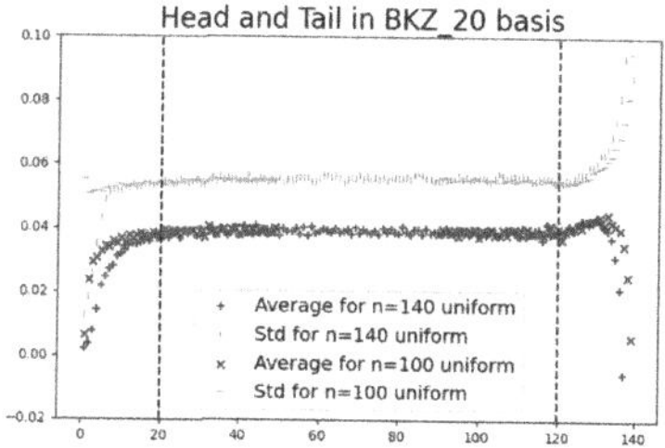

Fig. 1. Average value and standard deviation of r_i as a function of index i based on over 5000 samples with dimension $n = 100, 140$. First halves $\{r_i\}_{i \le (n-1)/2}$ are left-justified while last halves $\{r_i\}_{i \ge (n-1)/2}$ are right-justified in order to observe heads and tails. The blue curves and red curves denotes the mean and variance of r_i respectively. Dashed lines mark indices β and $n - \beta$. Plots look similar for various β and thus are omitted.

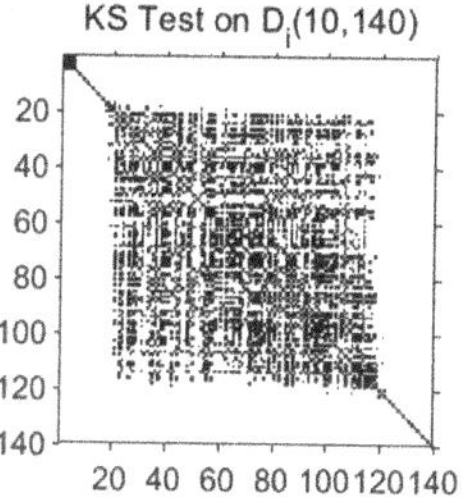

(a) Circulant NTRU lattices

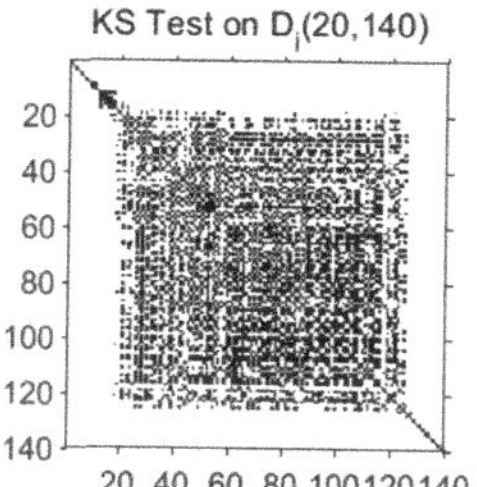

(b) Random q-ary lattices

Fig. 2. Kolmogorov-Smirnov test with significance level 0.05 on all $\mathbb{D}_j(\beta, 100)$'s calculated from 5000 samples. Plots look similar for various β and thus are omitted.

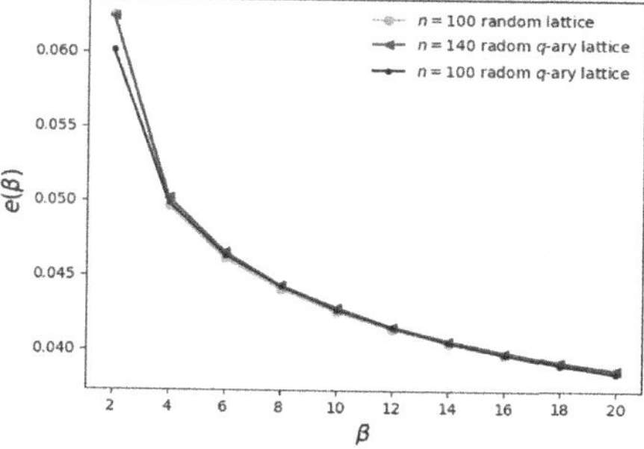

Fig. 3. Experimental measure of e(β)

In [26], the expectation of r_i inside the body is denoted by $e(\beta)$. The experimental measure of $e(\beta)$ from 5000 random 100-dimensional and 5000 random 140-dimensional q-ary BKZ $_\beta$-reduced bases are exhibited in Fig. 3. In order to compare actual BKZ behaviors between q-ary lattices and random lattices, we also plot the experimental measure of $e(\beta)$ from [26] from 5000 random 100-dimensional BKZ$_\beta$-reduced bases. The curves of the experimental measure of $e(\beta)$ almost coincide.

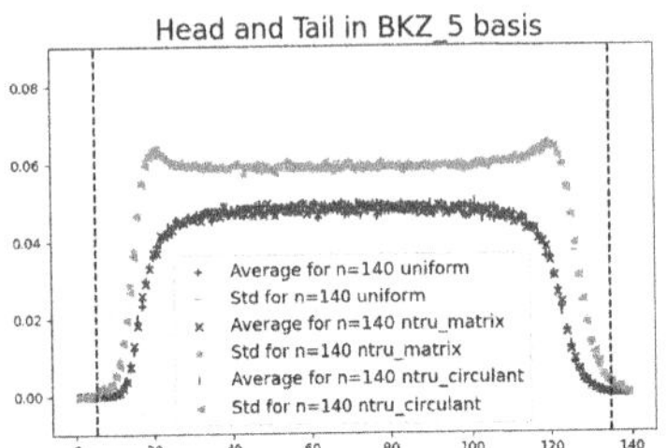

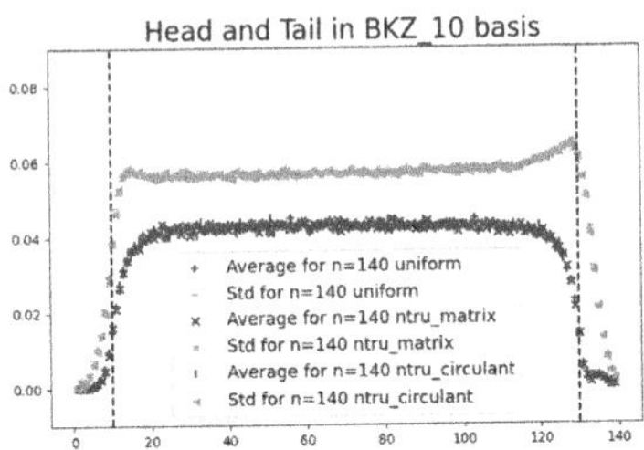

Fig. 4. Average value and standard deviation of r_i as a function of index i based on over 5000 samples with three types of 140-dimensional q-ary lattices. The blue curves and red curves denotes the mean and variance of r_i respectively. Dashed lines mark indices β and $n-\beta$. (Color figure online)

From Fig. 4, the curves for three types of $q-$ary lattices nearly coincide and exhibit Z-shape. Meanwhile, the range of r_i is divided into five pieces: the initial horizontal part, the head, the body, the tail, and the final horizontal part. But in Fig. 1, when Z-shape is destroyed for large block-size β, the range of r_i can be divided into three pieces: the head, the body and the tail. This is similar to the cases in random lattices. This observation is utilized to simulate further the behavior of BKZ algorithm for q-ary lattices in Sect. 4.2 when Z-shape is destroyed.

3.2 Local Correlations and Global Variance

From $\mathrm{rhf}(\boldsymbol{B}) = \left(\frac{\|b_1\|}{\mathrm{vol}(\mathcal{L})^{1/n}}\right)^{1/n}$, we have $\ln(\mathrm{rhf}(\mathbf{B})) = \frac{1}{n^2}\sum_{1\leq i\leq n-1}(n-i)r_i(\mathbf{B})$. So

$$n^4\,\mathrm{Var}(\ln(\mathrm{rhf}(\mathbf{B}))) = \sum_{i=1}^{n-1}(n-i)^2\,\mathrm{Var}\left(r_i\right) + 2\sum_{i<j}(n-i)(n-j)\,\mathrm{Cov}\left(r_i, r_j\right).$$

To compute the variance of the root Hermite factor (which is called the global variance), one needs to calculate the covariance matrices $\mathrm{Cov}(\boldsymbol{r})$ with $\boldsymbol{r} = (r_1, \ldots, r_{n-1})$ and variance of r_i computed in Sect. 3.1. The covariance matrices of $\boldsymbol{r}$ is exhibited in Fig. 5. The diagonal entries $\mathrm{Cov}\left(r_i, r_i\right)$ are equal to the variance of r_i and thus are set to 0 to enhance contrast. The entries on the second diagonals seem different when other entries seem very close to 0. Thus we shall pay more attention to covariance $\mathrm{Cov}\left(r_i, r_{i+1}\right)$ between r_i and r_{i+1}, and call it a local correlation.

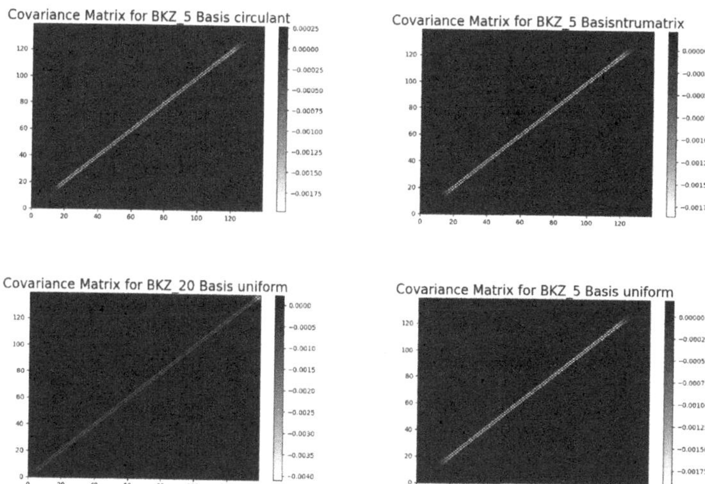

Fig. 5. Covariance matrices of $\boldsymbol{r}$. Experimental values measured over 5000 samples with three types of 140-dimensional q-ary lattices with block-size $\beta = 5, 20$. Plots look similar for various β, n and thus are omitted.

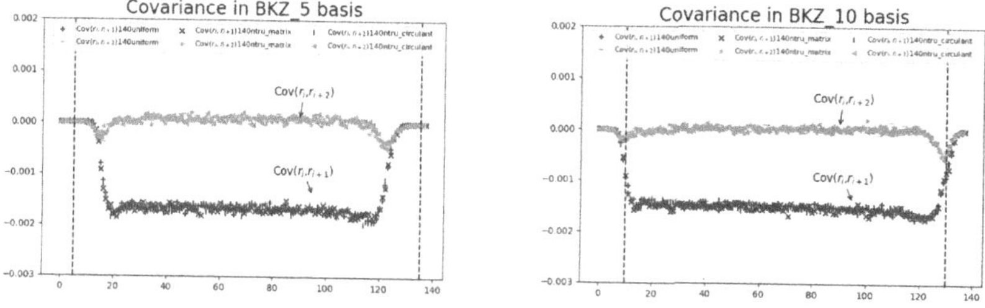

Fig. 6. Cov (r_i, r_{i+1}) and Cov (r_i, r_{i+2}) as a function of i, are denoted by blue curves and red curves separately. Experimental values measured over 5000 samples with three types of 140-dimensional q-ary lattices. Dashed lines mark indices β and $n - \beta$.

The experimental measure of Cov (r_i, r_{i+1}) and Cov (r_i, r_{i+2}) are plotted in Figs. 6, 7. For other Cov (r_i, r_{i+d}) with large $d > 2$, the curves always are observed as a horizontal asymptote at $y = 0$ and thus are not plotted for readability.

Our experiments verify that many claims remain valid for q-ary lattices. The curves for three types of q-ary lattices nearly coincide in Fig. 6. In Fig. 7, the curves of Cov (r_i, r_{i+1}) and Cov (r_i, r_{i+2}) inside the body is nearly complete overlap and almost horizontal for the various n but same β, that it depends on β only. Thus two functions of $v(\beta)$ and $c(\beta)$ are introduced to denote the expectation of Var (r_i) and Cov (r_i, r_j) in the body respectively.

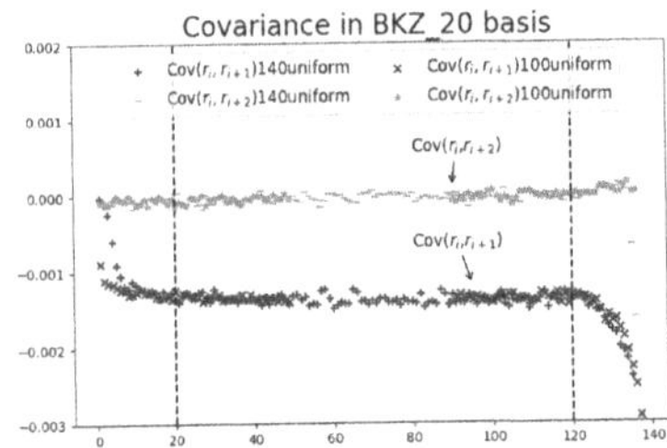

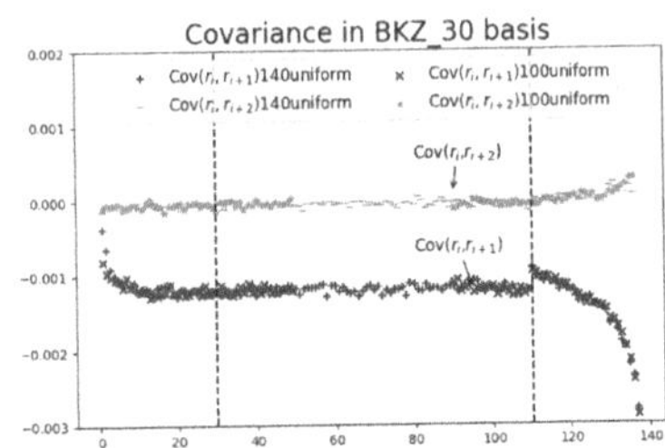

Fig. 7. Cov (r_i, r_{i+1}) and Cov (r_i, r_{i+2}) as a function of index i based on over 5000 samples with dimension $n = 100, 140$, are denoted by blue curves and red curves separately. First halves are left-justified while last halves are right-justified in order to observe heads and tails. Dashed lines mark indices β and $n - \beta$.

But some experimental measure of Cov (r_i, r_{i+2}) might have something different between random lattices and q-ary lattices. For random lattices, Cov (r_i, r_{i+2}) is 0 for all i. It is entirely true inside the body for q-ary lattices, but Cov (r_i, r_{i+2}) has a slight deviation in the tail when Z-shape is destroyed and also in the head and the tail when Z-shape remains, shown in Fig. 6, 7. But it doesn't influence their corollary. Following is a brief description of the corollary.

Corollary 3. *For a fixed block-size β and as the dimension n grows, it holds that*

$$\mathrm{Var}(\ln(\mathrm{rhf}(\mathbf{B}))) = \frac{1}{3n}v(\beta) + \frac{2}{3n}c(\beta) + O\left(\frac{1}{n^2}\right)$$

Proof.

$$\begin{aligned} n^4\,\mathrm{Var}(\ln(\mathrm{rhf}(\mathbf{B}))) &= \sum_{i=1}^{n-1}(n-i)^2\,\mathrm{Var}\,(r_i) + 2\sum_{i<j}(n-i)(n-j)\,\mathrm{Cov}\,(r_i, r_j) \\ &= \sum_{i=1}^{n-1}(n-i)^2\,\mathrm{Var}\,(r_i) + 2\sum_{i=1}^{n-2}(n-i)(n-i-1)\,\mathrm{Cov}\,(r_i, r_{i+1}) \\ &+ 2\sum_{i\le h, i\ge n-t}(n-i)(n-i-1)\,\mathrm{Cov}\,(r_i, r_{i+2}) \end{aligned}$$

Since both h and t are constant, all Var (r_i), Cov (r_i, r_{i+1}) and Cov (r_i, r_{i+2}) inside the head and tail are of size $O(1)$. Thus the two sums in the head and tail are $O(n^2)$, then:

$$2\sum_{i\le h, i\ge n-t}(n-i)(n-i-1)\,\mathrm{Cov}\,(r_i, r_{i+2}) = O\left(n^2\right)$$

$$\sum_{h<i<n-t}(n-i)^2\,\mathrm{Var}\,(r_i) = \sum_{i=1}^{n-1}(n-i)^2\,\mathrm{Var}(r) + O\left(n^2\right) = \tfrac{n^3}{3}v(\beta) + O\left(n^2\right)$$

$$\sum_{h<i<n-t} (n-i)(n-i-1)\,\mathrm{Cov}\,(r_i, r_{i+1}) = \sum_{i=1}^{n-2} (n-i)(n-i-1)c(\beta) + O\left(n^2\right) = \tfrac{n^3}{3}c(\beta) + O\left(n^2\right)$$

A straightforward computation then completes the proof. □

4 A Simulator Tailored for q-ary Lattice

In this section, we start by describing the Albrecht-Li BKZ simulator tailored for random q-ary lattices, and then propose a new simulator that captures the head concavity phenomenon when Z-shape is destroyed. It is remarked that the Albrecht-Li simulator misses this phenomenon.

4.1 The Albrecht-Li BKZ Simulator Tailored for Random q-ary Lattices

Albrecht and Li [3] has made some progress in simulating the random q-ary lattice by extracting heuristic analogues of Hermite's constants are tailored for BKZ-reduced random q-ary bases. It is referred to in **line 1–3** and is applied in **line 11** of Algorithm 4. The heuristic analogues of Hermite's constants is computed by extensive experiment and the fact that BKZ algorithm first pre-process each projected block $\mathbf{B}_{[i,n_i)}$ using BKZ recursively with a smaller block size (say, β_i - 20) and then invoke an SVP-solver on it, so that $\mathbf{B}_{[i,n_i)}$ indeed becomes approximately HKZ-reduced at the end of the i-th BKZ iteration. We call the Algorithm 4 and compare it with the actual behavior of BKZ algorithm in Fig. 8 and Fig. 9 as implemented in fpylll.

Algorithm 4. The Albrecht-Li BKZ simulator tailored for random q-ary lattices

---

Input: (k, n, q, ξ), where $q \geq 17$ is the prime modulus, k is the number of $q\mathbf{e}_i$-vectors, n is the dimension, and the scale $\xi \in \mathbb{Z}^+$ such that $q/\xi \geq 37/4$

Output: A prediction of the Gram-Schmidt log-norms $\left\{\widehat{\ell_i} = \log \|\mathbf{b}_i^*\|\right\}_{i\leq n}$ after running N tours of BKZ-reduction with block size $\beta \in [50, n)$

1: **for** $i = 1$ to β **do**
2: By equation, extract the heuristic analog r_i of Hermite's constant Υ_i in the context of BKZ-reducing random q'-ary bases with scale $\xi' \in \mathbb{Z}^+$ s.t. $q'/\xi' \geq 37/4$
3: $c_i \leftarrow \log \sqrt{r_i}$
4: **end for**
5: **for** $i = 0$ to $k-1$ **do**
6: $\ell_i \leftarrow \log q$; $\ell_{i+k} \leftarrow \log \xi$
7: **end for**
8: **for** $j = 0$ to $N-1$ **do**
9: **for** $i = 0$ to $n-2$ **do**
10: $g \leftarrow \sum_{p=i}^{n_i-1} \ell_p$
11: **if** $\ell_i > c_{\beta_i} + g/\beta_i$ **then**

```
        for s = i to n_i − 1 do
            ℓ_s ← c_t + (g − Σ_{p=i}^{s−1} ℓ_p) /t where t = n_i − s is the rank of local
    block B_[s,n_i)
        end for
      end if
    end for
end for
return (ℓ_0, ..., ℓ_{n−1})
```

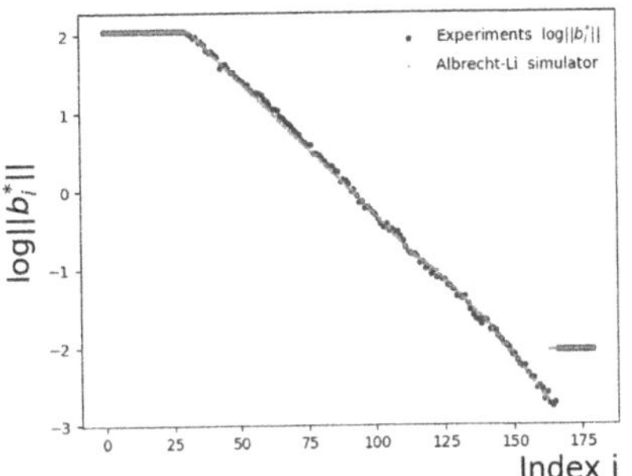

Fig. 8. Gram-Schmidt log-norms for BKZ_{50} 2.0 at tour 16.

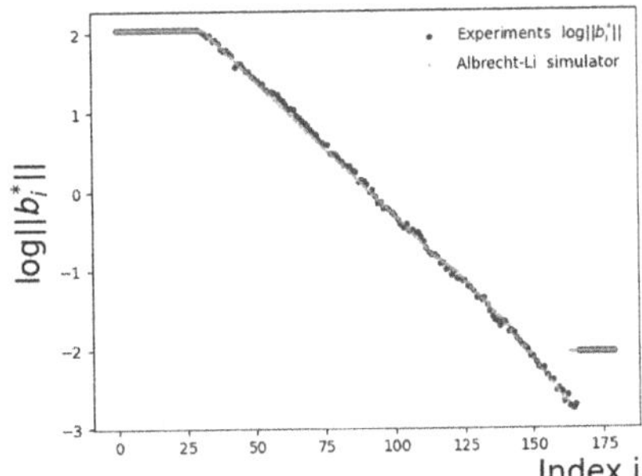

Fig. 9. Gram-Schmidt log-norms for BKZ_{60} 2.0 at tour 16.

4.2 A New Simulator for Random q-ary Lattices

In our experimentation with the method from [3], some discrepancies are observed, especially in the head region when Z-shape disappears. To solve this problem, we utilize the emulation of the probabilistic nature in Theorem 1. It is noted that this theorem has been applied in Bai-Stehlé-Wen simulator for the random lattice to capture the head regions. Meanwhile, we choose the Heuristic ZGSA as an estimator. The disappearance of Z-shape is accepted when $m = \frac{1}{2} + \frac{\ln(q)}{2\ln(\alpha_\beta)} > n$, and we bring in the probabilistic nature in **line 17** and heuristic analogues of Hermite's constants in **line 1–3, 17, 31** of Algorithm 5. Otherwise, when Z-shape exists, we directly invoke Algorithm 4. The new simulator is described in Algorithm 5.

Algorithm 5. A new simulator tailored for random q-ary lattices

Input: (k, n, q, ξ), where $q \geq 17$ is the prime modulus, k is the number of $q\mathbf{e}_i$-vectors, n is the dimension, and the scale $\xi \in \mathbb{Z}^+$ such that $q/\xi \geq 37/4$

Output: A prediction of the Gram-Schmidt log-norms $\left\{\widehat{\ell_i} = \log \|\mathbf{b}_i^*\|\right\}_{i \leq n}$ after running N tours of BKZ-reduction with block size $\beta \in [50, n)$

1: **for** $i = 1$ to β **do**

By equation, extract the heuristic analog r_i of Hermite's constant Υ_i in the context of BKZ-reducing random q'-ary bases with scale $\xi' \in \mathbb{Z}^+$ s.t. $q'/\xi' \geq 37/4$
  $c_i \leftarrow \log \sqrt{r_i}$
end for
if $n/2 - 1/2 - \frac{\ln q}{2 \ln \alpha_\beta} > 0$ **then** call Algorithm 4; **break**
for $i = 0$ to $k-1$ **do** $\ell_i \leftarrow \log q$; $\ell_{k+i} \leftarrow \log \xi$ **end for**
for $j = 1$ to N **do**
  $t_1^{(i)} \leftarrow$ **false**, $\forall i \leq n$
  for $k = 1$ to $n - t$ **do**
    $d \leftarrow min(\beta, n-k+1)$; $e \leftarrow k + d$; $\tau \leftarrow$ **false**
    for $k' = k$ to e **do** $\tau \leftarrow \tau \| t_0^{(k')}$ **end for**
    $\log \mathrm{vol}\left(\Lambda_{[k,e]}\right) \leftarrow \sum_{i=1}^{e-1} \ell_i - \sum_{i=1}^{k-1} \widehat{\ell}_i$
    if $\tau =$ **true then**
      $X \hookleftarrow \mathrm{Expo}[1/2]$; $g \leftarrow \left(\log X + \log \mathrm{vol}\left(\Lambda_{[k,e]}\right)\right)/d + c_d$
      if $g < l_k$ **then**
        $\widehat{\ell}_k \leftarrow g$; $\widehat{\ell}_{k+1} \leftarrow \ell_k + \log(\sqrt{1 - 1/d})$
        $\gamma \leftarrow (\ell_k + \ell_{k+1}) - \left(\widehat{\ell}_k + \widehat{\ell}_{k+1}\right)$
        for $k' = k + 2$ to e **do**
          $\widehat{\ell}_{k'} \leftarrow \ell_{k'} + \gamma/(d-2)$; $t_1^{(k')} \leftarrow$ **true**
        end for
        $\tau \leftarrow$ **false**
      end if
    end if
    $\{\ell_k, \cdots, \ell_{e-1}\} \leftarrow \left\{\widehat{\ell}_k, \cdots, \widehat{\ell}_{e-1}\right\}$
  end for
  $\log \mathrm{V} \leftarrow \sum_{i=1}^{n} \ell_i - \sum_{i=1}^{n-tl} \widehat{\ell}_i$
  for $k' = n - 50$ **to** n **do**
    $\widehat{\ell}_{k'} \leftarrow \frac{\log \mathrm{V}}{n-k'} + c_{n-k'}$; $\log \mathrm{V} = \log \mathrm{V} - \widehat{\ell}_{k'}$; $t_1^{(k')} \leftarrow$ **true**
  end for
  $\{\ell_1, \cdots, \ell_n\} \leftarrow \left\{\widehat{\ell}_1, \cdots, \widehat{\ell}_n\right\}$; $\left\{t_0^{(1)}, \cdots, t_0^{(n)}\right\} \leftarrow \left\{t_1^{(1)}, \cdots, t_1^{(n)}\right\}$
end for

4.3 Impact of New Simulator Tailored for Random q-ary Lattices

In this subsection, we measure the quality of our new simulator for random q-ary lattices when Z-shape disappears by comparing with the Albrecht-Li simulator and the practical behavior of the BKZ algorithm using two quantities: the Gram-Schmidt log-norms and the root Hermite factors. Experiments show that our simulator fits better with the practical behavior of BKZ algorithm. We point out that a similar, such improvement was reported in [5] for comparison between Chen-Nguyen simulator and Bai-Stehlé-Wen simulator.

(a) Graph of Gram-Schmidt Log-Norms. In reality, measuring the entrie sequence of Gram-Schmidt is important for assessing the quality of a reduced basis. We consider the following experiments: the input lattice are random q-ary lattices with dimension 120, and we use BKZ_{50} 2.0 [8] in fpylll [24] to measure the average value of the full sequence of Gram-Schmidt basis. As shown in Fig. 10, our new simulator can capture the head regions (Fig. 11).

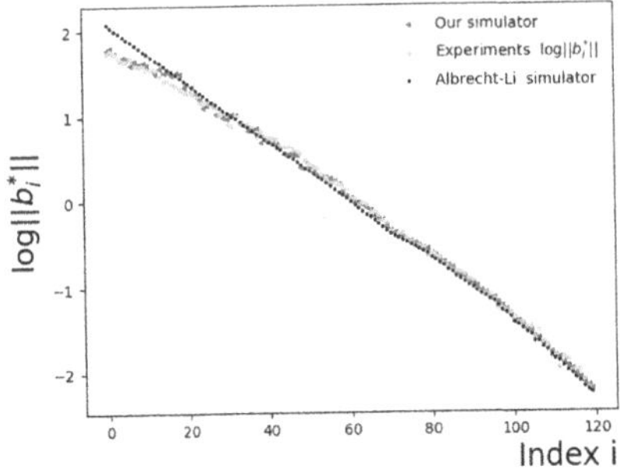

Fig. 10. Gram-Schmidt log-norms for BKZ_{50} 2.0 at tour 3000.

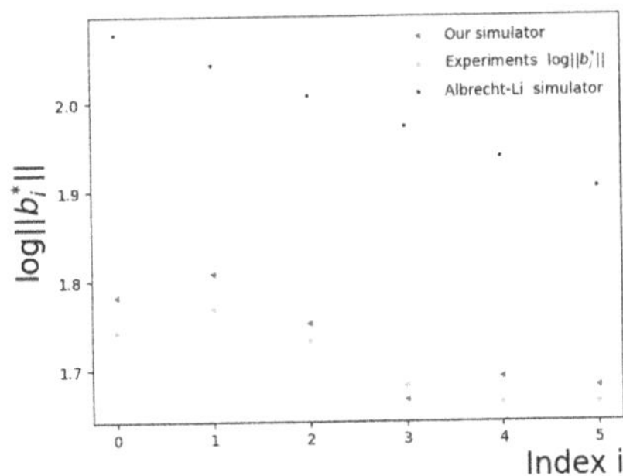

Fig. 11. Same as left hand side, but zoomed in.

(b) Root Hermite Factor. By measuring and recording the root Hermite factors in Fig. 12 obtained with our new simulator, the Albrecht-Li simulator and the BKZ algorithm, we can observe our new simulator predict the experimental data more accurately. As the number of tours increases, asymptotic lines of root Hermite factors obtained by our new simulator and by the BKZ algorithm are getting closer, but asymptotic lines of root Hermite factors obtained by Albrecht-Li simulator and by the BKZ algorithm are at a distance away.

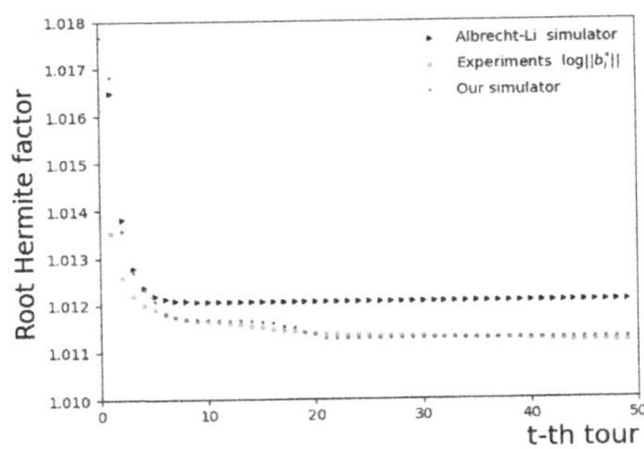

Fig. 12. The root Hermite factor during the execution of BKZ_{50} 2.0 with 120-dimensional q-ary lattices

5 Conclusion

The second order statistical behaviors of BKZ algorithm had been measured for random lattices in the literature. In order to better observe and understand the q-ary lattices, this paper gives a study of these behaviors for three types of q-ary lattices. Comparison to that of the random lattices is made, similarities and differences are briefly analyzed. The results lead to a new simulator tailored for random q-ay lattices to better capture the head phenomenon and maintain a pretty good approximation in other regions when Z-shape is destroyed.

Acknowledgements. We are very grateful to Dr. Yang Yu for helpful discussions. We also thank the anonymous reviewers for their valuable comments. This work is supported by the National Natural Science Foundation of China (No. 12271306), and by the National Key Research and Development Program of China (No. 2018YFA0704702).

References

1. Albrecht, M.R.: On dual lattice attacks against small-secret LWE and parameter choices in HElib and SEAL. In: Coron, J.-S., Nielsen, J.B. (eds.) EUROCRYPT 2017. LNCS, vol. 10211, pp. 103–129. Springer, Cham (2017). https://doi.org/10.1007/978-3-319-56614-6_4
2. Albrecht, M.R., Ducas, L.: Lattice attacks on NTRU and LWE: a history of refinements. Cryptology ePrint Archive (2021)
3. Albrecht, M.R., Li, J.: Predicting BKZ Z-shapes on q-ary lattices. Cryptology ePrint Archive (2022)
4. Aono, Y., Wang, Y., Hayashi, T., Takagi, T.: Improved progressive BKZ algorithms and their precise cost estimation by sharp simulator. In: Fischlin, M., Coron, J.-S. (eds.) EUROCRYPT 2016. LNCS, vol. 9665, pp. 789–819. Springer, Heidelberg (2016). https://doi.org/10.1007/978-3-662-49890-3_30
5. Bai, S., Stehlé, D., Wen, W.: Measuring, simulating and exploiting the head concavity phenomenon in BKZ. In: Peyrin, T., Galbraith, S. (eds.) ASIACRYPT 2018. LNCS, vol. 11272, pp. 369–404. Springer, Cham (2018). https://doi.org/10.1007/978-3-030-03326-2_13
6. Brakerski, Z., Vaikuntanathan, V.: Efficient fully homomorphic encryption from (standard) LWE. SIAM J. Comput. **43**(2), 831–871 (2014)
7. Chen, Y.: Réduction de réseau et sécurité concrete du chiffrement completement homomorphe. Ph.D. thesis, Paris 7 (2013)
8. Chen, Y., Nguyen, P.Q.: BKZ 2.0: better lattice security estimates. In: Lee, D.H., Wang, X. (eds.) ASIACRYPT 2011. LNCS, vol. 7073, pp. 1–20. Springer, Heidelberg (2011). https://doi.org/10.1007/978-3-642-25385-0_1
9. Ducas, L., et al.: Crystals-dilithium: a lattice-based digital signature scheme. IACR Transactions on Cryptographic Hardware and Embedded Systems, pp. 238–268 (2018)
10. Ducas, L., van Woerden, W.: NTRU fatigue: how stretched is overstretched? In: Tibouchi, M., Wang, H. (eds.) ASIACRYPT 2021. LNCS, vol. 13093, pp. 3–32. Springer, Cham (2021). https://doi.org/10.1007/978-3-030-92068-5_1
11. Gama, N., Nguyen, P.Q.: Predicting lattice reduction. In: Smart, N. (ed.) EUROCRYPT 2008. LNCS, vol. 4965, pp. 31–51. Springer, Heidelberg (2008). https://doi.org/10.1007/978-3-540-78967-3_3

12. Genise, N., Gentry, C., Halevi, S., Li, B., Micciancio, D.: Homomorphic encryption for finite automata. In: Galbraith, S.D., Moriai, S. (eds.) ASIACRYPT 2019. LNCS, vol. 11922, pp. 473–502. Springer, Cham (2019). https://doi.org/10.1007/978-3-030-34621-8_17
13. Gentry, C., Peikert, C., Vaikuntanathan, V.: Trapdoors for hard lattices and new cryptographic constructions. In: Proceedings of the Fortieth Annual ACM Symposium on Theory of Computing, pp. 197–206 (2008)
14. Hoffstein, J., Pipher, J., Schanck, J.M., Silverman, J.H., Whyte, W., Zhang, Z.: Choosing parameters for NTRUEncrypt. In: Handschuh, H. (ed.) CT-RSA 2017. LNCS, vol. 10159, pp. 3–18. Springer, Cham (2017). https://doi.org/10.1007/978-3-319-52153-4_1
15. Hoffstein, J., Pipher, J., Silverman, J.H.: NTRU: a ring-based public key cryptosystem. In: Buhler, J.P. (ed.) ANTS 1998. LNCS, vol. 1423, pp. 267–288. Springer, Heidelberg (1998). https://doi.org/10.1007/BFb0054868
16. Howgrave-Graham, N.: A hybrid lattice-reduction and meet-in-the-middle attack against NTRU. In: Menezes, A. (ed.) CRYPTO 2007. LNCS, vol. 4622, pp. 150–169. Springer, Heidelberg (2007). https://doi.org/10.1007/978-3-540-74143-5_9
17. Lenstra, A.K., Lenstra, H.W., Lovász, L.: Factoring polynomials with rational coefficients. Mathematische annalen **261**(Article), 515–534 (1982)
18. Massey, F.J., Jr.: The kolmogorov-smirnov test for goodness of fit. J. Am. Stat. Assoc. **46**(253), 68–78 (1951)
19. Micciancio, D., Walter, M.: Practical, predictable lattice basis reduction. In: Fischlin, M., Coron, J.-S. (eds.) EUROCRYPT 2016. LNCS, vol. 9665, pp. 820–849. Springer, Heidelberg (2016). https://doi.org/10.1007/978-3-662-49890-3_31
20. Regev, O.: On lattices, learning with errors, random linear codes, and cryptography. J. ACM (JACM) **56**(6), 1–40 (2009)
21. Schnorr, C.P.: Lattice reduction by random sampling and birthday methods. In: Alt, H., Habib, M. (eds.) STACS 2003. LNCS, vol. 2607, pp. 145–156. Springer, Heidelberg (2003). https://doi.org/10.1007/3-540-36494-3_14
22. Schnorr, C.P., Euchner, M.: Lattice basis reduction: improved practical algorithms and solving subset sum problems. Math. Program. **66**(1), 181–199 (1994)
23. Södergren, A.: On the poisson distribution of lengths of lattice vectors in a random lattice. Math. Z. **269**(3), 945–954 (2011)
24. Fpylll, a Python wraper for the Fplll lattice reduction library, Version: 0.5.7 (2021). https://github.com/fplll/fpylll
25. Wunderer, T.: A detailed analysis of the hybrid lattice-reduction and meet-in-the-middle attack. J. Math. Cryptol. **13**(1), 1–26 (2019)
26. Yu, Y., Ducas, L.: Second order statistical behavior of LLL and BKZ. In: Adams, C., Camenisch, J. (eds.) SAC 2017. LNCS, vol. 10719, pp. 3–22. Springer, Cham (2018). https://doi.org/10.1007/978-3-319-72565-9_1
27. Zhang, Z., et al.: NTRU-technical report, national institute of standards and technology. NIST National Institute of Standards and Technology (2020)

Inferring Sequences Produced by the Quadratic Generator

Jing Gao[1,2], Jun Xu[1,2](✉), and Lei Hu[1,2]

[1] State Key Laboratory of Information Security, Institute of Information Engineering, Chinese Academy of Sciences, Beijing 100093, China
xujun@iie.ac.cn

[2] School of Cyber Security, University of Chinese Academy of Sciences, Beijing 100093, China

Abstract. The Quadratic generator is one of the number theoretic pseudorandom number generators. It works by iterating an algebraic map $F(V_i) = V_{i+1} = aV_i^2 + b \bmod p$ on a secret random initial seed V_0. In this paper, we use the iterative relation of the Quadratic generator to reconstruct the relevant modular equation and improve the security bound from $\frac{1}{5}$ to $\frac{1}{4}$ in the case of multiplier a known and shift b unknown, based on Coppersmith's method for finding small roots of the modular equation. That is, in the case that the bit size of the unknown variable is $\frac{1}{4}$ of the modulus, we can recover the initial seed V_0, the map F, and the subsequent sequence.

Keywords: Nonlinear pseudorandom number generators · Quadratic generator · Coppersmith's method

1 Introduction

Pseudorandom number generators play an important role in cryptography, and they have various uses in many places, such as public-key signatures, encryption schemes, etc. A pseudorandom number generator is a deterministic algorithm that expands an initial random seed into a longer number that is indistinguishable from a uniform random number. It works by iterating over a secret random initial seed V_0, with each iteration outputting some consecutive bits of the intermediate value V_i, where $V_i = F(V_{i-1}) \bmod p$, and F is an algebraic map. Therefore, its security is closely related to the number of output bits.

When F is an affine function, the pseudorandom number generator is called a linear congruential generator, which is efficient and has good statistical properties. However, it is insecure in cryptography. One after another, it has been shown that one can recover the seed V_0 in polynomial time about p, even knowing

The work of this paper was supported by the National Natural Science Foundation of China (No. 61732021 and No. 62272454) and the National Key Research and Development Project (No. 2018YFA0704704).

Y. Deng and M. Yung (Eds.): Inscrypt 2022, LNCS 13837, pp. 483–494, 2023.
https://doi.org/10.1007/978-3-031-26553-2_26

only the most significant bit of each output V_i, when the pseudorandom sequence is long enough [7,8,16,17]. Therefore, it has been suggested to use nonlinear map F to avoid these attacks. However, the works [2–5,11,12] demonstrated that a nonlinear pseudorandom number generator is also insecure when the output bits during the iteration exceed a certain bound, i.e., the generator is polynomially time predictable when a sufficient number of consecutive output values of the pseudorandom sequence are known, even if the degree of F is known but no specific F is known.

The work in this paper focuses on the Quadratic generator, which corresponds to the map $F(x) = ax^2 + b \bmod p$. There has been a lot of work as well as improvements in inferring sequences for the Quadratic generator. The table below shows the work in various cases of the multiplier a and shift b, known or unknown, where the number of known outputs is limited. The symbol – indicates that the corresponding cases were not considered in that paper.

The Quadratic generator	[4]	[2]	[11]
a, b known	$\frac{1}{4}$	$\frac{1}{4}$	$\frac{1}{3}$
a known, b unkonwn	–	$\frac{1}{5}$	–
a, b unkonwn	$\frac{1}{19}$	–	$\frac{1}{12}$

The Coppersmith method is a powerful tool in the field of cryptanalysis. In 1996, Coppersmith introduced a lattice-based method for finding small roots in polynomial time on univariate modular polynomial equations [10] and bivariate integer equations [9]. The Coppersmith method works by finding linear combinations of equations with common roots that have small coefficients such that the new equations hold on the integers. Thus, the desired root can be found by standard root-finding algorithms. In general, the Coppersmith method we usually use now is a simple reformulation given by Howgrave-Graham [13] that has been widely adopted. As these techniques have a wide range of cryptanalytic applications, some generalizations to more variables have been proposed [1,6] with some heuristic assumptions to find the desired roots by computing the resultants or Gröbner basis algorithms.

In 2006, Jochemsz and May [15] described a general strategy to construct polynomial sets as well as matrices more simply and analyzed the bounds of the small roots. In 2014, Huang et al. [14] introduced a technique to completely separate a variable from the original equation, which is used in this paper.

Our Contributions. We reconstruct the modular polynomial equation based on the iteration relation of the Quadratic generator. In the previous work, they used the equation $V_i = 2^k w_i + x_i$, with x_i as the unknown variables, where w_i is the known $\pi - k$ bits of the output, x_i is the unknown k bits, and π is the length of the modulo p. Instead, we construct the polynomial equations by making the combinations $x_i - x_{i+1}$ and $x_i + x_{i+1}$ as unknown variables. This construction simplifies the equation form and allows for an easier separation of variables.

We first show how to solve the modular polynomial $f(x_1, x_2, y) = x_1x_2 + ax_1 + bx_2 + cy + d \bmod p$ with bounds on the root in Sect. 3. Then in Sect. 4, the problem of attacking the Quadratic generator is transformed into the problem of solving for the modular polynomial $f(x_1, x_2, y) = x_1x_2 + ax_1 + bx_2 + cy + d \bmod p$, and we can infer the sequence produced by the Quadratic generator in the case that the multiplier a is known and the shift b is unknown, provided that the root bound $X < P^{\frac{1}{4}}$. This result is better than the best result $X < P^{\frac{1}{5}}$ in the previous work [11]. Section 5 gives experiments about the attack on the Quadratic generator when $\pi = 1024$. Section 6 is a conclusion.

2 Preliminaries

The Coppersmith method is a lattice-based technique that can efficiently solve the small roots of modular polynomial equations. Hence, we first introduce some basic definitions and necessary knowledge about the lattice. Then we give a brief overview of the coppersmith method, estimate the bounds of the small roots by the LLL algorithm and Howgrave-Graham's lemma. Finally, we will introduce the Quadratic generator.

2.1 Lattice

Given n linearly independent row vectors $\vec{b}_1, \vec{b}_2, \cdots, \vec{b}_n \in \mathbb{R}^m$, the lattice $\mathcal{L}$ generated by them is defined as follows, that is the set of all integeral linear combinations of the b_i's:

$$\mathcal{L}(\vec{b}_1, \vec{b}_2, \cdots, \vec{b}_n) = \{\sum x_i\vec{b}_i | x_i \in \mathbb{Z}\}.$$

The lattice $\mathcal{L}$ is a discrete subgroup of $\mathbb{R}^m$. We often denote B as the $n \times m$ basis matrix of $\mathcal{L}$ that its rows are the basis vectors $\vec{b}_1, \vec{b}_2, \cdots, \vec{b}_n$. Then the lattice can be written as

$$\mathcal{L}(B) = \{\vec{x}B | \vec{x} \in \mathbb{Z}^n\},$$

where $B = [\vec{b}_1^T, \cdots, \vec{b}_n^T]^T$.

We call $\dim \mathcal{L} = n$ the dimension of $\mathcal{L}$, m its rank and $\det \mathcal{L}$ its determinant. Then the determinant of $\mathcal{L}$ can be computed as

$$\det \mathcal{L} = \sqrt{\det BB^T}.$$

When $n = m$, the lattice is called full rank and $\det \mathcal{L} = |\det B|$.

In 1982, Lenstra et al. presented the most famous deterministic polynomial time algorithm for lattice basis reduction, called the LLL algorithm, to output a reduced basis satisfying the following property.

Lemma 1 (LLL). *Let $\mathcal{L}$ be a n-dimensional integer lattice. Within polynomial time, the LLL algorithm outputs reduced basis vectors $\vec{v}_1, \ldots, \vec{v}_n$ that satisfy*

$$\|\vec{v}_1\| \leq \|\vec{v}_2\| \leq \cdots \leq \|\vec{v}_i\| \leq 2^{\frac{n(n-1)}{4(n+1-i)}} (\det \mathcal{L})^{\frac{1}{n+1-i}}, 1 \leq i \leq n.$$

2.2 Coppersmith's Method

In this subsection, we will review the specific steps of the Coppersmith method.

The first step is to construct more modular polynomials with the same desired roots. Let $f(x_1, \cdots, x_m) \bmod p$ be an multivariate polynomial with a root $(a_1, \cdots, a_n)$ satisfying $|a_1| < X_1, \cdots, |a_m| < X_m$. We generate a collection of polynomials $f_1, \cdots, f_r$ with the same modular root $(a_1, \cdots, a_m)$. Usually, the form of f_i is $x_1^{\alpha_{1,i}} \cdots x_m^{\alpha_{m,i}} f^{k_i} p^{t-k_i}$ which satisfy the relation $f_i(a_1, \cdots, a_m) \equiv 0 \bmod p^t$.

The second step is to construct a matrix with coefficients of these polynomials. Every row of the matrix is the coefficients of $f_i(x_1X_1, \cdots, x_mX_m)$.

Finally, utilize the lattice reduction algorithms such as the LLL algorithm to obtain integer polynomials over $\mathbb{Z}$ with the desired roots. In the process, the following lemma, reformulated by Howgrave-Graham [13], is needed. It states that under which condition a modular equation holds over the integers.

Lemma 2 (Howgrave-Graham). *Let $f(y_1, \ldots, y_m)$ be an integer polynomial that consists of at most ω monomials and $(x_1, \cdots, x_m)$ is the root of f. Let t be a positive integer and the X_i be the upper bound of $|x_i|$ for $i = 1, \cdots, m$. Suppose that*

1. *$f(x_1, \ldots, x_m) = 0 \pmod{p^t}$,*
2. *$\|f(x_1X_1, \ldots, x_mX_m)\| < \frac{p^t}{\sqrt{\omega}}$,*

then $f(x_1, \ldots, x_m) = 0$ holds over $\mathbb{Z}$.

The norm of a polynomial $f(x_1, \cdots, x_m) = \sum c_{i_1,\cdots,i_m} x_1^{i_1} \cdots x_m^{i_m}$ is defined as $\|f(x_1, \cdots, x_m)\| = \sqrt{\sum |c_{i_1,\cdots,i_m}|^2}$. Therefore, according to Lemma 1 and Lemma 2, in order to obtain at least m polynomials with the common desired root $(a_1, \ldots, a_m)$, there is the following condition:

$$2^{\frac{\omega(\omega-1)}{4(\omega+1-m)}} \cdot (\det L)^{\frac{1}{\omega+1-m}} < \frac{p^t}{\sqrt{\omega}}. \tag{1}$$

In order to find the desired root $(a_1, \ldots, a_m)$ by utilizing the Gröbner basis technique, we expect the obtained integer polynomials to satisfy the following assumption, which is often used by Coppersmith-type cryptanalysis [15].

Assumption 1. *Let $g_1, \cdots, g_m \in \mathbb{Z}[x_1, \cdots, x_m]$ be the polynomials that are found by Coppersmith's method. Then the variety of the ideal generated by $g_1(x_1, \cdots, x_m), \cdots, g_m(x_1, \cdots, x_m)$ is zero-dimensional.*

2.3 The Quadratic Generator

For a prime p, $\mathbb{F}_p$ denotes the field of p elements $\{0, 1, \cdots, p-1\}$. For fixed $a \in \mathbb{F}_p^*$ and $b \in \mathbb{F}_p$, the Quadratic generator [11] is given by the recurrence relation occurring on $\mathbb{F}_p$,

$$V_i = aV_{i-1}^2 + b \bmod p,$$

where V_0 is the initial value, the coefficient a is multiplier and b is shift.

3 Solving $f(x_1, x_2, y) = x_1x_2 + ax_1 + bx_2 + cy + d \bmod p$

For p an integer of size π, we denote by $\mathbb{Z}_p$ the residue ring of p elements. In this section, we will give the method for solving the modular polynomial equation $f(x_1, x_2, y) = x_1x_2 + ax_1 + bx_2 + cy + d \bmod p$ on $\mathbb{Z}_p$, as well as the bound X on the small roots x_1, x_2, y, where these roots have the same bound.

Since the variable y is independent of the other variables x_1, x_2, we will consider the equation f in two parts, following the approach of [14].

Let $g(x_1, x_2) = x_1x_2 + ax_1 + bx_2 + d$, then the original equation can be rewritten as $f = g + cy \bmod p$. For any positive integer m, we have the binomial expansion

$$f^m = (g + cy)^m = (cy)^m + \binom{m}{1}(cy)^{m-1}g + \binom{m}{2}(cy)^{m-2}g^2 + \cdots + g^m.$$

Therefore, f^m is divided into $m + 1$ parts and the monomials are sorted in the order of the monomials in the term $(cy)^m$, the monomials in the term $(cy)^{m-1}g$, $\cdots$ and the monomials in the term g^m.

According to Coppersmith's method, we need to construct the set of modular polynomials $h_{i,j_1,j_2,j_3}(x_1, x_2, y) = y^{t-i}x_1^{j_1}x_2^{j_2}f^{j_3}p^{t-j_3} \bmod p^t$ with the same root, where t is some positive integer and i, j_1, j_2, j_3 are non-negative integers. In the following we present the simple case at $t = 2$.

3.1 Solution for $t = 2$

To compute the small root (x_1', x_2', y) of $f(x_1, x_2, y)$, we first consider the following collection of polynomials:

$$P = \{h_{i,j_1,j_2,j_3}(x_1, x_2, y) = p^{2-j_3}y^{2-i}x_1^{j_1}x_2^{j_2}f^{j_3}$$
$$|i, j_1, j_2, j_3 \geq 0 \text{ and } 0 \leq j_1 + j_2 + j_3 \leq i \text{ and } j_1 + j_2 = \max\{j_1, j_2\}\}.$$

It is clear that the polynomials $h \in P$ all satisfy $h(x_1', x_2', y') = 0 \bmod p^2$. Next, we construct the lattice spanned by the coefficient vectors of the polynomials

$$h_{i,j_1,j_2,j_3}(x_1X_1, x_2X_2, yY),$$

where X_1, X_2, Y are the bounds of x_1', x_2', y', respectively. In order to ensure that the basis matrix of our constructed lattice is lower triangular, we first consider the construction of $g(x_1, x_2) = x_1x_2 + ax_1 + bx_2 + d$. In the set P, the highest degree of f is 2, then the highest degree of g is also 2, so we denote G_l as the set of polynomials about g constructed when the highest degree is l.

$$G_l = \{x_1^{j_1}x_2^{j_2}g^{j_3} | j_1, j_2, j_3 \geq 0 \text{ and } 0 \leq j_1 + j_2 + j_3 \leq l \text{ and } j_1 + j_2 = \max\{j_1, j_2\}\}.$$

Obviously, $G_{l-1} \subseteq G_l$. We can simply obtain the set of polynomials corresponding to G_0, G_1 and G_2.

$$G_0 = \{1\},$$
$$G_1 = \{1, x_1, x_2, g\},$$
$$G_2 = \{1, x_1, x_2, g, x_1^2, x_2^2, x_1g, x_2g, g^2\}.$$

The matrixes corresponding to G_0, G_1 and G_2 are lower triangular.

Now, we return to the original polynomial construction.

$$
\begin{aligned}
&p^{2-j_3}y^{2-i}x_1^{j_1}x_2^{j_2}f^{j_3} = p^{2-j_3}y^{2-i}x_1^{j_1}x_2^{j_2}(g+cy)^{j_3} \\
=&p^{2-j_3}y^{2-i}x_1^{j_1}x_2^{j_2}g^{j_3} + p^{2-j_3}x_1^{j_1}x_2^{j_2}\left(\sum_{k=1}^{j_3}\binom{j_3}{k}c^k y^{2-i+k}g^{j_3-k}\right).
\end{aligned} \tag{2}
$$

For $i = 0$, the monomial y^2 can be constructed as a diagonal matrix that corresponds to y^2G_0.

For $i = 1$, if $j_3 = 0$, (2) can be written as $p^2yx_1^{j_1}x_2^{j_2}$, indicating that the resulting matrix adding these monomials is also diagonal. If $j_3 = 1$, (2) is $pyg + pcy^2$, and the latter monomial y^2 has already appeared in the case of $i = 0$. The new monomial in pyg is only pyx_1x_2. Thus, for $i = 1$, the added monomials correspond to the monomials in yG_1 and the newly composed matrix is lower triangular.

For $i = 2$, (2) can be written as

$$
p^{2-j_3}x_1^{j_1}x_2^{j_2}g^{j_3} + p^{2-j_3}x_1^{j_1}x_2^{j_2}\left(\sum_{k=1}^{j_3}\binom{j_3}{k}c^k y^k g^{j_3-k}\right).
$$

The monomials in the latter part $p^{2-j_3}x_1^{j_1}x_2^{j_2}\left(\sum_{k=1}^{j_3}\binom{j_3}{k}c^k y^k g^{j_3-k}\right)$ have already appeared in G_0 and yG_1. The new monomials are the terms in the first part $p^{2-j_3}x_1^{j_1}x_2^{j_2}g^{j_3}$ that correspond to the polynomials in G_2.

We show the matrix L constructed by $h_{i,j_1,j_2,j_3}(x_1X_1, x_2X_2, yY)$ at $t = 2$ as follows.

	y^2	y	yx_1	yx_2	yx_1x_2	1	x_1	x_2	x_1x_2	x_1^2	x_2^2	$x_1^2x_2$	$x_1x_2^2$	$x_1^2x_2^2$
p^2y^2	p^2Y^2	0	0	0	0	0	0	0	0	0	0	0	0	0
p^2y	0	p^2Y	0	0	0	0	0	0	0	0	0	0	0	0
p^2yx_1	0	0	p^2YX_1	0	0	0	0	0	0	0	0	0	0	0
p^2yx_2	0	0	0	p^2YX_2	0	0	0	0	0	0	0	0	0	0
pyf	0	pdY	$paYX_1$	$pbYX_2$	pYX_1X_2	0	0	0	0	0	0	0	0	0
p^2	0	0	0	0	0	p^2	0	0	0	0	0	0	0	0
p^2x_1	0	0	0	0	0	0	p^2X_1	0	0	0	0	0	0	0
p^2x_2	0	0	0	0	0	0	0	p^2X_2	0	0	0	0	0	0
pf	0	pcY	0	0	0	pd	paX_1	pbX_2	pX_1X_2	0	0	0	0	0
$p^2x_1^2$	0	0	0	0	0	0	0	0	0	$p^2X_1^2$	0	0	0	0
$p^2x_2^2$	0	0	0	0	0	0	0	0	0	0	$p^2X_2^2$	0	0	0
px_1f	0	0	$pcYX_1$	0	0	0	pdX_1	0	pbX_1X_2	paX_1^2	0	$pX_1^2X_2$	0	0
px_2f	0	0	0	$pcYX_2$	0	0	0	pdX_2	paX_1X_2	0	pbX_2^2	0	$pX_1X_2^2$	0
f^2	c^2Y^2	$2cdY$	$2acYX_1$	$2bcYX_2$	$2cYX_1X_2$	d^2	$2adX_1$	$2bdX_2$	$2(ab+d)X_1X_2$	$a^2X_1^2$	$b^2X_2^2$	$2aX_1^2X_2$	$2bX_1X_2^2$	$X_1^2X_2^2$

The dimension $\dim L$ and determinant $\det L$ of this matrix L can be directly obtained as $\dim L = 14$ and $\det L = p^{22}Y^6X_1^{11}X_2^{11}$. Substituting $\omega = \dim L = 14$ and $\det L = p^{22}Y^6X_1^{11}X_2^{11}$ into the inequality (1). Since the dimension is small, we can treat the condition simply as $\det L < p^{t\omega}$ when p is sufficiently large. That is consistent with the experimental results. Then, the result can be approximated as follows:

$$
Y^6X_1^{11}X_2^{11} < p^6.
$$

Let $X_1 = p^{\delta_1}$, $X_2 = p^{\delta_2}$ and $Y = p^{\delta_3}$. Then the bound of the roots need to satisfy the following condition, $11\delta_1 + 11\delta_2 + 6\delta_3 < 6$. When $Y = X_1 = X_2 = p^{\delta}$, there is $\delta < \frac{3}{14}$.

In the following, we will consider the case where t tends to infinity.

3.2 Solution for $t \to \infty$

As t tends to infinity, the idea is similar to that for $t = 2$. Below we detail that the basis matrix of the constructed lattice is lower triangular, and the calculation of the dimension and determinant of the matrix.

We construct the set of polynomials in the general case:

$$P = \{h_{i,j_1,j_2,j_3}(x_1, x_2, y) = p^{2-j_3} y^{2-i} x_1^{j_1} x_2^{j_2} f^{j_3} \\ |i, j_1, j_2, j_3 \geq 0 \text{ and } 0 \leq j_1 + j_2 + j_3 \leq i \text{ and } j_1 + j_2 = \max\{j_1, j_2\}\}.$$

The polynomials $h \in P$ satisfy $h = 0 \bmod p^t$. Next, we construct the lattice L spanned by the coefficient vectors of the polynomials $h_{i,j_1,j_2,j_3}(x_1X_1, x_2X_2, yY)$. We still consider the construction of the polynomial g first. Let G_l denotes the set of polynomials about g^k that $k \leq l$.

$$G_l = \{x_1^{j_1} x_2^{j_2} g^{j_3} | j_1, j_2, j_3 \geq 0 \text{ and } j_1 + j_2 + j_3 \leq l \text{ and } j_1 + j_2 = \max\{j_1, j_2\}\}.$$

This is a general construction on a bivariate equation, and previous work has shown that matrix constructed through the set G_l is lower triangular [15].

We arrange the monomials in the order of i from 0 to t and use mathematical induction to prove that the matrix is lower triangular. When $i = 0$, the monomial y^t can be constructed as a diagonal matrix that corresponds to $y^t G_0$. Assuming that the constructed matrix is lower triangular at $i = m - 1$, then the newly added polynomials at $i = m$ can be written as $p^{t-j_3} y^{t-m} x_1^{j_1} x_2^{j_2} f^{j_3} = p^{t-j_3} y^{t-m} x_1^{j_1} x_2^{j_2} g^{j_3} + p^{t-j_3} x_1^{j_1} x_2^{j_2} \left(\sum_{k=1}^{j_3} \binom{j_3}{k} c^k y^{t-m+k} g^{j_3-k} \right)$.

Note that the monomials in the second half after the plus sign $x_1^{j_1} x_2^{j_2} y^{t-(m-1)} g^{j_3-1}, \cdots, x_1^{j_1} x_2^{j_2} y^{t-(m-j3)}$ have already appeared before for $i \leq m - 1$. Because of $j_3 \leq m$, the new monomials in the first half part $p^{t-j_3} y^{t-m} x_1^{j_1} x_2^{j_2} g^{j_3}$ correspond to the monomials in $y^{t-m} G_m$. Since the matrix constructed by the polynomials in G_m is lower triangular, and $y^{t-m} G_m$ is equivalent to multiplying each monomials in G_m by a y^{t-m}, which does not affect the property of triangular, the matrix remains lower triangular after adding the new polynomials. To sum up, the matrix we construct using the polynomials $h_{i,j_1,j_2,j_3}(x_1X_1, x_2X_2, yY)$ is triangular.

Next, we analyze the dimension and determinant of L. The dimension can be showed by the sorting process of the monomials:

$$\dim L = \sum_{l=0}^{t} \#G_l, \tag{3}$$

where $\#G_l$ is the number of elements in the set G_l. Based on the fact that the constructed matrix is lower triangular, $\#G_l$ is the number of monomials.

$$\#G_l = \sum_{j_1=0}^{l}\sum_{j_2=0}^{l} 1 = (l+1)^2.$$

Substituting $\#G_l$ into (3),

$$\dim L = \sum_{l=0}^{t}(l+1)^2 = \frac{1}{3}t^3 + \frac{3}{2}t^2 + \frac{13}{6}t + 1 = \frac{1}{3}t^3 + o(t^3).$$

Since L is a triangular matrix, only the elements on the diagonal need to be considered when calculating the determinant. According to the way we construct L, the diagonal elements can be divided into $t+1$ parts, each corresponding to $y^{t-l}G_l$ is lower triangular, so we first look at the diagonal product in matrix $L_{y^{t-l}G_l}$ constructed by $y^{t-l}G_l$. From the entries on the diagonal $p^{t-j_3}Y^{t-l}X_1^{j_1}X_2^{j_2}$, we get that the determinant of $L_{y^{t-l}G_l}$ is

$$\det\left(L_{y^{t-l}G_l}\right) = p^{w_p}Y^{w_Y}X_1^{w_{X_1}}X_2^{w_{X_2}},$$

where

$$\begin{aligned}
w_p &= \sum_{j_3=0}^{l}\sum_{j_1=1}^{l-j_3}(t-j_3) + \sum_{j_3=0}^{l}\sum_{j_2=1}^{l-j_3}(t-j_3) + \sum_{j_3=0}^{l}(t-j_3)\\
&= -\frac{1}{3}l^3 + \left(t-\frac{1}{2}\right)l^2 + \left(2t-\frac{1}{6}\right)l + t,\\
w_Y &= (t-l)\times \#G_l = (t-l)(l+1)^2,\\
w_{X_1} &= w_{X_2} = \sum_{j_1=0}^{l}\sum_{j_2=0}^{l} j_1 = \frac{1}{2}l^3 + l^2 + \frac{1}{2}l.
\end{aligned}$$

Then the power of P, Y, X_1 and X_2 corresponds to the determinant of L is the summation of l from 0 to t, respectively.

$$\begin{aligned}
\sum_{l=0}^{t} w_p &= \sum_{l=0}^{t}\left(-\frac{1}{3}l^3 + \left(t-\frac{1}{2}\right)l^2 + \left(2t-\frac{1}{6}\right)l + t\right) = \frac{1}{4}t^4 + o(t^4),\\
\sum_{l=0}^{t} w_Y &= \sum_{l=0}^{t}(t-l)(l+1)^2 = \frac{1}{12}t^4 + o(t^4),\\
\sum_{l=0}^{t} w_{X_1} &= \sum_{l=0}^{t}\left(\frac{1}{2}l^3 + l^2 + \frac{1}{2}l\right) = \frac{1}{8}t^4 + o(t^4).
\end{aligned}$$

The determinant of L can be expressed as follows:

$$\det L = p^{\frac{1}{4}t^4+o(t^4)}Y^{\frac{1}{12}t^4+o(t^4)}X_1^{\frac{1}{8}t^4+o(t^4)}X_2^{\frac{1}{8}t^4+o(t^4)}.$$

Substituting $\omega = \dim L = \frac{1}{3}t^3 + o(t^3)$, $\det L$ and number of variables $m = 3$ into the inequality (1) $2^{\frac{\omega(\omega-1)}{4(\omega-2)}} \cdot (\det L)^{\frac{1}{\omega-2}} < \frac{p^t}{\sqrt{\omega}}$, we also ignore the parts of 2 and ω for a sufficiently large p,

$$\det L < p^{t(\omega-2)},$$

and the result is approximated:

$$Y^{\frac{1}{12}t^4+o(t^4)} X_1^{\frac{1}{8}t^4+o(t^4)} X_2^{\frac{1}{8}t^4+o(t^4)} < p^{\frac{1}{12}t^4+o(t^4)}.$$

Let $X_1 = p^{\delta_1}$, $X_2 = p^{\delta_2}$ and $Y = p^{\delta_3}$. We can obtain the relation on the bound δ_1, δ_2 and δ_3, $2\delta_3 + 3\delta_1 + 3\delta_2 < 2$. When $Y = X_1 = X_2 = p^{\delta}$, there is

$$\delta < \frac{\frac{1}{12}t^4 + o(t^4)}{\frac{1}{12}t^4 + \frac{1}{8}t^4 \times 2 + o(t^4)} \stackrel{t\to\infty}{\longrightarrow} \frac{1}{4}. \tag{4}$$

Result 1. *Given a modular polynomial equation* $f(x_1, x_2, y) = x_1x_2 + ax_1 + bx_2 + cy + d \bmod p$. *Under Assumption 1, we can find the modular root* (x_1', x_2', y') *when the bound* $X = p^{\delta}$ *that* $x_1', x_2', y' < X$ *satisfy*

$$\delta < \frac{1}{4}.$$

4 Application: Attacking the Quadratic Generator

The Quadratic generator corresponds to the map $F(x) = ax^2 + b \bmod p$. If the multiplier a is known, the shift b is unknown and the three consecutive outputs of the Quadratic generator are known, we can transform the relevant equation into the modular polynomial equation in Sect. 3. Therefore, the subsequent sequence of the Quadratic generator can be obtained under the condition given in Sect. 3 about the bound of root.

Given three consecutive equations

$$\begin{cases} V_1 = aV_0^2 + b \bmod p \\ V_2 = aV_1^2 + b \bmod p \end{cases},$$

the unknown shift b can be eliminated

$$V_1 - V_2 = a\left(V_0^2 - V_1^2\right) \bmod p. \tag{5}$$

Assume that the Quadratic generator outputs the k most significant bits of V_i at each iteration, i.e. V_i can be written as $2^k w_i + z_i$, where w_i is output by the generator, $z_i < 2^k = p^{\delta}$ stays unknown and π is the bit length of the modulo p. Our goal is to recover z_i and the subsequent sequence with δ as large as possible.

Substituting $V_j = 2^k w_j + z_j$ into $V_i - V_{i+1}$ and $V_i + V_{i+1}$,

$$\begin{aligned} V_1 - V_2 &= 2^k(w_1 - w_2) + (z_1 - z_2), \\ V_0 - V_1 &= 2^k(w_0 - w_1) + (z_0 - z_1), \\ V_0 + V_1 &= 2^k(w_0 + w_1) + (z_0 + z_1), \end{aligned}$$

where let $\alpha_1 = 2^k(w_1 - w_2)$, $\alpha_2 = 2^k(w_0 - w_1)$ and $\alpha_3 = 2^k(w_0 + w_1)$ be the known part, and $\beta_1 = z_1 - z_2$, $\beta_2 = z_0 - z_1$ and $\beta_3 = z_0 + z_1$ be the unknown part. Replacing V_k in the Eq. 5 with α_i and β_j, we get $\alpha_1 + \beta_1 = a(\alpha_2 + \beta_2)(\alpha_3 + \beta_3) \bmod p$. Then, by three consecutive outputs of the Quadratic generator, the following modular polynomial equation can be obtained

$$f(x_1, x_2, y) = x_1 x_2 + \alpha_3 x_1 + \alpha_2 x_2 + (-a^{-1})y + \alpha_2\alpha_3 - a^{-1}\alpha_1 \bmod p, \quad (6)$$

where $(\beta_2, \beta_3, \beta_1)$ is its root.

Based on the result in Sect. 3, in the case of $\delta < \frac{1}{4}$, we can solve for the small root $(\beta_2, \beta_3, \beta_1)$. Then it can be calculated that $z_0 = \frac{1}{2}(\beta_2 + \beta_3)$, $z_1 = \frac{1}{2}(\beta_3 - \beta_2)$ and $z_2 = \frac{1}{2}(\beta_3 - \beta_2) - \beta_1$. Thus we can recover the algebraic mapping $F(V_i) \bmod p$ of the Quadratic generator, where the shift $b = 2^k w_1 + \frac{1}{2}(\beta_3 - \beta_2) - (2^{\pi-k} w_0 + \frac{1}{2}(\beta_2 + \beta_3))^2 \bmod p$. That is, we can recover all its subsequent sequences.

Result 2. *Given three consecutive outputs of the Quadratic generator, we can predict the entire sequence and recover the initial seed V_0 and the shift b under the condition that at least $\frac{3}{4}\pi$ most significant bits are output at each iteration, that is*

$$\delta < \frac{1}{4}.$$

Remark 1. In the case where the multiplier a is known and the shift b is unknown, the best result of the existing work is $\frac{1}{5}$ of [11]. We improve the bound to $\frac{1}{4}$ by the construction method of splitting out an independent variable.

5 Experimental Results

Let us take the Quadratic generator with $\pi = 1024$ and $\pi = 256$ as examples for the attack. We ran each case over 500 times in SageMath 9.3 on a PC with an Intel(R) Core(TM) i7-9750H CPU @ 2.60 GHz, 16 GB RAM, and Windows 10 to retrieve the algebraic mapping $F(V_i) \bmod p$.

Because the bound $\delta < \frac{1}{4}$ is reached when t approaches infinity, we choose $t = 2$ and $t = 3$ for our experiments. It can be seen that the corresponding bound δ increases when t increases, and it is verified that the practical attack bound has been better than $\frac{1}{5}$ (Table 1).

Table 1. Attack of the Quadratic generator

π	t	k	δ	Running time	Success rate
1024	2	218	0.213	5.78 s	100%
		219	0.214	3.34 s	58%
	3	226	0.221	63.2 s	100%
		227	0.222	62.0 s	75%
256	2	53	0.207	0.27 s	100%
		54	0.211	0.27 s	95.8%
	3	55	0.215	9.61 s	100%
		56	0.219	9.23 s	97.6%

6 Conclusion

In this paper we first give a specific method for solving the modular polynomial $f(x_1, x_2, y) = x_1x_2 + ax_1 + bx_2 + cy + d \bmod p$, and then apply this method to the Quadratic generator to improve the upper bound on the unknown output. Next, we will explore whether the upper bound on the unknown output can be continued to improve when more than three consecutive outputs are known, and whether the attack can be improved for the both multiplier and shift are known or unknown.

References

1. Bauer, A., Joux, A.: Toward a rigorous variation of coppersmith's algorithm on three variables. In: Naor, M. (ed.) EUROCRYPT 2007. LNCS, vol. 4515, pp. 361–378. Springer, Heidelberg (2007). https://doi.org/10.1007/978-3-540-72540-4_21
2. Bauer, A., Vergnaud, D., Zapalowicz, J.-C.: Inferring sequences produced by non-linear pseudorandom number generators using coppersmith's methods. In: Fischlin, M., Buchmann, J., Manulis, M. (eds.) PKC 2012. LNCS, vol. 7293, pp. 609–626. Springer, Heidelberg (2012). https://doi.org/10.1007/978-3-642-30057-8_36
3. Blackburn, S.R., Gomez-Perez, D., Gutierrez, J., Shparlinski, I.E.: Predicting the inversive generator. In: Paterson, K.G. (ed.) Cryptography and Coding 2003. LNCS, vol. 2898, pp. 264–275. Springer, Heidelberg (2003). https://doi.org/10.1007/978-3-540-40974-8_21
4. Blackburn, S.R., Gómez-Pérez, D., Gutierrez, J., Shparlinski, I.E.: Predicting nonlinear pseudorandom number generators. Math. Comput. **74**(251), 1471–1494 (2005). https://doi.org/10.1090/S0025-5718-04-01698-9
5. Blackburn, S.R., Gómez-Pérez, D., Gutierrez, J., Shparlinski, I.E.: Reconstructing noisy polynomial evaluation in residue rings. J. Algorithms **61**(2), 47–59 (2006). https://doi.org/10.1016/j.jalgor.2004.07.002
6. Blömer, J., May, A.: A tool kit for finding small roots of bivariate polynomials over the integers. In: Cramer, R. (ed.) EUROCRYPT 2005. LNCS, vol. 3494, pp. 251–267. Springer, Heidelberg (2005). https://doi.org/10.1007/11426639_15

7. Boyar, J.: Inferring sequences produced by a linear congruential generator missing low-order bits. J. Cryptol. **1**(3), 177–184 (1988). https://doi.org/10.1007/BF02252875
8. Boyar, J.: Inferring sequences produced by pseudo-random number generators. J. ACM **36**(1), 129–141 (1989). https://doi.org/10.1145/58562.59305
9. Coppersmith, D.: Finding a small root of a bivariate integer equation; factoring with high bits known. In: Maurer, U. (ed.) EUROCRYPT 1996. LNCS, vol. 1070, pp. 178–189. Springer, Heidelberg (1996). https://doi.org/10.1007/3-540-68339-9_16
10. Coppersmith, D.: Finding a small root of a univariate modular equation. In: Maurer, U. (ed.) EUROCRYPT 1996. LNCS, vol. 1070, pp. 155–165. Springer, Heidelberg (1996). https://doi.org/10.1007/3-540-68339-9_14
11. Gomez, D., Gutierrez, J., Ibeas, A.: Cryptanalysis of the quadratic generator. In: Maitra, S., Veni Madhavan, C.E., Venkatesan, R. (eds.) INDOCRYPT 2005. LNCS, vol. 3797, pp. 118–129. Springer, Heidelberg (2005). https://doi.org/10.1007/11596219_10
12. Gómez-Pérez, D., Gutierrez, J., Ibeas, Á.: Attacking the pollard generator. IEEE Trans. Inf. Theory **52**(12), 5518–5523 (2006). https://doi.org/10.1109/TIT.2006.885451
13. Howgrave-Graham, N.: Finding small roots of univariate modular equations revisited. In: Darnell, M. (ed.) Cryptography and Coding 1997. LNCS, vol. 1355, pp. 131–142. Springer, Heidelberg (1997). https://doi.org/10.1007/BFb0024458
14. Huang, Z., Hu, L., Xu, J., Peng, L., Xie, Y.: Partial key exposure attacks on Takagi's variant of RSA. In: Boureanu, I., Owesarski, P., Vaudenay, S. (eds.) ACNS 2014. LNCS, vol. 8479, pp. 134–150. Springer, Cham (2014). https://doi.org/10.1007/978-3-319-07536-5_9
15. Jochemsz, E., May, A.: A strategy for finding roots of multivariate polynomials with new applications in attacking RSA variants. In: Lai, X., Chen, K. (eds.) ASIACRYPT 2006. LNCS, vol. 4284, pp. 267–282. Springer, Heidelberg (2006). https://doi.org/10.1007/11935230_18
16. Joux, A., Stern, J.: Lattice reduction: a toolbox for the cryptanalyst. J. Cryptol. **11**(3), 161–185 (1998). https://doi.org/10.1007/s001459900042
17. Stern, J.: Secret linear congruential generators are not cryptographically secure. In: 28th Annual Symposium on Foundations of Computer Science, Los Angeles, California, USA, 27–29 October 1987, pp. 421–426. IEEE Computer Society (1987). https://doi.org/10.1109/SFCS.1987.51

Correction to: Practical Multi-party Private Set Intersection Cardinality and Intersection-Sum Under Arbitrary Collusion

You Chen, Ning Ding, Dawu Gu, and Yang Bian

Correction to:
Chapter "Practical Multi-party Private Set Intersection Cardinality and Intersection-Sum Under Arbitrary Collusion" in: Y. Deng and M. Yung (Eds.): *Information Security and Cryptology*, LNCS 13837, https://doi.org/10.1007/978-3-031-26553-2_9

The original version of this chapter contained errors on page 8,9,10 & 11 in chapter 9 which is indicated in our final book. This is now corrected.

The updated original version of this chapter can be found at
https://doi.org/10.1007/978-3-031-26553-2_9

Y. Deng and M. Yung (Eds.): Inscrypt 2022, LNCS 13837, p. C1, 2023.
https://doi.org/10.1007/978-3-031-26553-2_27

Author Index

Y. Deng and M. Yung (Eds.): Inscrypt 2022, LNCS 13837, pp. 495–496, 2023.
https://doi.org/10.1007/978-3-031-26553-2

Printed in the United States
by Baker & Taylor Publisher Services